We have never heard the devil's side of the story,
God wrote all the books.
Anatole France

BOOKS BY TROY TAYLOR

DEAD MEN SO TELL TALES SERIES
Dead Men Do Tell Tales (2008)
Bloody Chicago (2006)
Bloody Illinois (2008)
Bloody Hollywood (2008)
Without a Trace (2009)
Blood, Guns & Valentines (2010)
Murdered in Their Beds (2012)

HAUNTED ILLINOIS BOOKS
Haunted Illinois (1999 / 2001 / 2004)
Haunted Decatur (1995 /2000 / 2006/2009)
More Haunted Decatur (1996)
Ghosts of Millikin (1996 / 2001)
Where the Dead Walk (1997 / 2002)
Dark Harvest (1997)
Flickering Images (2001 / 2011)
Haunted Alton (2000 / 2003 / 2008)
Haunted Chicago (2003)
The Haunted President (2005 / 2009)
Mysterious Illinois (2005)
Resurrection Mary (2007)
The Possessed (2007)
Weird Chicago (2008)
Illinois Hauntings (2011)

HAUNTED FIELD GUIDE BOOKS
The Ghost Hunters Guidebook
(1997/ 1999 / 2001/ 2004 / 2007 / 2010)
Confessions of a Ghost Hunter (2002)
Field Guide to Haunted Graveyards (2003)
Ghosts on Film (2005)
So, There I Was (with Len Adams) (2006)
Talking with the Dead (2009)

HISTORY & HAUNTINGS SERIES
The Haunting of America (2001 / 2010)
Into the Shadows (2002 / 2012)
Down in the Darkness (2003)
Out Past the Campfire Light (2004)
Ghosts by Gaslight (2007)

HELL HATH NO FURY SERIES
1. Legacy of Evil (2012)
2. Murderous Medium (2012)
3. The Lost Girls (2012)
4. Mercy Brown (2012)
5. Come Prepared to Stay Forever (2013)

OTHER GHOSTLY TITLES
Spirits of the Civil War (1999)
Season of the Witch (1999/ 2002)
Haunted New Orleans (2000)
Beyond the Grave (2001)
No Rest for the Wicked (2001)
Haunted St. Louis (2002)
The Devil Came to St. Louis (2006)
Houdini: Among the Spirits (2009)
And Hell Followed With It (with Rene Kruse) (2010)
Suicide & Spirits (2011)
A Pale Horse Was Death (with Rene Kruse) (2012)

WHITECHAPEL OCCULT LIBRARY
Sex & the Supernatural (2009)
The Devil & All His Works (2013)

STERLING PUBLICATIONS
Weird U.S. (Co-Author) (2004)
Weird Illinois (2005)
Weird Virginia (Co-Author) (2007)
Weird Indiana (Co-Author) (2008)

BARNES & NOBLE PRESS TITLES
Haunting of America (2006)
Spirits of the Civil War (2007)
Into the Shadows (2007)

HISTORY PRESS TITLES
Wicked Washington (2007)
Murder & Mayhem Series:
Chicago's North Side (2009)
Chicago's South Side (2009)
Chicago's West Side (2009)
Downtown Chicago (2009)
Chicago Vice Districts (2009)
Wicked New Orleans (2010)
Haunted New Orleans (2010)
Wicked Northern Illinois (2010)
Wicked Decatur (2011)

STACKPOLE BOOKS TITLES
Haunted Illinois (2008)
True Crime Illinois (2009)
Big Book of Illinois Ghost Stories (2009)
Illinois Monsters (2011)
Haunted Missouri (2012)

THE DEVIL AND ALL HIS WORKS
A History of Satan, Sin, Murder, Mayhem & Magic
BY TROY TAYLOR

- A Whitechapel Press Publication from Apartment 42 Productions -

The devil's voice is sweet to hear.
Stephen King

Original Cover Artwork Designed by
© Copyright 2013 by April Slaughter & Troy Taylor
Back Cover Author's Photo by Janet Morris

This Book is Published By:
Whitechapel Press
A Division of Apartment #42 Productions
Decatur, Illinois / 1-888-GHOSTLY
Visit us on the internet at http://www.whitechapelpress.com

First Edition -- March 2013
ISBN: 1-892523-80-9

Printed in the United States of America

An apology for the Devil: it must be remembered that we have heard only one side of the case. God has written all of the books.
Samuel Butler

It is a revenge the devil sometimes takes upon the virtuous, that he entraps them by the force of the very passion they have suppressed and think themselves superior to.
George Santayana

The Devil pulls the strings which make us dance;
We find delight in the most loathsome things;
Some furtherance of Hell each new day brings,
And yet we feel no horror in that rank advance.
Charles Baudelaire

If the Devil does not exist, and man has therefore created him, he has created him in his own image and likeness.
Fyodor Dostoyevsky

We are each our own devil, and we make this world our hell.
Oscar Wilde

The devil is an optimist if he thinks he can make people worse than they are.
Karl Kraus

TABLE OF CONTENTS

INTRODUCTION:
PLEASE ALLOW ME TO INTRODUCE MYSELF...

Satan.

The Devil, Lucifer, Old Nick, the Tempter, the Dark Prince, the Lord of Darkness, Old Scratch, the Deceiver, the Adversary, Prince of the Air, His Satanic Majesty, the Evil One, Father of Lies, the Devourer, the Dragon and Mephistopheles... Pick any name; they all refer to the same thing, or person, or being, or whatever the Devil is supposed to be. Feared, worshipped, laughed about or dismissed, he (or it) remains a presence in our world. Satanism, Black Magic, Sex Magic, fear, hatred, works of evil, incantation and curses, rituals and ceremonies – we hear of them all. Each of them connects to Satan, but what does it all mean?

Is Satan an actual person? Is evil an essence, an objective reality? Or is it all just a metaphor for the good and evil sides of man? Does Satan rule the world? Is there an absolute evil set against absolute good? Is Satan roaming the Earth "seeking whom he may devour?"

What is Satanism? Who are the true worshippers of Satan? Does demonic possession exist? Were the witches executed during the Middle Ages really worshippers of Satan? Have people really killed in the name of Satan?

Some of these questions have been raised by medieval and modern theologians, others by philosophers, psychologists and sociologists. They have never been fully answered, in spite of centuries of study, discourse and experience. All of them will be addressed in this book but, while I can't provide concrete, cut-and-dried answers to the mysteries that have plagued us for generations, I can provide an examination of the Devil and his works throughout the centuries. By examining the occult, we may gain an understanding of its practitioners. This idea is best stated in the words of 17th-century English philosopher John Locke: "The improvement of the understanding is for two ends: first, our own increase in knowledge; secondly, to enable us to deliver and make out that knowledge to others."

And that knowledge can sometimes be dangerous.

Our subject is Satan, to some the embodiment of evil, to others merely a symbol of the dark side of humanity. The figure of the Devil permits us to create a personification of the otherwise elusive concept of evil, which we must do if we are to understand the needs and drives of those who have become embroiled in the worlds of black magic and Satanism. The existence of evil has always been man's central problem. God may be in his Heaven, but all is not right with the world.

The structure of being is composed of two battling opposites: light and dark, day and night, positive and negative, good and evil. With the dawn of man's imagination ages ago, came the concept of evil as a terrifying external force. Different cultures had different names for it. Even today, with our modern technology and sensibilities, the external force is still often said to be Satan, the Devil and the Evil One. We like to think that we have come a long way from pagan times, from the idea that Satan is a real force in our world, but the stories and accounts in this book will shatter that illusion. Our rational age of science and reason is marked by a staggering number of tales of supernatural events, horrific discoveries and nameless horrors that all have their roots in antiquity – and all of which are connected to a solid belief in the Devil.

Most of us have never met a witch, have never had coffee with a black magician, witnessed a ritualistic orgy, or encountered Satan. And yet, we are painfully aware of widespread nefarious and infernal activities. We read about them in books and newspapers or see them on television. Back in the 1980s, stories of Satan worshippers were everywhere. Were all the stories true, or were they merely part of the hysteria spread by fundamentalist Christians, bewildered parents of rebellious teenagers and ratings-hungry talk show hosts? It is hard to decipher even now, more than two decades later, what was real and what was elaborate fiction, but if the stories did anything, they strengthened the public's belief in evil. And, by extension, they strengthened the belief in the Devil.

When we explore the "Devil and all his works," we can never truly understand the Devil. However, we can uncover the history and reveal "his works," which are carried out by the hand of man. Keep this in mind as you read the following pages, for Satan rarely ever acts directly. He has a lot of help. When we look upon the evil that has been associated with the Devil, we have to remember who is actually responsible for his vile and evil "works." Fodor Dostoyevsky pointed out that man created the Devil and "he had created him in his own image and likeness." When we look upon the face of Satan, we cannot help but see our own reflections looking back at us. Even if you believe that Satan is a physical being, he requires the hand of man to carry out his evil deeds.

And if that doesn't frighten you, I don't know what will.

Troy Taylor
Winter 2012-2013

1. THE ORIGIN OF THE DEVIL

Many of us believe that we have an idea of who the Devil is, but the question of who (or what) this elusive creature might be is a very complex riddle. Some believe that they know what he looks like – a Faustian character with cloven hooves and a tail; a tall, gaunt man, dressed in black; or a horned demon that is terrifying to look upon. None of these descriptions are true, or perhaps they all are. Hellfire and damnation preachers have their own ideas of the Devil, but the writings on which they base their faith call Satan an "angel" and a "bringer of light" – or at least that's what he started out to be. Or did he? There seems to be some confusion about that too, as you'll see from the pages ahead.

The true nature of the Devil is a confusing and exasperating subject to explore, but to understand the works that have been carried out in his name, it's necessary for us to paint a vivid picture of what he actually might be. Satan has been worshipped, hated, and feared over the centuries. But do those who have used his name actually know how this being came into existence? Is he merely the opposite of God? Is Satan just a dark side to counter the light? Or is there more to him than we can imagine?

Prepare yourself. It's a long, strange, and often bloody road ahead.

The word "satan" comes from a Hebrew verb that means primarily to "obstruct or oppose." Satan was traditionally translated as the "accuser" or the "adversary" and was a title bestowed on a being, rather than the name of a being. Prior to the Babylonian exile of the Jews in the sixth century B.C., "the satan" was no more than an opponent. There was nothing supernatural about "satan" in those days. Usually, when biblical writings referred to "satan" it was taken to mean either humans or obedient angels of God. In the Bible, Davis was a "satan" to the Philistines. Solomon was bothered by a "satan" named Hadad the Edomite. A man named Rezon was a "satan" to Israel in the days of Solomon.

In this sense of the word, the gods of other people with whom the Israelites (who worshipped one god) came into contact were "satans." It was when the Israelites' Jehovah was developed into the one and only God, sole creator of the universe, that other gods – the "satans" – were reinterpreted as "sons of God" on an angelic level and became members of the Divine Council of Jehovah. In other words, they became subordinates who assisted God in his governing over the world.

It is in the Book of Job that the Satan first makes an appearance, but he's not exactly the character that modern-day theologians would like us to believe. Rather than being a sinister persecutor of Job, Satan is a member of God's Divine Council, the so-called "sons of God," who are subservient to the Lord. In this capacity – sort of as a prosecutor – he is given the task of tempting humans and reporting back to God about any of them who go against his decrees. At the beginning of the book, Job is a good person "who feared God and turned away from evil." Thanks to this, he had been rewarded by God. When the Divine Council meets, God informs Satan about Job's blameless, morally upright character. Satan, however, remarks that since Job has been given everything he wants, it's no surprise that he's loyal to God. He states that if it was all taken away, Job's faith would collapse. In a kind of cosmic chess game, Satan dares God to test Job and see if his faith holds up or if it fails. Here's how the story starts out:

Now there was a day when the sons of God came to present themselves before the Lord, and Satan came also among them. And the Lord said unto Satan, Whence comest though? Then Satan answered the Lord and said, From going to and fro in the earth, and from walking up and down in it.

And the Lord said unto Satan, Hast though considered my servant Job, that there is none like him in the earth, a perfect and upright man, one that feareth God, and escheweth evil?

Then Satan answered the Lord and said, Doth Job fear God for nought? Hast thou not made a hedge about him, and about his house, and about all that he hath on every side? Thou hast blessed the work of his hands, and his substance is increased in the land. But put forth thine hand now, and touch all that he hath, and he will curse thee to thy face.

In the story, Satan prods God into causing bad things to happen to Job, just to see what happens. It's a cruel sort of game and one that shows the devious nature of the Devil. If looked at in a certain way, it almost appears

that Satan tricked God into bedeviling Job. This is almost apparent in the epilogue to the story (during which, in spite of plague, financial ruin and the death of his family, Job stays true to God). When God, who sounds more than a little sorry for practically destroying one of his most faithful followers over what was basically a wager, tells Satan, "You have incited me against him, to destroy him for no reason."

The story of Job is a strange one and, let's face it, not exactly the kind of tale that puts God in a good light. But we can't help but notice that Satan seems to have a fairly cordial relationship with God. The story of Job is supposed to take place long after the fall of Satan from Heaven (more on that in a moment), but yet he was still on good terms with

The rather cruel story of Job marks Satan's first appearance in the Bible in a role that most would come to known him for -- a devious figure.

God. He acted almost as God's agent and, in fact, at one point, God actually puts his power into Satan's hands. One passage reads: "And the Lord said unto Satan, behold, all that he hath is in thy power." Satan tried to break Job, but

Job stayed true.

Centuries later, the Inquisitors and the witch hunters of the Middle Ages would use a portion of the story of Job for their own devices. It was not the story of the unlucky Job that they used, but rather the passage that noted that Satan had been traveling the Earth. They used these words to prove that Satan is the "ruler of the world." History attests that they used the fear of Satan to drag countless men and women to torture chambers or to be burned at the stake.

But in the days of the Old Testament, there was no tradition of any fear of the Devil, an evil presence that was the enemy of God. The figure of that Devil came about much later. In the Book of Job, Satan was still considered one of the sons of God, enjoying cordial relations with Jehovah. Only after the rise of Christianity did he become God's adversary. In Jude 9, for example, there is a story that clearly indicates that Satan was in good standing with God. When Satan audaciously lays claim to the corpse of Moses, even Michael, the Archangel and captain of the heavenly host, responded in a surprising manner, politely telling Satan that he couldn't have the body. The same Michael – who allegedly had once battled Satan in Heaven – is docile and polite when dealing with his old enemy. Michael's mildness confirms the idea that, contrary to later Christian beliefs, Satan still commanded respect after the fall.

As with all angels, Satan often did God's dirty work. With God's complicity, he murdered Egyptian children in Exodus, incited treachery against a Prince of Israel in Judges, prompted King Saul to dishonorable behavior, sent plague to Israel, entices Ahab into military disaster – all with God's permission, and usually according to his orders. Only once, in the Book of Zechariah, did God rebuke him for punishing Jerusalem too severely. Satan wasn't evil; he was just doing what God told him to do.

If the Israelites didn't believe in Satan as the originator of evil, then where did evil come from? The answer lies in the fundamental idea of God, or Jehovah. They considered him the sole creator of all things – which meant he was the source of all good, as well as all evil.

In Christian tradition, in which God is entirely good, Satan is presented as the antithesis of God. In early Jewish tradition, however, in which God is both good and evil, Satan is comparatively insignificant. He is merely an adversary, nothing more. Only God could create, and he created evil. Amos asked: "Shall there be evil in a city, and the Lord hath not done it?" And to Isaiah, the Lord said: "I form the light, and create darkness. I make peace, and create evil. I the Lord do all of these things."

The Jewish belief that God is the origin of evil is also reflected in the story of David numbering Israel. It's a bit of a stretch to see how anyone could think that taking a census of Israel is an evil act, but many thought so. There are actually two accounts in the Bible about the census-taking – one inspired by God, and the other inspired by Satan. This difference is pertinent to our understanding of the Israelite's shift from regarding God as the source of everything, including evil, to regarding Satan as the only source of evil. In one account, which may have been written in the eighth century B.C., God deals directly with David: "The anger of the Lord was kindled against Israel and he moved David against them to say, "Go, number Israel and Judah." In the second account, written about four centuries later, it is Satan who is responsible for the census-taking: "And Satan stood up against Israel, and provoked David to number Israel."

No matter what some might say, the disparity between these two accounts does not prove that the Bible contradicts itself; it simply illustrates that at one time the Israelites believed that God created evil, and at another point in time they believed that Satan created evil. Their ability to shift the responsibility for evil from God to Satan tells us more about human nature than it does about evil itself. The Israelites changed their minds about evil in the same way that the early Christians would. It may be said that the evolution occurred in defense of God. The very idea that God could author evil had some ramifications that were painfully felt by later Jews and Christians. The belief, however, is not without foundation.

In early Hebrew traditions, "the satan" is the direct instrument of God, performing a useful purpose, functioning as God's emissary or agent. From this, it followed that there must have been two tempters in the Garden of Eden. True, the temptation of Eve was Satan's work, but some Israelites wondered if it was possible that Satan, in whatever form, could have entered Paradise secretly and against the will of God. He had to have been in on the scheme. All that Adam possessed he had received from God, which included his susceptibility to lust and disobedience, also the weakness of the will and of the flesh. God then, appeared as a tempter from the very start of creation, fortifying the belief that God is the creator of evil as well as good.

But such ideas would eventually change. In later Jewish writings, the figure of Satan emerges as the great opponent of both God and man. God was recognized as entirely good. Good and evil were now separated, dividing the light and dark between God and the Devil. But how did "the satan" become Satan? How did a member of Jehovah's council fall so far from grace that he became a creature destined to be hated and feared by mankind?

St. Augustine, along with other Christian scholars, believed that his fall from grace was caused by the sin of pride. Lucifer, which meant "bringer of light" or "morning star," was God's chosen angel, favored above the other heavenly host. Filled with pride, Lucifer began to believe that he was equal to God and when he rebelled against God's instructions, war broke out in Heaven. Others would later insist that it was not pride that doomed Lucifer, but envy. He became jealous because God favored man over the angels. When he created man, he gave him dominion over the Earth and all its creatures. Lucifer believed that demonstrated that God loved mankind more that he loved his heavenly host.

Lucifer cast out of heaven in the Biblical accounts

Whatever the cause of his rebellion, Lucifer was joined by other angels and they fought a ferocious battle against the forces of Michael the archangel. The war ended with Lucifer's defeat and he and his angels were cast out of Heaven. After the fall, Lucifer became as hideous as he had been beautiful and his name was changed to Satan.

The Gospel of Luke reports that Jesus told his followers, "I beheld Satan as lightning fall from heaven." In his second letter to the Corinthians, Paul warned against false prophets, saying, "Satan himself masquerades as an angel of light." By these statements, it became clear that Satan – the adversary, obstructer and servant of the Old Testament – had become the fallen Lucifer, the deceitful angel.

12

Lucifer's fall was accompanied by other angels who also joined in his rebellion. By the time of the Christian era, there were numerous stories of fallen angels. It is to these angels that traditional sources refer to as "giants in the Earth." According to the Book of Genesis: "And it came to pass, when men began to multiply on the face of the Earth, and daughters were born unto them, that the sons of God saw the daughters of men that they were fair, and they took them wives of all which they chose... There were giants in the earth in those days; and also after that, when the sons of God came in unto the daughters of men, and they bare children to them, the same became mighty men which were of old, men of renown. And God saw that the wickedness of man was great in the earth, and that every imagination of the thoughts of his heart was only evil continually." This wickedness, started by the fallen angels, was followed by a devastating flood that wiped out most of humanity. To later ages, the

"I beheld Satan as lightning fall from heaven."
Gospel of Luke

point of the story was that evil came to Earth with Lucifer and his angels, who had sexual relations with mortals, producing giants and mighty men. This forbidden sexual union so enraged God that he wiped out everyone on the planet except for Noah and his family. Thanks to this story, good and evil were separated permanently, making God a being of light and Satan, a creature of the dark.

But it should be noted that these stories are widely open to interpretation. Satan never appeared in the Old Testament as the being that we think of today. In fact, the legend of Lucifer can be traced to a date long after the books of the Bible were written. The legend is one that is largely of medieval origin, "borrowed" from the story of the fall of the morning star in Isaiah, with elements of Ezekiel and the New Testament tale of Satan's fall in Luke all mixed together.

In the New Testament, Satan the tempter is recast as the Evil One, the merciless host of hell where the souls of the damned burn for eternity if they do not repent and accept Jesus Christ as their savior. However, Jesus never claimed to be able to save man from original sin. The doctrine of vicarious atonement was the invention of St. Paul.

It was not until the thirteenth century that the name of the Devil came into common use. The name derives from the Greek world "diabolos," meaning slanderer, which was adopted when the Old Testament was translated from Aramaic. From "diabolos" came the Old English word "deofol," which eventually became "devil."

The idea of the Devil became popular in those days because the Church needed him badly. In the Dark Ages, and even today in some devout religious sects, the threat of eternal torment was sufficient to keep the faithful on the straight and narrow. It also ensured that the Church never lacked for donations.

The early Christians faced a fierce fight on two fronts as they struggled to establish their new order. As an essentially pacifist movement, they rejected violence as a means of overthrowing their Roman oppressors. Instead, they used persuasion as a tool for converting unbelievers and putting an end to persecution. But the message of brotherly love was not likely to soften the hearts of the Roman emperors, who believed themselves to be gods incarnate. It also was unlikely to convince ordinary Roman citizens to abandon their faith in the pantheon of gods that they had been worshipping for generations. The promise of eternal life in paradise and the blessings of a benign being were not a sufficiently attractive incentive for the materialistic populace, so the Christian leaders invoked a new deity – the Devil. He was designed to frighten followers of the "old religions" into adopting an itinerant Jewish mystic as their messiah – once they had abandoned their pagan practices, of course. As a recruiting tool, the Devil had no equal. Fear, not love, drove legions of converts into the open arms of the Church. It was a crude, but highly effective, form of propaganda.

Reading between the lines of religious allegory, however, raises the interesting possibility that some of the compilers of the Christian gospels might have been familiar with the older Jewish concept of Satan as a symbol of our darker side and therefore did not expect their references to Satan to be taken literally. Several of Jesus' disciples, such as Paul (born Saul of Tarsus), were Jews and were likely familiar with the older teachings. If this was true, it could explain the references to Satan as "the prince of this world" and "the lord of this word" in the Book of John and in the Second Book of Corinthians. The Gospels seem to have been alluding to man rather than to his supernatural adversary. A closer scrutiny of the Gospels produces suspiciously few allusions to the existence of Satan and these references are pretty ambiguous. Matthew, for example, mentions him only as the "prince of demons" and "the tempter."

But perhaps the most revealing reference in the Gospels is found in the words of Jesus, which were recorded in both Mark and Matthew, when he addressed Peter by that name. "He rebuked Peter saying, 'Get thee behind me Satan, for thou savorest not the things that be of God, but the things that be of men.'" The meaning is clear. Peter is being admonished for his doubts by being called an adversary. And when Jesus is offered the world by Satan in Matthew, it is his own fallible human nature that is tempting him to renounce the self-discipline of the spiritual path at the moment of crisis, not a supernatural villain.

But the bulk of the Bible's satanic lore comes from the allegorical Book of Revelation, a bizarre, hallucinogenic trip taken by a religious visionary, in which Satan appears as a shape-shifter who can turn into a serpent or a dragon at will. But in the final apocalyptic battle, he is known as Apollyon, and is demoted to a mere functionary that St. John predicts will be cast into a lake of fire with the other defeated enemies of the Lord.

Obviously, the New Testament is as inconsistent about the true nature of Satan as its predecessor was. Things were so confusing that the Church fathers were forced to acknowledge the problem. In 563 A.D., eight bishops took part in the Council of Braga, during which they defined Satan's role as if they were creating a fictional character in a play – which is, more or less, what many have since accused them of doing. They decided that Satan was not an equal to God, but a disgraced subordinate that had no part in the creation of the universe, forever reversing the beliefs of dualistic religions which long believed in two gods, one good and one evil.

ANCIENT EVIL

Throughout history, other cultures have had their own versions of the Devil, or at least the evil spirits who provided a dark side to a wise and magnanimous god. Every faith, culture and religion has a light side-- the side of good-- and because of this, nature demands that it be balanced with a dark side. Since the earliest history of man, our ancestors scurried for safety when darkness descended on the land. It was a matter of survival, which is our most fundamental impulse. Spiritual needs were not of great importance to early man. Reflection, contemplation and introspection came much later, with the gradual awakening of self-awareness and a curiosity about the meaning of life. In the beginning, our ancestors did not pause to admire the sunset as darkness fell across the land; they hurried to find a place to hide, stopping only to find a weapon with which to arm themselves against what might be lurking in the shadows.

Even after the founding of the first great civilizations in Sumeria and Egypt around 4,000 B.C., man's first instinct was not to worship a creator but rather to appease the dark gods of death and destruction. The ancient world was a harsh and hostile place. Daily life was an ongoing battle against the whims of nature, not to mention the threat posed by predators, disease and mortal enemies. They knew pain and death very well and the dark, cruel gods held dominion over all.

It comes as no surprise that humanity's fears found expression in legends about mysterious beings that fought amongst themselves in the skies and under the surface of the Earth. These beings created storms, floods, famine, earthquakes and all manner of natural disasters. In their effort to explain the mystery of death, which was often violent and random, a belief formed in the immortality of the soul and an afterlife in which the good were rewarded and evil was punished. This nether world of souls and spirits varied from civilization to civilization and yet all of the cultures, produced strikingly similar accounts of what could be found beyond this world – and the dark beings that often lurked there.

One of the earliest records of such a figure was found in the Caverne des Trois-Frères in France. The cave painting dates back to prehistoric times and shows a man in animal skins with a headdress of antlers. Some have suggested that the figure represents the Horned God of a fertility cult that survived in Europe until the Middle Ages and may have been the origin of the Greek god, Pan. Others have proposed that it was from this source that the Christian Devil acquired his hooves, horns and tail.

The Horned God of the pagans of Europe had its counterpart in the Sumerian deity of Marduk, who was neither good nor evil, but who allowed evil to exist in his guise as the god Bel, whose name means "Lord." In time, the two deities became one, Bel-Marduk, and this new being demanded human sacrifice. With the decline of the Sumerian empire, the people of Babylonia and Assyria degenerated into idol worship and their ritual magic became corrupted and selfish. The cultural achievements of the early empire, which included astronomy, astrology and architecture, were abandoned in favor of blood sacrifice, superstition and murder.

Anthropologist Ivar Lissner dates the earliest appearance of black magic to this era. The Sumerians had come up with the idea that if they could lure animals to death by magic, they might be able to defeat their human enemies by disfiguring their likenesses. Bizarrely, at this same state of human evolution, people all around the world suddenly stopped making images in human form – all except for the practitioners of what we now refer to as the Black Arts.

The scriptures of Islam have their own version of the Devil – "Shaitan," which roughly translates as "enemy" and can refer to either a man or a spirit. In the Koran's re-telling of the Creation story, the Devil is named Iblis. He was a fallen angel who was punished by Allah for refusing to bow to Adam and to acknowledge his divinity. Iblis considered man his inferior because man was fashioned from mud, while angels were born of fire. The exiled Iblis was given the name Shaitan, and was allowed to roam the Earth to test the moral fiber of the faithful.

In addition to their own Jesus-like figure (Osiris), the ancient Egyptians also had their own version of Satan. They called him Set, and he was one of the earliest embodiments of evil to appear in the world. Set was the personification of the arid desert, a cursed place that was naturally dreaded by a people who depended on the Nile for their lives. Originally, Set seems to have been the Lord of Upper Egypt and the evil side of his character was never accentuated. Paintings exist that show the heads of Horus (the god who ruled the living) and Set growing out of the same body, embodying light and darkness, life and death, good and evil. According to text found in the pyramids, Horus banished Set to the desert in the same way that Lucifer was banished from Heaven. Later, as Osiris gained prominence in Egyptian religion, Set was made his eternal enemy. Osiris, the son of Horus, became the personification of physical and moral good while Set became the personification of evil.

Set became the enemy of both gods and men. He is purportedly the originator of the sin of fratricide. This crime – the killing of one's

The Egyptian God, Set

brother – appears in both Egyptian and Hebrew tradition. Driven by envy and malice, Set killed his brother Osiris. Having organized a conspiracy of 72 accomplices, he invited his brother to a feast during which he had a wooden chest brought in. The chest, he stated, would belong to anyone who could fit into it exactly. Osiris promptly climbed in. As soon as he was inside, Set and his companions locked the chest and tossed it into the Nile. When Isis, the sister-wife of Osiris, heard of the cruel murder, she wept and mourned. But Set was not yet satisfied. Isis succeeded in finding the corpse of Osiris, but Set cut the body into 14 pieces and scattered them throughout the land. The rest of the story – the retrieval of the body and the revenge carried out by Horus and Isis --- is not part of this tale. Instead, we should focus on the pattern of fratricide that Set established that came to be followed by others, notably in the Biblical story of the murder of Abel by his brother, Cain.

Set is portrayed as the god of darkness, the sworn enemy of the gods of light. He is represented as having "the features of a fantastic beast with a thin, curved snout, straight, square-cut ears and a stiff forked tail." This last may have also influenced later depictions of Satan as a demon with a forked tail.

The Hindu triumvirate of gods is comprised of Brahma the Absolute, Vishnu and Shiva. Brahma is the creator of the universe and Vishnu is its preserver, but Shiva's role is to destroy the universe in order that it can be re-created, this time without all of its imperfections. Shiva is sometimes represented as having both male and female aspects. Alternatively, he has a consort, the Mother Goddess, who can take on many forms. One of them is Kali, the multi-armed goddess of death. She is traditionally depicted as naked and dripping with blood, wearing a necklace of skulls and armed with a sword, a trident, a severed head and a cup made from a skull that catches the blood that drips from the severed head. Her role, powers and significance varied among the different sects of Hinduism. For the Shaktas, she was to be worshipped with rituals involving sex orgies, while the Thugees venerated her through ritual murder by strangulation. But while all of the Hindu gods were simply aspects of Brahma, Kali was the closest thing in their belief system to a devil-like figure.

At some point after the old Babylonian period, the Middle East produced a prophet named Zoroaster (Zarathustra) who founded a long-lasting religion adopted by virtually the entire region, stretching up into southern Russia and the eastern Balkans and eastward as far as India. The faith persisted until the Muslim invasions of the seventh century, which were followed by severe persecutions. It still survives today in India, especially in Mumbai, and, until recently, in Iran.

The art of writing had been lost to the region by the time of Zoroaster and was religiously forbidden for many centuries afterward, so we know practically nothing about him, not even when he lived. Modern scholars speculate that he was raised among Bronze Age nomads in the southern mountains of Russia, perhaps as long as 1,000 years before Christ. The Avestra, the sacred book of Zoroaster, was not written down until the fifth century A.D., and then it was scripted in an invented sacred language that was never used again. For these reasons, it's safe to say that what we know of this faith may not be exactly what Zoroaster had in mind when he founded it. This is probably true of all religions, even if their sacred books were allegedly dictated by God. What we do know is that the word "magician" derives from Magi, the name of the Persian priests of Zoroastrianism, who were said to be skilled in the interpretation of dreams and astrology. Interestingly, the Magi made an appearance in the New Testament, when three of them brought symbolic gifts to the infant Jesus.

In many ways, Zoroastrianism had an enormous influence, directly and indirectly, on Christianity. It was based on the early Vedic faith, from which Hinduism and Buddhism also developed. Instead of relying on a pantheon of gods, Zoroaster taught a dualistic religion: The divine force of good, Ohrmazd (Wise Lord), who lived above with his angels, is pitted against Ahriman (Evil Spirit), the Lord of Lies, who dwells in the darkness of Hell beneath the Earth's crust, sending out his demons to torment the world. Among those demons was Pazazu (which will be familiar to fans of *The Exorcist* as the demon encountered by Father Merrin), who would display many of the characteristics of later Christian demons.

Law, order, and light were opposed to darkness, filth and death. It was a scenario that would play itself out in countless religions throughout history.

The many tribes of northwestern Europe fell into three general groupings: the Celts or Gauls, the Germans or Teutons, and the Scandinavians, which were known as the Vikings or Norsemen. These were Roman classifications, which meant nothing to the tribes of nomadic warriors, farmers and seamen who were categorized, but the names have largely remained over the centuries. Generally speaking, the Celts were west of the Rhine; Germania was the area between the Rhine and the Danube, reaching east and north to include Denmark, southern Norway and Sweden, and the Vikings were farther north. Because the Vikings were the last group to be converted to Christianity, we know more about their religious beliefs than the others, but those of the Germans and Celts were similar, although with local variations.

By the mandate of Pope Gregory, Christian missionary monks were sent north and west from Rome to combat the beliefs of all of those they encountered. Thus "Hel" was originally the name of the Scandinavian death goddess, and the word came to refer also to her realm, just as Hades meant both the god and the place to the Greeks. Helia was Hel's name in Germania.

A Viking warrior bows before the Viking Goddess Hel

The Viking Hell was also called Niflheim. It was thought to be the northernmost land beneath the roots of Yggdrasil, the World Tree. To the east was Jotunheim, the land of giants, and to the south, across the great void Ginnungagap, was Muspell, a fiery region ruled by the giant Surt. Midgard, or Middle Earth, was our own world. Niflheim was the lowest point of Hell and was a place of utter darkness and stagnation. Niflheim was cold, dark, dreary and full of shadows, but it was not a place of punishment. Nastrond, on the other hand, a hall with a roof formed by venomous snakes, was a place of after-death torment, although probably for enemies rather than for sinners. Contrasted with these unpleasant places was Valhalla, Odin's banquet hall, where Valkyrie maidens escorted the souls of brave warriors to enjoy huge feasts where there was an endless supply of mead and a chance to battle one another forever.

The goddess Hel was the daughter of Loki, an elusive figure who has been compared to both Satan and Prometheus. Like Prometheus, Loki is not exactly a god but is represented as a giant. He is not entirely wicked, either; Christians are thought to have blackened his reputation. Originally, he was just a trickster and a thief, but he went on to cause the death of Balder, a Norse god whose name has been interpreted to mean "the good." Like Satan, Loki was bound after his crime and was to remain so until the Last Days, when he was to unleash the fury of Ragnarok, the final battle of gods and giants.

Celtic mythology is far from clear, but it seems to have been largely positive and to have included reincarnation. The Romans once stated that the Celts were so reckless in battle because they were not afraid to die. One of their underworld gods was called Donn, but little information about him survives today. There is also little knowledge available about a trio of enigmatic Germanic underworld goddesses called "the Mothers," whom Goethe would later use in his own writings about Hell.

The other worlds of most cultures are far away or inaccessible, but the Celts and Germans believed in a parallel world of earth spirits that were more or less a part of our own. Many tales survive of encounters with giants, trolls, elves, dwarves, goblins, fairies, pixies, leprechauns, werewolves and vampires. These creatures managed to survive Christianity. To a degree, many of them became Christian demons, which was a common way for the Church to dispose of the old beliefs of the people they converted to the faith.

The mythology of Satan as the evil counterpoint to all that is good continued to develop during the early days of the Christian era and in the centuries that followed. But much of this development came in conjunction with the development of the place over which Satan would have absolute dominion – Hell.

THE HISTORY OF HELL

There is perhaps no single place that is as dreaded and feared as much as Hell. It is in this place of pain and torment where the Devil and his fallen angels – now demons – hold captive those souls who died in sin and were denied entry into Heaven after death. It is Hell – also known as Hades, the Underworld and other names – that has most shaped the image of the Devil that we know today.

Hell was around for a long time before the early Christians got ahold of it and made it their own, so to speak. The first accounts of the underworld of the dead were written about 4,000 years ago on clay tablets in the Tigris-Euphrates Valley north of the Persian Gulf in Iraq. It is an area that came to be called Sumeria. After it was conquered by the Semitic Akkadians, it became Babylonia, named for is principal city of Babylon. The Sumerians, Akkadians, Babylonians and the neighboring Assyrians have been frequently grouped as Mesopotamians and shared many of the same beliefs and myths as the Greeks and Romans did later on.

These very early stories of gods and heroes were extraordinarily pervasive in later religious thought, myth and literature. Many of the elements of the underworld first appeared in these original writings, including a mountain barrier leading to the land of the dead, a river, a boat piloted by a boatman, a bridge, and gates and guardians. These elements from the Greek and Roman tales were already present in Mesopotamian mythology. Four Mesopotamian stories, including *Gilgamesh*, that still exist today, were set partly in the underworld. The dead spirits in these early stories lead a grim, bleak, and completely unhappy experience. As far as the Mesopotamians were concerned, the underworld was a dark and frightening place.

Another ancient region to leave a record of the world beyond the grave was Egypt. Some Egyptian hieroglyphic writings date back more than 4,000 years and the ritual spells and incantations recorded in the earliest papyruses that made up the *Book of the Dead* may have already been in use for centuries before they were written down. Unlike the Middle East, which seems always to have been

The god Anubis, waiting with the Scales of Justice in the afterlife

embroiled in wars and clashing religious beliefs, Egypt had relative peace and prosperity throughout most of its history. As we know from the splendid tombs of the pharaohs, the carefully prepared mummies, the abundance of burial goods, and from the illustrated papyrus rolls, which contain protective survival spells to ensure a safe trip to the next world, the Egyptians were deeply concerned about the afterlife.

To reach the afterlife, the dead person's *ka*, or vital life-force, and their *ba*, or soul, would embark in the boat of Ra (the sun), which traverses the river of the sky during the day to arrive at the West at night with its cargo of the newly dead. After disembarking, the dead must go through seven gates, each with a Gatekeeper, Watcher and Herald, who names had to be invoked after consulting the Book of the Dead. After that, they had to pass through the many portals of the house of Osiris before the doors would be opened to let them pass.

Anubis then escorted them to the Hall of Justice. Anubis was usually characterized as the "jackal-headed" god, but in truth, he was meant to be an Egyptian hound. A jackal has sinister connotations, especially when linked with corpses, but Anubis was meant to be the faithful dog that was to guide the dead to the other side.

Much less agreeable was the horrible monster, Ammit, who squatted below the Scales of Justice, where the dead were given the chance to plead for their former and continuing existence. Thoth, the god of Wisdom, acted as prosecutor while Osiris, the Judge, sat on a throne attended by the goddesses Isis and Nephthys. No matter how long or how eloquently the dead might speak, Anubis would eventually place the heart of the dead on the scale to weigh it against a feather from the headdress of Maat, goddess of Truth. If the dead person's heart sank low under its burden of sin, Ammit would gobble it up and that was the end of them.

But if the dead survived this trial and were admitted into the Field of Rushes, their troubles were not yet over. The Book of the Dead contained spells to protect them from crocodiles, snakes, giant beetles, suffocation, decay, turning upside-down and being forced to eat excrement. The aim now was for the dead to transform into a bird -- a golden falcon, a phoenix, a heron or a swallow – a crocodile, a snake, or even a farmer, tasked with providing sustenance for the underworld.

According to the beliefs of Zoroastrianism, a dead person's soul first hovers around the head of the corpse for three days and then it is judged by Rashnu, the angel of justice, and Mithra – who, in Hellenistic times, started a new career as a god of soldiers. All of the dead man's good deeds were entered into a great ledger as credits and all wicked actions as debits. At the foot of the bridge to the underworld, a reckoning is made. If a man is deemed to be good, a beautiful maiden accompanied by two guardian dogs escorts his soul across the bridge into the House of Song. If he is found lacking, the soul falls into Hell, which is ruled over by Yima, the first man to die. If the balance is even, the soul passes into a kind of limbo, quite similar to the old Babylonian underworld, where it will stay until the apocalypse.

Eventually, there will be a cosmic final battle between good and evil and, according to Zoroaster, evil will be conquered forever. A savior named Soshyans, born of a virgin impregnated with the seed of Zoroaster, will open the doors to Hell, sinners will be forgiven and there will be a universal resurrection of the body, which will reunite with the soul. Hell will be destroyed and the kingdom of God will begin on earth.

As any reader familiar with the Christian faith can see, many of the ancient Zoroastrian ideas had extraordinary staying power. Orthodox Christianity's debt to them is never formally acknowledged, though by bringing the Magi into the Christmas nativity story and putting a new star in the east. Matthew, by far the most mystical of the four Gospel writers, seems to have wanted to make sure his Messiah was firmly linked to the resurrection and immortality promised by Zoroastrianism. In addition, some scholars say, he sent the infant Jesus off to Egypt to imply his connection with ancient wisdom.

For more than 1,000 years before the fifth century A.D., when the whole world changed, the religion of Greece and Rome, with its array of gods on Mount Olympus, was what shaped our vision of the "classical" world of the Mediterranean peoples. This was the religion that decent people believed in; anything else was considered exotic, barbaric or radical. The Greeks fought the Persians and the very idea that the Zoroastrian religion would ultimately have more effect than their own upon the Mediterranean world would have struck them as irrational. That the peculiar customs of the Jews would have even more influence would have seemed even more ridiculous.

The Greek writers whose names and works still exist today wrote poetry, plays, history and philosophy. They did not, as was the custom of the time, spend their days dutifully transcribing sacred writings. They saw no harm in presenting their own ideas and opinions and tales spun from their imaginations. It was a new kind of writing and a departure from the orthodox nature of the written word up until that time. Thanks to this, the gods of Greece were a different sort of creature than had been seen before. There was no separation of good and evil in the Greek pantheon of gods. Each Greek god was capable of both righteous and vindictively destructive behavior.

By tradition, Homer and Hesiod, whose poems were first written down in the new alphabet borrowed and adapted from the Phoenicians, lived in the eighth century A.D. Hesiod is less read than Homer today, but his *Theogony*, which relates Greek creation myths and legendary history and lists the gods and minor deities, became the essential foundation for a huge body of literature.

Homer's *Odyssey* is the earliest well-known story of a visit to the land of the dead. It is so well known that most people forget that it never happened. Odysseus and his shipmates, who are told by the witch Circe that they must go to the underworld, never actually get there, though Odysseus does manage to see many of the famous sites of Hades.

The underworld was the source of several of the Greek cults of the period, including one that surrounded Persephone, the "Bringer of Destruction." The story of her abduction became the basis for the Eleusinian mysteries, an important religious faith of the ancient Greek world. In the story, a young girl gathering flowers is seized by Hades, the master of the underworld, and she is taken below, where she becomes Hades' bride. Persephone refuses to eat or drink, knowing that if she does, she can never return to the world of the living. Meanwhile, her mother, Demeter, the goddess of the harvest, neglects the crops as she wanders the world in mourning for her lost daughter. When at last Persephone is found, she turns out to have eaten some pomegranate seeds, and thus must spend part of each year in the underworld. The rest of the time, she stays with her mother, who rejoices by making the flowers bloom and the crops grow. This is a fertility myth, and long after worship of other Olympians became perfunctory, men and women went through the Eleusinian initiation rites, which are thought to have featured a ritualistic symbolic journey to the netherworld – in imitation of Demeter – ending in triumph with spring and rebirth.

Classical Hades and its inhabitants have left an enduring mark on history. The few mortals to enter this shadowy place traveled there by way of the Taenarus cave. The dead emerged at least once by another cave on an island in Persephone's magic grove. The newly dead souls are guided by the god Hermes to the River Styx to meet Charon the boatman, who had to be paid to ferry the dead across the river.

The Titans were chained in lower Tartarus, except for Tityus. For his crime of attacking Leto, the mother of Apollo and Artemis, he is tied down over nine acres of Hades while vultures eat his liver. Because he tried to trick the guardians into letting him out of Hades, Sisyphus is condemned to forever roll a rock up a steep hill, even though it always rolls back down before it reaches the top. Next to him is Ixion, bound to a burning wheel for attempting to rape Hera, Queen of Olympus. Nearby is Tantalus, who served up his own son to the gods in a stew. He now hangs from a tree over a lake, tormented by hunger and thirst, but unable to reach either the water in the lake or the fruit on the tree. Trying vainly to draw water from the lake in leaking containers are the Danaides, sisters who murdered their husbands with hairpins.

Monsters and demons live in Hades: the snake-haired Medusa; the Alastor, which like the Christian Devil, tempts men toward evil or folly and then punishes them for it; the Furies, spirits of vengeance; the Keres, frightening winged death spirits, one for each living soul; Lamia, a vampire-like creature, and others.

Charon the boatman, crossing the River Styx into Hades

But punishment for wrongdoing in the old Greek stories was not generally an after-death affair, except in the cases of crimes against the gods themselves. It has been suggested that the early Greeks, unlike the Egyptians and the Zoroastrians, had no after-death accounting for their sins simply because classical Greece never developed a centralized judicial system. But all that began to chance in the fifth century B.C., when the Greeks began adopting some of the Persian and Egyptian ideas and turning the afterlife into a place where evil-doers endured "toil which is terrible to behold."

Thanks to traveling merchants, mercenaries and armies that pushed the Persians back to the Middle East, Greek culture became the dominant force in the Mediterranean region from at least the fifth century, B.C. Their only real rival was the old and static civilization of Egypt. But when Alexander the Great set out to conquer the world in the fourth century, Greeks quickly formed a network of cities and Greek civilization stretched from India to Spain. Their power was only eclipsed by the Romans who, while battling barbarians through Gaul to the northwest all of the way to Britain, brought the civilization of their empire with them.

But carrying culture always worked both ways. Soldiers married native girls and took them home after leaving the army, bringing practices from the native culture with them. The upper class of a far-off city aspired to the Hellenic ways of their conquerors, while the local peasants taught native traditions to the newly arrived soldiers. Slaves from Asia, Africa, Scandinavia and the Slavic countries brought more strange customs with them. Never before the in the history of the world, and never again until the twentieth century, was there such an astonishing cross-fertilization of languages, cultures, customs and beliefs. The old religions were assaulted by new gods, rituals and faiths.

Romans, although faithful to their gods, were not much for myth-making. Their native religion was a form of animism: groves, streams and even individual trees had their own gods, and so did households and courtyards and each aspect of daily life. Each man had his own *genius* and each woman her *juno*, a concept that passed into traditional Christianity as that of a guardian angel. For the more important gods, of the sky, sun, moon, sea and harvest and the concepts of love, war, marriage, wisdom and so forth, they adopted the Greek myths wholesale, giving them new names for their own stories.

Roman soldiers in foreign lands did the same thing with local shrines. A statue of a maiden thus marked the shrine as that of Diana, no matter who the resident Gauls had in mind, and she would be honored accordingly. The practice worked well. Since the armies displayed respect and piety, they managed to avoid religious conflict with the locals. Even in the later empire, the Roman attitude remained the same. It would be the controversial Christians who violated that code, refusing to concede unto Caesar what was by that time his divinity. Their behavior was, by Roman standards, disrespectful and disorderly.

The widespread Roman mystery cults heavily influenced early Christianity. For example, the Seven Deadly Sins, which Christians appropriated in their own views of Hell, were formed by a worship of Mithra, which looked back at the Zoroastrian mysticism connected to the number seven. As the dead soul journeyed to the underworld, it passed through seven heavenly spheres, shedding in each one the appropriate vice: the Sun – Pride, the Moon – Envy, Mars – Anger, Mercury – Greed, Jupiter – Ambition, Venus – Lust, Saturn – Sloth. Mithra's worshippers referred to him as "the Good Shepherd" and "the Son of God." He was born of a virgin on December 25, which the Christians also appropriated, along with a persistent interest in astrology and numerology.

The poets of Rome embellished the older Greek stories and contributed a few of their own additions to the mythology of the underworld. The changed a few names, but overall, it was still the Hades envisioned by the Greeks. Virgil, the poet who wrote *The Aeneid*, used Homer as his model for the underworld and his epic undoubtedly contains one of the best descriptions of the Land of the Dead from the era.

Virgil's description of Hell had a great impact on later writers, especially Dante, who used him as a guide into the depths of the underworld in his epic poem.

The hero of the story is Aeneas, a Trojan who fought in the war. Like Odysseus, he is on a journey, but his is to find a new home, since Troy has been destroyed. He goes to the underworld to seek advice from his dead father. Virgil sets the scene with macabre effects like howling dogs, noxious fumes, earthquakes and eerie cries. Limbo appears for the first time in this epic, a place where some souls have to wait for 100 years, or until they have been properly buried, before continuing their journey. Aeneas encounters scores of ghosts, fiery rivers and clanking chains to which the sinful have been linked in punishment for their wrongdoings.

Virgil presented the first thoroughly graphic description of Hell, and one of the best. His impact was enormous, not only on later poets and storytellers like Dante, who would evoke him as a guide and mentor, but on the men who hammered together the early guidelines of Christianity, especially St. Augustine, who quoted him frequently.

But it would be during the time of the early Christian church that Hell would truly come into its own. Those early writers, leaders and missionaries would use the words of Jesus – whether he really said them or not --- to paint a vivid and terrifying portrait of the underworld that would finally be realized as a masterpiece in the hands of Dante during the Middle Ages. But the "creation" of the Christian Hell would come about in an odd and perhaps questionable way.

Saul of Tarsus, the Jewish persecutor of early Christians who converted and became one of the first and most important Christian missionaries to the Roman world, became the first writer of Christian thought. Paul, as he renamed himself, never actually met Jesus, but his letters in the New Testament of the Bible predate the composition of the earliest Gospel, written by Mark, and were written more than 20 years before Luke wrote the Acts of the Apostles, about the founding of the church.

The Christian doctrine of Hell did not originate with Paul. However, he did put together lists of those who would not make it into Heaven. They included unrepentant fornicators, idolaters, adulterers, homosexuals, thieves, drunkards, slanderers, swindlers, sorcerers, the envious, the quarrelsome, the indecent and the greedy. Instead of condemning these wrongdoers to Hell, he taught that the "wages of sin is death," and this is what he meant by "destruction." The good would live, the sinners would die. Death could be avoided through God's grace. Other disciples, like Peter and Jude, also warned of after-death punishments in their writings, though not of flames.

Mark, who first told stories of Jesus in a continuous form, probably didn't know Jesus either, but he may have known Peter. Mark does speak of "eternal damnation" for anyone who slanders the Holy Spirit, but he only made one brief mention of Hell in his writings.

Paul's traveling companion, Luke, an educated man said to be a doctor, based his own Gospel on Mark's and left out the passage that Mark wrote about Hell in chapter nine. Luke's Jesus urges repentance in order to achieve the kingdom of God, rather than to avoid retribution. He does, however, tell the significant story of the rich man and the beggar, which will be related later. And, whether or not the Gospel according to John was written by the same John who was Jesus' disciple, it nowhere mentions Hell. The Book of Revelation, once erroneously credited to John, is something else entirely.

This leaves us with Matthew. Matthew's Gospel relies heavily on the one written by Mark, but when it comes to the subject of Hell, it goes off the rails and it is on this book that much of the Christian proof of Hell's existence – and what's waiting for sinners there – depends. What makes Matthew's book different than the other Gospels is the way that he tacked dire warnings onto the parables that Mark attributed to Jesus. That this was his own idea is clear when his writings are compared to the same stories that appear in the Gospel of Luke. In Luke's book, he relates the same incidents, but without the warnings.

Matthew's Jesus always takes the time to drive home two points: that salvation is possibly only through God, represented by his son, and that not to be saved is desperately perilous. When he tells the parable of the wheat and the chaff, he adds that at the end of the world, "The Son of man shall send forth his angels, and they shall gather out of his kingdom all things that offend, and them which do iniquity: And shall cast them into the furnace of fire: there shall be wailing and gnashing of teeth." Matthew particularly likes this graphic image. When Jesus talks about good men who, like good fish, can be caught in nets, he mentions that the worthless ones will be tossed "into the furnace of fire: there shall be wailing and gnashing of teeth." He keeps this one going on the Mount of Olives, where Jesus talks of the Last Days and then relates a string of parables – the wise servant, the wise and foolish virgins, the ten talents, the sheep and the goats – all of which have the same theme: that the deserving will gain eternal life. Of course, we know what happens to the rest – they are cast "into the outer darkness: there shall be weeping and gnashing of teeth." They are also in store for the "everlasting fire that is prepared for the Devil and his angels."

The Gospel of Luke told the story of a beggar named Lazarus who went to heaven, while a rich man suffered in Hell.

Only Matthew stresses these dire warnings. Mark and Luke do well without them and Paul, who also relied on Luke's Gospel, would not likely have approved. Curiously, though, the essentially incontrovertible evidence that the early Christians believed that Hell existed as a place for after-death punishment for evil-doers comes not from the grim pen of Matthew, but from the Gospel of Luke. Mark had told the story of a rich man who came to Jesus to ask about the secret of eternal life and was dismayed to find that it hinged on giving everything away to the poor, which prompted Jesus to offer the analogy of a camel passing through the eye of a needle being easier than a rich man getting into Heaven. But Luke expanded on Jesus' insistence that the rich were socially responsible for the less fortunate with a number of parables and cautionary examples on the subject of wealth and property. The most colorful, for our purposes here, was the story of the rich man and the beggar named Lazarus.

The rich man had a fine house, lavish clothes and he ate well each day. At his gate was a beggar named Lazarus, whose sores were licked by dogs as they all waited in vain each day for the rich man's table scraps. Lazarus died and was carried away by the angels to Heaven, where he was greeted by Abraham. The rich man died a short time later, but he ended up in Hell. Looking up from the flames, he begged Abraham to send Lazarus with a drop of water to cool his tongue, but Abraham reminded him that he had already had "thy good things." Also, there was a "great gulf fixed," so that the trip was impossible. The rich man begged to be able to warn his five brothers of the fate that awaited them if they continued the sort of selfish life he had lived, but Abraham refused, telling him that since they didn't heed to words of the prophets then they wouldn't be persuaded by their brother.

The parables of Jesus in all of the Gospels are filled with metaphoric allusion, but Luke's later audience chose to take this particular fable quite literally. For whatever reason, this story chilled more hearts than Matthew's spooky references to places of "weeping and gnashing of teeth."

In addition to the obvious moral of the story, the tale also illustrated the claim that part of the payoff for the religiously saved was to be able to contemplate the torments of the damned. The early Church taught that this view proved God's justice and the hatred of sin and other passages in Revelation and Isaiah seemed to agree, telling of the wicked being tormented in the presence of the Lamb and the angels, and the faithful smugly looking down on the carcasses of transgressors. Watching the wicked burn in Hell was supposed to be some sort of "prize" for those who lived a good life. Not surprisingly, modern mainstream churches removed this grim "bonus" from the table, but centuries of religious artwork embraced the idea.

Artists were also fond of representing the wild, even insane, ideas presented by the Book of Revelation, a hallucinogenic trip that barely made it into the New Testament at all. It only did so because of a mistake in attribution. Its author is now usually called John of Patmos to distinguish him from the John of the Gospels. The apocalyptic work was thought to have been written in the latter part of the first century as a protest against Roman rule and particularly against the imperial cult of emperor worship. Domitian, the Roman emperor of the day, was a cruel and dangerous man who insisted on always being addressed as *dominus et deus*, "master and god."

Without a doubt, the prophetic visions of Revelation seem stranger to us now than they did at the time, since the writing form looked back to traditional Jewish apocalyptic literature like Daniel and Ezekiel, also written in response to imposed tyranny. The dramatic conflict presented is between the powers of good and evil, with evil being represented by the Roman Empire symbolized by a great, red, seven-headed dragon. The scene is the end of the world, following scorched earth, the poisoning of the water supply, volcanic eruptions, earthquakes, plagues, and the slaughter of two-thirds of mankind. Seven angels have blown their trumpets and God's "temple in heaven" is laid open, amid thunder, more earthquakes and a hailstorm.

A pregnant woman, "clothed by the sun," appears and the red dragon tries to devour her son as she gives birth but instead, he is snatched up by God. Michael and his angels attack "that old serpent called the Devil and Satan, which deceiveth the whole world: he was cast out into the earth, and his angels were cast out with him." The dragon transfers its power to the grotesque "beast" rising from the sea, which is blasphemously worshipped by men. Further calamities hit the Earth, until the Great Whore of Babylon (which represents Israel's ancient enemy of Babylon, just as the dragon represents its current enemy, Rome) is overthrown and Heaven opens up.

The great war of the Book of Revelation

In Chapter 20, Revelation reads:

Then I saw an angel coming down from heaven with the key of the abyss and a great chain in his hands. He seized the dragon, that serpent of old, the Devil or Satan, and chained him up for a thousand years; he threw him into the abyss, shutting and sealing it over him, so that he might seduce the nations no more till the thousand years was over. After that he must be let loose for a short while.

When Satan is eventually released, he will come out to muster the forces of "Gog and Magog, countless as the sands of the sea." Fire from Heaven will consume them, and the Devil will be flung into the lake of fire and sulphur, together with a "false prophet" to be tormented forever. At Judgment Day, the sea gives up its dead, and so do Death and Hades. They will be judged according to their deeds in life. Death and Hades are flung into the lake of fire, which represents the "second death," and so are those who are judged unworthy.

And there it was, all written down in the Bible, the appalling Hell that man had envisioned and a portent of things to come at the "end of times." Revelation became the book of choice for the radical Christian fringe, the millenarians, revivalists, mystics and visionaries who used it for their own purposes for the next 2,000 years. Christianity would have had a much easier time without Revelation, but it would have been a lot less colorful religion.

Jesus tempted by Satan

What Revelation achieved with regard to Satan – despite or because of the confusion and incoherence of its text – was to offer plenty of room for interpretation of a number of allusions and legends, leading to a new mythology for Satan.

Satan had gone from meaning "adversary" in Old Hebrew to achieving autonomy as "prince of his world" by the time the Gospels were written in the first century. It was in the Gospels that his character was most fully formed when he tempted Judas into betraying Jesus to the authorities, and most notably when he lures Jesus into the wilderness to test his mettle – although many would argue that he acted as an agent of God in that situation. Really, his motives didn't matter. What mattered is that Satan was finally given a real personality and substance as a being that man needed to fear.

According to the story, after he was baptized, Jesus went out into the Judean desert in order to fast and pray for forty days. While he was there, the Devil came to him and tried to tempt him into giving up his public mission to save souls. In the first temptation, Satan came to him after he had not eaten for many days and basically suggested that if Jesus could really perform miracles, he should turn some stones into bread and have something to eat. Of course, Jesus replied with the proverbial, "Man shall not live by bread alone," and refused to allow Satan to take advantage of his human weaknesses. After that, Satan spirited Jesus away to the top of the temple in Jerusalem, where he said that if Jesus was really the Son of God, he should throw himself off. After failing again, Satan took Jesus to the top of a high mountain and showed him all of the kingdoms of the world. Satan said that everything Jesus saw could be his, if only he would bow down and worship him. It was a telling passage for the early Christians. When Jesus refused this final temptation, it put him on the path that would lead to his arrest and crucifixion. He went to his death willingly, dying as a sacrifice for the sins of his followers. But the passage also revealed that Satan was indeed the "prince of the world." From the seas to the mountains, east to west, north to south, all of the kingdoms were his – and he could offer dominion over such things to anyone who agreed to worship him. This belief would play a prominent role when ferreting out those who allegedly made "pacts with Satan" during the Middle Ages.

The Gospels also provided more devilish works for Satan by way of his minions. Jesus' chief recorded activity, aside from preaching, was the exorcism of minor demons. There were many other healers, magicians and exorcists in business at the time; the difference was that Jesus was supposed to be operating through the power of God. The word *demon* comes from the Greek *daimon* and it came to be identified with *diabolos*, a word which, in the New Testament, refers only to Satan himself. By the first century, there was some indication among Jews that ordinary, trouble- and disease-making demons were subordinate to an arch-demon. Inevitably, as the mythology of Satan grew, pagan gods were added to his roster of lieutenants. One man's god is always another man's devil.

But, as mentioned, it was Revelation that gave the Devil an even bigger name, so to speak. The fallen angel was identified with the red dragon thrown down from Heaven with his angels – "one third of the stars in the sky" – who were now identified as demons. The dragon was linked to a beast like the fearsome and supernatural beasts of the Hebrew Bible: the Leviathan, Behemoth and Rahab, the sea-dragon. He was also linked with "that serpent of old" responsible for the banishment of Adam and Eve from Eden. The Gospels had shown Satan to be the tempter of Jesus and Judas, but Revelation displayed him as the tempter and seducer of all mankind, the cause of our subsequent sorrow and even of death itself. By showing Satan in power with "the forces of Gog and Magog," his position as "prince of this world" was further established, at least until his eventual defeat. The story of the final battle between good and evil, already familiar from Zoroastrian writings and from Jewish apocalyptic literature, confirmed the apocalyptic prophecy in Matthew and identified Satan as the adversary of God.

Finally, unbelievers (those who worship the beast), the beast itself, and its "false prophet" (associated with, though not always identical to the Antichrist) are all to be thrown into the lake of fire. After a term of being bound in the abyss, the Devil joins them and so do Death and Hades, pagan figures of death. After judgment, so do the sinners among the dead formerly in their keeping. This is a significant grouping of what had formerly been very disparate figures. By the Middle Ages, the beast, the dragon, Death and Hades all merged into the person of Satan.

Early theologians labored over their difficult "factual" texts, seeking to define the role of the Devil and his relation to God and man. On a simpler story-telling level, it all happened with writings that weren't exactly in the Bible. It began to come together around the fifth century, when St. Augustine began putting all of the pieces into place but it was not until the Middle Ages that that the attributes of Hell and even the name of the Devil became a conventional part of Christianity.

The richest period in the history of Hell and the Devil came in the millennium that followed the fall of Rome, the middle period between the classic world and the one that began with the Renaissance, or the rebirth of the classical approach to learning. All of the foundations of Hell were already in place when Rome fell, but its mythology was vastly elaborated during the Middle Ages.

Medieval theologians continued to refine doctrine made by the Church fathers, but made few advances in their intellectual thoughts about Hell. These theologians, intent on believing that Hell was a literal place, discussed matters that were anything but literal. If these men had been born centuries later, they would have spent their time discussing quantum physics, but in those days, they focused their attention on such things as to whether food consumed during a lifetime would be part of the body at the resurrection. (The answer was yes, by the way) "How many angels can dance on the head of a pin?" is the question theologians are supposed to have pondered, but they counted devils too, and tried to calculate the size of Hell and define where it was – under the earth or somewhere else.

Hell became a theme of books, visions and medieval theater. Theatrical shows called "mystery plays" were used to teach the Bible to churchgoers, but they soon escaped their solemn beginnings. The Hell scenes were enlivened with devilish pratfalls, firecrackers and crude dialogue. The mystery plays became beloved popular theater and when, after many centuries, they were eventually banned, they mutated into forms that still exist today.

Medieval plays were not "literary," but an astonishing amount of literary tradition focused on Hell and much of it was thrillingly attractive. Writers blocked by the frightful picture presented by the Church from the ancient theme of the underworld quest inventively managed to displace Hell with bizarre underworld regions taken from classical and Norse mythology, folklore and poetry, where Hell strangely merged with fairy lands and allegorical knights went adventuring.

This era was also marked by the rise of "vision literature," which became a sort of mass-market genre. In surviving manuscripts that describe more than sixty different visions, someone is taken by a supernatural guide to the infernal regions and then on to Heaven. Though visions were transcribed by the literate clergy, they were often experienced by quite ordinary people, who certainly believed in them. Their modern equivalents might be reports of UFO abduction. It should be remembered that this was an age of obsessive piety, self-imposed fasting and flagellation. There were no antibiotics to treat fevers, and people who became delirious were educated to believe there was a religious message behind any odd sights and sounds they experienced as the result of illness. Some accounts, on the other hand, were undoubtedly concocted by storytellers for the astonishment of the pious and credulous.

Visions and stories of journeys into Hell were made popular by writers like Gregory the Great (later Pope Gregory), who related stories that were recounted to him in his *Dialogues*, which were written about 590 A.D. The Venerable Bede, an English monk whose *Ecclesiastical History of England*, written in 731, was a classic source for later historians, recorded two visions of Hell in his writings. He told of two men who died and whose journeys into Hell were meant to be used as a warning to the unfaithful. Another popular book (hand-lettered and widely circulated) was *The Vision of Tundal*, written by an Irish monk in 1149. Nearly 250 of these manuscripts still survive today. The vivid story and illustrations made it one of the most famous stories of a journey into Hell during the Middle Ages. *The Vision of Alberic* is a story that was thought to have been read by Dante. Alberic of Settefrati was a monk at the famous monastery of Monte Cassino. After an illness that left him in a coma for nine days, he dictated his vision to a fellow monk around 1115 A.D. During this vision of Hell, he was guided by St. Peter and two angels, not to mention a dove that flew off with his soul. He saw many of the standard sights that appeared in other vision writings, including children roasting in flaming gas, a frozen valley, woods filled with thorns, serpents, a fiery ladder, a cauldron of pitch, a sulfurous oven, a lake of blood, a basin of molten metal and a lake and river of fire. Novelties in the story included an enormous chained dragon near the pit that holds Judas, Herod and other terrible sinners and a great bird that first drops the monk into the pit, and then thoughtfully picks him back up again.

Old English was the earliest European language to have a literature of its own and a number of its earliest surviving works refer to Hell and the Devil. *Genesis A* and *Genesis B*, together with *Christ and Satan*, present Lucifer's biography, including the story of his fall and of the angels who fell with him. The account is a familiar one but with more detail and with a distinctly feudal approach. The rebellious Satan raises his own throne in the north of Heaven. God, angry at this challenge to his authority, prepares Hell and flings him down with his followers. All become demons. Satan, still very much the leader, delivers a speech to his followers: not only is God unjust in his condemnation, he is planning something even more unfair: the creation of a usurping pair of contemptible creatures on Earth. Satan is bound in Hell, but a subordinate is conscripted to subvert God's plan, which he does – but not quite in the usual way. Like any proper knight, he approached Adam, the head of the household, first. Rebuffed, he pays court to Eve by flattering her with lies, which, of course, leads to success.

The Middle Ages had a tremendous effect on the hierarchies of both Heaven and Hell. It was a time characterized by feudalism, a form of decentralized government administered by the local lords who owned large areas of farmland and forest. Taxes, legal problems, religious appointments, charitable dispositions, and all of the minutiae of daily life were governed by these lords. At the center of the structure was the lord, the leader of the tribe and the "father" to those who swore to be faithful to him. The great noble families lived in fortified castles and oversaw armies of knights. These men in turn were supported by an even larger number of serfs who performed agricultural duties and manual labor in return for the right to earn a living on the land.

The monasteries of the era employed an almost exact clerical counterpart to the secular feudal system: The abbot played the part of the lord, friars were the knights and foot soldiers and the brothers were the serfs. Just as the abbot owed a greater fealty to the pope, the lord owed formal homage to a king.

For this reason, it's not surprising that the heavenly hierarchy was often portrayed as having its own lord and a prince in the person of Jesus, with his retinue of apostles. The lady of the manor was the Virgin Mary. There was a senior household of saints, and a foremost knight represented by the archangel Michael, who was typically portrayed suited in armor, wielding a sword, and leading angelic troops.

When Lucifer fell, he took his own knights with him. His sin, the betrayal of faith and fealty to the Lord by a highly placed knight, meant a great deal in the Middle Ages. Betrayal was the greatest sin of feudalism. The lowest circle of Dante's Inferno is reserved for the faithless and, apart from Satan himself, the lowest of the faithless is Judas, who betrayed his honor and his own Lord with a terrible parody of the kiss of fealty. The popular term for Muslims or Saracens in those days was "infidels," the unfaithful. They were considered to be worse than Jews or simple heathens who knew no better, for they, too, were "people of the book," the Bible, who had fallen away from the true faith. Christians considered Muslims "servants of Satan," and the Muslims returned the insult.

In stories of deals with the Devil, it is fealty that Satan demands. Pledge yourself to me, he says, and I will give you power, fortune, wealth and all the things that the Christian asks from God or the saints. The kiss of homage, though, was to be administered to the buttocks of the Devil.

The one writer of the Middle Ages who most defined the popular vision of Hell was Dante Alighieri, whose *Divine Comedy* would forever shape the design and engineering of the dark regions. His landscape of Hell has always fascinated readers. Modern editions have included maps and diagrams of Hell, and rich illustrations of wonderful underground embankments, moats, castles, paved trenches, winged creatures and terrifying punishments that awaited the sinner. Writing his great poem in exile, Dante was concerned with a great many issues beside theology, including history, Florentine politics, the corruption of the clergy, the moral position of his contemporaries, and most of all with the state of his own psyche. After seven centuries, we can no longer appreciate any of these things except the last – Dante is generous with his emotions. But anyone reading the

Dante Alighieri

Inferno "just for the story" can still marvel at not only the stories the Pilgrim is told, but also at the sights, sounds and even the smells of the underworld.

Dante took every theme covered in this book – philosophical, mythic, repulsive, fantastic, allegorical, comic and psychological – and put them together with meticulous care. His religious views were conservative and orthodox, but his imagination was unbridled. Even if his artistic contribution had been limited to the radical step of combining the classical attributes of Hades with those of the Christian Hell, it would have been a great achievement. But his influence went far beyond that.

Dante led a complicated life. He was orphaned as a very young boy and was raised by wealthy relatives in the city-state of Florence, where he received an excellent education in both the classics and the poetry of the time. At various times, he worked as a businessman, a soldier, a politician and a professor of philosophy. Because he ran afoul of the tangled politics of the era, he was forced to spend the last twenty years of his life in an unhappy, although not uncomfortable, exile.

The most famous event of Dante's childhood was his encounter with Beatrice Portinari when he was nine and she was a year younger. Theirs was a model of courtly romance, for they seldom met and each married someone else. Dante was so infatuated with Beatrice that he continued to write poetry to her all his life. She died in 1290, a date remembered because Dante set the *Comedy* in 1300, just ten years later. In the poem, she appears as Divine Love or Grace, which inspires and guides the Pilgrim after Human Reason, represented by the poet Virgil, can go no farther. Dante had other reasons for choosing 1300. He was thirty-five at the time, "midway along life's journey." It was a centennial year, and numbers are essential to the scheme of the poem. It was also the year that his political troubles began.

To imagine what Dante's imaginary universe looked like, picture the round ball of the Earth with a large hole in it the shape of a cone or a funnel. The center of that hole is Jerusalem, and its diameter, the width of the circle around Jerusalem, is equal in size to the radius of the earth, about 3,950 miles, though Galileo's calculations showed it to be a few hundred miles less. This hole was formed by the force of Lucifer and his angels striking the Earth as they fell from Heaven. The matter displaced by the impact, forced upward and backward along the tunnel that Virgil and Dante use to escape, formed the mountain of Purgatory that rises in an inverted cone to an isolated island in the southern hemisphere. On top of Purgatory is the Earthly Paradise. The opening to Hell is covered by a vault of earth that Galileo calculated to be a little over 405 miles in depth, although there are obviously irregular shallow openings such as the one by which the poets enter. In the Dark Wood of the *Inferno's* first section, where the Pilgrim flees from the leopard, the lion and the she-wolf, is a hill that must be climbed to reach the entrance to the lower depths, where the famous words were inscribed: *Abandon hope, all ye who enter here.*

To complete the picture, remember that for Dante, though notoriously not for Galileo, the Earth was at the center of the universe around which circled nine heavenly spheres: the moon, Mercury, Venus, the sun, Mars, Jupiter, Saturn, the fixed stars and the *primum mobile*, or "first mover," which keeps the universe in order. (The outer planets had not yet been discovered at that time) Beyond the spheres was the vast Empyrean, home of God, the angels, and saints, but Dante's heavens are lodged in the spheres. The nine circles of Hell are a direct inversion of the heavens.

Dante's love of precise structure and symbolic numerology extends to the poetry itself. It is written in *terza rima*, in which the first and third lines of each three-line stanza rhyme while the second rhymes with the first and third line of the next stanza. Each of the three sections, the *Inferno, Purgatorio* and *Paradiso*, is further divided in thirds, of thirty-three cantos each, with an introductory canto to make an even one hundred in all. To have carried off this structure in a way that is so readable is truly amazing.

When the two poets enter the Gates of Hell in Canto III, they find themselves in the vestibule, an area where Dante places the "indecisive," those who have never committed to anything, including life, and because of this, have not earned Hell but get no real death either. This vestibule slopes down to the river Acheron, the first of three circular rivers, each of which flows into the next and which finally empty in Cocytus, the frozen lake at the center of the Earth.

The entire underground cone is terraced in descending ledges or circles of narrowing size down to the deepest well or pit at the center of the Earth, where the frozen lake is found. Between the Acheron, across which Charon the boatman ferries the poets, and the Styx, are Hell's first four circles, the highest of which is technically Limbo, the residence of virtuous unbaptized souls, mostly pagan. No one is punished in the First Circle. Virgil himself inhabits this circle, together with Homer and other famous pagans.

The next four circles punish the Incontinent, those who, in life, gave in to their passions. The Second Circle holds the lustful, whirled forever in the winds of desire. The Third traps gluttons in a cold, smelly, garbage heap. The Fourth pits misers and spendthrifts, many of them priests, against one another. The Styx itself, a filthy marsh, forms the Fifth Circle, as well as a boundary between Upper and Lower Hell. In the swamp, the angry fight with one another, while under the mud, the slothful gurgle to the poets incoherently.

The poets are ferried across the Styx to the City of Dis (or Satan), the capital of Hell and home to the fallen rebel angels – who will not permit the poets to enter until an angelic messenger forces the gate. All of Lower Hell lies within the walls of the city, which is guarded by the Furies and Medusa. Immediately beyond the gate is the Sixth Circle of heretics, who burn in fiery graves. In Dante's Inferno, despite its name, the traditional punishment of fire is used only inside the walls of the citadel.

Down a steep slope guarded by the Minotaur, the poets head toward the Seventh Circle and the Phlegethon, the river of boiling blood that is guarded by centaurs, one of whom, Nessus, takes them across. The Seventh Circle, which punishes the sins of Violence, is divided into three rounds, the first being the boiling river itself. Immersed in the bloody stream are the murderous: warmongers, tyrants, predators and psychopaths. The next round, guarded by Harpies, is the Wood of Suicides. At the edge of it, the wastrels are condemned to dwell. Next was the Burning Plain of usurers, blasphemers and homosexuals, which the poets can only cross by following the banks of the paved conduit along which the end branch of the Phlegethon flows to a great waterfall at the edge of a cliff.

A sampling of the terrifying images created by nineteenth-century artist Gustave Dore to illustrated Dante's *Divine Comedy.*

The monster Geryon flies them down the cliff's edge to the most elaborate circle of all, and the beginning of a new and final set of sins, those of Fraudulence and Malice. Malebolge is shaped like a great stone amphitheater with a spoke-like series of stone bridges leading down to a central well over ten concentric ditches. Each ditch holds a group of sinners: in the first, horned demons torture pimps and seducers. In the second, flatterers wallow in excrement; in the third, corrupt men of faith, including at least one pope, are plunged upside down into something resembling a baptismal font while their feet are burned with flames. False prophets and soothsayers trudge through the fourth ditch, their heads twisted entirely around so that their tears flowed down to their buttocks.

At the fifth ditch, Dante introduces us to the Malebranche, a band of antic devils who gleefully toss grafters and swindlers into boiling oil. The mood becomes one of grotesque comedy and Canto XXI actually ends with breaking wind. Dante chose to inject comic relief at this particular point because of his own troubles at the time. He had been exiled from Florence on the grounds of political corruption, as well as on charges of intrigue and hostility to the pope. His response to the charges was grim burlesque and it is no accident that the next ditch of Hell holds the hypocrites with whom he must actually consort.

The poets find that the bridge over the sixth chasm has been broken by an earthquake. In order to escape the hungry Malebranche, they must slide down the rubble into the realm of the hypocrites, who shuffle in single file, weeping from the weight of heavy, lead-line cloaks that they are forced to wear. The two climb up the ruins to the opposite bank to regain the bridge, from which they look down into the seventh ditch, where thieves and reptiles shape-shift back and forth into one another.

Deceivers burn in flames in the eighth chasm and in the ninth are the sowers of discord, horribly mutilated by a demon with a sword. Among them is Mohammed, the "infidel," whom Dante considered a heretic. The last chasm is where the falsifiers (impersonators, perjurers, counterfeiters, alchemists) lie stricken with horrible diseases. It rests just above the tip of the inverted cone. Below it, in a well at the bottom, stand the Giants, each about fifty feet high. They are Dante's version of the ancient world's Titans. They stand here to guard the Pit, their heads and torsos protruding above it. One of them lowers the poets in his huge palm to a point about midway down the Ninth Circle.

Three rings around the center of Cocytus, the icebound lake that is the realm of Treason, hold traitors. Caina

(named for Cain, biblical murderer of Abel) holds those who betrayed their families. Antenora imprisoned traitors to their countries and Ptolomea was for traitors to guests. Ptolomy was a captain of Jericho who arranged a banquet for his father-in-law, Simon the high priest, and his two sons, and then murdered them. In the absolute center – of the Inferno and of the Earth – is Judecca (named for Judas, of course), for traitors to their lords. In its center was the greatest traitor of all – Satan himself. He is frozen there, mindlessly weeping as he devours the ghosts of Judas Iscariot, Brutus and Cassius. It is across his body that the poets must climb to find their exit to clean air and starlight.

As with his vision of Hell, Dante's picture of Satan combines the convention and the original. Most literature of this type tended to offer a quick, thrilling glimpse of Satan but Dante gives us a prolonged, grotesque version with three faces – one red (Judas) in the middle, a black one (Brutus) on the left, and a yellow one (Cassius) on the right. Below each was a pair of wings, which fanned the frozen wind of Coctyus.

The three heads were inspired by artists' conceptions. Dante, like most of Florence, likely saw the spectacular Last Judgment mosaic on the cupola of the baptistery of the cathedral of San Giovanni, which was completed in 1300, two years before he was banished from the city. Dante was a close friend an artist named Giotto who painted his own Last Judgment at Scrovegni Chapel in Padua in 1307. In both of these depictions, Satan is a bestial creature with a pair of sinner-swallowing snakes emerging from where his ears should be. Dante rearranged the image to parallel the Holy Trinity. Both Last Judgments had humanoid devils with soul-eating serpents emerging from Satan's throne, implying that they were excrement since Satan was in a seated position. But what was new in Dante's portrait was the fact that Satan was utterly defeated and locked away, mindlessly eating the dead and oblivious to the escape of the poets, even though they managed it by walking across his body. Dante's vision of Satan is brief, but it leaves an impression.

The *Inferno* was a sensation as soon as it was circulated and made available to copyists. This was about 1314, while Dante was still working on the later sections of the *Comedy*. Illustrated copies began to appear almost immediately, and the *Inferno*'s influence also extended to public art. This was an era of great cathedral building in Italy, and the Last Judgments that were commissioned for them quickly began to reflect Dante's vision. His version of Hell absolutely fascinated artists.

With Dante, the history of Hell entered a new stage. His new work killed off the earlier "vision literature." Dante made it possible to think of Hell in fictional and allegorical terms. He abandoned the old pretense of truth in vision literature and invited readers to join him and Virgil in a fictitious story, an artistic creation written to intrigue the reader and examine real world problems using an imaginative setting. "Real" visions of Hell ended with Dante --- but this did not stop the Church from insisting that it was a real place, one that was ever more frightening than was depicted in the works of fiction.

Artists like Jan Van Eyck, Hieronymus Bosch, Hans Memling, Pieter Brughel the Elder and even Peter Paul Rubens painted terrifying and horrific images of Hell and the tremendous suffering that awaited sinners when they died. Unlike painters like Bosch, who spent his entire life creating hallucinogenic and grotesque scenes of punishment, Michelangelo painted Hell only once. His *Last Judgment*, on the wall of the Vatican's Sistine Chapel, is one of the world's most famous paintings, and his Hell, though far from the dominant element, is unforgettable.

Michelangelo was perhaps the greatest artist of the Italian Renaissance. During his life, he always considered himself a sculptor rather than a painter, but not only did he excel at both, he also designed the dome of St. Peter's in Rome. Although a Christian, he was also devoted to the ideas of Plato, which he had studied as a young man. It is obvious that the spirit of Classical Greece can be found in all of his work, including the *Last Judgment*.

Michelangelo had completed the ceiling and vault of the Sistine Chapel during the years between 1508 and 1512, a grueling work marathon that forced him to lie on a scaffold, facing upward, for long, uncomfortable sessions. He was not pleased when, in 1534, Pope Clement summoned him back for more work. The great end wall above the Sistine altar was at that time covered with frescoes, but the pope wanted the Last Judgment to be depicted there and he insisted that Michelangelo be the one to paint it. Even though he was nearly sixty by that time, there was no way for the great artist to refuse. Clement soon died, but his successor, Paul III, was equally adamant that Michelangelo do the work. The great fresco took seven years to complete and ironically, Michelangelo painted himself, exhausted and limp, into the picture. It was likely an accurate portrayal of how he felt.

Michelangelo's only painting of Hell was a command performance in the Sistine Chapel. It covered an entire wall and became mired in controversy.

Even when the painting was finished, his trials were not over, for the pope, listening to the complaints of one of his assistants, Biagio De Cesena, ordered Michelangelo to cover the genitals of all of the male nudes. Michelangelo refused. Instead, he angrily painted Biagio's face on Minos in Hell. When Biagio protested, Paul III told him, "Had the painter sent you to Purgatory, I would use my best efforts to get you released, but I exercise no influence in Hell; there you are beyond redemption." Later, his successor, Pope Paul IV, ordered the genitals concealed by another painter, Daniele da Volterra. Even in the massive cleaning effort of the 1990s, the painted diapers were not removed: the Vatican claimed that after so much time, it was impossible.

Michelangelo dispensed with all of the supernatural accoutrements of halos and wings. The only wing in the painting seems rather mysteriously attached to Charon's boat, or perhaps to a creature underneath it. Demons and angels are human-looking and fully sexed (or they were, anyway), though the demons have donkey ears or small horns, and Minos has a serpentine tail. One beast-demon attacks perhaps the most famous figure in the painting – other than the virile and implacable Jesus – that of the man who has realized for the first time that he is really going to Hell.

Discontent with the Church swelled after the twelfth century. The perceived corruption, ignorance and hypocrisy distressed people with genuine religious convictions. The great wealth of the monasteries, their huge holdings of untaxed lands (between one-half and one-third of all Europe), and their insistence on tribute, their right to interfere politically and to have their own courts of law exasperated the secular rulers. The growth of the middle-class mercantile towns made the old feudal system obsolete. In the fourteenth century, there were two popes, sometimes three, simultaneously, which encouraged contempt for the office. The savagery of the Inquisition (more about that later) outraged people of sensibility, even in an age when a public burning was entertainment for the masses and heretics, Jews, lepers and witches were considered fair game.

During the middle years of the fifteenth century, the printing press was invented, which would immeasurably aid in the protest against the religious authorities. The Church had long held that it was heretical for a layman to read the Bible even in Latin, let alone in translation. Copies of translations had, however, been quietly circulating for more than a century and, though the Church tried to burn them (and the translators, too), the new printing presses made the task hopeless. New books with fresh ideas soon began to circulate to a larger reading public.

The leader of the age turned out to be a monk named Martin Luther, a man of passionate intensity who gambled with his life when he nailed his ninety-five theses against indulgences to the door of the Wittenberg church in 1517. He argued against metaphysical ideas, wanted to abolish indulgences and other corruptions and return to the strict teachings of the Bible. He did not believe there was any accommodation possible with the current Church. He was a man of tremendous energy and strong will who believed himself to have been called to the monastery and then to his reformist mission directly by God. To appeal directly to the people and the German nobility against the Church, as he did, was extremely dangerous, but he had faith in his destiny.

In the monastery, Luther studied St. Augustine and became convinced that the scholars of the Middle Ages had strayed from the true path. The idea that struck him most forcefully from his reading was that of predestination. Only God could elect men to salvation or damnation, Luther believed that St. Augustine said. Therefore the entire structure of the Church interference in the afterlife was false and had been concocted by bad men for no end other than greed. He quickly came to regard the Church rulers in Rome "as possessed by Satan and as the throne of the Antichrist."

St. Augustine

(Below) Martin Luther

Luther threw out the idea of Purgatory and all that went with it, including the Virgin Mary as an intercessor and a deity. His Hell was St. Augustine's Hell, dire and eternal, constructed by God to punish the wicked. No one could be saved but by God's grace, and there was no way to influence the outcome – good works were only an indication of grace and had no effect in themselves; prayers for the dead were useless. The Devil was God's servant, created by him and destined to fall. Like one of the old desert prophets, Luther believed himself to be plagued by demons and, like a proper medieval man, he associated them with his bowels – he evidently had severe problems with both flatulence and constipation. Luther also believed in witches and their pacts with the Devil, which explains why the Protestant record on the subject of witch hunts is worse, if possible, than that of the Catholic Church.

John Calvin, the second leader of the Reformation, came into contact with Luther's ideas when he was still a student and became a convert in his early twenties. He agreed with Luther's principles but went much further with regard to predestination. From the beginning of time, Calvin thought, God's preordained plan had been in effect. He believed that all men and angels were predestined to either eternal life or damnation, so Christ had not died for all men, only for the already selected. Satan acted at God's command to punish the wicked. Prayers, good works, deathbed confessions and absolutions could do nothing to change fate.

Luther and Calvin, together with Huldereich Zwingli, the third leader of the Reformation, rejected Purgatory, but conceded to a Limbo for unbaptized babies and an interim state between death and the Final Judgment. About resurrection, the Devil and eternal Hell, they had no doubts.

By the middle of the seventeenth century, the religious wars were finally over. Hardly a European country had been untouched. Italy, perhaps because its cultural renaissance happened early, or because it was closely connected to classical antiquity which had revived such interest, or because the papal rulers had close family links to Italian aristocracy, remained Catholic. Even so, there were reformist rumblings in Venice and Florence and some had departed for Protestant countries like Switzerland. The Inquisition kept Spain in line and Portugal and Ireland remained Catholic, as did Austria, Eastern Europe and, uneasily, France.

All of the Scandinavian countries adopted Lutheranism as a state religion and by the middle sixteenth century it was legalized in Germany, which was divided between Lutherans and Calvinists. Switzerland followed Calvin, as did Scotland, led by John Knox who adopted the French Huguenot "Presbyterianism." Phillip II's attempt to impose the Inquisition on the Netherlands led to a bitter struggle to tear them apart, leaving Holland Protestant and Belgium Catholic.

In England, Henry VIII broke with Rome for reasons of politics, not faith, and his Church of England was intended to be "the papacy without the pope." He burned heretics who subscribed to the new Protestant ideas and beheaded bishops who opposed his unity of church and state. He dissolved the monasteries and seized their land and wealth. He encouraged an authorized English Bible and a Book of Common Prayer that was purged of Catholic "idolatry," but upheld the old values. His son, Edward VI, continued Henry's policies through his short reign, and though his successor, "Bloody Mary," made notorious efforts to return the country to Catholicism, she ultimately failed.

England's great fortune was the long reign of Elizabeth I, from 1558 to 1603. The queen seemed to understand the arts of both negotiation and compromise, a skill that was unknown to most of her fellow rulers. The Church of England continued as the state religion with Queen Elizabeth as the "Supreme Governor" in all spiritual matters. Catholics were fined but not persecuted, nor were John Knox's Scottish Presbyterians, who rejected the mass and papal authority in 1560, a year after the English parliament did so. The Elizabethan Age is synonymous with the English Renaissance, and fortune smiled on England by giving it so reasonable a ruler at so critical a time.

One of the great glories of the Elizabethan period is its dramatic literature, especially the plays of William Shakespeare. It may seem surprising that Shakespeare never attempted the subject of Heaven and Hell, but in fact he was forbidden to do so. Religious plays were forbidden nearly everywhere at the time and the last such production was held in 1589 and became known as the "last straw" for the English parliament. No further plays of this sort were allowed and were banned in Britain around the time that Shakespeare's career began. With religious plays off the table, it was up to Shakespeare and his fellow Elizabethans to construct a new form of secular entertainment.

The play that forced a change in the law was the *Tragicall Historie of Doctor Faustus* – a play about the Devil. It

Christopher Marlowe, creator of Doctor Faustus

was a controversial play and its author, Christopher Marlowe, was a controversial young man. His enemies accused him of atheism, blasphemy, espionage and immorality and it's likely that they were right on all accounts. He was the son of a shoemaker who, with scholarship aid, was able to attend Cambridge. Although various misdemeanors nearly cost him his degree, he finally achieved it in 1584. He went on to achieve a Master of the Arts three years later. As a playwright, Marlowe was immediately successful. With *Tamburlaine*, produced when he was only twenty-three, he received rave reviews, but his most famous play was *Doctor Faustus*. It was based on a 1587 German book that had been translated into English, and Marlowe's play was produced two years later.

The story of the philosopher who sells his soul to the devil was an old one, dating back in Christian legend to Simon Magus of Samaria, the first-century Gnostic sorcerer who was often picture flying magically into the Roman Forum before Peter caused him to fall, break his head and die. Simon lived with a former prostitute named Helen and he became the epitome of the "false prophet" and was considered to be the father of all Christian heresy. Dante placed him far down in the Eighth Circle of Hell. Another, similar story from the Middle Ages was that of Theophilis, a church deacon who was dismissed by his bishop and turned to a Jewish sorcerer to contact the Devil, with whom he signed a pact in his own blood agreeing to trade his soul for success and wealth. This tale had a happy ending. Theophilis was plagued by his conscience and tried and failed to re-bargain with the Devil. While praying to the Virgin Mary, he fell asleep and dreamed that she appeared to him, carrying the pact that he had signed. She told him that she had descended into Hell and seized it from the Devil's hands, and that Theophilis was pardoned. He awoke to find the pact beside him, made a confession and died in peace. This was the most famous of all of the "rescue tales" pitting Mary against the Devil.

A real Doctor Faustus received a degree from Heidelberg in 1509. One story about him is supposedly historically confirmed: when in prison he offered to show the chaplain how to remove the hair from his face without a razor in return for free wine. The wine arrived and Faustus gave the chaplain a salve of arsenic, which not only removed his hair but his skin. Apparently, this sadistic would-be humorist set up shop as an astrologer, alchemist, magician and "philosopher," a job description that fits all of the figures that we think of today as early Renaissance scientists, like Nicolaus Copernicus, John Dee, Francis Bacon and Galileo. Well into the seventeenth century, Newton studied alchemy and, a century later, so did Goethe.

Both the Protestants and Catholics of the era had a problem with learned men. It was easy to believe that all of them were somehow in partnership with the Devil, pursuing "forbidden" knowledge. The first great wave of witch hunts swept across Europe from 1590 to 1620 and the notion of pacts with the Devil was very much in the air when Marlowe was writing *Doctor Faustus*.

Marlowe made a lasting mark on history with his play and it was a good thing that he did for he was stabbed to death in a duel before he was thirty. Mercutio, the eloquent jester of *Romeo and Juliet* to whom Shakespeare gave his extravagant Queen Mab speech, was said to be based on Marlowe. If this is not true, it ought to be.

It was during this era that the Church launched its defense against the Reformation and in so doing, gave stature to a group that would long be associated with both Hell and the Devil. The Society of Jesus was founded in 1540 by Ignatius Loyola, the youngest son of an old Basque noble family. A war wound forced Ignatius into a long convalescence, during which he read about the lives of the saints and courtly romances, like those of King Arthur. He began dreaming about the feudal ideal of holy chivalry. When healed, he decided to obtain an education of a greater degree than what he had received as a young knight. He entered the university at Barcelona at the age of thirty-three. Harassment by the Inquisition drove him to Paris, where he finished his schooling at age forty-five and gathered friends to help him found his new religious order. It quickly developed an effective leadership network of Catholic reform and resistance to stand up to the Protestant encroachment.

The Jesuit ideal was not only to save one's own soul but one's neighbor's soul as well. It was founded to be a teaching and missionary order. Jesuits carried the faith to Asia, the Indies and the Americas. They brought sincerity, vitality and fresh ideas to the old Catholic establishment. Within prescribed limits, they were up to date in the sciences too. By the early 1600s, Jesuit missionaries to China were correctly predicting eclipses. They later sidestepped the Galileo debacle by declaring that the soul revolved around the immobile God as the Earth moves around the sun. (It wasn't until 1992 that the Vatican formally admitted that the Church might have been wrong in persecuting Galileo for saying that the Earth circled the sun)

In the early age of printed books and changing educational standards, the teaching Jesuits were shrewdly positioned to change society, since most of their pupils were the children of the rich and powerful – most of whom held the outdated tenets of the Church in contempt. The Jesuits were eager to bring about change and one effective approach was to change Hell again. Horrid as the old Hell was, it was lively. It had variety, activity, scenery and a certain entertainment value – too much entertainment, in fact, for the Jesuits. It might serve to frighten the uneducated into good behavior, but it was not taken seriously by the people who counted. So, the Jesuits dispensed with all of the frills. They eliminated all of the imaginative tortures, except for fire, and all of the monsters, except possibly "the worm that never sleepeth," although there remained some doubt about how the worm and the fire were supposed to co-exist. What they added to Hell was unnervingly apt for the times – they added urban squalor.

The Jesuit Hell was repulsively suffocating and a place of unbearable crowds, likely because of all of the new Protestant arrivals. In the dank, dungeon-like cesspool, sinful aristocrats and prosperous merchants were jostled together, cheek to jowl, buttocks to belly and mouth to mouth. The rich were pressed together with coarse, foul-smelling peasants, lepers and slum-dwellers. Just as the bodies of the saved were to be glorified at the Resurrection, those of the damned would be deformed, bloated, diseased and repugnant. There were no latrines, no baths and no water. Hell stunk and it was disgusting and permanent, composed of filth, feces, pestilence, running sores, foul breath and everything else the creative Jesuits came up with to make their wealthy clients promise to mend their ways. Whether this scenario would have frightened the urban sinners who already lived in unspeakable poverty is unknown, but it had the desired effect on the upper and middle classes.

The Jesuits retained fire within their Hell – it was one of the most fearsome properties of the age of alchemy – but mostly ousted the old demons. They weren't needed in the Hell of "other people," who turned on one another in their pain and terror. At any rate, demons now had a new task, which was tempting and corrupting people here on earth, especially destitute old women. The Jesuits became the greatest terror to "witches" during the witch-hunting craze, which began during the Renaissance and lasted intermittently until almost the nineteenth century – and not only, it should be emphasized, in Catholic countries. Satan, or done of his demonic lieutenants, was supposed to be the master of witches, but his association with them, which including night flights and diabolical orgies and evil spells and all sorts of other things that people confessed to under torture, was very much of this world, not the next.

Demons also had time for heretics, atheists and philosophers, according to the Jesuits, who burned Giordano Bruno at the stake. Bruno was a Dominican friar, philosopher, mathematician and astronomer who proposed that the universe contained an infinite number of inhabited worlds populated by intelligent beings. Galileo only escaped a similar fate by lying and John Dee faced serious accusations of sorcery. As last as the mid-seventeenth century, Descartes found it advisable to move to Holland and live among the Protestants. Even later than that, Voltaire and Rousseau sought sanctuary in Switzerland.

The Jesuits asserted that they could summon demons when needed. Now that religious plays performed by laymen were forbidden, the Jesuits took over religious theater. In 1597, the church of St. Michael was consecrated in Munich with an astounding festival with brass bands and hundreds of players portraying dragons, sinners and heretics. The final curtain featured a tumultuous spectacle in which 300 masked devils were hurled into what must have been the largest mouth of Hell stage set ever designed.

While the painters and artists of the era were understandably not very interested in the Jesuit version of Hell, the terrors of the Devil were still fascinating to the writers that followed. John Milton, for one, had little interest in the images conjured up by the Church, but he was convinced that Hell was a very real place. Milton, who was born in 1608, was a very different man than Christopher Marlowe, who had also attended Cambridge a generation earlier. He was the younger son of a Protestant convert. At Cambridge, Milton was nicknamed "The Lady," more for his high-minded prudishness than for his unquestioned good looks. His family considered him suited for the ministry, but he thought otherwise. Poems written during his seven years at the university brought him local fame and the confidence to dream of a literary career.

His father's wealth allowed him to travel to Italy to continue his studies and spend twenty years writing tracts in favor of religious liberty in answer to the Stuart kings bringing religious dissension and civil war back to England. In addition, he worked as a translator, editor and occasional politician in the government of Oliver Cromwell. He married three times, had three daughters by his first wife, and lost his eyesight gradually over time, becoming completely blind by 1652 – before even a single word of his great epic had been written down. It was his blindness that saved him from hanging when Charles II was restored to the throne. Andrew Marvell, the metaphysical poet and politician who sat in the House of Commons at various times between 1659 and 1678, was said to have pleaded on his behalf.

Milton is sometimes referred to as the "Puritan Poet," but, at least in his greatest work, nothing could be further from the truth. He was raised an Anglican at a time when Calvinism ruled the Church of England, but the entire point of *Paradise Lost* is to dispel the idea of predestination and demonstrate free will. Satan chooses to rebel in Heaven and deliberately decides to commit further acts of wickedness. Eve, beguiled and foolish, might be excused from listening to the serpent and taking a bite from the forbidden fruit, but Adam certainly understands the issues, if not the consequences, when his love for Eve

John Milton

overwhelms his love for God. Actually, Milton seems to have become quite independent in his religious views by the time that he began to dictate *Paradise Lost*, which was published in 1667. In this, he was in step with other intellectuals of the day, though most of them wisely kept their opinions largely to themselves. Milton deliberately made his ideas about religion ambiguous in his poetry, and generations following him have co-opted *Paradise Lost* for their own often-opposed points of view.

The character of Satan is tremendously oversized in Milton's work. After the war that he waged in Heaven, during which the Son of Man is sent in to back up Michael and his angelic troops, Satan was hurled headlong from the heavens and fell nine days through the chaos with his followers. They splashed down into a burning lake, no longer in the bright, angelic form that they once had. They manage to escape from Hell (Milton never

fully explains how they accomplished it) and set to work building a palace on the side of a volcano. To the reader, it was supposed to conjure up the worst excesses of Rome, Byzantine Constantinople and of course, sinful Babylon. The architect is Mulciber, another name for Vulcan, the craftsman of pagan Olympus, and the builder is Mammon, the incarnation of greed. Their combined efforts result in Pandemonium ("All-Demons"), the most palatial structure in Hell's history, grander than anything conjured up by Dante.

In the meeting hall, Satan called an infernal council, to which demons flocked by the thousands. Moloch counsels war – he represents Anger. Belial, representing Sloth, argues against going to war. Mammon, who is willing to put up with the fiery inconveniences for Hell's gems and gold, is Greed. Beelzebub, second in rank to Satan, is Envy. He convinces the council of his plan to seduce mortal men to join them in Hell and they vote to adopt it. Satan himself is Pride. After the council is dissolved, the demons disperse, some to engage in heroic games, others to play the harp, to philosophize, and to explore the depths of Hell.

Meanwhile, Satan travels to the gates of Hell – three of brass, three of iron and three of adamantine rock.

The warrior Satan in *Paradise Lost*

They were guarded by two formidable shapes who turn out to be Sin and Death personified. It is eventually established that Sin is Satan's daughter, sprung full-grown from his forehead like Athena from the head of Zeus, and Death is his incestuous son with her. Sin unlocks all of the gates, and for a moment, they all contemplate the region beyond, called Chaos.

At this point, the reader might understandably wonder just where Milton's Hell is located. It is certainly not in the center of the Earth, the traditional site. Earth had not yet been created when Milton's rebel angels fell. It is not the claustrophobic, stinking Jesuit prison, but a vast world that is unpopulated except for the rebels, Sin, Death and a handful of monsters. It seems to be on, or rather inside, another planet altogether. When Sin unlocked the gates, it was as though Satan was about to step out into space, though here it is called Chaos. And Chaos is outside the universe, as the universe was generally understood.

In Chaos, the elements noisily battle one another while Satan is knocked back and forth until he reaches his first stop, the pavilion of Chaos and his consort, Night. There it is learned that Hell is "beneath" and that the new "world" hangs over "Chaos," which is linked to Heaven by a golden chain. However, the "world" is not a single planet, but the old idea of the universe, with nine spheres circling the Earth. Even though he was acquainted with the theories of Galileo, Milton found it more poetic to abandon them in favor of earlier ideas.

Satan looks back to see Sin and Death building a bridge behind him, then he looks ahead to the opal towers and the sapphire battlements of Heaven. Satan climbs to the outermost sphere of the "world" that dangles from the golden chain and finds that it houses a limbo called the Paradise of Fools, which is reserved for unreconstructed Catholics. He finds a stairway to Heaven, but heads away from it through the sphere of the fixed stars, past Jupiter, Saturn and Mars to the sphere of the sun, ruled by the archangel Uriel. Disguised as an angel, Satan asks directions and Uriel points him toward Paradise, the home of Adam – which, of course, leads to the fall of man.

Time marched on. Poets, philosophers and religious men came and went, wooed the masses and fell out of favor. Writers like John Donne offered satirical looks at Hell, while others, like John Bunyan, took it quite seriously in his massively popular *Pilgrim's Progress*. The book had gone through 160 editions by 1792, and remained, after the Bible, the best-selling book in the English language through the nineteenth century. Hell entered only peripherally, but it left quite an impression. *Pilgrim's Progress* became the book most often presented to Puritan children.

During the Age of Enlightenment of the eighteenth century, thinkers, writers and critics began to embrace a belief in rationality, science and freedom from oppression, which included freedom from the heavy hand of organized religion. They began an assault on the teachings of the various churches, including the belief in Hell and the Devil. They believed that Hell was here on Earth and the Devil was inside of all of us. They considered the old idea of the Devil as an independent being as a quaint tale of antiquity, one they largely dismissed as another part of the way that the Church used the threat of the fiery torments of Hell to control its followers.

But not everyone felt this way. In fact, most people in the eighteenth century were not engaged in the pursuit of reason, nor had they abandoned religion and the old concept of Hell. Catholics and Protestants alike began preaching thunderous sermons from church pulpits, promising dire after-life punishments for sinners.

Protestant dissenters and extremists flocked to the American colonies. Anglicans settled in the Virginia colonies. The grim Puritans of Massachusetts were Congregationalists who were in revolt against the Anglican hierarchy and the pleasure-loving court of England's King Charles II. The Baptists broke away at about the same time, establishing themselves in Rhode Island. Persecuted in England, the Quakers settled in Pennsylvania and Scottish Presbyterians joined them there and in New Jersey. John Wesley founded Methodism in the eighteenth century, and it took root in New York, though the main church splintered into many branches.

Beginning in the 1730s, a wave of evangelical revivalism swept across the colonies. The so-called Great Awakening started in New Jersey with the Presbyterian evangelist Gilbert Tennent, but was quickly taken up in New England by the famous Congregationalist theologian Jonathan Edwards. Their avowed purpose was "to drive the nail of terror into slumbering souls." Audiences responded with tears, shouts, convulsions, fainting fits and mass conversions.

Jonathan Edwards, the son and grandson of New England clergymen, studied Newton and Locke at Yale, where he received his degree in 1723. He endeavored, with considerable success, to draw natural sciences into the fold of Puritanism. He was a strict believer in predestination, considering evil and its punishment to be part of the grand design, but he was also something of an ecstatic and was skilled in "preaching of terror." His first great revival meeting was in Northampton, Massachusetts, in 1734 and 1735. One of his most celebrated sermons, "Sinners in the Hands of an Angry God," was preached in 1741 when the Great Awakening was in full swing.

The first Great Awakening (others followed throughout the nineteenth century) had two distinct effects on American history. The intense emotions that it unleashed surely contributed to the revolutionary fever that soon swept through the colonies.

Jonathan Edwards

The second effect was more subtle, and was not one that revivalist leaders anticipated. The mass controversy -- and religious fervor caused by the revivalists -- was not lost on the Founding Fathers. Distaste for religious zeal pushed men like Benjamin Franklin and Thomas Jefferson, both of whom thrived in the Age of Enlightenment, away from the moderate Christianity to which they might have otherwise subscribed. Franklin became an out-and-out deist (the belief that reason and observation of the natural world are sufficient to determine the existence of a creator, accompanied by the rejection of organized religion) and Jefferson leaned in the same direction. Both saw that America's religious pluralism had to be supported in order to preserve its independence from fanaticism and so, in the Declaration of Independence, written by Jefferson with help from Franklin, there is only reference to "the Laws of Nature and Nature's God." In the Constitution, the name of God is never mentioned and the church is firmly separated from the state.

A new era dawned in the early nineteenth century when Napoleon's forces fell at Waterloo, ending a quarter century of political upheaval. In October 1815, the former emperor was exiled to Saint Helena, there to end his life almost inevitably mythologized as a powerful and fearful symbol, a Satan in exile who had appeared like a fallen angel out of nowhere to take charge of a demoralized, bloodied and bankrupt France and lead her on a terrifying crusade of world conquest.

The French Revolution had far more impact in Europe than it did in America. The tyranny, corruption and injustice that had rallied the French lower classes also had offended liberals and reformists in the surrounding countries of Europe. Primed by the Enlightenment, people thrilled in sympathy to the Declaration of the Rights of Man (1789). Poetry at the century's turn was full of hope and excitement, and many came to believe that France was to lead the way to the promised kingdom of God on Earth. Disillusionment, when it inevitably came, was profound.

The "Spirit of the Age," a series of articles by John Stuart Mill in the 1830s, had a tremendous impact. On one level, the century moved straight ahead, accelerating ever faster. Industry prospered, science, exploration, conquest, trade and railroads advanced, and great fortunes were made by men who came to be known as "robber barons." But underneath the progressive surface, things were uneasy. The earlier philosophers used wit and reason to attack what they considered to be the tottering superstructure of superstition. But a dawning new age swept tradition aside, bringing uncertainty, and a sense that reason had failed. The metaphysical began to be embraced and in the early eighteenth century, a new kind of German ideology came along that was a strange mixture of Roman Catholic, primitive Greek and Germanic folklore that became a sort of Teutonic paganism. By the end of the century, the strange mixture had produced Gothic and Romantic literature and music, a strong

The infamous Marquis de Sade

interest in fantasy and folklore, the mysterious faith called Spiritualism, and dozens of occult and mystical sects, including some that worshipped the Devil. There was also a secular approach to soul-searching that would become psychoanalysis, as well as a morbid fascination with death and dying such as had not been seen since ancient times.

The prose novel was developed in the eighteenth century with the traditional characters of Don Juan and Faust serving as models for cautionary tales against lust and greed. Virtue was rewarded in most cases, but what drove the plots in almost every case was, emphatically, vice. The machinations of the hero-villains bent on sin do not, however, lead then to their just rewards below. Something new was in the air and nowhere was that more clear than in the writings of the notorious and demonic aristocrat, the Marquis de Sade. He spent much of his life either in prison or an insane asylum, which gave him plenty of time to fantasize.

He claimed that his pornographic inventions of bizarre rapes, tortures and murders in the name of pure sexual pleasure were legitimate extensions of Enlightenment ideas. If there was no God, he argued, then there was no accountability, no social responsibility, and everything was permissible, including the wanton destruction of others. If people were merely objects, their wills counted for nothing in a world were morality was subjective.

De Sade's influence was considerable. He stretched sex and sensationalism beyond all previous limits of taste and his violent scenarios went beyond apocalyptic visions of Hell, the Catholic Church's gruesome accounts of martyrdom, or the most lurid revenge melodramas. No moral was attached to de Sade's writings – quite the opposite, in fact. The heavens themselves, enraged by the heroine's obstinate attachment to virtue throughout her many degradations, strike her dead in *Justine*, written while de Sade was imprisoned in the Bastille. *Justine* and a follow-up book called *Juliette* so revolted Napoleon Bonaparte that he had de Sade arrested and incarcerated for the last thirteen years of his life. The Marquis became, in later imagination, a kind of underground hero and the personification of the romantic, doomed aristocrat. In truth, he was anything but heroic or romantic. De Sade was a depraved, perverse member of an entitled family, whose fevered imagination led to his downfall.

The Gothic novel was born at about this same time. Horace Walpole was arguably the inventor of the genre with his book *The Castle of Otranto*, published in 1764. He continued the Don Juan character theme, but added to it with dark, forbidding castles, thunder storms, gloomy heroes, persecuted heroines, and the creaking torture devices of the Inquisition, all of which set the stage for the horror genre and for the Romantic poetry that followed.

Horace Walpole

Despite the trappings, the early horror settings of the Gothic novels had less to do with Hell and the Devil than one might think.

What happened at this time – it seems almost inevitable after de Sade – was that Gothic authors began to re-create Hell on Earth. They employed terror – both natural and supernatural – for thrills instead of for moralizing. Punishment was almost always the lot of the innocent; the guilty did the punishing.

In Matthew Lewis' *The Monk*, the sadistic Gothic novel hit its stride. Written before he was twenty-one, the book was a scandal and a sensation, winning the author lasting fame as "Monk" Lewis. Conventional opinion held that it was "poison for youth and a provocative for the debauchee." Lewis created a messy mixture of Roman Catholicism with rape, orgies and hair-raising violence. Lucifer shows up at the end to tear the sinful monk to pieces. The action never descends into Hell, but the claustrophobia, imprisonment, torture and underground gloom provides a hellish atmosphere and the characters who are not victims behave in a demonic way.

The trend toward Hell on Earth is even more apparent in Charles Maturin's *Melmoth the Wanderer*, published in 1820. *Melmoth* is a Faust-type story set in a murky world of decadence, despair and corruption. It was another tale for a world that was increasingly embracing the uncanny and the supernatural.

This school of thought set the stage for the Romantic writers who, rebelling against the past, created a new mythology that overturned and discredited the old ones. As the years progressed, their new myths become more perverse, more occult and fantastical, more dependent on drug-induced visions, and more self-consciously decadent. A new point of view soon emerged all over Europe and, in turn, filtered across the sea to America.

This radical perspective began at the start of the nineteenth century in the writings and illustrations of William Blake. Blake, the son of a London stocking maker, was apprenticed to an engraver as a boy. At age twenty-one, he set up shop for himself and worked all of his life in the trade, assisted by his wife, Catherine. He had no higher education, though he was a great reader. Despite the fact that he invented his own theology, he can accurately be called a profoundly religious and visionary man. In a series of complex epic poems, he replaced the classical mythologies of the Christian church, and of Milton and Dante, with inventions of his own. While these poems were scarcely known in his lifetime – and he is still better known for his short poems and stylized paintings today – Blake's poems reflect his sensitivity to everything that happened during his time. He responded to the American and French revolutions with apocalyptic poems and echoed the occult and mystical stirrings of the era. It was in his poetry that a negative picture of the industrial revolution first emerged. In his poem "London," the city slums are portrayed as Hell for the neglected poor. Like an Old Testament prophet, he spoke out against the hypocrisy and cruelty of the age but in his epics, he presented his Satan figure as a heroic rebel, fighting back against an oppressive tyrant. No other theme is so central to high Romantic poetry.

William Blake

Percy Bysshe Shelley

No later poet attempted so complex a mythology as Blake's, though *Prometheus Unbound* by Percy Bysshe Shelley also presents a tyrannical Jupiter as a figure who maintains the universe and who must be overthrown to achieve a new Heaven and Earth. Opposed to him is Prometheus, the suffering Titan chained to his precipice. Shelley's preface to the poem holds up Prometheus directly, and favorably, to Milton's Satan as "susceptible of being described as exempt from the taints of ambition, envy, revenge, and a desire for personal aggrandizement." Prometheus' immovable position, chained to the rock, complicates his movements, which Shelly solves by sending Asia, a spiritual avatar of his hero, down to the Deep, the otherworld "underneath the grave," where among "terrible, strange, sublime and beauteous shapes, she will find the gods of nameless worlds, phantoms, heroes, beasts and "Demogorgon, a tremendous gloom."

The Deep portrayed in Shelley's work is not Hell or even Hades, which the poet associated with the established authority of the Church and the state. Demogorgon is a great, dark, formless being which Shelley identified with the force of the inarticulate masses. Overthrown, Jupiter falls into what seems like a Christian Hell. When it's all over, there is a great celebration of Love, joined by a newly articulate Demogorgon, as everyone cheers freedom from "Heaven's despotism."

John Keats chose Hyperion, the sun god overthrown by Apollo, as his Titan. In his first attempt at allegorical mythology, *Hyperion*, Keats ran into Shelley's technical problems of the fallen Titans being paralyzed in the underworld – almost literally turned to stone – by grief and gloom, making any kind of action difficult. Keats solved this problem in *The Fall of Hyperion* by sending himself (in a dream) into the underworld. Obviously influenced by Dante, he found himself before what appear to be the steps of Purgatory, which he is ordered to climb. Fearfully, he obeys, shrieking from the icy cold. This is what it feels like, he is told, to die. The poet had to suffer, die and then conquer Hell in order to be re-born as Hyperion's successor, Apollo, who is not only the sun god, but the god of poetry. The poem was never completed. It remains today as an early look at the decent into Hell motif as a metaphor for creative ambition and the artist's struggle with the looming figures of his artistic predecessor and father-figures. Sometimes, the entire artistic community of the nineteenth century seemed to be just waiting for Freud to arrive.

In his day, George Gordon, Lord Byron, was widely seen as the central figure of Romantic poetry, as much for the Romantic anti-hero that he himself represented as for what he wrote. Byron was handsome, daring and greatly popular with the ladies. He was, as one of his lovers, Lady Caroline Lamb, famously put it, "mad, bad, and dangerous to know." A rumor of incest with his half-sister had blackened his reputation, his marriage had foundered amid reports of sexual sadism and various scandals had driven him out of England. His sardonic response was to publish *Manfred*, a Faust-type drama about Satan featuring a dashing nobleman steeped in incestuous sin. Manfred refused allegiance to either God or the Devil and at the end, he even refused to go to Hell, scornfully treating the traditional demons that appear to drag him off like his lackeys.

Byron's contempt for the British bourgeois could not have been clearer, or more successful. He represented himself, not without irony, as the solitary Promethean rebel against tyranny, the exiled artist, the doomed Don Juan whom women longed for, the Gothic anti-hero, exploiting his dark reputation to the hilt. The public bought his act – and his books. His eventual "poetic" death at thirty-six from a fever contracted in Greece, where he went to join the fight for independence against the Ottoman Empire, firmly entrenched him in literary history.

In addition to Byron's colorful personal reputation, his works added to the Romantic era's personification of the Devil. He returned to his demonic theme in *Cain*, in which, predictably, the Devil himself is the Byronic hero. Byron's version of Hell in the story is interesting in that the poet had recently been reading the works of the French geologist and paleontologist Baron Georges Cuvier, a figure who gained attention shortly before Charles Darwin emerged on the scene. The baron had come to the conclusion that a catastrophe, or a series of them, had killed off the creatures whose huge bones were being increasingly collected by nineteenth-century fossil hunters. Byron used the biblical account of "giants in the earth in those days" to propose the "poetical fiction" that these included bones of "rational beings much more intelligent than man and proportionately powerful to the mammoth..." With the spirits of these lost beings, he populated a sort of science-fiction Hell – located somewhere in space. Lucifer transports Cain there in the story and shows him a weird underworld of monsters and portrays a brontosaurus as the serpent in Eden.

George Gordon, Lord Byron

Although it sounds horribly confusing, the poem was branded as blasphemy, largely due to the theme of incest (again) and the celebration of rational disobedience to mindless orthodoxy. The poem was denounced, just as Byron wanted it to be. Its message was obvious: knowledge and love are worth having, according to Lucifer, and any God or government that prevents them may be fairly called evil.

The Romantics were the first artists to live the "rock star" lifestyle. They were lauded as celebrities, practiced free love and experimented with drugs. Byron and Shelley both started trying out drugs in Italy, but other nineteenth-century poets went beyond experimentation into a region that they very naturally equated with Hell. Although there was not yet a medical concept of addiction, Samuel Taylor Coleridge and Thomas De Quincey began taking doses of laudanum (tincture of opium) early in the century. By doing so they were making their own Faustian bargains – they received a dose of magic, but it came at a heavy cost.

Visions have always had their price and some men and women have always been willing to pay it. In the Middle Ages, that price included marathon hypnotic prayers, fasting, flagellation, fever, induced sleeplessness and sometimes worse. For some people, like Blake or Bosch, visions seem to have come naturally. But drugs, more readily available in the industrial age, made visions easy to achieve. A brave new world of discovery lay inside of the mind. It was a brilliantly colored and poisonously seductive place, and a dangerously poetical and allegorical "Hell."

Drug-related experiences so often take the form of journeys into the otherworld that psychedelic experimenters of the late twentieth century frequently referred to them as "trips." Coleridge's *The Rime of the Ancient Mariner* is the prototype for such hallucinatory forays. The Mariner's vessel bursts into a strange sea where, under an unnatural tropical sun, it is at once becalmed and surrounded by uncannily bright waters filled with "a thousand, thousand slimy things" and hostile spirits. A spectral ship manned by Death and "the Nightmare Life-in-Death" appears, and one after another the sailors die until the Mariner is left alone, out of his mind with thirst and desperate for water. For seven days and nights of private penance (for having killed an albatross), he yearns for death to no avail until, by moonlight, he looks down at the "slimy things" he has despised and sees their "rich attire" in the eerie light. When love for the creatures gushes from the Mariner's heart, the spell is broken and rain comes, followed by a wind that blows the ship, now manned by angels inhabiting the dead crewmen's bodies, back to the real world.

The Rime of the Ancient Mariner, a drug-like version of a trip through Hell

It has been said that the *Ancient Mariner* does not make a great deal of sense. And why would it? It's a hallucinogenic poem, written under the influence of opium. It's not really supposed to "make sense," but it's not completely out of control either. The drug-induced visions are far from random. The *Ancient Mariner*, along with Coleridge's other drug-induced, supernatural pieces like *Cristabel* and *Kubla Khan* have never lost their appeal.

Like the English, the French Romantics fought with Milton's Satan, but Napoleon had been one of their own, and their attempts at rebellion were not as successful. Author and diplomat François-René de Chateaubriand transported Hell to North America in his 1826 work *Les Natchez*, and Victor Hugo wrote an unfinished trilogy about Satan, whom he intended to redeem. Meanwhile, young French poets made their own way, washing down opium and hashish with absinthe, and indulging in sexual debauchery. The syphilis contracted by Charles Baudelaire brought him close to madness before he was forty. Baudelaire, an admirer of both Byron and Edgar Allan Poe, called his first collection *Les Fleurs du Mal* (The Flowers of Evil) in 1857. In it, nearly every poem refers in some way to the Devil, Hell's inhabitants, corpses, vampires or some ominous vice. The poet does not exactly identify with them, but he feels the attraction to the dark side. He has freely, if somewhat ironically, chosen to wander in Hell, with drugs as his guide and his downfall. At its worst, Hell is a change from the drab, everyday world and at its best it defies the God that he, too, has rejected. The mixture of good and evil, an erotic celebration of "cold and sinister beauty," is complete. There was a public outcry following the book's publication. The author and his publisher were taken to court and charged with *Les Fleurs* being "an insult to public decency." Baudelaire was fined 300 francs and six of the poems were banned. The ban was not lifted in France until 1949, but *Les Fleurs du Mal* was too much of a sensation not to remain popular with a certain segment of the public.

Arthur Rimbaud was Baudelaire's disciple, emulating him even to the point of similarly contracting syphilis. His poetic career only lasted for three years, between the ages of sixteen and nineteen, and he was said to have made a virtual religion of drugs. *Une Saison en Enfer* (A Season in Hell) is less about drugs than about his affair with Paul Verlaine, a third poet who embraced narcotics, but Rimbaud also wrote perhaps the most famous "trip" poem of all, "Le Bateau Ivre" (The Drunken Boat). It told of a wild ride down a hallucinatory river in which the poet lost control of his vomit-stained body and boat. Drink and drugs carried him higher and faster until he left the planet. Bosch-like landscapes were described, mixing strangeness with memories, so that the experience becomes one of exhilarating terror – a Hell that he both loathes and loves.

Drugs were frequently associated with late Victorian occultism, especially with diabolist groups like the Hermetic Order of the Golden Dawn, whose members include William Butler Yeats, Algernon Swinburne (in whose poetry erotic sadomasochism of the Hell-on-Earth kind was extreme), and Oscar Wilde. Yeats, a lifelong believer in the occult, took on the "spiritual name" of Demon Est Deus Invernus – "The Devil is God Reversed." Devil worship was *en vogue* during the period, as often portrayed in the illustrations of artist Aubrey Beardsley.

The Victorians, fascinated with Spiritualism, mesmerism and theosophy, made a fetish out of mourning and the cult of the dead, especially if the corpse was an attractive young person. They also loved ghost stories, tales of horror, and fantasies, few of which were notably Christian, though some had saccharine morals slapped on at the end. Like American horror stories, which were more or less invented by Edgar Allan Poe, the European authors avoided Hell in favor of spooks and apparitions, revenants from the occult and mysterious spirit worlds that lay "beyond the grave."

Out of all of the rich available material, three Gothic novels provided the essential popular fantasies of the twentieth century. They have been adapted and copied over and over again throughout the years. These are, of course, Mary Shelley's *Frankenstein* (1818), where science brings to life and then heartlessly abandons a monster; Robert Louis Stevenson's *The Strange Case of Dr. Jekyll and Mr. Hyde* (1886), in which science creates life not from the dead but from the inner being of man, and Bram Stoker's *Dracula* (1897), the ultimate Gothic demon-lover story.

Hell has no place in any of these novels. Dracula and his minions are demons, but they are not Christian demons, despite their aversion to the crucifix. They are night creatures from the darkest corners of folklore and no one thinks for a moment that when their physical bodies turn to dust and crumble away that the vampires' spirits are destined for Hell. Hyde is a demon, too, but despite some conventional Victorian hand-wringing on the part of the narrator, he is an important modern metaphor, not a supernaturally damned soul. His counterpart is Dorian Gray in Oscar Wilde's short novel, who like Dr. Jekyll, also hides a diabolical soul behind the handsome face. Mary Shelly was a progressive who was far ahead of her time, while Stoker and Stevenson were both very much the products of theirs, but none of them found any need for a punitive Hell for any of their monstrous creations.

Thus, by the end of the nineteenth century, Hell had virtually vanished from popular culture.

There have been four figures that have been generally regarded as the "prophets" of the modern world: Charles Darwin, for his scientific theories and discoveries about the evolution of mankind; Karl Marx, who brought theories about labor and wages, and the conflict between social classes to the economic forefront; Friedrich Nietzsche, who believed that human beings were far too conformist and mediocre and lobbied for change, and Sigmund Freud, whose modern view of Hell is central to the discussion here.

Metaphorical, or "poetical," thinking advanced in the nineteenth century, but Freud's ventures into mental sciences threw new light into dark areas and permanently and importantly changed the modern vocabulary. Questions of predestination versus free will are peripheral to an age preoccupied with the struggle between human nature and free will. Today, we speak of anxiety, inhibition, and repression, not of Original Sin, although Freud (unlike many of his followers) was as determined as St. Augustine to link all of these problems to sex.

Freud was opposed to religion, which he considered to be a form of institutionalized neurosis. His younger colleague, Carl Jung, who had a somewhat mystical turn of mind, differed with him on that point, and added the notion of a collective unconscious, drawing upon archetypal figures with significance to the entire human race as well as to the individual. He called the despair that resulted from the repression of the unconscious the "shadow." Jung's influence on artists and writers may be even greater than Freud's for they certainly understand the "shadow."

Far from disappearing in the twentieth century, Hell became one of its most important and pervasive metaphors. Hell appeared in a variety of places, from Thomas Mann, who set his *Doktor Faustus* in Hitler's Germany, where his obsessed and despairing musician-hero goes mad. Fyodor Dostoevsky, in a series of novels exploring the nature of good and evil, sanity and madness, made a strong case for what Nietzsche called the "death of God."

Modern writers have used the Hell metaphor with great imagination in a number of ways. It appeared in various ways in everything from James Joyce's *Ulysses*, William Gaddis' *The Recognitions* and more. A journey into dangerous territory paralleled Dante's journey into the underworld with Joseph Conrad's *Heart of Darkness* as a prime example. Joseph Heller used the technique in *Catch-22*, as did Gunter Grass in *The Tin Drum*.

Another modern version of Hell is that of the wasteland, which first appeared in the "starved ignoble nature" of Robert Browning's *"Childe Roland to the dark tower came."* Browning claimed not to know where the blighted nightmarish imagery of the poem came from or what it meant, but T.S. Eliot readily admitted that he appropriated images of Hell for *The Waste Land* in 1922. Eliot borrowed from, and added to, the entire tradition. Eliot's Hell is a place of exhaustion and derangement, an arid void where emptiness of the heart and a lack of meaning lead to "rat's alley, where dead men lose their bones." He returned to the same landscape in other poems, notably "The Hollow Men," and "Little Gidding," where his guide to the underworld is a ghost that is made up of a mixture of long-dead poets like Dante and Yeats.

Hell remains a constant fixture as a metaphor in scores of books, films and television shows today, but the Hell of yesterday – a place or torment, punishment and dark landscapes of madness in the tradition of Dante – has long vanished from most forms of modern culture. It's become increasingly hard to find, outside of a few horror books and films and from the pulpits of fundamentalist Christian churches. In those houses of worship, the Devil is alive and well and Hell is a place that awaits anyone whose beliefs differ from the congregation's own.

IN THE NAME OF SATAN..

One has to wonder, after discussing the mythology of Hell and the creation of Satan, as to what really amounts to an opposite number to God – is the Devil real, or merely a legend? And is Hell a real place, or merely a metaphor for our own inner demons?

If the Devil isn't real, and we are our own worst enemy, how can we account for the people who worship him, pay homage to him and even murder in his name? This is a complex and confusing question – more complex than most can even imagine. It seems that true Satanists (as opposed to the mixed-up high school students and black-robed goofballs who use horror film settings to justify their orgies) do not actually worship a dark deity but merely assert their right to indulge their innate desires, instincts, and impulses free from guilt, a philosophy that conflicts with the Judeo-Christian concept of morality. It is the condemnation of unrestrained sexual self-indulgence by orthodox religion and society that they see as oppressive, unnatural and the root of all of the problems that seem to plague our modern society. Their core belief and guiding principle is the credo adopted by occultist and mystic Aleister Crowley from the works of William Blake: "Do what thou wilt, shall be the whole of the law."

Apparently, real Satanists do not harbor an insane need to invoke the legions of Hell to fight an apocalyptic battle on their behalf so that they can dominate the world. That nightmarish scenario is entirely the creation of horror films and Christian theologians. The mythology of Satan didn't originate with the Satanists. It started with the early Christians, who imposed their own fears and prejudices upon an indefinable group of unbelievers in much the same way that Islamic fundamentalists have demonized the "infidels" to justify their extremist beliefs.

Many have suggested that we have a need to believe in the existence of evil because it absolves us of responsibility for our actions. Unable, or unwilling, to acknowledge our failings and those of our fellow human beings, we created a bogeyman to take the blame. Lucky for us, he is conveniently invisible and can never be exposed as anything more substantial than a shadow. The pagans created their own bogeyman of sorts, a straw man that they ceremonially burned at the summer solstice to banish evil from their villages. But they, unlike

Christians, admitted that their burning man was purely symbolic. Unfortunately, the Devil of the Christians proved more persistent and has been behind some of the most heinous crimes ever committed.

But is the Devil merely a figment of our overactive imaginations? Many of the figures that you'll find in the pages of this book, from Aleister Crowley to Anton LaVey, Adolph Hitler and the numerous satanically-inspired murderers, all claimed that some sort of malevolent forced could be summoned to do their bidding. But did they invoke anything but their own inner demons? And if not, does this force come from within – or without? Can it possess us against our will? Can it be invoked by perverse rituals and blood sacrifices?

Is the Devil real? Does he walk among us? Or is what we think of the Devil really just a malevolent force that has had a calamitous effect on our civilization? I'm not sure that the pages ahead can answer these questions completely, but we will take a walk through "Hell" of sorts – the long, blood-soaked history of the Devil and all his works.

2. THE DEVIL'S OWN

SATANISM, WITCHCRAFT AND THE RISE OF THE BLACK MASS

Satanism and witchcraft have been loosely tied together for centuries. When the great witchcraft trials began in the Middle Ages, accused witches were often said to have engaged in sexual intercourse with the Devil as part of their pact with Satan, who gave them their evil powers. In most cases, though, it should be noted that witchcraft and Satanism are two very different things. While they have become synonymous in popular culture over the years, they actually constitute two vastly divergent philosophies. For our purposes here, we will steer clear of the Wicca-style, nature-worshipping form of witchcraft and focus on witchcraft's darker side.

Witchcraft had its origins in primitive nature worship and was a means by which people sought to control the forces of nature and the elemental forces of both the visible and invisible world. In essence, the power of witchcraft had always been the effective exercise of mind over matter, although it was often carried out by way of potions, spells, rituals and ceremonies, which were used to focus energy in achieving the wants and needs of the witch.

Stories of witches – those who cast spells, commune with the Devil and conjure up the dead – are much older than Christianity. In the Old Testament, King Saul is said to have consulted the Witch of Endor so that she could ask the dead prophet Samuel how he might defeat his enemies. Samuel responds that it is the fate of all men to surrender power to another. The witch in the story is not evil; she is merely a medium who uses a talisman to summon a benign spirit on the king's orders, although Saul has expressly forbidden his subjects to dabble in the occult. It is the king who attempts to deceive the witch by disguising himself and flaunting his own law when it suits him. Even so, the Old Testament writers took a dim view of anything connected to witchcraft. In Exodus, it was written, "Thou shalt not suffer a witch to live." Or at least that's how it was translated in the 1500s, when persecuting witches was one of the major goals of the Church.

The Greeks also told stories of witches, seers, sorcerers and enchantresses. They consulted oracles and practiced forms of magic. In the *Odyssey*, Homer's hero summons the spirit of the seer Tiresias and encounters the witch Circe, neither of whom was evil. Later, the poet Theocritus conjured up the image of a broken-hearted girl who was driven to praying to Hecate, the goddess of Hell, in order to have her faithless lover back in her arms. She was not evil, and neither was Glaukias, the hero of a passage in Lucian's *Philopseudes*, which is the oldest known text to refer to the witches' love spell known as "drawing down the moon." Glaukias was so in love with the beautiful Chrysis that he feared he would die of grief if he could never see her again. So, he consulted a magician who invoked Hecate, the goddess of Hell and the dead. Glaukias was instructed to make a clay image of his beloved and stick bronze needles into it while speaking the words, "I pierce thee that thou should think of me." The spell proved successful, for Chrysis ran to the lovesick young man and threw her arms around him, swearing undying devotion. Lucien's fable suggests that although the radical thinkers of Greek society were advancing the idea of free will and pushing their gods to the poetic past, they were still chained to the idea that one individual could influence another by use of the dark arts.

It was the Roman scribes Horace, Ovid, Petronius, Lucan and Apuleius who created the iconic image of the witch as a withered old hag who mixed up vile potions in a huge pot and skulked around graveyards with her familiars. Lucius Apuleius wrote the first full-length story of witchcraft, *The Golden Ass*, in the second century. Although it was a satire that followed the author's misadventures after he had smeared himself with a witch's ointment, there was a serious lesson to be learned from it – that the dark side, or Left-Hand Path as it would come to be called – was fraught with danger. Wise man and women would do well to steer clear of it or risk making an ass of themselves.

There was no moral to be drawn from the description of a necromantic ritual in Lucan's fable *Pharsalia*, just pure terror from the idea that such practices might be possible. In this account, Sextus Pompey, son of Roman General Pompey the Great, consulted the most formidable necromancer of the classical world, Erichto, to learn if his father would be successful against Caesar. Erichto, who Lucan described as "foul with filthiness" and dreadful to look upon, lived in a cemetery in Thessaly and slept in a tomb surrounded by relics of the dead that had been plundered from nearby graves. When Sextus approached her and asked if she could predict the future, she told him that she could only learn what she needed to know from a fresh corpse, because the spirit of the dead lingered near the body for a short time and could be persuaded to return to it. She stipulated that the corpse had to be one that had not been gravely wounded in the mouth, throat, or lungs as that would prevent the reanimated corpse from speaking. She then led him to a battlefield where they could find a suitable specimen in a recently slain soldier. While Sextus was filled with revulsion about what had to be done, Erichto pierced the corpse's jaw with a hook and dragged it to a nearby cave. She brewed a noxious concoction of menstrual blood, spittle from a mad dog and the flesh of a hyena and then poured it into a wound above the dead man's heart in order to reanimate him. Amid the deafening rumble of thunder and the crying of wild animals, she called upon the dark gods Hermes, Charon, Hecate, Prosperine and Chaos to surrender the soldier's spirit, which was lingering above the lifeless body. But the spirit refused to obey her summons to re-enter the corpse until she promised to burn the body afterwards so that it could never be used again. Only then did the soldier's ghost return into his body. The ghastly creature rose shakily to its feet and foretold the future. After that, the body was burned and the spirit was released.

The strange tale was certainly fiction, and such stories were not intended to be accepted as fact. They were created to preserve the faith of a people who needed to believe that the spirit survived after death. A tale of a benign ghost returning to reassure its loved ones that all was well in the world beyond would not have gripped the imagination in the same way that the gruesome story of Erichto did. In addition, its description of a witch as a hideous crone would remain to haunt the world for many centuries to come.

The true melding of Satanism and the black arts of witchcraft began during the Middle Ages, at a time when the Christian Church held most of the religious world in the grip of both devotion and fear. Christianity spread outward from Rome nearly 2,000 years ago, marching along with the Roman legions as they conquered the far-flung lands of the empire. In many places, like Britain, Christianity shared equal status with the gods of the Norse invaders who came to the isles after the departure of the Romans and with the ancient pagan rites that had been passed down for generations. England saw the arrival of St. Augustine and the building of the Canterbury Cathedral hundreds of years later but this did little, at first, to convert the Britons to Christianity. Kings, Queens and the greater part of the nobility accepted the new religion and, in most cases, blackmailed by a fanatical and militant priesthood with threats of hellfire and damnation, they handed over much of their wealth for the building of churches, abbeys and priories.

By the height of the Middle Ages, the Church had succeeded in imposing the Christian faith on the upper classes and a large portion of those who came into close contact with them. Many sites that were considered sacred to the pagans, often marked by monolithic stone circles and monuments, were built over by the Church. The land, once venerated as the womb of the Mother Earth, was plundered without regard for the nature that had provided it. Pagan festivals were gutted of their potency and significance by being re-imagined as harmless communal celebrations of the seasons, like Christmas and Easter. At the Church's insistence, celebrations to mark the summer solstice and the winter equinox were condemned as witches' gatherings so that rural communities would be dissuaded from reviving them. As the cult of Christianity swept across Europe, the Church attempted to eradicate the "old religion" by assimilation. It also adopted its myths, such as the concept of the virgin birth, which had been the traditional method of endorsing prophets since the time of Zoroaster, and the physical resurrection – despite the fact that no mention of those events was made in contemporary accounts of Jesus' life. The birth date of the Christian messiah, December 25, came from the cult of Mithra and the Roman feast of Saturnalia. Even the iconic image of the Madonna and Child was taken from the Egyptian story of Isis and Horus.

At first, the new edicts of the Church had little effect on the common people and they continued their pagan beliefs for many years to come, often being baptized as Christians, but continuing their worship of the old gods. They attended church because the lord of the manor ordered them to do so, but they continued to rely on the old gods when they needed rain, good harvests, protection from misfortune or other blessings. As Christian churches were built on the ancient sites, the people sought to appease the fertility gods by slipping the images of phalluses under the altars. Many old churches still bear stone effigies of naked women exposing their sexual organs, which were overlooked by the clergy who attempted to erase such things from the hearts and minds of the people.

At first, the Church allowed some slack when it came to the old religion. Many of the rules that were created in the years to come had not yet been placed into effect. Perhaps the greatest of these would be when Rome decreed that all of its priests should remain celibate. When it expected the tens of thousands of priests who were then officiating throughout Europe, most of whom were young, virile men, all to lead a life of chastity, it was asking the impossible. Many of them doubtless suppressed their urges by fasting, self-flagellation and other methods. But, based on the literature of the time, it cannot be doubted that many gave in to temptation and managed to seduce their pretty, young parishioners. Before the decree, most priests had lived normal lives as married men and had not unduly condemned their flocks for their pagan festivals and celebrations. Some of them even joined in. They knew about the old religions and, as it did not menace their own, they allowed the pagan rites to continue.

But all of that began to change as the power of the Church grew and its tolerance for the old gods began to disappear. Pan, the playful woodland sprite and granter of sexual potency, was demonized as a purveyor of sin and his followers were condemned as servants of an unholy master. Had the Church possessed the strength of its own convictions, it might have waited patiently for the old ways to die out, but it saw its authority challenged by a rural tradition that saw nothing sinful in sex. The Church retaliated by decreeing that sex could only be sanctioned by marriage, and only then for the purpose of producing children.

Satan became a symbol of anything or anyone who opposed the Church's authority, but in exercising its authority with brutality while turning a blind eye to the excesses and indulgences of its own officials, it could be argued that the Devil was the shadow of Christianity and that is why the zealots feared him so much. Christianity became a dark and morbid religion, obsessed with sin and evil and far from the teachings of Jesus, who spoke of love and forgiveness.

Much of the increase in the Church's power was due to the Crusaders. The adventure of going to the Holy Land on an armed pilgrimage in order to capture Jerusalem from the infidels (and to bring back gold, jewels and other plunder) appealed to thousands of ordinary soldiers. The Crusades, where the soldiers were constantly reminded that if they put their faith in God they would return home safely, led to many of them being converted to Christianity. When they returned home, their families were converted to the faith, as well.

During the age of the Crusades, it was not only knights, squires, and soldiers that went to the Holy Land. Many of the thousands of people who made the arduous journey were devoted pilgrims, anxious to see the land where Christ walked. To protect them from thieves, killers and infidels, the Order of the Knights Templar were formed. The Knights were drawn from several countries and each man was sworn to celibacy and poverty – although this did not stop them from freely indulging in vice or from becoming immensely wealthy. They made their headquarters in Malta, and for many years, they dominated a large portion of the world.

The order was founded in Jerusalem in 1119 by Hughes de Payns and his comrade, Geoffrey de St. Omer. It was officially endorsed by the Church in Rome in 1129 and after that, became a favorite charity throughout Christendom, growing rapidly in membership and power. Templar knights, in their distinctive white mantles with a red cross, were among the most skilled fighting units of the Crusades. The Templars' success was tied closely to the Crusades and when the Holy Land was lost, support for the order faded, although most believed it would

The Knights Templar were formed during the Crusades to protect pilgrims to the Holy Land

continue, thanks to the vast business and banking dealings that the Templars had created across Europe.

However, it was not long before their enemies began to plot against them. Rumors quickly spread about the Templars having distinctly anti-Christian leanings. Reports claimed that the Order worshipped Baphomet, a bizarre pagan deity that had been envisaged by Arab mystics. The figure of Baphomet had the head and hooves of a goat with a black candle placed between its horns. It had human hands, one pointing up and one down. Each hand pointed to a crescent moon, one white and one black. The belly was green and had scales like a fish. It had female breasts and sexual organs of both a man and a woman. A pentagram, symbol of magical power, was on its forehead. When initiated, a Templar allegedly had to renounce Christ and pledge his allegiance to this idol. If that weren't bad enough, it was rumored that he would next be stripped naked and all of the Knights present would engage in a homosexual orgy.

These scandalous stories were soon acted upon by King Phillip IV of France, who was deeply in debt to the Templars after his war with England. The Templars disputed the charges, but Phillip managed to get assistance from Pope Clement V, who was based in France, in starting an investigation into the Templars' activities. He then began to pressure the Church to take action against the order as a way of freeing himself from his debts.

On Friday, October 13, 1307, Phillip ordered the Templar Grand Master Jacques de Molay and scores of other French Templars to be simultaneously arrested. The Templars were charged with a number of heresies and were tortured to extract false confessions. The confessions, despite having been obtained under duress, caused a scandal in Paris. After more pressure from Phillip, Pope Clement issued an order instructing all of the monarchs of Europe to arrest the Templars and seize their assets. He called for papal hearings to determine the guilt or

The Templars became associated with the symbol of Baphomet, a deity that represented the dual nature of man and sexuality.

innocence of the Templars. Once freed from torture, the knights recanted their confessions. In spite of this, dozens of them were burned at the stake in Paris. Phillip then threatened military action unless the Pope disbanded the order, and in 1312, the Templars officially ceased to exist and their assets were taken by the Church and by governments across Europe.

Grand Master of the Templars Jacque de Molay had confessed under torture to being a high priest of Satan, but he later retracted his statement. He was burned at the stake in 1314, but remained defiant until the end. According to legend, he called out from the flames that both Pope Clement and King Phillip would soon meet him before God. Pope Clement died just one month later, and King Phillip died in a hunting accident before the end of the year.

The Middle Ages advanced, and while an increasing number of people began to put their faith in the Christian God, the Holy Virgin, and the saints, the Church was still not powerful enough to suppress the pagan feasts, so it began to simply replace them. In many cases, though, the old traditions remained. On the eve of May Day, the day of Beltane, young men still jumped over bonfires and carried young women off into the darkness. On May Day itself, young people kept up the custom of dancing around a phallus – now disguised under the new name of the Maypole. Christmas was substituted for the old Roman holiday of Saturnalia and, although attendance was required at church on Christmas day, the people had until Twelfth Night, on January 6, for merry-making. And during these feasts, the Church usually overlooked at least two of the deadly sins – gluttony and lust.

With the coming of the Black Death, peaking in Europe between 1348 and 1350, things took a turn for the worse. Where formerly even the poor and middle class had access to public baths with soap and warm, scented water in which to bathe, the pandemic made public gatherings obsolete and standards of hygiene fell.

It was a canon of the Christian Church that dirtiness was next to godliness in those days. In Roman times, visiting the baths had been a daily event, but times had changed. In the Christian nations alone (Muslims had great concern for physical cleanliness), the people worshipped a god whose priesthood insisted upon the deliberate cultivation of dirt and misery. The rich and poor alike lived in stench and squalor. They stayed in inns infested with bed bugs, lived in homes coated in filth and even their bodies were dirt- and sweat-covered breeding places for every type of disease imaginable.

Their God, they were told, would reward them for their suffering, so penances were given that forced people to whip themselves, crawl through the streets on their knees and wear shirts made from hair. Whatever sin had been committed, there at least a dozen punishments by which they could atone.

And perhaps the greatest of these sins was sex. By the Middle Ages, sex had come to dominate the Church's thinking in a way that can only be seen today as pathological. The Christian sexual code was comprised of many regulations but its basic law was that sexual intercourse was to be performed as seldom as possible (and if you were a priest, not at all) and then only for the purpose of procreation. For the weak members of the Church, who fell to their natural impulses, a constant recitation of the need for abstinence was drummed into them, creating guilt and confusion. It was not actually the sex act itself that so dismayed the Church, but the pleasure that might be derived from it. Joyless sex for the sole purpose of procreation could be tolerated, but the warm-blooded enjoyment of sexual love was something that could damn a soul for eternity.

54

In addition, to desire a member of the opposite sex, even though no actual physical contact occurred, was also a sin. Marriage, as already noted, provided no sanctuary for physical love. To desire one's wife was just as sinful as desiring a buxom young woman in the marketplace. One theologian stated that if a man loved his wife too passionately, he had committed a sin that was worse than adultery.

The Church eventually put together a strict system of morality in a series of "penitential books," which explored the subject of sex in every possible detail. Every conceivable misdeed was discussed and analyzed and appropriate penalties were listed for each. The basic code of the Church stated that all were urged to accept the idea of complete celibacy, meaning that virginity was better than marriage. There was also a ban on all forms of sexual expression, other than relations between a married couple, which could occur only on a set number of dates per year. All other sex was forbidden.

The codes also created the mystical concept that all virgins were "brides of Christ," and that anyone who seduced a virgin not only committed the sin of fornication, but, at the same time, committed the more serious crime of adultery. God was cast in the role of the outraged husband and the Church, as his earthly representative, was empowered to exact a terrible vengeance on the perpetrator. The violated virgin, unless she had been forcibly raped, had also committed a mortal sin and she could be charged with adultery.

It was not only for the sexual act that the church prescribed punishments for sinners. Kissing, fondling, attempting to fornicate and even thinking about sex could have dire consequences. Dreams were held equally suspect, and if a young man should experience an involuntary nocturnal emission, he was instructed to get out of bed at once, sing seven psalms and then sing an additional thirty in the morning before breakfast.

Masturbation was another sin with which the Church was obsessed and it held the greatest number of penalties. In five brief codes, there were twenty-two paragraphs dealing with various types of sodomy and bestiality, but there were twenty-five paragraphs dealing with masturbation committed by laymen and several more that dealt separately with member of the clergy who indulged in it. St. Thomas Aquinas stated that masturbation was a greater sin than fornication – for not only was this enhancing the sin of lust, it was also considered murder because a man's spilled seed would never be used to impregnate a woman and create a child.

The sex act itself – when it was permitted to be performed – was strictly regulated and controlled. No position other than the "missionary position" of a man on top of the woman was permitted. Women were not allowed to be on top and a rear entry position was regarded with the greatest amount of horror because it was thought to offer the greatest amount of pleasure. Confessors were instructed to specifically ask married couples if they had dared indulge in this position and if they admitted to it, they were made to do penance for seven years.

When the Church proclaimed that intercourse was illegal on Sundays, Wednesday and Fridays, it effectively removed the equivalent of five months of the year from the possible taint of sexual pleasure. The Church then decided to enforce abstinence for forty days before Easter and another forty days before Christmas, removing the equivalent of eight months from the sexual calendar of the year. It also seemed sensible to the clergy to prohibit intercourse for three days prior to Holy Communion, at which regular attendance was required. From the remaining four months of possible sexual activity, another month had been removed. Then, of course, sex was forbidden during pregnancy and at any time during a penance that had been invoked by the clergy.

The frustrated populace was left with the equivalent of about two months during the year in which they might, for the purpose of procreation alone, have sex without any sensations of pleasure. If a child had been born to them, and had been delivered at a particular time of the year that would fit into the wrong time of the Church calendar, their faith would prevent them from having sex for a year or more.

Depictions of witches in the Middle Ages by Martin van Maele. The Church considered women to be the source of all evil, tempting men into sin with their carnal nature.

It has been said that the Church passed such stringent and ruthless codes of behavior in order to save the souls of the weaker brethren in its midst. Such an extreme ban on sexual activity was certainly never preached by Christ and was not supported by anything in the Bible. The Middle Ages were simply a time of intolerable sexual frustration and obsession – making it possible for a sexual revolution to occur. The traditions of the old gods, which had lain dormant but had never died, were made all the more attractive thanks to sexual frustrations and the enforced sexual repression of the people by the Church. As people began to compare the old ways and new ways the beginnings of Satanism began to emerge in the troubled era of the Middle Ages.

One can easily see how appealing the tales of the old ways, the old customs and the old religion, with its emphasis on fertility and communal sex rituals, could be to the young as they listened to the older folks tell stories about the past. Wild stories described orgies in the woods when everyone present "mixed" their bodies and joined at the loins. Tales told of the bodies of women past child-bearing age serving as "living altars" for young and inexperienced bachelors.

The sexual repressions of the Church placed special emphasis on women as the source of all fleshly evil. In the past, women had been regarded as property but in the Middle Ages, they bore the additional burden of being held responsible for all sexual guilt. It was a woman, after all, who had caused the fall from grace when she had tempted man, who would have otherwise surely remained pure. The mere presence of a woman was liable to attract evil. It was Saint Chrysostom of Constantinople, who was likely more tolerant that most of his contemporaries, who declared that women were, "a necessary evil, a natural temptation, a desirable calamity, a domestic peril, a deadly fascination, and a painted ill."

In the infamous *Malleus Maleficarum*, the authors stated:

A woman is beautiful to look upon, contaminating to the touch, and deadly to keep. She is a foe to friendship, a necessary evil and a natural temptation. She is a domestic danger and an evil of nature, painted with fair colors. A liar by nature, she seethes with anger and impatience in her whole soul. Since women are feeble in both mind and body, it is not surprising that they should come under the spell of witchcraft more than men would succumb. A woman is more carnal than a man. All witchcraft comes from carnal lust, which in a woman in insatiable.

Witches satisfy their filthy lusts not only in themselves, but even in the mighty ones of the age, of whatever sort and condition, causing by all sorts of witchcraft the death of their souls through the excessive infatuation of carnal love.

And the so-called "witch-finder's manual" was not referring just to witches – it meant "good" women too, which is how "woman" and "witch" became largely synonymous in the Middle Ages and even into the so-called enlightenment of the Renaissance era. St. Augustine declared that mankind had been sent to destruction by the actions of Eve, who was, of course, a woman. Women had been offered equal roles in the early days of Christianity. The early Church leaders permitted women to preach, heal, exorcize and baptize. By the Middle Ages, women had lost all vestige of legal rights. The Church leaders seemed to hate women – perhaps because they lusted after them so much.

The penitential books were suffused by an obsession with sex. The Church reformers expressed a horror and hatred of sex that seems to hide a fascination with the temptation and delights of the flesh. The works of the Christian writers of the time literally throb with the sensual agony of devout men who sought to banish desire from their bodies by prayer, scourging and fasting. And it was primarily these men who won positions of power in the Church.

Eventually, the Church's repressive ways provided the catalyst for the old religions to return and to lead to the loss of hundreds of thousands, perhaps millions, of innocent lives during the witch hunts and inquisitions of the Middle Ages. To the Church, the old religion was inhabited by devils that were personified as Satan, the enemy of the Church's work on Earth. To the people, who didn't care about such things, the old gods offered a release from oppression and unrelenting punishment. The Church soon began to try and combat the "evil" influence of the resurrected Pan, the god of fertility, nature and freedom. The Church scholars began to consult ancient manuscripts to determine how best to deal with the formidable adversary who had returned to torment their parishioners. They saw it as the Devil's establishment of power and began to declare that the old religion was henceforth satanic and the women who kept the old traditions were witches. The traditional gatherings, festivals and feasts became witches' sabbaths and the broom, once a symbol of the sacred hearth, became an evil tool. The sexual rites of old, created to stimulate fertility in nature, were now manifestations of forbidden carnal lust.

The peasants felt quite differently about the old traditions that had been revived. Their lords had conditioned them not to feel jealousy if they or their knights should desire a village woman for the evening. The noblemen had long considered the villages as large, informal harems, and no peasant's wife or daughter was safe if she was desired by a lord or one of his men. Now, the peasant protested, he was being threatened with torture and death as a witch if he freely shared his wife or daughter with someone whom he considered an equal during a fertility rite. But he did not let his fear of punishment forbid him from embracing the old ways. He could not experience pleasure without the interference of the Church, which sought to control and repress human emotions. The rebellion took hold and swept across Europe and the old religions once again found their place again among the common people. But eventually, even the natural instincts of the old ways began to darken and change into something else.

THE SABBATHS

It was obvious by the height of the Middle Ages that, despite the best efforts of the Church, the old horned god had not died, because the people still had need of him. They found no satisfaction in a religion that failed to provide an outlet for their carnal needs. Many of them had more faith in the old gods as providers of good harvests and healthy babies than they did in a sad figure that hung pitifully from a cross. After all, no amount of fasting, chanting of dirges, and sexual abstinence had put a stop to the Black Death until the terrible plague had killed off millions of people.

As the old ways returned, the Sabbaths became a regular feature of country life throughout Western Europe and for many years, there was nothing wicked about them. In those days, there was little in the way of enjoyment in the lives of the common people. They were poor and they often worked from dawn to dusk. Very few of them could read or could afford candles to light indoor amusements during the winter months. Apart from fairs and the feasts of the Church, their only form of relaxation was the Sabbath of the old religion. Sabbaths were usually held during a full moon and, four times each year, there were

A depiction of the Sabbaths of the Old Religion

Grand Sabbaths at which several villages might join together to celebrate the feasts of the old gods. These were February 2 (Candlemas), April 30 (Walpurgisnacht), August 1 (Lammas), and October 31 (Halloween).

Those who attended these celebrations contributed poultry, game, fruit, cakes, honey and home-brewed drinks to their gatherings in open fields or in forest clearings. The man who represented the horned god dressed for the part as a goat or stag, and received homage in the god's name. When homage had been paid, he and a village elder would give advice about problems that the villagers did not care to share with a priest and provide herbal remedies for those in need of them. He then assumed the role of a reveler and led the party in the celebration that followed. Those who brought instruments formed a band and everyone joined in to dance and play games. After the feast was over, and everyone had gotten plenty to eat and likely had too much to drink, the sexual rituals began in earnest. Fornication was a sin according to the Christian Church, but the old religion taught that sexual intercourse aided in the fertility of crops and cattle. When it was all over, the villagers returned, tired and happy, to their homes, facing another day of grueling work, but knowing that another Sabbath was just around the corner.

But time changes all things and early in the sixteenth century, the nature of the Sabbaths began to take on a different character. Many believe that this was caused by the coming of the Reformation. Before this, the peasants had no love for the wealthy priests and abbots, but the vices of the clergy kept them from doing anything about the carnal escapades of their flocks. They knew all about the revels of the old religion, yet they rarely interfered. The only people tried and condemned for heresy in those days were those foolish enough to publicly deny Christ or to commit an act of sacrilege in a church. The Reformation changed all of that. The movement began as an attempt to reform the Catholic Church. Many Catholics were troubled by what they saw as false doctrines and malpractices within the Church, particularly involving the buying and selling of church positions and what was seen as considerable corruption within the Church's hierarchy, even reaching as high as the Pope. The Reformation swept away many of the tolerant priests, or forced them to become zealots. A new type of clergy came along, earnest, vociferous, puritanical men, who took their religion very seriously and were determined to force their beliefs on everyone else. It was they who stigmatized the old god as the Devil, and threatened with eternal torment in Hell any of their parishioners who attended a Sabbath.

This must have scared many worthy folks into ceasing their attendance at the pagan celebrations. Moreover, this new type of priest spoke with real conviction about the goodness of Christ and of how he had sacrificed himself to redeem mankind. Services were not always conducted in Latin, but in the language of the common people. The printing press was invented and books began to circulate, allowing many peasants to learn how to read. Much of the literature of the period was religious, telling inspiring tales of saints and martyrs, and offering horrifying accounts of worshippers of the old gods being carried away by demons.

In the course of just two generations, the bulk of the population had changed from being nominal Christians who also still worshipped in the old ways, to devout believers in the Church. This change in attitude was not solely accomplished by prayer and priests – it was largely inspired by fear. Not only would those who followed the old ways find torment in Hell, they could also find it on Earth because the witch trials and Holy Inquisition had now arrived. Sheer terror was felt at the thought of being denounced as having attended a Sabbath. The threat of being burned alive at the stake caused the greater part of the people to abandon the old gods and become devout Christians; they simply had no other choice.

Soon, only the worst elements of the population still followed the old ways. They were the outlaws and robbers who lived in the woods, those who felt the need to defy authority, and the greedy and unscrupulous who were prepared to risk discovery and punishment in order to obtain the secrets of casting spells and making potions and poisons that they could sell for money. There were also those who had a pure, burning hatred for the Church and all that it stood for, and believed that only the powers of darkness could provide them with complete satisfaction.

It was these groups who changed the midnight gaiety of the Sabbath to a blasphemous parody of the Christian faith. Anyone who wanted to attend had to first be initiated into a coven, and the chief of the coven ruled it by terror. The initiate had to deny Christ, spit on the cross and, in a token of submission to Satan, kiss the bared rump of the leader of the coven. They also had to sign a blood oath to Satan in which they surrendered their souls to him in return for a life of prosperity. Such signed pacts could also be used as blackmail if the initiate ever decided to leave the coven or pass along its secrets to someone outside of the group. It was also customary for worshippers to present their children to the coven and have them baptized in the name of the Devil.

The new Black Sabbaths (or Black Mass, as they came to be called) were always held away from populated areas on a tract of flat ground. Wherever the rituals were held, it was essential that they take place in wooded areas. The clearing would serve, according to tradition, as the imitation of the sanctuary of a church. At the far end, worshippers erected an altar of stones and placed an image of Satan on top of it. The idol's torso was that of a man, but its bottom half was like a goat. Its head was also goat-like and sometimes had a small torch between its horns. The central feature was a prominent penis of large and lusty proportions.

The tortures of the witchcraft trials brought forth all manner of obscene versions of the Black Sabbath, but scholars believe that each began with the ceremonial entrance of the naked worshippers, led by the leader of the coven. After the procession and the completion of an opening prayer, the female leader of the coven delivered a kiss to the hindquarters and the erect penis of the satanic image on the altar. Some reports state that after the ceremonial kiss, the priestess would then mount the oversized penis of the effigy and offer herself to the dark god. After that, a banquet would take place with all of the members of the coven taking part. The only steadfast rule of the Black Sabbath was that there be an equal number of participants of both sexes. Every worshipper had to have a mate. Under torture, many told their confessors that Satan would conjure up male or female demons to

The New Sabbaths – The Black Mass

take the place of a missing member of the human company. While many are skeptical of this, there is some evidence to suggest that freshly interred corpses were sometimes dug up and used as cold, uncomplaining partners for some male worshippers.

Each member of the coven was required to bring something for the banquet, and attendees were encouraged to eat and drink their fill. In the opinion of many scholars, the food and drink was likely sprinkled with liberal does of trance-inducing herbs, which would break down the inhibitions of the worshippers. It was important that everyone take part in the Sabbath dance or, as it was commonly known, the "witches' round." The round was performed with the dancers in a back-to-back position with their hands clasped and their heads turned so that they might see one another. The wild, circular dance resulted in an ecstatic condition where, as movement became more frenzied, the group was united as if in one body. A mass sexual communion followed the dancing and it became the responsibility of the coven's leader to make sure that he had sex with each of the female participants using a large, oversized phallus during the orgy. Such a ritual likely caused the women a great amount of pain, and may have been responsible for those who were tortured to elicit confessions to say that had they had sex with Satan during the drug-addled Sabbath.

Acts of sodomy were also reported under duress but both the Church and the worshippers were in agreement that the semen of Satan was sterile. At a time before any birth control methods, other than withdrawal, were used, sexual intercourse without fear of becoming pregnant would have been an exciting and pleasurable aspect of the Sabbath.

The rituals of the Black Sabbath were flexible, and most authorities believe that they changed and developed over time. In the sixteenth century, a priest Florin de Raemond described the Black Mass:

The presiding deity is a black goat with two horns. A man dressed as a priest is attended by two women servers. A young initiate is presented to the goat who makes the sign of the cross with the left hand and commands those present to salute him with a kiss to the hind-quarters. Between his horns, the creature carries a black lighted candle from which the worshippers' tapers are lighted. As each adores the goat, money is dropped into a silver dish.

De Raemond added that when a new female witch was initiated to the coven, she gave the goat figure, which personified Satan, a lock of her hair as a token of allegiance. She then went "apart with him into a wood," where she offered him her body. He also went on to write:

The Sabbat dance follows in the familiar back-to-back positions and the Mass proper begins. A black cape without any cross embroidered upon it is worn by the celebrant. A segment of turnip, dyed black, is used in place of the Host for the elevation. On seeing it above the priest's head, the congregation cry, 'Master, save us!' Water replaces wine in the chalice. Offensive material is used a substitute for holy water in the black asperges.

An asperges or aspergil was the sprinkler filled with holy water used by priests during Mass.

Other accounts of the Black Mass from the sixteenth and seventeenth centuries vary only slightly in their descriptions. In other cases, the leader of the coven would read the litany of Satan out of a black book, followed by a report from every member of the evil acts that he or she had committed since the last meeting. Anyone who had not caused trouble or grief for someone was savagely whipped. The leader was always dressed as some sort of animal. When the feast was held, filthy brews were consumed, loaded with drugs and aphrodisiacs that could arouse the members into a sexual frenzy. Some accounts said that the revelers ate human waste and others went so far as to say that the flesh of a murdered child would sometimes be consumed. The orgies were not encounters of joyful lust, but were dark tangles of sweaty flesh that deteriorated into every type of depravity possible.

The Black Sabbaths that occurred during this time period established the pattern that would continue into the modern era and create what we commonly think of Satanism today. British author Dennis Wheatley, whose espionage novels helped inspire Ian Fleming's James Bond stories, also wrote a number of best-selling supernatural thrillers, among them *The Devil Rides Out* and *To The Devil, A Daughter*. Several of his books that were written during the Cold War had Satanists joining forces with Communists in an attempt to achieve world domination. Wheatley claimed that his lurid descriptions of contemporary Black Masses were based on first-hand research. He wrote:

A Black Mass in Paris -- 1926

At a Black Mass, everything possible is done the opposite way to the correct procedure. The cross on the altar is upside down, crooked or broken. The acolytes should be youths who readily give themselves to sodomy. In the censers that they swing, instead of incense, opium and other drugs are burnt. The celebrant wears a black cape embroidered with serpents and other satanic emblems. He is naked beneath it, and it is open down the front, exposing his genitals. The congregation should, preferably, be wearing animal costumes and masks. The litany and prayers are recited backwards. The congregation's responses are animal howls, snuffling and grunts. The ceremony is performed on the body of a naked woman, preferably a virgin, on her bottom and later on her belly. On the altar is a mattress covered with a black cloth. She lies on this with her head on a pillow below a broken crucifix; her arms spread out and in her hands she holds two black candles made from human fat. Her legs dangle down over the edge of the altar, and each time during the ritual that the priest should kiss the altar, instead he kisses the vagina of the woman. Sacramental wafers stolen from a church are scattered on the floor. The congregation tramples, then urinates, on them while repudiating Christ and vilifying the Virgin Mary. Some of the broken wafers are put into a chalice. The celebrant is handed an infant. He cuts its throat on the belly of the woman who is lying on the altar, and catches its blood in the chalice. Having drunk some of the blood, he sprinkles the rest of it on the congregation, who, by then, incited to a frenzy by the smoke from the drugs in the censers, are howling imprecations and blasphemies. Finally, the celebrant copulates with the woman, while the congregation, as though possessed by demons, frantically slakes their lust on one another in every way possible to perceive.

By the sixteenth cemetery, most scholars believe, the remaining practitioners of the old religion went completely underground, while a hardened few turned the Sabbaths into something more macabre and much darker than those who revived the belief in the old gods ever intended. The Black Mass also gained the attention of many members of the decadent aristocracy of the day, who seized upon its sinister indulgences as sort of a hedonistic parlor game, expressing their sexual fantasies and cavorting about in the nude.

But no matter what the actual beliefs of those who began practicing these horrific rituals, the fact that they were occurring, and spreading across Europe, was proof that the power of darkness was coming into its own.

SATANISM, TORTURE AND THE GREAT WITCH HUNTS

It was not long after the revival of the old religion that the rival faiths – the old ways and the Church – began to clash. In 1303, the Bishop of Coventry was accused of paying homage to a deity in the form of an animal, but he managed to escape punishment. So did Dame Alice Kyteler, who in 1324 was accused of sacrificing animals to the Devil. Even the Carmelite friar Pierre Recordi, who was placed on trial in 1329, was only imprisoned for life, even though he admitted to having seduced three women by making wax images of them that were mixed with his own blood and spittle and burying them under the women's windows. When he achieved success, he celebrated by making a sacrifice to Satan.

It's possible that such statements and confessions were not taken seriously at the time, but all of that was about to change. It was around this time that the Church started to find that such stories were not to be taken lightly. The change occurred when Pope John XXII sanctioned a witch hunt in the belief that his enemies were plotting to murder him by magical means. His suspicions were well-founded. Three bishops, led by Hugh Geraud, Bishop of Cahors, admitted to testing the potency of the powers of the plotters by putting a curse on a wax image of the pope's nephew. The boy subsequently died.

Encouraged by their success, they anointed images of the pope and two leading members of the papal court at Avignon and entrusted their servants to smuggle them into the court by hiding them inside loaves of bread. But the servants were searched at the entrance and the plot was uncovered. Among the incriminating items found on them were poisons, herbs, toads and the hair of a hanged man. Bishop Geraud protested his innocence but was found guilty. He was flayed alive and his body was burned.

In 1335, Catherine Delort and Anne-Marie de Georgel were tried in Toulouse, France, and confessed that, over a twenty-year period, they had attended satanic Sabbaths and had given themselves to the Devil. Catherine claimed that she had first been taken to a Sabbath by her lover, a shepherd, and had submitted sexually to a man dressed as a goat in front of the assembled company. She said that they drank horrid liquids and ate the flesh of infants, and were rewarded by being taught spells that would harm the people they disliked.

Anne-Marie testified that when she was washing the family laundry one day she had seen a huge dark-skinned   man with glowing eyes and dressed in animal skins coming toward her from across a river. He had blown into her mouth, thereby possessing her. On the following Saturday, she was carried to a Sabbath by the sheer force of his will. It was presided over by the man in the animal skins, who urged those present to do all of the harm they could to Christians. He instructed them on magic incantations and showed them how to make potions from poisonous plants.

In 1441, astronomer Roger Bolingbroke, along with Thomas Southwell, a Canon of St. Peter's Westminster, and a woman named Margery Goodmayne, were all charged with having conspired against the life of England's King Henry VI by sorcery, carried out under instructions by Dame Eleanor, daughter of Lord Cobham. Southwell died in the infamous Tower of London. Goodmayne was burned at the stake and Bolingbroke was dragged through the streets behind a horse before being hanged, drawn, and quartered. Dame Eleanor was pardoned for her role in the "assassination attempt" after doing a public penance. Charges of black magic were now being seen as a much more serious offense than they had been previously.

During the reign of Edward IV, the Duchess of Bedford was accused of having employed a sorcerer named Thomas Wake to bewitch the king into marrying Elizabeth Woodville, by whom he had the two princes who later disappeared and were reported to have been murdered in the Tower. The charges against the duchess were later dropped. After Edward's death, his one-time mistress, Jane Shore, was convicted of using witchcraft against his Edward's successor, Richard III. However, the common people, who loved her, refused to believe the charges. She was forced to walk the streets with a sign around her neck that declared that she was a harlot, but she was met with nothing but sympathy and affection by the crowds.

In 1477, a witch named Antoine Rose was brought to trial. She had told a neighbor that she badly needed money, so he took her to a Sabbath, where she was persuaded to give homage to the Devil. He took the form of a large, black dog and everyone present kissed his hindquarters. Then the men had sexual intercourse with all of the women in rear-entry style, as further satanic tribute. They were told to take the communion host, hold it in their mouths, and then spit it out and trample it. They were given potions for making people and cattle ill and told to do as much harm to their fellow man as possible.

These accounts, and others, appeared over the course of almost a century before Pope Innocent VIII declared open war on Satanism on December 5, 1484. He published a decree that led to the formation of the Holy Office, as the Inquisition was officially called. It empowered inquisitors that were appointed by the Church to participate in trials for heresy, to override the decisions of local courts, to proceed against persons of any rank, and to punish all those who were found guilty of practicing witchcraft and black magic.

The object of the decree was to stamp out the lawlessness that was believed to be affecting society. Practitioners of what became known as the "Left-Hand Path" had become so numerous that, by casting spells, inciting rebellion and endorsing other nefarious activities, they had become a menace to the Church and to the Christian way of life. In 1487, a Dominican friar named Tomas de Torquemada was appointed as the Grand Inquisitor of Spain. Under the patronage of the fanatical Queen Isabella, he began a reign of terror that is still remembered today as one of the darkest periods in the history of the world.

The persecution of witches in Europe lasted for nearly 300 years. The surprising, and generally unknown, feature of the witchcraft that attracted the attention of religious and civil authorities during this period is that it was largely invented by the Inquisition and developed by the Church. Soothsaying, divination of all kinds, sorcery, the use of charms and spells – all of these rank with prostitution and espionage as the most ancient institutions in the world. It is nevertheless a fact, however, that such features of witchcraft of this period like incubi and succubi (sexual demons), pacts with the Devil, Devil's marks and witch's marks, and flying through the air on brooms were all thought up by the witch's inquisitors. By a gradual process of indoctrination, over time they were believed and put into practice by self-styled witches. The creations of these maniacal religious figures were to have a deadly effect on the history of the world.

The Inquisition was endowed with exceptional powers. It followed no rules of evidence; it rejected the basic principle of Anglo-Saxon common law that a man is innocent until the prosecution proves him guilty, and it allowed no denial to be entered nor legal representation. Worst of all, even when it proved to its own satisfaction that a victim was guilty, he or she could not be executed until a full confession had been made. If a confession was not voluntarily offered, the Inquisition had the authority to extract one by torture, and this it did not hesitate to do, using the most heinous means imaginable. A confession was followed by the most painful of deaths: burning alive at the stake. On the bright side (if there could be any bright side to being burned alive) since they had confessed, the witches' souls had a chance to enter Heaven.

For more than three centuries, hundreds of thousands of men and women in Europe met their deaths at the executioner's hands, victims of the witch-hunters. Witchcraft persecution swept over the continent in recurrent waves. Many of those dragged before the Inquisition had been denounced by their neighbors out of spite or because they were old or mentally ill. Some might have been heard talking to themselves or to their cat or some animal "familiar" – a sure sign of being in league with the Devil, according to their accusers. Others were "put to the test" because they were known to use herbs and roots to make natural remedies or for telling

MALLEVS
MALEFICARVM,
MALEFICAS ET EARVM
hæresim frameâ conterens,
EX VARIIS AVCTORIBVS COMPILATVS,
& in quatuor Tomos iustè distributus,
TOMVS PRIMVS.
Sumptibus CLAVDII BOVRGEAT sub signo Mercurij Galli.
M. DC. LXIX.
CVM PRIVILEGIO REGIS.

The infamous *Malleus Maleficarum* (Witches' Hammer), an instructional manual for the depraved torture and execution of accused witches. Thousands went needlessly to their deaths because of this horrific book.

fortunes. But many were put to death simply for looking at their neighbors in the wrong way, for cursing them with the "evil eye." To justify their barbarity, the leaders of the Inquisition quoted the biblical edict of "Thou Shalt not Suffer a Witch to Live," but they were ignorant that a more accurate translation had been published in 1584 as "Thou Shalt not Suffer a Poisoner to Live."

The tortures of the Inquisition were dark and brutal, and believe it or not, they had a sort of "instruction manual" to go by. The initial decree to create the Inquisition had been aimed at Germany, where Satanism was particularly rife at the time. It inspired Jacobus Sprenger, the prior of the Convent of Cologne, and Prior Heinrich Kramer, to write the previously mentioned witch-finder's book *Malleus Maleficarum.* It was first published in 1486 and it ran for many editions. The book was written with great care as an examination of witchcraft and it offered a lengthy analysis on the best methods of dealing with the menace. The authors took extreme care to correct errors, to instruct against ignorance, and to carefully direct action. In spite of this, it remains one of the most appalling texts ever written, leading to the deaths of hundreds of thousands of people during the terrifying era of the Inquisition.

As was the standard with Church writings of the time, the authors were obsessed with sex. The inquisitors of the Church followed the writings in the book as they directed their tortures of accused witches to target the private areas of the body, mutilating female breasts and running red-hot pokers into vaginas. Once an accused woman found herself in prison because of the testimony of those who had seen her alleged evil powers in action (which could include jealous neighbors, a rejected suitor or even a relative who wanted her money), she was as good as dead. At the height of the Inquisition, an accusation was the same as guilt in the eyes of the judges. And no lawyer would dare to come to the accused person's aid for fear that he might also be accused of heresy if he pled her case too well.

The Inquisition charged that no witch could be condemned to death unless they convicted themselves by their own confession. This left the judges with no choice but to torture the accused in ways that were so horrific that they would admit to anything to end the pain, even if it meant being put to death for the imaginary acts that they confessed to. The judges turned the accused over to black-hooded torturers who hacked, burned, branded, stretched, starved and raped them in order to obtain confessions.

The tortures began with a search of the witch's body for the alleged "Devil's Mark," a red blemish that Satan placed on all of those who swore allegiance to him. Often, the women had all of their hair shaved off to search for such a mark – which could be anything from a pimple to a scratch, a cut or even a birthmark. They were also stripped naked for the search, which made the abuses that followed even easier for the torturers. Long sharp pins were inserted into the victim's flesh as the sadistic questioners searched for insensitive spots of flesh that Satan left behind on his chosen ones. The pins were stabbed into breasts, cheeks, and groins and if a woman did not scream in pain, then she was obviously a witch. The accused were often raped, were branded with hot irons, had their nipples torn away with iron pincers, were stretched and broken on the rack, had their feet crushed by the iron boot, had sulphur inserted in their anus and vagina, and were scalded with boiling oil, among other things. It's not surprising that many so-called "witches" confessed to anything their accusers suggested to them, preferring death over the continued agony of the torture chamber.

Once a confession was made, the admitted witch was made to stand before the judges and confess to them of her own free will. According to law, the judges were unable to hear confessions unless they were made freely, which is why the accused had to be tortured into admitting that they practiced the black arts. Once they confessed, they were eligible to be reconciled to the Church, absolved of sin, and burned at the stake. Even those

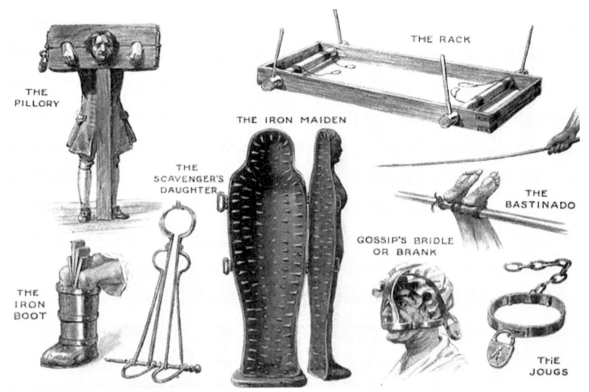

An array of devices used to torture confessions from accused witches.

who managed not to confess were burned anyway – for merely the accusation was enough to make a person guilty in the eyes of the Inquisition. The difference, as far as the Church was concerned, was whether a person died as guilty but penitent, or guilty and not sorry for the things they had done.

In addition to those who were dragged kicking and screaming into the courtroom, there were also those who came and proudly boasted of their intercourse with Satan and of the times that they roasted children alive and ate them. The confessions of these pathological people were eagerly recorded by the court's secretaries and were readily accepted by the Inquisition as an admission of guilt. But even these foolish wretches didn't escape the horrors of the torture chamber. Torture, in cases where a witch confessed readily, was considered to be good for their soul and was prescribed as a way to get into Heaven.

One of the most horrific –and hypocritical – stories from the era of the Inquisition is the grisly account of Joan Bohorquia, a noblewoman and the wife of Lord of Higuera of Seville, who was brought to trial as a witch during her sixth month of pregnancy. Although she was confined in a cell, Lady Bohorquia was not mistreated or abused until after her baby had been born. Eight days later, she was taken into the torture chamber. She was placed on the rack and stretched so tightly that the ropes that bound her cut into the bones of her arms, thighs and lower legs. Not satisfied that she would confess, the priests instructed the torturers to tighten the device and as they did, Lady Bohorquia's bowels burst, sending a torrent of blood from every orifice of her body. She died eight days later, never having confessed to being a witch. This proved embarrassing to the court and after her husband expressed outrage, it was declared that Lady Bohorquia had been found innocent of all charges of witchcraft. She was pronounced absolved from any further process and any damage done to her reputation was

The cruel and sexually depraved methods of torture were carried out against young women by priests and hired torturers.

ordered restored. This was small comfort to her grieving husband, whose wife had been murdered in one of the cruelest and most hideous ways imaginable. Even after the dust had settled, the Inquisition believed that it could not be blamed for the travesty of justice that had occurred.

Persecution of "witches" soon became a thriving industry. The attack on the forces of the Devil depended on judges, jailers, torturers, exorcists, woodcutters, scribes and a legion of experts on the forces of darkness. The livelihoods of many depended on the continued rooting-out of witches and minions of Satan. It was not long before the torturers discovered a foolproof method of continuing their profession: Under torture, nearly any witch could be forced to name a long string of her fellow Satanists, thereby causing one trial to turn into hundreds.

But not everyone in the Church approved of what was going on. Jesuit scholar Friedrich von Spree became an opponent of the trials when the Duke of Brunswick brought him and a fellow priest into a torture chamber. As the Duke and the two Jesuits, who were believers in the Inquisition, stood beside a confessed witch who had been tortured further for the good of her soul, the Duke asked the Jesuits if they truly believed the Holy Tribunal was doing God's work. The priests replied that they did and so the Duke asked the poor woman who was tied to the rack to look closely at his two companions. He told the woman that he suspected the two priests of being witches. With this, he indicated to the torturer that the ropes that stretched the woman should be turned even tighter. At once, she began to scream that the two Jesuits were agents of Satan, that she had seen them having sex with demons and dining on the flesh of a roasted baby. After this, Father von Spree became a dedicated opponent of the Inquisition. He wrote: "Often I have thought that the only reason why we are not all wizards is due to the fact that we have not all been tortured. And there is truth in what an inquisitor dared to boast lately, that if he could reach the Pope, he would make him confess that he was a wizard."

In 1584, Reginald Scot wrote *The Discovery of Witchcraft*, which served as opposition to the earlier *Malleus Maleficarum*. In it, Scot wrote that the Inquisitors were sexually obsessed madmen, who took delight in inflicting sadistic tortures on their victims. He chastised the Holy Tribunal for spending so much time examining the naked bodies of young women for marks of Satan, which they claimed could only be found in the most secret curves and hollows. When one catalogued the terrible agonies that were inflicted, Scot asked, who would not confess to any crimes that their accusers chose to name? Scot was one of the few who dared to rail publicly against the sexual mania that had provided one of the strongest reasons behind the horrible witchcraft persecutions.

The Inquisition eventually died away, but it was only one of the abominations that wreaked havoc during the sixteenth and seventeenth centuries, when religious figures took it upon themselves to try and uncover and destroy the followers of Satan.

THE WITCH FINDER GENERAL

According to legend, in 1591, a Grand Sabbath was held by three covens in England for the purpose of destroying King James IV of Scotland, later King James I of England. The king was about to travel to Demark to bring back his new bride, Princess Anne. The Grand Master at this Black Sabbath, John Fane, assigned specific duties to all of those who were present. Some of them arranged to bring a piece of the king's clothing, then made a wax image of him, wrapped it in the cloth, and slowly burned it. Others attempted to poison him while others tried to use magic to make storms that would destroy his ship at sea. A storm did succeed in delaying his departure for three weeks, and it was later learned at trial that after he sailed, a witch name Agnes Simpson named a cat after him and drowned it in the ocean. This was said to have aroused another terrible storm, but King James, owing it to his great piety, managed to survive and return safely to Scotland. Not surprisingly, he initiated the first great witch hunt in the land, hoping to gain vengeance on those who had attempted to kill him.

Matthew Hopkins

Fane, Simpson, and many others were arrested, tortured, brought to trial and burned at the stake. The confessions that were extracted revealed numerous satanic practices in the country. Fane admitted that he had broken into a church one night by means of a "hand of glory." This was the hand of a murdered man that was cut from his corpse, then dipped in wax and used as a candle. All locks were supposed to open for this charm, and everyone in the building would fall into a deep sleep under its power. Fane had then performed a Black Mass inside of the church, desecrating the holy place. Simpson claimed that she often foretold the future by devilish means and had caused sickness to fall upon more than one hundred people during her allegiance with Satan.

By the early seventeenth century, scores of witches had been put to death in Scotland. In Pendle Forest, a ruin that was known as Malkin Tower was a favorite place for holding Sabbaths. Two rival witches caused so much trouble in the region that the local magistrate had them arrested. On the night of Good Friday 1612, their two covens met at the tower to cast spells and try and free their leaders. Unfortunately for them, a child named Janet Device had been brought along, and she betrayed all she saw and heard that night. Nearly the entire group of witches was seized and burnt at the stake a short time later.

In Scotland, and soon in England, professional witch-hunters began to be employed, with each man receiving a fee for every witch that he detected. There is no doubt that these unscrupulous fanatics sent many innocent victims to their deaths. Many of these men were known as "prickers." They employed a method that involved stripping their prisoners, blindfolding them, and then feeling all over the bodies for some place where, perhaps after an accident, the skin had grown hard. A pin was then pushed into the skin at that spot. If the prisoner did not cry out, or did not bleed, they were told to find the pin and pull it out. If their hand went to some other part of the body, it was accepted as proof that the place where the pin had been stuck into them had been touched by the Devil – so the accused was most definitely a witch.

Perhaps the most infamous of the witch hunters was Matthew Hopkins, who with his assistant John Stearne, began a reign of terror during the time of the English Civil War. Hopkins held, or claimed to hold, the office of "Witch-Finder General," although this title was never bestowed upon him by Parliament. He conducted witch hunts in Suffolk, Essex, Norfolk and other eastern counties of Britain.

Hopkins was a Puritan and a religious fanatic who started out in life as a shipping clerk, not as a lawyer, as some have suggested. According to his book *The Discovery of Witches*, he began his career as a witch-finder when he overheard various women discussing their meetings with the Devil in March 1644 in Manningtree, a town near Colchester, where he was living at the time. Hopkins brought this to the attention of the authorities and as a result of his accusations, nineteen alleged witches were hanged and four more died in prison.

Hopkins recognized this as a message from God, and soon began traveling all over eastern England, claiming to be officially commissioned by Parliament to uncover and prosecute witches. His witch-finding career spanned only two years -- from 1645 to 1647 – but they were busy years. Hopkins and Stearne were well paid for their work, earning £20 from one visit to Stowmarket, Suffolk, which was then more than a year's wages for most people.

While torture was technically illegal in England, Hopkins used various other methods to extract confessions from his victims. He often employed sleep deprivation, a tactic that is still used by interrogators today, and also used a "swimming test" to see if the accused would float or sink in the water. The theory behind this was that witches had renounced their Christian baptism, so water would supernaturally reject them. If a prisoner floated on the surface of a pond or river, then she was likely a witch. If she sank to the bottom and drowned, she was innocent. Of course, a finding of innocence would be of little comfort to the dead.

Matthew Hopkins' career was cut short by an illness, possibly tuberculosis. He died in his home in August 1647 – perhaps saving scores of innocent lives.

Hopkins' career as a witch-finder was made possible by the events of the era, most notably the English Civil War. The victory by the Parliamentarians in the Great Rebellion greatly intensified the witch hunts because Oliver Cromwell's "Roundheads" were Puritans, who strongly believed in the rooting out of evil from the country. All of the fanatical sects that thrived in England at the time continued the witch trials and during the sixteen years that Britain was a republic, hundreds of men and women, mostly innocent, were drowned, whipped, and hanged as Satanists.

On May 8, 1660, the great civil war came to an end and 30-year-old Charles II was proclaimed king. With his landing at Dover, the worst period of repression in England's history came to an end. History has regarded him as the "merry monarch," and a kind and forgiving man. He even called a halt to the hangings of the men who had carried out the murder of his father after ten of them had been executed. "I am weary of hanging, let it rest," he said, and spared the lives of the rest of the conspirators.

The indiscriminate witch hunts were brought to an end, but random trials and burnings continued up until the nineteenth century. Witches continued to assert that they could not be induced to give up the Devil as their lover, even though his embrace was said to be as agonizing as childbirth. In 1662, a woman named Isobel Gowdie told her accusers that the Devil's scrotum was as heavy as a malt sack and his huge member was as cold as ice but he was "abler than any man can be." Another accused witch, Jeannette d'Abadie claimed that Satan's member was enormous and that it, and his semen, were as cold as ice. Although she said that she suffered severe pain whenever she joined with him, that pain was mingled with such exquisite delight that she was nearly driven mad by the ecstasy of it.

There can be no doubt that, during this period in history, many thousands of wretched people were accused of witchcraft and unjustly sent to their deaths at the end of a rope or were burned at the stake. But there were also a great number of people who died who were unquestionably guilty – of something. While many were executed for nothing more than being different, angering a neighbor or engaging in sexual practices not approved of by the Church, there were also many burned at the stake who were murderers of children, poisoners, blackmailers, and worse. But were a few legitimate punishments enough to justify all of the innocent lives that were swept away, as well? No – because the crime of which the Church was most guilty was that, while claiming devotion to God, they inflicted unspeakable cruelties on those who could not defend themselves.

THE AMERICAN WITCH

That there is a Devil, is a thing doubted by none but such as are under the influences of the Devil.
Cotton Mather

Much of the settlement of the early American colonies remains shrouded in mystery today. Records are few and while we know a good deal about the leaders of this era, their broad goals and strategies, we have little that illuminates the lives of ordinary folk.

We do know some things about them from the stories and letters that survived. We know they came to America in sailing ships, crammed with people, animals and whatever belongings that could bring with them. Sickness, including near-constant nausea from being tossed to and fro by the waves, plagued them. Many died on the way, never reaching the New World at all. They brought with them their Old World heritage, ideas and beliefs. They were Europeans from all parts of the continent: English (by far the largest number), French, Dutch, Swedish, Spanish and a scattering of others. They were Protestants (again, the largest number), Catholics (mostly headed to Maryland), and a handful of Jews. In a great many ways, they reflected the traditional stock from which they had sprung. To be sure, they did not constitute an entirely representative example of European culture: Puritans for example, were disproportionately included and persons of high rank and privilege were scarcely to be found at all. Still, when considered from the broadest possible perspective, their values and opinions, their habits of thinking and doing, fell within the usual range for European people of the era.

The first of several waves of immigration to America occurred in the early seventeenth century, a time that coincided with the peak of the great European witch craze. Hence, the new arrivals would have surely known about witchcraft – and feared it, and maybe experienced it, or even practiced it – firsthand. They would have carried their beliefs in the supernatural with them to their new home across the sea. Indeed, the Devil troubled them, both figuratively and literally. One elderly New Englander, reflecting late in his life about his decision to come to America fifty years before, stated that he felt that he would be freer from temptations in the New World than in England, but to his dismay, "I found here a Devil to tempt, and a corrupt heart to deceive."

Were there passengers aboard those first ships suspected of performing witchcraft? That does seem a reasonable presumption, given the state of affairs in Europe at the time. Evidence from a generation or two later suggests that ocean travel may have actually primed witchcraft suspicion in special ways. In 1654, on a ship traveling from London to Maryland, sailors spread a rumor that a woman on board named Mary Lee was a witch. The captain ignored their demand that she be put on trial – at first anyway. Then, when gale-force winds began to blow and the ship began to leak, his attitude changed as the situation started to become desperate. The sailors were permitted to search her body, and they quickly discovered "the mark of a witch upon her." She was hanged as a witch and according to legend, the voyage proceeded in safety. A similar scene was enacted a few years later on board a boat sailing to Virginia. Few details exist today, but surviving records state that an old woman named Katherine Grady was accused of witchcraft and was hanged from the yardarm of the ship. The sentence was allegedly carried out at the urging of the passengers after the arrival of a violent storm. Like a latter-day "Jonah," fearing she was bad luck, the passengers and crew sacrificed her to the sea.

Stories, rumors, legends and gossip about witches spread from farm to farm, and village to village, throughout the colonies. Witches could be found among the settlers, but worse, there was real terror with regard to the Native American populace, a fear that stretched all of the way back to the Old World. In Europe, a large and constantly expanding amount of literature about travel in America had cast American Indians as "Devil worshipers." The notorious English explorer and pirate Francis Drake, for example, reported seeing a native group dance in "hellish" costumes on a beach with plans (or so he believed) to destroy his ships. Similarly, Captain John Smith (of "Pocahontas" fame) regarded Virginia's Powhatan tribe as being in "league with Satan." And Reverend Alexander Whitaker, an early visitor to the same region, wrote a letter home to describing the strange "antics" of the Indians. He concluded, "All these things make me think there be great witches among them, and that they are very familiar with the Devil." Farther to the north, Governor William Bradford of Massachusetts recalled how Indian "pow-waws" had greeted the small band of settlers at Plymouth by gathering "in a horrid and devilish manner... to curse and execrate them with their conjurations." Even Roger Williams, long regarded as uncommonly sympathetic to native cultural ways, declared flatly that Indian priests were "no other than our English witches."

The same opinion continued among the colonists long after the initial arrival of European settlers. Indians were "minions of Satan," "conjurers," and consorters with "evil angels." However, there is always something missing in these stories, which is that the Indians never appear as inflicting injury on the colonists by diabolical means. It was the key to the image of witches elsewhere, but its absence in portrayals of native culture is striking. In fact, the activity that the colonists were identifying as Indian witchcraft was what we could now call shamanism. The practitioners of traditional medicine might have been "witch doctors," but they were certainly not witches in the classic European sense. One early colonist noted that their main role was "curing diseases of the sick and the wounded." Another described them as "partly wizards and witches, and partly physicians." In their latter capacity, "they seem to do wonders." What made them objectionable, in European eyes, was their apparent "familiarity with Satan," their propensity to "cure by the help of the Devil" – in short, their methods were the problem, not the end results. Observations of their rituals confirmed their "Satanism." A typical account of an Indian ritual spoke of "hideous bellowing and groaning," "foaming at the mouth like a chased boar, smiting his naked breast and thigh with such violence as if he were mad." Such "fiendish rites" – bizarre, awesome and terrifying -- could only be inspired by the Devil himself.

Despite the claims of fraternizing with the Devil, it seems significant that no native people were ever prosecuted in colonial courts on charges of witchcraft. They could be, and sometimes were, prosecuted on other charges – like drunkenness, theft and murder – but not on this one. Moreover, the colonists, while harboring a deep revulsion against native rituals, seem to have felt that they had no power to affect them, either for good or for ill. Nor, for that matter, could the magic have much effect on the native converts to Christianity. They, too, had some sort of cultural immunity. This made the overall picture sharply mixed. Europeans were predisposed to associate the Native Americans with Satanism and witchcraft and were deeply troubled by this connection. Yet absent the diabolical intent, Indian witchcraft seemed a different, distinctly lesser, problem than the dark arts practiced by the settlers themselves. As time and experience would repeatedly confirm, for the colonists, the most dangerous witches were those found within their own ranks.

As the years passed, another culture intersected with the native people and the European colonists – the Africans. Small groups of Africans began arriving in the British colonies as early as 1619. Of course, they were immigrants of a very different sort since they had been kidnapped from their homelands and transported to America against their will. Their numbers grew at a gradual pace throughout the rest of the seventeenth century, and then they increased quite explosively in the century that followed. The single most important element in their lives was, of course, slavery; especially after about 1660. From that time on, almost all Africans in America were held in bondage by white settlers. But perhaps the second most important element was the persistence, in various forms, of their own traditions.

In their homelands, magical practice, including witchcraft and sorcery, had been central to the supernatural belief systems of the people. When transferred to America, these beliefs became both truncated and, in many ways, distorted but even so, they encompassed a host of "spirits" who influenced the various details of daily life. At the same time, these beliefs would gradually shift away from the benevolent (fertility, healing and the like) and toward the more directly harmful (loss, injury and death). This, one imagines, reflected the darkened and desperate circumstances into which the Africans had been so cruelly transported.

Evidence of such things came directly from the pens of the white colonists. Many writings of the era referred to "conjurors" and "poison doctors" among the slave population. They made frequent reference, also, to specific episodes of magical practice, and even to the particulars of method and technique: charms, invocations and substances such as "powders, roots, herbs and simples." A different, literally more solid sort of evidence comes from under the ground. Archaeologists have been able to recover some of the artifacts of African-American magic – amulets, beads, objects made of glass, ceramic, wood and even, in one instance, a raccoon's penis bone on a string, which may have been used to promote fertility. Words survive as well, found both in African and American dialects like *juju* (for evil spirit), *mojo* (for witchcraft or magic), *ubio* (for charm), and, most famously, *wudu* or *vodun* (for what we now call Voodoo). Taken together, this combines to reveal a distinctive African-American presence in the colonies, especially in the southern colonies, where slavery expanded greatly after 1700.

As to the matter of how the magic was actually used, most of it was confined within the black population but slave owners, and other white folk, expressed fear of harm from the "sorcery" of their slaves. Most of all, they feared "poisoning." This was a word that seemed to have multiple meanings in the documents of the day. In some cases, it described a straightforward ingestion of a deliberately administered lethal substance, but in others it apparently referred to a supernatural power – poisoning by way of spirits or diabolical magic. Dozens, if not hundreds, of slaves were suspected, accused, convicted and put to death for alleged acts of poisoning.

Slave sorcery, real or imagined, directed against their masters and other white people were an exception. The largest source of "diabolical" danger – or so most colonists believed – remained with and among their own kind. And such belief was prevalent throughout the entirety of British America during the colonial years.

But prevalence was one thing, intensity was another. In some regions – the central colonies along the Mid-Atlantic, for example – concern about witchcraft rarely led to any official action. In others, especially Puritan New England, it was a deeply rooted, malevolent presence. There, formal accusation, involving whole communities and generating full-blown legal proceedings, remained plausible, even likely. The most relentless persecution of witches in England took place when the country was dominated by the Puritans, so it's no surprise that most American witches were hunted down in New England. The courage and endurance displayed by the founding members of the colonies unquestionably came from their absolute faith in God, but this faith sometimes veered into fanaticism. Their religious beliefs forced a strict adherence to the word of God and they would not tolerate anyone who questioned even a single passage in the Bible – including the Old Testament verse about not "suffering a witch to live."

Few other regions were so fanatical and yet, witchcraft was still reported elsewhere in the colonies. Virginia was the site of the first British settlement in America. And Virginia was also the source of the earliest surviving report of witchcraft. In 1626, the colony's general court heard charges against a woman named Joan Wright. During several years at the Kickotan plantation, Wright had earned the reputation of a "very bad woman" by telling fortunes (usually about impending death), "railing" at neighbors and, most ominously, uttering mysterious threats of harm to any who "crossed" her. Her targets included two men who had subsequently failed in hunting despite "coming to good game and very fair to shoot at," and another whose "plants were all drowned." She was also accused of having made an entire family "dangerously sore." In 1641, another court settled a dispute between two women, Jane Rookins and the wife of George Busher (her given name was not recorded). They had fallen into a loud quarrel, at the height of which Rookins denounced Busher as a witch. Busher's husband then brought suit for defamation on her behalf. Rookins claimed not to recall the alleged accusation, but apologized anyway. The court took this as a sufficient resolution of the matter, adding simply that the defendant had to pay all of the costs of the prosecution.

Versions of this same sort of story were repeated many times in other communities across the region. Indeed, most recorded references to witchcraft in early Virginia actually come from defamation cases. There were about twenty of these, with roughly even splits between acquittals and convictions. Punishments, when ordered, typically involved paying a fine. Often, as with the case previously mentioned, a public apology was ordered. In one case, a plaintiff stated that, after she was accused of being a witch, her neighbors refused to "keep company" with her. There is evidence, too, that some of the individuals thus defamed had been subject to physical assault and felt their lives to be in danger.

The surviving records afford a glimpse of the particular suspicions that were aroused at the time – of curses, for example, and of "spells." One woman was said to have uttered "a kind of prayer" against her neighbor that "neither her nor any of his family might prosper." Shortly after, sickness overtook the neighbor's family. Another man claimed "bewitchment" of his cow; another, injury to his horse; yet another, the sudden and mysterious death of some chickens. Several described experiences of being "ridden" like a beast of burden by supposed witches, over long distances, usually at night. One incident left the victim "wearied nearly to death." There were occasional references to the Devil's "imps" and also to shape-shifting – people changing into a black cat or some other animal. There were also elaborate stories of counter-magical activity. In one instance, a woman who "thought herself to be bewitched" ordered a servant to "take a horseshoe and fling it into the oven, and when it was red-hot to fling it into her urine." According to the servant, the remarkable tactic produced immediate, and telling, results: "So long as the horseshoe was hot, the witch was sick at heart, and when the iron was cold she was well again."

A smaller group of cases involved the prosecution of witchcraft itself, not simply its link to defamation. Juries were sworn in, witnesses called, defendants interrogated, all along the lines of traditional English legal practice. By the same token, the suspect's body was carefully examined by "ancient and knowing women" who searched for "teats, spots and marks not usual on others." If found, these dermatological imperfections were attributed to the Devil and understood to be flesh that was used to suckle his imps. The result of one such examination was recorded in detail: "She is like no other woman, having two things like teats on her private parts of a black color." In addition, the homes of defendants were searched "for all images [witch dolls] and such like things as may strengthen the suspicion." And at least a few suspected witches were ordered to be "tried in the water by ducking." This time-tested method of discovery meant that the accused would be immersed in a pool or a stream. If she floated too easily, the Devil was presumed to be at work on her behalf. If she sank – or better yet, she drowned – then she was obviously innocent of the charges that had been brought against her.

Virginia was the first colonial site for court proceedings over witchcraft, and it also turned out to be among the last. Some trials occurred as late as 1706. Meanwhile, there were similar cases in nearby Maryland. Most of these, though, revolved around slander. A typical case involved a man named Peter Godson who was confronted by his neighbor, Richard Manship, who had heard Godson was saying that Manship's wife was a witch. Godson said that he had gone to Manship's home and his wife, in a jesting way, placed two straws on the floor and told Godson that if she was a witch, then he would not be able to step over them. Godson did step over them, but was struck lame the following day – which he claimed proved that Mrs. Manship was a witch. Manship sued him for libel. Godson later retracted his accusation and the court case against him was dismissed, but it's likely his friendship with Manship was never the same again.

New York witnessed occasional witchcraft trials, including a lengthy one in 1665 that charged a Long Island couple named Ralph and Mary Hall with using certain "detestable and wicked arts, commonly called witchcraft and sorcery," to cause the illness of a neighbor, George Wood, and his infant child. In the end, though, there were no convictions. A jury found "some suspicions of guilt" in the woman, but not enough "to take away her life." Her husband was acquitted outright. Other, more casual implications of witchcraft are scattered through New York legal records until the late 1600s, with only a few rising to the level of legally actionable slander and one involving the banishment of a witch who had moved there from Connecticut.

Pennsylvania was founded in 1682, later than many of the other colonies, so it had a briefer involvement with the witchcraft of the era. The Quakers, who made up the majority of the population in those days, had little to do with such things, but a handful of cases did surface. In 1684, William Penn and his council conducted a full-blown prosecution of charges against members of the colony's Swedish minority. Two women, Margaret Mattson and Greta Hendrickson, stood accused of bewitching cows and practicing other "sorceries" over a span of at least twenty years. The jury returned an unusual form of split verdict: "guilty on the common fame of a witch, but not guilty in manner and form as she stands indicted." In 1701, a Philadelphia butcher and his wife were charged with slander for identifying a neighbor couple as the cause of a "very sudden illness in a certain strange woman lately arrived in town." The plaintiffs claimed as a result to be "suffering much in their reputation, and by that means in their trade." The strange woman, perhaps their lodger, had been found with "several pins in her breasts," and other seeming indicators of witchcraft. The case, however, "being inquired into, and found trifling, was dismissed."

The word "trifling" that appeared in the record was one not found in any other case of the preceding century. By this point, concern with witchcraft – at least *official* concern with witchcraft – was beginning to fade. Indeed, in all places outside of New England, it had never amounted to a great deal. It was certainly a part of local culture and it certainly could, for short periods of time, around particular persons, attract a great deal of attention, but the sum of its effects was modest. There were few executions, few clear-cut findings of guilt, and only occasional prosecutions (and the majority of those for slander only, with the roles of the accused witch and

The Puritans brought their strict religious beliefs to America, leading to the numerous witchcraft trials that still haunt us today.

accusing victim turned around). For the most part, America was a mere shadow of the witchcraft frenzy that had been seen in the Old World.

But then we turn to the history of witches in New England.

The Puritans of New England hold a special place in American history. This group of settlers – actually two groups, the *Mayflower* pilgrims who arrived at Plymouth in 1620 and the much larger contingent that arrived at Boston about a decade later -- were defined from the outset as religious reformers of a strict and radical nature. They were the leading social reformers of their time and yet they took a fundamentally reactive and backward-looking stand. The English church as they knew it was "corrupt" and in response, they wanted to "purify" it by returning to the habits and principles of the early Christians. English society was no less compromised, they believed, and they wanted to restore it by recapturing the "brotherly" spirit of a simpler age. Their social criticism is of special importance here. They saw themselves, not without reason, as being born at a time of unprecedented change. They saw rapid population growth, runaway inflation in prices and rents, the development of trade and industry, the swelling of towns and cities (spectacularly so in the case of London), the disruption of the ancient manorial and parochial systems in the countryside and felt that the stays of traditional culture were truly coming apart. To the Puritans, the accompanying social costs seemed enormous – with vagabonds roaming the highways, beggars infesting the cities, disease, fire and crime running rampant – all of it seemed to predict an ultimate breakdown. Their writings were a litany of outrage and sorrow about the evil surrounding them.

Puritans lived with a terrible fear of disorder and chaos. They found in their religious faith a vital measure of reassurance, offering strength, hope and the promise of a "new life." It was centered precisely in the values that history seemed bent on destroying. Puritanism enshrined, above all, the principle of *control*, both inner control of the individual person and outward control among the community of "saints." Intense and unrelenting discipline was the appropriate answer to disorder.

Having crossed the ocean and established homes along the New England coast, Puritan leaders seized a unique opportunity to start fresh – to found communities were the law of God and the law of man would become one in the same. That they expressed their goals in theological terms should not mislead us; there were, after all, no other terms available to them. In contrast to what they had encountered in England, they would strive to re-create an organic connection among God-fearing folk. In contrast to disorder, they would establish harmony, peace and the subordination of individual interest to the "commonwealth." Countless New England sermons would later bear witness to the importance of these values. It was, for Puritans, the true meaning of Christian love. In a famous shipboard sermon, Governor John Winthrop encouraged his followers to "knit together, as one man, and delight in each other, make others' condition our own, rejoice together, mourn together, labor and suffer together, always having before our eyes our commission and community in the work."

The pursuit of Winthrop's goals involved strenuous work by the Puritans in the area of self and collective improvement. Individual striving for holiness was an important element of life, as was an attitude of unflinching "watchfulness" toward one's family and neighbors and a community-wide commitment to consensual decision-making. But being and acting "knit together" proved to be a most difficult ideal, one they would never fully realize. They often disappointed themselves as, all across the new land, towns and villages fell into "controversy" and divided into "factions" around matters both large and small. To some extent, Puritanism itself was to blame for this. In rejecting the established ecclesiastical hierarchy, it had also relinquished many traditional checks on the possibility that individuals might plot their own course, in religion and otherwise. Because of this, various factions formed and flourished in early New England. Some of these had the potential to split entire communities." Moreover, New England's special brand of Puritanism was challenged from outside as well, by Anglicans (members of the official established church of the realm), by Baptists and by Quakers.

Governor John Winthrop

But perhaps the most sinister challenge came from another source altogether. This was not a competing sect or even a religion in the strictest sense of the term, but rather the ancient traditions of "folk magic." Interest and belief in magic had crossed the ocean with the first wave of New England settlers and had firmly taken root in the cultural soil of American communities. Its traces are numerous and varied but early ministers often referred to it in their sermons and writings. Cotton Mather, for instance, declared that "in some towns it has been a usual thing for people to cure hurts with spells, or to use detestable conjurations, with sieves, keys, peas, nails and horseshoes, and I know not what other implements." Courts inquired into it, most often as part of witchcraft prosecutions. Ordinary people mentioned its use – and often its success – in their diaries and in letters to one another. Its pervasiveness, even in the most religiously oriented of colonial regions, is beyond doubt.

As in the Old World, the term "magic" covered a wide range of beliefs and practices. So-called "high magic," including alchemy, astrology, numerology, and other arcane disciplines was the province of learned men and as such, it was respected and even admired. Some of New England's foremost magistrates and ministers were among its devotees and practitioners. Folk magic, however, was a different and far more controversial matter. For this, there were specialized adepts, "cunning" men and women, who were prepared to assist those who came to them in times of need. The largest group of recorded cases involved "divining," which was the use of occult methods to foretell the future or to find lost or stolen objects. Fortune-telling, using all manner of devices, was a commonly held custom of that era and for many years after.

Folk magic was truly a matter of folk – ordinary individuals – who knew something of traditional lore and sought to apply it the best way they could. Besides divining, their efforts frequently embraced healing, in response to illness or injury. One man reportedly had "an effectual remedy against the toothache," another "a cure for the ague" (fever, perhaps malaria), still another had a quick fix for a broken leg.

A detailed look at the folk magic being practiced at the time comes from the testimonies given in court cases, like a case against a "doctor woman" named Ann Burt of Lynn, Massachusetts, filed by several of her erstwhile patients. According to one, Burt had prescribed potions from a certain "glass bottle," and after he drank it, he was even sicker. The same man claimed to then have frightening encounters with "familiar" animals, and then with Burt herself, seated "upon a gray horse." A second witness went to Burt to cure a sore throat and was told to smoke a pipe, after which she "fell into fits." Still others claimed that she invoked a force they called "her god" as an apparent part of the treatment process. For example: "She said that her husband did not believe in her god and could not be cured, and that her maid did believe in her god and was cured." This suggestion of a supernatural being – separate from the Christian tradition – is rare, if not unique, in the annals of New England folk magic. It may have appeared in other cases as well, but if so, the records have been lost over time.

A case of folk magic going wrong can be found in a New Hampshire witchcraft case from 1680. A little boy fell ill and a neighbor, thought to be adept at healing, offered to try a cure. Coming to the child's bedside in strange garb, "her face dabbed with molasses," she proceeded to carry out a ritual. "She smote the back of her hands together sundry times and spat in the fire. Then, having herbs on her hands, stood and rubbed them and strewn them about the hearth. Then she sat down and said, 'Woman, the child will be well,' and then she went out of the door." Outside of the house, the ritual continued. According to the parents of the sick child, she turned back to face the house and stood "beating herself with her arms, as men do in the winter to heat their hands, and this she did three times while stooping down and gathering something off the ground in the interim." As it transpired, the child did not get well, but died within a few days. The would-be healer was held responsible, and her supposed "remedy" was condemned as witchcraft.

There was a fine line between beneficial magic (including healing) and diabolical magic. One could easily be construed as the other, and in many cases the difference was in the eye of the beholder. Some magic, meant to be helpful, could easily be turned another way. Image magic was considered especially potent and dangerous – for example, the use of "poppets" (another name for witch dolls) to represent particular human targets. Treat the dolls with kindness and the intended recipient of the magic thrives. But pinch, prick or twist the poppet and the intended victim might fall ill, break into fits or perhaps even suffer a mortal injury. Records exist of the authorities searching a suspect's house for evidence of these dolls and occasionally, they found what they were seeking. One case file from Boston noted the discovery of "several small images made of rags and stuffed with goat hair and other ingredients."

Many believed the "poppets" used by folk magic practitioners were the work of the Devil.

Closely related to image magic practiced by a witch were various forms of counter-magic that were directed against her. For example, urine might be taken from a witch's victim, poured into a special container, infused with pins and nails and heated over a fire. This was supposed to cause an immediate reaction – scalding, burning or some other painful sensation – in the suspected perpetrator, wherever she might be. This same trick might also force her to return to the scene of the crime. In one such case, a suspect was seen "walking to and fro" near her victim's house for several hours – after a certain urine-filled bottle was opened. In this way, both revenge and identification were achieved in one stroke. The key element in every instance was a powerful line of influence that was believed to connect the witch to her victim – a sort of invisible tether – with effects that could travel in either direction.

To these methods of magic and counter-magic were added many more. Palmistry was one of them and it was learning about "the future condition of a person by looking into their hands." This was something of a learned discipline in New England and skilled palm-readers would occasionally claim to have consulted books in which "there were rules to know what should come to pass." One diviner was skilled at not only reading hands but also in scrutinizing the "veins about the eyes," apparently as a way to predict longevity. Astrology was also practiced, and there were many fortune-tellers throughout New England who consulted the stars as a way of measuring both a man's past and his future.

Palms, eyes, and the stars; crystal balls, and obscure manipulations of keys, nails, scissors and tea leaves: the accoutrements of folk magic went on and on. It seemed that everyday objects of various sorts might, under the right circumstances, be associated with powers of the occult, though the particulars of how many of them were used have been lost. There were charms, too, involving the use of mysterious words and letter combinations – sometimes written and sometimes spoken. There were secret healing phrases as well as spoken curses with "ill words" that were designed to injure.

Toward all of this – the interest, the beliefs and of course, the actual practice of magic – the orthodox clergy of New England maintained an unswerving, vehement opposition. For them, it was nothing less than sacrilege, an affront to their own authority and, most of all, to God's. If the common people needed protection from the bad things in life, it must come from God – and no one else. Suffering should be relieved through "solemn prayer" and not by the workings of a witch. The difference between folk magic and "true religion" lay in that one was manipulative and human-based, and the other was divinely ordained. Wherever magic had apparently succeeded in achieving some intended effect, its source could only be the Devil himself.

Christian clergy all over Europe had long condemned magic, and this was true for Catholics and Protestants alike. But to the extent that Protestants, more than Catholics, stressed the absolute sovereignty of God and the utter fallibility of man – to that extent magic was an even greater, more blasphemous challenge. As it turns out, though, some could even say that Protestantism *invited* such a challenge. Protestants, unlike Catholics, were effectively disarmed against such things, since their faith denied them the "intercessory" means that the Catholics had. There was no more saying of rosaries, no use of holy water or holy relics, no elaborate church rituals, no potentially comforting doctrine of salvation by works. Instead, they had inherent sin and irrefutable weakness in the face of an all-powerful deity. For Protestants, the human situation was a stark and desperate one. Men and women could only wait, pray, hope and fear. Is it any wonder that some found this predicament too great to bear, and the temptation of magic became too hard to resist?

Cotton Mather

In the Protestant belief system, nothing evoked more anxiety, more agonized speculation, that "predestination," the idea that God had already decided the salvation or damnation of every living person. One's destiny was certain and beyond all possibility of change – and yet one could never know its nature. Such a belief within some faiths seems to have fostered an attitude of particular concern with the future – with the afterlife and with the immediate matters of everyday existence. This, in turn, may help to explain the popularity of divining and fortune-telling in early New England.

But if there was anything that the Puritan clergy knew about folk magic, it was that they did not like it – not at all. Reverend Cotton Mather wrote, "Tis in the Devil's name that such things are done, and in God's name I do this day charge them as vile impieties." Just to make sure that he got his point across, he added, "They are a sort of witches who thus employ themselves." Reverend John Hale stated, "Magic serves the interest of those that have a vain curiosity to pry into things God has forbidden, and concealed from discovery by lawful means." Indeed, Puritan ministers particularly emphasized folk magic's links to witchcraft and the Devil, which, of course, caused it to be fatally compromised.

As this controversy – folk magic versus orthodox religion – simmered in New England, ordinary folks were often caught in the middle. Resisting the clergy's pressure to choose, these people would remain Christians, remain churchgoers, remain adherents of the Puritan doctrine – yet would also avail themselves of magical "remedies" when need and opportunity presented themselves. They were inclined to move back and forth between doctrines at their convenience. Sometimes, to be sure, they paid a price in loss of reputation or feelings of guilt. A case in point was Reverend John Hale's experience in dealing with a woman parishioner who was involved in fortune-telling. She admitted to consulting a "book of palmistry," and professed her sorrow and "great repentance." Hale told her that this was, most assuredly, "an evil book and an evil art," after which she appeared to "renounce and reject all such practices." But it didn't last. A few years later, she went back to palm reading, likely until she was chastised for it again.

However, certain forms of magical practice seemed to be able to bridge the gap to religion. The charms used in healing rituals could include "scripture words" along with others. Most of these "scripture words" were Latin from the Roman Catholic Mass, which for devout Puritans would create a special objection. The Bible itself was subject to magical deployment, with its aura of sanctity harnessed to efforts of healing or divination or counter-magic. The touch of a Bible on the forehead of a sick child might serve to encourage healing. A key placed between its pages would help reveal the location of objects that had gone missing. Such methods came as much from the magical side of traditional culture as from the formally religious one.

It was against this cultural backdrop that New England's notorious role in American witch-hunting began. Of course, the most notorious incident in this diabolical history took place in Salem, Massachusetts, in 1692-1693, but there was a considerable amount of controversy that swirled around witchcraft in the region for four or five decades before the events at Salem took place.

There are records of witchcraft being practiced in Massachusetts as early as 1637. Although, honestly, this case seemed to have more to do with the fact that the accused was a woman, rather than that she was a witch. Anne Hutchinson, at the center of the controversy, seemed to challenge the very foundations of the Puritan establishment. The daughter of an Anglican minister, she was a unique presence: deeply thoughtful, eloquent, visionary and charismatic. The mother of fifteen children, she was an amazingly energetic woman who worked as a midwife and held Bible study groups in addition to running a large household. Hutchinson gathered a large following composed of Boston folk who attended her special worship meetings, and this served as another element about her that attracted attention. Governor John Winthrop, her chief antagonist, referred to her as a "prophetess," and the term does seem apt. Such a woman invited admiration, but great suspicion as well. She was, in a sense, too "nimble" of wit, for her own good. Her prophesying, in particular, would be held against her as her gifts seemed to some to be "beyond nature." Two years after she arrived in Massachusetts, she was brought before the authorities in a trial because, as Winthrop wrote, her doings "gave cause of suspicion of witchcraft."

As it happened, she was never formally accused of being a witch. Her trial, conviction and subsequent banishment focused instead on her "heretical opinions" and "traducing authority." She was also charged with being "deluded by the Devil." In addition, two of her "confederates," Jane Hawkins and Mary Dyer, were also accused. Hawkins, like Hutchinson, was a midwife, whose practice allegedly included the use of traditional fertility potions. As a result, according to Winthrop, she became "notorious for familiarity with the Devil." Dyer and Hutchinson both experienced problematic childbirths. In Dyer's case, the baby was stillborn and was badly deformed. Hutchinson, too, gave birth to a severely deformed baby, which never had a chance at life. Such "monstrous" births – as they were regarded at the time – were a clear sign of some demonic connection.

That these suspicions did not immediately lead straight to prosecution for witchcraft was probably due to a couple of different factors. First, heresy was considered a serious crime, especially to New England folks, and second, the usual prelude to a witchcraft trial – the gradual, piece-by-piece buildup of suspicion and doubt, over many years, accompanied by neighborhood gossip – was lacking in the case. Hutchinson, Hawkins and Dyer were relatively recent arrivals to Boston and so were their adversaries. In a sense, neither side knew the other well enough to support a full measure of witchcraft allegations. In fact, there were no witchcraft trials in New England at all during the quarter-century following the landing of the Mayflower in Plymouth Harbor in 1620. People needed to get to know one another better before they could start accusing each other of frolicking with the Devil. Once they started, though, the trials went on until almost the end of the century.

The earliest record of an American proceeding against witchcraft comes from the town of Windsor, Connecticut, in 1647. On May 26 of that year, a woman named Alice Young had the unfortunate distinction of being New England's first legally certified witch – and the first to be punished by hanging. Few facts are known about Alice Young, other than that she was married, probably to a carpenter named John Young, and was the mother of at least one daughter. She was probably middle-aged when she was charged and convicted. She and her husband settled in Windsor around 1640. Young sold his land and moved away after his wife's hanging.

Barely a year after Alice Young's execution at Windsor, the nearby town of Wethersfield began its own involvement with witch-hunting. Again, little remains of the official record. It states only, "The jury finds the bill of indictment against Mary Johnson, that by her own confession she is guilty of familiarity with the Devil." Later writings by Cotton Mather offer a little more

information. Mary was evidently a domestic servant and Mather noted that the Devil often played tricks on her master at Mary's request. He wrote, "She said that her first familiarity with the Devil came through discontent, and wishing the Devil to do that and t'other thing, whereupon the Devil appeared unto her, tendering what services might best content her." From this, she progressed to "uncleanness [sexual contact] both with men and devils" and somewhere along the way, she allegedly murdered a child. Such a confession, rare in the record of American witch trials, left no room for doubt and a death sentence was assured.

After the events in Connecticut, the record of witch trials traveled north and east to the communities surrounding Massachusetts Bay. A little-known case, possibly as early as 1648, resulted in the execution of a woman referred to only as Goodwife Kendall. Another proceeding in 1648 against Margaret Jones of Charlestown brought the same outcome. Jones had been acting as a healer and fortune-teller and details of her methods aroused suspicions about her. Her medicines "though seemingly harmless had extraordinary violent effects." Worse, she showed "such a malignant touch as many persons who she stroked or touched with any affection or displeasure were taken with deafness or vomiting or other pains or sickness." When searched for the Devil's Mark, she was found to have "an apparent teat in her secret parts." A witness to her nights in prison as she awaited her trial noted the comings and goings of a "familiar" spirit in the shape of a "little child."

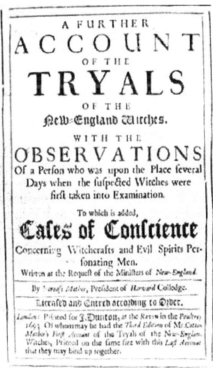

Over the course of the next few years, a number of slander cases emerged in Massachusetts communities that were filed on behalf of women against neighbors who had defamed them by intimating, or openly charging, that they were involved in witchcraft. Several of them had been accused of conducting meeting with the Devil at their homes.

In 1652, a more substantial and serious case took place in Springfield, Massachusetts. At the center of the events was a married couple, Hugh and Mary Parsons. Mary was accused of murdering her infant son. Numerous accounts and depositions were filed against them and the list of supernatural events of which they were accused included mysterious disappearances, strange illnesses and injuries, "threatening speeches" (especially by Hugh Parsons), and perhaps most important, "fits" in several apparent victims. Mary seems to have admitted her guilt and her own testimony recounted startling details of "a night when I was with my husband and Goodwife Merrick and Bessie Sewell in Goodman Stebbins' lot... We were sometimes like cats and sometimes in our own shape, and we were a-plotting for some good cheer." Her conviction and execution shortly followed her confession. Hugh Parsons, although he denied all of it, was convicted and condemned to death. However, the verdict was later reversed and he fled to Rhode Island. Whatever happened to the other suspects was never recorded. What is clear, though, is that Springfield was in great upheaval during the many months of the unfolding events, since participants in the Parsons trial came from over half of the households in town.

Another striking case occurred in Boston in 1656. The defendant, Ann Hibbens, was a person of unusually high social status as her husband, William, was a not only a wealthy merchant but an admired civic leader, a magistrate and member of the Court of Assistants, the colony's highest governing body. Ann doubtless shared in the prestige of her husband's position and yet her abrasive personality frequently caused her grief. In 1640, she had engaged in a long and bitter dispute with a group of carpenters who had been hired to refurbish her house, accusing them of cheating her. A resultant lawsuit in civil court went was resolved in her favor but the manner in which she pursued the case was so aggressive that the Boston church called her to account in a widely publicized ecclesiastical inquest. When she refused to apologize for her actions, the church first admonished, and then excommunicated her. Her husband pleaded on her behalf, yet he also acknowledged that she could be "uncharitable" and "un-Christian-like." Church authorities accused her of wronging him also – admonitions that Ann mostly ignored.

As the years passed, Ann had other problems with the townspeople of Boston, but little could be done about her because of her husband's standing in the community and the fact that he was so well-liked. But when William died in 1654, Ann lost her protective barrier and within a few months she was accused, and arraigned as a witch. The details of her final trial have been lost, but its outcome is known – she was convicted of witchcraft and hanged.

Around this same period, suspicion was aroused toward several people against whom rumors of being witches would circulate for decades. Eunice Cole of Hampton, New Hampshire, was one of them. There was also Elizabeth Godman of New Haven, Connecticut, Jane James of Marblehead, Massachusetts, and John Godfrey of Andover, Massachusetts. These individuals all fit a classic pattern in which a reputation for practicing witchcraft might never be escaped from and thanks to this; they were subject to repeated court prosecutions.

John Godfrey's story was particularly remarkable. In one respect it was unusual in that he was male. Within the relatively small subgroup of accused men, most were husbands of previously suspected women. Their guilt was always one of association. But Godfrey was different in that he was unmarried and in fact, had no identifiable kin at all. He had arrived in Massachusetts sometime around 1642, and had almost immediately become mixed up in a number of legal proceedings. Before he was through, he would set a new standard for litigiousness in what was a very litigious society. Suits and countersuits piled up around him by the dozens: for debt, for breach of promise, for defamation, for "abusive carriages" and "contempt to authority," among others. He often appeared as the plaintiff in cases against one or more of his neighbors, and he won more cases than he lost. However, he was also a frequent defendant and the charges against him often involved criminal conduct. He was accused of theft, arson, of suborning witnesses, of physical assault. And he was accused again and again of practicing witchcraft. The testimonies generated by his seemingly non-stop legal issues are both lengthy and consistent in quality. Taken together, they depict a man continually at odds with his peers over a score of personal and usually mundane affairs. They also reflect his unlikable manner: angry, rough and threatening. He directly epitomized the character that New Englanders expected of their "witches" and served, in effect, as an extreme example of a typical pattern. In other words, if you made enough people angry with you in that time and place, you could expect as some point to be accused of being a witch – it seemed like the best way to put some people in their place.

It is notable that Godfrey remained at large to fight with his Essex County neighbors for more than three decades until his death in 1675. Five times he stood in court under formal indictment for witchcraft, which was a capital crime. And five times he (more or less narrowly) he escaped conviction. At least once, a jury declared him "suspiciously guilty of witchcraft, but not legally guilty according to the law and evidence we have received." Put on notice again and again, he just kept coming back for more. No one can ever truly explain the motives behind Godfrey's constant antagonism, but he simply refused to go away.

Eunice Cole was the female version of John Godfrey. She, too, was repeatedly accused and often prosecuted for witchcraft, but never convicted. She was also uncommonly rough and abrasive, given to "unseemly speeches" and physical brawls. Her reputation was widely known and it would long outlive her. Tales of her supposed witchcraft entered into local folklore and was told to generation after generation. Even today, centuries later, children in Hampton know her name and tell of her supposed misdeeds – and even shudder a little when they pass near her old home site.

The stories of Elizabeth Godman and Jane James were variations on the same theme. In both cases, there was years of suspicion, occasional court trials, and acquittals each time, often accompanied by a stern warning. In these cases too, though, the women lived next door to the same people who accused them of being witches for years. They became fixtures of local culture, almost as familiar as Sabbath services, autumn harvests and barn raisings.

The decade of the 1660s saw nearly as many witchcraft trials as the one that preceded it with twenty-five trials in all. Thirty-two people were charged, five convicted, and four executed. However, a new element was added in the years 1662-1664 when New England's first experience of "witchcraft panic" occurred. It was the sort that spread and multiplied in a contagious fashion, with one accusation feeding another. It began in Hartford, Connecticut, and while its exact origin remains obscure, it seems to have begun with the "very strange fits" of a young woman in town. As they developed, "her tongue was improved by a demon to express things which she herself knew nothing of." She apparently also began to speak in a "Dutch-tone" and then revealed "mischievous designs by such and such persons" against several neighbors.

One of the "persons" was a certain "lewd and ignorant woman" named Rebecca Greensmith, who was already in jail on suspicion of witchcraft. Going by the established procedures, the accused was examined by a group of magistrates and ministers, who managed to get her to put together a pretty impressive confession. She described all sorts of familiarity with the Devil, including "carnal knowledge of her body," and described witch meetings that occurred near her house. Some of the witches appeared in one shape, others in another, and "one came flying amongst them in the shape of a crow." No one knows why she confessed to the things that she did, although one witness to her interrogation stated that Rebecca felt "as if her flesh had been pulled from her bones and so she could not deny her guilt any longer." This seems to suggest that some sort of torture took place. Regardless, her statements were more than enough to bring about her conviction and a sentence of death. Her husband was also executed, even though he claimed to be innocent until the end.

Since the "fits" experienced by the young woman pointed to a self-confessed witch who confessed to having had sex with the Devil and met with other witches from around the area, there was every reason for the authorities to continue their investigation. Accusations spread out across Hartford and into neighboring towns like Wethersfield and Farmington. The details of everything that happened have been lost to history, but a few things are still known. Suspicion fell on a particular married couple, and a group of townspeople decided to try the notorious "ducking" test. The husband and wife were both tied at their hands and feet, and then thrown into the water. When they appeared to float "after the manner of a buoy," bystanders concluded that the Devil must be holding them up. The ministers, including Increase Mather, who reported on the use of this procedure, regarded it as an ignorant superstition and may have even tried to intervene. One way or another, the couple managed to escape. Others were not so lucky. Among the additional suspects, four were acquitted, six were

Reverend Samuel Willard

convicted and at least two were executed. It made for a death toll unrealized during any other single period until the Salem witch trials.

The 1670s began with no sign that the number of new witchcraft cases would slacken. There were incidents in Massachusetts, Connecticut, and even in rarely affected Rhode Island. One case, even though it did not produce an actual court proceeding, was focused on "diabolical possession." Accounts say that the Devil apparently invaded a woman and took control of her. This was always a possibility with witchcraft, and while it rarely happened, when it did, it could be sensational.

And sensational it was, thanks largely to the written account kept by the town's minister, Samuel Willard. He wanted to keep a record that might be useful to other clergy confronting similar situations. The possession occurred in the town of Groton, Massachusetts, in late 1671. A teenage girl named Elizabeth Knapp had been working as a servant in the home of the Willard family for some time. That autumn, Elizabeth suddenly began to experience fits of increasing intensity. At one point, Reverend Willard's meticulous account described Elizabeth being "seized in such ways that six persons could hardly hold her; but she leaped and skipped about the house perforce, roaring and telling extremely and fetching deadly sighs as if her heartstrings were broken, and looking with a frightful aspect, to the amazement and astonishment of all the beholders." On another occasion, "she was suddenly thrown down in the midst of the floor and with much ado, kept out of the fire from destroying herself." In another entry, "she was hurried into striking those that held her and spitting in their faces." Willard also noted how, "her tongue would be for many hours drawn into a semicircle up to the roof of her mouth and not to be removed, for some tried with their fingers to do it." And he made frequent mentions of the times when she "barked like a dog and bleated like a calf, in which her organs were visibly made use of." By the time his record was complete, incidents like these filled dozens of pages.

As both her minister and employer, Willard had both a special responsibility and fondness for Elizabeth and he sought repeatedly to calm her by talking to her and praying over her. He, and many others who came to lend a hand or simply stare at the spectacle, wished most of all to discover the cause of Elizabeth's troubles. Near the start of things, she "seemed to impeach one of the neighbors" as a witch – and her presumed tormentor. But, for reasons the minister did not explain, this accusation was disregarded. Some time later, she accused another person, but this accusation also failed to convince anyone. After that, suspicion shifted to the possibility of her own guilt. Pressed hard by Willard, she admitted that she had met with the Devil and "given of her blood and made a covenant with him." She quickly regretted these admissions and tried unsuccessfully to retract them, but no one believed her denials. Her fits grew stronger and bystanders crowded into the Willard house in ever-increasing numbers. The shattering climax occurred on a Sunday in front of a large, frightened, and utterly fascinated group of townspeople. Her body took on a number of "amazing postures" and then a strange voice – nothing like her own – erupted from somewhere inside of her, reviling the minister and uttering blasphemous and obscene words and phrases.

In Willard's mind, this appalling development resolved any doubt about "whether she might property be called a demoniac, or person possessed by the Devil." As far as he was concerned, there could be no other explanation. Elizabeth's troubles continued for several more weeks with the "same voice" returning at least one more time. "Thus she continues to this instant to be followed with fits," wrote the minister but then his narrative abruptly broke off. Sooner or later, Elizabeth must have recovered. She remained a resident of Groton and within a few years, she married and began to have children. Her notoriety was eventually forgotten and she settled into the life of an ordinary resident of the community.

The middle part of the decade brought new challenges to the American colonies, and turned attention away from witchcraft for a time. The greatest calamity was King Philip's War, a horrific race war that pitted the white colonists and their Mohegan and Pequot Indian allies against Indians from five other tribes. The human toll was unparalleled before or since in American history, with a casualty rate approaching 10 percent of the total colonist population, and even higher among the natives. As a result, in the four years between 1675 and 1679, only one accusation of witchcraft drew an indictment. But at the war's end, the pace increased again with six witch trials over the next four years. There were additional indictments in the half-dozen years after that, none of which resulted in convictions. It is worth noting that no one was executed for witchcraft anywhere in New England between 1663 and 1688.

Was the witchcraft craze finally running its course and gradually fading away? At the time, it might have seemed so. But in 1688, an especially strong prosecution developed in Boston against an alleged witch named Glover (her first name was not recorded). She was Irish, Gaelic-speaking and likely a Catholic, all of which would have cast her in a dubious light for most New Englanders. Her leading accusers – and supposed victims – were the residents of a neighboring farm, who hired her as a laundress. The course of events was a familiar one: dispute, angry words, fear of retaliation and then, of course, "fits" among the neighbor's children. The result was a full-blown trial, ending in Glover's conviction, confession and execution. Other suspects were linked to Glover and the people of Boston became more and more alarmed. The local clergy was involved, especially Cotton Mather. Eventually, the children's fits stopped and a kind of normalcy returned to the community. Glover's was the first New England witchcraft case to end in capital punishment in twenty-five years. Of course, it would not be the last.

As the final decade of the seventeenth century began, New Englanders were feeling upset and frightened by events taking place at home and at distant corners of the colonies. On the political and military front, the major European powers, together with their various colonial possessions, were at war. In America, this meant New England was at odds with New France (Canada) and violent, though sporadic, bouts of fighting occurred throughout the wilderness borderlands. Many of the targets included villages in Maine, New Hampshire, and New York, several of which suffered from devastating surprise attacks.

But perhaps more frightening was the renewal of the witchcraft panic that had seized the region in years past. Accusations surfaced in Boston, New Haven, and Northampton. In 1692, a significant outbreak gripped the coastal Connecticut towns of Stamford and Fairfield. These events began in March, in the home of a locally prominent family, when a servant girl named Katherine Branch suddenly "fell into fits." The details followed a long-established precedent: wild physical contortions, trances, fainting spells, cursing and blasphemies, suggestive sexual acts, spectral confrontations with the Devil, and finally, the naming of her supposed witch "tormentors." Once again, it all happened in the presence of numerous enthralled onlookers, all of whom were willing to carry the tales to family and friends. After names were given, now fewer than six women were brought under suspicion. A special court was convened and dozens of witnesses offered testimony about their dealings with the accused. They all spoke of quarrels, threats made and received, cows that died mysteriously and strange "injuries" of every sort. The proceedings continued throughout the summer and the atmosphere surrounding them was both angry and circus-like. Local townspeople divided into opposing factions, with some supporting and others doubting (or dismissing outright) the various charges. The doubters included several members of the court and a group of ministers whose opinion was given about the ridiculousness of the entire charade. In the end, their viewpoint prevailed with only two of the suspects being indicted. They were tried before a jury who found one of the women guilty. She was eventually "reprieved" by a committee of magistrates.

But at almost exactly the same moment that Katherine Branch was seized by "fits," something similar was taking shape about 100 miles to the north, where a group of impressionable young girls had a notion to "try fortunes," hoping to learn the identity of their future husbands by using an old divining trick of dropping an egg white into a glass to see what patterns it formed. Instead of news about their matrimonial prospects, the girls allegedly saw a sure sign of death – leading to shock, terror, strange antics and whispered accusations.

The horror of Salem was about to be unveiled in New England.

THE SALEM WITCH TRIALS

The events that began in the village of Salem started at the home of the Reverend Samuel Parris. He had a nine-year-old daughter named Betty, a quiet, nervous child. Also living in his household was an 11-year-old niece, Abigail Williams, who was much bolder and who dominated her cousin. Of the reverend's wife, we know little, except that she was a devout woman who spent most of her time doing charitable work in the village. Parris had lived for a time in Barbados and had brought two black slaves to Salem with him: John Indian, who did outside work, and his wife, Tituba, who cooked and cleaned. The children were mostly cared for by Tituba, who loved them. Often, to entertain the girls, she told stories about her island home, usually involving Voodoo, and showed how to cast harmless spells. The girls were very proud of this secret knowledge and they boasted about it to some of their older friends - Mary Walcott, Elizabeth Booth, and Susanna Sheldon – and later, to several others, including Ann Putnam, the malicious daughter of a neurotic, gossipy mother who was largely responsible for the ignorant rumors that began to spread.

After the ill-fated conjuring session with the egg white and the glass of water, both Betty and Abigail, and later other girls, were "possessed." They began to suffer from seizures that Reverend Parris claimed went far beyond anything that might have been caused by epilepsy. They were said to suffer from vacancy of mind, fits of dizziness and spells during which they crawled about on all fours and make horrible animal noises. Prayer proved to be of no avail and doctors could find nothing physically wrong with the girls. Accounts stated that the girls screamed as though touched with burning coals whenever sacred words were said over their bodies. Reverend Parris appealed for help and two ministers, Nicholas Noyes and John Hale, arrived in the village.

Many modern scholars believe the whole thing was a hoax, while others have suggested that perhaps the girls were poisoned, or accidentally drugged, by something that Tituba had brought with her from Barbados. It's believed that a herb that caused hallucinations, used during Voodoo ceremonies, could have been the culprit in the case. Still others support the theory that the girls' hallucinations and bizarre behavior were caused by their having eaten bread made from grain that was contaminated by the ergot fungus. Ergot poisoning – or ergotism -- leads to hallucinations, seizures, vomiting, and prickling sensations under the skin, all of which the girls experienced. Of course, that doesn't explain why only the girls and their friends experienced the strange symptoms, and not the others in their households. More likely, they were simply seized that the same witchcraft hysteria that had run amuck in New England for the better part of the last seven decades.

However, the faithful Puritans of Salem quickly came to believe that the Devil was at work in their village. They reportedly asked all of the girls who their tormentors were but could not get a straight answer from any of them. Mary Walcott's aunt, who suspected Tituba, persuaded the slave to make a "witch cake" from an old country recipe, consisting of rye meal and the urine of the afflicted children. The idea was that if the family dog ate the cake made with the urine of the "possessed" girls, the dog would begin to act as if it were bewitched if the girls were truly under the influence of witchcraft. When Parris learned of this and accused his daughter of being involved with the making of the cake, she went into such terrible hysterics that he feared she would die. Betty and the other girls soon accused Tituba of witchcraft. Two other women, Sarah Good and Sarah Osbourne, were also charged.

Two magistrates, John Hathorne and Jonathan Corwin, were sent to examine the alleged witches. The prisoners were allowed no defense counsel. It was enough for a witness to declare that he had seen the "shape" of the accused riding through the air on a broomstick for his word to be believed. It didn't matter how much the poor soul on trial protested the testimony.

During the trials that were held in Salem, the accusers had seizures and spells in the courtroom, sealing the fates of those they claimed were witches.

Tituba, who was considered Parris' property, was thoroughly beaten by her master as he tried to obtain a confession from her about her evil acts. Eventually, hoping to avoid further punishment, she gave him what he wanted – and confessed to anything that she could think of. Once started, she was nearly impossible to stop. She claimed that a "tall man" had come to her, told her that he was God, and ordered her to serve him for the next six years. He had brought her a book that contained nine names and among them were those of Sarah Good and Sarah Osbourne. She had flown to Sabbaths with the "tall man," accompanied by a hog, two red cats and the winged head of a cat that belonged to Sarah Osbourne. The "shapes" that belonged to the two witches had tried to force her to harm Betty and Abigail, but she had resisted.

The court readily accepted her testimony. It was evident to them that the uneducated slave had been deceived by the Devil and was an innocent victim of the witches. Evidence of this was given as Tituba also became "possessed," rolling her eyes, frothing at the mouth, and screaming that she was being attacked by a demon for having spoken out against the forces of darkness. Her husband also got involved in the ruse and he roared, blasphemed, and threw himself onto the floor of the courtroom, also apparently in agony. The court believed that he, too, was also another victim of the horror that had come to Salem.

Hysteria soon gripped the village. A dozen people came forward, including some who may have honestly believed what they were saying, who claimed that they had seen the "shapes" of others sticking pins into dolls and taking a diabolical sacrament of red-colored bread and wine mixed with blood. Rebecca Nurse, a formerly respected old woman, was dragged from her sick bed to be charged as a witch. A farmer named John Proctor had the courage to declare that the girls were liars and that their "possession" was self-induced in order to draw attention to themselves. The result was that he was arrested as a witch and his property was confiscated before he had even been tried.

During each of the trials, the girls were brought into the courtroom. Their behavior had an unsettling effect on the accused. If the prisoner lifted his eyes, the girls all lifted theirs; if he rubbed his face, the girls did the same; if he coughed, the girls all coughed; and so on. If the prisoner denied the charges brought against him, the girls went into a frenzy, howling and throwing themselves on the floor. Still worse, they became the jury and executioner of the accused. One by one, the girls were carried to the prisoner and he was forced to take each of their hands. If she continued to rave and thrash about, he was innocent, but if she became quiet, it was assumed that he had removed the demon that he had sent to torture her, and so was obviously guilty.

The girls had a terrifying effect on not only the trials, but on the people of the village, as well. They were constantly seeing "shapes" all over the place, and so unshakable had the belief in them become that, at the children's direction, the villagers stabbed with swords and pitchforks at the empty air where the "shapes" were supposed to be.

A new governor arrived from England, Sir William Phips, who came to the village with Increase Mather, the father of Cotton Mather and later president of Harvard University. Mather had been prominent in the earlier witch trials in Boston, but Phips was only interested in getting together a military expedition against the French in Canada. After decreeing that all of those who had been accused of witchcraft be left chained in their cells, he left the business of trying them to the courts. A special court was formed with Deputy Governor William Stoughton as president, and six other judges.

People in Salem who feared being accused or "cried out," as it was called, began to leave the village. Among them was John Willard, the deputy constable, who had arrested several of the accused witches. In a sudden fit of disgust, he turned on the girls, accused them of being fakes, and said that they should be hanged for what they had done. The girls retaliated against him by claiming that they had seen his "shape" strangling his own nephew, a young man who had recently died. Willard tried to flee but was captured and chained up in prison, accused of having witched to death a number of other people.

Around this time, the "possessed" girls finally announced the identity of the man who had played the part of

The grave of one of the Salem witch trial victims in the witches memorial section of the old Salem cemetery

the Devil at the local Sabbaths. It was, they declared, The Reverend George Burroughs, who had been a minister in Salem a number of years before. Even though they were shocked at the idea that a minister would be involved, the magistrates quickly dispatched officers to the parish where Burroughs now lived. They stormed into his home in the middle of a meal and dragged him back to Salem. To Burroughs' amazement, he was accused of murdering a number of soldiers who had been killed near his parish while fighting Indians – not physically, of course, but as a sinister "shape," just like the other alleged witches. What possible defense could he offer to prove his innocence?

Rebecca Nurse was brought to trial. Her good reputation served her well – at first. Her numerous friends and family were brave enough to testify on her behalf and she was found to be not guilty of the crimes for which she was accused. Instantly, the courtroom was plunged into chaos. The girls howled, pulled their hair, and rolled around on the floor screaming that the woman was guilty. Unbelievably, she was brought back into court and the jury was ordered to think things over again. This time, they reversed their verdict and she was found guilty. On Tuesday, July 19, she was one of five women hanged as witches in Salem.

The terror continued to spread. Scores of people were "cried out" and the court continued its travesty of justice. Prisoners who confessed could hope for clemency, but those who denied their guilt were condemned. On September 22, eight more were hanged, including a woman named Mary Esty – which led to one of the most bizarre incidents to occur during these hysterical times. According to a servant girl named Mary Herrick, the ghost of Mary Esty appeared to her on the day that she was hanged. She said to her, "I am going upon the ladder to be hanged for a witch, but I am innocent and before a twelve-month be past you shall believe it." Shortly afterwards, Herrick claimed that the ghost told her to denounce the wife of minister John Hale as a witch.

Reverend Hale knew the charge to be false, and he suddenly realized how many others of the accused might also be innocent.

This event marked the beginning of the end of the insanity. The governor returned from the Canadian border and was shocked to find that 150 people were chained up in prison, waiting to be put on trial for witchcraft. He decreed that in the future, supernatural evidence would be inadmissible in his courts. This made trying the other defendants impossible. They were found to be not guilty, and the Salem witch hysteria came to an end.

What really happened in that small New England village? Was it fraud, class conflict, village factions fighting against one another, repression, accidental poisoning, actual witchcraft or merely a product of the hysteria of the times? It's a question with many possible answers. Many can be discarded completely because the evidence is too weak. Several others seem obvious but are not very helpful in getting to the bottom of things. Yes, a few of the "afflicted" may have been acting or lying, even while their fellow accusers were in the grip of a true psychopathology. And yes, Puritan beliefs and practices could be hard on young children. It seems likely, too, that some of the individual suspects did actually attempt the practice of witchcraft, but there is no way to distinguish them from the ones who were falsely accused.

While the list is trimmed down, a number of possibilities remain. In the end, there are likely a number of reasons why things turned out the way they did. Witch-hunts, like most social and historic phenomena, almost always show a pattern of multiple causes. And the case of Salem, because it is well-documented, allows the identification of a number of causes.

They begin in 1675, a time when Salem was already showing signs of growing conflict between the different factions within the town. There are the small farmers, geared toward old-style "subsistence" production. There are other farmers, somewhat more prosperous and forward-looking, who are beginning to produce for the market. There are tradesmen and artisans, who operated on a community-wide basis. Finally, there are the merchants, whose economic horizons extend all over the region. Each of these groups represented a different way of being in the world. They continue, of course, to share a great deal – they live in small area, they often interact and cooperate with one another on a regular basis. But they actually feel, and truly are, quite different from one another. Soon, Salem began to see bitter conflicts between these groups that stretched for almost two decades. The underlying issues were social standing and change. New modes of production and trade created new interests, new values, new expectations and new lifestyles. But the old ways died hard. Some wanted change, others did not. In places like Salem, there were many defenders of both sides of the argument.

As part of the changes affecting the community, Salem began to feel a deep moral reproach toward new arrivals in the community who did not speak the same language or share the same religious beliefs as the earlier residents. Leaders and ordinary folk alike felt they were losing touch with the religious strength that once shaped the town and gave them purpose. Meanwhile, too, a political crisis loomed as administrative changes enacted by the royal authority overseas steadily eroded the self-governing traditions that were once part of colonial life. Indeed, when New England's official charters were revoked between 1684 and 1691, title to the very lands they lived on was potentially at risk. Yet another crisis came with an outbreak of smallpox in 1689, perhaps the most severe of the many epidemics to strike the region. Combine all of this with a rising fear of the Indian populace, which was spread through stories of massacres, rumors and threats, and the result was nothing less than an overwhelming and toxic climate of fear. With all of these things affecting the hearts and minds of the people, the New Englanders of the late 1680s and early 1690s must have felt the hand of "Divine Providence" was turning against them.

As the entire region teetered on the edge, all of these factors converged on the village of Salem. As panic overwhelmed the people, Salem became the center of early America's most far-reaching, deadly and lastingly famous American witch-hunt.

3. THE BLACK ARTS

MAGIC, EVIL AND RAISING HELL

I hereby promise the Great Spirit Lucifer, Prince of Demons, that each year I will bring unto him a human soul to do with as it may please him. And in return Lucifer promises to bestow upon me the treasures of the earth and fulfill my every desire for the length of my natural life. If I fail to bring him each year the offering specified above, then my own soul shall be forfeit to him.

Signed _____
[Invocant signs pact with his own blood]

"The Completed Book of Magic Science"
Unpublished manuscript in the British Museum

Who, in their right mind, would deliberately invoke the Devil?

Who would call up infernal powers and then hope, once the demons were conjured, to able to control them?

If the history of black magic tells us anything, it is that the desire to harness the powers of evil and bend them to human will is as old as mankind itself. Men and women of every age have believed that there is another world – invisible, eternal and essentially unknown – that co-exists with the one we inhabit every day. It is a world of spirits, demons, gods and monsters, and in this world can be found all of the answers to life's greatest questions: Is death truly the end? Is there a Heaven? And is there, perhaps more important for our purposes here, a Hell?

Magic, the mystical precursor to religion, professed to have all of these answers. But where "white magic" looked for answers from a divine, or holy, source, black magic looked in another direction – enlisting the aid of Satan or his spawn. Using such dark methods, sorcerers and magicians claimed to be able to probe the mysteries of the universe. They made pacts with demons, promising their immortal souls in exchange for a lifetime of riches or a godlike glimpse at what awaited humanity on the other side. The raised the souls of the dead to ask them where they had gone and how they had gotten there. They searched ancient and sacred texts, searching through the cryptic words for clues and advice.

Along the way, these occult pioneers often stumbled upon real and verifiable truths. Astrologers mapped the heavens and paved the way for the astronomers that followed. Alchemists, in their futile quest to turn lead into gold, performed thousands of experiments that led to the discovery of everything from phosphorous and sodium sulfate to the manufacturing of steel. Even the seers, who read palms and interpreted dreams, contributed to a future that included psychology and hypnosis.

What made their efforts all the more surprising were the dangers, both real and imagined, that these explorers of the dark side faced. First, there was the ever-present threat of religious or royal condemnation. Dabbling in the occult could get you interrogated, excommunicated, tortured, hanged and burned at the stake or, in some cases, all of the above.

Then, there was the imagined danger implicit in the act of conjuration – if you summoned a demon from Hell, there was always a good chance that he might take you back with him. In all of the *grimoires* of black magic, there were repeated warnings and explicit instructions about what to watch out for. Demons, according to all of the books, were dangerous creatures who didn't like taking orders from humans and if given the slightest chance, they'd do their best to kill the conjurer and make off with his soul. When at long last it came time for Faust to make good on his deal with the Devil, for instance, his body was found torn to pieces in an open field and his soul, according to most accounts, was carried off to Hell.

Even so, the occult arts have never disappeared and have even flourished through the centuries. Though many of them had their origins in the ancient Middle East (where they formed the basis of the faiths of Babylon and Egypt), during the Middle Ages and Renaissance they reached their peak in western Europe. In those days, the old practices were revived, revered, refined and combined with the latest discoveries in medicine, metallurgy, astronomy, anatomy, botany and zoology and subjected to the spirit of inquiry that distinguished the era. What started as magic occasionally became fact.

And though the Devil and his minions were pushed from the scene, they were never altogether banished. They were always waiting, just offstage, ready and willing to offer, to anyone foolhardy enough to accept it, whatever unholy bargain they could concoct.

THE MAGICIAN

The magician has gone by many names over the centuries – magus, sorcerer, wizard and magician. He is thought of as the master of the occult, able to call up storms, cast spells, defy nature and cause people to do his bidding. The true origin of the magician lies in the ancient empire of Persia. There, the "magi," or wise men, were the high priests and the interpreters of the wisdom of Zoroaster. The word "magic" is derived from their name. They were revered for their learning and for their gift of prophecy. Rulers consulted them for everything from personal matters to affairs of state. The magi searched for truth, studying the sky and the stars and making sacrifices to the elements.

The wise men who brought gifts to the infant Jesus were magi from the Orient. Caspar, Melchior and Balthazar were, according to some theologians, master astrologers who followed the star to Bethlehem and then gave up their pagan beliefs.

As centuries passed, and with the decline of the Persian empire, the wisdom of the magi made its way to the west. Soldiers who survived the Crusades brought back with them stories and bits of arcane lore from the eastern lands. Trade routes were forged, making their way east beyond the Mediterranean and then back again. What the magi had begun, Europeans adopted and developed and added their own mystical philosophies from the Jewish Cabala and early Christian beliefs. It became a curious, but potent, mixture of alchemy and chemistry, metallurgy and medicine, astrology, divination and metaphysics. All of this was thrown together and turned into a weird brew from which magicians hoped to draw the answers for all things mysterious. Paracelsus wrote: "Magic has power to experience and fathom things that are inaccessible to human reason. For magic is a great secret wisdom, just as reason is a great public folly."

It was believed that every man was a tiny universe unto himself, replicating in his own mind and body a natural order that affected the larger universe that he inhabited – the motions of the stars and planets, the wind, the rain and the changing of the seasons. The magician, it was thought, could work wonders in two ways. First, by controlling and directing his inner forces, he could project his will and desires outward, influencing the actions of others. At the same time, he could call upon, or invoke from the outside, powers that he could then use to achieve his own aims.

In 1855, Eliphas Levi, often considered the last of the magi, wrote, "To attain the *sanctum regnum*, in other words, the knowledge and power of the magi, there are four indispensable conditions – an intelligence illuminated by study; and intrepidity which nothing can check; a will which nothing can break; and a discretion that nothing can corrupt and nothing intoxicate. To know, to dare, to will to keep silence – such are the four words of the magus."

But success in the magical field could turn out to be dangerous. Even if the magician met all of the requirements, both personal and professional, he could still find himself in deep trouble. If, for example, he summoned up infernal forces that he was not able to control, he ran the risk of being overpowered by them. The spirits of the dark were never known for their charity. In a moment, the magician could lose his life, and if he wasn't careful, lose his soul along with it.

THE MAGIC CIRCLE

The best protection that magicians had from the dark forces they conjured up was something as simple as – and often complex as – a circle. The circle has always held great meaning for magicians, mystics, philosophers, priests, alchemists and astrologers. The simple act of drawing a circle around someone or something was often considered a means of protection from outside forces of evil. In ancient Babylon, a circle was drawn around the sickbed of anyone who became ill, hopefully to keep away the demons that were trying to prey on him. In medieval Germany, Jews did the same thing for women who were giving birth. The circle would protect the mother and her baby. When Roman messengers were sent to deliver news (or warnings) to foreign rulers, they drew a circle around themselves in the sand to symbolize that they were immune from retribution. Even prehistoric societies revered the circle, as circular monuments at places like Stonehenge and ancient Native American cities like Cahokia in current-day Illinois can attest.

But what gives the circle such a powerful reputation? In part, it is its simplicity. The circle is, at once, capable of surrounding anything and everything while at the same time, it contains nothing. At the center, it is a

hole. Over time, and in many different cultures, the circle has become a symbol of unity, of oneness, of all things. A circle is a single line that has no beginning and no end. It is a figure that can represent everything from the eternal to the idea of perfection.

Alchemists used a symbol they called the *ourobouros*, a circle formed by a snake swallowing its own tail. The mystical symbol sometimes carried the Greek phrase *En to Pan*, or "All is One." Using the kind of numerology at which the alchemists were skilled, they counted the three words in the Greek phrase and came up with the number "10" --- thought to mean "all things."

Magicians used the circle for a couple of reasons. On the one hand, by drawing a circle and remaining inside of it, the magician believed he could gather and concentrate his personal powers. The circle kept the unseen energy from draining off and going every which way. But more important, the circle provided a protective barrier against the diabolical forces that the magician's incantations might summon up. The demons outside of it could try and get to him, but as long as the magician stayed inside of the circle, the danger could be kept at bay.

If, that is, the circle had been created correctly.

Although the recipe differed in many details, the general instructions were fairly consistent. The circle was drawn on the floor (or in the dirt if it was outside) with the tip of a sword, a knife or a staff. Sometimes charcoal, chalk or even blood was used. A French grimoire from the 1700s suggested that the circle should be fashioned from strips of skin, cut from a young goat, and secured to the floor with four nails pulled from the coffin of a dead infant.

It was also important when drawing the circle to do so in the correct direction. If it was drawn in a clockwise manner, it was designed to perform white, or benevolent, magic. If it was drawn counterclockwise, its purpose was one of evil. Going to the left in this way was called *widdershins*, a word derived from an Anglo-Saxon phrase that meant "to walk against." The sun moved from east to west, from right to left, and anything that went in the opposite direction was thought to be moving against nature and, consequently, against the powers of light and goodness.

As to the size of the circle, nine feet was generally considered the proper diameter of the outer circle, with another, smaller circle – eight feet in diameter – drawn inside of it. In that narrow space between the two circles, the magician not only etched a number of magical symbols, but he also often placed objects and talismans that were thought to ward off evil forces. Most important of all, he had to make sure the circle was completely closed. If there was any little gap, a demonic spirit might be able to slip through and wreak havoc.

The magician had so much to do and so much to prepare for a ritual that it was a miracle that he could remember it all. Among other things, there was a number of clothing requirements. The standard garb included a long robe of black cloth, to which two drawings on virgin parchment were attached, depicting the two seals of the Earth. Under this outer robe, a ceremonial, apron-like vestment known as an *ephod* was worn. The *ephod*, which was held up by two shoulder straps, was made of fine, white linen. Around his waist, the magician wore a wide girdle that was inscribed with magic words. On his feet, he wore shoes decorated with crosses and on his head, a sable silk hat with a high crown. In his hands, he held a wand and a bible, either written or printed in the original Hebrew. Once he was dressed and equipped, he was ready to start his incantations.

Standing safely inside the two magic circles – and within a smaller triangle that was often etched inside of the inner circle – the magician was about as protected as he could be from the demonic forces that he was about to summon. The arrival of such beings was said to be accompanied by dreadful and harrowing sounds – shrieks, growls, howls, anguished cries and angry barking. Long before they could be seen, the spirits and devils ranted and roared around the perimeter of the circle, trying to frighten the magician and trying to get him to abandon whatever schemes he had concocted.

If the sounds didn't work, they took on visible shapes that were also designed to intimidate and terrify. They appeared as animals and dark shapes, breathing fire, snapping, snarling and clawing at the magician. If he faltered in his resolve, if he tried to run away in fright, he would be ripped to pieces the moment he left the confines of the circle. But if he remained strong and held onto his wits, continuing to recite the necessary conjurations, the demons would eventually be drawn close to the outer circle and settle down. They would shed their beastly shapes and reconfigure themselves as naked men of a peaceful demeanor.

At this point, the magician could relax a little, but not much. Even though the demons had taken on a gentle appearance and were quiet for the moment, they were still a deadly and antagonistic force, simply waiting for their first opportunity to put doubt or fear in the mind of the magician and trick him into making a mistake. The smartest thing that the magician could do was to make his demands of the demons, or ask for the information that he sought, as quickly as possible, while his senses were still intact.

As soon as that was finished, and he had gotten what he was after, he could begin the rituals that dismissed the spirits. Once these rites were performed, the demons would go backwards through all of the same stages and transformations that had announced their coming, until they finally vanished in a sulfurous cloud. Then --and only then -- was the magician allowed to emerge from the magic circle.

THE PENTAGRAM

In addition to the magic circle, there was another shape that provided the magician with a powerful measure of protection – the pentagram. A five-pointed star, the pentagram was to drawn around the rim of the larger circle and again, just inside it. Demons, it was believed, had a fear and loathing of the pentagram.

Why was this? With demons, it's never easy to say why they felt of behaved in the way that they did. But according to some early theologians, the five points of the pentagram stood for many things that evil spirits had a natural aversion to – the living, breathing world of nature, for one. The five points could be thought to represent the four elements of which the world was composed – earth, air, fire and water – plus the combination of them all. Or the four points of the compass and its center. Or the five wounds inflicted on the body of Christ. Or – and this was considered very significant – man himself. With arms and legs extended, a human could be viewed as a five-pointed star (the head being the fifth point), and man was often said to be the embodiment of all nature. And what could be more repulsive to a demon bent on destroying order and goodness at every opportunity?

If, however, a magician was intent on channeling evil, the pentagram was perfect for that, too. All that he had to do was to turn it upside down, so that the two lower points were now on top, symbolizing the reversal of the natural order and pointing upward like the Devil's horns. The magician Eliphas Levi wrote: "It is the goat of lust,

attacking the heavens with its horns." This particular configuration was also known as the Goat of Mendes, because the inverted star resembled the shape of a goat's head. When used for nefarious purposes, the pentagram was sometimes called the footprint of the Devil or the sign of the cloven hoof.

In the manuals of the Order of the Golden Dawn, a mystical order of the nineteenth century, the upside-down pentagram was recommended whenever "there may arise an absolute necessity for working or conversing with a spirit of evil nature." Even so, it was a good idea to write the names of power – like those in ancient Hebrew, or Hallya, Ballater, Soluzen, Bellony and Hally – inside the pentagrams so that once devils did appear, they didn't get out of hand.

To ensure even greater protection, a magician might also construct a hexagram. Created by laying one triangle upside down on top of another, this six-pointed star was also known as the Seal of Solomon. Solomon himself, a great king of Israel, was said to have worn a ring with the seal on it, engraved with the real name of God, which gave him the power to control the spirit world. Using the ring, he was able to get the demons to help build his temple for him. Furthermore, the ring allowed him to travel, each day at noon, up into the skies, where he would listen to the secrets of the universe. Legend has it that the Devil was able to persuade him to take the ring off his finger one day and Solomon had to wander in distant lands for three years until he could get his throne back. For alchemists, the two triangles of the hexagram symbolized fire (an upward-pointing triangle) and water (a downward-pointing triangle), making the figure the ideal sign for the elusive philosopher's stone, which was thought to be a combination of the two elements.

THE GRIMOIRES OF BLACK MAGIC

Every sorcerer of note had a grimoire, or book of black magic, on which he relied for all the necessary instruction and advice. Raising spirits (evil or otherwise) was a devilishly difficult and dangerous task: First, you had to conjure them up, then you had to keep control of them long enough to do your bidding, and finally you had to make sure you got rid of them safely so that you could hang onto your immortal soul. It was not an easy thing to do.

The great grimoires (which meant, literally, "grammars") were weighty and seemingly unreadable books, often written in ancient languages, filled with confusing, arcane lore and meant by their very obscurity to frustrate amateurs and reward the true magician that was willing to put in the required time and effort. If you could make it through the grimoire, then you were halfway to calling up a demon.

Two of the most famous of these books were known as the *Key of Solomon* and the *Lesser Key of Solomon*. Some believed the Keys were written by King Solomon himself; others believed that they were written by demons and entrusted to the king. They came to be called the Keys after the lines in the Book of Matthew, chapter 16, in which Jesus says to Peter, "And I will give unto thee the keys of the kingdom of heaven: and whatsoever thou shalt bind on earth shall be bound in heaven: and whatsoever thou shalt loose on earth shall be loosed in heaven." These books, it was believed, held the power to lock all of the world's occult wisdom.

Solomon was the ruler of Israel in the tenth century, B.C. and was widely regarded as a master magician, one who could control the spirits and make them do what he wanted. It was even said that he had marshaled their

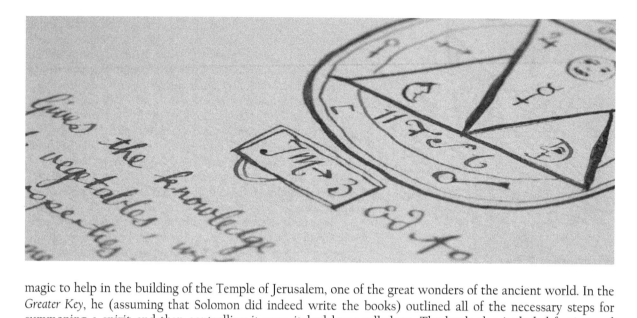

magic to help in the building of the Temple of Jerusalem, one of the great wonders of the ancient world. In the *Greater Key*, he (assuming that Solomon did indeed write the books) outlined all of the necessary steps for summoning a spirit and then controlling it once it had been called up. The book also included fasting and purification rituals to which the magician must submit before attempting any conjurations, along with practical advice on what to wear, what equipment to use, the proper etching of magic circles, and more. In short, it was a "how-to guide" for magicians.

In the *Lesser Key*, which was often thought of as even more useful, Solomon didn't offer much general advice. It was a more detailed look at magic. In the first section, entitled "Goetia" ("magical arts"), he described how to conjure up seventy-two chief demons and their respective assistants. In the second, "Theuriga Goetia," he discussed spirits and their main characteristics. The third, "Pauline Art," spoke of angels of the hours and the days and the signs of the zodiac. In the fourth, "Almadel," he described the angels that presided over the altitudes, as the compass directions of north, south, east and west were then called.

According to legend, both of the Keys were buried under Solomon's throne, where they would have stayed forever if it hadn't been for the intervention of some problematic demons. After Solomon died, the demons revealed where the books were hidden to some of the king's courtiers, who promptly dug them up and unleashed all kinds of trouble on the world.

In addition to the two Keys of Solomon, there were other grimoires, which were also considered must-have books for occultists. They shared a great deal of common advice on the proper ways to call up diabolical powers, along with words of wisdom on how to thwart the evil intentions of devils.

One book, the *Grimoire of Honorius*, was a veritable catalog of fallen angels and it gave detailed information on how to raise them. The book was credited to Pope Honorius III, who succeeded Innocent III in 1216. It claimed to be approved by the papacy and was published in Rome in 1629. Filled with Christian formulas and benedictions, it not only instructed priests in the arts of demonology but virtually ordered them to learn to conjure and control demons as part of their job. The introduction to the book, which promised to offer information on controlling the spirits, was followed by an edict from Pope Honorius addressed to all of the brethren of the Holy Roman Church. "In times when Jesus, the Son of God, the Savior, of the tribe of David, lived on this earth we see what power he exercised over Demons. This power he passed on and communicated to St. Peter with these words: 'Upon this rock I shall build my Church, and the Gates of Hell shall not succeed against it.'"

The edict goes on to explain that although the power over infernal spirits had traditionally only resided with the pope, Honorius now felt that every priest, cardinal and bishop ought to know how to perform such feats. That said, the book conferred on its readers not only the power of exorcism and invoking demons, but a sort of papal permit for doing so. This wasn't something that was going to stay permissible with the Church for very long.

The *Grimorium Verum*, or *True Grimoire*, was printed in 1517 and it claimed to be a translation from the Hebrew and borrowed heavily from both of the Keys of Solomon. Its publisher was listed as "Alibeck the Egyptian" and its place of origin was given as Memphis in Egypt. It was divided into three sections, but the organization wasn't very strict. Overall, the book was another outline for invoking demons. The book stated: "In the first part is contained various dispositions of characters, but which powers the spirits or, rather, the devils are invoked, to make them come when you will, each according to his power, and to bring whatever is asked and that without any discomfort, providing also that they are on their part content, for this sort of creature does not give anything for nothing."

There were two kinds of pacts, the grimoire explained, "the tacit and the apparent," and only by reading the book would the magician be able to know one from the other. "It is when you make a pact with a spirit, and have to give the spirit something which belongs to you, that you have to be on your guard."

As for the spirits themselves, there were many that could be called on, but only three that were referred to as the superiors. They were Lucifer, who was in charge of Europe and Asia, Beelzebub, who resided in Africa, and Astaroth, who controlled the New Worlds of the Americas. In appearance, these spirits were quite changeable. This was because, the grimoire explained, they didn't actually exist in a corporeal form of their own and had to find a body to inhabit. They always looked for one that suited their intended manifestation and appearance. Lucifer, the great deceiver, often chose to appear as a handsome man or young boy with "nothing monstrous about him." But if he got angry – a not uncommon occurrence – he turned bright red. Beelzebub, on the other hand, opted for the more conventional, frightening look. He often appeared as a gigantic cow or as a male goat with a long tail. When he became angry, he had a tendency to vomit flames. Astaroth appeared as a human man, cloaked in black. Once an angel in Heaven, Astaroth had fallen with Lucifer and had been made a ruler of the infernal regions.

Each of these demons had a couple of lieutenants that they could dispatch to do their dirty work and in addition, there were dozens of freelance demons that the well-versed magician could call upon for specific tasks.

The third part of the *Grimorium Verum* was made up of invocations and rituals that the magician had to go through in order to raise spirits and get them to do his bidding. In order to do this, and remains safe, he had to follow all of the instructions to the letter – which wasn't always easy. The instructions were convoluted, time-consuming and often confusing. But even so, the *Grimorium Verum* was considered the most precise and authoritative of all manuals on ceremonial black magic.

To begin with, the magician had to purify himself. The "Ablution of the Sorcerer," as it was called in the *Grimorium Verum*, began with instructions on how to wash with blessed water and then told how to prepare the instruments that would be needed to perform magic.

There were a lot of instruments involved. First, there was the knife, which had to be made "on the day and hour of Jupiter with the Moon crescent" (or, in other words, it had to be new). The magician then had to recite a lengthy conjuration over it, followed by the Seven Psalms. Then there was what was known as the Sacrificial Knife, which had to be "strong enough to cut the neck of a kid with one blow." It also had to be new and had to have a wooden handle made at the same time as the steel. Four magical characters were to be engraved on the handle. Once you had the knife, it was necessary to cleanse it in blessed water and cauterize it over a coal fire. Aromatic branches and perfumes were added to the blaze so that the knife was made fragrant. Again, there were prayers to be recited over the blade.

A virgin parchment, made from the skin of a lamb, goat or other animal, was also essential. The creature was laid on a flat surface before having its throat cut "with a single stroke... do not take two strokes, but see that he dies at the first." After the animal was skinned, "take well-ground salt, and strew this upon the skin, which has been stretched, and let the salt cover the skin well." Needless to say, the salt, too, had to have an extensive benediction performed over it before it was used.

When the skin was dried and blessed (again), it was ready for use – provided that none of the preparations had been observed "by any women, and more especially during certain times of theirs, otherwise it will lose its power." The parchment was used for writing spells and for the holy names of power that would keep the magician safe from the demon that he summoned. The quill pen, the inkwell, and the ink itself all had to be newly made, too, and then, of course, blessed and cleaned.

As for the magician's wand, it had to be cut from a hazel tree, on a Wednesday, during a crescent moon and engraved with the seal of the demon Frimost, whose specialty was controlling the bodies and minds of women and young girls. Then a second wand had to be made, also of hazel wood. This one had to be engraved with the seal of Klepoth, a demon that provided men with insightful visions and dreams. The magician's wand was so important to his conjurations that it was essential for him to have a spare on hand.

"All this [and there was a lot more] having been done correctly," the *Grimorium Verum* advised, "all that remains is to follow your invocations and draw your characters..." It was time to pick your demon and tell him what to do. Once the ritual was completed, all that remained was to dismiss the infernal spirits who might still be hanging around, wondering what to do next. As they were known to be of a volatile nature, it was wise to dismiss them with care and graciousness.

Besides his grimoire, the magician had another, handmade volume in his library – the *liber spirituum* (the book of spirits). As the reader might expect, it had to be made from virgin parchment and the magician had to fashion it himself. On each left-hand page, he inscribed the name and seal of one of the spirits that he was planning to conjure. On the right-hand page, he wrote the words of the incantation that would summon – and, of course, control – the spirit. This information included the spirit's full name, its ranking in the spirit world, the particular area that the spirit controlled, and the times and places at which it could be most successfully invoked.

The object was to get each spirit to manifest itself and then to sign the guest book, so to speak. Once a spirit had done that, it could be called back whenever the magician summoned it.

Once the magician had compiled his personal book of spirits, he had to consecrate it with a powerful, all-inclusive conjuration. In the *Grimoire of Honorius*, the conjuration was followed by a command that would allegedly force the spirit to obey the "rules" set by the magician. It warned the spirits not to interfere with the body or the soul of the magician, or to stir up any unnecessary storms or trouble. And if the spirits weren't able to fulfill their obligations for some reason (a prior commitment?), they were required to "send other spirits, who have been empowered to act for you, and they, too, shall swear equally to perform everything that the reader of the book may command." There was even a final clause that threatened the spirits with "torture for a millennium" if they were hesitant or unwilling to do what the magician told them to do.

When all of this was finished, the signs written, the conjurations made, the book was sealed and only opened again when the magician was standing inside of a pentagram or magic circle where he would be protected from the demons and spirits that the book could invoke. It was only then that he recited the Conjuration of Spirits, in which he called on "all the spirits of Hell" to appear before him, place their marks in the book and do his bidding whenever he commanded them to do so.

A PACT WITH THE DEVIL

There is no doubt that the magician's trade was a dangerous one. Dealing with unholy spirits and angry demons could be like putting out fires in a gunpowder factory. But the most dangerous element of all was the pact that many demons insisted that the magician sign before they would do his bidding. Although the terms and wording varied, the general agreement was that the demon would deliver the goods – wealth, women, forbidden knowledge – for a period of years, but that at the end of that period the demon would claim the soul of the magician for eternity. As one-sided as that bargain seems, many magicians apparently agreed to it.

In the grimoire known as *Le Dragon Rouge* (the "Red Dragon," which was largely based on the two Keys of Solomon), the contract was offered as stated:

Emperor Lucifer, master of all the rebellious spirits, I beseech thee be favorable to me in the calling which I make upon thy great minister Lucifuge Rofocale, having desire to make a pact with him. I pray thee also, Prince Beelzebub, to protect me in my undertaking. O Count Ashtoreth, be propitious to me, and cause that this night the great Lucifuge appear unto me in human form and without any evil smell, and that he grant me, by means of the pact which I shall deliver to him, all the riches of which I have need. O great Lucifuge, I beseech thee leave thy dwelling, in whatever part of the world it may be, to come and speak with me; if not, I will thereto compel thee by the power of the mighty words of the great Clavicule of Solomon, whereof he made use to force the rebellious spirits to accept his pact. Appear, then, instantly, or I will continually torment thee by the might words of the Calivcule.

If carried out correctly, this would bring the demon but he would assent to the magician's demands only "on condition thou give me thyself at the end of twenty years, so that I do with thee, body and soul, what shall please me."

In my humble opinion, this should have been the moment when the magician decided to re-think the whole deal. Was twenty years of fame, fortune, and lavish living really worth an eternity of pain? But many magicians believed that they could have what they wanted and then cheat the demon when it came time for them to pay up. They could sign the bargain, they believed, and then slip out of the deal later. Assuming he was thinking this way, the magician would scrawl on a piece of virgin parchment, in his own blood, the words, "I promise great Lucifer to repay him in twenty years for all he shall give me. In witness whereof I have signed..." followed by the magician's name.

The magician, still enclosed in the magic circle or pentagram, would then toss the parchment to the waiting demon, who'd look it over, scanning for loopholes. [At least this is how I imagine this situation taking place] If he was happy with it, he'd take it back with him to Hell and file in the archives. Of course, this is the reason that so few of these documents have ever been found – that, and the fact that if such a pact had ever been discovered by Church authorities, the magician whose name was on it would have been in very big trouble. Making deals with the Devil was considered heresy at its worst, a renunciation of God, the Virgin Mary, the saints and the Church itself. This was not the kind of contract that you wanted left around for anyone to find.

Grandier's alleged pact with the Devil

One of the few such documents that do exist, now housed in the Bibliotheque Nationale of France, claims to be a pact that Urbain Grandier made with the Devil in 1634. Grandier, a powerful priest of the era, known for his oratorical skills, arrogance and vanity, was accused of having bewitched a convent of Ursuline nuns in Loudon. The nuns, who showed signs of being demonically possessed, offered up the names of the demons that possessed them in court. Their testimony was corroborated by a sheet of parchment on which Grandier had supposedly written out a pact with the Devil.

After a great deal of torture, Grandier was taken on a stretcher to the public square – his legs had been broken by the inquisitors – and was burned at the stake. According to a monk who was present at the execution, a big black fly buzzed around Grandier's head. In the monk's opinion, the pest was actually the devil Beelzebub, the Lord of the Flies, there to make sure that the pact was observed and to carry off the black priest's soul to Hell.

From the moment a deal with the Devil was signed, both participants kept a close eye on each other. The Devil knew that the magician would try to renege on the deal when it came time to collect, and the magician knew that the Devil would be always lurking nearby to make sure that his prey didn't escape. By one account, the two black dogs that accompanied the magician Agrippa von Nettesheim everywhere that he went were, in fact, demons who were assigned to keep an eye on him. The French historian Palma Cayet had purportedly signed a pact that guaranteed that he would win any disputes that he had with Protestants. The contract was found after he died, and although there was a public funeral, the stories claimed that his coffin was filled with rocks. Demons, it was said, had already made off with his body.

Le Dragon Rouge included a prayer that was supposed to serve the magician as sort of an insurance policy – or more accurately, as a way to cheat the Devil. Right after signing his unholy pact, the magician was supposed to state (out of the demon's hearing, of course): "Inspire me, O great god, with all sentiments necessary for enabling me to escape the claws of the demon and all of the evil spirits."

Whether or not this prayer worked is still a mystery.

BELL, BOOK AND CANDLE

In the practice of the black arts, magicians needed more than just grimoires, knives and wands. There were other devices that became something like staples of their art. If they couldn't manufacture these items, then they could hardly be expected to perform the more elaborate rituals.

One such standard was the Magic Candle, which was used to find hidden treasure. A recipe for making the candle could be found in a 1722 book called *Secrets merveilleux de la magie naturelle et cabalistique de Petit Albert* (the book, very popular with the sorcerer crowd, was usually referred to more simply as *Le Petit Albert*). The candle had to be made from human fat and wedged upright in a curved piece of hazel wood. A diagram on the proper placement of the candle was included in the book – but there were no instructions on how to get the human fat. If you took the candle underground and lighted it there, presumably in a cave, burial vault, or castle basement, it would sputter noisily and give off a bright light whenever treasure happened to be buried nearby. The closer you got to the treasure, the brighter the candle would burn. When you reached the spot, the candle would suddenly go out; that's how you knew where to start digging.

Hand of Glory

This type of candle was almost essential to the magician's box of tricks. Buried treasure often made up the majority of the wealth that sorcerers used to finance their art. Obviously, all of the books of magical instructions, types of clothing that had to be worn, objects with which to make knives (not to mention the human body fat needed) all required a great deal of money.

But wandering around looking for treasure was not all there was to it; there were also precautions that had to be taken. For one thing, it went without saying that the magician should always keep several candles or a lantern burning in addition to the Magic Candle. That way, he would not be plunged into pitch darkness when the treasure was found. More importantly, if he thought there was even the slightest chance that the treasure might be guarded by the souls of the dead, these extra candles had to be made from wax that had been blessed. If he did run into guardian spirits, it was wise to ask them if there was anything he could do to "help them to a place of untroubled rest." Whatever they asked him to do, he was advised to do it, without fail.

The Magic Candle usually had a companion piece – the Hand of Glory. Together, they usually occupied a place of honor on the magician's mantelpiece. But the hand was used for far more nefarious purposes than simply searching for treasure, as is evident by its preparation alone. The first thing that the magician had to do was to go to a gallows near a highway and cut off the hand – either one would do – of an executed criminal. Using a strip of burial shroud to wring out any remaining blood, he then put the hand into an earthenware pot filled with a mixture of herbs and spices, where it would be left for two weeks. The next step was to take it out and leave it in the bright sunlight until it was good and dry. If the weather was not cooperating, it was permissible to dry it out in the oven, like beef jerky.

What the magician now had was a perfect, if macabre, candlestick. If he stuck into it a candle made from human fat, virgin wax, sesame and horse manure, he could cast a spell over the inhabitants of any house that he chose, rendering them insensible and unable to move. The advantages to this – burglary being the main one – are pretty clear. For as long as the candle burned outside of their house, the residents would be powerless to protect themselves or their belongings. In some accounts, it was also said that the Hand of Glory could be used to open any lock. Once again, it was a handy tool for the black magician when he wanted to raise the necessary funds to conduct his magic.

But it wasn't always foolproof. According to one account, from sixteenth-century demonologist Martin Del Rio, a thief once lit a Hand of Glory outside of a family's home but he was spotted by a servant girl. While he was busy ransacking the house, she desperately tried to put the candle out. She tried blowing on it and dousing it with water, but neither worked. Then, for some reason, she tried putting it out by pouring milk on it. It worked and the moment the candle was extinguished, the family revived and caught the thief in the midst of the burglary. The servant girl was rewarded for her bravery and quick thinking.

Apparently, there was also a sort of home security system that could be devised against a Hand of Glory. During the hottest days of summer, you had to prepare a mixture of bile from a black cat, blood of a screech owl and the fat of a white hen, and then smear it over the doors, window frames, chimney and any other place that someone might use to gain entry into your house. Once it was in place, the house was impenetrable to anyone with a Hand of Glory.

CURSES AND INCANTATIONS

With all the previous discussion about preparations for casting spells and practicing black magic, there should be some details about the variety of spells, culled from manuals and experiments, that the magician had with which to achieve his desired goals. Sometimes these goals were truly diabolical – raising the dead, conjuring demons – but often they were more mundane, such as predicting a change in the weather or helping someone find a lost object. Selling their services, a magician could be called upon to inflict a curse or remove one, to do evil or to protect someone from it. In a way, they were something like brokers, making money off a transaction, no matter which direction it went. An unscrupulous magician – which were easy to find – could even place a curse on someone, rendering him impotent or his business ruined or his fields barren, and then offer to put things right again – for a small fee, of course.

If a person was very unlucky, he might find himself caught between two competing magicians, one placing a curse on him and another trying to get it off. Such things could cost a man a lot of money.

And then, on occasion, magicians found themselves in direct conflict with one another, testing their powers against another member of their own secret brotherhood. In a case that was recounted by Olaus Magnus in 1555, a magician named Gilbert challenged his master, a powerful magician named Catillum, who responded by imprisoning Gilbert in an underground chamber, where he was "shackled by two wooden bars inscribed with certain Gothic and runic characters in such a manner that he could not move his limbs." According to the story, Gilbert would remain a prisoner there until another magician, more powerful than Catillum, was able to break the spell. There was no follow-up as to the eventual outcome of the story, although the moral clearly was not to challenge another magician unless you were sure you were more powerful.

Magicians had a tendency to specialize, to some extent based on where they lived. Those who lived near the sea, for example, were often called upon to do something about the wind, currents or a fisherman's catch. They were asked to speed some ships on their journey, sink others, stir up storms or calm turbulent waters. In seafaring nations, particularly the Scandinavian countries, magicians did a lively trade selling favorable winds. It was thought possible by many to tie up the winds in a knotted rope. A ship's captain could buy such a rope, and when he needed a gentle west-southwest breeze, he only had to undo the top knot. A northerly wind could be found in the second knot, a storm in the third, and so on. In Scotland, the wives of sailors thought they could conjure up favorable winds on their own. They would slip into the church after the regular service was over and then blow the dust on the floor in the direction their husbands' ships were traveling.

Magicians who lived in rural areas were called upon to do everything from improving crops to sweetening the milk of a farmer's cows. In times of plague, they would be accused of causing the epidemic or would be begged to make it go away. In times of war, they would be asked to place curses on the enemy or to heal soldiers' wounds. Many magicians were thought capable of staunching the flow of blood from a wound or magically removing an arrowhead or a bullet. They could start a fire, or they could put one out. They could be, at the same time, a community's most dreaded enemy or its greatest ally. To stay on the safe side, ordinary people were advised to give them a wide berth and always treat them politely.

This was especially true if the magician had unpleasant friends that he could call upon to do his bidding.

In his *Sententiae*, Thomas Aquinas stated in no uncertain terms that "magicians perform miracles through personal contracts with demons." If that wasn't' clear enough, Ebenezer Sibley, author of the 1787 book *The New and Complete Illustration of the Occult Sciences* warned his readers that while sorcerers and witches could call upon all sorts of spirits and apparitions, there were three types in particular that were most likely to do the magician's bidding.

First, Sibley said, there were the astral spirits, who haunted mountaintops, dark forests, ancient ruins and any spot where someone had been killed. Then, there were the fire spirits. These monstrous creatures, with a nasty turn of mind, were particularly receptive to skilled conjurers. Last, there were the terrine spirits, who seemed to have a deep hatred of mankind – perhaps because of where they lived. Confined to the "chasms of the earth" -- caves, mines and tunnels -- they were locked away and anxious to get loose and cause some real mayhem. Some of their attacks were recorded in a 1549 work by German metallurgist Georgius Agricola. According to one of his accounts, the workers in a mine called Rosy Crown, in the district of Saxony, were suddenly surprised by a dreadful apparition, a "spirit in the similitude and likeness of a horse, snorting and snuffling most fiendishly with a pestilent blast." Its breath was so foul that a dozen miners died on the spot, while others escaped to safety, screaming in terror. And despite the fact that the mine was rich with ore, no one would go back down into it again. Another Saxony mine, the mine of St. George, was also haunted by a terrine spirit. This one took the shape of a man in a great, black cowl. When the miners encountered him, he grabbed hold of one of them and hurled him up against the ceiling of the mine. He came back down, battered and bruised, to find that the other miners had fled in a panic.

All of these spirits, in Sibley's opinion, existed in a state of "continual horror and despair." He wrote, "That they are materially vexed and scorched in the flames of fire is only a figurative idea, adapted to our external senses, for their substance is spiritual, and their essence too subtle for any external torment. The endless source of their misery is in themselves, and stands continually before them, so that they can never enjoy any rest, being absent from the presence of God; which torment is greater to them than all the tortures of this world combined together."

The magicians that called upon such spirits, for whatever purpose, ran the risk of sharing their grim fate.

LOVE, DEATH AND OTHER HORRORS

It should come as no surprise, based on what we know about human nature, that there were two areas of life that the magician was most often called upon to influence – one was love, the other death. And the magician had a whole arsenal of potions, talismans and incantations to deal with both of them.

When it came to winning a woman's love, there were a variety of methods. Among the easy ways to capture her heart, there was what might be called a horoscope ploy. As outlined in a French manuscript from the eighteenth century, "To gain the love of a girl or a woman, you must pretend to cast her horoscope – that is to say, when she shall be married – and must make her look right into your eyes. When you are both in the same position, you are to repeat the words, '*Kafe, Kasita non Kafela et publia fili omnibus suis.*' These words said, you may command the female and she will obey you in all you desire." If you are skeptical about this as this, you might try something even easier: Rub the juice of a vervain plant on your hands and then touch the one you love. Still doubtful? You can also try touching her hand while saying, "*Bestarberto corrumpit viscera ejus mulieris,*" which is supposed to make her "inward parts" burn with desire.

If these simpler methods failed to work, a man could resort to a love potion made from wine mixed with assorted herbs and drugs. The recipe for such a potion was included in a seventeenth century manuscript called the *Zerkerboni*, written by a self-styled "Cabbalistic philosopher" named Pietro Mora. It included "the heart of a dove, the liver of a sparrow, the womb of a swallow, the kidney of a hare," all reduced to an "impalpable powder," and added to an equal portion of the manufacturer's own blood. The blood, too, must be dried to a powder. If a dose of this concoction is added to the intended victim's wine, Mora assured his readers, "marvelous success will follow."

A simpler, although just as unappetizing, recipe was offered by Albertus Magnus in his "Of the Vertues of Hearbes." After taking some leaves of the periwinkle and mashing them into a powder with "wormes of the earth," the recipe then called for a dash of a succulent commonly known as houseleek. If it was used as a condiment with a meat dish, sparks were guaranteed to fly.

According to the magicians, plants offered a number of different aphrodisiacs – lettuce, jasmine, endive, purslane, coriander, pansy, cyclamen and laurel. The ancient Greeks included carrots – thanks to their shape. The poppy and deadly nightshade plants were also said to be helpful in the search for love, but less because they inspired ardor and more because they could render a woman unconscious and vulnerable to assault.

In the Middle Ages, mirrors were recommended to lovesick young men. The idea was to use the looking glass to create a link between the owner of the mirror, the woman he desired, and the act of making love. The method was fairly simple. First, the man had to buy a small mirror (without haggling over the price) and then write the name of the woman he was in love with on the back of the glass three times. Then, he had to seek out a pair of copulating dogs and hold the mirror in such a way that he captured their reflection in the act. Finally, he would hide the mirror in a spot where he was sure that the woman would pass by it frequently. It had to be left there for nine days. After that, he would pick it up and carry it in his pocket. Without knowing why, the woman would find herself irresistibly attracted to him.

In reverse, if a woman had her eye on an elusive male, she would win his love by serving him a dish made up of, well, herself. First, she had to take a very hot bath and then, as soon as she got out, cover herself with flour. When the flour had soaked up all of the moisture, she would wipe if off with a white linen cloth and then shake out the cloth over a baking dish. She then would cut her fingernails and toenails, pluck a few hairs from every part of her body, burn them all to powder and add the powder to the dish. Stirring in one egg, she would bake the whole concoction in the oven and serve it to the object of her affections. Assuming that he would actually eat this, he would be her lover forever.

As the reader might imagine, casting a death spell was a much more dangerous affair. If the magician tried it, and was found out, the penalty could be his life. As a result, death spells were often reserved for games of the highest stakes – most notably, royal thrones and titles. If you were a king or a queen, there was a very good chance that some malcontent in your kingdom was sending a death spell in your direction.

In 1574, Cosmo Ruggieri, a Florentine astrologer at the French court of Charles IX, was accused of creating a wax image of the king and then beating it on the head. He might have gotten away with this if he had not made the mistake of asking around if the king had been having any pains in his head lately. He was quickly placed under arrest, but was his magic successful? The king died later that same year.

In 1333, Robert III of Artois was banished from France by Philippe VI for forging land deeds to support his claim to the title of count. In revenge, Robert tried to cast a death spell on the king, but his plot was revealed to the authorities by Robert's priestly confessor.

Around 1560, the Privy Council of England was thrown into a panic when a waxen image of Queen Elizabeth, with a long needle through its heart, was discovered. Her advisers quickly called in Dr. John Dee for an immediate consultation with the young queen, who was dreadfully worried. Dee met with her, explained the mechanics of a death spell and reassured her that it would be counteracted. As she reigned until 1603, Dee clearly did a good job of reversing the diabolical spell.

Although there were plenty of ways to cast death spells, using a wax figure was one of the oldest and the most popular. A little wax doll was made, representing the person that the magician wished to do harm. It was then pierced with needles to inflict, by magical transmission, actual physical damage or death. If possible, it was a good idea to dress the figure up in the style of the intended victim and, better yet, to obtain bits of his clothing, hair, blood or nail clippings.

An alternative to the wax doll was an actual human heart. If the right incantations were said over it, this dead heart could serve as an occult substitute for the one that was still beating (for the moment anyway) in the victim's chest. Again, a needle or two inserted in the right place, according to the lore, could kill the magician's enemy.

For skilled magicians who wanted to enlist a demon to do their dirty work, there was a specific ritual to perform. It was known as the Ceremony of Mars, named for the god of violence and war. To start the ceremony, the magician draped the room in red and put on red robes. The instruments that he used were made of iron, and the wand that he wielded was an unsheathed sword. Conjuring up Asmodeus, the "arch-devil of the Fifth Infernal Habitation," the magician offered himself as a conduit for the malignant force of the demon, which he would then direct toward the intended victim.

To make sure what direction he pointed the demon, though, he needed a link with his intended victim – perhaps something he wore, a cup he drank from, or hair or nail clippings. If he couldn't lay his hands on any such item, he had two options. One was to channel his lethal thoughts toward an object that he'd purposely left in the victim's house or buried in a spot where he knew the victim would step over it; the other was to make his own artificial connection to the victim by formally identifying something with him, before inflicting harm on it. Usually, an animal that belonged to the victim was chosen for this. It would be baptized with the victim's name, then tortured and slain.

If a magician had sufficient powers of imagination, he could even conjure up an elemental spirit on his own, sending it forth to go and do his bidding. Elementals were minor spirits of earth, air, fire and water and thought to invisibly exist all around us. By creating one of his own, which would hold only a temporary lease on life, the magician had the perfect accomplice – once that ceased to exist once the murder was committed. Sometimes these creatures manifested themselves in animal form, as wolves, snakes and toads, and sometimes they appeared as half human and half animal. Either way, they could only be seen by those who were being attacked or by someone with great magical gifts, like the sorcerer who sent them in the first place.

Signs of an attack by an elemental included feelings of dread and anxiety, not to mention more visible signs like thick, foul-smelling slime, and bruises that looked like they had been inflicted by a goat's hooves. Sometimes an invisible bell could be heard ringing when the spirit was on the prowl. Francesco-Maria Guazzo, the Italian friar who wrote *Compendium Maleficarum* in 1608, listed other symptoms like pricking pains in the chest, convulsions, fever, inexplicable sweating and sexual impotence. The skin, he stated, could take on a yellowed cast and the victim would be unable to look his priest in the eye. When confronted by his tormentor, "the patient is at once affected with great uneasiness and seized with terror and trembling."

In 1538, a case of psychic malevolence was reported in the English town of York. The perpetrator, Mable Brigge, was hauled into court under suspicion of having made an occult attempt on the life of Henry VIII. She was accused of performing a ritual called the Black Fast. While concentrating all her mental powers on the king's demise, she had abstained from eating any meat, milk or dairy foods. While in court, she admitted to having earlier "fasted upon" a thief, who had broken his neck while she was working her spell. Brigge was convicted of witchcraft and executed.

As evidence that magical spells are still very active in modern times, British witches in 1940 reportedly focused their psychic powers on Adolph Hitler, in this case to convince him not to bring his armies across the English Channel. In light of the fact that he never did, perhaps those witches were on to something.

Another method of bringing pain, horror and death to a victim was by way of the "evil eye." In Italy, it was known as *malocchio*, in Germany the *boser Blick* and in France, the *mauvais oeil*. In Scotland, it was thought that a glance from the evil eye could sicken cattle. In England, it was considered powerful enough to kill a person. Among colonial Americans, the evil eye was sometimes thought to be the source for soured milk and butter that turned sour in the churn. No matter how far back into history we go, to the ancient Mesopotamians and the Greeks, the eye has been considered much more than merely an organ of sight. Compared to the sun by the Egyptians, the eye was considered a powerful source of energy and a repository of the will, capable of sparking love on one hand and wreaking havoc on another. The evil eye has always been something that has been feared.

Warding off the Evil Eye, or really loving a rock band – take your pick.

What powers did the evil eye have? Depending on what country a person lived in and its particular customs, the evil eye could affect anything from childbirth to the failure of crops. It could cause minor irritations like headaches and hiccups, along with diseases that would eventually cause death. Sexual afflictions (especially impotence) were especially prone to being caused by the evil eye. Often, during childbirth, the expectant mother's house would be sprinkled with urine as a preventive measure.

During the sixteenth and seventeenth centuries, when the witch craze was sweeping through Europe, invoking the evil eye was a charge that was often leveled at the accused during trial. It was generally believed that when a witch made her pact with the Devil, in return for doing his bidding, one of the things she received was the ability to cast spells with her eyes. According to the *Malleus Maleficarum*, the witchcraft manual compiled by two Dominican friars (and containing helpful instructions on how best to torture, interrogate, and execute the accused), "there are witches who can bewitch their judges by a mere look or glance from their eyes, and publicly boast that they cannot be punished." As a result of this claim, many of the people who were charged with witchcraft were led into the courtroom backward.

In theory, the evil eye did the most damage when it first landed on the object of its intent. In other words, if a person could avert a direct gaze for an instant, he might be able to deflect its power. For this reason, people in some parts of Europe wore amulets, often in the shape of a toad, which were thought to soak up the "venom" of the evil eye's attack. In ancient Greece, they wore talismans of the Medusa; Romans wore beads made to look like an eye or gold, silver, or bronze phallic shapes, symbols of the life force. Even such seemingly innocuous customs as wearing a bridal veil and a boutonniere can be traced back to the belief in the evil eye – by wearing a veil, a bride is protected from the envious gaze of her enemy, while the colorful flower in the man's lapel was designed to draw the eye first to the colorful flower and away from the face of the man wearing it.

There were other ways to ward off the evil eye. Spitting three times was a good precaution, as was carrying salt, a symbol of life and purification, in one's pocket. Touching iron or carrying iron keys was another method, since iron was supposed to possess supernatural powers. The color red was also useful. In England, homeowners sometimes nailed a red ribbon to their front door, and in Scotland, farmers tied red ribbons on the tails of their cattle.

There were also some hand gestures that were thought to protect from the evil eye. One, called the *mano fica* (roughly translated as "fig hand"), was made by inserting the thumb between the second and third fingers while making a fist. Another, the *mano cornuta* ("making devil's horns"), involved holding down the two middle fingers with the thumb while sticking up the index and little fingers. This still popular gesture – now mostly used at rock concerts – was originally invented to protect from magical attacks.

Parents could protect their children by making the sign of the cross with their tongues on the children's foreheads or by tying little bells around their necks. The jingling of the bells was a sign of good luck. In one account, a Yorkshire man who was cursed with the unwanted ability to cast the evil eye was very careful, first thing every morning, to look out the window at a pear tree in the yard. That first look of the day is considered the most lethal. Even though his pear tree withered and died, his friends and family were spared from his deadly gaze.

NECROMANCY

Of all the black arts, there was no question that the most dangerous was necromancy – the summoning of the dead. In a way, it was the highest example of the magician's art, the most extreme and impressive feat that he could add to his professional skill set. In part, this was due to its difficulty – the ritual's requirements were extraordinarily elaborate – and in part it was due to the great risks that any magician was expected to encounter the moment that he summoned ghosts and demons from the underworld. In almost every case, their spirits were very unhappy about being forced to make the trip.

So, why were so many conjured up? Necromancers had a variety of motives, some of them more pure than others. Spirits were often called up out of affection – the magician missed a loved one who had died. They were sometimes conjured up because the magician wanted the arcane knowledge that only the dead were reputed to possess. And sometimes – perhaps most often – spirits were called upon to reveal the whereabouts of hidden treasure. It was generally understood that the dead had gained the ability in the afterlife to uncover secrets and see into places that the living could not. According to folklore, spirits remained near their burial places for up to a year after their bodies were interred. After that, getting in touch with them became much harder, if not impossible.

Not that summoning the dead was ever an easy task. First, the proper location had to be found to perform the magic ritual. Some of the preferred locations for necromancy were underground chambers, hung with black cloths and lighted with torches, or forest clearings, where no one was likely to intrude. Crossroads were also popular, perhaps because of the belief that many souls, both living and dead, were accustomed to passing through them. Ruined castles, monasteries and churches were all considered worthy locations, as were, of course, cemeteries.

The best time for necromancy was, not surprisingly, at midnight. If it happened to be a night of the full moon, that was even better. Better still was a night of wind, rain, lightning and thunder – and this wasn't just for atmosphere. Spirits, it was thought, had trouble showing themselves and remaining visible in clear weather.

The necromancer had many preparations that had to be made. In the nine days preceding any attempts to raise the dead, he and his assistants were required to literally take on the personas of the dead. They took off their normal, everyday clothing and put on faded, worn clothes that had been stolen from corpses. As they put them on for the first time, they had to speak funeral rites over themselves. Until the actual necromancy was performed, they were forbidden to take these clothes off.

There were many other restrictions, too. They were not allowed to even look at a woman, let alone have sexual relations with her. The food that they ate had to be without salt, because salt was a preservative – and in the grave, the body decomposed and did not remain intact. The only meat that they could eat was the flesh of dogs, for dogs were the creatures of Hecate, goddess of ghosts and death, whose appearance was so terrible that no one could look at her. If they did, their minds would be destroyed. And in a kind of black version of the Holy Communion, the bread that they ate had to be black and unleavened and their drink was the unfermented juice of the grape. These items symbolized the emptiness and despair of death. In all of these preparations, the goal was to try and create a kind of sympathetic bond between the necromancer and the spirits that he hoped to summon.

Once everything was in order, the necromancer and his assistants went to the churchyard and, by the light of their torches, drew a magic circle around the grave they were planning to disturb. Next, a fire was built out of henbane, hemlock, saffron, aloeswood, mandrake and opium. After unsealing the coffin, the body was exhumed and then laid out with its head to the east (the direction of the rising sun) and the limbs outstretched like those of the crucified Christ.

Next to the right hand of the corpse, the necromancer placed a small dish in which he burned a mixture of wine, mastic and sweet oil. Touching the body with his wand three times, the magician recited a conjuration from his grimoire. Though the wording of these conjurations differed from book to book, one of them read, "By virtue of the Holy Resurrection, and the agonies of the damned, I conjure thee and command thee, spirit of [name of person] deceased, to answer my demands and obey these sacred ceremonies, on pain of everlasting torment. Berald, Besroald, Balbin, Gab, Gabor, Agaba... arise, arise, I charge and command thee."

In a slight variation, if the spirit being summoned had committed suicide, the magician was required to touch the corpse nine times and invoke it using other powers, including the "mysteries of the deep" and the rites of Hecate. He would also ask it why it had cut short its life, where it resided now, and where it was likely to go after its service was completed. The spirit was compelled to answer the magician's queries, "As thou hast hope for the rest of the blessed and the ease of all thy sorrow."

If all went well, the spirit re-entered its former body and it would slowly rise to its feet. In a weary voice, it would answer each question the necromancer put to it – what waited in the next life, which demons caused the most harm, where a buried treasure might lie, and more. When the interrogation was over, the magician rewarded the spirit for its cooperation by assuring that its rest would not be disturbed in the future. The body was then

The witch of Endor raises the spirit of Samuel for King Saul, one of the first stories of necromancy.

burned or buried in quicklime. Either way, the spirit knew the body would be gone and it would never be forced to return again.

Necromancy had a macabre place in the history of the black arts. Norse magicians were reputedly so skilled at the art that they didn't even need to wait for a body to be buried before they could summon its spirit. In some cases, they were known for calling up the spirits of hanged men still swinging from the gallows in order to speak to them. In medieval Spain, necromancy was often taught, just like any other discipline, in Toledo, Seville and Salamanca – except the classrooms for such knowledge were deep caverns, often lying beneath cemeteries and tombs. When Queen Isabella, a devout Catholic, took the throne, she sealed up these subterranean "lecture halls."

One of the earliest stories of necromancy appears in the Bible's First Book of Samuel, when King Saul turned to the Witch of Endor to find out the fate of his kingdom. Worried over the outcome of a battle that he faced against the great army of the Philistines, he begged his servants to find someone who could raise spirits to give him a glimpse of the future. He visited the witch in disguise (which was especially important since he had recently decreed that all witches and magicians were to be banished) and asked her to summon a spirit for him. At first, she was reluctant; she knew the law and was afraid of being tricking into breaking it. But she finally agreed after Saul swore that she would not be punished. She asked who Saul wanted to see and he told her the prophet Samuel.

Fearful, the witch performed the necessary rites and the ghost of Samuel, an old man in a long robe, soon appeared. At first, Saul could only bend low and press his face to the ground. The spirit demanded to know why he had been summoned and Saul summoned the courage to ask his questions. The news that he received in reply was not good. Samuel told him, "Tomorrow, shalt thou and thy sons be with me; the Lord also shall deliver the host of Israel into the hands of the Philistines." Saul realized that he and his army were doomed.

But the dead were not merely the bearers of grim news – they could also be dispatched on errands of evil.

According to a Greco-Egyptian text, a clever necromancer could use the dead to seduce whatever woman he desired. First the magician had to make a wax doll and pierce it with thirteen needles through the eyes, ears, mouth, hands, feet, stomach, brain, anus and genitals. At sunset, he was to go to the cemetery and place the doll on the grave of someone who had died young, or by violence. To summon the corpse from the grave, he then called upon the spirits of everyone who had ever died a premature death, along with the powers still held by an eclectic group of gods and spirits that included Persephone, Ereshkigal (queen of the underworld in ancient Sumerian lore), Adonis, Hermes, Thoth and Anubis.

The corpse, now reanimated, was ordered to march to the door of the woman that the magician desired. The incantations stated, "And bring her hither and bind her... Let her sleep with none other, let her have no pleasurable intercourse with any other man, save with me alone. Let her neither eat nor drink nor love, nor be strong or well, let her have no sleep except with me..." and so on. It's hard to believe that any woman could possibly resist the seduction of having a corpse show up at her front door.

When it wasn't love or lost treasure that the necromancer was after, it was often just the cadavers themselves. In ancient Egypt, magicians bought dead bodies from embalmers and kept the corpses on hand for future rites. In the Middle Ages, magicians haunted tombs and gravesites in search of pieces of corpses, which were thought to have occult properties. Most prized, of course, were the bodies of people who had died suddenly, in accidents or by violence. It was generally thought that such bodies left a large amount of their life force still unused.

Paolus Grillandus, a sixteenth-century witch trial judge wrote, "Some take a small piece of buried corpse, especially the corpse of anyone who has been hanged or otherwise suffered a shameful death," and employ it for occult purposes. Very little of the corpse went to waste – "the nails or teeth, the hair, ears or eyes, sinews bones, and flesh," all of these, according to Grillandus, were put to use. In an even grimmer note, the flesh of unbaptized infants was also sought after, and their graves were desecrated as a result. Isabel Gowdie, the accused Scottish witch, once dug up the body of a freshly buried infant and re-buried it in a farmer's manure pile as a way of putting a curse on the man and his crop.

It should come as no surprise that the Christian Church took a very dim view of all of this. The Bible spoke out against such practices – Saul and the Witch of Endor as a case in point – and the third-century theologian Tertullian condemned anyone who would disturb or desecrate a grave. In the sixteenth and seventeenth centuries, the Church was even arguing that these spirits were nothing more than demons taking on a human disguise. William Perkins, in his 1608 *Discourse on the Damned Art of Witchcraft*, wrote that "the Devil being sought unto by witches appears to them in the likeness of a dead body."

PHILOSOPHY OF THE DAMNED

Over the centuries, from almost the start of recorded history and continuing into modern times, there have been a number of names, personalities, societies and philosophies linked to the practice of the black arts and association with the Devil. Many of them are regarded as some of the wisest men and women in history, while others are among the most feared – and most evil. But each of them has left a strange and indelible mark on the study of the occult and the history of black magic.

SIMON MAGUS

Although the Gnostic sect by no means created "Satan," they certainly influenced the worship of the figure and many of their beliefs, most notably the idea that there are opposing gods of good and evil, and two worlds, one of light and one of darkness, definitely offered Satan the chance to grow and take hold in the imagination of mankind.

The Gnostic sects first emerged in the early centuries A.D., in and around the Middle East, and offered rival views to the Judaic and early Christian theologies. The word "Gnostic" meant "one who knows," and what the Gnostics knew, the secret knowledge they possessed, wasn't something that was easily demonstrated or proved. What the Gnostics knew was that the world, as they saw it, was unquestionably evil and that no supreme deity could possibly have made it that way. Consequently, they argued, such a god must be far, far away, pretty much existing on his own in a Heaven of his own making. What we were left with here was something created by proxy, a world fashioned by lesser deities, who had really botched the job.

It was these lesser gods who, for instance, created man. They'd gotten the image of a perfect man sent to them by the supreme deity but had been unable to hang onto it. Working from memory, they'd tried to re-create the image, but the man they made was so badly build, according to some Gnostic teachings, that he couldn't even stand up on his own. He squirmed around on the ground like a lizard until God caught a glimpse of him and flicked the divine spark in his direction and this was how man began to stand on two feet.

In the views of some Gnostic teachers, the lesser gods were in fact rebel angels. In the second century A.D., Saturninus of Antioch taught his followers that the world had been created by seven of these fallen angels, whose leader was the God of the Jews. These seven had deliberately misled Moses and the Old Testament prophets so that they, in turn, would lead mankind astray. In the opinion of many Gnostic followers, the God of the Old Testament was a brutal, evil deity. Some of them even equated this God with the Devil. They praised his enemies, condemned the prophets and made other, equally volatile arguments. In some Gnostic sects, the serpent was worshipped and the serpent in the Garden of Eden was proclaimed a friend of Adam and Eve. Why? To the Gnostics, the serpent was doing its best to open Adam and Eve's eyes to the difference between good and evil. And when it came to Cain and Abel, the Gnostics (predictably) sided with Cain. Only an evil deity, they said, would prefer Abel's blood sacrifice to Cain's nonviolent fruits and berries.

All in all, the Gnostics turned every traditional Judeo-Christian value upside-down. In a world created and governed by evil, it was thought best to simply throw caution to the wind and do whatever they pleased. You could not get to Heaven by following the rules laid down by the lesser, rebel gods. You got there by having the true knowledge of how things really were. Some of the Gnostics interpreted this as a virtual license to steal, embarking on wild lives of sexual abandon and forbidden magical practices. In many cases, normal man-woman sex was frowned on, because there was a good chance it would wind up creating another human being who would become just one more slave for the lesser gods.

Other Gnostics, however, went in the opposite direction, freeing themselves of the world by leading the lives of hermits and mystics, focusing themselves on the purification they would need to undergo if they ever hoped to transport themselves above the sin and evil around them. For the Gnostic, the afterlife was a long way off and the soul had to undergo many trials before getting there. It had to lead a life on Earth that was free of worldly appetites, and it had to rise up through the spheres of Heaven ruled by the seven angels. That was the only way to get to the Heaven of the supreme deity.

To get past these seven angels, the soul had to know their respective names and powers. It also had to know how to address them and what symbols had to be shown to them in order to move past them to the next level. There were hostile spirits to contend with, too, who might try to waylay the rising soul. The Gnostic road to salvation, as with many other mystic religions, was long and difficult. Anyone setting out on it had to make sure that he had a bag filled with holy secrets, sacraments and signs.

A famous painting of Simon Magus trying to bribe his archenemy, St. Peter

And there was no Gnostic with a bag more filled with miracles and revelations than the magician who came to be known as Simon Magus. In the first century A.D., Simon built up such a following of believers, from his native Samaria to the city of Rome, that he posed a significant challenge to the fledgling cult of Christianity. It was a challenge that Simon lost, quite badly, in the end.

Often credited with being the founder of Gnosticism, Simon was in fact one of many who spread the word of the Gnostic principles, and in so doing, according to the Christians, committed unforgivable heresies. He claimed to be, at various times and at various places, the Son of God, the Redeemer and the transcendent God of the Gnostic universe. He was said to have been born, like Jesus and other past prophets, of a virgin. Among the miracles he purportedly performed were the raising of the dead, healing of the sick, and the magical creation of spirits. He could control legions of demons, make himself invisible, or take on any shape that he wanted. He could pass unscathed through curtains of fire, pass through solid stone and animate statues so that they sang and danced. The list of miracles went on and on, but when his magic ran up against the greater power of Christ's disciples, Simon Magus came up short over and over again.

He had received his early training in Egypt, from a man named Dositheus, who claimed to be the living incarnation of something called the Standing One. One day, in front of Dositheus' disciples, Simon challenged him to a battle of the magicians. When Simon won, Dositheus swung his staff at him, but the staff passed right through Simon's body. At that moment, Dositheus knew that his entire existence had been a fraud – Simon was the true Standing One. He handed over leadership of his sect to Simon and he died a short time later.

Wherever Simon went, he performed miraculous feats, and according to the biblical account in Acts, it wasn't long before he was venerated as a god – which, of course, he encouraged the public to do. The only problem that Simon seemed to have was being caused by the Christian evangelists who were traveling around the region performing miracles that were getting bigger notices than his own. The one called Phillip had cured palsies, made the lame to walk, and chased away unclean spirits from those who were possessed. Two of the apostles, Peter and John, had come from Jerusalem and laid hands on people, pouring the Holy Spirit into them.

Simon was impressed with not only their works, but with the relative ease that they displayed doing them. He confessed that his own effects took large amounts of preparations and incantations. In fact, he was so anxious to learn the magic words that the apostles used that he offered Peter money to share the secret of his powers. Peter refused in no uncertain terms, telling him that the gift of God could not be purchased with money. Simon could never do what the apostles could, Peter told him, "for thy heart is not right in the sight of God."

From that time on, Peter became his bitter enemy, repeatedly foiling Simon's attempts to win over new converts and make a living. Afraid that Peter might even accuse him of sorcery, Simon took his books of magic and threw them into the sea. He then set off for Rome, where he was sure that the emperor Nero would still give him a warm welcome.

He was right. In Rome, Simon was a resounding success, becoming even more so after he faked his own death and resurrection. But it wasn't long before Peter turned up again, this time accompanied by the apostle Paul. Nero saw this as the perfect opportunity for a face-off between Simon, who claimed to be a god, and Peter, who was merely representing one. Peter readily agreed and proposed a simple test. He said that he would whisper something in Nero's ear and Simon, after reading their thoughts, would tell the emperor what was said. Simon, always unnerved by Peter, refused and instead began to rattle off a series of incantations. He summoned up a pack of wild dogs and set them to attacking his enemy. The dogs raced toward him and Peter stretched out his hands in prayer. The snarling dogs suddenly disappeared.

But Simon wasn't finished. He asked the emperor to give him one day to prepare for an even larger trick that he wanted to do. In front of the crowds, he said, he would fly off into the heavens. The following day, Simon climbed to the top of a tall tower, stepped off and then sailed unharmed through the air. Nero asked Peter what he thought of the stunt and Peter simply began to pray. He prayed in the name of the God who created all things, in the name of Jesus, who had truly risen from the dead, that the invisible agents of Satan, who were keeping Simon aloft, should let loose their hold and let Simon fall to the earth.

The powerful prayer worked. The demons dropped Simon and he plummeted to the ground, landing so hard that his body was shattered. This ended the contest – and Simon's life.

AGRIPPA THE MAGICIAN

Written in 1510 by the German magician Heinrich Cornelius Agrippa von Nettesheim, the three-volume set of books *De Occulta Philosophia*, or *The Occult Philosophy*, was one of the most important and most authoritative tomes on the black arts. The books were not published until 1531 and even then, it brought the author far more trouble than praise.

Even though Agrippa was only in his early twenties when he wrote it, *The Occult Philosophy* was a mature compendium of magical practice and theory. A brilliant young scholar born in Cologne in 1486, Agrippa started out by studying approved subjects like Greek philosophy and Latin, but his interests were so far-reaching that he became fascinated with the mysterious and the unknown. Like many young men, he wanted to make his mark in the world and since his mind veered toward the occult. He immersed himself in everything from theology to alchemy before eventually settling on magic.

Despite its increasing bad reputation, Agrippa stated that he felt magic had nothing to do with devils and demons. It wasn't a means to do evil or to invert the natural orders. If anything, he argued in his book, magic was a way to understand the cosmos, as God had created it, and, by extension, to understand God. The occult, in Agrippa's view, was a science all its own, using the more traditional branches of knowledge in a new and different fashion. It employed physics, as it was then understood, to study the nature of things. It used mathematics to plot the movements of the planets and stars and theology to cast a light on the human soul, and on the spirit world inhabited by angels and demons.

In addition, Agrippa believed that all things, animate or not, had a soul, or spiritual essence, and that all of these souls, such as they were, contributed to one vast "oversoul." This, he believed, explained the miraculous properties he attributed to everything from garden herbs to precious stones. They contained powers that, however dormant, could be called forth and put to use by a skilled magician. There were harmonies between all sorts of things, which, if properly understood, could solve a whole host of problems and cure almost any illness.

Almost everything was bound up in Agrippa's great theory: "The stars consist equally of the elements of the earthly bodies and therefore the ideas (power and nature) attract each other. Influences only go forth through the help of the spirit but this spirit is diffused through the whole universe and is in full accord with the human spirit. Through the sympathy of similar and the antipathy of dissimilar things, all creation hangs together; the things of a particular world within itself, as well as the congenial things of another world." It was up to the magician to comprehend, interpret and manipulate this fantastically complicated web of life.

But for all his protestations to the contrary, Agrippa managed to cultivate quite a reputation as a practitioner of the black arts and sorcery. Although he claimed to be firmly on the side of angels, throughout his lifetime he was dogged by reports that he had consorted with demons and used his powers for diabolical purposes – stories that he didn't go out of his way to deny. Some of the stories about him inspired Goethe, who attributed them to his character Faust, who famously sold his soul to the Devil.

The stories were unusual, to say the least. At many inns where Agrippa stayed, for instance, there were stories that he paid the bill in perfectly good coins, which, once he departed, turned to worthless shells. Agrippa had a magic mirror that could conjure up images and visions. And, of course, there were reports that Agrippa had contacted the dead. Once, to please a crowd gathered by the elector of Saxony, he summoned the shade of the great orator Cicero, whose eloquence moved the members of the audience to tears.

It was said that he was also capable of divination. By spinning a sieve on top of a pivot (or rod), he could discover someone's guilt. He claimed to have used the method three times in his youth. He wrote: "The first time was on the occasion of a theft that had been committed. The second on account of certain nets or snares of mine used for catching birds, which had been destroyed by some envious ones; and the third time, in order to find a lost dog that belonged to me and by which I set great store." Although the system worked perfectly all three times, he claimed that he had given it up "for fear lest the demon should entangle me in his snares."

This wouldn't be the only time that Agrippa reportedly stepped back from the dark side. Everywhere he went, for instance, he was accompanied by a large black dog (in some accounts, it was two dogs), which many claimed was his demonic familiar. Legend has it that one day Agrippa decided that he had fallen too deeply into the clutches of the Devil and so he ordered the dog to leave his side and it was never seen again. There were other explanations of the mysterious dog, the most famous being that it was a demon in the form of a dog, keeping watch over Agrippa because he had sold his soul to the Devil. When his time was up, it was said, the demon could collect his soul.

But the most famous story involved Agrippa's student lodger, who waited until Agrippa went out one day, then managed to get the key to the master's workroom from Agrippa's unsuspecting wife. The student couldn't wait to sit down at Agrippa's desk and look through the books of magic stacked on top of it. He was in the middle of one of the books, reading passages under his breath, when a knock came at the door to the workroom. The student didn't answer, the knock came again – and the door was opened by a demon. "Why have you summoned me?" the demon asked and when the terrified young man couldn't come up with an answer, the demon, furious at being called up for no reason, leapt on top of the student and choked him to death.

When Agrippa got back and found the body, he was afraid that he would be accused of murder even though it didn't take him long to figure out who had done it. He summoned the demon back to his study – only this time, the demon was given explicit orders by a master magician. Agrippa told him to revive the student and walk him up and down the town market for a short while, just long enough for everyone to see him looking well and healthy. The demon did what he was told, then allowed the boy to fall over dead from an apparent heart attack. It was only on closer inspection of the body that the marks of strangulation were seen on his throat. The people, in an outrage, chased Agrippa out of town.

Despite the fact that he occasionally stirred up crowds against him, there is no evidence that Agrippa was seriously accused, much less persecuted, for his interest in or practice of magical or occult arts during his lifetime. According to some sources, Agrippa rejected magic totally around 1533, two years before his death. Others disagree, while still others claim that any rejections that he made were merely to save his own skin became of his pact with the Devil. Obviously, no one knows for sure. It is believed that the magician died in Grenoble, in southeastern France, in 1535.

ROGER BACON

When it came to writing about the dangers of conjuring up demons, no one was more persuasive than a Franciscan friar named Roger Bacon. In his book, *Discovery of the Miracles of Art, Nature and Magick*, written in the thirteenth century, Bacon stated that "there is a more damnable practice, when men despising the Rules of Philosophy, irrationally call up wicked spirits, supposing them of energy to satisfy their desires. In which there is a very vast error, because such persons imagine they have some authority over spirits, and that spirits may be compelled by humane authority, which is altogether impossible, since humane energy or authority is inferior by much to that of spirits." It was much easier to get what you wanted, Friar Bacon went on, by invoking "God or good angels" – but it seems he didn't follow his own advice.

During his lifetime, Bacon wrote many learned tracts and essays, extolling the virtues of art and nature, praising science over superstition and prayer over magic. But if there is any truth to the many legends that have been told about him, he never really gave up on the practice of magic. He studied alchemy, astrology and necromancy and believed strongly in the power of magical incantations, wrting that "all the miracles since the world began, almost, have been wrought by words." And he warned often that the Antichrist would one day come, and use these powers – both natural and magical – to bring about the destruction of the world.

Born in 1214, near the town of Ilchester in Somerset, England, Bacon studied at Oxford. He later taught there, before moving to Paris. It was in France, when he was a member of the Franciscan order, that he first ran into trouble. In a letter to the Pope, he complained that, "the Prelates and Friars have kept me starving in close prison nor would they suffer anyone to come to me, fearing lest my writings should come to any other than the Pope and themselves." This missive piqued the interest of the papal office – what could this unknown friar be writing that was so dangerous? Bacon was asked to send a copy of his work so that the pope could see what was causing the problem. Bacon did so, sending on his *Opus Majus*, *Opus Minus*, and *Opus Tertium*.

In these works, Bacon described a world of wonders, of instruments, experiments and techniques that could be used to explore the vast reaches of the natural world. He described something that sounded like a diving suit for exploration of the ocean floor, and recounted experiments with niter that foretold the discovery of gunpowder. In the *Opus Tertium*, a kind of overview of the first two books, he predicted the use of "burning glasses which operate at any distance we can choose, so that anything hostile to the commonwealth may be burnt – a castle, an army or city or anything; and the flying machine, and a navigating machine by which one man may guide a ship full of armed men with incredible speed; and scythe-bearing cars which full of armed men race along with wondrous machinery without animals to draw them, and break down and cut through all obstacles." It's easy to see why such ideas were considered so volatile. Weapons like these, in the wrong hands, could indeed do the Devil's work.

Although Bacon was released from his confinement and permitted to return to Oxford in 1268, his life remained one of trial and turmoil. He was imprisoned again ten years later, once more because of his writings, and he spent the next fourteen years under arrest. This makes it all the more amazing that by the time he died, most likely in 1294, he left behind such a vast legacy of stories and adventures. In sixteenth-century England, there was what could only be a called a "Bacon revival" that generated a huge interest in his work.

Among other things, he was credited with having invented, while at Oxford, two magical mirrors. One of them could be used day or night to light candles. The other was far more astonishing – it could reveal what someone

Bacon at work at his marvelous and magical inventions -- often weapons that were far ahead of their time.

else was doing, anywhere in the world, at that precise moment. Legend has it that two young noblemen asked to see their fathers in the mirror, and when they did, they saw them with drawn swords, fighting a deadly duel with each other. The two sons instantly drew their own swords and engaged in their own battle – much to Friar Bacon's dismay.

Bacon was also a great patriot and he dreamed of one day building an entire wall of brass around England to defend it from its enemies. But since the engineering techniques of the time (or of today) did not allow for anything so monumental, he started small by building a talking brass head that would tell him how to accomplish his greater goal. (Strangely, these talking brass heads were more common than you might think – Robert Grosseteste, bishop of London was said to have made one; Albertus Magnus is said to have had another, and even the ancient Roman philosopher Boethius reportedly had one) Bacon made his according to all of the specifications, but for some reason it wouldn't talk. Frustrated, Bacon and his trusted assistant, Friar Bungay, went out to the woods one night and raised a demon to ask it what the problem might be. After hesitating at first, the demon finally told them what to do and said the head would talk in one month's time, though he couldn't specifically say what day or hour. He warned the friars that if they didn't hear it before it finished speaking, all would be lost.

Consequently, the two men went on a round-the-clock vigil. After several weeks of constantly watching the head, they decided to get some rest one night and delegated the responsibility for watching it to their servant, Miles. And, of course, that night turned out to be the one they had been waiting for. The head opened its brass jaws and said two words: "Time is..." Miles didn't think this was important enough to wake his masters for. A short time later, it again intoned, "Time is..." but Miles figured this was pretty inconsequential stuff. In fact, the head had so little to say that he started to jeer at it and sing bawdy songs.

Another half hour passed and the head, unhinging its jaws one last time, pronounced, "Time is past," and exploded into hundreds of pieces. Bacon and Bungay, awakened by the terrible sound, raced into the room, but it was too late for them to learn anything from the smoldering ruins of the brass head.

On a different occasion, Bacon was able to come to the aid of his country – or so legend has it. Using one of the burning glasses that he created, the English army was able to set fire to a French town that they were attacking. The French garrison surrendered, a treaty was signed, and a grand party was held to celebrate the generous terms of newfound peace. As part of the festivities, a magic contest was held and Bacon pitted his skills against a renowned German magician named Vandermast. The German kicked things off by conjuring up the spirit of Pompey, in full battle dress. Bacon, not impressed, summoned the spirit of Caesar, who engaged and, once again, defeated Pompey. The English king was pleased with Bacon's skill.

But Vandermast was not ready to admit defeat. Bacon allowed Friar Bungay to handle the next round. Bungay waved his wand, uttered some incantations, and made the tree of Hesperides appear before the celebrants, adorned with its golden apples and watched over by a dragon. Vandermast knew just what to do – he summoned up the shade of Hercules, who had once slain the dragon and plucked the fruit. The famous warrior was ready to enact his victory all over again when Bacon stepped in to save the day. He waved his wand and Hercules stopped dead in his tracks. Vandermast furiously shouted at Hercules to carry on but the mighty warrior, trembling, was unable to move.

Vandermast cursed the spirit and Bacon laughed at him. Then, to seal his victory, Bacon said that since the spirit wouldn't be following the German's instructions, he should follow his own – and carry Vandermast back home to Germany. The spirit obligingly tossed Vandermast over his shoulder and started to march away. When the crowd cried out, sorry to lose one of the competitors, Bacon relented and said that Vandermast would only be in Germany long enough to say hello to his wife, and then he'd be back at the celebration.

This pleased the crowd – but not Vandermast. Angry and humiliated, he swore revenge. He later paid an assassin 100 crowns to travel to England and kill the friar but Bacon, who had consulted his books of magic, knew that the killer was coming and was ready for him when he sprang out of the shadows, sword in hand. Bacon decided to terrify the man by conjuring up the spirit of Julian the Apostate – a frightening specter covered in blood and burning flesh, scorched by the fires of Hell. The ghost told the assassin that he was in eternal torment for his sins. The assassin fell to his knees in terror and became a convert to Christianity.

Despite Bacon's insistence that he was a good Christian friar, he as commonly thought to have come by his magical powers by making a deal with the Devil. How else, it was often asked, could he perform all of his magical feats? But even there, Bacon's genius is said to have prevailed. In return for his magical powers, Bacon was said to have promised the Devil his eternal soul, but on one condition – that he died neither in nor out of a church. The Devil, thinking this was a safe bet, agreed. And Bacon, during the last two years of his life, built and lived inside of a tiny cell in the outer wall of a church – neither in the church nor out of it.

In that small cell, he spent his time praying, meditating, having meals delivered to him and talking to visitors through a small window. When he died, his bones were interred in the grave that he had dug, inside the cell, with his bare hands.

DR. DEE AND MR. KELLEY

In the annals of the occult, there is no more unusual pair than Dr. John Dee, the unofficial astronomer and consultant to Queen Elizabeth I, and Edward Kelley, the unscrupulous crystal gazer with whom he formed a long and often tempestuous alliance. For this reason alone, their story is one that should be told together.

Dr. John Dee, by every account, was a serious and devoted scholar throughout this life. Born in 1527 to a minor functionary at the court of Henry VIII, he soon distinguished himself at his studies, attending Cambridge University at the age of fifteen (where he recorded in his diary that he studied up to 18 hours a day) and graduating with a Bachelor of Arts degree two years later. Already an avid student of astronomy, in subsequent years he traveled through all of Europe, learning everything that he could, and meeting with other scholars, scientists and astronomers to study every new discovery that they were willing to share with him.

Among his most valued souvenirs from his travels were two Mercator globes, which he acquired from the Flemish cartographer Gerardus Mercator himself, and a treatise on magic that he came across, quite by chance, while browsing through bookstalls in Antwerp. Written by Trithemius, a Benedictine abbot, the treatise on natural magic, called *Steganographia*, made a powerful impression on Dee. He was so impressed that he wrote an enthusiastic letter about it to statesman Sit William Cecil, in which he claimed that the book's "use is greater than the fame thereof is spread." Inspired by what he found in the pages, he created his own work on magic, *Monus Hieroglyphica*, in just twelve feverish days. Dee's work delved into the correlation between numbers and various arcane magical practices. Although no one has ever been able to decipher the book's true meaning, Sir William solemnly declared it to be "of the utmost value for the security of the Realm."

John Dee

But for all of his intellectual gifts and his growing reputation as an astronomer, Dee hungered after knowledge that he could not discover – the secret of the philosopher's stone, for instance – and talents that he could not acquire, most notably second sight. He became terribly interested in crystal gazing and spent numerous hours gazing into a convex mirror – his "magic glass"—that he believed had been a gift to him from the angel Uriel. Only once did he catch a glimpse of something, barely discernible, in the glass. He became convinced that if he was ever to make any headway in the unseen world, he would need an assistant – someone with the powers that he did not have and whose visions and conversations with the angels could be recorded and interpreted by Dee.

And this is when Edward Kelley came into his life. Dee had already been through a few assistants, of insufficient ability, before Kelley introduced himself to the scholar. Up until that time, Kelley, a young Irishman, had not had the most illustrious career. At one time, he had been an apothecary's apprentice, but he soon turned his hand to forgery and counterfeiting. Convicted for those crimes, he'd had his ears cut off. When he presented himself to Dee in 1582, it was as a scryer – crystal gazer – who could see and hear the denizens of the other world. Dee, wanting to make sure that this new applicant understood exactly what kind of service he was entering into, explained that he did not consider himself a magician – the term carried many evil connotations and, depending on the views of the authorities at the time, grim penalties – and that before he made any attempts at crystal gazing, he always asked for divine assistance. Kelley put Dee's mind at rest on that subject, dropping to his knees and praying for the next hour, before looking into the magic glass and describing what he saw.

Dee was thrilled with his abilities. Kelley claimed to see a child-like angel trapped in the glass, struggling but unable to make its voice heard. From the description that Kelley gave, Dee identified the figure as Uriel. Dee, who was 55

John Dee was one of the most respected men in England, advising even the Queen herself when her life was in danger.

Dee and Kelley try their hands at necromancy

years old at the time, and beginning to despair about ever making a big breakthrough into the occult world, welcomed Kelley not only into his employment, but into his home. Dee's much younger wife (whom he married after his first wife died of the plague) was unhappy with the arrangement, but for the sake of her husband, she was prepared to go along with it. Later, though, she would come to regret it.

Kelley, who always wore a black cap to hide his missing ears, spent the next several years communicating with angels and spirit guides for Dee and the many wealthy patrons that they were able to acquire. Among the spirits that Kelley spoke for was Madimi, who was, as Dee described her, "a spiritual creature like a pretty girl of seven or nine years of age." While Kelley relayed Dee's questions and related Madimi's answers, Dee made a careful transcription of their conversations. She was always willing to chat, but in truth, none of her pronouncements were all that revealing. In most every case, she brushed off questions and failed to provide direct answers, which aggravated both Dee and the notable patrons who hoped that she could provide them with knowledge of the future.

Kelley then decided to try necromancy. In the graveyard of Walton-le-Dale in Lancashire, he went with an assistant named Waring to elicit information from a freshly buried corpse. But his luck in this was not much better than it had been with Madimi. He drew a magic circle and inscribed its border with the names of several helpful angels – Raphael, Rael, Miraton, Tarmiel and Rex. Standing inside of it and using a torch to read from a book of incantations, Kelley was purportedly successful in coaxing the corpse, still wrapped in its burial shroud, to rise from the grave and speak to him. To his dismay, the corpse had little to say.

Interestingly, there was one subject on which the spirit Madimi's instructions were quite explicit. According to Kelley, he was consulting her one day when she advised him that he and Dr. Dee should "share all things in common, including their wives." Jane Dee, likely seeing this one coming, flew into a rage. Mrs. Kelley's reaction was never recorded, but it's safe to say that she wasn't too pleased about it either.

After encountering this unexpected opposition, Kelley quit his position. And even though Dee was very unhappy with the idea of sharing his wife, he found himself missing the best scryer that he'd ever known. Later, when Kelley came back, he again consulted the magic glass and learned that the angel Uriel also advocated the wife-swapping plan. Dee gave in and he wrote, "There is no other remedy but as hath been said of our cross-matching, so it needs to be done." According to Dee's diary entry on Sunday, May 3, 1587, the two couples "covenanted with God, and subscribed the same for indissoluble and inviolable unities, charity and friendship keeping between us four, and all things between us to be common, as God by sundry means willed us to do."

The new, wife-sharing peace didn't last long. The wives fought bitterly, the husbands ran out of cash and Dee decided that the partnership was not working out after all. Kelley packed his bags, filling with them magic powders and trinkets, and traveled through Bohemia and Germany, telling fortunes and selling his wares. He was arrested twice as a heretic. The second time, afraid that he might actually end up in a dungeon sentenced to death, he tried to climb over the prison wall, lost his grip and fell. He broke both legs and two of his ribs and died of his injuries in February 1593.

As for John Dee, he set up shop in his ancestral home in Mortlake, where he gradually slid into poverty. A couple of the crystal gazers that he employed turned out to be incompetent and his pursuit of the philosopher's stone – an alchemical substance said to have the power to turn base metals like lead into gold – proved fruitless. He wrote voluminously, but with little effect or public acclaim. The queen came to his rescue with a minor appointment, but she died and was replaced by James I, who was no friend to any man with a reputation for sorcery. Dee had run out of luck. The lonely and impoverished old man had lost his second wife years before, and his health grew steadily worse. He died in 1608, surrounded by arcane books, magic mirrors and the other strange instruments of his trade.

ELIPHAS LEVI

Although he was better known as a writer about magic than an actual maker of magic, Eliphas Levi did indeed conjure up at least one important soul and left a full record of the experience in one of his many books, *Transcendental Magic, Its Doctrine and Ritual*. It became one of the most important incidents in his career.

Levi had been born Alphonse Louis Constant in February 1810. "Eliphas Levi", the name under which he published his books, was his attempt to translate his given names "Alphonse Louis" into Hebrew, although he was not Jewish. The son of a shoemaker in Paris, he attended the seminary of Saint Sulpice and began to study to enter the Roman Catholic priesthood. However, while at the seminary he fell in love, and left without being ordained. He wrote a number of minor religious works, as well as some political writings during a time of revolution, which led to two brief prison sentences.

In 1853, Levi visited England, where he met the novelist Sir Edward Bulwer-Lytton, who was interested in the occult and was the president of a minor Rosicrucian order. Levi wrote his first treatise on magic in 1855, followed a year later by a second, and then combined into a single volume, *Dogme et Rituel de la Haute Magie*. It was translated into English by Arthur Edward Waite as *Transcendental Magic, its Doctrine and Ritual* in 1910. The opening lines of the book became famous in occult circles:

Behind the veil of all the hieratic and mystical allegories of ancient doctrines, behind the darkness and strange ordeals of all initiations, under the seal of all sacred writings, in the ruins of Nineveh or Thebes, on the crumbling stones of old temples and on the blackened visage of the Assyrian or Egyptian sphinx, in the monstrous or marvelous paintings which interpret to the faithful of India the inspired pages of the Vedas, in the cryptic emblems of our old books on alchemy, in the ceremonies practiced at reception by all secret societies, there are found indications of a doctrine which is everywhere the same and everywhere carefully concealed.

In 1854, Levi, a large man with a great forked and devilish beard, was already known for his mastery of magic, although none of his occult writings had been published at the time. He was approached in London one day by a young woman, a magical adept who was dressed all in black. Claiming to be a friend of Bulwer-Lytton, she asked Levi if he could summon the spirit of Apollonius of Tyana, an ancient philosopher, and ask the specter two questions. Levi, who was never able to resist a beautiful young woman, decided to abandon his writing and take on the task. There's no record of it, but it's possible that the impoverished magician was also tempted by a large commission.

Eliphas Levi

To prepare for the necessary ritual, Levi put aside his usual appetites for women and food and practiced fasting and abstinence for twenty-one days. The little food that he ate during this time was strictly vegetarian, and for the last seven days, he claimed to eat nothing at all. All the while, he meditated deeply upon the life and writings of Apollonius, even going as far as to have imaginary talks with him so that he could create a strong mental bond between the two of them.

Then, on July 24, Levi outfitted himself in a white robe. Around his brow, he put a wreath made of the herb vervain, entwined with gold. Vervain, also called verbena, was purported to be able to keep demons away. Taking a new sword in one hand and a manuscript of the ritual in the other, Levi entered the "magical cabinet," which the mysterious woman had obligingly prepared for the ceremony.

The cabinet consisted of a room with four concave mirrors on the walls, and a white lambskin rug on the floor. There was an altar made from white marble with a pentagram carved into its top. A copper chafing dish, filled with charred alder and laurel wood, was placed on the altar, and another chafing dish was placed on a tripod to one side. Around it all was a magic circle, formed from a chain of magnetized iron, to ward off any hostile spirits.

Filled with trepidation, Levi lit the two chafing dishes so that a pall of smoke filled the room. The spirit of Apollonius was supposed to use the smoke to give itself some definition. For hours, he recited the necessary invocations to the dead: "In unity the demons chant the praises of God, they lose their malice and fury... Cerberus opens his triple jaw, and fire chants the praises of God with the three tongues of the lightning... the soul revisits the tombs, the magical lamps are lighted..."

Gradually, as the smoke swirled about him, Levi thought he could discern a shape. He tossed more twigs into the chafing dishes and he recited the prayers more loudly. In the mirror opposite, he saw a vague figure approaching him, as if coming from a great distance. He closed his eyes and summoned the spirit three times, asking it to appear before him. When he opened his eyes again, "there was a man in front of me, wrapped from head to foot in a species of shroud, which seemed more gray than white; he was lean, melancholy and beardless."

Terrified by his success, Levi found himself almost unable to speak. He was chilled to the bone and he slapped one hand down on the pentagram to reassure himself. Then, making his first mistake, he tried to order the ghost to obey him by pointing the sword at it. The ghost, not pleased, promptly vanished.

Levi ordered it to return, but instead of seeing the spirit materialize again, he felt something touch the arm holding the sword. Instantly, the arm went numb, from elbow to the hand, and the point of the sword drifted downward. The figure then reappeared, and though it never spoke, answers to the two questions that Levi planned to ask came into his mind -- one answer was "death" and the other was "dead." Weakened by fear, no doubt intensified by his weeks of fasting, Levi fainted and fell to the floor.

For days after the ritual, his arm remained sore. He wrote, "Something of another world had passed into me. I was no longer either sad or cheerful, but I felt a singular attraction towards death, unaccompanied, however, by any suicidal tendency." On two subsequent occasions, he claimed to have raised the spirit again, each time learning a great secret of magic. But he could never be certain how, or why, the operation worked. He wrote, "I do not explain the physical laws by which I saw and touched. I affirm solely that I did see and that I did touch, that I saw clearly and distinctly, apart from dreaming, and this is sufficient to establish the real efficacy of magical ceremonies."

He also added one bit of warning: "I commend the greatest caution to those who propose devoting themselves to similar experiences; their result is intense exhaustion, and frequently a shock sufficient to occasion illness."

The events of 1854 had an intense effect on Levi, and his first works on magic appeared the following year. He began to write in even greater succession in 1860, starting with *Historie de la Magie*. The following year, he published *La Clef des Grands Mystères* ("The Key to the Great Mysteries"). Further magical works included *Fables et Symboles* ("Stories and Images"), 1862, *Le Sorciere de Meudon* ("The Witch of Meudon") 1865, and *La Science des Esprits* ("The Science of Spirits"), 1865. In 1868, he wrote *Le Grand Arcane, ou l'Occultisme Dévoilé* ("The Great Secret, or Occultism Unveiled"); this, his final work, was published posthumously in 1898.

Levi's version of magic became a great success, especially after his death in 1875. By the 1850s, Spiritualism was becoming popular on both sides of the Atlantic, and this contributed to his popularity. More than anything, his writings were free from obvious fanaticisms. He had nothing to sell, and did not pretend to be the initiate of some ancient or fictitious secret society. This made his work even more credible and some of his ideas have had a lasting impact on the occult. He was really the first to incorporate tarot cards into his magical system, and as a result, the tarot has been an important part of magic ever since. He was also the first to popularize the idea that an inverted pentagram could be used for evil. Such ideas – as well as his other magical writings – strongly influenced many of the magicians and secret societies of the late 1800s and early 1900s. Thanks to the occultists that were inspired by him, Levi is remembered as one of the key founders of the current revival of magic.

THE BROTHERHOOD OF THE ROSY CROSS

Although its earliest documentation dates back to 1614, this mysterious organization, which claimed to be in possession of the elixir of life (along with other great secrets of the universe), traced its origins back to the fourteenth century and a wandering magician (almost certainly fictitious) named Christian Rosencreutz. His last name – which translated as "rosy cross" – followed in the footsteps of many great magic seekers before him, from Apollonius of Tyana to Cyprian, in having traveled from the West to the ancient East in search of occult wisdom.

According to lore, Rosencreutz began his studies at the age of five in a convent school in Germany. When he turned fifteen, his education was continued when he embarked, under the care of a monk, on a trip to the Holy Land. Soon after arriving at Cyprus, the monk took ill and died. But young Rosencreutz, eager for knowledge, set out alone for Arabia, where he was told that the great magical adepts still lived. When he eventually found them, they welcomed him with open arms, claiming that his coming had been foretold. They taught him all that he learned about the occult sciences. Three years later, they sent him on to Egypt, where he was instructed on the invocation of elemental spirits.

His next stop was Spain, where the adepts offered him no respect or help. In fact, the Spanish magicians claimed that they'd learned the secrets of the Black Arts from the master himself – the Devil – who'd taught them the finer points of necromancy in a lecture hall at the University of Salamanca. Rosencreutz moved on to other countries, but gaining little, he returned to Germany, where he spent the next five years in solitude, writing down the secrets that he had learned during his travels.

When that was done, he slowly and carefully began to gather the assistants and students who would form what came to be called the Rosicrucian fraternity. They created a magical language that was only spoken among themselves, an equally cryptic written language designed for magical incantations, and a dictionary containing all of the occult wisdom that had been accumulated to date. They also started to put their knowledge into practice, using it, or so they claimed, to heal the sick. They also built what they called their House of the Holy Ghost, a headquarters that no one has ever found, to serve as a repository for all of their records and wisdom.

When Rosencreutz died, he was buried in a secret vault, the walls of which were inscribed with magical etchings. When all of the original Rosicrucians died out, the location of the vault was lost. But 120 years later, when one of the brotherhood's lodges was being rebuilt, the door to the tomb was rediscovered hidden behind a large bronze tablet. Inside of the seven-sided vault, the Rosicrucians found not only the perfectly preserved body of their founder but a number of magical items, like mirrors, bells and books. After debating among themselves, the brothers decided that the time had come to make their order, and its miraculous discoveries, available to other worthy initiates in a public fashion.

Thanks to this, we have *The Fama of the Fraternity of the Meritorious Order of the Rosy Cross Addressed to the Learned in General and the Governors of Europe*. As a book, it was kind of an open letter, published in 1614 in Germany. It called for a reformation in science equivalent to that which had already occurred in religion. It was time, the booklet insisted, that men of science stopped relying on the authorities handed down from antiquity and looked instead to a new synthesis, based on moral renewal and the mysteries of the Grand Orient, which the children of light, the illuminated ones, the Rosicrucians, had obtained. Their symbol became a rose crucified on a cross.

Not surprisingly, the booklet created quite a stir. Many were anxious to know what this mysterious order had to offer. Others, who considered themselves adepts in the magical arts, were offended by the suggestion that their own skills were lacking. By the following year, the book had gone into three printings and two additional editions in Dutch. Capitalizing on their initial success, the brotherhood put out another booklet, *Confession of the Rosicrucian Fraternity*, which advertised for new members. Selected applicants, it said, would be gradually initiated into the mysteries, and into the ranks, of the secret brotherhood. But there was nowhere to apply. All you had to do was publicly state your interest, perhaps by posting an advertisement or printing a booklet of your own, and wait to be contacted about membership. Needless to say, it was a frustrating process for many.

However, the rewards were so tantalizing that scholars, magicians and philosophers continued to line up. After all, the Rosicrucians professed to know the secrets of making gold and becoming immortal. Their members were required to go about their business – which was mostly healing the sick – without dressing in special garments or standing out in any obvious way. They looked like everyone else, and were forbidden to accept payment for their medical treatments. They were to remain anonymous at all times, never telling anyone that they were members of the secret fraternity. As a result, it's difficult to know for sure who was actually a member, but signs point to Roger Bacon, Agrippa, Paracelsus, Descartes, and others.

The writings of the Rosicrucians inspired other works, all of them detailing ideas and philosophies about magic, alchemy and even politics. Michael Maier was ennobled with the title Pfalzgraf (Count Palatine) by Rudolph II, Emperor and King of Hungary and King of Bohemia. He was one of the most prominent defenders of the Rosicrucians, clearly transmitting details about the "Brothers of the Rose Cross" in his writings. Maier made the firm statement that the Rosicrucians existed to advance arts and sciences, including alchemy. He never claimed to produce gold, though. His writings point toward a symbolic and spiritual alchemy, rather than an operative one. He (along with other writers) conveyed the nine stages of an evolutionary transmutation of the threefold body of the human being, the threefold soul and the threefold spirit, along with other esoteric knowledge.

In a booklet written in 1618, it was said that the Rosicrucians left for the East due to the instability in Europe caused by the start of the Thirty Years' War. In the years that followed, many Rosicrucian societies arose. They were based on the occult tradition and inspired by the mystery of what came to be called the "College of Invisibles." This Invisible College, an order exemplified by the network of astronomers, professors, mathematicians, and natural philosophers in sixteenth-century Europe, was a precursor to the Royal Society, which was founded in 1660. It was made up of a group of scientists who began to hold regular meetings to share and develop knowledge acquired by experimental investigation.

The Rosicrucian brotherhood was also believed to have a great effect on Freemasonry during this period. According to Jean-Pierre Bayard, two Rosicrucian-inspired Masonic rites emerged towards the end of eighteenth century, the Rectified Scottish Rite, widespread in Central Europe where there was a strong presence of the "Golden and Rosy Cross," and the Ancient and Accepted Scottish Rite, first practiced in France, in which the 18th degree is called Knight of the Rose Croix.

The Gold und Rosenkreuzer (Golden and Rosy Cross) was founded by the alchemist Samuel Richter in Prague in the early eighteenth century as a hierarchical secret society composed of internal circles, recognition signs and alchemy treatises. Under the leadership of Hermann Fictuld, the group reformed itself extensively in 1767 and again in 1777 because of political pressure. Its members claimed that the leaders of the Rosicrucian Order had invented Freemasonry and only they knew the secret meaning of Masonic symbols. The Rosicrucian Order had been founded by an Egyptian who had immigrated to Scotland. Then the original Order disappeared and was supposed to have been resurrected by Oliver Cromwell as "Freemasonry."

Led by Johann Christoph von Wöllner and General Johann Rudolf von Bischoffwerder, the Masonic Lodge (later, Grand Lodge) Zu den drei Weltkugeln (The Three Globes) was infiltrated and came under the influence of the Golden and Rosy Cross. Many Freemasons became Rosicrucians and the order was established in many lodges. After 1782, this highly secretive society added Egyptian, Greek and Druidic mysteries to its alchemy system. There are many who believe that the Gold and Rosenkruezer order inspired many later occult groups, including the Nazi party in Germany in the 1930s.

During the late nineteenth and early twentieth centuries, various groups styled themselves Rosicrucian. The diverse groups who link themselves to a "Rosicrucian Tradition" can be divided into three categories: Esoteric Christian Rosicrucian groups, which profess Christ; Masonic Rosicrucian groups such as Societas Rosicruciana; and initiatory groups such as the Golden Dawn and the Ancient Mystical Order Rosae Crucis.

Esoteric Christian Rosicrucian schools provide esoteric knowledge related to the inner teachings of Christianity, which present the mysteries, in the form of esoteric knowledge, of which Christ spoke in Matthew 13:11 and Luke 8:10. The fellowship seeks to prepare the individual through harmonious development of mind and heart in a spirit of unselfish service to mankind and an all-embracing altruism. According to their history, the Rosicrucian Order was founded in 1313 and is composed of twelve exalted beings gathered around a central, thirteenth figure, Christian Rosenkreuz. These great adepts have already advanced far beyond the cycle of rebirth; their mission is to prepare the world for a new phase in religion—which includes awareness of the inner worlds, and to provide safe guidance in the gradual awakening of man's latent spiritual faculties during the next six centuries toward the coming Age of Aquarius.

THE FREEMASONS

A mystical order, which for many years became sort of a safe haven for astrologers, alchemists and magicians, the Freemasons have a long and mysterious history. Although scattered records do exist, and legends abound, its origins seem to lie in the Middle Ages with the freemasons – itinerant stoneworkers – who raised the great cathedrals and other edifices of western Europe. As each great structure was built, it attracted a score of skilled builders, the architects and engineers of the day, who understood stone and structure, and who formed close bonds with one another over the years that it took to complete each building.

What began as an operative guild made up of men trained in the art of building became a more speculative order over time, one that embraced all religious faiths in a quest for universal brotherhood. The instruments of the stoneworker's trade – gauge and tool aprons, compass and chisels – became symbols of more arcane practices and wisdom. A complex mythology evolved, claiming that the Freemasons had existed for thousands of years, and that members of their order had been instrumental in building the Great Pyramid of Giza and the Temple of Solomon in Israel.

The Freemasons flourished in England, where the Grand Lodge was founded in 1717 and served as the society's powerful central hub. It was in London that fundamental tenets of the society were drawn together, codified and sent out to lodges all over the world. New applicants underwent an elaborate initiation ceremony,

An illustration of a Freemason Initiation -- published at the time to show the bizarre and mysterious workings of the group, which originally started with strong links to magic and mysticism.

which gained them the status of Apprentice. Later, they would move on to Fellow Craft, before eventually graduating to Master Mason. Often, in France and Germany, for instance, these ceremonies took on a decidedly occult appearance.

In the eighteenth-century French rite, the initiate was held aloft, and then slowly lowered to the floor by several members. This was a way to symbolize him being lowered into the grave. Then, while he was on the floor, a bloody cloth was thrown over his face and the members gathered around him, pointing swords at his body. Finally, the grand master of the lodge would clasp the new apprentice by the hand, using the Mason's grip, and raise him up from the floor. The Masonic handgrip, a handshake with the thumb cocked, was a way for Masons everywhere to recognize each other without having to say a word. They also had various symbols and signs that achieved the same thing. There is no way that I can overstate the importance of the Freemasons during the eighteenth and nineteenth centuries, particularly in England and in the British colonies. Members of the society would do almost anything for a "fellow traveler." It was a display of brotherhood that would have repercussions in politics, crime, war, and some of the most poignant events in history.

As a Mason progressed through the different levels of the lodge, he was allowed to share more and more of the secret knowledge and power that the order was reputed to possess. The lodges grew and prospered, making inroads in places like Colonial America, where Founding Fathers like George Washington and Benjamin Franklin were Masons and Master Masons.

But thanks to all of the claims of extraordinary knowledge, coupled with the shroud of mystery with which the society purposely surrounded itself, the Masons drew suspicion and later, outright hostility, from a number of institutions, including governments and the Catholic Church. For example, in 1822, the Russian minister of the interior closed down all of Russia's Masonic lodges, and the pope issued an edict in 1884 that condemned the brotherhood. Even today, as Masons across America grow older and fail to attract many younger members, they still continue to instruct apprentices in the hidden mysteries and secret signs that have been preserved and handed down through many generations.

The Freemasons remain the best-known of the scores of secret societies that have sprung up over the years and perhaps for this reason, they have inspired more than their share of would-be magicians, weird organizations and infamous characters.

ALEISTER CROWLEY

The true face of notorious magician Aleister Crowley is shrouded in myth and misinformation, most of it of his own making. He was a master of manipulation, a shameless self-promoter who took a perverse pleasure in shocking polite society with his boasts of drug abuse and debauchery. He relished his role as the "wickedest man in the world," and did everything he could to enhance that reputation. His fame – or infamy – lives on. In 1967, twenty years after his death, Crowley was among those pictured on the album cover of the Beatles' *Sgt. Pepper's Lonely Hearts Club Band*, causing some fundamentalist Christians to accuse the Beatles of being Satanists. A BBC poll conducted in 2002 described him as the seventy-third greatest Briton of all times. Cynics said that Crowley's claims to be a seeker of

Aleister Crowley as a young magician. He became fascinated with the occult as a young man and became involved in the new Order of the Golden Dawn before striking out on his own. He would later be dubbed "the wickedest man alive".

occult wisdom were entirely fabricated to enable his debauchery. But merely thinking of him as a fraud and attention-seeker does not take into account his considerable influence on the occult world or his reputation as one of history's most notorious practitioners of practical and sex magic. No matter what, he was a remarkable and fascinating figure whose views on magic permanently changed the occult world.

He was born Edward Alexander Crowley in England on October 12, 1875 – that much we know. Beyond that, much of Crowley's life remains shrouded in mystery. This is not because documentation of his life does not exist, but because most of that documentation was provided by Crowley himself. Crowley undoubtedly "invented" whole sections of his life, magnifying the occult aspects of his existence to appeal to his followers. We'll never know for sure just how much of his biography is fact, and how much is fancy, but the following has been pieced together from the most reliable sources that could be found.

His father, Edward Crowley, had made his fortune from Crowley's Ales, and had retired to the small town of Leamington Spa to become a protestant minister, preaching the conservative evangelical doctrine of the Plymouth Brethren. Crowley made it clear that his "diabolism" later in life was a revolt against the religious repression of his childhood. However, his youth was not a bitter one and his parents were affectionate and indulgent. Crowley admired his father and imitated his leadership abilities, a skill that would serve him well as

123

A young Aleister Crowley

an adult. His father died when Crowley was eleven. Perhaps predictably, the boy began getting into trouble. He was sent to a private, religious school and it was there that his seeds of rebellion began to be sown in earnest.

As Crowley became a teenager, his interest in sex began to grow. His mother was so straitlaced that she once argued violently with Crowley's cousin Agnes because the younger woman had a book by Émile Zola in her house. Zola was a nineteenth-century French author. His novel *Nana*, the story of a streetwalker who became a high-class prostitute, was generally considered to be scandalous, which made it all the more popular. As an outright revolt against such puritanical attitudes, Crowley lost his virginity to a female servant on his mother's bed when he was 14 years old.

Just a year later, Crowley's career almost came to a premature end on Guy Fawkes Night in 1891. Guy Fawkes Night (or Fireworks Night) is an annual celebration on the evening of November 5 to mark the foiling of the Gunpowder Plot in which a number of Catholic conspirators, including Guy Fawkes, attempted to blow up the Houses of Parliament. As Crowley tried to light a ten-pound, homemade firework, it exploded, knocking him unconscious for ninety-six hours. His followers believe that the accident may have awakened some sort of latent psychic abilities, which they used to explain the dark career of his adulthood, and the powerful influence that he obtained over the occult community of the day.

After recovering from the fireworks accident, Crowley began attending public school at Malvern, and then went on to Trinity College at Cambridge, where he lived lavishly on his inheritance. While at Cambridge, he published a book of his own poetry. Crowley was not a gifted poet, but he certainly believed that he was. At one point, he referred to the proximity of the small town where he grew up to Stratford-on-Avon, birthplace of William Shakespeare. He noted that it was "a strange coincidence that one small county should have given England her two greatest poets."

As a student, the first inklings of what lay ahead of him in life began to surface, especially after his discovery of A.E. Waite's compilation on ceremonial magic, *The Book of Black Magic and of Pacts*. Crowley continued to pen his own poetry, including a cycle of poems about a sexual psychopath who becomes a murderer, but his writings began to take on a more supernatural feel.

Through a fellow student, Crowley was introduced to alchemist George Cecil Jones, and through Jones to the Order of the Golden Dawn, a magical cult that practiced arcane rituals for the purpose of spiritual development. The Order had been founded by retired physician Dr. William Robert Woodman; Dr. William Wynn Westcott, a London coroner, and Samuel Liddell MacGregor Mathers. They were Freemasons who were also members of the Societas Rosicruciana, an offshoot of the Masons. Westcott, also a member of the Theosophical Society, appears to have been the initial driving force behind the establishment of the Golden Dawn.

The Order of the Golden Dawn was founded by (Left to Right) retired physician Dr. William Robert Woodman; Dr. William Wynn Westcott, a London coroner, and Samuel Liddell MacGregor Mathers.

The Golden Dawn was formed along the lines of a Masonic lodge; however, women were admitted on an equal basis with men. The Golden Dawn is technically only the first, or the "outer," of three orders, although all three are often collectively described as the "Golden Dawn." The First Order taught esoteric philosophy based on the Kabbalah, as well as the basics of astrology and tarot reading. The Second, or "Inner," Order, the Rosae Rubeae et Aureae Crucis (the Ruby Rose and Cross of Gold), taught magic proper, including scrying, astral travel, and alchemy. The Third Order was that of the "Secret Chiefs," who were said to be powerful adepts who were no longer in human form, but who directed the activities of the lower two orders through spirit communication with the chiefs of the Second Order.

In October 1887, Westcott began working to translate the legendary Cipher Manuscripts, which allegedly gave the specific outlines of the Grade Rituals of the Order, and organized a curriculum of specifically graduated teachings that encompassed the Kabbalah, astrology, occult tarot, geomancy, and alchemy. He wrote to a woman in Germany named Anna Sprengel, whose name and address he said he received through the decoding of the Cipher Manuscripts. Sprengel was said to be an adept of the Order of the Golden Dawn. She reportedly replied to Wescott's letter with a letter of her own that contained much in the way of supernatural wisdom, and also bestowed honorary titles on Westcott, Mathers and Woodman. She also supposedly gave Westcott the task of establishing the first Golden Dawn temple in England.

In 1888, the Isis-Urania Temple was founded in London and the order's rituals began to be developed and practiced. The original lodge did not actually teach magical practices, except for basic "banishing rituals" and meditation, but was rather a philosophical and metaphysical teaching group. This was called the "Outer Order," but the "Inner Order" that became active in 1892 was comprised of a circle of adepts who had completed the entire course of study and initiations of the "Outer Order," detailed in the Cipher Manuscripts. This group eventually became known as the Second Order.

A short time later, the Osiris Temple in Weston-super-Mare, the Horus Temple in Bradford, and the Amen-Ra Temple in Edinburgh were founded. A few years after this, Mathers started the Ahathoor Temple in Paris.

In 1891, correspondence with the mysterious adept Anna Sprengel suddenly stopped, and Westcott allegedly received word from Germany that she was either dead or that her companions did not approve of the founding

Crowley in the Golden Dawn

of the order and demanded that she cut off contact with them. If the founders were to contact the Secret Chiefs, they would have to do it on their own, without the help of their benefactor. It was about this time that Woodman died, never having seen the Second Order come into being. In 1892, Mathers (not surprisingly) claimed that a link to the Secret Chiefs had been formed and supplied the rituals for the Second Order.

By the middle 1890s, the Golden Dawn was well established in England, with members from every class of Victorian society. This was considered the heyday of the order and many celebrities of the time boasted membership within its ranks, including actress Florence Farr, Annie Horniman (who sponsored the Abbey Theatre in Dublin), occult novelist Arthur Machen, William Butler Yeats, Evelyn Underhill, and many others.

Aleister Crowley was introduced to the Golden Dawn during this period, but he was disappointed with the mediocrity of most of the members and found the ceremonies boring. Nevertheless, he was admitted to their ranks, and was given the name Brother Perdurabo (one who endures to the end). He was among the lowest of the order's levels, and he began working hard to rise in status.

Around 1897, Westcott broke off all ties to the Golden Dawn, leaving Mathers in complete control. It was speculated that Westcott left the order after some papers were found in a hansom cab, outlining his connection to the Golden Dawn. His affiliation came to the attention of his superiors and he was told to either resign from the Order or be relieved from his position as a coroner. Rumors claimed that Mathers planted the papers to drive Westcott out, but there has never been any proof of this. It was noted that any public relationship between the two men ended at this point, although it's possible that Westcott continued with the order in secret. Lodge documents bearing his signature have since been found, dated years after his "resignation." After Westcott departed, Mathers appointed Florence Farr to be Chief Adept in Anglia. This left Mathers as the only active founding membe, and in charge of the order. Thanks to personality clashes with other members, and his frequent absences from the center of order activity in England, challenges to Mathers' authority as leader began to develop among the members of the Second Order.

By late 1899, leaders of the Isis-Urania and Amen-Ra Temples had become very unhappy with Mathers' leadership, as well as his growing friendship with Crowley, whom they saw as a disturbing influence. They were anxious to make contact with the Secret Chiefs on their own, instead of receiving their wisdom through Mathers. To make matters worse, when Crowley was denied entry into the Second Order in London, Mathers overrode the decision and initiated him at the Ahathoor Temple in Paris on January 6, 1900. For the London leaders, this was the last straw. Crowley's initiation led to a general meeting that called for Mathers' removal as chief and his expulsion from the order. A committee of three was formed to temporarily govern the order, which included P.W. Bullock, M.W. Blackden and J. W. Brodie-Innes. After a short time, Bullock resigned, and Dr. Robert Felkin took his place. In 1903, A.E. Waite and Blackden joined forces to retain the name Isis-Urania, while Felkin and other London members formed the Stella Matutina. J.W. Brodie-Innes continued the Amen-Ra Temple in Edinburgh.

Once Mathers realized there would be no reconciliation among the members of the order, he began trying to establish himself again in London. Members of the Bradford and Weston-super-Mare temples remained loyal to him, but their numbers were few. He appointed Edward Berridge as his representative, who proceeded to begin working the ceremonies and rites of the Golden Dawn in West London in 1903.

Brodie-Innes, who had continued the Amen-Ra Temple, eventually reached the conclusion that the revolt against Mathers was unjustified. By 1908, the two men were again in complete accord. Brodie-Innes assumed command of the English and Scottish temples, while Mathers concentrated on building up the Ahathoor Temple and extending his connections in America. The first Golden Dawn temple had been established in Chicago around 1900. It was located in a small building on Halsted Street, which is now home to a bar. Renovations in the building in recent years revealed ritual paintings in the basement and a dagger that had been buried under the floor to purify the location.

The Order of the Golden Dawn (at least in its original incarnation) eventually faded out of existence. Most of the temples closed down by the 1930s, with the exception of the Hermes Temple in Bristol, which operated sporadically until 1970. The group has been revived several times over the years and a modern version still survives today.

Crowley abandoned the Golden Dawn after Mathers' initial banishment and after a public disagreement that Crowley had with W.B. Yeats -- who Crowley maintained was jealous because Crowley was a much better poet. The problem emerged over money, of which Crowley had plenty, thanks to his inheritance. Crowley shared with Mathers a habit of pretending to be an aristocrat. Mathers was given to dressing in kilts, and calling himself the Chevalier MacGregor or the Comte de Glenstrae, both of which were titles he created himself. Crowley started speaking with a Russian accent, and called himself

Crowley's Boleskine House on the shores of Loch Ness. The house was later owned by Led Zeppelin's Jimmy Page, who maintained that it was still "tainted" by Crowley's tenancy in the mansion.

Count Vladimir Svareff. He explained later that he did this in the interests of a psychological experiment. He had observed how tradesmen deferred to him because of his wealth, and he wanted to see how they behaved with a Russian nobleman. This may, or may not have been the case because Crowley continued such charades long after the "experiment" in London.

When he moved to Boleskine House, overlooking Loch Ness, he dubbed himself Lord Boleskine, or the Laird of Boleskine, and imitated Mathers by adopting a kilt. While living in the house, he concentrated on the magic of Abra-Melin the Mage, whose ultimate aim was to establish contact with one's guardian angel. Crowley claimed that in London, he and George Cecil Jones, his alchemist friend, succeeded in materializing the helmeted head and left leg of a spirit called Buel, and that on another occasion, a group of semi-formed demons spent the night marching around his room. At Loch Ness, the lodge and terrace of his house allegedly became haunted by shadowy shapes. The lodge keeper went mad during Crowley's tenancy and attempted to kill his wife and children. Crowley claimed that the ritual room of the house became so dark while he was trying to copy magical symbols that he would have to light lamps, even when the sunshine was blazing outside.

Crowley's friend, Allan Bennett

Boleskine House was later purchased by Robert Plant, best known as the lead vocalist of the English rock band Led Zeppelin. Plant owned a collection of Crowley's work, including manuscripts and artwork. Inscribed on the vinyl of the 1970 album *Led Zeppelin III* were the words, "Do what thou wilt," part of Crowley's famous edict.

After his quarrel with Yeats, Crowley went to Mexico, where he claimed that his concentrated effort almost made his reflection vanish from a mirror. In the dry, hot climate of Mexico, Crowley continued to work to create his own mystical religion, greater than any that he had encountered before, but he was at a loss as to how to continue. He said that he put out a great call for help from the Masters and a week later, he received a letter from George Cecil Jones, suggesting a new course of study. Oddly enough, it was an old mountain climbing companion of Crowley's who suggested his next move. He advised him to give up magic and simply develop a power of intense concentration. Crowley followed his friend's suggestion and spent months involved in what constituted yoga training.

More mountain climbing followed, as well as travels to San Francisco, and Ceylon (now Sri Lanka), and a love affair with a married woman that resulted in his book *Alice, An Adultery*. In Ceylon, he found his close friend Allan Bennett, a colleague from his Golden Dawn days, and a student of Buddhism. Crowley's generosity to his friend had resulted in Bennett's trip to Ceylon. Bennett later became the founder of the British Buddhist movement, and he was one of the few people of whom Crowley remained consistently fond. He spent months teaching Crowley everything he knew about Eastern mysticism, and after his recent period of intense thought control, Bennett's teachings came as a revelation to him. Crowley now believed that he could harness all of his psychic energies to do amazing things.

Meanwhile, Bennett, who had been working as a private tutor to the solicitor-general in Ceylon, decided that he was going to renounce the world and become a Buddhist monk. With his friend out of commission, Crowley went on a big game hunt, penetrated a secret shrine at Madura, explored the Irrawaddy River in a canoe, and finally visited Bennett at his monastery, where he claimed to see Bennett levitating during a period of intense meditation.

Crowley, now in his middle twenties, was still basically a rich playboy and sportsman, not much different from the Golden Dawn members whom he held in such disdain when he first joined the order. In 1902, he was one of the party that attempted to reach the summit of the Chogori (now known as K2), the world's second-highest mountain, (after Everest) in India's Karakoram range. Bad weather and illness prematurely ended the expedition.

Crowley returned to Paris and called on Mathers, hoping that his mental accomplishments would earn him respect. Mathers was not in the least bit interested in yoga and dismissed his one-time ally, which greatly cooled Crowley's respect for him. Crowley set about becoming an eccentric character in the artistic circles of Paris and W. Somerset Maugham wrote about him in his 1908 novel, *The Magician*. In this tale, the magician, Oliver Haddo, a caricature of Aleister Crowley, attempts to create life. Crowley wrote a critique of this book under the pen name Oliver Haddo, where he accused Maugham of plagiarism.

After a time in Paris, he returned to Boleskine House at Loch Ness, where he became friendly with a young painter named Gerald Kelly (who later became Sir Gerald Kelly, president of the Royal Academy). Crowley soon met Kelly's unstable sister, Rose, an attractive young woman with a score of emotional issues. Already a widow, she had involved herself with a number of men who wanted to marry her, and she encouraged them all. Crowley's odd sense of humor offered her a solution to her dilemma: marry him and she could leave the marriage unconsummated if she wished. She could have his name and be free of her admirers. They were married by a lawyer the next morning.

Crowley had pretended to be uninterested in sex with Rose, but he could not pass up the opportunity to work his "sexual magic." In addition, there was something about Rose's mental weakness that appealed to the sadist in him and he couldn't help but take advantage of her. Their decision to keep the marriage platonic lasted for only a few hours. He ravished her over and over again, much to his new bride's delight. However, Kelly and the rest of Rose's family were not happy about the marriage, which delighted Crowley, who loved drama of any sort. He took Rose to Paris, and then they traveled on to Cairo, where they spent a night inside the Great Pyramid. In Ceylon, Crowley took his new wife hunting. He shot a bat, which fell onto Rose's head and dugs its claws into her hair. That night, Rose had a nightmare in which she was the bat, and clung to the frame of the mosquito netting over the bed. When Crowley tried to detach her from it, she howled, spat, scratched and bit at him. He later admiringly described it as "the finest case of obsession that I have ever had the good fortune to observe."

In 1903, Crowley married the unstable sister of his friend George Kelly. Rose became pregnant a short time later, beginning a strange new era in Crowley's life.

Soon after that night, an event occurred that Crowley would call the most important in his life: Rose became pregnant. Her behavior, already bizarre, became even stranger. Crowley didn't blame hormones on her personality change, but stated that the spirits of the air that he had invoked for her benefit put her into a peculiar mood. She told him that she had offended the Egyptian god Horus, of whom, Crowley said, she knew nothing. In a museum, she showed him a statue of Ra-Hoor-Khuit, one of the forms of Horus. Crowley was impressed to find that the number of the exhibit was 666, the number of the Beast in the Biblical Book of Revelation. Rose, whom he began calling Ouarda, now began to instruct him on how to invoke Horus. The ritual did not seem to make sense, but he tried it anyway, and later claimed that it was a complete success. Horus allegedly told him that a new epoch was beginning, a statement that many other occultists also believed. Crowley was ordered to write, and a disembodied "musical voice" from out of the corner of the room dictated *The Book of the Law* to him. The voice assuring him that the volume would solve all religious problems, and would be translated into many languages.

The Book of the Law, with its fundamental theme of "Do What Thou Wilt," became what Crowley considered one of his central pieces of writing. He attached enormous importance to it. It was his own bible and he was the chosen prophet. For the rest of his life, he began all of his letters with the assertion "Do what thou wilt shall be the whole of the Law." He believed that the old era of gods and demons was over and that a new epoch was beginning that would force man to stand on his own and come into his own power. Crowley saw himself as a potential new god, gradually coming to understand his own powers. The book became Crowley's major achievement, and when he had finished it, he likely felt that he had at last produced his masterpiece, a work that towered above everything that he had previously written, and one that was worth devoting his life to making known.

As Crowley began attracting disciples, he shaved his head to attain a more sinister air.

The next portion of Crowley's life was filled with anger and perhaps even madness. After he completed *The Book of the Law*, he wrote Mathers from Paris and told him that the Secret Chiefs had appointed him the head of the Order of the Golden Dawn. The letter was obviously meant to antagonize Mathers (Crowley said that he "declared war on him") and it succeeded. According to Crowley, malevolent magical currents swept from Mathers in Paris to Loch Ness, where he had taken Rose to give birth to their child. He believed Mathers was out to get him and was responsible for killing off his dogs and causing a workman to go insane and try to attack Rose. In response, Crowley invoked forty-nine demons, which Rose allegedly saw, and sent them off to torment Mathers. Soon, Rose gave birth to their daughter, whom Crowley named Nuit Ma Ahathoor Hecate Sappho Jezebel Lilith.

After his daughter was born, Crowley returned to traveling. He took on another mountaineering expedition, this time to Kanchenjunga in Nepal, at 28,160 feet the world's third-highest mountain. In 1905, he led the group that attempted to scale the peak. His narcissistic personality soon set the others on edge. After the party had reached a height of about 24,000 feet on the main peak, a conference was called to formally depose Crowley as the leader of the team, thanks to his sadistically cruel treatment of the porters. One of the expedition members, noticing the porters were climbing the icy mountain barefoot, accused Crowley of failing to provide them with shoes, as he had agreed. Crowley insisted that he had given the "economical natives" footwear but they preferred to pack them away for future use rather than wear them "unless there is some serious reason for putting them on." Crowley refused to accept the demotion, and the expedition was called off. Everyone but Crowley and a Swiss climber named Reymond started down the mountain toward the lower camps. Then someone slipped, setting off an avalanche. The entire party was swept down the mountain, where they were buried under the snow. A few of

Crowley traveled widely around the world, climbing mountings, experimenting with drugs and creating his unique magical philosophy.

the men managed to dig themselves out and called to Crowley to come and help as they searched for the porters and the other climbers, who later turned up dead. Reymond ran to help, but Crowley refused to leave his tent, where he was drinking tea. That evening, he wrote a letter, which was later printed in English newspapers, commenting that he "was not over-anxious in the circumstances to render help. A mountain accident of this kind is one of the things for which I have no sympathy whatever." The next morning, he descended the mountain, avoiding his former companions, and proceeded to Darjeeling by himself.

He went on to Calcutta, where he described an incident in which he was attacked in the street by a gang of thieves. Crowley claimed that he fired his revolver at them and then "made himself invisible." He explained that this was not literally true; it was simply that he possessed an odd power that caused a blank spot in the minds of those who were looking at him.

The next day, Rose and the baby arrived in India. Crowley had fallen out of love with her, he said, and had little interest in the child. Regardless, he took his family with him to China, where he tried opium for the first time. After four months, he sent Rose back to England by way of Calcutta, so that she could pick up some luggage they had left there. Crowley, meanwhile, returned through New York. When he arrived back in Liverpool, he learned that his daughter had died of typhoid in Rangoon.

Rose gave birth to another child not long after, Lola Zaza, who almost died of bronchitis soon after she was born. The birth and illness caused a permanent falling out between Crowley and Rose's family. Shortly after, the marriage fell apart. Rose became an alcoholic and later went insane. Strangely, this was a pattern that seemed to occur over and over again with people who became too intimate with Crowley.

Left to his own devices, Crowley began seeking disciples. His first was Lord Tankerville. Together, they traveled in Morocco and Spain. Tankerville footed the bill for these trips because Crowley's fortune was finally beginning to run out. They parted ways, but Crowley soon found another follower, a poet named Victor Neuberg. Crowley published more of his own poetry; a

Crowley and his magical symbols

book praising himself called *The Star in the West*. He also started a bi-annual journal about magic called *The Equinox*. Crowley also decided to start his own magical society, which he called the Silver Star, which made use of some of the rituals from the Golden Dawn. He knighted himself, claiming that he had received the title in Spain and shaved his domed head. Rose was, by now, completely insane, and he divorced her.

In 1910, he began using mescaline and, probably with assistance from the drug, devised a series of seven rituals, which he called the Rites of Eleusis. He hired a hall for their performance on seven successive Wednesdays. Admission was five guineas. The aim of the rituals was to induce religious ecstasy. Crowley's mistress, Austrian violinist Leila Waddell, provided musical accompaniment. Newspapers and magazines were harshly critical of the performances. One magazine devoted three issues to attack Crowley personally. This was the beginning of what Crowley referred to as the "persecution" that plagued him until his death in 1947.

At the same time, he again began having trouble with his former friend Samuel Mathers. Crowley was being sued to try and stop the publication of the third issue of *The Equinox*, because it contained a full description of the secret rites of the Golden Dawn, which Crowley had taken an oath never to reveal. The judge found in favor of Mathers but Crowley later claimed that he performed a series of magic rituals before appealing the case. This time, he won. The issue was published and Mather's secrets were revealed, affording Crowley a small bit of revenge.

Crowley was now beginning to fear that the best part of his life was over. His existence was becoming a series of repetitive events – magical ceremonies, mistresses, frantic efforts to raise money, and newspaper attacks on him, followed by attempts to justify himself in the press. But everything changed in 1912, when Crowley met German occultist and Ordo Templi Orientis leader Theodor Reuss. At first, Reuss was angry with Crowley because he had revealed in his *The Book of Lies* that sex could be used magically. When he realized that Crowley's revealing of the secret had been inadvertent, he authorized him to set up his own branch of the O.T.O., an idea that Crowley heartily embraced. He launched his branch of the order by sodomizing disciple Victor Neuberg as part of a magical ceremony in 1913.

Crowley's need for debauchery now had an outlet and he began practicing sex magic (or "magick" as he began to call it -- he explained that the "k" stood for *kteis*, meaning "vagina" in Greek) with a new diligence. One of his companions in this was a friend of Isadora Duncan's, Mary D'Este Sturges. They rented a villa in Italy for a lengthy bout of rituals. He also took a troupe of chorus girls, the Ragged Ragtime Girls, to Moscow and became involved in a violent affair with a young woman who needed to be beaten in order to achieve sexual satisfaction. Crowley claimed this was his first relationship of this kind, but it was not the last. He developed a taste for sadism and began incorporating it into his rituals.

He opened a Satanic Temple in a studio on London's Fulham Road. The newspapers had a field day, especially after an American journalist was allowed to visit the Temple and wrote an article about the number of rich British women who frequented it. Crowley had filed his canine teeth to sharp points, and when he met women, he was inclined to give them the "serpent's kiss," biting them on the wrist, and occasionally the throat, with his fangs. He also developed a new kink: defecating on carpets. He explained to a man who was offended that Crowley had done this in his home, that his waste was sacred, like that of the Dalai Lama.

When World War I broke out, Crowley, now age thirty-nine, was caught in Switzerland. He claimed that he tried to get the British government to employ him as a spy, but was refused. He decided to go to America and after a year of unsuccessful magical activities (apparently the Americans were not yet ready for Crowley's version of weird), he developed a new role: the anti-British Irishman. He was not, of course, Irish, nor had he ever been to Ireland, but this didn't appear to matter to him. He made a speech at the foot of the Statue of Liberty, and tore up what he claimed was his British passport. After this, he began to write anti-British propaganda for a German-leaning newspaper; a bit of treason that he later explained was actually to help the British cause during the war. He said that he tried to make his propaganda so absurd that it would provoke the opposite effect. The British were not impressed, but they dismissed Crowley as an annoying but essentially harmless attention-seeker who would do anything to keep his name before the public. But was this the truth? Some researchers don't think so, nor do they accept Crowley's later version of events. They believe that he was becoming increasingly disgusted with England, a country which he felt had been rejected him. He had never been given the recognition that he felt he deserved there, and he struck out in the only way that he could.

It is interesting to note that late in his life, during World War II, Crowley was approached by members of British intelligence, who asked his advice on how to deal with Hitler's deputy, Rudolf Hess. Hess had been arrested after he had flown to Scotland to try and negotiate peace with Britain. Knowing that Hess was interested in the occult, the intelligence officers tracked Crowley down in Torquay, where he was writing patriotic poetry. They asked his advice on how best to get Hess to tell them about the inner working of the Nazi hierarchy. It is not known whether Crowley's suggestion that British planes drop propaganda literature written by him on Germany was ever taken seriously (whether the purpose of the pamphlets would be to put the Germans under a magical spell to make them surrender or to simply confuse them is not clear). Crowley had previously written to Ian Fleming, director of Naval Intelligence, to offer his help with the war effort. The pair met several times, and Crowley seems to have made quite an impression. When Fleming went on to write his first James Bond novel, *Casino Royale*, he included an arch-villain whom he modeled on Crowley.

Crowley described his period in America as a time of poverty and humiliation. Humiliated or not, he managed to live quite well in the states. A report in a New York newspaper, *The Evening World*, described him living in a fairly luxurious studio in Washington Square, most likely provided for him by his followers. Crowley was an expert at cadging money from his disciples. American writer on witchcraft and Voodoo, William Seabrook, who was introduced to Crowley, said that Crowley had a retinue of followers and disciples around him at all times. He witnessed several of the group's rituals and admitted that some of the invocations were "quite beautiful." Seabrook also remarked that Crowley seemed to be a "man of power" and a person of great inner strength. He recalled that Crowley would eat and drink until he became bloated and then starve himself down to a healthy weight again. Seabrook recounted an amusing story of how Crowley one day announced that he was going off to spend forty days and nights in the wilderness. Seabrook and some other friends decided to fund his trip, since Crowley was broke. They gave him some money and found him a canoe and a tent. When they went to see him off, they discovered that he had spent all of the money on fifty gallons of red paint, brushes and rope. He told them that, like the prophet Elijah, he would be fed by the ravens. Crowley spent the forty days and nights camping on Esopus Island on the Hudson River, about six miles south of Kingston, N.Y. When Crowley wasn't bewildering passersby by sitting by the side of the road in the lotus position, he spent his time painting in huge red letters on the nearby cliffs the inscriptions EVERY MAN AND WOMAN IS A STAR and, of course, DO WHAT THOU WILT SHALL BE THE WHOLE OF THE LAW. He was fed by local farmers, who periodically brought him eggs, milk and sweet corn. He returned to Manhattan looking fit and well.

Seabrook told another story about Crowley, an incident that

Author William Seabrook

marked one of the strangest examples of his powers. After his return from the "wilderness," Crowley told him that he had gained strength during his time away. Seabrook asked for a demonstration of this. Crowley took him along Fifth Avenue, on a sparsely populated stretch of the sidewalk, and fell into step with a man, walking behind him and imitating his walk. Suddenly, Crowley buckled at the knees, squatted on his haunches for a moment and then stood upright again. At the same time, the man in front of him collapsed onto the pavement as his own knees gave out. Seabrook and Crowley helped him to his feet and the man nervously went on his way, unable to explain why he had fallen. Was this a real example of Crowley possessing a supernatural power? Was it merely the power of suggestion? Or did Crowley stage the event for Seabrook's benefit, knowing that he would write about it and generate publicity for the charismatic cult leader?

Toward the end of his time in America, Crowley discovered yet another "Scarlet Woman" (which is what he called his female acolytes). An acquaintance named Renata Faesi called on him one day in the company of her younger sister, Leah, a thin girl with a wide mouth, strangely sharp teeth, a bony, angular body and no breasts to speak of. But something almost magnetic occurred when she and Crowley saw one another. Crowley immediately seized Leah and began to kiss her violently, much to Renata's astonishment. Within hours, Leah was agreeing to be painted in the nude, and Crowley created a ghoulish picture that he called "Dead Souls." In due course, Leah, whom Crowley called Alostrael and The Ape of Thoth, in reference to the companion of the god Tahuti, became pregnant.

In December 1919, Crowley finally returned to England, but was not happy there. His periodic binging on all kinds of drugs, from mescaline to hashish, cocaine and opium, had lowered his physical resistance to the British cold and dampness, causing him to suffer from asthma and bronchitis.

He had lost many of his English friends and contacts during the war. His former disciple, Victor Neuberg, had married and settled down, but he remained obsessed with Crowley for the rest of his life. Crowley had cursed him when they separated before the war and Neuberg was very nervous for years after, blaming a number of health problems on Crowley's incantations. There was no one else in London from whom Crowley could get money, but as luck would have it, he received a fairly large sum of money around this time and decided to leave England for a warmer climate. Crowley and Leah found a farmhouse in Sicily and were accompanied there by a Ninette Shumway, who doubled as a nursemaid for Crowley and Leah's children and Crowley's mistress; Ninette's young son, Hermes, and the two children that Crowley had with Leah: a boy named Dionysus and a newborn girl named Anne Leah. Crowley, now in his middle forties, seemed to have developed a few normal human feelings. He wrote of his family: "I love Alostrael; she is all my comfort, my support, my soul's desire, my life's reward..." He also expressed deep affection toward Anne Leah, whose health had been poor since the time she was born.

Leah, one of Crowley's abused and manipulated "Scarlet Women"

At first, life in Sicily was idyllic, with swimming in the ocean, long hours of meditation and magical sex rituals. Crowley covered the walls of the farmhouse with paintings of people having sex in every position, and painted his studio, which he called the Chamber of Nightmares, with pictures of demons. He became convinced that one could only free one's self from the need for drugs by taking them freely so piles of cocaine were left around the house for anyone to take, and Crowley arranged for opium to be supplied to him by a trader from the mainland.

The only thing that seemed to spoil the scene was the jealousy of his two "Scarlet Women." One peace-shattering incident occurred on the day that the sun entered the sign of Taurus (April 20, 1920). Crowley celebrated the event with a sex ritual in which both women participated. In the middle of the proceedings a violent argument broke out between Leah and Ninette. The latter, bursting into tears, snatched up a cloak and ran out into the dark, rainy night. Crowley wandered all over looking for her, afraid that she had fallen over one of the nearby cliffs. After calling her name for almost an hour, he found her and dragged her back to the house. Meanwhile, Leah had opened a bottle of brandy and was now raging drunk. She cursed at Ninette when Crowley brought her back, and the fight started all over again. Crowley managed to get Ninette to go to bed, and then Leah vomited and passed out.

Crowley tried hard to convince the two women that possessiveness was wrong, and that they should rise above such a trivial thing, but they were unconvinced. However, they continued to take part in his magic sex rites, including one ceremony when Leah allowed herself to be penetrated by a goat. The animal's throat was then cut as a sacrifice.

Visitors, both disciples and curiosity-seekers, began to arrive at the Sicily farmhouse, which Crowley had dubbed the Abbey of Theleme. American film star Elizabeth Fox was among the first to call. Crowley looked forward to introducing her to sex magick, but she turned out to be a disappointment. The mathematician J.N.W. Sullivan arrived with his wife, Sylvia. He found he liked Crowley, and staying up talking with him all night. Sylvia liked him too, and stayed on for another day to practice sex rituals after her husband left. But life at the Abbey was becoming too complicated with personal issues, arguments and tragedies – something that visitors were becoming aware of. Crowley's daughter, Anne Leah, died after a long illness and Crowley was shattered. Soon after, a young American, an ex-naval officer named Godwin, arrived and Crowley named him Brother Fiat Lux. The strain of life around Crowley and his mistresses became too much for Godwin after another disciple, Australian businessman Frank Bennett, arrived at the Abbey. Crowley asked Godwin to let Bennett have his room. This resulted in a violent argument. Godwin returned to America and in 1931, he founded the Chortonzon Club, which was named for a demon. Godwin rejected Crowley's magic rituals and invented his own type of sex magic, which involved sexual intercourse that would be continued indefinitely without orgasm.

The aim of it was to produce long and drawn-out ecstasy and intoxication. Godwin operated in California for many years.

Another rebellious Crowley disciple was Jack Parsons, a brilliant rocket scientist and one of the founders of the Jet Propulsion Laboratory at the California Institute of Technology. Parsons was obsessed with the sexual side of ritual magic. He was an early follower of Crowley who went on to become fascinated with the idea of incarnating the Whore of Babylon described in the Book of Revelation. He believed this creature would be the bride of the Antichrist and the Mother of All Abominations. His chosen method of doing this was known as "Babylon Working," which essentially involved him impregnating his wife, the artist and actress Marjorie Cameron, under occult conditions. Parsons hoped that the resulting "moonchild" would be the Whore's incarnation on Earth. Parsons lived in a house called the Parsonage, in Pasadena, California, where one of his roommates was L. Ron Hubbard, the founder of Scientology. The two men collaborated in magical exercises, some of which included Parsons having sex with Cameron while Hubbard "magically" described what was happening on the astral plane. Parsons claimed that his "Left-Hand Path" magic had been successful in creating the moonchild, not as a physical being but as a spiritual entity. In his later years Parsons legally changed his name to Belarion Armiluss Al Dajjal Antichrist. He was killed in an explosion in his garage laboratory in 1952 caused by his dropping a container of fulminate of mercury. His death was ruled an accident.

But Crowley did succeed with some of his disciples, especially Frank Bennett. Like Crowley, Bennett had had a repressive childhood. When Crowley explained to him that the sexual organs were the image of God, and the best way to free the hidden powers of the subconscious mind was through sexual magic, Bennett found the revelation so startling that he ran out into the ocean and began to swim frantically up and down the beach. After further discussion that same night, he walked barefoot into the mountains. Then, after a day of bewilderment, he lapsed into a trance-like state of pure delight as he began to grasp the idea of allowing the subconscious to free itself. After all of this, Bennett departed and went back to Australia, filled with the gospel of the "Beast."

Crowley's health and finances began to suffer. The doses of heroin that he had begun to take would have killed a normal man. Periodically, he would force himself to go "cold turkey," going without all drugs for days. After a period of intense depression and misery, he would begin to paint and write again with his old excitement. He always returned to the drugs, though, claiming that he could take them or leave them however he wanted. The result was long periods of listlessness and increasing insomnia, which troubled him for years. In addition to his drug problem, he was broke again. In Sicily, there were no rich disciples to sponge off; on the contrary, his steady stream of visitors sapped his finances. J.N.W. Sullivan suggested that he write his memoirs, but Crowley wanted to write a novel first and managed to get a small advance for a book called *Diary of a Drug Fiend*. The novel was about an aristocratic couple who become slaves to heroin. They meet a charismatic and mysterious character who uses "magickal" techniques to cure them of their addiction. The book appeared in 1922 and was violently attacked by newspapers that denounced Crowley as a seducer of young people. Crowley was not entirely displeased by the publicity, but the publisher allowed the book to go out of print and balked at the idea of publishing Crowley's autobiography, even though he had been given a good-sized advance.

While in London for the release of his book, Crowley met an enthusiastic, but slightly unbalanced, young man named Raoul Loveday, who was married to a pretty model. Loveday had read Crowley's works, and within hours, he was an enthusiastic disciple. When Crowley returned to Sicily, Loveday and his wife, Betty May, followed. Loveday's wife had strong misgivings about Crowley. She hated the Abbey, hated the food, the lack of bathrooms, the obscene paintings, and most of all, she hated her husband's infatuation with Crowley.

Loveday's stay at the Abbey lasted three months – and ended with his death. Both he and Crowley came down with the same ailment, similar to hepatitis, caused by bad water. In February 1923, Crowley decided that a cat should be sacrificed. He hated cats and chose one to kill that had scratched him badly when he threw it out of a room. Allegedly, he found the animal in a pantry and made the sign of a pentagram over it with his staff, and ordered it to stay there until the hour of sacrifice. Crowley claimed that the animal never moved. Even when

Betty May took it somewhere else in the house, it came back to the same spot, petrified and refusing food. Loveday was selected to perform the sacrifice. The cat was placed on an altar, incense was lit, and incantations were performed for two hours. Finally, Loveday slashed the animal's throat with a knife, but the cut was too shallow and the cat ran from the room. It was captured and slain and then Loveday was made to drink a cup of its blood. He subsequently collapsed and was taken to his bed. Crowley consulted his horoscope and predicted that Loveday was going to die, on February 16.

A number of terrible arguments with Betty May followed. One day, she stormed out of the Abbey after calling Ninette a whore, but returned the next day at her husband's request. On February 16th – the day that Crowley had predicted – Loveday died. Betty May was stunned. She recalled that on their wedding day, he had dropped the ring as he was about to put it onto her finger, a bad omen. She also remembered a photograph of the two of them that had been taken at St. John's College, Oxford, in which the ghostly outline of a man appeared, his arms stretched out over his head. This was the same position that Loveday had been in when he died.

Betty May returned to England where she gave newspaper interviews about her disastrous visit to the Abbey. The British public was both shocked and delighted with more gossip about the infamous Crowley. More newspaper attacks followed, and by the time they appeared, Crowley was taken ill with the same sickness that had killed Loveday. He was semi-conscious for three weeks before slowly recovering. But the adverse publicity over Loveday's death had its effect on Italy's new ruler. A short time later, Mussolini ordered Crowley to vacate the Abbey and leave the country.

Once again, a strange turn of events saved Crowley from poverty and homelessness. Norman Mudd, who had known Crowley since 1907, during their student days at Cambridge, came back into his life. Mudd had been introduced to the Beast through Neuberg but when Crowley's unsavory reputation and pornographic books got him kicked out of Trinity College, their friendship cooled. Mudd had become a professor of mathematics in South Africa, but was unable to forget about Crowley. As Crowley was being attacked by the British press, and being expelled from Sicily, Mudd appeared at the Abbey. He presented Crowley with his life savings, and begged to be accepted as his disciple.

Crowley moved to Tunis, hoping that the Italian government would change its mind. Leah went with him, as well as his five-year-old son, who reportedly smoked cigarettes all day long and declared that he would become the Beast when his father died. Ninette had borne Crowley another daughter, and Crowley's horoscope for the child ended with the prediction, "She is likely to develop into a fairly ordinary little whore." Norman Mudd accompanied the party and he and Leah became lovers, a development that Crowley did not mind. He was too preoccupied with recovering his health, and with his drug addiction, which he realized he was unable to shake.

When Crowley became bored, he abandoned the group and went to Paris, leaving Leah and Mudd to get by as best they could in Tunis. Crowley was faring no better in the City of Lights. Drug-addled, he wandered the city in a daze. Eventually, he was kicked out of the hotel where he was living on credit. Leah and Mudd followed him to Paris and then Mudd moved on to London, where he took refuge at the Metropolitan Asylum for the Homeless Poor. Crowley and Leah stayed together for a few months, but Crowley was growing tired of her and her inability to survive under any conditions, as he was able to do. When a rich American woman named Dorothy Olsen fell under his spell, Crowley named her his new "Scarlet Woman," and deserted Leah. Leah's sister, Renata, had already taken her son from her and had gone to America. Leah was furious and hysterical. Mudd returned to her, and they lived on the streets of Paris together while Crowley and his new mistress traveled in North America.

Crowley's abandonment of them seemed to break something inside of Leah and Mudd. Leah worked as a prostitute for awhile, then as a waitress. Mudd remained in a state of despair. Even after all that had happened, his main concern seemed to be whether or not Crowley would remain faithful to *The Book of the Law*. Crowley's new lover soon ran out of money after a few months of supporting him in the luxurious style to which he was accustomed and had to write to friends in America to borrow money.

But Crowley, once again, had another stroke of incredible luck. Theodor Reuss, his old friend from the Ordo Templi Orientis, died and his successor turned to Crowley as one of the elite members of the Order. The O.T.O. paid off all of Crowley's debts in Paris, and even gave money to Dorothy Olsen, Mudd and Leah. Both Mudd and Leah eventually grew to hate Crowley, and Leah wrote him a letter renouncing her vow of obedience to him. What eventually happened to her is unknown. In 1934, Mudd committed suicide in the Channel Islands by drowning himself. He closed the bottom of his pants with bicycle clips, filled them with rocks, and walked into the sea.

Crowley still enjoyed his reputation as the "wickedest man in the world," but this was a double-edged sword for him. He loved the infamy, but it meant that no major publisher would touch the autobiography that he had been working on. Eventually, a small press put out the book, but they were unable to get bookstores to place orders for it.

Crowley and Maria Teresa de Miramar, who he married in 1929. She, like so many others who passed through his life, later went insane.

In 1929, Crowley was ordered to leave France. He tried to go back to England but his two chief disciples, an American secretary whom he called "The Serpent" and his latest mistress, Maria Teresa de Miramar, were not allowed to enter the country. It was to get Maria into England that Crowley took the startling step of marrying her in August 1929. He was due to lecture at Oxford in early 1930, but found himself banned from the college. He tried to present an exhibition of his paintings at a rented house in Langham Place, but bad newspaper publicity caused the owner to cancel his lease. His marriage to Maria became a series of vicious arguments and it soon fell apart, but there were plenty of other women who were eager to be his "Scarlet Woman."

Crowley took a new mistress, a 19-year-old German girl named Hanni, whom he called "The Monster." They went to Lisbon together but Hanni soon became disenchanted with Crowley and his sex magic rituals. She deserted him and returned to Berlin. To be abandoned was a new and shattering experience for Crowley. He pursued Hanni to Berlin, where a reconciliation took place. Before leaving, he left a suicide note at the top of a high cliff called Hell's Mouth. The result was a flattering uproar in the press, which delighted in the fact that the "world's wickedest man" had taken his own life. After lying low in Berlin for a few days, Crowley attended the opening of an exhibition of his paintings, ending the speculation about his death. Hanni became Crowley's magical assistant and Crowley maintained that she became a skilled "scryer" who once saw the Devil's face looking up at her from inside a crystal. Their sex magic was so successful that she became pregnant, but she left him soon after.

Crowley's wife, Maria, went insane and was hospitalized for the rest of her life. At least one Crowley biographer claims that Hanni also went insane. While some might claim a supernatural cause behind the reports of insanity and suicide among those who were close to Crowley, there is a simpler explanation. Crowley's powerful, dominant personality attracted people to him who were much weaker than he was. In many cases, they were already mentally unstable. Crowley's eventual rejection and abandonment of them, or perhaps simply their exposure to his magical rituals, often sent them over the edge and drove them to suicide and into asylums.

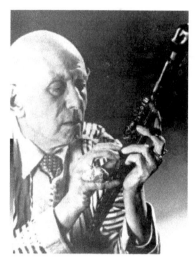

An elderly Crowley, who played the role of the world's "wickedest man" to the very end.

As far as magic is concerned, the remainder of Crowley's life was anticlimactic. In the 1930s, Crowley became involved in a court case against his old friend Nina Hammett. He got a taste for litigation when he saw a copy of his novel *Moonchild* displayed in a bookstore window with a sign next to it stating that his earlier novel, *Diary of a Drug Fiend*, had been withdrawn from publication after a newspaper attack. This was not true; it had simply gone out of print. Crowley sued the bookseller and received a small settlement.

This legal victory gave him the idea to raise money by suing Nina Hammett, a flamboyant Welsh artist and writer who was known as "the Queen of Bohemia." Hammett had referred to Crowley as a "black magician" in her autobiography. She had hinted that a baby (possibly used as a sacrifice) had disappeared from the Abbey while Crowley was living there. Crowley knew that Hammett had no money, but her publisher, Constable & Co., certainly did, and they would have to pay. Whether he expected to win the case, or merely thought that it would garner him more publicity remains a matter for speculation, but he hired lawyers to pursue it. Unfortunately, none of his friends would appear for the defense and his attorneys warned him that if the court got a look at any of his pornographic writings, the case would be thrown out. As it turned out, things never got that far. When several witnesses appeared on the stand and described Crowley's magical activities, the judge halted the trial and declared that he had "never heard of such dreadful, horrible, blasphemous and abominable stuff as that which has been produced by a man who describes himself as the greatest living poet in the world." The jury found against Crowley and he was bankrupted, although he really had no assets anyway. The publicity for the case, though, was absolutely tremendous – and that might have been what Crowley wanted in the first place.

Crowley spent his last days living in a Hastings guest house called Netherwood, where he played chess, injected heroin, and spent much of his time in his room, snacking on sardines sprinkled with curry powder and writing late into the night. Photographs of him from the years after World War II show a thin old gentleman dressed in tweeds, smoking a pipe and looking more like an affable retired British military officer than one of the most infamous men in history. He lived on the generosity of old friends and fading disciples, who couldn't bear to see the Great Beast starve during his final days on Earth. He continued, as he had throughout his life, to impose on the kindness of friends, taking whatever he could get from them. The irate wife of one of his disciples pointed out to him in a letter that he had spent £15,000 of her money on expensive cigars, cognac, cocktails, taxis, dinners, and mistresses. She concluded "God Almighty himself would not be as arrogant as you have been, and that is one of the causes of all of your troubles." And she was right. Until the very end of his life, Crowley possessed a withering arrogance, and a lofty view of his own worth. This explained why he could so easily turn on faithful disciples like Norman Mudd and his mistress, Leah, totally convinced in his own mind that some action of theirs had forfeited their rights to his divine presence.

But there were positive aspects to Aleister Crowley, as well. It cannot be denied that, no matter what his shortcomings, his over-the-top self-promotion, his haughty arrogance and his exaggeration (or perhaps outright lies) about his magical abilities, Crowley managed to change the course of occult history with his ideas, theories, sex rituals, and by the fact that he existed at all.

It seems almost tragic to say that he died from something as mundane as pneumonia on December 1, 1947. He was 72 years old at the time and unrepentant about his life of sin and scandal. The novelist Louis Wilkinson read aloud Crowley's *Hymn to Pan* at the funeral service, as gleefully and shamelessly as Crowley would have

138

expected it to be read for such an occasion. According to author Colin Wilson, the Brighton City Council angrily stated that it would take steps to see that such an incident was never, ever repeated again.

It was a fitting, scandalous end for the "wickedest man in the world."

ORDO TEMPLI ORIENTIS

The Ordo Templi Orientis (O.T.O.) was founded by German occultist, Carl Kellner, who made his fortune as a paper manufacturer. Kellner was a student of Freemasonry, Rosicrucianism and Eastern mysticism, and traveled extensively in Europe, America and Asia. During his travels, he claimed to come into contact with a trio of ancient masters or adepts, consisting of a Sufi and two Hindu Tantrics, and an organization called the Hermetic Brotherhood of Light.

In 1885, Kellner met the Theosophical and Rosicrucian scholar Dr. Franz Hartmann, and the two men later collaborated on the development of an inhalation therapy for tuberculosis. During the course of his studies, Kellner believed that he had discovered a "Key" that offered a clear explanation of all of the complex symbolism of Freemasonry and, Kellner was convinced, opened the mysteries of nature.

Kellner soon began working to found the Academia Masonica, which would enable all Freemasons to become familiar with all existing Masonic degrees and systems. In 1895, he began to discuss this idea with his friend and associate, Theodor Reuss, and decided that the Academia Masonica should be called Ordo Templi Orientis (which translates to mean "Oriental Templar Order"). The inner circle of the order would be organized parallel to the highest degree of the Masonic Rite of Memphis and Mizraim and would teach the mysterious Rosicrucian doctrines of the Hermetic Brotherhood of Light and Kellner's "Key" to Masonic symbolism. Both men and women were to be admitted to all levels of the O.T.O., but possession of the various degrees of Craft and High-Grade Freemasonry would be required in order to be admitted to the inner circle. Unfortunately, due to regulations of the established Grand Lodges, which governed regular Freemasonry, women could not become Freemasons and therefore, would be excluded from the O.T.O. This may have been one of the reasons that Kellner and his associates decided to try and obtain control over one of the many rites, or systems, of Freemasonry in order to reform the system so that women could be admitted.

Carl Kellner

Despite plans and lengthy discussions between Kellner and Reuss, nothing came of their attempts to launch the O.T.O. Reuss was busy at that time trying to revive the eighteenth-century Order of the Illuminati with his friend Leopold Engel, a sect that Kellner did not approve of. The revival of the Illuminati failed and in 1902, Kellner contacted Reuss again and they agreed to proceed with the establishment of the Ordo Templi Orientis by seeking authorization to work the various rites of Freemasonry. Kellner and Reuss prepared a manifesto for the Order in 1903 that was published the next year in the obscure Masonic periodical, *The Oriflamme*. In short, the group claimed, "Our Order possesses the key which opens up all Masonic and Hermetic secrets, namely, the teachings of sexual magic, and this teaching explains, without exception, all of the secrets of Freemasonry and all systems of religion." The O.T.O also claimed a direct spiritual link to the original Knights Templar, with all of that order's mystical trappings intact.

In spite of all that Kellner claimed his "Key" possessed, the secret of longevity somehow eluded him and he died just three years after organizing the O.T.O., leaving the order in the hands of Reuss. The order expanded soon after, starting new chapters in Denmark, France and England. It was around this time that Aleister Crowley became involved in the order, enhancing the initial promises of sexual magick. He took over leadership

Jack Parsons

L. Ron Hubbard

of a British branch and soon added a homosexual "eleventh degree" to his chapter, sodomizing one of his followers in celebration. Doctrinal differences led to a rift between Crowley and the German home office in 1916, but Crowley later patched things up and succeeded Reuss as international head of the O.T.O. in 1924.

Meanwhile, the order's brand of magic had crossed the Atlantic with O.T.O. disciple C.S. Jones starting chapters in Los Angeles, Washington, D.C., and Vancouver, British Columbia. Crowley himself visited the Vancouver lodge in 1915, meeting Winifred Smith and giving him permission to start his own lodge. Excited, Smith went straight to the fledging film colony of Hollywood, where he set off a chain of events that were bizarre, even by the standards of the Ordo Templi Orientis.

Smith caused quite a stir in Hollywood, luring celebrities to special, invitation-only "Gnostic Masses," which typically featured Smith's heroic attempt to have sex with as many new women as possible. No one seemed to mind that his Agape Lodge was little more than a front for group sex; if anything that might have been the Hollywood order's main selling point. One of the women that Smith seduced was the wife of occultist John Parsons, an explosives expert at the California Institute of Technology and Smith's ultimate successor at the lodge. Apparently untroubled by his wife's infidelity, Parsons took up with his sister-in-law, soon rising in prominence in the lodge and moving it to his home in Pasadena. There, he renamed it the Church of Thelema. By March 1946, Parsons was involved in a series of sexual experiments with his newest recruit L. Ron Hubbard. According to Aleister Crowley, they were trying to produce a supernatural being called a "moonchild." Crowley had little patience for these antics, writing, "I get fairly frantic when I contemplate the idiocy of these louts."

The "moonchild" never materialized, but Hubbard showed his true colors by skipping town with Parson's mistress and $10,000 in O.T.O. funds. He used the money to found his own Church of Scientology a few years later. In the meantime, Parsons busied himself with a "black pilgrimage" and changed his name to Belarian Armiluss Al Dajjaj Antichrist and made plans to continue the work of the Great Beast (Crowley) to make way for the coming of the apocalypse. Parsons died four years later in an explosion in his garage laboratory, where he made nitroglycerine for private sale.

In 1947, Crowley died and the leadership of the order was passed to Karl Johannes Germer, who had been living in California since his expulsion from Germany in 1941. Germer died in 1962, creating a divide in the order. In Switzerland, Karl Metzger aspired to the leadership position, but his rule was disputed in England by Kenneth Grant, and in America by Grady McMurty, who possessed several letters from Crowley that supposedly gave him the position. The letters were enough for most of the order's faithful and McMurty carried the day, though Grant persisted with his opposition in England and a renegade chapter in Virginia chose Robert E.L. Shell as their leader. Under McMurty's guidance, the O.T.O. experienced dramatic growth, expanding across the United States and into several other countries. McMurty retired in 1982 and a new – anonymous – leader was elected from the ranking disciples. The headquarters moved from Berkeley, California, to New York City. By 1988, the O.T.O. claimed forty-eight chapters in the United States, nine in Canada, two each in Australia, Norway, and Germany and one each in England, France, New Zealand, and Yugoslavia.

Likely thanks to the strange nature of many of the candidates drawn to the order over the years, a number of lodges and individual members of the O.T.O. have been linked to crimes ranging from child abuse to ritual murder. One renegade faction of the order, the so-called Solar Lodge, was organized in California during the mid-1960s by Richard Brayton, a professor of psychology at USC, and his wife, Georgina. Devoted to the prospect of a coming race war between blacks and whites, Georgina sent her disciples as far as Utah and New Mexico in search of hideouts where the faithful could hunker down and weather the storm. One such location, acquired by the order in 1966, was a ranch near Blythe, California. The Solar Lodge earned its income from bookstores in Los Angeles, from a service station that it owned, and from the sale of drugs allegedly procured from contacts at the USC medical school. Within the order, Georgina maintained strict discipline, commanding one follower to slash his arms each time that he experienced sexual desire. Another member – a dentist from Palm Springs – called in sick one morning and vanished without a trace, his fate still unknown to this day. Discipline went out the window at the desert ranch, where members of the order freely indulged in drugs, sacrificed animals, and drank blood during their rituals. Aleister Crowley would have approved.

It was Georgina Brayton's love of power that finally destroyed the Solar Lodge. On May 20, 1969, one of the ranch buildings burned down with two goats trapped inside. Georgina blamed Anthony Gibbons, the six-year-old son of a cult member, for the fire and punished him by burning his hands, forcing him to bury the dead goats, and ordering other members to beat him all day with bamboo poles. Still unrepentant, the boy was chained in a packing crate and kept outside in the brutal sun from May 23 to July 26. Finally, some visitors noticed his plight and called the county sheriff's office. The Braytons and three members escaped before the police arrived but eleven other O.T.O. members – including the boy's mother – were arrested at the ranch and later confessed to felony child abuse. A search of the ranch also turned up a corpse, the victim of an accidental drug overdose. FBI warrants were issued for the Braytons, but they remained at large for a year before finally surrendering. Years later, a number of informants revealed to author Ed Sanders that the leaders of the Solar Lodge had often been in contact with Charles Manson in 1968 and 1969 and that Georgina's "race war" theory may have inspired Manson's obsession with the apocalyptic vision that he called "Helter Skelter."

DION FORTUNE

Although the debauchery and excess of Aleister Crowley seems to dominate the history of occultism and magic in the twentieth century, there is another figure that should demand an equal amount of attention, and yet many have never heard of her. Author and occultist Dion Fortune was responsible for disseminating the theory and practice of ceremonial magic to a much wider circle that anyone before her. The information that she dispensed had previously only been available to initiates of secret societies like the Golden Dawn. Encoded in her novels – *The Winged Bull, The Sea Priestess, The Goat-Footed God* and others – were rites and rituals that magicians and modern-day Wiccans have been able to adapt and incorporate into a magical system that revolves around the worship of the Goddess, or the feminine principle. This was a departure from the "old religion," in which the patriarchal figure of Pan dominated. Her many treatises on ritual magic and occult philosophy, including *The Cosmic Doctrine, The Mystical Qabalah* and *Sane Occultism* were serialized in *The Occult Review*, a magazine that was circulated around the world in the 1930s. Her writings would have a direct influence on the modern witchcraft revival of the 1950s.

It is arguable that without Dion Fortune's contribution to magic, the modern Wiccan movement would not have flourished and the New Age movement would not have evolved into the widely accepted state that it enjoys today.

Dion Fortune was born Violet Mary Firth in Llandudno, Wales, in 1891. She was raised in a Christian Science family, where her marked propensity for daydreaming was a subject of some concern. Even as a young woman, she seemed to show less interest in the material world than in the supernatural one. It was perhaps not a great

Dion Fortune

surprise that her life took a strange and important turn when at age twenty, and working as a teacher in a private girl's school, she suffered a nervous breakdown. It was no ordinary mental disorder. She believed that she was the target of a sustained "psychic attack" by another woman, one who used her superior will to break down Violet's resistance and destroy her self-confidence.

Unknown to her, Violet had managed to unintentionally antagonize the principal of the school, a cold and arrogant woman who was known for her highly developed skills in yoga, which she had studied in India. That woman, she later came to believe, had twisted the yogi energies into something malign, and had focused those energies at her. The power of the assault left Violet physically devastated and mentally drained – but it also pointed her toward her true vocation in life.

"I entered a strong, healthy girl. I left it a mental and physical wreck," she later wrote. "But it was this experience which led me to take up the study of analytical psychology, and subsequently of occultism." Trained as a psychologist, she was determined to learn all that she could about latent power of the mind, which she suspected was the source of all occult phenomena. She began looking for alternate theories about the mind and became interested in the occult practices of the Order of the Golden Dawn. It was only after her initiation into the group in 1919 that she felt the damage done to her by the school principal was finally repaired. She became determined to help others who found themselves under the same kind of attack.

During her time with the Golden Dawn, she acquired a working knowledge of ceremonial magic, but by then, the order was in decline. The squabbling elder members of the group spent more time arguing over points of procedure than they did practicing and studying magic. During the three years that she spent with the order, she acquired her magical name of Dion Fortune, a contraction of *Deo Non Fortuna* ("by God, not by chance"), and formed the opinion that modern occultists could not afford to ignore the insights offered by modern psychology. Magical orders like the Golden Dawn were doomed to extinction, she believed, because their members were determined to preserve an arcane knowledge instead of developing it, making the same mistake that organized religion had already made.

She outlined her philosophy in *Sane Occultism*, the first of several books on the practical aspects of magic and psychic development, but it was in her novels that she made it clear that realigning oneself with nature is the path to psychological integration and self-realization. Religion asked the believer to take the promise of the afterlife on trust, to submit one's life to the service of God and resist temptation, whereas philosophy offered the afterlife only as a possibility, and asked the individual to take responsibility for their own destiny. Fortune wrote that only occultism revealed the true nature of the "greater reality" and our purpose within it. She believed that occultism empowers the individual with the ability to create that reality.

In the 1920s and 1930s, it was almost unheard of for anyone – especially a woman – to criticize religion. Any author who did so would have been pilloried in the press. So Fortune made her views on Christianity known through the voices of the fictional characters in her novels. Thanks to this, as well as her serialized occult writings, she became not only a famed practitioner of many occult practices, including scrying and astral travel, but as a kind of psychic physician to others who got into trouble on the etheric plane. In one case she recounted, a clumsy magician tried to employ a magic circle, but did it wrong. Every night thereafter, he suffered nightmares and unexplained anxiety. Finally, one night, he actually caught sight of the creature that was tormenting him – a bearded figure with long flowing hair that he sensed had a sort of terrible force that was just starting to awaken. On a subsequent night, he saw a red snake slithering out from beneath his bed. In terror, he jumped out of the window of his room. When the first creature appeared again, the hair on his head had turned, Medusa-like, into a nest of writhing serpents.

Fortune believed that the actual forces of evil in the world had created evil intelligences, entities that had "probably originated through the workings of black magic, which took the essential evil essence and organized it for purposes of its own." The presence of these creatures could be detected by sinister sounds, strong odors, and flickering balls of light. Their effects on people could range from hallucinations to physical decay.

Throughout her career, she made some of the most significant additions to the occult canon of the twentieth century, but she always resisted the Left Hand Path – the path of evil-doing – and used her research and beliefs to simply explore and explain the unseen world. But she could have done it if she had chosen to. On one occasion, she was lying on her bed, thinking about a woman who had done her harm, and becoming increasingly angry and vengeful. As she grew angrier, her mind wandered to the ancient Nordic myths and to a great wolf that tore men apart. Fortune claimed that she felt a drawing sensation in her solar plexus, and a large wolf materialized next to her on the bed. It was so real that she could actually feel its hairy back pressed against her. She later wrote, "I knew nothing of making elementals at the time, but had accidentally stumbled upon the right method – the brooding highly charged with emotion, the invocation of the appropriate natural force, and the condition between sleeping and waking in which the etheric double readily extrudes."

But she still had to do something about the accidental wolf. Summoning up her courage, Fortune ordered it down off the bed – and it went. Changing into more of the shape of a dog, it slinked to the corner of the room. But Fortune knew the creature was still loose in the world, carrying that explosive psychic charge aimed at the woman who had angered her. She mentally asked her mentor (who may have been Aleister Crowley) what she should do because she really didn't want to cause the woman harm. His advice was to reabsorb the creature into her body, which she could do by forgiving the woman and destroying the need for the creature to exist.

Using all of her powers of concentration, she called the wolf to her. By then, she wrote, it appeared "in quite a mild and domesticated mood." A shadowy line of ectoplasm stretched from the wolf's belly to Fortune's solar plexus. She wrote, "I began by an effort of will and imagination to draw the life out of it along the silver cord, as if sucking lemonade up a straw. As the wolf-form began to fade, the cord thickened and grew more substantial. A violent emotional upheaval started in myself; I felt the most furious impulses to go berserk and rend and tear anything and anybody that came to hand." Eventually, the wolf faded away, vanishing in a gray mist.

Dion Fortune died in 1946; her career spanning a lifetime that almost mirrored that of Aleister Crowley and yet made a very different mark on the history of magic and the occult.

THEY USED DARK FORCES: THE NAZIS AND THE OCCULT

If something profoundly evil does not lurk behind Germany's present tyranny, where, indeed, is evil to be found?
Lewis Spence

The public history and genocidal horror of Adolph Hitler's Nazi Germany are too well known for repetition here, but most historians of the Third Reich tend to ignore the significant links between Nazism and the occult. When the Third Reich collapsed in May 1945, the victorious allies saw the surrender of Germany as the climax to an apocalyptic battle between the forces of good and evil. It was a terrible panorama that had played itself out on the world stage and led to the horrifying consequence of millions of lives lost, countries destroyed, and civilization changed forever. At the end of the hostilities, all agreed that the Allied victory signified much more than just the military defeat of a merciless dictatorship that had threatened to drag the world into a dark age.

Adolph Hitler

Religious, political, and even military leaders spoke of evil having been vanquished and of the Devil himself having been consumed by the diabolical forces that he had unleashed. But no one at the time thought such statements were anything more than rhetoric.

But there's a very good chance that there was something truly satanic at the black heart of the Nazi state.

The occult roots of German fascism can be traced back to the middle nineteenth century, when Guido von List began mixing his worship of "Wotan" (the Germanic spelling of Odin) and other Nordic deities with heavy doses of Teutonic racism. By 1875, von List and his disciples had a symbol for their bigotry, adopting the swastika, which had previously served as an innocuous good-luck symbol on everything from Grecian pottery to Hindu texts and Native American rock paintings. By 1908, von List's disciples had spread throughout western Europe, carrying the message of a Nordic master race that had been spawned by ancient magicians.

A year earlier, German occultist Georg Lanz von Liebenfels had founded the Ordo Novi Templi (Order of the New Templars) and placed a racial twist on the old legend of the Knights Templar. A friend and fellow traveler of von List, by 1909 von Liebenfels was advocating imprisonment and forced sterilization of "socially inferior elements" such as Jews, "mongrel" races and mental defectives. One of von Liebenfel's early admirers was a young man of dubious ancestry named Adolph Hitler, who came to the Ordo Novi Templi office in 1909 for a personal conference with his new mentor. Only one meeting between von Liebefel and Hitler was ever documented, but there are many reasons to suspect a more enduring association. Years later, in 1932, von Liebenfels wrote to another member of the order, "Hitler is one of our pupils. You will one day experience that he, and through him we, will one day be victorious and develop a movement that will make the world tremble."

There are other occult links in the foundation of the Nazi party as well. They include two secret fraternities known as the German Order and the Thule Society. Founded by Theodor Fritsch in 1912, the German Order offered a strain of "pure Nordic" occultism to counter the menace of "Jewish" Freemasonry, conducting rituals with its members dressed in white robes and Viking helmets, their leader brandishing the sacred "spear of Wotan." When Fritsch died in 1933, Nazi newspapers mourned the passing of the "old teacher," but his beliefs continued on in the racist rants of men like von List and von Liebenfels.

The Thule Society, meanwhile, was created in 1917, while World War I was still in progress. Its founder, Walter Nauhaus, was a wounded veteran, and a member of the German Order who adopted a swastika with sword and wreath as his society's official emblem. Generally regarded as a front group or recruiting body for the German Order, the Thule Society created an activist Worker's Political Circle in November 1918. Two months later, Circle leaders organized the German Workers' Party – a right-wing, anti-Semitic group that later added "National Socialist" to its title, thereby becoming the Nazi Party. Adolph Hitler joined the movement in 1919, while other early recruits included occultists and sexual deviants in roughly equal numbers. Another Thulist group, the German Socialist Party, officially merged with the Nazis in the summer of 1922. Marthe Kuenzel – head of the German Ordo Templi Orientis and a confidante of Rudolph Hess – introduced Hitler to the writings

144

of Aleister Crowley in 1927. Unfortunately for Kuenzel, her personal devotion to Hitler as the satanic messiah or "magical child" did not prevent Hitler from banning the O.T.O a few years later.

As a symbol of his new order, Hitler reversed von List's "right-handed" swastika in favor of the "left-handed" version, generally regarded by occultists as a signature of evil, on par with the inverted crucifix. The Nazi battle flag finally approved by Hitler was designed by Frederick Krohn, a longstanding Thule disciple and a member of the German Order since 1914.

Another early Nazi fascinated by the black arts was Heinrich Himmler, who was appointed to lead the dreaded Schutzstaffel (SS) in 1929. From his vantage point, Himmler sought to create his own pagan religious order, adopting runic lightning bolts as the official SS insignia, requiring all initiates to participate in Wotan ceremonies of his own design. The SS was originally intended to serve as Hitler's personal bodyguard, but it became the brutal right hand of the regime, and a powerful force that answered only to itself.

By creating the distinctive rituals, oaths and insignia, Himmler was able to instill into every member the belief that they were part of an elite unit. Each man was to consider

Heinrich Himmler -- like so many of the Nazi leaders, he was a far cry from the "Aryan elite" that their views espoused. The unassuming chicken farmer would become one of the most feared men in the Reich.

himself an initiate in a secret religious order, whose sacred duty it was to subjugate the "inferior races" by any means necessary. A New Order would then be established in which the Aryan "master race" would rule the world. SS members were indoctrinated with the idea that they were superior beings in an amoral universe and so they operated beyond the human concepts of good and evil.

It's hard to say if any SS officers shared Himmler's romantic vision or whether they just saw the Nordic "lightning flash" SS rune, which decorated banners, helmets, uniforms and armored vehicles, as simply a distinguishing accessory of their dark brotherhood. For Himmler, the runes had a supernatural significance. He had borrowed the idea from occultists who believed that runes were the true expression of the ancient Aryan culture. According to Norse legend, the "runic" alphabet predated the written word, and therefore the symbol embodied natural and magical forces.

When the SS was originally formed in 1922, as an elite bodyguard for Hitler, the order numbered fewer than two hundred men. Himmler took over leadership of the group in 1929 and within a few years, his organizational skills had swelled the ranks to nearly 50,000. But it was the "Night of the Long Knives" on June 30, 1934 that truly made the SS a unit to be truly feared.

The "Night of the Long Knives" was a purge that took place when the Nazi regime carried out a series of political murders. Leading figures of the left-wing Strasserist faction of the Nazi Party, along with its figurehead, Gregor Strasser, were murdered, as were prominent conservative anti-Nazis (such as former Chancellor Kurt von Schleicher and Gustav Ritter von Kahr). Many of those killed were leaders of the *Sturmabteilung* (SA), the paramilitary "brown-shirts." Hitler moved against the SA and its leader, Ernst Röhm, because he saw the independence of the SA and the penchant of its members for street violence as a direct threat to his newly gained political power. Hitler also wanted to conciliate leaders of the *Reichswehr*, the official German military who feared and despised the SA. Hitler used the purge to attack or eliminate critics of his new regime, especially those loyal to Vice-Chancellor Franz von Papen, as well as to settle scores with old enemies.

An SS Wedding, 1936 -- Himmler not only recruited "pure-blood" men for the SS, he also took complete control over their family and reproductive plans. On December 31, 1931, he issued the so-called Engagement and Marriage Order, which called on SS members to protect their "racial potential" by marrying and producing offspring with women of so-called equal value. SS members who were married to women of "lesser value" were threatened with expulsion from the organization. This photograph shows Heinrich Himmler to the right of the bride.

At least eighty-five people died during the purge, although the final death toll may have been in the hundreds, and more than 1,000 perceived opponents were arrested. Most of the killings were carried out by the SS and Gestapo (*Geheime Staatspolizei*), the regime's secret police. The purge strengthened and consolidated the support of the *Reichswehr* for Hitler. It also provided a legal grounding for the Nazi regime, as the German courts and cabinet quickly swept aside centuries of legal prohibition against extra-judicial killings to demonstrate their loyalty to the regime.

Ironically, Himmler, the slight, unassuming chicken farmer, and son of a Catholic schoolteacher who rose from petty party bureaucrat to command one of the most feared military orders in history, was said to turn pale and feel faint at the sight of blood. His sadistic streak had to be satisfied vicariously by others who willingly tortured and killed on his behalf. As with many in the upper echelons of the party, he considered himself a man of culture and high ideals. He had studied agriculture at the University of Munich and dreamed of establishing an agricultural academy that would lead to a rural revival. If his ideas had prevailed, Germany industry would have been dismantled and the nation would have been forcibly regressed to the Middle Ages, centered around a feudalistic self-sufficient peasant economy with himself as a ruling lord.

According to his adjutants, Himmler envisioned himself as the reincarnation of King Heinrich der Vogler, King of Saxony and the founder of the First Reich, whom he described as the "noble peasant of the people." It is unclear if he took this idea literally as, according to his personal physician Felix Kersten, he was also in the habit of conversing with the spirit of the former king in the dead of night. This apparent contradiction is explained by the fact that Himmler subscribed to the theory put forward by the mystic Karl Eckhart, who believed that each individual is part of a soul group and so is drawn to reincarnate within the group. By this way of thinking, a man night return as his own grandson, or a father and son might be reborn a century later as brothers in order to resolve the differences that divided them in their previous life.

Himmler was never ashamed to express his belief in such unconventional ideas in public. In Dachau, on the thousandth anniversary of King Heinrich's death in 1936, he told an audience of high-ranking SS officers that they were part of an esoteric order who had known each other in a previous lifetime, and had been brought together again to fulfill a special mission after which they would meet again in a future life. The following year, he ordered 20,000 copies of Karl Eckhart's book *Temporal Immortality*, to be distributed among SS troops. The order was canceled after several members of Hitler's inner circle convinced the Fuhrer that Himmler's embrace of bizarre Eastern philosophies was undermining the Nazi party's relationship with the Church.

Ancestry, heritage, culture and the sacred nature of the land loomed large in Himmler's mythos, giving rise to the Nazi belief that the Aryans were *Ubermenschen*, the Master Race, to be served by slaves like the pharaohs of ancient Egypt. Clearly, his concept of German peasant life was not the pastoral ideal of the German romantic poets. He envisaged the fields of the Fatherland being tilled by Slavic slave laborers who would toil from dusk to dawn until they dropped dead from starvation and overwork, while their Nazi masters looked on. Tragically, this vision became a reality for hundreds of thousands of people.

But with his unimposing physique, poor

Nazi SS Officers

eyesight and chronic digestive disorders, Himmler made a pretty pathetic example of the so-called "Master Race." Nevertheless, entry requirements for the SS were initially stringent in the extreme, although they were later relaxed to accommodate suitable candidates in the occupied countries, especially after the defeat at Stalingrad when the ranks of the SS were severely depleted. In addition to qualifying as exceptional physical specimens of Nordic manhood, officers had to prove their Aryan ancestry back to 1750, while the lower ranks only had to prove that their lineage was "untainted" by Jewish blood back to 1900. Exceptions were made for Himmler's favorites who were suspected of having Jewish ancestors. Reinhard Heydrich was one of them, of whom Himmler said, "He had overcome the Jew in himself by intellectual means." The whole Nazi concept of a pure Aryan race was as ridiculous as it was tragic, for even Himmler had to admit to having Jewish relatives by marriage.

Once accepted, a typical SS inductee underwent a lengthy period of training and indoctrination during which he was permitted to wear the uniform but without the collar patches. These were awarded on November 9 of each year, the anniversary of the Nazis' rise to power in 1923. On the following January 30, the anniversary of Hitler taking command of the party, the candidate would receive his provisional SS identity card, but he had to wait until Hitler's birthday on April 20 before he was given his full identity card.

In addition to his military training, during which he was instructed in "how to kill and how to die," as Himmler said, candidates were subjected to indoctrination in the SS credo, a perversion of the Catholic catechism that demanded that every man memorize the answers to questions like: "Why do we believe in Germany and the Fuhrer?" (The required answer was: "Because we believe in God, we believe in Germany, which he created in his world and in the Fuhrer, Adolph Hitler, whom he has sent us.) Once the credo was learned, the candidate was required to attend a pagan initiation ceremony that ended with him taking an oath that would bind his fate to the Fuhrer, even unto death.

Such an oath exploited the German trait of unquestioning obedience to authority and in this way, the Nazis ensnared thousands of young people into blind obedience. In that era, obedience was equated with religious observance and authority with Divine Will. To question the state and its leaders was tantamount to questioning the will of God. Hitler and his minions were well aware of this and by using this tactic, they convinced the German people to go along with things that they would not have even considered in the past. This is why the SS was such an effective tool of terror.

After an obligatory stint in the Labor Corps or the Army, a successful candidate was then entitled to wear full SS insignia and carry a ceremonial dagger was engraved with runic symbols that were intended to bestow magical powers of protection on the owner. Since ancient times, the dagger was considered a sacred weapon and was used in ceremonial magic. Prior to 1939, all ranks also received a silver death's head signet ring, but during the war it was given only SS commanders who had held a senior rank for more than three years. The ring was also intended to be a counterpart to the magic rings worn by pagan priests of ancient Germany.

After serving their time in the Labor Corps or the Army, the SS novice was assigned to whichever branch of the service that his superiors deemed most suitable for his particular skills. The SS had a regular army unit, the Waffen SS, who were considered Hitler's loyal shock troops. In the concentration camps, the SS doubled as guards and executioners, or they could be transferred to duties supervising and assisting the Gestapo as they rounded up and interrogated members of the resistance in occupied countries. The most notorious unit of all was the *Einsatzgruppe*, or death squads, who sole duty was to act as an extermination unit, instigating Hitler's policies of genocide in the wake of advancing troops.

Every aspect of the SS soldier's life – from induction into the corps to his funeral – was controlled by the state. If an SS man had children, his first-born son would receive a baptism gift from Himmler in the form of a silver mug that bore the inscription "You are but a link in the endless chain of the clan." Himmler even issued instructions about how his men should commit suicide so as not to bring dishonor to the regimen. Even in death, the SS were distinguished from the regular troops by a wooden stake with runes inscribed on it at their grave, instead of a conventional cross.

A dossier was kept on each member detailing every aspect of their public and private lives, including their finances. Their prospective marriage partners were screened to ensure "the conditions of race and healthy stock were fulfilled." Once they had been approved, the marriage ceremony was purged of Christian elements, and was officiated by a local SS leader, who stood in place of a religious figure. Himmler had no use for religious celebrations of marriage and made plans for after the war, when monogamy would no longer be forced on the Nazi population. All men would be allowed as many wives as they wanted, as long as they produced pure Aryan stock. His obsession with procreation led to the formation of *Lebensborn*, SS stud farms to which every unmarried woman over twenty-nine was required to report and to "put herself at their disposal to be made pregnant." *Lebensborn* means "wellspring of life." Ironically, Himmler's human breeding farms proved unproductive. The infant mortality rate was twice the national average, despite the use of calming herbal teas made from ingredients that were cultivated in gardens at the concentration camps.

One of the most bizarre practices of the SS was one advocated by the SS magazine *Die Schwarze Korps* (The Black Corps), which encouraged readers to have sex in graveyards where German heroes had been buried. Lists of suitable sites were published only after they had been approved by the *Ahnenerbe* department of the SS, whose job it was to ensure that the cemeteries had not been "polluted" by non-Aryan spirits. Jewish cemeteries were systematically desecrated and the sites redeveloped – with one significant exception. The ancient Jewish cemetery at Worms was spared because Himmler believed that the magical geology of the site, which dated back to the eleventh century, would be disturbed if the alignments were altered. Some have also suggested that he feared some sort of divine retribution if any of the 2,000 graves should be disturbed, as the bodies were buried in sand that had been brought from Jerusalem.

Perhaps Himmler's greatest contribution to occult lore was his choice of Schloss Wewelsburg as the headquarters for the SS. He discovered the castle near Paderborn, in Westphalia, in the summer of 1934 and was immediately taken by it. Although it would require several million Reichmarks to restore it to its former glory – and considerably more to furnish it in a manner befitting the spiritual haven of the SS – there was no doubt in Himmler's mind that it would be money well spent. Legend has it that the castle would be the last surviving stronghold against a furious future assault by hordes from the East and the Himmler planned to be safe within its walls. Furthermore, according to occult experts in Himmler's *Ahnenerbe* bureau, the fortress was situated at the intersection of several ley lines, which meant that the Earth's energies were concentrated at the spot, and these energies could be invoked during magical rituals to be directed toward whatever end the practitioner desired.

The castle was leased from the reluctant local authority for the nominal fee of one mark per year, and after receiving a government grant, renovation work quickly began. Each suite was furnished in a style befitting a German hero, with richly-embroidered tapestries, heavy drapes, ornate

Schloss Wewelsburg -- Himmler's occult castle

furniture carved from solid oak and plush carpets to keep out the bone-shilling cold of the stone walls. At the heart of the castle was a banquet hall with an imposing, Arthurian-style round table. At the table were thirteen large oak chairs, each bearing the name of the Nazi official who was to be honored with a place in Himmler's inner circle. The number of guests coincided with the twelve signs of the Zodiac, with Himmler at the head.

Directly below the Great Hall lay the hushed stone circular vault known as the "realm of the dead." The vault housed twelve black pedestals, each in a niche arranged around a hollow shaft. This was the crypt in which the fallen "knights" of the SS leadership were to find eternal rest. In the event that their bodies could not be recovered from the battlefield, their coat-of-arms were to be burned in their place, and the ashes placed in a porcelain urn. It was hoped that future generations would come to the castle to venerate the founders of the 1,000-year Reich.

The official word was that Wewelsburg was to serve as an SS training school, but reports claimed that magical rites were performed in the antechamber of the castle. In his memoirs, SS Brigadefuhrer Walter Schellenberg stated that he inadvertently walked in on a psychic circle whose members had been instructed to project their mental

(Below) Himmler's ritual room beneath the Great Hall

149

energy into an adjacent room, where a suspect (General Von Fritsch) was being questioned. He wrote, "[Himmler had] ordered them all to concentrate their minds on exerting a suggestive influence over the General that would induce him to tell the truth... to see these twelve SS leaders sitting in a circle, all sunk in deep and silent contemplation, was indeed a remarkable sight."

Through distinctive rituals, oaths and insignia, every SS man was made to understand that he was more than merely a soldier in an elite fighting unit – he was an initiate in a secret, magical order, and a superior being that was above the concept of good and evil. He was above the law and no court could judge him. Only his superiors had dominion over him and he was conditioned to act without mercy toward his enemies and those condemned by the state as unworthy of life. Once he put on that black uniform, he no longer had a conscience or a thought of his own. He was a man who killed with impunity and was to consider every brutal act as one committed in service to Germany.

The SS may have been the most overtly occult unit of the Nazi regime, but the Nazis had many strange beliefs. They linked themselves to bizarre supernatural theories, and badly desired to be considered the Aryan "master race," which was nothing more than Nordic folklore. But in their vain quest to prove their superiority, they distorted the esoteric teachings of the Theosophists, perverted Christian doctrine and steeped themselves in the occult. Undesirables were put to death under the guise of "natural selection," and fruitless expeditions were funded to prove crackpot theories. Had the Nazis succeeded in their plans for world domination, they would have plunged civilization into an age of superstition, insanity and barbarity. They were not above going to any lengths – magic included – to carry out their horrific plans.

The Nazis believed that if they captured the spiritual center of a country, their enemy would lose their will to resist, and they could be overtaken. The same would be true if its symbols of power were taken -- its regimental flags, icons of culture, and crown jewels. The enemy would lose their sense of national identity, they believed, and their morale would crumble. In Vienna, they looted the Hapsburg crown jewels; from Prague they stole the treasures of the Bohemian kings, and in Warsaw, they stole the Polish royal regalia. In his defense, Hitler cited the precedent established by Emperor Napoleon and by the British, who looted the tombs of the pharaohs in Egypt. Hitler regarded the emblems of royalty – and the royals themselves – with disdain, but he understood their symbolic value, conferring power and authority on those strong enough to take them.

Even greater than the taking of a country's symbols, Hitler believed, was the possession of their sacred centers, a distortion of the esoteric science of geomancy. The ancients believed that certain locations were sources of psychic energy and that this force could be drawn upon for communicating with the forces of nature and the gods. For this reason, they built their megalithic monuments and temples over underground streams, near natural magnetic fields or at the point of converging ley lines, all of which could be divining by shamans and magicians.

The Nazi fascination with sacred sites can be traced back to the theories of William Henry Black, an Englishman who proposed in 1870 that many of the world's ancient monuments conformed to a grand geometrical pattern, perhaps more coincidentally than by design. However, the fact that these sacred stone circles and temples were located at a focal point of a natural energy source suggested that early civilizations and communities may not have been as primitive as nineteenth-century science assumed they were. Between the two world wars, the idea found enthusiastic support among amateur antiquarians in Germany, who discovered that the distances between many monolithic structures revealed that their ancestors possessed a remarkably sophisticated understanding of mathematics and astronomy. In his book *The Cosmology of the Indies*, Willibrod Kirfel argued that the Aryan tribes of India had developed a complex cosmology which they had documented in stone at their most sacred sites. The following year, Otto Reuter galvanized the German academic establishment with a book called *The Riddle of the Edda*, which legitimized the beliefs of German occultists by demonstrating that there was a historic basis for the Norse myths. Reuter stated that there was a previously unknown Indo-

European culture that had encoded their knowledge of the constellations in their creation myths. Then, in 1929, Wilhelm Teudt published his exhaustive study of the subject, *Ancient German Sanctuaries*, drawing on years of painstaking research and thousands of detailed measurements that he had personally made at sites all over Germany. He claimed to have discovered a national astronomical cult based on "extensive scientific foundations," which cemented the growing belief among mystically minded German nationalists that the Aryans were far more civilized than their non-Aryan counterparts around the world.

Basically, they were books about pseudo-science that could have been written at the behest of the Nazi party. In such idealism, the myth of the "master race" began to take shape.

In the 1920s, a German lawyer named Josef Heinsch began promoting the idea that many of the major ley lines around the world (notably in Germany) originated

Heinrich Himmler was an advocate of Aryan myths, occultism, and esoteric ideas. Himmler regarded his SS as an ancient Germanic clan, and endowed it with a series of pagan or pseudo-medieval symbols and rituals. This photograph shows Himmler (center), SS Colonel Weisthor and others at a quarry in the Palatinate. At the time, Weisthor was head of the department of early pre-history and early history at the Main Office of Race and Settlement; he was also considered an expert on ancient German runes. Weisthor, whose real name was Karl Maria Wiligut, was later unmasked as a charlatan and an escapee from a mental hospital. He was expelled from the SS in 1939.

under hills and mountains that had been deemed sacred as dwelling places of the gods. Such sites were said to be courses of energy that could be harnessed by magical means.

Legend had it that the pagan priests of ancient Britain used this energy to reduce their enemies to ash, which led to it being known as the "lightning of the druids." The Nazi mystics renamed it *vril*, adopting the name from *The Coming Race*, a novel by British author and magic adept Sir Edward Bulwer-Lytton, best known for beginning one of his novels with the infamous words, "It was a dark and stormy night..." The force itself was not entirely a literary creation. During the same time period when Heinsch was tracing the source of the ley lines, two scientists from Stuttgart were attempting to find a common factor linking cases of cancer within the city. The scientists thought there might be a geological cause for the reported cases, but could find nothing out of the ordinary until dowsers demonstrated that the cases were clustered around the region's five major underground fault lines. Nazi scientists were brought in to follow up on their research and they discovered that the velocity of the radiation that was detected by dowsing traveled at a median rate of 44 meters per second, which was the same number as the Germanic geomantic measure, the *raste*. It appeared that there might be a link between the magnetic radiation emitted by the Earth at ancient sacred sites and the standard unit of measurement used by the ancient astronomical cults in the construction of their sacred sites.

The potential power to be unleashed by those who tried to focus such a force can be found in a description given in 1895 by A.P. Sinnett, a member of the London Theosophical Society, whose members were fervent believers in the existence of such forces. He wrote, "There are great etheric currents sweeping over the surface of the earth from pole to pole in volume which makes their power as irresistible as the rising tide; and there are methods by which this stupendous force may be safely utilized, though skillful attempts to control it would be fraught with frightful danger."

When Heinrich Himmler learned of such a force, he became determined that Germany would be the first to control it. And based on the other acts carried out by the Nazis, it would not be used for the benefit of mankind.

While the validity of geomancy continues to be debated today, its more bizarre Nazi companions of the World Ice Theory and the Hollow Earth elicit nothing but derision. But during the Hitler years, in the vacuum created by the defection of Germany's intellectual elite, ideas like these threatened to replace mainstream science in the Nazi state. With the loss of scientists of renown like Albert Einstein, crackpot scientists and philosophers moved in to fill the void, introducing the Nazis to the most outlandish oddball theories imaginable.

Austrian engineer Hans Horbiger was typical of the eccentric "scientists" that were sponsored by the state. In turn, he learned the benefits of threats and intimidation. In 1925, he recruited Nazi thugs to disrupt meetings and lectures held by orthodox physicists, and he wrote threatening letters to scientific journals and academics who disagreed with him. One such letter read, "The time has come for you to choose whether to be with us or against us. While Hitler is cleaning up politics, Hans Horbiger will sweep the bogus sciences out of the way. The doctrine of Eternal Ice will be a sign of the regeneration of the German people. Watch out! Come over to our side before it is too late."

The core of Horbiger's theory was that the solar system was formed millions of years ago when a massive chunk of space ice collided with the sun. The resulting explosion threw molten matter into space, and it eventually cooled to form the planets. He had come to this conclusion after witnessing the violent reaction caused by molten metal being poured onto snow in the foundry where he worked. According to Horbiger, this cosmic accident accounted for the existence of the North and South Poles and the Great Flood that was mythologized in the Bible and in Nordic accounts. But what really intrigued the occult-minded Nazis was the idea that *Welteislehre* (World Ice Theory) offered a scientific basis for their belief in the antediluvian age of supermen, which Horbiger explained was made possible by gravitational changes caused by one of the three moons then orbiting the Earth. The increasing proximity of this moon resulted in a mutant race of giants who were rendered almost extinct when the moon finally collided with the planet about 150,000 years ago, leaving their human slaves scavenging for survival. The few remaining giants established several advanced civilizations, like Atlantis and Lemuria, for a superior race of humans – the Aryans. They nurtured the Aryans as their successors until they were hunted down by their vengeful slaves, giving rise to the legends of gods and heroes that endured into modern times. It only remained for the Nazis to implement a selective breeding program from pure Aryan stock for the race of Aryan supermen to be regenerated and take their place as the rightful rulers of the world.

However, it was never satisfactorily explained how the regular-sized Aryans had inherited the "pure" blood from their oversized mentors – or why no real evidence had ever been found of Atlantis, the existence of a race of giants, or any of the other flaws in the story. When challenged to explain these glaring anomalies by "Jewish Liberal scientists," Horbiger retorted in the tone of a true Nazi, "Trust me, not equations! When you will learn that mathematics is valueless!"

It is unknown whether or not Hitler was converted to Horbiger's Aryan fantasy, but there is evidence that he was willing to act on it. He wrote in 1942 that he was "quite inclined to accept the cosmic theories of Horbiger." Himmler was (not surprisingly) an ardent supporter of *Welteislehre* in the 1920s and remained so throughout the war. He noted, "Hans Horbiger's monument does not need to wait a hundred years before it is built; one can employ these ideas even today."

Unfortunately for the Nazis, Hitler did put Horbiger's theories into practice in the late summer of 1941. He ordered the Central Army Group to halt within sight of Moscow while several mechanized divisions broke off in an ill-fated effort to capture Leningrad, and another raced toward the oil fields of the Ukraine. When snow began to fall in the first week of October, Hitler shrugged off warnings that his troops were not equipped for a Russian winter. He had complete faith in his meteorological department, which had forecast an unusually mild winter using Horbiger's principles and predictions. It turned out to be a fatal error. Within weeks, the front lines of the German Army found themselves in the terrible grip of a fierce Russian winter, stuck with summer uniforms, without gloves, hats, boots or even dark glasses to protect the men from snow blindness. German newsreels made light of the situation, filming naked soldiers braving ice water baths, but the reality was far grimmer. By early November, the oil was freezing in the guns, and synthetic fuel was separating into its component parts in the gas tanks of their trucks and tanks. By Christmas, one million of Germany's finest troops – the same men who had marched proudly through the streets of Paris after the fall of France just two years earlier – perished in the snow, their weapons frozen in their fingers.

Hitler was shaken but unapologetic, for his belief in his own infallibility would not allow for defeat. Fate had conspired against him, but he was right and so was Horbiger. The "master race" had to be forged anew in a trial of fire and ice, the two elements that had forged the world centuries before. He ordered the army at Stalingrad to stand and fight to the last man, but even the most fervent soldiers lost their resolve in the sub-zero weather. After weeks of bitter hand-to-hand fighting, the remnants of the German army surrendered to the Russians.

A curious postscript to this story occurred in 1943 when Hitler inexplicably ordered the end to the secret V2 rocket project. He was said to have had a dream in which his saw his potential war-winning weapon shatter huge chunks of ice floating about the Earth, bringing them crashing down and triggering a cosmic cataclysm. By the time Hitler was persuaded that the rocket posed no danger to the world, it was too late to pursue this technological advantage. The war had already been lost.

The Nazi belief in the Hollow Earth had a curious proponent – Reichmarshall Hermann Goering, a man that no one would dare call a fool. And yet, the fact that he subscribed to a concept even more outlandish that Horbiger's World Ice Theory seemed completely out of line with his usual coldly rational way of thinking. For some reason, though, Goering became a rabid believer in the idea that our world existed inside of a great hollow sphere.

Hermann Goering

The idea of the Hollow Earth dates back to the seventeenth century, when English astronomer Edmund Halley (the man for whom the comet is named) published a paper in which he postulated a theory to explain the variance in the Earth's magnetic poles. He envisioned the Earth's crust as the outer layer of a hollow sphere within which two inner players spun at different speeds. The poles were supposedly situated on one or both of these inner layers and the variation of speed between the revolving spheres accounted for the day-to-day variances.

Three centuries later, a variation on the idea was embraced by a former World War I German fighter ace and friend of Goering named Peter Bender. Some have laughingly suggested that Bender must have suffered from shell-shock during the war because his idea bordered on insane. He believed that the human race was living inside of a large sphere, and that the sky was its inner skin and the stars were merely glimmers of light that could be seen through it. He called this notion "the phantom universe." Incredible as it might seem, Goering was not the only high-ranking Nazi to consider this theory plausible – many other German officers believed it as well. In April 1942, a group headed by Dr. Heinz Fisher succeeded in commissioning a full-scale test in the Baltic Sea where a prototype radar station was established and equipped to send beams of infrared light up into the sky at 45-degree angles. The hope was that the rays would bounce off the roof of the larger sphere, and then back down to Earth, where they would produce a radar image of ships that would be out of the visual range of the vessel conducting the experiment. In this case, the target was the British fleet anchored off the Orkney Islands in northern Scotland.

Needless to say, the experiment was a failure. The expedition returned to face the wrath of Hitler, who considered the venture a serious waste of time and resources at a critical point in the war. Bender and the most vociferous advocates of his theory were dispatched to concentration camps. Even Goering was too embarrassed to speak in his friend's defense. Only Fisher escaped with his life. After the war, he was taken to American where he became a significant contributor to the development of the hydrogen bomb.

In March 1939, a mystery rippled through the ranks of the Nazi party. When the frozen body of SS Obersturmfuhrer Otto Rahn was discovered on Kustein Mountain on March 13, it was assumed that he had died from exposure after falling or getting lost in a blizzard. But, as some of his friends pointed out, it would take up to two weeks to die from the cold at that time of year and at the altitude at which his body was found. Rahn was fit, trained in survival techniques, and was an experience climber. To many, it seemed highly suspicious that he had died just a few weeks after "resigning" his commission in the SS – the very same month that his colleague,

The mysterious Otto Rahn, seeker of the Holy Grail, which Himmler desperately wanted in Nazi hands.

Karl Maria Willigut was also forced to resign his commission and then put under the "protection" of the Gestapo. Was it possible that Rahn, an occult scholar, and Willigut, a half-mad visionary, shared a secret that put both of their lives at risk?

Some historians believe it likely that Rahn committed ritual suicide by starving himself to death on his beloved mountain in the manner of the thirteenth-century Gnostic sect, the Cathars, with whom he believed he shared a spiritual bond. It is surely no coincidence that his death occurred on the anniversary of the fall of Montsegur, the Cathars' mountain stronghold in southern France, which occurred on March 14, 1244. Months before the Cathars came to be regarded as heretics by the Church, and were besieged by over 10,000 troops. When they finally surrendered, more than two hundred of them were burned to death at the bottom of the mountain when they refused to renounce their faith.

Rahn's connection to the Cathars seems to be the key to the mystery, for it also ties into Himmler's fervent quest for the Holy Grail, the cup that Jesus was said to have used at the Last Supper, and which, legend claims, caught drops of his blood at his crucifixion. Himmler believed that the Cathars were the custodians of the Grail, and that it had been smuggled out of Montsegur before the fortress was overwhelmed. While it might seem unlikely that one of Hitler's leading Nazis would scour the Earth for an iconic Christian symbol, it is around this central theme that the whole strange affair seems to revolve.

Himmler believed that the Grail was not only a symbol of Christianity, which made it a powerful icon to have in Nazi hands, but he believed that Jesus was a member of the Aryan race. The Nazis held that orthodox Christianity bore no relation to the true teachings of Jesus or the original sect that his disciples had founded. Nazi doctrines asserted that the Catholic Church had appropriated the names and principles of the true Christians in order to enrich itself at the people's expense. The Nazis justified their plans to replace Christian symbols and rituals with their own brand of paganism because they believed that as Aryans, they were reviving the "true religion." For this reason, Himmler was intent on finding the Grail as a part of his revitalization of the one true church.

Although it was commonly believed (since it was one of the symbols the drove the various Crusades to the Holy Land during the Middle Ages) that the Holy Grail was an artifact of Christian origin, others believed that the Grail was a sacred stone that contained the secrets of the alchemists. Himmler likely didn't care what form it took so long as it was a vessel of occult power through which he could channel forces that would ensure the invincibility of the SS.

Rahn, however, was convinced that the object of his lifelong obsession was a sacred stone, and he traveled throughout Europe during 1931 in search of proof. He claimed to have found it in a small French town called Ussat-les-Bains under the guidance of a fellow seeker named Antonin Gadal, a member of a historical society known as the "Friends of Montsegur and the Grail." He had founded a small private museum filled with artifacts and documents that Rahn found invaluable.

After transcribing the ancient documents and deciphering the instructions on the relics provided by Gadal, Rahn concluded that Montsavat, the legendary mountain of the Grail, was in reality the Cathar stronghold of Montsegur. He decoded the sacred geometry of the site, and its relation to other sites, and became convinced that the Cathar treasure would not have been removed from such a holy place but must have been hidden in a secret location. It had been most likely hidden underground, where it would have remained unharmed when the pope's soldiers burned the fortress.

The result of his research was published in a 1933 book called *Krezzug gegen den Graal* (Crusade Against the Grail). Inevitably, the book came to the attention of Reichsfuhrer SS Himmler.

It was said that Rahn only agreed to accept a commission in the SS because it guaranteed him food, lodging and unlimited funds with which to continue his research. Whatever the reason, he certainly lived to regret it, as it put him under intolerable pressure to produce results and introduced him to the eccentric and unpredictable Karl Maria Willigut.

Willigut, who had designed the Death's Head ring for the SS, was often referred to as "Himmler's Rasputin." At one time he had been certified as insane, which perhaps made him an ideal Nazi expert on the occult. Himmler was suitably impressed with the wild-eyed rune scholar and clairvoyant, to the extent that he gave him the title of Head of the Department of Prehistory at the SS Race and Resettlement Office. Willigut's qualifications for the posting were his knowledge of runes and his ability to access 20,000 years of Aryan history from the collective memory of every human being – which he did psychically, of course. According to information gathered during his trances, he learned that Christianity was of German origin and that Jesus was in fact the Teutonic god Baldur, who fled to the Middle East after surviving a murder attempt by devotees of his rival, Wotan. Exactly what Otto Rahn, a more or less conventional historian, thought of his new colleague is not known, but he likely wondered what sort of madhouse he had gotten himself committed into.

Whatever misgivings that Rahn may have had, he kept them to himself. His correspondence with Willigut concerning his search for the Holy Grail, which took him as far afield as Iceland, was restricted to basic reports on the symbolic significance of ancient place names and little else. When he returned from his travels in 1936, Himmler made his displeasure known about Rahn's lack of progress and gave him until October 31 to provide a publishable manuscript that documented proof of Aryan superiority and Germany's right to the lands to the east, specifically Russia. Or better still, evidence that there were underground passages at Montsegur that contained the Grail and perhaps other occult artifacts, as Rahn had originally suspected.

Rahn produced the ordered book, which he called *Luzifers Hofgesind* (Lucifer's Court). It contained some very interesting information, which no doubt pleased Himmler and showed just how far the researcher had fallen under the SS leader's spell. Once passage read:

The ancient god of love is also the lord of the Spring, as personified in the Greek myth of Apollo, who brought back the light from the sun, he is the light-bearer, or Lucifer. According to the Apocalypse of John, Apollo was identified with the Devil... There is much more light in the world than in the houses of God – cathedrals and churches – where Lucifer is neither able nor desirous of entering because of the somber stained-glass windows on which the Jewish prophets and apostles, the Roman gods and saints are depicted.

In essence, Rahn was attempting to legitimize the Nazis' rejection of orthodox Christianity by claiming that the early Church demonized Lucifer, the true god. While the idea seems nonsensical, Rahn appears to have been sincere in his beliefs. A newspaper report of a lecture that he gave on the subject in January 1938 revealed his continuing loyalty to the Cathars, as well. Speaking on the fall of Montsegur, he noted, "205 leading followers of Lucifer were burnt on a huge pyre by Dominicans in the south of France after a large-scaled priestly Crusade in the name of Christian clemency. With fire and sword the Lucifer doctrine of the Light-Bearer was persecuted along with its followers. They are dead, but their spirit lives on."

There was more in the book in a similar vein – a lot more. Himmler loved it and ordered 5,000 copies to be bound in the finest leather and distributed to the Nazi elite. By now, Rahn had to realize that he was trapped within the Nazi circles, especially when he read the proofs of *Lucifer's Court* and found that one blatantly anti-Semitic passage had been inserted by someone else. What made this especially grave is that there is evidence to suggest that Rahn himself was of Jewish ancestry. However, it's not clear that he was aware of it. What was clear, though, was that Rahn was openly homosexual.

As far as Himmler was concerned, this was not his greatest sin. Himmler's disenchantment began when Rahn came back empty-handed from Montsegur – no Grail, no occult artifacts. Himmler planned to mount the Grail on a marble pedestal at Wewelsburg Castle, giving it a place of honor in the Realm of the Dead underneath the Great Hall. Bravely, if naively, Rahn also began to move in anti-Nazi circles, and while he did voice some rebellious sentiments, he was always fairly discreet about it. Himmler turned a blind eye to this, and to Rahn's homosexuality, but after his failure to find the Grail, his tolerance wore thin.

In 1937, Rahn was punished for a drunken homosexual scrape by being assigned to a three-month tour of duty as a guard at Dachau concentration camp. What he saw there appalled him. Clearly in a state of anguish he wrote to a friend, "I have much sorrow in my country... impossible for a tolerant, liberal man like me to live in a nation that my native country has become."

He also wrote to Himmler resigning from the SS. This, too, was as naive as it was brave. Although Himmler accepted Rahn's resignation, he had no intention of letting him escape. What happened next is unclear. There are stories that Rahn was threatened with having his homosexuality exposed, also that he had links with British intelligence. Told that his life was in danger, Rahn was apparently offered the option of committing suicide. One evening in March 1939, he climbed up a snow-covered slope in the Tyrol Mountains and lay down to die. He is believed to have swallowed poison, although no cause of death was ever given. The following day Rahn's body was found, frozen solid, looking up toward the mountains as if gazing off into the distance.

And there the story might have ended – except that Hollywood has conferred a strange kind of immortality on Otto Rahn by naming him as the inspiration for another adventurer on a search for holy artifacts – Indiana Jones, made famous in *Raiders of the Lost Ark* and its sequels. Thanks to this, stories of Otto Rahn have remained alive over the years. Predictably, there are stories that Rahn was murdered, or that he didn't die in the Tyrol but faked his death to fool the Nazis. Instead, he is said to have survived, changed his first name to Rudolf, and went on to become the German ambassador in Italy. As for the Grail, that too lives on, with claimants and contenders continuing to turn up in the most unlikely places.

But one place where it probably did not turn up was in the hands of the Nazis.

Perhaps the most sinister element of Himmler's fascination with the occult was the so-called "Occult Bureau." Its official name was the *Ahnenerbe*, or the Department of Ancestral Heritage, an innocuous title that masked some of the most perverse activities ever conceived by the human mind, including sadistic experiments on concentration camp inmates. The bureau's senior administrator, SS Colonel Wolfram Sievers, with his dueling scar and menacing gaze, resembled the perfect stereotypical Nazi. He cultivated a sinister manner that put people who met him in mind of the Devil. Some writers have suggested that when he went to the gallows of Nuremberg Prison in 1945, he likely did so in the belief that Satan was waiting for him to arrive in Hell.

Prior to its assimilation into the SS in 1935, the *Ahnenerbe* had been a pseudo-scientific institution staffed by academics studying an array of innocuous subjects like the nutritional value of various forms of honey, the occult symbolism of British hats, and the mystical significance of the Celtic harp. These studies had been presided over by Sievers' predecessor, Hermann Wirth, a man whose sanity was as questionable that of Karl Maria Willigut. At the entrance to his home, Wirth had posted a notice that read, "No Smoking. A deep breather lives here." It referred to his wife, a medium, who remained in a permanent trance-like state, while he husband waited patiently to record the profound cosmic truths that he claimed she was able to channel from the spirit world.

Hermann Wirth

Wirth had secured his post at the head of the bureau after impressing Himmler with his knowledge of prehistory, but he was gullible in the extreme, and embraced every crackpot theory that came along. He trusted his intuition to inform him whether a questionable source was genuine or not, rather than demanding any scientific proof. His unshakeable belief in the mythical German homeland of Thule, for example, was based entirely on "evidence" offered by the patently fake *Uralinda Chronicle*, a supposed ancient Nordic document that had obviously been printed in the nineteenth century. When its authenticity was questioned, he justified his belief in it by saying that it was a copy, and that he trusted the original would surface when the owner felt the time was right.

Himmler was forced to defend Wirth's reputation on more than one occasion, if only to save his own. In 1933, he ordered Hermann Rauschning to strong-arm dissenting scholars and academics into silence, so that Wirth's claims would go unchallenged.

Eventually, though, Himmler grew tired of having to defend Wirth's unsubstantiated claims and replaced him with the staunchly loyal Wolfram Sievers. From the day he took office, Sievers implemented a restructuring of the entire institute, expanding it to fifty separate departments, including the notorious *Institut für Wehrwissenschaftliche Zweckforschung* (Institute for Military Scientific Research), which instigated human experiments at Dachau Concentration Camp.

Prior to that, the *Ahnenerbe* focused strictly on the occult, and with proving Aryan superiority. In 1935, Himmler contacted author Yrjö von Grönhagen, after seeing one of his articles about folklore that was published in a Frankfurt newspaper. Grönhagen agreed to lead a voyage through the Karelia region of Finland to record pagan sorcerers and witches. One of the trip's successes was in finding Miron-Aku, a soothsayer believed to be a witch by locals. Upon meeting the group, she claimed to have foreseen their arrival. The team persuaded her to perform a ritual for the camera and tape recorder in which she could summon the spirits of ancestors and "divine future events."

In 1936, Wirth had convinced Himmler to launch an expedition to Bohuslän, a region in southwestern Sweden. The area was known for its massive quantity of petroglyph rock carvings, which Wirth believed were part of an ancient writing system, predating all other known systems. While his studies were largely based on personal belief, Wirth made interpretations about the meaning of ideograms carved in the rock, such as a circle bisected by a vertical line representing a year, and a man standing with raised arms representing what Wirth called "the Son of God." His team proceeded to make casts of what Wirth deemed to be the most important carvings, which were then crated and sent back to Germany.

In 1937, the *Ahnenerbe* sent archaeologist Franz Altheim to study prehistoric rock inscriptions. He returned to Germany claiming he found traces of Nordic runes on the rocks supposedly confirming that ancient Rome was originally founded by people of Nordic descent. The following year, Altheim requested sponsorship to travel to the Middle East to study an internal power struggle of the Roman Empire, which he believed was fought between the Nordic and Semitic peoples. Eager to credit the vast success of the Roman Empire to a Nordic background, the *Ahnenerbe* agreed. The expedition was far from successful, as were expeditions to the Antarctic, where the Nazis hoped to find evidence of the Aryan race.

In 1937 and 1938, *Ahnenerbe* archaeologists excavated burial mounds and ancient forts but the greatest discovery in Germany was in the southern Jura mountains of Bavaria. During an excavation of the Mauern caves, R.R. Schmidt had discovered red ochre, a common pigment for cave paintings made by the Cro-Magnon. In the fall of 1937, Dr. Assien Bohmers took over the excavation. His team proceeded to find artifacts such as Stone Age tools called burins, ivory pendants, and a woolly mammoth skeleton. They also discovered Neanderthal remains buried with what appeared to be throwing spears and javelins, a technology thought to have been developed by the Cro-Magnons. Bohmers interpreted this to mean Cro-Magnons had left these stones in the caves over 70,000 years before, and this was therefore the oldest Cro-Magnon site in the world. To validate his claims, Bohmers travelled throughout Europe speaking with colleagues and upholding the German belief in Aryan superiority, now going back to the dawn of man.

More expeditions followed, including an extended trip to Tibet in 1939. Himmler had decided that he could increase the visibility of the *Ahnenerbe* by investigating Nazi scientists' claims that the early Aryans had conquered much of Asia. The search for relics and artifacts – including holy and sacred objects – continued and thousands of items were collected. Many of them were permanently lost at the end of the war.

But it was not the expeditions and the looting that gave the bureau its greatest notoriety.

The Institute for Military Scientific Research, which conducted extensive medical experiments using human subjects, became attached to the Ahnenerbe during World War II. It was managed by Wolfram Sievers, who had founded the new branch of the organization on Himmler's orders.

It all seemed scientific on the surface. Dr. Sigmund Rascher was tasked with helping the Luftwaffe study pilot safety — because aircraft were being built to fly higher than ever before. He applied for and received permission from Himmler to requisition concentration camp prisoners to be placed in vacuum chambers that simulated the high-altitude conditions that pilots might face.

Rascher was also told to discover how long German airmen would be able to survive if shot down above freezing water. His victims were forced to remain out of doors naked in freezing weather for up to fourteen hours, or kept in a tank of ice water for three hours, their pulse and internal temperature measured through a series of electrodes. Warming of the victims was then attempted by different methods, most usually and successfully by immersion in very hot water, and also with less conventional methods, such as placing the subject in bed with women who would try to sexually stimulate him, a method that was suggested by Himmler.

Rascher also experimented with the effects of a substance made from beets and apple pectin on coagulating blood flow to help heal gunshot wounds. Subjects were given a tablet made from these ingredients, and then shot through the neck or chest. Sometimes their limbs were amputated without anesthesia. Rascher published an article on the use of the substance, without detailing the nature of the human trials. He also set up a company to manufacture the substance, staffed by prisoners.

Similar experiments were conducted from July to September 1944, as the *Ahnenerbe* provided space and materials to doctors at Dachau to undertake "seawater experiments," chiefly through Sievers. Sievers was known to have visited Dachau on July 20, to speak with the doctors who ultimately carried out the experiments.

At the end of the war, some of the men responsible for these heinous acts were punished for their crimes – while others were not.

Dr. Sigmund Rascher escaped Allied justice but was shot by SS guards on Himmler's orders during the last weeks of the war. He had endorsed Rascher's sadistic treatment of prisoners but had drawn the line at being lied to by the scientist, who had accepted a gift from Himmler for having fathered three children in late middle age. In fact, Rascher and his wife had kidnapped three babies from an orphanage and claimed them as their own.

Director Wolfram Sievers was captured at war's end. A slew of documents found by American troops played a large part in finding him guilty at his trial. He had been charged with ordering the human medical experiments at Dachau, as well as creating a macabre skeleton collection from the bodies of murdered Jews. Jurors found him guilty in August 1947, and he was hanged the following June. A Tibetan chant was performed upon his corpse.

A founder of *Ahnenerbe*, Richard Walther Darré was tried in for his crimes. He received seven years imprisonment after being found not guilty on more serious charges.

Although he was the president of the *Ahnenerbe* from 1937 until the end of the war, Walther Wüst claimed that he was unaware of any medical experiments that took place. Evidence seemed to show this was the case, and in 1950, he was classified as a "fellow traveler" and released. He returned to the University of Munich as a professor.

In 1948, *Ahnenerbe* official Bruno Beger was also exonerated for his crimes, although the tribunal had been unaware of his part in the skeleton collection that had been organized by Sievers. In 1960, investigators began looking into the details of the collection and Beger was taken into custody in March. He was released four months later, but the investigation continued, leading to his trial on October 27, 1970. Beger claimed that he was unaware the Auschwitz prisoners he measured were to be killed. While two others indicted in the trial were released, Beger was convicted on April 6, 1971, and sentenced to three years in prison for being an accomplice in the murder of eighty-six Jews. Upon appeal, however, his sentence was reduced to three years of probation.

It was the last gasp of the Nazi's "Occult Bureau," coming almost three decades after the end of the war.

In 1940, British occult historian Lewis Spence published an anti-Nazi booklet called "Occult Causes of the Present War." In it, he voiced an opinion that many people had already suspected for several years: that Nazi Germany was the creation of satanic forces that were intent on ushering in a new Dark Age. Spence declared, "In this work, the author reveals the nature and existence of hidden powers at work behind the Nazi organization, which he believes is but the outward, though appropriate, manifestation of satanic and diabolic agencies which employ it for their own malignant purposes." Spence was firmly convinced that socio-economic factors, militant nationalism and the power of Hitler's personality alone could not account for the emergence of what turned out to be an evil empire.

And it was not merely the Nazis' vociferous opposition to Christianity and organized religion that convinced Spence and other writers that they were aligned with the Devil. He also pointed to the deep-rooted practice of witchcraft and magic in Germany to prove that the country was a breeding ground for the black arts. Their fascination with the dark lore of the forests proved that the population was predisposed to paganism. Or so he believed, but he may have been right in one respect. The German psyche could be said to be inclined to morbid romanticism, and the Nazis had conditioned the population to see themselves and their enemies in terms of mythic archetypes. Propaganda portrayed the statuesque blue-eyed, blond men of the SS as Wagner's Siegfried personified, while the Jews were the dwarves of the underworld. Mistrust of the outsider was deeply rooted in the nation's psyche, and was clearly ripe for exploitation.

It was a time period when society had been reduced to survival of the fittest by the Great Depression. Racial stereotypes were symptomatic of the times, and lawlessness and extremism were on the rise in the world. Evil, in all its forms, seemed to be fighting for a foothold in the twentieth century. Even Germany's elderly Kaiser was reported to be looking to blame his nation's defeat in World War I on malign and faceless forces, namely the Freemasons and the occult brotherhood known as the Illuminati, who were reputedly behind every conspiracy in history.

In his country retreat at Doorn, Kaiser Wilhelm was said to have pored over volumes devoted to the occult and the arcane in a vain search for answers that haunted his waking hours and disturbed his sleep. How could he have been tricked into gambling the destiny of his people in a war that Germany had blundered into? And why did he squander his opportunities during the stalemate on the Western Front, which gave the Americans the time to decisively enter the war on the side of the allies? Moreover, how did Germany lose the war after having won several significant battles?

Such matters would soon preoccupy his successor, Adolph Hitler, whose initial aim was to avenge the "betrayal" of 1918 and restore national pride, but whose inherent flaws made him a more suitable vessel for malevolent spirits who were drawn by the aura of resentment and repressed aggression surrounding the wounded German psyche and, once admitted, would come to possess it. Hitler was sufficiently shrewd not to lay blame on imaginary secret societies. His choice of scapegoats proved to be targets that were more conveniently out in the open, readily identifiable according to Nazi racist ideology, and could be eliminated without the fear of protest by the population. The Jews had been portrayed in propaganda films, and even in children's school books, as vermin who spread disease and corrupted the pure Aryan soul. German capitalists had been blamed for the rampant inflation of the 1920s, while communists had been demonized for organizing industrial unrest that threatened the stability of the state. The average German was convinced that he would be glad to see them all gone. The communists might put up a fight, but they were vastly outnumbered by the *Sturmabteilung* "brown-shirts." The Jews could be persuaded to accept "resettlement," but they would have to surrender their wealth in exchange for the promise of safe passage.

That was how it all began, and in this way, evil crept insidiously into German society.

Whether one believes in evil as a conscious entity or defines it as a lack of empathy – the denial of the divine in oneself and others – evil always searched for itself, for its own reflection in the faces of others. It is doomed to work with tools whose temper is as unsound as its own. Evil people are capable of wreaking havoc and causing suffering on a vast scale, but they are by definition self-centered and eventually, self-defeating. In this way, they are fated to fail. Evil can only succeed in the short term and only if there is a lack of determination to limit the damage that its agents can do. The allies sorely lacked this resolve when Hitler began to assert the German people's need for conquest in the middle 1930s. The French in particular were tired of war and the British believed more in appeasement than confrontation. It was no secret that certain elements of European society –as well as many influential people in America – admired Hitler for the "miracle" he had been able to work on the Germany economy (by excessive borrowing with no intention of repaying the loans) and for his firm stance against the Jews, who had been the world's scapegoats for centuries. In this atmosphere of grudging respect, the Nazis were able to tear up the punitive Versailles Treaty from World War I, start a massive rearmament under the noses of the allies, and take back the Rhineland in 1936 without a single shot being fired. Tragically, World War II could have been averted at this point if France had opposed the re-occupation of the Rhineland. German officers had orders to withdraw their troops if the French army had deployed their forces to the region, but the French never returned.

After testing the resolve of the allies in this way, Hitler went on to successfully demand the annexation of Austria, the return of the Sudentenland and the Danzig corridor, and finally, neutral Czechoslovakia before the allies realized how foolishly naïve they had been and announced they would stand with Poland in the event of a German invasion. By then, short of starting an all-out war, it was too late to stop the Nazi aggression.

While it's true that the deeply evil nature of the Nazi regime was not fully realized until after the liberation of the concentration camps in 1945, only the most ignorant and callous individual could say that they had no idea what a fascist dictatorship could be capable of. It is often been said that for evil to exist, it only requires good men to do nothing, but is the notion of evil merely a convenient explanation for abhorrent human behavior? Do we simply use evil as an excuse for not taking responsibility for things because we imagine them to be out of our control? Or is there evidence that evil exists as a malign and conscious influence that uses tyrants, killers and criminals as its agents? To some people, like Lewis Spence, Nazi Germany was the personification of Faust, selling its soul to Satan for temporal power. He did not believe that Nazism started out as a hive of Satanists, but he believed the regime was infiltrated by them so that it could become their instrument for chaos and destruction.

Spence and his occultist colleagues were not the only ones to think so. Many others expressed the belief that Germany was in league with the Devil, so to speak. The most vociferous critics of the Nazi regime repeatedly spoke in apocalyptic terms. The exiled Queen Wilhelmina of Holland described the war as being "between God and conscience and the forces of Darkness," while Cardinal Hinsley, Archbishop of Westminster, told his congregation, "You are on the side of the angels in the struggle against the pride of rebellious Lucifer." The Anglican Bishop of Ipswich, Dr. W.G. Whittingham, was equally convinced of the righteousness of the Allied cause and the nature of the threat posed by their enemies, "We are not fighting flesh and blood, but the Devil, in the persons of Hitler and his gang."

Were such warnings merely rhetoric? Many didn't believe so. People living under Nazi occupation were sincere in their belief that they were resisting evil incarnate. It was only later, when they learned of the true scale of the Nazi atrocities, that they realized the terrible truth – that human beings were capable of truly evil acts even without the urging of external influences. Many of the concentration camp commanders and bureaucrats who ordered the Jews to be transported to Auschwitz and Dachau lacked the imagination to realize the terrible consequences of their actions. Others simply didn't care, being devoid of all conscience and compassion. A few even believed that they were acting for the greater good. This indifference to the suffering of others gave rise to what became known as the "banality of evil," and explains the otherwise incomprehensible actions of serial killers today, just as it did the actions of those who took part in the genocide carried out by the Nazis.

Was that all there was to it? Were the stories of Hitler and the Nazis being "black magicians" and invoking dark forces merely tales spread by occultists and religious leaders? Was it a case of Nazis stooges simply "following orders" and allowing evil deeds to occur on their watch? Or was there more to it than that? Did Hitler truly invoke the forces of black magic to carry out his plans for worldwide domination? Those who believe this to be the case would ask you to judge for yourself.

To the uninitiated, the Nuremberg Rallies of the 1920s and 1930s represented a celebration of German nationalism, an adoration of the Fuhrer, and an impressive display of military might. But they were much more than just elaborately staged spectacles. They were a "triumph of the will," to borrow the title of Leni Riefenstahl's film that documented the 1934 Nazi party rally – and according to some, they were also an invocation to Mars, the pagan god of war.

Hitler may have been a poorly educated Bohemian, driven by the basest human instincts, but he instinctively knew how to manipulate the masses into a mindless mob. He was also shrewd enough to understand that the power of his personality was not enough to induce even his most fervent followers to swear undying allegiance to their flag, their Fuhrer or the Fatherland. He needed to involve them in a formalized ritual so that their fate would be connected to his – no matter the outcome.

This was, many occultists still believe, the true purpose of the Nuremberg Rallies. They acted as an insidious form of magic ritual, a perversion of both the Catholic sacrament and a pagan consecration of the weapons with which Nazi Germany would wage war, with Hitler as the High Priest and his inner circle in the role of acolytes. It was not necessary for the participants to be aware of the part they were playing. They were simply swept along on a tide of heightening emotion expertly stage-managed by Hitler's architect, Albert Speer, who understood the power of making every person in the crowd feel like they were participating in a heroic pageant, and had become a part of something greater than themselves. All of the elements for invoking the dark side of the psyche were harnessed by Speer to focus the ranks of Hitler's followers on a single purpose: the awakening of the collective will.

The stadium formed a magic circle from which non-believers were excluded. Within this space, the crowds were whipped up into ecstasy by ritual drumming, blaring fanfares, colorful banners and the sight of the massed ranks of black-shirted SS troops and brown-shirted SA storm troopers, all marching in automated precision. This was designed to impress upon the onlookers the idea that they were privileged to be allowed to participate, that they were initiates of a special order and were invincible as long as they stayed loyal. The basic need to confirm was ruthlessly exploited with each section offered their own uniforms, awards, ritual ceremonies and insignia, down to the League of German Girls and the Hitler Youth.

As the crowds waited in the sunlight, music by Wagner was played to evoke "racial memories" of Nordic heroes and the mythical traditional of Aryan supremacy, after which stirring marches boasted of military victory yet to come. Banners of red, white and black – the traditional colors of war, terror and death – fluttered overhead. The late arrival of the Fuhrer was designed for maximum impact, his appearance triggering a release of tension and idol worship normally reserved for the world's greatest celebrities. Overlooking the ceremony stood the high priests of the black order, Hitler's inner circle. This hierarchy was designed to give the illusion of order and of unity. In truth, Hitler's acolytes were a self-serving rabble who would have turned on each other had it not been for the overbearing personality of Hitler – and the threat of death, ruin and shame that would follow if they failed the regime.

As darkness descended over the stadium, two hundred searchlights were aimed at the sky to form what Speer called a "Cathedral of Light." His words were well chosen, for his purpose had clearly been to create the illusion of a magic temple. It only lacked the climatic act, a blood sacrifice, to seal the pact with the dark forces that had been invoked. In its place, Hitler consecrated the flags of new SS battalions by bringing them together with the sacred "blood banner" that had been carried in the failed Munich Putsch of 1923, and which was stained with the blood of Nazi martyrs. It wasn't quite what the Devil demanded as his due, but there would be time enough for blood sacrifices in the years to come that would be undreamed-of by even the Nazi's most bloodthirsty forebears.

Finally, though, we have to ask one more question – was Hitler's evil anything so grand, was it truly his intent to call down the forces of darkness to aid the Nazis in their quest to conquer the world. No one can say, for while Hitler and his minions certainly bore similarities to the black magicians of this chapter, it's not clear that they were truly active disciples of the Devil. But then, of course, neither were many of the others documented in these pages. Just because Hitler and his minions were not practitioners of black magic, they did indulge their basest instincts and satiated their sadistic appetites to the detriment of their higher selves. What these men did was to become the very definition of evil. They suppressed their own humanity and refused to see it in their victims. Moreover, they corrupted others, some by force, some by simply sanctioning their acts of brutality on fellow countrymen who were deemed unworthy of the right to life. Some of the worst excesses of the Nazi era were carried out by ordinary people who were encouraged to allow their spite and vindictiveness to run wild, free of threat of reprisal or the prospect of being held accountable for their actions. This was possible because both the perpetrators of these crimes and their Nazi masters considered themselves to be beyond good and evil.

In short, the Nazi regime was capable of unleashing the torments of Hell without assistance from supernatural forces. But that does not meant that such forces were not at work in the world at that time, only in a form that we might not understand or recognize as demonic.

The aim of ceremonial magic is the focusing of the magician's will to bring about change in consciousness or effect a change in the environment. The Nazis were practitioners of magic in its truest and purest sense, but whether or not they did this consciously is unknown. But perhaps because they were unaware of what they were doing or of the nature of the forces they unleashed, they were unable to control it. Eventually, they were consumed by the dark forces they invoked.

Esoteric doctrine states that every individual has the opportunity to make their own Heaven or Hell on Earth. Hitler chose the latter and in so doing, proved to the world that evil can be created by man, and those who succumb to it are doomed to failure.

4. DEMONS AMONG US

POSSESSION, HORROR AND THE WORKS OF SATAN'S MINIONS

The demons among us have many names.

Traditionally, the term for a spirit that interferes with the affairs of human was known by a term derived from the Greek word *daimone*, which meant "replete with wisdom." These spirits were originally both good and evil, but in time demons began to be considered more troublesome than helpful. In the history of the early Church, demons gained a reputation for serving Satan, and were often designated as the rebellious angels that fell with him to Earth after he was cast out of Heaven. They were said to be servants of the Devil, and their sole purpose was the subverting of souls.

But even before the Church emerged as a powerful religious force in the early centuries A.D., demons were among us. They were universally considered to be the cause of all mankind's problems: disease, misfortune, poor health, bad luck, ruined relationships and even death. Since ancient times, demons have had sex with some humans, tormented others, and were controlled by the magicians among us after being summoned in arcane rituals. The people of old had numerous ways to protect themselves against demons, and to banish them from people, places and animals.

The lore of the ancient Babylonians, Assyrians and other Middle Eastern cultures teemed with demons. The greatest demonic problem seemed to be illness, and demons had to be cast out of a person in order to heal them. In Mesopotamian lore, demons took the form of human-like animals that were controlled by the gods.

For the ancient Jews, their stories of demons evolved with influences from the lore of the Babylonians, Persians and Egyptians. In Talmudic tradition, demons were always-present entities that posed constant dangers to humanity. They were created by God on the first Sabbath eve at twilight. Dusk fell before he finished them, so they had no bodies. According to another story, they were spawned by Lilith, the first wife of Adam. She demanded equality with Adam, and when she did not receive it, she left him in anger. King Solomon was said to have used magic to summon and control demons, which, under his command, built the great temple at Jerusalem.

The Jewish "middle world" was filled with scores of demons and angels. Demons were said to be less powerful than angels, and frequented uninhabited and unclean places. By the second century, the Hebrews had developed complex systems of both angels and demons. Rabbinical teachings frowned on demon magic, but beliefs and practices concerning demons were tolerated. Specific demons were identified with every kind of

calamity known to man, and Jewish writings dealt with various types of magic and causes for bad luck and terrible events.

Other writings that following – including the fifteen or so Apocryphal books – have more to say about angels and demons than do the canonical works of the Bible. The Apocrypha (or "hidden") consists of a number of books or portions of books that were written between about 200 B.C. and 200 A.D. For whatever reason, they were not included in the standard books of the Bible. Demons have minor roles in most of these books, with the exception of the Book of Tobit, in which a young man named Tobias is instructed on how to cast out demons by the archangel Raphael, disguised as a man.

More information about demons is given in other religious works of the same period, like the books of Jubilees and Enoch. According to Jubilees, evil originated with bad angels, not with Adam and Eve. Angels were created by God on the first day, according to the book, and while it does not say when demons followed, it implies that it was later on the same day, "along with all of the spirits of his creatures which are in Heaven and on earth."

Angels are described only by their classes and duties. One class was the "Watchers," good angels who were assigned the task of watching over humanity. Unfortunately, though, the Watchers began to lust after human women. They descended to Earth and their offspring became the cannibalistic "Nephilim." God sent a great flood to cleanse the planet, but not all of the Nephilim were destroyed. When the demonic figures began to bother Noah and his sons, Noah appealed to God, who agreed to send angels to bind them all into the place of judgment. Mastema, the prince of evil and the only demon to be named in Jubilees, stepped forward and asked God to allow one-tenth of the demons to remain on Earth under his jurisdiction. The angels then taught Noah the lore he needed to restrain the remaining demons.

The three books of Enoch also tell the story of the Watchers and the Nephilim, in more detail. Again, evil came into being with the fall of the angels.

In Christianity, demons had their origins in the fallen angels who allied themselves with Lucifer and were cast out of Heaven by God. By the end of the New Testament period, demons were synonymous with fallen angels, and were under the direction of the Devil. Demons gained a major role in the development of the early Church.

From its beginnings, Christianity was beset with contention and violence arising within and outside of the faith. The world at large was not stunned by the story of Jesus, or its shocking climax. Very few people outside of Jerusalem even heard about it. His disciples were simple men, with limited skills and intelligence, and they were not equipped to spread the message to the world. It was nearly twenty years after Jesus was killed before a powerful, eloquent man called Paul of Tarsus gave voice to the movement. He was an intellectual, long familiar with Grecian theology and the ancient Jewish teachings. He had never met any of Christ's early disciples, and although skeptical at first, he created a theological system and a doctrine of belief on which the Church was founded.

It seems unlikely that the followers of the pagan gods were disturbed by the arrival of a strange new sect that had come from the old Hebrew legends. However, to the authorities, the new church had a revolutionary air about it. The real cause of the persecution of the early Christians was not their belief in Christ's existence, but their refusal to acknowledge either the pagan gods or the divinity of Caesar. The emperor, his patience exhausted, issued an edict with an aim to have them exterminated. The Christian churches were to be razed, their holy writings destroyed, assembly for worship became punishable by death, and the followers lost all of their rights under the law. Tortures and executions followed, much to the approval of the general public.

But the policy didn't work. In fact, the persecution of the Christians unified them, and their numbers began to grow. Two decades later, the Emperor Constantine turned the now disturbingly large movement into a national asset by granting the Christians complete religious freedom. It was from perhaps this moment that the spirit that marked the Christians' defiance of an outside enemy turned inward, becoming a series of fierce theological dissensions that often threatened to tear the Church apart.

Nevertheless, the Church survived and lived on while the Roman Empire crumbled under the Goths and the Vandals. When the "Holy Roman Empire" rose again, it faced a new enemy that had been created by Mohammed, stretching eastward along the entire North African shore to the Holy Land and beyond, where men prayed five times each day to the One and Only God of Islam. The Crusades against this new threat began with an enthusiasm that suggested that Christianity had regained its defiant soul, but after two centuries, the effort ended in failure and disillusionment. The Church was now lost in the moral vacancy of its leaders. However, it held its position of power, for within the kingdoms of Christendom, it had become a state within a state, with its own legal system and prisons, and with the Pope as the supreme law-giver of the Christian world.

Money was always needed, and it was the duty of the lowly priests who were closer to the parishioners to find it. Any success that they had was probably due as much to their own devotion as to the brew of truth, garbled theology and superstition that was now being served by the Church. Even the poor were forced to provide funds in any way they could. If they refused, this was seen as a statement of disbelief, which might be followed by an accusation of heresy – a crime punishable by torture, or even death.

In the beginning, charges of heresy were only made against professed Christians who committed "religious error," but that began to change. When a person was accused of being a heretic, he was first excommunicated and then handed over for execution. His worldly goods were confiscated by the Church, a rule that became an important source of revenue. By the fourteenth century, "religious error" was not the only thing that could earn a charge of heresy. By that time, witchcraft was deemed to be the work of heretics, as well.

The Church was now seeking its victims among the humble people whose magic worked through rites and charms intended to cajole the old nature spirits into actions that were either favorable to the supplicant or unfavorable to someone else. There were, of course, many signs to detect a witch, from a skin blemish to the

166

A possessed woman sees the face of a demon in the mirror.

sickness of a neighbor's cow, but one of the most popular accusations in those sex-obsessed times related to sexual intercourse with the Devil or one of his minions – the incubi or succubi. Such beings were part of the demonology of Christianity and were accepted without question by all but a few practical folks, who doubted whether devils, who had no actual substance, could achieve a sexual act with someone of flesh and blood.

Church officials worked quickly to ensure that having sex with a demon was truly a punishable act. To do this, they called upon the most learned theologians of the day. The most eminent of these, Thomas Aquinas, was quite specific on the matter, making it clear that human sexual intercourse with devils was not only possible but could result in pregnancy. The objection that devils had no seed was met with a convoluted explanation. A human male might copulate with a female demon, who having received his seed, would change into a male so that it could have sex with a woman and impregnate her. Aquinas also provided a simpler explanation stating, "Because the incubus demon is able to steal the semen of an innocent youth in nocturnal emissions and pour it into the womb of a woman, she is able to conceive an offspring whose father is not the demon incubus but the man whose semen impregnated her. Therefore, it seems that a man is able without a miracle to be at one and the same time both a virgin and a father." He also noted that a man, equally unknowingly but less innocently, could also provide a demon with semen through the act of masturbation.

A torrent of demonological literature appeared during the course of the next few centuries, but it was Thomas Aquinas' conception of man's sexual association with demons that laid the foundation for the witchcraft mania that followed – and provided a powerful influence on the thinking of the Church during the next five centuries.

Aquinas did not invent the concept of a sex demon. Great thinkers from several faiths had been pondering their existence long before the creatures began conveniently ravishing the women that the Church accused of being witches. Even the mere concept of a sex demon was a perplexing problem for theologians. That God had created them directly was an unattractive idea, although it was one that was occasionally presented. However, it seemed more palatable to believe that while God might have created these monsters, they had become evil of their own free will.

In the early years of the Christian Church, theologians combined the legends of ancient times and created their own theology from it concerning sex demons. Justin Martyr declared that angels copulated with women and hence, demons were born into the world. These demons then introduced evil into the minds of men, including lust, murder, war, and the entire gamut of man's vices. The early Christians also decided that the ranks of demons included all of the gods of antiquity, especially those of the Greeks and Romans. A few variations on this idea appeared, including that some of the offspring between the angels and human women became the "giants" mentioned in biblical writings. In this part of the story, however, the giants could not be admitted to Heaven and were forced to wander the Earth, eventually being worshipped as the gods of the pagans.

A 1890s French postcard depicting a satirical look at sex with demons

While stories of people having sex with demons have been around for centuries, when most of us today think of demons, and the evil that they do, the idea of "possession" is usually the first thing that comes to mind. It's been portrayed in books for centuries, and has become commonplace in films and on television over the last several decades. Most people are aware of what happens when someone is demonically possessed: Heads spin around, furniture and people levitate, pea soup is vomited all over the room, along with all sorts of other scary and nasty stuff. But is any of this real, or are they only legends created years ago from the minds of Church officials, novelists and screenwriters? Do people really become possessed?

The state of "possession" had been defined as the presence of a spirit entity that occupies and controls the physical body of the subject. Belief in this phenomenon has long existed in most countries of the world. In the Christian religion it was once regarded as the exclusive domain of demons acting in the interest of Satan. This belief comes from a number of references in the Bible, including a passage from Mark that states: "In my name shall they cast out devils;" from Luke that reads: "Then he called his twelve disciples together and gave them power and authority over all devils," and also from Luke: "And the seventy returned again with joy, saying Lord, even the devils are subject unto us through Thy name." There is also the story of when Jesus confronts a man who is possessed by so many demons that they call themselves "Legion." He exorcizes the spirits and banishes them into a herd of pigs, which commit mass suicide by throwing themselves off a cliff. Thanks to references such as these, demonic possession remains a tenet of the Catholic Church, as well as fundamentalist sects.

But possession, as such, has many faces. The symptoms can include agonized convulsions, often with writhing and twisting, the mouthing of obscenities, vomiting, reports of poltergeist-like happenings, terrible violence and even a state of unnatural calm. No unanimous opinion exists today as to the cause, or causes, of possession and the subject has involved such varied disciplines as religion, medicine, psychiatry, spiritualism and demonology. As in most cases of possible supernatural activity, the possibility of fraud cannot be

Illustrations from Dr. Richter's work, depicting the throes of hysterics -- which might be mistaken for possession.

overlooked. Many cases of possession that were once thought to be genuine have later been questioned or disproved. However, it is clear that in many cases, the symptoms, sometimes of deep distress or of mental and even physical torment, are genuine, no matter how controversial the cause. This does not dismiss the possibility that the symptoms may be the result of suggestion, either external or self-induced, and that victims may be better served by a psychiatrist rather than an exorcist.

As far as most physicians and mental health specialists are concerned, the diagnosis of demonic possession is one that reeks of medieval superstition and ignorance. The symptoms, they believe, are subject to either a wide range of medical and psychiatric interpretations or can be dismissed as misperceptions and hallucinations. They feel that the cases of possession in the past were nothing more than conditions like epilepsy, hysteria, or what has been referred to as multiple personality disorder.

During a convulsive seizure, a person with epilepsy can experience extreme muscular rigidity, foaming at the mouth, and rapid back-and-forth head movements. His face may be distorted and he may produce strange, guttural noises that are caused by a spasm of the throat muscles. During the period just before a seizure, the patient may experience hallucinations, seeing things that aren't really there, and hearing weird sounds and voices.

These are all things that are sometimes attributed to people who are thought to be possessed, but there are also distinguishing characteristics of the "real thing." The first of these is that a demonic attack may last for hours at a time, as opposed to the five minutes or so that an epileptic seizure usually lasts. Extreme movements, rather than rigidity, are more characteristic of a possessed person, and muscular reflexes tend to be strong. According to Church records, other signs of a possession include "the ability to speak with some familiarity in a strange tongue or to understand it when spoken by another; the faculty of divulging future and hidden events; and the display of powers which are beyond the subject's age and natural condition."

A condition called hysteria also produces many of the symptoms of possession. The following description of a female hysteric was recorded in the early 1900s by Professor Paul Richter, a doctor at La Salpetriere, a famous mental hospital in Paris:

Suddenly, we heard loud cries and shouting. Her body, which went through a series of elaborate motions, was either in the throes of wild gyrations or catatonically motionless. Her legs became entangled, then disentangled, her arms twisted and disjointed, her wrists bent. Some of her fingers were stretched out straight, while others were twisted. Her body was either bent in a semi-circle or loose-limbed. Her head was at times thrown to the right or left or, when thrown backward with vehemence, seemed to emerge from a bloated neck. The face alternately mirrored horror, anger and sometimes fury; it was bloated and showed shades of violet in its coloration...

Two of the most striking details in Richter's description are that of the woman's entangling and disentangling legs and that of her body "bent in a semi-circle." The description of what is referred to as the "hysterical arch" appears in some texts describing characteristics frequently seen in cases of possession. All of the other symptoms described above have been observed by exorcists over the years. In addition, the appearance of livid marks on the skin – sometimes resembling bites, symbols or even letters – is also known to be produced by hysterics.

Given this partial duplication of symptoms, how does the Church distinguish between hysteria and genuine cases of possession? The determining factor is the context in which they occur. If the symptoms come about at the same time as an aversion to religious objects, and if they are accompanied by paranormal phenomena (the ability to detect religious items that have been hidden, understand languages that the subject never learned, levitations, and so on), the Church is much more likely to consider the symptoms to be manifestations of possession.

As mysterious as hysteria, and as likely to be confused with possession, is multiple personality disorder, in which a person can manifest several different personalities. Each personality may have its own likes, dislikes, and speech patterns, and may be opposed to the others or indifferent of them. If one, or more, of them seems diabolical in nature, it's possible that the disorder could be mistaken for possession. It should be noted, however, that true cases of multiple personality disorder are extremely rare. They are usually connected to repressed memories of traumatic events, such as sexual molestation, and often emerge to protect the victim from facing what happened. For this reason, labeling cases of possible possession as multiple personality disorder can be problematic at best.

Even so, doctors are usually violently opposed to even considering the idea of demonic possession when a medical or psychiatric disorder might explain the symptoms being exhibited by a patient. With only a hatred of religious objects and instances of paranormal phenomena (which most of them do not believe in anyway) standing as the criteria for a case to be considered to be one of possession rather than hysteria, most doctors and psychiatrists are likely to reject these incidents as misperceptions and hallucinations on the part of the witness. A few, less skeptical medical professionals might concede that something strange appears to be going on, but they will probably steer toward parapsychology rather than possession.

In cases where objects are reported to move about without anyone touching them, many will point toward poltergeist phenomena rather than the work of demonic spirits. The word "poltergeist" is German for "noisy ghost, and for many years, researchers believed that boisterous ghosts were causing the phenomena reported in haunted house cases of a violent and destructive nature. The variety of activity connected with such cases can include knocking and pounding sounds, doors slamming, and violent, physical actions by sometimes heavy objects. Despite what some believe, many cases like this have nothing to do with ghosts --- or with demons either.

The most widely accepted theory in many "poltergeist-like" cases is that the activity is not caused by a ghost, but by a person in the household. This person is usually (but not always) an adolescent girl, and normally one who is troubled emotionally. It is thought that she is unconsciously manipulating the items in the house by "psychokinesis," the power to move objects using energy generated in the mind. It is unknown why this rare ability seems to appear in some females around the age of puberty but it has been documented. Most of these disturbances are short-lived because the conditions that cause them often pass quickly. The living person or "agent" subconsciously vents her repressed anger or frustration in ways that science has yet to explain. An unhappy or emotionally disturbed young person might exhibit symptoms of this type, which match some of the criteria of a possession but again, is something else entirely.

As the reader has undoubtedly discovered by now, modern science is quick to try and explain away the idea of spiritual or demonic possession. There are many possible explanations as to why a person cannot be possessed and yet, the explanations fail to account for all of the symptoms that a possessed person is alleged to

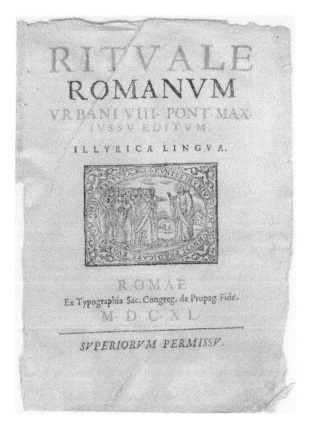

exhibit. Does this mean that possession can be real – or is it simply that science has not yet found a reason as to why some so-called "possessions" defy explanation?

One thing is certain, whether possession exists or not, there are people all over the world who believe that it does – and they have whole-heartedly believed this for centuries. The belief in possession dates back to the years of the early Catholic Church but it gained prominence due to a number of famous cases during the Middle Ages. Instances of nuns possessed by satanic influences affected convents in France, Italy, Spain, Germany and elsewhere. Commonly beginning with a single nun, the possession proved to be highly contagious, and whole groups became involved. Coinciding with the relentless years of the Spanish Inquisition, the cases often had tragic consequences for anyone who might be accused of causing a person to become possessed. Usually the victims themselves were not considered to be responsible for what had occurred to them, and their treatment was confined to the expulsion of the demons by exorcism. The exorcists, who formed one of the minor orders of the Church, were priests who specialized in the work using methods that had been outlined in the *Rituale Romanum*.

The *Rituale Romanum*, which is still used in the Catholic Church today, was issued in 1614 at the behest of Pope Paul V. It was designed to formalize practices that had developed during the early days of the Christian Church, and it placed special emphasis on identifying diabolical possession, selection of the exorcist, and defining the setting and texts to be used during an exorcism ritual. The ritual has retained its central features over the past centuries, although recent revisions were made in 1952 and 1999. Today, the text is initially designed to establish the actual presence of demonic possession. For this, it specifies:

First of all, one should not easily assume that someone is possessed by a demon unless he shows signs that distinguish the possessed person from those who suffer from melancholy [mental illness] or some [physical] disease. The signs indicating the presence of a possessed person are as follows: speaking in an unknown tongue or understanding someone who speaks in a language unknown to the person; revelation of distant and unknown matters; manifestation of powers beyond one's natural age and condition; as well as other such matters, all of which, when taken together, compound such indications.

However, as noted by Monsignor Carlo Balducci in 1959, parapsychology widened the possibility of natural phenomena (such as psychokinesis and precognition) being interpreted as demonic in origin. Combine that with mental illness and some types of medical conditions and it becomes much harder to determine if a possession is genuine. For this reason, the exorcist's first task was to confirm that the victim was indeed possessed by a Christian devil, who existed only by the permission of God. In that way, the demon was subject to the authority of the priest. Numerous manuals covered not only the discovery and expulsion of demons from

171

humans and animals but many techniques for countering demonic offenses, both small and large. There was, it was believed in the past, scarcely any evil that a demon was not capable of, from the drying up of the milk of cows to the more serious grievance of inhibiting the sexual intercourse of married couples.

Once a satanic origin was established, the exorcist's next problem was to find the manner of the demon's entry into the possessed, which might be due to the demon's own initiative, invitation by the possessed person or, as believed in past centuries, by the incantations of a witch. The latter was usually preferred because it meant an easier expulsion and when the witch was discovered, she could be tried, hanged or burned. The most difficult process of discovery involved situations when there seemed to be no clear reason for the victim to become possessed. In many historic cases, pious and religious people were often reportedly possessed by demons. In these cases, it was often believed that the possessions occurred as a test of the victim's faith or that of the exorcist himself.

From the records, it is clear that an exorcism had the nature of a contest between the exorcist -- armed with the authority of God and the Church -- and the demonic intruder. An exorcist could fail, he could even be destroyed if the battle went against him. The fact that several exorcists died prematurely – and several went insane – seems to lend credence to the horror of the exorcism itself. The prayers, adjurations and commands of the exorcist, along with the ritual acts prescribed, were in themselves dramatic, and when they provoked, as they were intended to do, a dialogue between the exorcist and the demon, they could be overwhelming and fantastic. For it was here that the drama of the confrontation reached its height as the demon's bestial voice belched out its obscenities while the priest answered with commands and prayers.

While we think of an exorcism as "driving out" the demon, it is really more of a case of forcing the demon to make a binding agreement. In some instances, there may be more than one demon possessing a person. The word "exorcism" is derived from the Greek "*ek*" with the verb "*horkizo*," which means "I cause [someone] to swear" and refers to "putting the spirit or demon on oath." To put it simply, it means invoking a higher authority to bind the entity in order to control it and command it to act contrary to its own will. In the Christian sense, this higher authority is Jesus Christ, based on the belief that demons and evil spirits fear Christ. This belief hearkens back to the story mentioned earlier when Jesus cast out a legion of devils from an afflicted man. Not only did Christ exorcize demons and unclean spirits but he gave the power to his disciples as well. "...He gave the power against unclean spirits, to cast them out, and to heal all manners of sickness, and all manner of disease." (Book of Matthew)

Thanks to passages in the Bible that mention the expulsion of demons, Catholics and Protestants alike believe they have the power to cast out devils and to heal the sick. The Catholic Church uses the *Rituale Romanum* as an outline for exorcisms but the ritual may vary as determined by the exorcist performing the expulsion. The code of Canon Law allows authorized ministers (exorcists) to perform solemn exorcisms over not only the faithful but also over non-Catholics, and those who have been excommunicated from the church.

The greatest danger to the exorcist during the ritual is becoming possessed by the demon himself. This is the reason why the exorcist must be as free from sin as possible, and to feel no secret need for punishment. Many priests will fast and pray for some time before taking part in the ritual. During a prolonged exorcism, while they continue to fast, some will report extreme weight loss. Only a priest who is convinced that he is right with God can be safe during an exorcism. Otherwise, the demon can easily entrap him.

The *Rituale Romanum* has its own special qualifications for the priest who served as an exorcist. He has to lead a genuinely religious and virtuous life; must adhere to the rules and regulations governing exorcism as defined by the Bishop of his diocese; must have a profound knowledge of the theory and practice of exorcism, and has to make sure that the location and manner of exorcism is selected in accordance with faith and human dignity. In other words, there could be no undignified behavior during the exorcism, no idle talk with the entity, and no questioning of the demon about occult or future events.

The solemn "Great Exorcism Rite" in the *Rituale Romanum* covers twenty-three printed pages. During the ritual, a number of items are usually present, including salt, which represents purity, and wine, representing the blood of Christ. The victim will be asked to hold a crucifix during the rite, and the exorcist may also use holy water, religious medals, rosaries and relics, which may be physical items that were once a part of a saint (like a splinter of bone) or objects touched or blessed by saints. The reading of the ritual begins with a series of prayers, psalm readings, and an initial command for the unclean spirit. Next, biblical passages concerning possession are read. The priest's stole and his right hand are placed on the possessed person and the specific words of exorcism are spoken. Interspersed by the sign of the cross, made on the possessed person's forehead and chest, the two exorcism passages are as follows:

I exorcise thee, most evil spirit, direct embodiment of our enemy, the entire entity and its whole legion, in the name of Jesus Christ, to go hence and escape from this creature of God. He, himself, commands thee, who is master from the heights of heaven to the depth of the earth. He who commands the sea, the winds and the tempests, now commands thee.

Listen, then, be filled with fear. O Satan, enemy of the Faith, enemy of the human race, who creates death and steals life, who destroys justice and is at the root of evil, who stimulates vice, tempts men, betrays nations, originated envy and greed, causes discord and brings suffering. Why dost thou remain and resist, when thou knowest that Christ the Lord will destroy thy strength? Fear him who was sacrificed in Isaac, sold in Joseph, and slaughtered in the Lamb, crucified in man, and yet is triumphant over Hell.

Depart, therefore, in the name of the Father and the Son and the Holy Ghost. Make way for the Holy Ghost, by the sign of the cross of Jesus Christ, our Lord, who with the Father and the Holy Ghost lives and reigns, one God, forever and ever, world without end.

The second exorcism is as follows:

I adjure thee, thou old serpent, by the judge of the quick and the dead, by thy maker and the maker of the world, by him who has power to send thee to Hell, that thou depart quickly from this servant of God [name of the possessed individual], who returns to the bosom of the Church, with fear and the affliction of thy terror. I adjure thee again, not in my own infirmity, but by the virtue of the Holy Ghost, that thou depart from this servant of God [name again], whom Almighty God hath made in his own image.

Yield, therefore; yield not to me but to the Ministry of Christ. For his power compels thee, he who subjugated thee to his cross. Tremble at his arms, he who led the souls to light after the lamentations of Hell had been subdued. May the body of man be a terror to thee, let the image of God be terrible to thee. Resist not, neither delay to flee this man [woman], since it has pleased Christ to dwell in his [her] body. And although thou knowest me to be a sinner, do not think me contemptible.

For it is God who commands thee.
The majesty of Christ commands thee.
God the Father commands thee.
God the Son commands thee.
God the Holy Ghost commands thee.
The sacred cross commands thee.
The faith of the holy apostles Peter and Paul, and of all other saints, commands thee.

The exorcism cannot be expected to be achieved as the result of one rite, outlined in the *Rituale Romanum*, or without delays, frustrations and problems. When such a struggle occurs, the exorcist is advised to add a variety of prayers and readings from the Psalms. A "Prayer Following Liberation" may be said when complete success has been achieved. As mentioned earlier, the use of holy water, the laying on of hands and the placing of the priest's stole on the possessed person may also become part of the ceremony.

Exorcisms were always considered dangerous, dating back to the days of the early Church. According to the story from the Book of Acts, several "itinerant Jewish exorcists" began trying to expel demons from the afflicted, and their ritual included a phrase that cast out the demons "in the name of Jesus, whom Paul preaches, I command you to come out." During one such attempt, the evil spirit turned on the men and demanded of them, "Jesus, I know, and I know about Paul, but who are you?" The possessed man then turned and attacked them like a wild animal. He beat the men mercilessly and stripped them of their clothing, before throwing them into the street, naked and bleeding.

Exorcisms were never to be entered into lightly, but for several centuries during the Middle Ages, they became commonplace, for Satan seemed to be everywhere in those days.

EXORCISM IN THE MIDDLE AGES

Possessions and exorcisms were a part of Church theology from the very beginning. However, it would not be until the Middle Ages that demons began randomly possessing people on a grand scale, or so it was believed at the time. Exorcists who gained a reputation for success were in steady demand. Their first task in every case was to make sure that the possessed person was, in fact, a victim of a Christian devil and a minion of Satan. In that way, they were subject to the conjurations of a Christian priest, since a pagan demon could scarcely be expected to obey. Once satanic origin was established, the exorcist's next problem was to determine the manner of the demon's entry into the possessed, which might be due to its own initiative or the incantations of a witch. The latter was preferred because it was usually much simpler to drive the demon out and a witch to be identified, tried and burned.

Since the names of demons in Christian theology were widely known (there were about 6,000 of them listed!), they could sometimes be identified by the ravings of the afflicted and could be addressed by name. Questions that could only be answered by the demon – like how many demons were present and how long they planned to stay – were asked. As mentioned, an exorcism was a contest between the exorcist and the demon and if the priest failed, it could mean insanity or perhaps even death. The official prayers, adjurations and commands of the exorcist were dramatic and when they provoked, as they were meant to do, a dialogue between the exorcist and the demon, they could be sensational. Stories and legends surrounded the many exorcisms that were occurring, and never before the epidemic of possessions in the sixteenth and seventeenth centuries were the demons of the Church so well exposed to the public. Their names and individual characters, crimes, and vices became familiar to the most common and uneducated of people.

In the early days of the Church, exorcisms often consisted of nothing more than punching a possession victim in the nose, thus dispelling the demon. Unfortunately, though, possessing demons became much harder to handle by the Middle Ages and their victims became much more tragic – and much more public.

THE DEVIL IN THE CONVENT

During the Middle Ages, demons seemed drawn to convents and monasteries across Europe. Nuns and monks began to be possessed, causing them to act in ways that were completely the opposite of their normal behavior. All manner of sexual escapades began to be blamed on demons as the holy sisters discovered strange and unusual fires burning in their bellies while seductive voices whispered in their heads, exhorting them to uninhibited erotic acts. During the seventeenth century, epidemics of possession swept through the convents of France with dramatic outbreaks that have become the stuff of legend today.

In 1609, the first signs of a demonic infestation came to light at the Ursuline convent of Aix-en-Provence and involved a young woman, Sister Madeleine de Demandolx de la Palud. Only one other girl was actually claimed to be possessed but the contagion spread to other convents later and the consequences of Madeleine's possession were tragic.

An illustration of a possessed nun by
Felicien Rops

Madeleine was born into a wealthy family, and was always said to have religious inclinations. Perhaps for this reason, at the age of 12 she was sent to live in a small convent of six nuns at Aix, which was a sister establishment to one of the Ursuline order in Marseilles. Life there was apparently uncomfortable for a girl from a fine household, and after two years, she returned to her family in Marseilles. She was bored and depressed when she returned home but her personality began to change after she met Father Louis Gaufridi, a local parish priest. He began visiting her parents' home and Madeleine was immediately taken with the young, handsome man. And Madeleine was not alone. His lively personality had made him very popular with all of the women in the parish.

There is little doubt that many of the local women were in love with him and not surprisingly, Madeleine followed suit. Before long, rumors began to spread concerning the frequency and the length of the priest's visits to her home, especially when her parents were absent. The rumors came to the attention of the Reverend Mother of the convent in Marseilles, who dropped a hint to Madeleine's mother about the situation and warned Father Gaufridi about his conduct. The priest took heed of the warning and stopped coming to the house. And although Madeleine told her mother that he "had stolen her most beautiful rose," no lasting damage seemed to have been done.

The following year, Madeleine entered the Marseilles convent as a novice. She confessed to the Reverend Mother that certain intimacies had occurred with Father Gaufridi. There were no drastic actions taken, although the girl was transferred to the convent at Aix. Just before Christmas 1609, Madeleine began acting very strangely. She started suffering from cramps, convulsive tremors and fits. She had visions of devils and one day, during confession, she smashed a crucifix. She was believed to be possessed, and Father Jean-Baptiste Romillon, who had founded the convents at Aix and Marseilles, attempted an exorcism. Unfortunately, the ritual failed and three other nuns began to suffer from the same cramps that troubled Madeleine.

Anxious about what could have occurred to cause the girl to become possessed, Father Gaufridi was questioned about his contact with her. Although he denied having any sexual contact with the girl, Madeleine stated that she had, in fact, engaged in intercourse with him, starting at the age of 12. She said that as a precaution to divert suspicion away from him, he had given her a potion so that any baby she might have would not resemble him.

Father Romillon continued the exorcism, and five other nuns became infected by Madeleine's symptoms, although only one of them, Sister Louise Capeau, showed signs of also being possessed. In desperation, Father Romillon took both of the young women to the Grand Inquisitor in Avignon, Father Sebastian Michaelis, an aged and experienced priest who had burned eighteen witches at Avignon in the preceding months. His attempts at an exorcism were as fruitless as those of Romillon had been. Only a Dominican priest named Francois Domptius was able to make any progress toward saving the girls, but his attempt at exorcism was not without its share of drama.

During one ritual, Louise began to speak in a "deep bass voice" that named the various demons that possessed her. Her body was being tormented by three of the vile creatures, but Madeleine, she claimed, was inhabited by a legion of monsters. Madeleine began to blaspheme, "howling and crying with a loud mouth," and at one point, one of the possessing demons revealed that Father Gaufridi was the cause of her possession.

With the possession of the two young women beyond doubt, the Grand Inquisitor summoned the man accused of having caused it, ordering him to attempt an exorcism that would undo the damage. When the nervous priest arrived, he attempted to carry out the order. Unfortunately, he had no experience with exorcisms, and his attempts provoked cries of jeering laughter from the two nuns. His angry response made him appear all the more guilty to Church officials. He was locked in a cell to await trial.

Not only had Madeleine laughed at him, but she also charged him with a list of obscene acts that only devils could possibly accomplish. However, a search of his home in Marseilles produced no evidence of the kind of depravity of which he had been accused. On the contrary, the investigators found only indications of his good character and fine standing among his parishioners. Perhaps reluctantly, he was released and allowed to return to Marseilles. But this was not the end for him –

This painting from 1581 shows a lustful monk preying on a nun under his control. An epidemic of sex-crazed Church officials often to led to reports of "possession" as an excuse for what was going on behind convent walls.

Father Gaufridi wanted vindication. With the help of other clerics, he appealed to the Bishop and the Pope to suppress both of the convents and to have the two nuns placed in prison. In the end, he should have left the situation alone. His appeals led to further investigation. Once again, he was arrested.

While this was taking place, Madeleine began to develop a new assortment of symptoms. She behaved wildly, danced, sang lewd songs, and experienced bizarre erotic and often violent visions. She reportedly "neighed like a horse" and raved of Sabbaths involving sodomy and the eating of small children. She vomited strange objects and would stop anywhere she was standing to deposit unnaturally huge piles of steaming feces on the floor. After these torments, she would lapse into a deep, coma-like sleep.

Father Gaufridi's case went before the civil courts of the parliament of Aix in February 1611. The head judge, Guillame de Vair, was a superstitious man, and was quite ready to accept purely "spiritual evidence" as the basis of the trial. The events at the exorcisms were re-told and during the recital, the two girls experienced seizures and convulsions. Their behavior alternated between anger and penitence, but they were always insolent toward the clerical witnesses. On February 21, Madeleine confessed that her allegations toward Father Gaufridi were false – "all imaginings, illusions and not a word of truth to them." Later in the trial, she spoke raptly of her love for the priest, and then suddenly began to convulse into motions "representing the sexual act with violent movements of the lower part of her belly." While on the witness stand over the course of several days, she contradicted herself repeatedly. It was said that she twice attempted suicide while the trial was going on.

Father Gaufridi was not allowed to testify until March. He was sick and haggard by then, worn down by nearly a year of dealing with the Inquisition. His second arrest had landed him in a damp underground cell, where he was kept heavily chained. After months of torture and abuse, his health was broken. His entire body was shaved, and three "devil's marks" were revealed. At that point, he was ready to confess and sign anything that was placed before him. His confession was a lurid one, claiming that he had signed a pact in his own blood, and that he had gotten promises from the Devil that he could have any woman that he wanted, among other things. He was charged with fifty-two offenses, all of which he admitted – until his health improved. After that he denied everything, stating that his confession had been extorted through torture.

His retraction was, of course, ignored and in April he was found guilty on all charges, which included fornication since a medical examination had revealed that Madeleine was not a virgin. Her claim that he had stolen "her most beautiful rose" may have been one of the only truths that she spoke about the matter.

Father Gaufridi was sentenced to be burned alive in the most terrible way possible, with a pyre made from bushes, rather than wood. This had already proven to burn much slower and cause more torment to the condemned. Meanwhile, he continued to be tortured as the officials tried to learn the names of any accomplices that he might have had. He confessed to taking part in Black Masses (although his "confession" showed a genuine ignorance of what occurred during these rituals) but no matter what the torture inflicted upon him, he swore that he could name no names of fellow Satan-worshippers. The last five hours of his life were spent with him asking forgiveness from God before being taken by cart to the stake. Because of his final confession before God, the Bishop of Marseilles allowed him to be strangled before the pyre at his feet was lit.

On the day after Father Gaufridi was burned, Sister Madeleine was miraculously cured.

Nevertheless, a short time later, she was also accused of witchcraft. A few years later, a second charge was made. This time, she was condemned to life in prison, although her family's influence eventually allowed her to be released into the custody of relatives. She died at the age of 77.

Sister Louise Capeau was never cured. Within a year of Gaufridi's death, she accused a blind girl of witchcraft and helped to have her burned at the stake. After that, she vanished into history.

From about 1628 to 1647, nuns in Louviers alleged themselves to be possessed by demons that were in league with the father confessors of the convent. During that time, the nuns claimed that they had fornicated with black cats that had penises like those of large men. They said they had attended Black Sabbaths and participated in orgies with devils, clerics, and the ghost of the priest who had been their initial seducer. Every crucifix in the convent was supposedly turned upside-down.

According to reports from a trial that gained intense public interest, the priests involved instructed the women on lesbian intercourse, and then watched as they carried out the directions. Nuns wandered about the convent, proudly confessing their sins, were baptized in urine and took communion in the nude. During these ceremonies, a priest would place the communion host on his erect penis and encourage the nuns to place it in their mouths.

Most instances of possession in the convents of the seventeenth century arose from sexual yearnings aroused by a man who was brought by duty or routine into the confines of the cloister. A case that worried Church officials between 1658 and 1663 was different only because of the fact that the accusations of sexual bewitchment were not against some attractive or revered priest but against the mother superior of the Ursuline convent of Auxonne. Barbara Buvee, known as Sister St. Colombe, was the one who aroused, or attempted to arouse, the desires in question. This caused great concern because lesbian tendencies, although less common than heterosexual temptation, could never be ignored. The Church was well aware of how quickly outbreaks of demonic possession could spread, and the matter called for an immediate careful and quiet investigation. It was, in fact, so quiet that it took nearly two years for the scandal to become public, when Barbara Buvee was accused of having bewitched eight nuns.

All of the women testified that they were sexually excited by one of their confessors, the young Father Nouvelet. One of the nuns, Marie Borthon, claimed that she had suffered great temptations of the flesh for him, others had erotic fantasies during menstruation, and all were convinced that only witchcraft could be the cause

177

of their desires. The earnest young priest must have been relieved when he was not named as having contrived the possessions of the nuns, but as a safeguard, found it wise to suggest that he had also been bewitched. Two local women were accused of having cast spells on the priest, although in the absence of any evidence, they were merely sentenced to be banished from the region. Tragically, as they were ushered out of the court they were lynched by a mob that was waiting outside.

Father Nouvelet suggested that an exorcism be attempted on the nuns, and that he should be the one to carry it out. The idea was well received by all, including the nuns, who were documented to display some unusual happenings during the rituals that followed. Records say that, "Sister Denise, with only two fingers, lifted a heavy vase which two strong men could scarcely move, other nuns adored the sacrament by lying on their bellies, heads and arms raised off the ground and their legs bent backward to form an arc." Father Nouvelet initiated his own highly unusual form of exorcism, which involved either lying in bed naked with the women or conducting services during which they struck erotic poses before the altar.

There seemed to be little evidence to incriminate Barbara Buvee in any of this, but more was to come, which would suggest an immoral, but highly complicated, motive. It was said that Buvee had quarreled with Father Nouvelet's predecessor, Father Borthon, whose three sisters were members of the convent. She had been punished for her insubordination toward the priest with floggings and an enforced fast. After Father Nouvelet began his rather unique attempts at exorcism, Sister St. Colombe protested his methods – only to be met with anger by the nuns, who blamed her for their possessions and began making vile accusations against her. On October 26, 1660, Barbara Buvee, as Sister St. Colombe, was formally accused of witchcraft and held in solitary confinement until her trial began on January 5, 1661.

The nuns, including the three Borthon sisters, who had all been possessed of lustful desires for the young confessor priest, gave detailed testimony of Sister St. Colombe's sexual advances toward them. A Sister Henriette stated that Buvee had kissed her passionately and placed her hand on her breast. When Henriette protested, her superior replied that she thought she was kissing a holy statue. Sister Humberte had visions of Hell, in which the Mother Superior had embraced her and "lay down on her like a man on a woman." Sister Charlotte Joly testified that she had witnessed interaction between Buvee and Sister Gabrielle de Malo, including tongue kissing and reciprocal touching beneath their skirts. Sister Francoise Borthon said she had been made to sit across Buvee's lap, and the woman had "put her finger into her private parts just like a man would have done." Another sister said that she had a vision of the Mother Superior holding a sacred host in one hand and an artificial phallus in another, "with which she committed on herself impure acts." She was also said to have introduced the nuns to the pleasure of cunnilingus and masturbated them with her artificial penis. All of this, it was charged, was done with the aid of the Devil, who possessed the nuns, afflicting them with hot and aching vaginas and making them helpless to resist Sister St. Colombe when she wanted to have her way with them.

One of the most curious developments in the case was the way that it was handled by the court. On March 18, 1661, further investigation was ordered into the situation, and in August 1662, all charges were dismissed against Sister St. Colombe. During the months between, further medical and other reports had been obtained. They included fraud, sickness in a few cases, genuine demonic possession in others, but there was a sort of "not proven" verdict in regards to whether or not Sister St. Colombe had done anything to cause the situation.

Another famous possession was that of Angela de Foligny, who became a raging sex addict as a result of being influenced by demons. Later, she claimed to have copulated with Christ, a not uncommon craving for holy women of the time.

But France was not the only country to suffer from convent infestations. Another place that was overwhelmed with demons was the Diocese of Cologne in Germany. There, investigators searching for forbidden works on black magic found a packet of love letters in the belongings of a nun that had been written to an incubus, a demon in male form. Her bizarre appetites spread to the other nuns of the convent and they began reporting having sex with demons that were disguised as handsome young men, and being knocked to the ground by a large black dog that pounced on them and licked their vaginas. When this occurred, the Devil rendered them powerless and unable to stop it.

The nuns of Cologne were not alone. The holy sisters of Nimeguen were victimized by a black dog that raped them in their beds. Similar erotic manias, which included hallucinations of rapes by huge-membered demons, were rampant in the convents of Kentorp and St. Bridget.

It has been rumored that convents were still plagued by waves of erotic mania even in the nineteenth and twentieth centuries, though the epidemics may have taken a different form, and the Church was able to keep the embarrassing incidents quiet.

One of the most recent instances of convent infestation by demons was reported to have occurred in the late nineteenth century. It involved a young woman named Cantianille who had been placed in a convent of Mont Saint-Surplice at Auxerre. At the age of 15, the girl was alleged to have been violated by a local priest, who dedicated her to the Devil. The story added that the priest himself had been corrupted in early childhood by a nun who had belonged to a sect of possessed sisters that had been created on the day King Louis XVI was guillotined. Cantianille's possession caused a frenzy of other possessions in the convent, followed by reports of orgies, lewd behavior, and lesbian encounters. Cantianille was sent away from the convent, where she was exorcized by a priest named Father Thorey, who was apparently "contaminated" by the girl he was trying to assist. As the hysteria at the convent grew worse, the Bishop was forced to intervene. Cantianille was driven out of the country, Father Thorey was disciplined, and the entire affair had to be settled in Rome. The most curious after note to the case was that the Bishop, terrified by what he had seen at the convent, requested to be dismissed from his position soon after. He retired to Fontainebleau, where he died two years later – reportedly still disturbed by what took place behind the convent walls.

The strange affair at Auxerre was perhaps the most recent case of alleged possession involving cloistered nuns and the sexual obsessions of an isolated group of desperate women – but it not would be the most famous to emerge from the annals of the supernatural.

THE DEVILS OF LOUDON

One of the strangest, most notorious, and most terrifying cases of mass possession was the episode that involved Urbain Grandier and the nuns of Loudon in 1634. Few such cases have been more thoroughly documented, both in official records and in contemporary writings, and few have offered such a bizarre look into the minds of the people involved.

The Loudon case centered around one man, a priest named Urbain Grandier. He was born in 1590 and entered the priesthood as a young man. In 1617, he was appointed to the position of parish priest of St. Pierre de Marche in Loudon, France. Grandier was a handsome, cultivated man who, despite his avocation, had an eye for attractive young women. He was a worldly type of priest, which was not uncommon in seventeenth-century France. Unfortunately, he lacked discretion in the conduct of his numerous affairs, and his arrogance made him many enemies. As it would later turn out, many of those enemies eventually found themselves in positions from which they could engineer Grandier's downfall.

In time, Grandier's sexual affairs became so notorious that they attracted attention in high places. Perhaps most shocking was the news that came in 1630 that the priest was not only carrying on a relationship with Madeleine de Brou, one of his young penitents, but was also accused of being the father of an illegitimate child born to Philippa Trincant, daughter of the public prosecutor at Loudon. Grandier was arrested, charged with immorality, and found guilty. Somehow, he managed to persuade Archbishop Sourdis of Bordeaux to allow him to go free and to resume his clerical duties.

Grandier returned to Loudon to find that his enemies had joined forces with a Father Mignon, a priest who filled the post of confessor at a small Ursuline convent in Loudon. Mignon hated Grandier with a passion. Between Mignon and an assortment of Grandier's enemies, a scheme had been hatched to discredit Grandier further by persuading some of the nuns at the convent to say that they were possessed. They would confess during their exorcism that Grandier had bewitched them. The mother superior, Sister Jeanne des Anges, was involved in the conspiracy and she was the first to exhibit signs of demonic possession. Soon, other nuns began to mimic her symptoms. It was not long before a full-scale infestation was under way. The mother superior, along with several of the other sisters, began going into convulsions, acting out in lewd and erotic ways, holding their breath, and distorting their faces and voices. One of the nuns, at the height of the attack, whispered Grandier's name and soon several others began to claim that Grandier was to blame for their possession – they claimed that the demons that tormented them hissed his name into their ears. Sister Jeanne confirmed his guilt and gradually the story grew more elaborate. The motive that was given for Grandier's evil bewitchment was his thwarted ambition, along with a desire to exact revenge on the nuns because Jeanne des Anges was known to oppose his advancement.

Father Urban Grandier

Alarmed at the growing scandal, Archbishop Sourdis stepped in and came to Grandier's rescue again. He sent his personal physician to Loudon who, after examining the nuns, pronounced that they were not possessed. The archbishop forbade Father Mignon to continue with any further exorcisms and these sensible measures put a stop – as if by magic – to the nuns' strange behavior.

Although calm was restored at the convent, the conspiracy against Grandier continued to fester. Thanks to the priest's past behavior and penchant for making enemies, his opponents soon found other ways with which to continue their attack against him. A relative of Sister Jeanne des Anges named Jean de Laubardemont, who was an agent of the crown and a close supporter of Cardinal Richelieu, was sent to Loudon on business. When he arrived, Sister Jeanne apprised him of the situation with Grandier, whom he knew had once written a satire that infuriated the Cardinal. He realized that Grandier's demise could be worked to the advantage of everyone involved. He contacted Richelieu, who planned, for purely political motives, to revive the Inquisition. He wanted to stage great public exorcisms, which would bring fear to the Protestants and clear the way for the revoking of the freedom of religion act that had been recently passed. With Grandier's case, he would instigate a trial at Loudon and at the same time settle a personal score against Grandier, which dated back to the priest's embarrassing satire. He gave orders to de Laubardemont to form a hand-picked commission to arrest – and convict – Grandier.

To gain witnesses to support the original case against Grandier, Laubardemont appointed three priests to begin a public exorcism of the allegedly still-possessed nuns. Under the thrall of Father Surin, a Jesuit; Father Lactance, a Franciscan, and the Capuchin Father Tranquille, the women repeated their demonic accusations of possession, displaying new symptoms of even greater intensity than in the previous attack – the one that had been halted by a medical doctor and common sense. They shouted, screamed, contorted their bodies in hideous

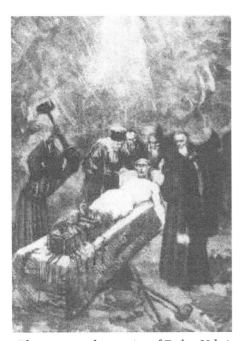

The torture and execution of Father Urbain Grandier. The real proof against him was the pact that he had allegedly signed with the Devil.

positions, masturbated publicly and entered convulsive trances as the exorcisms wore on. Various methods were attempted by the priests, including the use of a large brass enema syringe, which was supposed to flush the more stubborn demons out of the nuns' anuses. Grandier himself was coerced into taking part in the exorcism, since it was alleged that he was the one responsible for the nuns' condition.

Meanwhile, the charges against Grandier continued to pile up. Not only was he charged with causing the nuns to become possessed, but he was also accused of incest, sacrilege and a number of other crimes. Richelieu's agent was able to gather sixty witnesses who would attest to these crimes. But even at this stage, Grandier continued to underestimate the power of those who were working against him. He believed that he had little to fear since the charges that had been brought against him were imaginary. Much to his surprise, he was arrested on November 20, 1633, and thrown into prison in the castle of Angers. Proof of guilt was soon found in the form of a four "devil's marks" on his body, spots that were insensitive to pain.

Grandier went on trial in 1634, but the hearing was fixed against him right from the start. Richelieu had made a calculated choice to have an investigating committee handle the case, instead of a normal secular court. The committee denied Grandier's legal right to appeal to the courts in Paris, leading to a complete travesty of justice. When the bailiff of Loudon led a public protest (Grandier still had some friends left), the movement was quashed by Laubardemont, who portrayed the protest as being critical of the king, and hence an act of treason. All evidence in support of Grandier's innocence was disregarded, and pressure was applied on a number of his defense witnesses to keep silent – or face an accusation of witchcraft. Several of the nuns had a change of heart and attempted to recant their previous accusations, but the court would not allow them to be heard. Jeanne des Anges herself was denied a hearing when it became evident that she wished to refute her earlier statements.

The "real" proof against Grandier was provided in the form of a written pact that the priest had allegedly made with the Devil. The document, hand-signed by Satan, Beelzebub, Leviathan and Astaroth, was seriously presented by the prosecution as having been stolen by the demon Asmodeus from the Devil's own files. When it was displayed in court, the words were shown to be written from right to left, in "mirror writing," following the widely held belief that devils performed most of their actions in reverse to show their hostility towards Christianity.

Judgment was found against Grandier on August 18 and, not surprisingly, he was found to be guilty of magic, *malefica* (attempting to do harm by witchcraft), and causing the nuns to be possessed by demons. Sentence was passed and the priest was to be tortured according to "first and last degrees," which was designed to force him to incriminate others. Then, on the day of his execution, he would be allowed to ask for God's pardon and then would be taken to the public square of St. Croix and burned alive.

Grandier showed great courage and dignity under torture. A writer of the time wrote that his torture was so extreme that marrow actually oozed out of his broken bones. His strength served to infuriate his torturers but he refused to obtain mercy by naming imaginary accomplices. In the end, although he was assured that he would be strangled before being burned, the knot was purposely tied in such a way that it could not be drawn tight enough to put an end to his suffering. Urbain Grandier was burned alive for a crime that he most certainly did not commit.

Even after the scandal has passed, the convent continued to be a tourist attraction of sorts for the town of Loudon. People traveled from all over the country to see the nuns, who continued to claim they were possessed. It seemed that fits of erotic abandonment might come on them at any time – especially when large crowds were at hand. One young nun, Sister Claire, would regularly fall onto her back in front of the spectators, lift her habit to expose her genitals, masturbate frantically with both hands and implore the men in the audience to have sex with her. Other nuns did the same, revealing knowledge of sex and depravity that seemed beyond their experience – although, of course, it was claimed that that it was a demon that was speaking, not the demure nuns.

The story of Loudon eventually faded into the pages of history, only to be revived again during the twentieth century as the subject of a fascinating book by Aldous Huxley and a strange, but compelling, film by Ken Russell starring Vanessa Redgrave as Sister Jeanne and Oliver Reed as Father Grandier. It's a story that does not seem to want to let us go, even centuries later, and provides a shocking look at the mystery of sex, Satan and possession in the seventeenth century.

DEMONS IN THE MODERN AGE

There are many who say that evil thoughts and actions cannot overpower the healthy brain of a normal person. The mind cannot be overtaken, except by physical impairment or mental disease. There are no spirits, no devils and demons that are waiting to claim the bodies and minds of individuals, causing them to behave in ways that they would not ordinarily, either conscious or subconsciously.

But there are many intelligent men and women who feel otherwise. They are convinced that devils and demons are real and that they can, and do, possess the living. Serious individuals claim to have witnessed and experienced fearsome ordeals in which ordinary people became the targets of vile entities that wanted nothing more than actual possession of a living body.

Is possession real? Skeptics will dismiss such stories as examples of psychological disorders and wild imaginations. But is a logical explanation for possession always the answer? Many don't believe so. There are dozens of what seem to be authentic cases of possession in the annals of the supernatural, cases that were witnessed by reliable people who were unable to provide an explanation for what they saw, heard and experienced, except to say that the Devil was at work.

A PACT WITH SATAN

At the age of 16, Clara Germana Cele told her confessor, Father Erasmus Horner, that she had made a pact with Satan. Not only was her soul promised to him, but her body, as well. She claimed that she had sex with the Devil on a nightly basis, and that he ravished her in her room when no one else was around. This confession occurred at the Marianhill Order mission school in Umzinto, South Africa, where Clara had been living since the age of four. In the weeks that followed the girl's chilling words, Clara began to behave wildly and on August 20, 1906, she terrified the nuns in charge of the school by tearing off her clothes, breaking one of the posts on her bed, growling and grunting like an animal and appearing to fornicate with an invisible being. In more lucid moments, she begged the sisters to call for Father Horner --- or Satan was going to kill her.

Before this strange confession, and the outbursts that followed, Clara had been considered a normal, healthy, although somewhat erratic young woman. As her condition worsened, she began to manifest signs of what the

Church considered to be a case of authentic demonic possession. Holy water burned her when she was sprinkled with it, but when she was sprinkled with ordinary water from the tap, she simply laughed. She complained loudly whenever a crucifix was brought into her presence and she could detect a religious object, like a rosary or holy medal, even when it was heavily wrapped or otherwise concealed.

One of the outstanding features of the possession was the great physical strength that the girl manifested whenever she was under demonic control. She battered those who tried to control her, and in the early days of the possession, she avenged herself brutally against two nuns who accused her of faking her condition. The two nuns were accompanied by three large assistants when they came to watch over Clara one evening. At first, Clara was quiet and subdued but soon, she began to ask "tricky questions," apparently of a theological nature, of the sisters and an argument began. Father Horner later wrote that before anyone could realize what was going on, Clara "stood before the sisters in blazing anger and upbraided them in a manner that would always remember for its lack of devotion and grace."

When the nuns tried to strike the girl, Clara ran for the door, locked it and put the key in her pocket. Then she grabbed the two nuns by their habits, shook them furiously and then, with incredible strength, slammed one into a corner and threw the other to the far side of the room. Clara severely beat one of the sisters, tore the veil from her head and then pushed her under the bed. With great speed, she jumped on top of the other nun, who was crouching in the corner in fear, and choked and beat her. The three brawny assistants cowered in terror during the assault, too afraid to come near the girl.

Mysterious fires also sprang up in Clara's presence. Once, when she entered a kitchen where a small coal fire was burning, a huge flame suddenly shot into the air. While others who were present screamed and ran away, Clara only laughed and seemed to bask in the heat. The room then seemed to fill with flames, even though only a few half-glowing pieces of coal had remained in the ashes. On another occasion, another fire broke out as the girls were going to bed and when Clara was surrounded by twenty other girls. The girls had just entered their dormitory room, where the room supervisor, Sister Juliana, was resting in a nearby chair. A few moments after Clara climbed into bed, the bed frame started to make a loud, creaking sound. Then flames rushed out from underneath it. They subsided when Sister Juliana sprinkled holy water on the bed. Upon examination, the bed and bedposts were found to be charred but the girl's bed clothes and blankets were completely untouched.

Strange sounds and unexplained noises were frequently heard around Clara. Often during the night, loud noises could be heard at the door of the dormitory where the girls slept. Father Horner and another priest armed themselves and began to guard the house, thinking that an outsider who was hostile to the mission school might be at work, trying to frighten the young women and the nuns. The two priests occupied an empty room close to the women's sleeping quarters, and as they began their vigil, they found everything to be quiet. Things did not stay quiet for long. Father Horner wrote:

Suddenly, at ten o'clock, there was a sound like a thunderclap at the door. Inside, everyone cried out in fear and horror. We hurried outside to find out what was going on. Then, once again, one, two, five tremendous blows. We went out once more, and again there was nothing in sight. Banging and pounding could be heard on several doors inside the house. We went to investigate and found nothing. The noise and pounding continued in the rooms of the brothers, in the smithy, in the storage section, and even in the shed where the animals had become restless, but nowhere was there anything to be seen. The noise stopped by eleven-fifteen.

The idea that Clara was engaged in some sort of hoax began to fade as the strange events continued, particularly when everyone saw how much she suffered during the times when she was allegedly under demonic control. Father Horner repeatedly reported to his superiors about the incredible speed with which Clara moved when she was visibly possessed. Another curious capacity that astonished the priests and nuns was her ability to transform into a snake-like creature. Her whole body seemed to become as flexible as rubber and she would writhe and slither, her neck seeming to elongate. Father Horner wrote that she "sometimes moved on her back,

183

at other times on her belly, with snake-like motions." He noted that "when she moved backwards, her head settled on the ground as if it were a foot and her whole body moved downward, snake fashion." On one occasion, while a nun was kneeling before her in prayer, Clara darted at her in "typical snake manner," and bit the woman on her arm. Where the girl's teeth had left their mark, a reddish point showed at the center where a small wound resembling a snake bite appeared.

In addition to being credited with the ability to run up a wall, two yards high, with such speed that "it seemed she was moving on solid ground," Clara was also said to be able to defy gravity while under demonic control. Although rarely seen outside of the realm of stage magicians and questionable accounts of spirit mediums, Clara was said to levitate during times of possession. Father Horner noted:

She floated often three, four and up to five feet in the air, sometimes vertically, with her feet downward, and at other times horizontally, with her whole body floating above her bed. She was in a rigid position. Even her clothing did not fall downward, as would have been normal; instead, her dresses remained tightly attached to her body and legs. If she was sprinkled with holy water, she moved down immediately, and her clothing fell loosely onto her bed. This type of phenomenon took place in the presence of witnesses, including outsiders. Even in church, where she could be seen by everyone, she floated above her seat. Some people tried to pull her down forcibly, holding on to her feet, but it proved to be impossible.

Father Horner's account should not leave the impression that Clara was in a state of relaxation as she levitated above her bed. On the contrary, levitation occurred during periods of such physical and verbal violence that she often had to be restrained and tied up to keep her from destroying property or hurting those who were nearby. He wrote about one of these incidents:

Everyone sought to help, but it still took another three hours before we were finally able to get handcuffs on the girl as she was in a state of violent anger. Both her arms were stiff and immovable. At the same time, and amid horrible noise and disturbance, she was, over and over again, levitated off the ground while sitting in her chair.

Permission to perform an exorcism on Clara, to rid her of diabolical possession, was issued by the local Bishop on September 10, 1906, slightly less than a month after the incidents began. Father Erasmus Horner was assisted in the rite by the house father of the mission, Father Mansuet. As is standard during exorcisms, the diabolical entity inside of the girl was asked to identify itself. Using a voice much different from Clara's, it identified itself and gave several names, such as "Yiminia" and either "Balek" or "Malek." When pressed for accuracy, the voice replied, "We do not all have names. Only the important ones have names, not those that are small and insignificant. I am small and insignificant."

The rites of exorcism began the following morning, ended at noon, and then began again at 3:00 p.m. that afternoon. The rituals lasted late into the night and then started once more the following morning. As with the days leading up to the exorcism, Clara had moments of clarity and peace during the process. Alternating between states of diabolical possession and her normal personality, she was able to take part in confession and communion. This however, involved great spiritual risks, of which Father Horner quickly became aware. She often asked him to hear her confession, just to have a few moments of respite from the possession. He said that hearing her confession was a difficult task because he could not be sure if it was Clara or the demon who spoke to him. In some cases, a self-dialogue seemed to be going on. It was as if two beings were speaking through Clara's mouth.

Father Horner also noted that he had to very careful during Holy Communion, as "Satan tempted her constantly." Clara seemed to be tempted to spit out the communion wine or to withdraw the wafer from her mouth and degrade it in some manner. At other times, she was unable to swallow at all. She gagged and strained but the back of her mouth remained rigid. When Father Horner placed two fingers on her neck, though, this difficulty disappeared instantly. She often trembled and shook during communion, spilling the wine, even when she had assistance. In many cases, though, she quieted down and listened to prayer. On these evenings, after a peaceful communion, the service was followed by the times of the most vicious attacks. As Father Horner wrote, "Those were the times of Satan's revenge."

In addition to the spiritual risks of Clara's exorcism, there were the physical risks to the girl -- and to the exorcists too. While in the midst of a severe possession crisis, while raving and acting destructively, Father Mansuet began the exorcism ritual. With his stole draped around his neck and across his shoulders, he began reading from the *Rituale Romanum*. He was soon interrupted by a voice speaking through Clara. When the priest commanded the voice to be silent, Clara began to react violently, straining at the bonds that held her to her bed. The voice raged at him, offering the body of the young girl to the priest for sex. Enraged, and momentarily losing control, the priest slapped the girl across the face. Instantly speaking in Clara's voice again, the young woman cried and asked why he was beating her – unaware of what she had been doing and saying just moments before.

Regretful, the priest leaned down to comfort the girl and as he did so, the demon returned. Snapping out of her restraints, Clara knocked the prayer book from his hands and in a quick movement, tore the stole from his neck and ripped it to shreds. As Father Mansuet tried to scramble away, Clara seized hold of him by the neck, choking him and throwing him to the ground. The priest tried to fight back but was no match for Clara's brutal strength. She hammered him against the bedpost and then shoved him under the bed. Moments later, the demonic rage vanished and Clara began to weep. She cowered into the corner as the priest gingerly crawled out from under the bed. His fingers were badly bruised, and his body was covered with scratches and abrasions. When Clara saw what she had apparently done, she began to weep. She was still sitting in the corner, apparently shattered with grief, when others came into the room to see what the commotion was about.

The exorcism rites continued with several hopeful days and a number of setbacks, like the one that occurred after Father Horner announced that he had to make a trip to Europe. Clara asked him not to go, or at least to postpone the trip, but he was unable to do so. While he was away, the girl experienced a relapse, announcing that she had made a new pact with the Devil. Horner was stunned and heartsick by this latest development, but he was encouraged by the fact that Clara wanted the exorcism to continue.

In April 1907, the rituals began again and were only interrupted by a visit from the Apostolic Vicar, Dr. Henri Delalle, Bishop of Natal, who came to the mission to see if Clara's possession was indeed genuine. Accompanied by others, Bishop Delalle checked the girl's condition and verified that she was authentically possessed. The new exorcism began on April 24.

Although Father Horner and the others continued to be discouraged by some of the problems they faced, Clara herself insisted that the exorcism continue. It lasted for only two more days and at last the demon departed, leaving behind a stench that "could not be compared with anything else."

The horrible events were now over. Clara began a normal life, unhampered by the threat of possession. She stayed on at the mission for the next seven years, living an ordinary and peaceful life. Sadly, though, she died on March 14, 1912 during a tuberculosis outbreak. She was only 23 years old.

THE POSSESSION OF EMMA SCHMIDT

The case of Emma Schmidt has become known as one of the most chilling and horrific cases of possession in American history. It is one that was well documented by those who were present. It was a case of possession that was said to be caused directly by a young girl's refusal to give into the sexual demands of her father, a ruthless, maniacal man who literally offered the girl to the Devil to use as he saw fit.

The events in the case began a number of years before their culmination in an Iowa convent. At that time, Emma was a young woman, living in Wisconsin. Following the death of her father, she began to develop a strangeness that no one recalled about her before. In later years, Emma would say that her father had cursed her upon his death because she had refused to give in to the incestuous demands that he placed on her after her mother had died. She was only a young girl when her mother had passed away, but her father didn't care. He constantly followed her about as she worked at her chores on the family's farm, stroking her legs and her breasts and trying to get her to put her hands on his stiffened penis. On more than one occasion, he had tried to force himself on her in the barn, and she always locked her door tightly at night to keep him away.

Just before his death, he had cursed at her, telling her that he hoped that all of the devils in hell crawled into her body and raped her in just the way that she always feared. The Devil himself could have her, he said, and he hoped that she would not have a moment's peace until the day she died.

Emma should have been freed from his hatred and lust when he died, but instead, she began to act very strangely. The once sensitive, quiet and religious young woman became increasingly angry, hurling obscenities and laughing inappropriately during church services and in public places. She became flirtatious and even downright brazen and lewd with young men in town. Many of the local people who had known the girl her entire life remarked on the bizarre changes in her personality. Doctors who examined her at first believed that she was either hysterical or prone to nervous spells and hallucinations, but they could find absolutely nothing wrong with her. They ran test after test, all of which proved to be negative -- but there was obviously something wrong.

After exhausting the doctors, Emma appealed to the Church for help. Several of the priests that she spoke with agreed with the findings of the physicians: that Emma was clearly hysterical and in need of psychiatric help. Others disagreed confounded by the fact that Emma appeared to understand languages that she had neither heard nor read. When a priest blessed her in Latin, she foamed at the mouth with rage. If she handled an object that was sprinkled with holy water, she would scream curses and blasphemies and throw it against the wall. Slowly, very slowly, it began to be realized that there was something going on with her that could not easily be dismissed. The Church did not take the rite of exorcism lightly, and only after intense study and observation, and the passing of a number of years, did the priests agree that Emma was actually possessed by evil spirits.

Father Theophilus Riesinger, a Capuchin monk who had past experience with exorcisms, agreed to take on the case. He knew Emma well, as she was a member of his parish in Marathon, Wisconsin, but he wanted to protect her privacy as much as possible. He made arrangements for her to travel to the small town of Earling, Iowa, where the ritual was to take place at the convent of the Franciscan Sisters. Joseph Steiger, the parish priest at Earling, was a long-time friend of Father Theophilus, but he was not eager for the exorcism to take place in his parish. It was only after urging from his friend and the mother superior of the convent that he agreed.

Emma traveled to Earling by train, passing the time alone, filled with desperate worry over what was about to take place. She knew that she wanted the demons to be banished, but she was also overwhelmed with anger and rage, brought on by the evil spirits that plagued her. When she stepped off the train at the station, she waved her arms wildly at the nuns who came to collect her. She screamed at them, calling them foul names before inexplicably going limp. The startled sisters gathered Emma and her belongings and helped her into their car. The group rode in silence to the convent.

Father Theophilus arrived later that evening, but the first signs of trouble had already begun. A well-meaning sister in the kitchen had sprinkled Emma's food with holy water, only to have the enraged woman throw it on the floor, screaming that the food smelled horrible. When unblessed food was substituted for the first tray, she devoured it, almost without chewing. There was no way that Emma could have known that either tray, containing the same items ---- save for the holy water ---- was different from the other.

The exorcism began early the next morning. Emma was brought into a room that had been set aside for the ritual and placed on the mattress of an iron bed. The sleeves and the skirt of her dress were tightly bound and Father Theophilus instructed several of the nuns to hold her firmly to the bed. The exorcist, with Father Steiger standing beside him, began to pray. Then, as she would on every day that followed, Emma sank into unconsciousness. Her eyelids closed so tightly that they could not be forced open.

Almost as soon as she blacked out, she tore loose from the sisters who were holding her. By some mysterious energy, she reportedly flung her body from the bed, into the air, and against the closest wall. She was pinned there by a force so strong that neither priest could pull her free. The nuns, now trembling with fright, tugged at her until they finally were able to pull her loose and return her to the bed. Moments later, the exorcism continued and Emma began to howl. But according to the statements of those present, her mouth never opened. Mewling, inhuman sounds and guttural growls issued from her throat, but her lips never moved.

News of the exorcism spread through the nearby community, and people came from all directions to find out what was happening at the convent. Crowds soon assembled beneath the windows of the room where Emma was kept but many of them left, reportedly unable to stand the excruciating sounds that issued from inside.

Over the course of the next few days, those inside the room endured the ordeal alongside of Emma. Twelve nuns took turns attending to her, afterwards leaving the building to get some fresh air, and often to weep. Only Father Theophilus remained composed. Emma, seemingly helpless to prevent what was happening to her, continually frothed at the mouth and spewed out torrents of stinking vomit that filled pitchers and pails. She had scarcely eaten for days, and yet was said to have thrown up as many as thirty times in one day. On several occasions, when the exorcist brought the Blessed Sacrament near Emma, he saw her flesh twist and contort, as though something was moving beneath her skin.

The exorcism continued from early in the morning until late at night, every day, hour after hour. The bellowing voices and cries continued to come from the stricken woman, shattering the usual stillness of the convent. At times, the voices became so frightening that Father Steiger and the nuns fled from the room. The priest persisted in his task, though, praying and screaming for the devils to leave Emma. His work was so strenuous that he often had to change his sweat-soaked clothing three times or more each day.

During the sessions, a number of voices allegedly came though Emma. They claimed to be various demons and evil spirits from her past, including her father, who had tried to force her to have sex with him, and her father's mistress, who according to the priest's report, had murdered her own children. During this manifestation, Emma was said to have vomited with such violence that Father Theophilus and Father Steiger had to use towels to clean the fluid from their clothing.

Whatever was expressing itself in these voices, it demonstrated an uncanny knowledge of things that could not have been known to Emma. On one occasion, as a test, a piece of paper with a Latin inscription was placed on Emma's head. The nuns, thinking the words were a prayer, were surprised to see that the demons tolerated its presence. In truth, the words had no religious content at all. However, when a second piece of paper, which had been secretly blessed, was placed on Emma's head, it was immediately ripped to pieces.

The exorcism continued day after horrible day. Emma was unable to eat, and the nuns were only able to get liquid down her throat. In a short time, it would usually come right back up again. Her now-emaciated body was said to no longer resemble anything human. Her head swelled and caused her features to distort. Her eyes bulged and her lips bloated to twice their normal size. Her face was flushed with heat as her skin stretched and took on an unnatural shine. The nuns feared that her limbs might actually burst, they were so badly swollen. They also claimed that her body seemed to take on such weight that the iron bedstead curved down to where it almost touched the floor.

As the exhausting days passed, a change came over Father Steiger. He developed a strong dislike for the entire procedure ---- almost hatred ---- and began to dislike Father Theophilus, his old friend. In one bout of anger, he raged at the exorcist but Father Theophilus took it in stride, explaining that the demons were using the priest as he tried to get the spirits to leave her. As the voices that came from Emma began berating Father Steiger, his friend commanded that they leave him alone. The battle was with him, he shouted. But the voices only laughed and continued to threaten Father Steiger. "Just wait until Friday..." they told him.

187

Sick of the constant howling, Father Steiger learned to ignore the voices but then on Friday, as promised, he nearly lost his life. It happened as he was returning from performing the last rites for the mother of a local farmer. On his return to Earling, as he crossed a bridge over a ravine, he would later claim that a large, black cloud suddenly descended on his car. Unable to see, he yanked the vehicle into low gear but it was too late to stop. The automobile veered to the side and collided with the steel railings of the bridge. Metal smashed and glass shattered as the car tore through the rails until it was left teetering on the edge of the ravine. A farmer who was plowing a field a short distance away heard the crash and came running. He managed to pull Father Steiger from the wreckage. The priest was stunned and numb with shock, but unhurt.

The farmer gave him a lift to the convent, and when he arrived, he went straight to Emma's room. As he walked in, she began laughing uproariously. A guttural voice from inside of her laughed at the priest and gloated at the destruction of his car. Father Theophilus and the nuns were shocked and asked if this was true. Father Steiger agreed that it was but added that the demon did not have the strength to hurt him personally. The voice cursed and stated that the priest's patron saint had saved his life.

On several occasions after this, Father Steiger continued to be bedeviled by the spirits. He was often awakened at night by knocking, scratching, and weird banging sounds coming from inside the walls of his room that would last throughout the night.

But none of this could match the suffering endured by Emma Schmidt. She continued to lose consciousness each day as the exorcism began, awakening late at night when it was over. She remembered nothing of what transpired during the day, the violent sickness that she suffered from, or the horrible curses that came from her mouth. As she became more and more frail from her daily ordeal, she was no longer able to walk. She had to be carried back and forth between her private quarters and the exorcism room. The nuns feared that she might die before the exorcism could end.

The records say that the events continued for more than two weeks before there was any indication that the spirits might be forced out of Emma's body. At that point, Father Theophilus doubled his efforts, and for three days and nights, he continued the exorcism without sleep and with very little rest. In addition to what must have been nerves of steel, the priest also seemed to have incredible powers of endurance. But even so, toward the end of the third night, he became so weak that he nearly collapsed. He prayed to God to spare his life and finally, the marathon session was finished.

The end seemed to be near. Later, the nuns would testify that a miraculous figure appeared to Emma one day and urged her not to give up hope. The nuns claimed that they saw a cluster of white roses appear on the ceiling of the room that disappeared before Father Steiger could be brought in to witness it. Regardless, the sign gave hope to the priest, and he and Father Theophilus both knew that the horror was finally reaching its climax.

More days of pain and exhaustion followed, but on the evening of September 23, 1928, Emma Schmidt jerked free from the hands of the nuns who held her and she stood upon the bed with only her heels touching the mattress. Fearful that she might be hurled against the wall again ---- or perhaps this time thrown against the ceiling ---- Father Steiger urged the sisters to pull her back down. As they reached for her, Father Theophilus blessed her and demanded once more that the demons depart from her. At that moment, Emma reportedly collapsed as the sounds of screams and piercing voices filled the room.

Everyone present froze as Emma contorted one last time and then opened her eyes and smiled. As she looked from one face to another, she began to weep. Her torment was over ---- the exorcism was finished at last. So happy were they about what had occurred that the witnesses did not at first notice the stomach-churning smell of human waste that filled the room. It was the final indignity left behind by the departing spirits, it was said. The nuns opened all of the windows and a fresh cool breeze blew across into the room, driving out the foul odor.

There was little to say in the aftermath of the Earling case. Had Emma Schmidt truly been plagued by demons? The exorcism caused a heated debate among members of the Catholic Church, as many of them continued to believe that she was merely a troubled woman who had been in the grips of hysteria. This may have been the case, but even if it was, Emma lived a quiet and peaceful life after the exorcism and was never bothered by her troubles again. For the rest of his life, Father Theophilus maintained that she had been possessed, and Father Steiger and the Franciscan sisters agreed. They only saw a young woman who had finally been freed from the lustful demands of a demented old man – and the legion of devils that he managed to conjure up.

ANNELIESE MICHEL

The ordinary person's idea of the horrors of exorcisms and possession largely seems to come from books and movies. And there have been few movies about possession that have chilled audiences in the way that the 2005 film, *The Exorcism of Emily Rose*, did. What many are unaware of is that the film was based on an actual case that occurred in Germany in the mid-1970s. It was a terrifying story of exorcism and death, for not only did the victim in the case die during her exorcism, but two priests were convicted of her murder.

Anneliese Michel was born on September 21, 1952, and was raised in a normal, happy family in the town of Klingenberg am Main, Bavaria. Her father, Josef, operated a profitable sawmill in town and he and Anneliese's mother, Anna, were strict Catholics who raised their daughter to be religiously devout. Her life changed one day in 1968 when she began

Anneliese Michel

shaking and found that she was unable to control her body. Her seizures were so extreme that she was unable to call out for her parents or her three sisters. They were terrified when they discovered her collapsed on the floor, and she was rushed to the hospital. A neurologist at the Psychiatric Clinic in Würzburg diagnosed her with epilepsy. Because of the seriousness of the seizures, and the severity of the depression that followed, Anneliese was admitted for treatment at the hospital.

Even though she was still suffering from seizures, and unknown to anyone was also experiencing visions of demonic faces during her daily prayers, Anneliese was able to return to school in the fall of 1970. She went on to the University of Würzburg in September 1973, where she began studying elementary education.

Anneliese was still experiencing the horrific visions that had started to plague her in the hospital and by now, she was hearing voices. She finally confessed to her doctors and her parents that the voices were starting to give her orders and threatening that they would take her to Hell. The medicine that she was given did not seem to chase away the eerie sights and sounds. Finally, possibly because of her strict Catholic upbringing, Anneliese became convinced that she was possessed. After four years of medical treatment, her condition and her depression continued to worsen to the point that her parents began to share her fears of demonic possession.

In the summer of 1973, her parents visited several different pastors, pleading for an exorcism for their daughter. Their requests were denied. Instead, the priests recommended that Anneliese continue with her treatment and medication. It was explained to them that the process by which the Church proves a possession is strictly defined, and until all of the criteria is met (including aversion to religious objects, speaking in a language that the victims does not know, paranormal powers, and more) a Bishop cannot approve an exorcism. Anneliese continued to suffer from her illness ---- as well as the visions and voices --- as she began her college studies.

In 1974, it seemed that Anneliese might finally be receiving some assistance from the Church. After supervising the young woman for some time, Pastor Ernst Alt, a local parish priest and a specialist in exorcism, requested permission to perform an exorcism from the Bishop of Würzburg, Josef Stangl. The request was denied. The Bishop suggested that Anneliese try and live a more religious lifestyle in order to find peace.

Attempts to intensify her already-religious lifestyle offered no relief. The attacks did not diminish and Anneliese's behavior started to become more erratic. At her parents' house in Klingenberg, she wreaked havoc on everything ---- and everyone ---- she came into contact with. She screamed insults at her family. She constantly assaulted them, hitting and beating her parents and her sisters, and biting them with savage force. She refused to eat because the "demons would not allow it." She slept on the stone floor in the basement, ate spiders, flies, and pieces of coal and even began drinking her own urine. She could be heard screaming throughout the house for hours, and ran about breaking crucifixes, destroying religious paintings and tearing apart rosaries. Anneliese also began mutilating herself, cutting her arms and legs, tearing off her clothes, and raising her skirts to squat and urinate on the floor without warning.

Although no details are available as to how it happened, Bishop Stangl was eventually worn down about his decision to allow an exorcism for Anneliese. He had consulted with a leading expert on demonic possession, Father Adolf Rodewyk, who had agreed with Father Alt about Anneliese's condition. Father Rodewyk recommended that the exorcism proceed, so in September 1975, Bishop Stangl verified the conditions of possession and assigned Father Arnold Renz and Father Ernst Alt to perform the ritual. For the next eleven months, all medical treatment of Anneliese was stopped, and the rites of exorcism were carried out secretly in a bedroom of her parents' home during one-hour sessions. The attacks that she suffered from during the exorcism were sometimes so forceful that she had to be held down by three men or even chained to the floor. During this time, Anneliese found that her life outside of the exorcism rituals had returned to a semblance of normalcy. She was able to go to church and return to school for a time, taking final examinations at the Pedagogic Academy in Würzburg.

As time passed, though, Anneliese either became sicker or continued to be possessed. Her symptoms began to return, not just during the exorcism sessions, and she would often find herself paralyzed or passing out. The exorcism went on, stretching over the weeks and months, always with the same prayers and readings from the *Rituale Romanum*. Anneliese refused to eat for days at a time. Eventually, her knees ruptured from six hundred genuflections (a respectful bowing on one knee while making the sign of a cross, which is usually done when entering a church) that she performed obsessively throughout the exorcism. Anneliese's parents, and the priests involved, made over forty audio tapes of the rituals, in order to preserve the details.

The last exorcism session was held on June 30, 1976. By this time, Anneliese had contracted pneumonia, was dreadfully emaciated, and was running a high fever. She was too exhausted to physically perform the genuflections of the ceremony but her parents held her up and walked her through the motions. "Beg for absolution", was the last statement that Anneliese made to the priests. To her mother, she said "Mama, I'm afraid." She died that night at the age of 23 from starvation. The autopsy report, which recorded her weight at only 68 pounds, stated that her death was caused by malnutrition and dehydration resulting from almost a year of semi-starvation during the exorcism.

Anna Michel reported the death of her daughter on July 1. Later that same day, Pastor Alt gave details of the events to the authorities in Aschaffenburg. Officials began an immediate investigation, but prosecutors took more than two years to file charges and bring the case to the courts. Anneliese's parents and the two exorcists, Father Alt and Father Renz, were accused of negligent homicide for refusing to bring a medical doctor into the case. According to the evidence, Anneliese had starved to death. Specialists claimed that if she had been force-fed even a week before her death, her life could have been saved.

The trial started on March 30, 1978. A series of doctors who testified all basically told the court that Anneliese had died from a combination of epilepsy, mental disorders, and an extreme religious environment that, in the words of Professor Hans Sattes of the University of Wurzburg, added up to "a spiritual sickness and heavy psychic disturbance."

Throughout the trial, Josef Michel sat impassively, listening to the testimony through a special amplifier that allowed him to hear. His wife, Anna, steadily took notes, pausing only to moan "Oh, dear God," whenever a doctor alleged that that her daughter was not possessed but had a mental disorder. Father Renz stayed quiet during the trial, but presented an imposing figure in his priest's robes, with his long gray hair swept straight back and an impassive expression on his face. Father Alt, who wore civilian clothing during the proceedings, was the one most involved in the trial. He offered advice to the attorneys that allowed nothing to pass that could be challenged.

The two priests were defended by lawyers paid for by the Church. Anneliese's parents were defended by one of Germany's top attorneys, Erich Schmidt-Leichner, who had made a name for himself during the Nazi war crimes trials following World War II. He claimed that not only was exorcism legal, but that the German constitution protected citizens in the unrestricted exercise of their religious beliefs.

The prosecution offered a number of psychiatrists as expert witnesses. They spoke about "Doctrinaire Induction," claiming the priests convinced Anneliese that demons were the cause of her psychotic behavior. They concluded that Anneliese's unsettled sexual development, along with a chronic neurological condition called temporal lobe epilepsy, had influenced her psychosis.

The defense countered their arguments with evidence they believed showed the girl had actually been possessed. The evidence, in addition to witness statements, included the audio tapes that were made during the exorcism sessions. The tapes were filled with the sounds of the young woman's screams and howls, as well as the exorcist's prayers and a number of strange voices that came from Anneliese and yet were clearly not her regular pattern of speech. In some segments, different voices argued with one another and the exorcists claimed that the voices were demons inside of Anneliese, fighting over which of them would have to leave her body first. No one involved with the exorcism had any doubt that Anneliese was genuinely possessed. Father Renz and Father Alt were convinced that she had been possessed, and that it had only been her death that freed her from her demons. She was now, they believed, with God.

In the end, the accused were found guilty of manslaughter resulting from negligence and were given a six-month suspended sentence. The jury had no choice but to find them guilty based on the evidence that was presented, but they were so unsettled by the audio tapes, along with the deep belief of the exorcists that they had been trying to help Anneliese, that a light sentence was handed down. The prosecutor dismissed this idea, however, and stated that he felt that the parents should not be punished because they had suffered enough.

Regardless of the reasons behind the verdict, the case was finally over. The trial, called the Klingenberg Case, became the basis for the film *The Exorcism of Emily Rose*. The film slightly deviated from the real events (for example, it is set in the United States and Anneliese was re-named Emily Rose) but it presented the most chilling aspects of the story and (like the real-life case) it allowed viewers to decide for themselves whether or not the main character was actually possessed or not.

This remains the biggest question to arise from the Anneliese Michel case: Was the young woman really possessed? Those who were directly involved maintain that she was, citing her visions and the voices that she heard, her aversion to religious objects and the terrifying recordings as evidence. But did the case really fit the criteria that were set forth by the Catholic Church? And if not, why was the exorcism suggested by an expert in possession, Father Rodewyk, and then sanctioned by Bishop Stangl?

For the Church, the death of Anneliese was a nightmare come true, demonstrating the dangers of becoming involved in exorcisms, and the murky responsibilities of the priest when it comes to spiritual and medical care. Father Rodewyk wrote a handbook on exorcisms in 1963 in which he urged priests to consider medical explanations for apparent possessions. He also outlined the bishop's responsibilities, saying that he "may appoint a commission of theologians and physicians to undertake a further investigation" and warns that exorcists "must guard against playing the role of physician when encountering psychological symptoms."

These were mere warnings, though, for the *Rituale Romanum* did not state that a doctor must be in attendance during the exorcism. This deficiency in church procedure was corrected, in Germany at least, after the conviction of the two priests in the Michel case. In May 1978, the German Bishop's Conference ruled that in the future, no exorcisms would be permitted unless a doctor was present.

While this may have protected future victims of possession, it did nothing for Anneliese Michel. Her death had been a

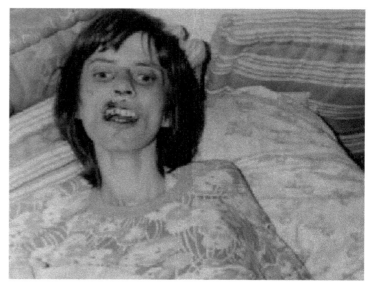

Anneliese at the height of the exorcisms -- and shortly before her death.

tragedy -- no matter what the cause -- and remains a mystery to this day. Was she a delusional young woman who, in the belief that she was possessed, starved herself to death? Were her parents and her priests, the people she trusted the most, ultimately responsible for her demise? Or was she truly possessed by demonic spirits? Did these demons break down her defenses to the point that only death could free her from their clutches?

The story of Anneliese Michel remains as mysterious as any within the annals of possession and exorcism. Those who can only read about the case, looking backward on history, will never really know for sure what really happened. Only those who were actually present can know what was heard, seen, and experienced. To make matters worse, we cannot even be sure that their perceptions can be trusted. Were their minds clouded by fear, by religion, or perhaps, simplest of all, by the confusing and convoluted nature of what was occurring?

THE DEVIL CAME TO ST. LOUIS

In 1949, the Devil came to St. Louis, Missouri.... Or at least, if you believe the stories that have been told for the last sixty-odd years, a reasonable facsimile of him did.

This is a story that has been told for three generations, one that has inspired countless books and films. It is, without question, one of the great unsolved mysteries of the occult in America. And, let's face it, a story that has become a confusing and convoluted mess over the years. There are so many theories, legends, tales and counter-stories that have been thrown into the mix that it's become very hard to separate fact from fantasy. So, let's see if we can get to the bottom of what happened in St. Louis in 1949, despite all of the unanswered questions that have been left behind.

What happened at the old Alexian Brothers hospital that still has former staff members whispering about it in fear today? What really happened to bring a young boy and his frightened family from Maryland to St. Louis? And most of all, was this boy really possessed by a demon?

The story began not in St. Louis, but in the small Washington, D.C., suburb of Cottage City, Maryland. As many readers already know, what has come to be known as the "St. Louis Exorcism Case" would go on to inspire William Peter Blatty's 1971 best-selling book and the movie based on it, *The Exorcist*. In the novel, a young girl is possessed by a demon and is subjected to an exorcism by two Catholic priests. In the true story, though, the

A photograph of the house in Cottage City, Maryland, where the events in the case began.

subject of the alleged possession was not a girl but a boy who has been identified in various accounts as "Roland" or "Robbie Doe." Robbie (as we will call him here) was born in 1935 and grew up in Cottage City. He was the only child of a dysfunctional family, and had a troubled childhood.

In January 1949, the family of 13-year-old Robbie began to be disturbed by scratching sounds coming from inside of the walls and ceilings of their small bungalow. Believing that the noises were being made by mice, the parents called an exterminator, but he could find no sign of rodents. To make matters worse, his efforts seemed to exacerbate the problem. Noises that sounded like someone walking in the hallway could be heard, and dishes and objects were often found to be moved without explanation.

The noises were disturbing, but they weren't nearly as frightening as when Robbie began to be attacked. His bed shook so hard that he couldn't sleep at night. His blankets and sheets were torn from the bed. When he tried to hold onto them, he was reportedly pulled off the bed and onto the floor with the sheets still gripped in his hands.

Those who have come to believe the boy was genuinely possessed feel that he may have been invaded by an invisible entity after experimenting with a Ouija board. He had been taught to use the device by a relative from St. Louis who was later referred to as "Aunt Tillie." Tillie took an active interest in Spiritualism and the occult and had died from multiple sclerosis on January 26, 1949, a short time before the noises in the house began. In the written accounts of the exorcism, it was noted that the family believed there was a connection between Tillie's death and the problems with Robbie.

William Peter Blatty

Many of the early events in the case were chronicled by the Jesuit priests who later performed the exorcism. One of them kept a diary, and it was this account of the exorcism that was heard about by author William Peter Blatty when he was a student at Georgetown University in 1949. He first became interested in the story after reading about it in newspaper articles and discussed it with his instructor, the Rev. Thomas Bermingham, S.J. The "diary" of the Robbie Doe case came to light in the fall of 1949 under rather odd circumstances. Fr. Eugene B. Gallagher, S.J., who was on the faculty of Georgetown, was lecturing on the topic of exorcisms when one of his students, the son of a psychiatrist at St. Elizabeth's Hospital in Washington, spoke of a diary that had been kept by the Jesuits involved in the Robbie Doe exorcism. Father Gallagher asked the psychiatrist, who may have been one of the professionals involved in the early stages of the case, for a copy of the diary and eventually received a 26-page document that was titled "Case Study by Jesuit Priests." It had apparently been intended to be used a guide for future exorcisms. Blatty asked to see it, but he was refused.

He later turned back to newspaper articles for information about the case and discovered that one of them listed the name of one of the priests involved. His name was Rev. William S. Bowdern, S.J. of St. Louis. Bowdern refused to comment on the case for the newspaper reports, as priests who perform exorcisms are said to be sworn to secrecy. Blatty tried contacting him anyway, but the priest refused to cooperate. Out of respect, Blatty changed the identity of the possession victim in his book to a young girl, but the exorcist of the novel remains a thinly veiled characterization of Father Bowdern. Father Bowdern died in 1983, never publicly acknowledging the fact that he was involved in the St. Louis case.

But the diary remained and revealed a series of bizarre occurrences reaching from Maryland to St. Louis.

The strange knocking, scratching and attacks on Robbie continued and soon, the family was desperate. They were Lutherans and turned for help to the Rev. Luther Schulze, the pastor of their church. Schulze tried praying with Robbie and his parents in their home, and then with Robbie alone. Nothing seemed to help and Schulze questioned whether the house was haunted – or if the boy was. He offered to let Robbie spend the night in his home and the boy's parents quickly agreed.

That night, Mrs. Schulze went to the guest room while Robbie and Reverend Schulze retired to the twin beds in the master bedroom. About ten minutes later, Schulze reported that he heard Robbie's bed creaking and shaking. He also heard strange scratching noises coming from inside the walls, just like the ones that had been heard at Robbie's house. Schulze quickly switched on the lights and saw that Robbie's bed was vibrating. When he prayed for it to stop, the vibration grew even more violent. He stated that Robbie was wide awake but was lying completely still.

Schulze then suggested that Robbie try and sleep in a heavy armchair in the room. While Schulze watched closely, the chair began to move. First, it scooted backward several inches, and then its legs jolted forward and back. It literally slammed against the wall and then it tipped over, depositing the boy unhurt onto the floor.

Trying not to be frightened or discouraged, Rev. Schulze made a pallet of blankets on the floor for Robbie to sleep on. As soon as the boy fell asleep though, the pallet began to slide across the floor and slipped under one of the beds. When Robbie was startled awake by the movement, he struck his head on one of the bedposts. Again, the minister made up the pallet, only to this time have it whip across the floor and slide under the other bed. Robbie's hands were visible the entire time, and his body was taut with tension. He was not making the blankets move.

Schulze was now both puzzled and a little afraid. He suggested that Robbie's parents take the boy to see a medical doctor and a psychologist to rule out any kind of physical or mental problems that might be causing the phenomena to take place. The minister also contacted J.B. Rhine, the founder of the parapsychology laboratory at Duke University. He explained what was going on and Rhine and his partner and wife, Louisa Rhine, drove from North Carolina to Cottage City to see the boy. Unfortunately, no activity took place while the investigators were present, but Rhine did deduce that it sounded like a classic poltergeist case in which the boy's unconscious abilities were influencing the objects around him. The details fit well with other experimental results that Rhine had been obtaining.

And while the explanation suggested by Rhine must have appealed to the minister, he did an abrupt about-face a short time later when the phenomena took another turn. A week or so after the incident at Schulze's home, bloody scratches began to appear on the boy's body. Perhaps startled by this new turn of events, Schulze suggested that the family contact a Catholic priest, telling the family, "Catholics know about these kinds of things."

After that, things get more confusing. According to some sources, Robbie's father went to the nearby St. James Church in Mount Rainier, Maryland, for help. There he met with a young priest named Edward Albert Hughes, the assistant pastor of the church at the time. Hughes was skeptical and reluctant to get involved in the matter, but he did agree to go and see Robbie. During the visit, Robbie allegedly addressed the priest in Latin, a language that he did not know. Shaken, Hughes was said to have applied to his archbishop for permission to conduct an exorcism. The sources go on to say that the ritual was performed at Georgetown Hospital in

"Robbie Doe" in high school, several years after the events in the case took place.

February 1949. Robbie seemed to go into a trance as he thrashed about and spoke in tongues. Hughes ordered the boy to be put into restraints but Robbie somehow managed to work a piece of metal spring loose from the bed and he slashed the priest with it. The stories say that Hughes subsequently left St. James, suffered a nervous breakdown, and during masses that he held later in life, he could only hold the consecrated host aloft in one hand.

This story turned out not to be true. The story about Father Hughes was not accurate. Father Hughes became assistant pastor of St. James Church under Rev. William Canning in June 1948, and he served without a break until June 1960. He was later reassigned to St. James in 1973 and stayed there until his death in 1980. Church records do not indicate that he ever suffered a breakdown, or that he ever made an attempt to exorcize Robbie at Georgetown University Hospital. However, Robbie was checked into the hospital under his real name for several days during the period when the alleged exorcism attempt took place. Records say that he underwent extensive medical and psychological evaluations, but there was no exorcism.

Father Hughes also never visited Robbie in his home. In truth, his mother brought him to St. James for the only consultation with the priest. There is nothing to suggest that Robbie spoke to him in Latin, and no evidence to say that Father Hughes was ever slashed with a bedspring. Those who knew Hughes personally remember him suffering no injuries during this period. The fact is, the church social calendar showed him to be quite busy during the weeks after Robbie's release from the hospital.

But strange things continued to occur. Robbie's hospital stay was documented as occurring between February 28, 1949 and March 2 of that year, but according to the priest's "diary," strange things began to happen on February 26. The statement records that "there appeared scratches on the boy's body for about four successive nights. After the fourth night words were written in printed form. These letters were clear but seemed to have been scratched on the body by claws."

At about this time, Robbie's mother began to suggest that a trip away from Maryland might free the boy from the strange happenings. She thought that perhaps they could leave their troubles behind by staying with her husband's brother and his family in St. Louis. The more she considered this, the better the idea seemed. And apparently, "something" agreed because the word *Louis* inexplicably appeared on Robbie's rib cage. When this "skin branding" occurred, Robbie's hands were visible and his mother specifically noted that he could not have scratched the words himself. He had been under observation at the time and the words, according to witnesses, had simply appeared.

The priest's diary even noted that the writing also appeared on Robbie's back. Later on, while in St. Louis, there was some question raised about sending Robbie to school while in the city but the message *NO* appeared on his wrists. A large letter "N" also appeared on each of his legs. His mother feared disobeying what she saw as a supernatural order. It has been suggested that perhaps Robbie created the writing himself with his mind, either consciously or unconsciously. With that in question, it should be noted that before his parents consulted a priest, they also had him examined by a psychiatrist. He reported that the boy was quite normal, as did a medical doctor who gave him a complete physical examination.

At this point, records do indicate that Robbie's mother took him to consult with Father Hughes at the St. James Church. During this one documented visit, he suggested that the family use blessed candles, holy water, and special prayers to try and rid the boy of his problems. Robbie's mother began the use of the blessed candles, and on one occasion, a comb flew violently through the air and struck them, snuffing out the flames. The kitchen table once overturned in the boy's presence and milk and food flew off the counters and onto the floor. Another time, a coat jerked from a hanger and a book landed at Robbie's feet. A chair that the boy was sitting in spun around so fast that he was unable to stop it. He eventually had to stop attending school because his desk refused to remain in place.

The priest's diary went on to add that "the mother took the bottle of holy water and sprinkled all of the rooms." She then took the bottle and placed it on a shelf, but it snapped into the air and flew onto the floor.

The relative's house in Bel-Nor, the North St. Louis suburb, where the exorcism actually began.

A 1975 newspaper report stated that attempts were also made to baptize Robbie into the Catholic faith in order to help him. The story mentioned that one of these attempts was made during Robbie's hospital stay (not an exorcism, as was later reported) and then later in St. Louis. Another baptism attempt was allegedly made in February 1949. It was said that as Robbie's uncle was driving him to the rectory for the ceremony, the boy suddenly glared at him, grabbed him by the throat and shouted, "You son of a bitch, you think I'm going to be baptized but you are going to be fooled!"

The Catholic baptism ritual usually takes about fifteen minutes, but for Robbie, it reportedly lasted for several hours. It was said that when the priest asked "Do you renounce the devil and all his works?" Robbie would go into such a thrashing rage that he had to be restrained.

In early March, after being released from the hospital, Robbie boarded a train to St. Louis with his parents. The family stayed in a home belonging to Robbie's aunt and uncle, a brick, three-bedroom, Colonial-style house in Bel-Nor, a north St. Louis County neighborhood. There, the boy's parents hoped that he might be freed from the strange and horrifying events. For those readers who are convinced that nothing was occurring in this case aside from overactive imaginations and silly superstition, they may want to consider the trip to St. Louis itself as evidence that something (supernatural or not) was taking place. The fact that Robbie's parents would uproot the boy from his home, that his father would take time off from his employment, and they would all travel halfway across the county in a last-ditch effort to find help is suggestive -- if not downright convincing-- that terrible things were indeed happening.

Father William Bowdern

(Below) Father Walter Halloran, who was a Jesuit student at the time of the exorcism.

Unfortunately, Robbie did not improve in St. Louis. His aunt and uncle, as well as various other relatives, witnessed more of the "skin brandings" and also saw his bed and mattress shaking on many occasions. On March 8, 1949, the shaking of the mattress and scratching continued. Robbie's cousin witnessed a stool that was sitting near the bed fly across the room. The boy was so concerned about Robbie that he tried lying down on the bed beside him to stop the mattress from moving. To his dismay, it didn't work. Finally, one of Robbie's cousins who had attended St. Louis University went to see her old teacher there, Rev. Raymond J. Bishop, S.J. She asked him if he might be able to assist Robbie. He agreed to look into the situation. It was Father Bishop who brought William Bowdern into the case.

Father Bowdern was not on the faculty of St. Louis University. In 1949, he was the pastor of St. Francis Xavier College Church on the St. Louis University campus. He was a native of the city and had served as a chaplain during World War II. He had many years of experience dealing with people and their problems and he listened carefully to the story that Father Bishop told him. Then, he and Father Bishop went to see Paul Reinert, S.J., the president of the university. All of them were skeptical about the case. They were concerned with bringing embarrassment to the church and the college, but decided that it might be well to have the boy say some prayers and to give him the priestly blessing.

Apparently, Father Bishop first went to see the family alone. He came to bless the house and the room in which Robbie slept. A holy relic of St. Margaret Mary was pinned on the boy's bed. But even after the blessing and in spite of the relic, the bed still shook and swayed, and the scratches still appeared all over the boy's body. Bishop then sprinkled holy water on the bed in the form of a cross and the movement suddenly ceased. It started up again after Father Bishop stepped out of the room. Then, a sharp pain allegedly struck Robbie in the stomach and he cried out. His mother pulled back the bed covers and lifted the boy's pajama top to reveal red lines that zigzagged across the boy's abdomen. During this entire time, Robbie was in clear view of at least six witnesses.

The next two nights passed in the same way, with the mattress shaking, scratching noises, and objects being thrown about. On March 11, Father Bishop returned to the home and this time brought Father Bowdern with him. The Jesuits were still skeptical about the case but they were open-minded enough to observe the boy and also to study the literature available about demonic attacks on humans. The priests came and prayed again, but this time, the activity did not respond. However, as soon as the two priests left, a loud noise was reportedly heard in Robbie's room and several family members rushed in to see what had happened. They discovered that a 75-pound bookcase had swiveled in a complete circle, a bench had turned over and a crucifix that one of the priests had left under Robbie's pillow had moved to the end of the bed. As they rushed into the room, the mattress was violently shaking and bouncing once more. Needless to say, the family was terrified.

Unfortunately, there is no reliable, clear-cut information about how the decision was reached by the Jesuits to perform an exorcism. According to church doctrine, there are a number of different conditions that have to be met to show that someone is truly possessed. Whether or not these conditions were met is unknown, but

Bowdern and Bishop went to Archbishop Joseph E. Ritter for permission to perform an exorcism on March 16. Ritter had a reputation as a down-to-earth progressive. Earlier in the decade, he had campaigned hard to integrate the St. Louis schools and parishes. Later, he would also have a large role in the sweeping reforms that came to the church as Vatican II. The Jesuits, who already had a tense history with the Catholic Church as a whole, had no idea how Ritter would respond to the request. Surprisingly, he prompted agreed.

And the exorcism began...

The chronology throughout the remainder of the case is extremely confusing. It is not clear how long Robbie stayed at his relative's house where portions of the exorcism took place, but it is known that he was taken to the Alexian Brothers Hospital in south St. Louis, possibly for as long as a month. Portions of the exorcism were also carried out in the rectory of St. Francis Xavier College Church. The rectory has since been demolished and replaced.

It also isn't clear how many people were actively involved in the exorcism. The names of the exorcists given out in St. Louis were Father Bowdern, Father Bishop, and Father Lawrence Kenny. Father Charles O'Hara of Marquette University in Milwaukee was also present as a witness (he later passed on information about what he saw there to Father Eugene Gallagher at Georgetown) and there were undoubtedly several hospital staff members and seminary students who were also in attendance.

One of these students was Walter Halloran, who I was able to personally interview before his death in 2005. At the time of the exorcism, he was a strapping young former football player who had been asked along to hold Robbie down. Exorcisms were known for being often-violent rituals and the Jesuits must have felt that a strong young man would prove to be very useful. After the exorcism, Halloran finished his studies and later became a Jesuit priest.

The exorcism started at the home of Robbie's St. Louis relatives. The priests came late in the evening, and after Robbie went to bed, the ritual began. The boy was said to go into a trance, his bed shook, and welts and scratches appeared on his body. Bishop was said to have wiped away blood that welled up in the scratches while Halloran attempted to hold the boy down. An exorcism is said to be a dire spiritual and physical struggle. The demon that takes control of the afflicted person also tries to break the faith of the exorcist involved. Father Bowdern had prepared himself for the exhausting events through a religious fast of prayer, bread and water. It is said that from the time he first learned of Robbie's plight until the exorcism had run its course, Bowdern lost nearly forty pounds.

As the prayers commanding the departure of the evil spirit began, Robbie winced and rolled in a sudden seizure of pain. Over the next two hours, the boy was branded and scratched thirty times on his stomach, chest, throat, thighs, calves and back. All the while, he reportedly cursed and screamed obscenities in a voice that "ranged from deep bass to falsetto." The ritual came to an end that night near dawn, but little progress had been made.

The ordeal continued for many weeks, and through many readings of the exorcism ritual. According to the witnesses, the boy's responses became more violent and repulsive as time went on. He allegedly spoke in Latin, in a variety of voices, in between bouts of screams and curses. He spat in the faces of the priests who knelt and stood by his bed, and his spittle and vomit struck them with uncanny accuracy and over great distances. He punched and slapped the priests and the witnesses. He constantly urinated, belched and passed gas that was said to have an unbelievable stench. His body thrashed and contorted into seemingly impossible shapes all through the night. Each morning, though, he would appear to be quite normal and would profess to have no memory of the events that took place after dark. He usually spent the day reading comics or playing board games with the student assistants.

The ritual continued with the prayers being recited every day, despite Robbie's rabid reaction to them. The exorcism seemed virtually useless, and so the priests requested permission to instruct Robbie in the Catholic faith. They felt that his conversion would help to strengthen their fight against the entity controlling the boy. His parents consented, and he was prepared for his first communion. During this time of instruction, Robbie

Scenes of an Exorcism: The old Alexian Brothers Hospital in South St. Louis

seemed to quiet somewhat and he was moved to the church rectory. He seemed to enjoy his lessons in the Catholic faith, but this time of peace would not last. As Robbie prepared to receive communion, the priests literally had to drag him into the church. He broke out in a rage that was worse than anything the exorcists could remember.

By this time, the family was exhausted and was ready to give up. Father Bowdern began searching for a new approach. He made arrangements to return Robbie to Maryland and continue the ritual there. It was said that during the train ride, Robbie became maniacal and attacked Father Bowdern. The priest and the others present wrestled with Robbie until he finally fell asleep.

Bowdern found no accommodations to continue the exorcism with Robbie in Maryland. No one would have anything to do with the boy, and so he returned with him to St. Louis. Robbie's instructions in the Catholic faith continued. It was now Holy Week, the week before Easter, and Robbie was taken to White House, a Jesuit retreat that overlooked the Mississippi River. It was there where the exorcism was continued.

Events now seemed at an impasse. Seeking a solution, Bowdern again plunged into the literature regarding possession. He learned of an 1870 case that took place in Wisconsin that seemed similar to Robbie's plight and he devised a new strategy. On the night of April 18, the ritual resumed. Bowdern forced Robbie to wear a chain of religious medals and to hold a crucifix in his hands. Suddenly, Robbie became strangely contrite. He began to ask questions about the meaning of certain Latin prayers. Bowdern ignored him, refusing to engage in conversation. Instead, he demanded to know the name of the demon and when he would depart. Robbie exploded in a rage.

Five witnesses held him down while he screamed that he was a "fallen angel" but Bowdern continued on with the ritual. He recited it incessantly for hours until Robbie suddenly interrupted in a loud, masculine voice, identifying himself as "St. Michael the Archangel." The voice ordered the demon to depart. Robbie's body went into violent contortions and spasms. Then, he fell quiet. A moment later, he sat up, smiled, and spoke in a normal voice. "He's gone," Robbie said, and then told the priests of a vision that he had of St. Michael holding a flaming sword.

The exorcism was finally over.

Robbie left St. Louis with his parents twelve days later and returned to Maryland. He wrote to Father Bowdern in May 1949 and told him that he

Scenes of an Exorcism: The White House, Jesuit retreat, located west of St. Louis – where the exorcism finally came to an end.

was happy and had a new dog. He is nearly 80 years old and, at last report, is still living in Maryland and is a devout Catholic with three grown children. He is said to have only dim recollections of what happened in 1949.

Father Bowdern believed until the end of his life that he and his fellow priests had been battling a demonic entity. His supporters in this maintain that there were many witnesses to the supernatural events that took place and that no other explanations existed for what they had seen. A full report that was filed by the Catholic Church stated that the case of Robbie Doe was a "genuine demonic possession." According to Father John Nicola, who had the opportunity to review the report, he noted that forty-one persons had signed a document attesting to the fact that they had witnessed paranormal phenomena in the case.

Was Robbie really possessed? Many people don't believe he was. Some have stated that they think Robbie's troubled childhood was to blame. The "possession" started as a way for him to get attention, or to get out of going to school, and then it snowballed into the mess that it became. Most of the debunkings of the case only deal with the inconsistencies of some reports; they never delve into the possible supernatural events that were witnessed, and only address the incidents that took place in Maryland.

And there are other theories. Some would agree that while Robbie was not possessed, he was afflicted with another unexplainable paranormal disturbance. They point to psychokinetic events, when physical objects move about, because of some sort of unconscious mental power that is generated by disturbed people, especially teenagers. While medical doctors have no interest in this, a few more adventurous scientists have grudgingly speculated that perhaps the human mind has abilities and energies that are still unrecognized. These energies just might be able to make objects move, writing to appear, and beds to shake. If it can really happen, it just might explain what happened to Robbie Doe.

Others feel that Robbie suffered from a mental illness, not demonic possession. He may have been hallucinating or suffering from some weird psychosomatic illness that caused him to behave so strangely, to curse and scream and to thrash about so violently.

It should be noted, however, that none of the people who have suggested that what happened to Robbie Doe was nothing more than a hoax or a mental illness were involved in the case. Even Father Walter Halloran later stated that while he was not an expert in exorcisms, and could not make the determination about whether the possession was officially genuine, he did feel that it was real. "I have always thought in my mind that it was," he said. He described seeing objects move, watching Robbie's bed lift off the floor, and other strange events. Since he was present during the events of 1949, his opinion has to be considered and acknowledged far beyond that of those who speculate, and yet were not even born when the exorcism occurred.

Skeptics aside, there are many who believe the events in St. Louis in 1949 were real. They believe that

Robbie truly was possessed. And perhaps they are right, because there is no question that memories of the exorcism remain vivid today in a variety of eerie ways.

After the exorcism at the old Alexian Brothers Hospital concluded, Brother Rector Cornelius, the monk in charge of the institution, went to the fifth-floor corridor of the old wing and turned a key in the door of the room that had been used for Robbie's exorcism. He gave orders that the room was to be kept permanently locked. From that day on, the Alexian Brothers in St. Louis maintained the secrets of the exorcism. The existence of Father Bishop's diary also remained a secret for many years. A copy of it was placed in a desk inside the room when it was sealed. Everyone who worked in the hospital knew why the room was locked.

For years after the exorcism, people who were involved in the case, or who worked at the hospital during that time, shared stories of things they heard and saw during the month-long ordeal that occurred in the psychiatric wing. Orderlies spoke of cleaning up pools of vomit and urine in the boy's room. Staff members and nurses claimed to hear the sounds of someone screaming and the echoes of demonic laughter coming from Robbie's room. More than anything, though, they spoke of the cold air that seemed to emanate from the room. No matter how warm the rest of the hospital was, the area around the door to the boy's room was always ice cold.

And even after the exorcism ended, something seemed to remain behind. Was it some remnant of the entity that possessed Robbie or perhaps the impression of the horrific events that occurred in the room? Whatever it was, the room was never re-opened. Electrical problems plagued the surrounding rooms, and it was always cold in the hallway outside the door to this particular room. That entire section of the hospital was eventually closed, but whether or not this had anything to do with the "exorcism room" is unknown.

As the years passed, tales about the locked room were passed on to new monks who came to serve at the hospital. They knew that the room was located in a wing for extremely ill mental patients but did not understand why the room was kept sealed -- until they heard about what had happened there. The Alexians who had been on the staff in 1949 would not soon forget what they had seen and heard.

In the early 1950s, one of the brothers was working at a summer camp for boys operated by the St. Louis archdiocese near Hillsboro, Missouri. He was a gentle, friendly man and was well liked by the boys. One afternoon, the burly monk was sitting at a table in the mess hall with several of the boys. They were talking and laughing and paying little attention to a radio that was playing in the background.

Then, a song came on that was the theme of the Woody Woodpecker cartoons -- a song that that featured Woody's jangling and rather maniacal laugh. The monk lunged across the table and roughly yanked the radio's electrical cord out of the socket. Trembling and breaking out in a cold sweat, he told his companions that he couldn't stand the song. Later on, he told them about the nights in the spring of 1949, when he and his fellow monks were kept awake by peals of wild, chilling laughter – laughter that sounded a lot like Woody Woodpecker -- coming from one of the rooms in the old wing of the Alexian Brothers Hospital.

Other Alexians had their own stories to tell. They spoke of banging sounds on their doors at night, voices calling in the darkened corridors, and more. Staff members would continue telling the stories in the years to come. I have personally spoken to more than a dozen nurses, maintenance people, orderlies and doctors who have dark and distinct memories of the old wing and the locked room on the psychiatric floor. Some of them have told me that sometimes, even after all of these years, they still dream about that wing and that one locked door.

The stories and tales about the "St. Louis Exorcism" have continued to circulate over the years. Many of the stories have involved the physical locations that were connected to the case. One of them, the old rectory of the St. Francis Xavier Church, was torn down many years ago. In 1978, the old Alexian Brothers Hospital became a memory as well.

In May 1976, work began on a new Alexian Brothers Hospital. In the first phase of the construction, some of the old outbuildings were torn down and a new six-story tower with two-story wings was built. In October

1978, the patients were moved out of the original hospital building and the contractor ordered the structure to be razed. It was done, but not without difficulty. Workers on the demolition crew claimed to be unable to control the wrecking ball when that floor was taken off. The ball swung around and hit a portion of a new building but luckily did no damage. This incident seemed to further enhance the legend of the room -- a legend which had continued to grow.

Before the demolition was started, workers first combed through the building for old furniture that was to be taken out and sold. One of them found a locked room in the psychiatric wing and broke in. The room was fully furnished with a dust-covered bed, nightstand, chairs and a desk with a single drawer. When the worker opened the drawer to see what was inside, he found a small stack of papers, which would turn out to be the priest's diary of the exorcism.

The furniture, including all of the items in the locked room, was sold to a company that owned a nursing home located a short distance away from the hospital. For some reason, everything that was salvaged from the hospital was locked in a room on the fourth floor of the nursing home and was never used. When the nursing home was later torn down, many of these demolition workers refused to go on the fourth floor -- but were never able to explain why. What became of the furniture from the locked room is unknown.

Or at least that's one version of the story...

In recent years, another, far stranger story about the fate of the items within the room has come to light. According to sources, the furniture was removed from the locked room at the time of the demolition but was never sold to the nursing home with the rest of the old hospital furnishings. The bed, nightstand, chairs and desk were instead locked away in the basement of a rectory in St. Louis. A number of years later, the rectory was scheduled to be torn down and movers were brought to haul away the items that were left in the basement. According to one of the movers, he arrived at the rectory with some other workers and they were taken down into the basement by a priest. The priest unlocked a door to one of the rooms in the rear of the basement and motioned the men to go inside. However, the worker distinctly remembered that the priest refused to set foot in the basement room. Inside, they found several pieces of furniture that they were directed to remove and then seal up into a wooden crate. After that, the crate was to be placed in a locked storage facility. The movers completed the task and then moved the crate to a storage warehouse across the river in Illinois. According to his story, the furniture from the "Exorcism Room," as it became known, is still there, sealed in a crate.

St. Louis legend has it that another strange thing happened when the locked hospital room was opened. According to workmen, "something" was seen emerging from the room moments before the wrecking ball claimed it. Whatever it was, the men are said to have likened it to a "cat or a big rat or something." I wouldn't begin to suggest what this creature might have been, but I will say that it has continued to add to the legend of the "St. Louis Exorcism Case" over the years.

In closing, I can only say that the St. Louis Exorcism case, whether you believe in possession, demons and exorcisms or not, remains unsolved. There is simply no way to adequately dismiss every unusual thing that was reported in this case without just saying that everyone involved was lying, drunk or insane. For myself, I can't say for certain that young Robbie Doe was possessed, or not possessed, but what I can say is that this is one of the few cases of alleged "possession" that has left me with many lingering questions.

The reader, of course, is advised to judge for himself but as for this author, well, I think there are certainly more things in Heaven and Earth than are dreamt of in our philosophies, and I'll leave it at that.

5. MASTERS OF MAYHEM

THE BLACK ARTS --- AND THOSE WHO DARED TO DABBLE IN THEM

Times have changed. According to those who know such things, modern magicians and practitioners of the black arts seek to master themselves, not the universe. The power these new magicians harness is the latent power of the mind and the elemental spirits that they subdue are not malevolent entities but their own inner demons of doubt and self-deception. They have dispensed with the physical trappings of altars, pentagrams and daggers. Instead, they achieve self-realization through inner workings. Gone are the grimoires with which the medieval magician sought to summon spirits to do his bidding. Gone too are the conjurations that were designed to reveal the mysteries of the universe. The modern adept knows that these abilities lie dormant within himself and that all of the arcane books of forbidden lore do not contain the knowledge that he can now access at will. He needs no spirits on the astral plane to awaken his powers, and no invocations to protect him from the legions of demons that his forerunners feared to unleash on the world. The sacred circle he draws is not to protect him from the forces that he invokes, but to contain the energy that he believes he summons from within his being. Magic is no longer a random mixture of science and superstition.

Or is it?

When the reader thinks of a modern-day black magician, his head is filled with images of pentagrams, black robes and magical appliances like daggers and chalices of blood. Is this merely the product of television and films, books and imaginative journalists? Perhaps – or perhaps these images come from those seeking attention, passing themselves off as Satanists and true practitioners of the black arts. Or perhaps not as much history has passed for the Left-Hand Path as some would have us believe.

The pages that follow chronicle the lives and careers of some of the modern-day figures and groups who have shaped our current picture of the black arts. Some of them claim to practice witchcraft. Some of them allegedly worship Satan. Others may be the real thing while still others write about the black arts, perhaps shaping our belief and knowledge of them in ways that those who actually practice them cannot.

MONTAGUE SUMMERS: THE CURIOUS CLERIC

In 1926, at the height of the Jazz Age, when books about frolicking flappers and lovelorn millionaires like F. Scott Fitzgerald's *The Great Gatsby* were all the rage, an obscure Roman Catholic cleric experienced overnight success with an unexpected bestseller. *The History of Witchcraft and Demonology* by Reverend Montague Summers was presented as a serious work of scholarship, with Latin and French quotations, extensive footnotes and a comprehensive bibliography. Even so, it immediately incurred the wrath of the foremost thinkers of the time, and it was equally condemned by the press. Author H.G. Wells vilified it as a catalog of superstitious nonsense, while several national newspapers asked if its publication was some sort of sophisticated practical joke. Summers, however, was quite serious about the book. He stated in his introduction that this was no mere antiquarian survey of quaint rural rites. Having separated fact from folklore, he had been able to cut through to the "core and enduring reality of Witchcraft and the witch cult throughout the ages" to conclude that "there were – and are – organizations deliberately, nay even enthusiastically, devoted to the service of evil."

Montague Summers

In order to support his argument, Summers cited case after case in which witches had freely confessed to communing with the Devil. He noted that many accounts were uncannily similar in substance despite the fact that they had come from different times and widely different places.

But it was not the depth of Summers' scholarship, not the believability of his arguments that made the book such a success – it was his habit of lingering over the sexual details of the satanic ceremonies described in the book. His barely repressed relish was combined with the righteous indignation of someone who didn't approve of orgies, but desperately wanted to see one. It was a feeling shared by many of his readers, who could only conclude that witchcraft was alive and well in the twentieth century. Montague Summers had almost single-handedly made the subject eerily seductive.

Augustus Montague Summers was as extraordinary and complex a character as his contemporary, Aleister Crowley, with whom he was acquainted. A cherub-faced eccentric, he appeared to have stepped out of an eighteenth-century novel by Henry Fielding or some other rural England writer. He compounded that impression by having a comic falsetto voice and a peculiar hairstyle that resembled a regency-era wig. He habitually dressed in a black cassock and a black cape. In order to complete the picture, he wore silver-buckled shores and twirled a silver-topped cane like a dandy from the days of antiquity.

Born in 1888, Summers was the youngest of the seven children of Augustus William Summers, a rich banker and justice of the peace in Clifton, Bristol. Summers was educated at Clifton College before studying theology at Trinity College, Oxford, with the intention of becoming a priest in the Church of England. In 1905, he received a fourth-class Bachelor of Arts degree, but as it turned out, the religious title that he used later in life was entirely fictitious. He was ordained as a Church of England deacon in 1908, and worked as a curate in Bath and Bitton in Greater Bristol, but he was never officially accepted as a cleric. Perhaps this was his rumored interest in Satanism or, more likely, the rumors that followed him about sexual misconduct with choirboys, for which he was subsequently tried and acquitted. Whatever the truth, he converted to Catholicism and passed himself off as a priest. He was a known "character," and was frequently caricatured by newspapers artists as a comical figure emerging from a library with a book on vampires tucked under his arm. But not everyone found him so funny...

The occult author Dennis Wheatley (more about him in this chapter) recalled being invited to Summers' Alresford home for the weekend, where he was entertained with stories of his host's struggles with the Devil. One particularly memorable incident saw the cleric performing an exorcism on a laborer's wife in Ireland. She was foaming at the mouth and had to be restrained while he carried out the ceremony. At the height of the struggle, he claimed to see a black mist come out of the woman's mouth. The strange mist then entered a leg of mutton that had been prepared for supper. When the time came to carve the meat, the exhausted host and his guest were horrified to see that the freshly prepared meat was now crawling with maggots. It was a good story, Wheatley knew, but the same events could have been attributed to a number of other occultists of the time. He wasn't sure that Summers was being truthful, but he didn't want to accuse him of lying.

During the visit, Summers took Wheatley into a room in his house that was piled high with books. He selected a small, leather-bound volume and offered to sell it to his guest for £50. He assured him that it was worth much more, but he wanted to do his new friend a favor. Somewhat embarrassed, Wheatley declined the offer, saying that he couldn't afford it at the time.

Wheatley later wrote, "Never have I seen a man's expression change so swiftly. From benevolent calm, it suddenly became filled with demonic fury. He threw down the book and flounced out of the room."

Unnerved, Wheatley sent himself a fictitious telegram that urgently called him back to London. He was packed up and on his way back to the city a short time later.

In the early 1900s, Summers joined the growing ranks of English men of letters interested in medievalism, Catholicism and the occult. He converted to Catholicism in 1909 and shortly thereafter began passing himself off as a Catholic priest. He styled himself as the "Reverend Alphonsus Joseph-Mary Augustus Montague Summers," even though he was never a member of any Catholic order or diocese.

Summers worked for several years as an English and Latin teacher at various schools before adopting writing as his full-time profession. He was interested in the theater of the seventeenth century, particularly that of the English Restoration, and edited the plays of Aphra Behn, John Dryden, William Congreve, among others. He was one of the founding members of The Phoenix, a society that performed those neglected works, and was elected a fellow of the Royal Society of Literature in 1916. But not all of his society memberships were so upstanding. He was also a member of the Order of the Chaerona, whose interest in young boys was neither platonic nor philosophical, and the British Society for the Study of Sex Psychology, for whom he wrote an essay extolling the virtues and vices of the Marquis de Sade.

He writing went in many directions. He wrote religious works about Saint Catherine of Siena and Saint Anthony Maria Zaccaria, but his primary interests were in horror and the occult. He produced important studies about the Gothic fiction genre and edited two collections of Gothic horror short stories, as well as an incomplete edition of two of the seven obscure Gothic novels, known as the *Northanger Horrid Novels*, mentioned by Jane Austen in her Gothic parody *Northanger Abbey*. He was instrumental in rediscovering those lost works, which some had supposed were an invention of Jane Austen herself. He also published biographies of Jane Austen and Ann Radcliffe.

When it came to the occult, He took cues from Aleister Crowley. While Crowley adopted the persona of a modern-day witch, Summers played the part of the learned Catholic witch-hunter. In 1928, he published the first English translation of Heinrich Kramer's and James Sprenger's *Malleus Maleficarum* ("The Hammer of Witches"), a notorious fifteenth-century Latin text on witch-hunting. In his introduction, Summers insisted that the reality of witchcraft was an essential part of Catholic doctrine. He declared the book to be a correct account of witchcraft and a manual on the methods necessary to combat it. The book was part of a horrific period of persecution during the height of the witch-hunting craze that ravaged Europe, and real Catholic authorities called the publication of the original book a "disastrous episode" in history.

The success of *The History of Witchcraft and Demonology* encouraged Summers to pen further volumes on related subjects, all boasting a similar degree of scholarship and research. He presented each book as documentary evidence, and seemed to believe every word that he had written. The titles included *The Vampire: His Kith and Kin* (1928) and *The Vampire in Europe* (1929), and later, *The Werewolf* (1933). To modern readers, Summers' work is often criticized for his old-fashioned writing style, his questionable display of erudition, and his purported belief in the reality of the bizarre subjects he treats. However, there is no question that the "curious and eccentric cleric" managed to almost single-handedly shape the way we treat the occult today.

THE DEVIL RIDES OUT: DENNIS WHEATLEY AND THE OCCULT

Dennis Wheatley

A nubile young woman writhes naked on a black satin cloth embroidered with an inverted pentagram, her wrists and ankles tied at each corner of the altar on which her virgin blood is about to be shed. Behind the altar, framed by two black candles and brandishing a ceremonial dagger, the high priest of the Satanic cult prepares to carry out the invocations to his infernal master...

The iconic imagery above could have been taken from any one of a number of Hammer horror films made in the late 1960s or early 1970s, when society's interest in black magic and the occult was at its peak. It was a time when the peace and love dream of the "Psychedelic Sixties" had been shattered by the shock of the Manson Family murders. An increasingly permissive society was threatening the moral order imposed by organized religion, whose authority was in rapid decline. Sex, drugs, and rock and roll were seen as symptoms of the Devil's increasing influence – but the unlikely "agent provocateur" at the center of this diabolical interest in the dark side of the occult was not a black magician but a middle-aged, former British Intelligence officer turned author named Dennis Wheatley.

When his writing career began, Wheatley had no first-hand knowledge or experience with the occult, but he thought that black magic and Satanism would be perfect ingredients for a "ripping good yarn." And he was right. His melodramatic prose style, lurching action scenes, and politically incorrect prejudices proved no barrier to his commercial success. Readers lapped up the pulpy thrillers with their wild mix of sadism, sex and Satanism, set in the world of British country houses and smoke-filled gentleman's clubs. Wheatley's heroes were all cross-carrying do-gooders whose faith, friendship, and fearlessness always carried the day against the shifty Satanists, who were almost invariably sleazy foreigners.

Although his books are little read today – especially in America, unless you were lucky to find his novels in second-hand shops like I was – Wheatley was once one of the world's bestselling authors. He had a huge impact on how millions of people saw satanic groups and cults. In fact, during the satanic sex abuse scare of the 1980s, it was discovered that many people with so-called "suppressed memories" of Satanic Ritual Abuse were actually generating false memories drawn from occult fiction – most specifically from the novels of Wheatley, who had been the first to come up with the idea of a worldwide satanic conspiracy.

As odd as it may seem, a fiction writer had perhaps more effect than anyone else on the way that we see practitioners of black magic today.

Dennis Wheatley was born in London on January 8, 1897 to a family of Mayfair wine merchants. His early education was varied and would come to make up the mixture of patriotism, epicureanism and love of adventure that was found in his novels. From 1908 to 1912, he was a Merchant Navy cadet aboard the HMS Worcester, after which he went to Germany to study wine-making. In September 1914, at the age of 17, he received a military commission and later fought at Cambrai, St. Quentin, and Passchendaele during World War I.

Injured after a chlorine gas attack, he was discharged from the army and went into the family wine business. Following the death of his father in 1926, he took control of the company. It was at this time that he began to write short stories. After a brief, first marriage failed, he wed Joan Younger in 1931, with whom he remained for the rest of his life.

Wheatley's business was badly affected by the general decline in the economy of the early 1930s and by 1932, he was forced to sell out and came close to bankruptcy. As a diversion from his financial worries, and with encouragement from his wife, he set to work writing a full-length thriller called *Three Inquisitive People*. His agent's reader considered the book weak, though, and it was not published until much later in his writing career. However, this book did introduce the character of the Duc de Richleau, a high-living French expatriate living in London, along with his friends, American adventurer Rex Van Ryn, English gentleman Richard Eaton, and Jewish financier Simon Aron, who went on to become Wheatley's most popular characters.

With his first book in the hands of his agent, he set about writing a second book with the same characters called *The Forbidden Territory*, which was immediately snapped up by a publisher. This adventure story, set behind the Iron Curtain, had the Duc attempting to rescue his friend Rex from a gulag in Siberia. It won immediate acclaim from both the press and the public, was reprinted seven times in as many weeks, and the film rights were bought by Alfred Hitchcock. As with most of the later adaptions of Wheatley books into film, it turned out to be a lackluster affair.

The book was followed by a string of thrillers and occult horror novels that, throughout the 1930s and 1940s, propelled Wheatley into the category of bestselling author. He used his popularity during World War II to speak on behalf of the war effort, and in 1941, he was re-commissioned to the military to become the only civilian member of the Joint Planning Staff. With the rank of wing commander, he worked in Churchill's basement fortress, producing papers for consideration by the Chiefs of Staff.

After the war, he returned to his writing and enjoyed a tremendous surge in popularity during the 1960s and 1970s. All of his many titles were returned to print, and he even edited a series of short story collections and a series of paperbacks known as the "Dennis Wheatley Library of the Occult."

In his private life, Wheatley was a charming man with a boyish sense of humor who was much loved by those who knew him. His religious convictions were unorthodox. Despite the conventional orthodoxy of his literary creations, he considered Christianity to be a joyless religion and his beliefs leaned more toward Eastern philosophies. He lived a life of quiet humility, and was genuinely touched by the praise that was heaped on him. It was only toward the end of his life that he had to stop replying personally to every letter written to him by his many fans. He did continue to reply to those that he considered were of a serious nature.

Wheatley died of liver failure on November 10, 1977, leaving behind an immense body of work – more than eighty books written and millions of copies in print. Of those books, only eight of them dealt with the occult. So, how did Wheatley become such an important part of the history of satanic cults and black magic?

The most famous novel that Wheatley ever wrote was the 1934 book *The Devil Rides Out*. It was the third book to feature De Richleau and his friends and it found the Duc attempting to rescue his friend Simon Aron from the clutches of Mocata, a Satanist based on Wheatley's real-life acquaintance Aleister Crowley. It was his first foray into the theme of black magic and it featured a relentless onslaught of spiritual warfare, Black Masses, orgies, magic circles, car chases, an air pursuit across Europe and even an appearance by the Devil himself. The book captured the public's imagination and it became an immediate hit. As mentioned, its popularity returned in the 1960s, especially after Hammer Films made a movie version of the book starring Christopher Lee as the heroic Duc De Richleau.

The occult was a subject that interested Wheatley tremendously, although he went to great pains to reiterate his belief that such forces were dangerous and not meant to be trifled with. He claimed to have never participated in an occult ritual himself. The one occasion on which he called on the Devil to help him win at cards was apparently sufficient to warn him away from such things for life. He claimed that he began winning hand after hand against the odds and had to make a conscious effort to lose in order to break the spell. For his books, Wheatley attributed his knowledge of black magic to conversations with contemporary practitioners and experts like Crowley and Montague Summers.

Although Wheatley could never be accused of playing fair with the beliefs of real-life ceremonial magicians, reducing their practices to a sort of Medieval Satan worship, he clearly relished the idea of adding their lurid presence to his novels. He frequently borrowed the terminology of existing occult societies. For example, his high-ranking Satanists often bore titled ranks from the Order of the Golden Dawn and Crowley's Argenteum Astrum, such as Magister Templi and Ipsissimus. To these flourishes he added lurid depictions of solemn rituals, human sacrifice, and sexual frenzy.

But how did borrowed material and fictional devices influence the real world of the occult? *The Devil Rides Out* spawned seven more black magic titles: *Strange Conflict, The Ka of Gifford Hillary, To the Devil – A Daughter, The Haunting of Toby Jugg, The Satanist, They Used Dark Forces* and *Gateway to Hell*. By the time of Wheatley's death, these books alone had sold more than fifty million copies. His descriptions of Devil-inspired debauchery became largely responsible for igniting the public consciousness and stimulating the imaginations of the already wildly imaginative tabloid press. If such theatrical cults appeared in Wheatley's books, then why couldn't they exist in real life?

Although Wheatley never claimed any in-depth knowledge of Satanism, he lent credibility to his tales by consulting serious experts on the subject. Consequently, his detailed descriptions of ceremonial magic, conjurations, curses and invocations offered any curious person a working knowledge of the black arts for the price of a paperback book. They had only to browse through their local shops and antique stores to find the required paraphernalia needed to conduct diabolical rites.

The secrets revealed in Wheatley's books were not harmless conjurer's tricks. If they were practiced by the uninitiated or the immature, they had the potential to wreak psychological havoc, especially if drugs (not uncommon in the 1960s) were also involved. Wheatley made his own views on the subject known during a radio interview in which he said, "Nine-tenths of them are phonies. To call down the powers of evil is a life-time's job. Most of the people are in it just for the sex orgies and the dope traffic. We should investigate the powers of the human mind, certainly, but this monkeying about with unknown forces is dangerous for the weak-minded. I've known people who neglect their wives and families and end up in the loony-bin."

Wheatley made quite a living writing about such things, but what caused his aversion to them? And most of all, did he believe in them? The answer would be yes – and his belief is what made him realize that strange forces were not to be tampered with.

As a child in preparatory school on the Kent coast, just prior to World War I, he saw a ghost – a "ghastly face" whose appearance he blamed on the housemaster, who had been conducting séances. After that, Wheatley vowed that he would never become involved in a séance or a magical ceremony. He chose instead to write about the subject, in order to warn every one of the dangers of dealing with unknowable – and uncontrollable – forces.

ALEX SANDERS: "KING OF THE WITCHES"

As Anton LaVey would do in America, Alex Sanders shocked the British public into the realization that witches were still living among them in the 1960s. They saw him on their television sets, behind the innocuous curtains of a modest home in the English seaside resort town of Bexhill-on-Sea, looking just like everyone else, hiding in plain sight, so to speak. A television crew filmed him as the self-proclaimed "King of Witches" as he donned a golden mask and a weighty feathered headdress before summoning an Aztec fire spirit to join him in his ritual. His assistants removed his robe, leaving the suburban witch to dance around his front room with a blazing flare in each hand. He became possessed by the entity, his followers explained, allowing him to offer wisdom from the next world. Sanders was invoking a spirit to "blaze a trail" for his people, protecting them

Alex Sanders – "King of Witches"

from persecution and from the eyes of the tabloid press. Like many magicians and occultists, Sanders was an unrepentant narcissist, with a larger-than-life ego and an insatiable need for attention. He courted controversy and plagued the press to publicize his activities -- publicity that rarely pleased his fellow witches, who feared the lurid reports would incite problems and ridicule. They also didn't appreciate his habit of embellishing the truth to make himself sound more interesting.

Understandably, this makes it a little hard to separate truth from fiction when examining Sanders' biography. Sanders was initiated into the "Craft" by a member of a Nottingham coven in the early 1960s, but according to Sanders' story, he insisted that his Welsh grandmother, Mary Bibby, had performed the ceremony when he was a child, after he had accidentally interrupted her while she was performing a ritual. He claimed to have walked into her house one day in 1933 and found the naked old lady drawing a magic circle on the kitchen floor. When she recovered from her surprise, she told him to remove his clothes and join her in the circle. Then she nicked his scrotum with a knife and declared that he was now a witch. After swearing him to secrecy, she informed him that he was a descendant of the Welsh chieftain and king of the witches, Owain Glyn Dwr. In time, young Alex would have the right to assume his title, she told him – or so he claimed.

As those with an interest in the occult would soon learn, it was hard to tell where legend ended with Alex Sanders and where truth actually began.

Whatever the truth of his beginnings may have been, Sanders was allegedly a natural-born psychic, as were his brothers. He was born on June 6, 1926 as Orrell Alexander Carter in Birkenhead, Merseyside. He was the oldest of six children. His father, Albert Carter, was an alcoholic dance hall performer who married Margaret Bibby in 1920. Later, the family moved to Manchester and unofficially changed their surname to Sanders.

As mentioned, there are several contradictory accounts about Sanders' initiation into witchcraft; even his own accounts were inconsistent. After the story that he told about his grandmother, he added that she let him copy her witchcraft book, *the Book of Shadows*, when he was nine and taught him the rites and magic of witches. He was taught clairvoyance first by scrying in inky water, then in his grandmother's crystal ball. Others would tell different stories. High Priestess Patricia Crowther said that, according to letters she received from Sanders in 1961, he did not then claim to be an initiate, but felt an affinity with the occult and had experienced second sight. In a 1962 interview, Sanders claimed to have been initiated for a year, working in a coven led by a woman from Nottingham. This claim was corroborated by Maxine Sanders, Alex's second wife. She maintained that although Sanders was later initiated into Wicca, he was indeed been taught a form of witchcraft by his grandmother when he was young. Three years later, the old woman allegedly took Sanders to London and left him with a certain "Mr. Alexander" – later identified as Aleister Crowley – who instructed Sanders in the so-called "Rites of Horus."

With that kind of background, it's no wonder that Sanders felt himself drawn to black magic in general and "sex magick" in particular. Over the course of the next several years, his interests in the occult grew darker.

Sanders often allowed journalists and cameramen to take lurid photos of his ceremonies, always looking for attention. This led to him being often criticized by other British witches.

Toward the end of World War II, he began working for a manufacturing chemist's laboratory in Manchester. He married a co-worker named Doreen Stratton in 1948. They had two children together. Sanders wanted more children, but Doreen didn't. The marriage quickly deteriorated as Doreen expressed her disapproval with her husband's continuing interest in the occult. She finally left him in 1952, taking their children with her. Grief-stricken, Sanders cursed her with a fertility spell so that when she remarried, she found herself burdened by three sets of twins.

But this was small consolation in the short term. Feeling isolated, lonely and dejected, Sanders drifted from one low-paying job to another, having sexual affairs with both men and women. It was at this point that he decided to pursue sex and wealth on the "Left-Hand Path," a seed that had been planted in his mind years before.

He almost immediately saw results. He wangled a free house and a monthly allowance from total strangers, a middle-aged Manchester couple who took Sanders for the "exact double" of their late son. He later wrote, "I held parties, I bought expensive clothes, I was sexually promiscuous; but it was only after a time that I realized I had a fearful debt to pay."

One of Alex's mistresses of whom he was particularly fond committed suicide. Then his sister Joan was injured in an accidental shooting and was shortly after diagnosed with terminal cancer. Alex, blaming himself, resolved to stop using magic for selfish reasons and instead teach it to others. He was dissuaded from walking any further on the "Left-Hand Path," and yet, while working as a healer, he couldn't resist ridding one client of warts by transferring them to someone he didn't like. He also claimed to have cured a man of drug addiction, and cured his daughter Janice of a deformed foot, which her doctors had said could not be treated. On the instructions of a spirit guide, Sanders bathed the girl's foot in olive oil, and worked on it until he was able to twist it painlessly back into the right position.

In 1963, on the advice of his spirit guides, he sought employment as a porter, book-duster and odd-job man in the John Rylands Library in Manchester, where he could access an original copy of the *Key of Solomon*. According to his own admission, he dismantled this book and borrowed it a few pages at a time for copying. He was threatened with prosecution when he was inevitably caught, but the librarians allowed him an amnesty on condition that the materials were safely returned. He brought everything back, but not before he'd made a handwritten copy of the most potent rituals.

Sanders' job was in trouble even before the discovery of what he had done with the book. Around this same time, he had attracted unwanted attention to himself by persuading the local newspapers to publish a front-page exposé of witchcraft. This publicity had several unfortunate side-effects for Sanders, including the loss of his job at the library and estrangement from the local coven that he had been trying to join. They considered him a troublesome upstart and refused to initiate him.

He was eventually initiated into another coven, and in time, most of the leaders of the group resigned, likely due to Sander's grating personality and need for publicity. When the press pestered him for salacious accounts of nude rituals and magical spells, he willingly obliged. And the more media attention he got, the more followers he attracted. By 1965, he claimed 1,623 initiates in 100 covens, who apparently elected him to the title of "King of the Witches."

Among his alleged magical feats was the creation of a "spiritual baby," who became one of his familiars. The birth is said to have resulted from a sacred act of masturbation, which occurred between Sanders and a male assistant. Shortly following its creation, the spirit disappeared to grow up on some unspecified spiritual plane, but reappeared later to take Sanders over in his channeling. Supposedly, this spirit forcibly made Sanders carry on at wild parties, insult people, and otherwise act abominably.

During the height of his popularity, Sanders met Arline Maxine Morris, who was twenty years his junior. He initiated her into his flock and made her a High Priestess. They were married in 1968 and moved into a basement flat near Notting Hill Gate in London, where they ran their coven and taught classes on Witchcraft. Their daughter, Maya Alexandria, was born that same year.

Sanders' launch into the national public spotlight resulted from a sensational 1969 newspaper article which led to the romanticized biography, *King of the Witches*, by June Johns in 1969, followed by the film "*Legend of the Witches.*" These led to greater publicity, guest appearances on talk-shows, and public speaking engagements. All of this was to the chagrin of other witches, who saw Sanders as exploiting their faith and dragging it through the gutter of the sensational press.

Not surprisingly, the 1969 news article that generated Sanders' fame had been written about a fraud. Sanders had told a reporter that he could raise the dead, a ritual that he would perform at Alderley Edge. When he arrived with a reporter and photographer, they found a bandaged figure lying on a stone altar. A friend of Sanders', posing as a doctor, certified that the man, another of Sanders' friends, was indeed dead. Sanders recited a "strange and ancient" invocation, which was in reality a Swiss roll recipe read backwards, and then, with great deliberation, the corpse slowly sat up. The reporter ran his story, which made front-page headlines. This made other witches furious. Again, it should come as no surprise that Sanders didn't care. He rode the wave of publicity, and alerted the public to the idea that witchcraft was alive and well in modern England.

In 1971, Sanders and Maxine separated. Alex moved to Sussex, while Maxine remained in the London flat, where she continued to teach and run the coven. Regardless, their relationship continued and they had a son, Victor Mikhael, in 1972.

In time, all of the anger that Sanders caused caught up with him. He was acutely aware of the criticism that had been leveled against him for years. In 1979, he made a full and sincere apology for the way that he had behaved. He announced to the witchcraft community that he wished "to make amends for some of the past hurts that I have given and many public stupidities I created for others of the Craft." He hoped that all of the new converts that he had brought to the movement could outweigh the negative attention he had attracted.

Sanders died from lung cancer on April 30, 1988. True to his form as a showman, it seems that he was still able to arouse controversy from the other side. A tape recording was played at his funeral in which Sanders declared Victor, his son, was to succeed him as "King of the Witches." Victor would lead the "Witchcraft Council of Elders," which the recording claimed had over 100,000 members. When word got out, other witches stated that the council was a fabrication, since it was highly unlikely that there were 100,000 witches in Britain, let alone that many elders. It didn't matter anyway. Victor had no interest in carrying on his father's business and had already moved to the United States.

Even after his many frauds and outrageous statements were revealed, there is no question that Sanders left an indelible mark on the practice of magic. After renouncing the "Left-Hand Path," he joined up with the Wicca movement, which was founded by Gerald Gardner in 1954. Of course, it wasn't good enough for Sanders. He subsequently revised the basic texts to create his own "Alexandrian" style of magic, which still exists today. Nude rituals were preferred and initiation into the "third degree" required performance of a special "Grand Rite" – better known as public sexual intercourse. With its nudity and sexual trappings, the Alexandrian cult was what made Sanders so popular with the tabloid journalists. In 1965, Sanders was helping out with a movie called *Eye of the Devil*, which starred David Niven and Sharon Tate – who was later murdered by members of the Charles Manson family. Sanders supposedly met Tate on the movie set and initiated her into his coven.

The Alexandrian cult continued after Sanders' death. In the United States, its headquarters was founded in Boston and active covens are still reported from coast to coast. While most Alexandrian witches claim to practice "white" magic, there is no question that the movement will always be tainted by the founder's failure to fully denounce his "black" magic roots or his devotion to witchcraft as a sexual tool.

ANTON LAVEY AND THE CHURCH OF SATAN

The traditional, or theistic, worship of Satan is a perversion of both black magic rites and orthodox religion, specifically Christianity. This type of Satanism mocks the rituals, priesthood, dogma, and liturgies of the Church. Over the centuries, it has created its own sex rituals to take the place of the form of worship practiced by Christians. This movement has never pretended to be anything other than an enemy of civil and religious establishment, a sworn enemy of the Church and the antithesis of the precepts of nature-based witchcraft. These types of Satanists are often referred to as "reverse Christians" because they practice what would be the opposite of the teachings of the Christian church. Satan is not a figure that is meant to be feared, but one that is embraced and upheld as the enemy of God.

But this is not always what comes to mind when we think of modern-day Satanism. Thanks to its very public face, which was first revealed in the 1960s, the so-called Church of Satan is usually the first thing that people think of when they hear about "Satan worshippers." Strangely, though, this isn't really correct. Members of the Church of Satan are atheists or agnostics who believe that Satan is simply a metaphor for the natural urges of mankind. The inspiration for these symbolic Satanists was Anton Szandor LaVey, the founder of the Church of Satan, who began publicizing the old Crowley motto of "Do What Thou Wilt" in the 1960s.

The Church of Satan was built entirely by the sheer force of LaVey's dynamic personality. He was a writer, occultist, musician, actor, and bona fide showman. He was brilliant, always controversial, and, in the end, more than a bit of a mystery since his autobiography was so mixed with legend that it's almost impossible to separate fantasy from the truth. His home, in a large Victorian house near San Francisco's Golden Gate Park, doubled as the organization's satanic chapel. His basement, which was a combination of chapel and nightclub, boasted a collection of grisly artifacts, including an Aztec sacrificial knife, a torture hook used by Spanish Inquisitors, a shrunken head from South America, and various objects from dead religions around the world. The house itself was painted stark black with purple trim, making it stand out among the pastel town houses that lined the street.

LaVey looked as startling as his house, with a shaven head, pointed beard, black attire and penetrating gaze. He was the very image of a sinister – albeit charming – Mephistopheles. He loved the attention the formation of the Church gave to him and he managed to keep his name in the headlines for decades. But was the Church of Satan merely a sideshow – a cynical con perpetrated by a former carnival showman?

Or was there more to the Church of Satan than LaVey ever revealed?

Anton Szandor LaVey – whose real name was Howard Stanton Levey – was born in Chicago on April 11, 1930. His father, Michael Levey, was a liquor distributor from Omaha. His mother, Gertrude, was a homemaker. The family later relocated to the San Francisco Bay area and Levey spent most of his early life in California. From his Eastern European grandmother, young Howard learned much about the superstitions that were rampant in her part of the world, which led to his interest in vampires, witchcraft, and the occult. He became an avid reader of dark literature and pulp magazines and later befriended writers of the day, like Clark Ashton Smith, Robert Barber Johnson and George Hass. According to his biography, he began developing his musical skills at an early age and tried his hand at various instruments, including the pipe organ and the calliope.

LaVey (as he would soon become known) dropped out of high school and began working in circuses and carnivals, first as a roustabout and cage cleaner, and later as a musician. He learned the ropes in the spook shows and became well versed in the rackets to separate rubes from their money. He played the calliope for the "grind shows" on Saturday nights, and played the organ on Sunday mornings for the tent revivals. He later noted seeing many of the same men attending both the strip shows on Saturday night and the church services on Sunday mornings, which reinforced his cynical view of religion. When the carnival season ended, LaVey began earning a living playing the organ in Los Angeles bars, nightclubs, and burlesque theaters. It was during this time that he claimed to have a brief affair with then-unknown actress Marilyn Monroe.

Moving back to San Francisco, LaVey worked as a police photographer for a time. A short time later, he met and married Carole Lansing, who bore him his first daughter, Karla Maritza, in 1952. They divorced in 1960 after LaVey began seeing Diane Hegarty. They never married, but she was his companion for many years, and bore his second daughter, Zeena Galatea LaVey in 1964. LaVey's final companion was Blanche Barton, who gave him his only son, Satan Xerxes Carnacki LaVey in 1993. Barton became the head of the Church of Satan after LaVey's death, but later stepped down to be replaced by Peter H. Gilmore.

During the 1950s, LaVey dabbled as a psychical investigator, looking into what his friends on the police force cheerfully referred to as "nut calls." LaVey soon became known as a San Francisco celebrity. Thanks to his paranormal research and his live performances as an organist (including playing the Wurlitzer at the Lost Weekend cocktail lounge), he attracted many California notables to his parties. Guests included Michael Harner, Chester A. Arthur III, Forrest J. Ackerman, Fritz Leiber, Dr. Cecil E. Nixon, and Kenneth Anger. He began presenting lectures on the occult to what he called his "Magic Circle," which was made up of friends who shared his interests. It was a member of the circle who suggested, perhaps jokingly, that he could start his own religion based on the ideas that he was coming up with.

LaVey took this suggestion seriously, and on April 30, 1966, Walpurgis Night, he launched his new religion. He shaved his head, declared the founding of the Church of Satan, and proclaimed 1966 as "the Year One," Anno Satanas - the first year of the Age of Satan. He exhibited a flair for self-promotion that would have impressed P.T. Barnum. In the years that followed, Satan rewarded him well. He acquired numerous properties, a fleet of classic cars, and even a yacht.

Once LaVey got the word out about the new "Church of Satan," he began receiving enormous amounts of publicity.

To create his personal version of Satanism, LaVey mixed together writings by Ayn Rand, Friedrich Nietzsche, Aleister Crowley, H.L. Mencken, and Jack London with the ideology and ritual practices that he created for the Church of Satan. He wrote essays that re-worked books on philosophy and "Satanized" versions of John Dee's Enochian Keys, turning them into books like *The Satanic Bible*, *The Compleat Witch* (re-released in 1989 as *The Satanic Witch*), and *The Satanic Rituals*.

LaVey had nothing but scorn for people who lived routine, monotonous lives – the "herd," as he called them – but he equally despised those individuals who killed in the name of Satan to obtain notoriety. He was acutely aware that his immoral ideology would attract more than its share of "crazies," as he referred to them. The Church of Satan appealed to the neo-Nazis, Charles Manson-types, and the countless eccentrics who saw conspiracies all around them or heard voices telling them to kill in the Devil's name. "These people are not Satanists," he once told a reporter. "They are deranged. But no matter how many they do, they'll never catch up with the Christians. We gave centuries of psychopathic killing in the name of God."

The majority of converts, LaVey claimed, were attracted to Satanism because they needed to belong to something that gave meaning to their lives. They were psychologically damaged products of broken homes, drug addicts crawling out from under the wreckage of their dead-end lives, or the jaded offspring of devoutly religious parents, who turned to LaVey in their adult lives to rebel against what they had been forced to believe in as children.

LaVey's philosophy was really pretty simple. According to him, Satan was not a malevolent entity but an "external projection of each individual's highest potential." He was the personification of our carnal nature, a primitive archetype of our selves, which should never be suppressed or denied. True Satanists, therefore, were not evil, but individuals who dedicated their lives to the pursuit of pleasure and a life free of the restrictions and limitations that were imposed on them by civilized society and organized religion. As such, all Satanists were responsible for their own actions and could not rely on some supernatural savior to redeem them if they were untrue to themselves and whatever code they chose to live by. LaVey argued that orthodox religion was created by man, not God, so no one was obligated to live by its rules, especially since the laws and customs of its founders were no longer relevant in the modern world. The Church created God in its own flawed image as a

LaVey got a lot of attention posing for men's magazines, which seemed to show that Satanism offered a bevy of naked and nubile young women for any man who embraced it. For LaVey, it did!

cruel and capricious patriarch who could never be placated because none of his followers could ever live up to the standards of perfection that the Church imposed upon them. But, LaVey said, no one ever actually gave the Church the authority to be a mediator between God and man or to impose its dogmas on society. It was, therefore, everyone's right to question this self-elected institution.

Unquestioning obedience and blind faith were contrary to the tenets of Satanism, which demanded that individuals think for themselves and act according to their own conscience. LaVey contended that organized religion did not have a monopoly on truth, and he suggested that its priests and ministers were just as capable of being cruel, self-serving and corrupt as the Devil that they claimed to be at war with. It was unrealistic and unnatural to live in the material world and resist the pleasures that it had to offer, in return for a mere promise of paradise.

Media attention followed the founding of the Church of Satan, leading to coverage in newspapers all over the country and the cover of *Look* magazine. The *Los Angeles Times* and the *San Francisco Chronicle* were among those that dubbed him the "Black Pope." LaVey performed satanic weddings, satanic baptisms (including one for his daughter Zeena) and satanic funerals. He released a record album entitled *The Satanic Mass*. He appeared on talk shows with Joe Pyne, Phil Donahue, and Johnny Carson, and in feature-length documentaries like *Satanis* in 1968 and *Speak of the Devil* in 1993. Since its founding, LaVey's Church of Satan has attracted scores of followers who shared a jaded view of organized religion, including celebrities like Jayne Mansfield, Sammy Davis, Jr., Marilyn Manson, director Robert Fuest, ufologist Jacques Vallee, author Aime Michel and many others.

But not all of the publicity was good...

One of the converts to Lavey's Church of Satan was Jayne Mansfield, one of America's top pinup girls. On June 29, 1967, she died a horrible and violent death along a lonely roadway near Biloxi, Mississippi. Her death had a sobering effect on the Hollywood film community and also strange repercussions in the occult community of the time, as well. Jayne's death was said to have been caused by a curse gone awry, and the tragic event opened up a side of the actress' life that few were aware of. Some believed that Anton LaVey was to blame.

Jayne had been born Vera Jayne Palmer in Bryn Mawr, Pennsylvania, on April 19, 1933. When she was three years old, her father died of a heart attack while driving in a car with his wife and daughter. After his death, her mother worked as a schoolteacher and in 1939, she re-married and the family moved to Dallas, Texas. Jayne's desire to become an actress started at an early age, and after high school, she studied both drama and physics at Southern Methodist University.

In January 1950, Jayne married to Paul Mansfield. Her show business aspirations were put on hold with the birth of her first child, Jayne Marie Mansfield, in November of that same year. Jayne was 17 at the time. She juggled motherhood and university classes, and spent the summer at Camp Gordon, Georgia, during her husband's service in the Army. She attended UCLA in the summer of 1953 and then went back to Texas for the fall quarter at Southern Methodist University. In Dallas, she studied acting and won many local beauty pageants, including Miss Electric Switch and Miss Potato Soup. Her physical beauty often hid the fact of how smart she was. Her IQ was said to be 163, she spoke five languages, and she was a classically trained pianist and violinist. But she admitted later in her career that the public didn't care about her brains, they were more interested in her looks and the size of her breasts.

Jayne Mansfield

Paul Mansfield had hoped that the birth of their daughter would discourage his wife's interest in acting. When he realized that it hadn't, he agreed to move to Los Angeles with her in late 1954 to help her start a movie career. Between working at a variety of odd jobs, Jayne studied drama at UCLA. Her film career began with bit parts at Warner Brothers, which had signed her after one of its talent scouts and seen her in a production at the Pasadena Playhouse. She got small roles in a low-budget drama called "*Female Jungle*" and "*Pete Kelly's Blues*," starring Jack Webb. Then in 1955, Paul Wendkos offered her the dramatic role of Gladden in "*The Burglar*," his film adaptation of David Goodis' novel. The film was done in film noir style, and Mansfield appeared alongside Dan Duryea and Martha Vickers. "*The Burglar*" was released two years later, when Mansfield's fame was at its peak. She was successful in this straight dramatic role, though most of her subsequent film appearances would be either comedic in nature or would take advantage of her sex appeal.

Her next role was on the stage, in which she first appeared wearing nothing but a towel, in "*Will Success Spoil Rock Hunter?*" After that, she starred in the camp, comic film "*The Girl Can't Help It*" in 1956. Her first real starring role featured her as the outrageously voluptuous, tone-deaf girlfriend of a retired racketeer. The film features some early performances by Fats Domino, The Platters and Little Richard, successfully introducing rock-n-roll to many movie audiences.

In May 1956, Jayne signed a long-term contract with 20th Century Fox, and then played a straight dramatic role in "*The Wayward Bus*," a 1957 film based on the book by John Steinbeck. She tried to move away from her "dumb blonde" image in this film and establish herself as a serious actress. The cast also included Dan Dailey and Joan Collins and enjoyed reasonable success at the box office. Jayne's performance in this film earned her a Golden Globe for New Star of the Year (Actress) beating out Carroll Baker and Natalie Wood.

216

In 1957, Jayne reprised her role in the movie version of *"Will Success Spoil Rock Hunter?"* co-starring Tony Randall and Joan Blondell. Jayne's fourth starring role was in *"Kiss Them for Me,"* in which she received prominent billing with Cary Grant. However, her part is little more than the usual "dumb blonde" comic relief. The movie turned out to be a box office disappointment and would prove to be her final starring role in a mainstream Hollywood film. Unfortunately, she missed out on a part opposite Jack Lemmon playing a free-spirited witch from Greenwich Village in *"Bell, Book and Candle"* because she was pregnant at the time. The role went to Kim Novak instead.

Jayne divorced Paul Mansfield on January 8, 1958. Five days later, she married actor and bodybuilder Mickey Hargitay. Their marriage lasted for five years, until Jayne got a Mexican divorce in Juarez in May 1963. The divorce was initially declared invalid in California, and the two reconciled in October 1963. After the birth of their third child, Mansfield sued for the Juarez divorce to be declared legal and won. Their acrimonious divorce battle had the actress accusing Hargitay of kidnapping one of her children to force a more favorable financial settlement. During this marriage, she had three children — Miklós Jeffrey Palmer Hargitay, Zoltán Anthony Hargitay, and Mariska Magdolina Hargitay, an actress currently known for her role as Detective Olivia Benson in *"Law & Order: Special Victims Unit."*

At the time of her divorce from Mansfield and her marriage to Hargitay, Jayne's career was still at its height. In addition to her movie roles, she also gained a lot of publicity for her repeated successful attempts to expose her breasts in carefully staged "accidents." Her breasts had become a huge part (pardon the pun!) of her public persona. Jack Parr, host of *"The Tonight Show,"* once introduced her by saying, "Here they are, Jayne Mansfield!"

In April 1957, her breasts were part of a notorious publicity stunt that was intended to deflect attention from Sophia Loren during a dinner party in the Italian star's honor. Photographs of the encounter were published around the world. One image showed Sophia Loren raising an eyebrow at Jayne, who was sitting between Loren and Clifton Webb, as she leaned over the table, allowing her breasts to spill out of her low-cut dress and exposing a nipple.

A similar incident occurred during a film festival in West Berlin. Jayne was wearing a low-cut dress and Mickey Hargitay picked her up so that she could bite a bunch of grapes that were hanging overhead at a party. The movement caused her breasts to spring out of her dress. The photograph of the incident became a sensation, appearing in newspapers and magazines all over the world with the word "censored" hiding the actress' exposed breasts.

Despite all of the publicity that she garnered, and her popularity with the public, good roles dried up for Jayne after 1959. She still managed to keep busy making a series of low-budget films, mostly in Europe. She appeared in a few films for Fox, but was usually relegated to a colorful, scantily clad supporting role. Jayne still commanded high prices as a live performer during this time, although she yearned to establish a more sophisticated image. She announced that she planned to study acting in New York, hoping this would rejuvenate her career, but it was too late. Her reliance on racy publicity had brought her notoriety, but it also proved to be her downfall. Fox did not renew its contract with her in 1962.

But Jayne continued to work. In 1963, Tommy Noonan persuaded her to become the first mainstream American actress to appear nude with a starring role in the film *"Promises! Promises!"* Photographs of a naked Mansfield on the set were published in *Playboy* magazine. The sold-out issue resulted in an obscenity charge for Hugh Hefner, which was later dropped. *"Promises! Promises!"* was banned in Cleveland, but it enjoyed box office success elsewhere and managed to land Jayne a spot on the Top 10 list of Box Office Attractions for that year. Later that year, she also appeared in the low-budget West German movie *"Homesick for St. Pauli."* She played a sexy American singer who was traveling to Hamburg by ship. She sang two German songs in the movie, though her speaking voice was dubbed.

Two photographs from the notorious photo session with Church of Satan founder, Anton LaVey. Both Jayne and LaVey were likely looking for some free publicity from the meeting.

Jayne remained a highly visible personality, despite her film career setbacks. However, good movie roles were getting harder and harder to find. Toward the end of her life, she appeared in a number of low-budget, forgettable films like *"Let's Go Bust!"* and *"The Las Vegas Hillbillies."* Her personal life was not going very well, either. In 1963, she had a well-publicized relationship with singer Nelson Sardelli, whom she planned to marry once her divorce from Hargitay was finalized. This marriage never took place. Instead, in September 1964, Jayne married Matt Cimber (whose real name was Matteo Ottaviano, né Thomas Vitale Ottaviano), an Italian-born film director. The couple was together less than a year and was divorced by July 1966. Jayne had worked with Cimber before, when he directed her in a widely praised stage production of *"Bus Stop"* He also worked with her on her last film, *"Single Room Furnished,'"* but work on the film was suspended when their marriage collapsed. It was later released in 1968, after her death.

In the middle 1960s, faced with a flagging career, Jayne began supporting herself doing burlesque and dinner theater. In late 1966, she took another step to revive her career, which many dismiss as nothing more than another of her infamous publicity stunts – Jayne joined Anton LaVey's newly created Church of Satan. According to LaVey, Jayne had a very real interest in exploring the philosophies of Satanism, although friends claim that she was simply curious about it. Others more cynically believed that she was merely attaching herself to LaVey for the publicity. The Church of Satan had recently been making headlines and appearing in magazines. LaVey cut a sinister and dashing figure. He had become quite notorious in a short time, and even those who disliked him respected him as being a great showman and promoter. Other celebrities, like Sammy Davis, Jr., were photographed with the country's leading Satanist and Jayne may have been looking to get a little free publicity for herself.

In November 1966, Jayne met LaVey for the first time. She and her current boyfriend and attorney, Sam Brody, drove with a press agent to meet with LaVey at his home. While the reasons for Jayne's visit may vary, one thing that all of the accounts agree upon is that LaVey and Sam Brody took an instant dislike to one another.

218

It was said that while Jayne was touring LaVey's home and church, Brody purposely touched a skull and two candles that LaVey stated were cursed. When Brody laughed at the notion that the objects were cursed, LaVey grew angry and asked them to leave.

Nevertheless, Jayne returned. She was hungry for the publicity that the Church of Satan could offer her and LaVey saw the chance to publicize himself through the actress, whether her career was on the downslide or not. Apparently, Jayne agreed to pose for a photo layout with LaVey as an apology for Brody's earlier offenses. LaVey brought out skulls, candles and trappings of the church and asked Jayne to pose in a bikini. She refused but wore a dress instead. Copies of the photo taken survive, showing Jayne drinking from a chalice with LaVey looming behind her in a black cloak.

Brody, who had accompanied Jayne to the photo session, had opposed her posing with LaVey but he promised to be on his best behavior. Then, he allegedly began fondling a statue of a nude woman and making jokes, causing LaVey to grow furious with him again. When he ordered Brody to leave, the attorney laughed at LaVey and began blowing out the black candles that were placed around the room. Infuriated, LaVey pronounced a curse on Brody, telling him that he would be dead within a year. Jayne's friend, May Mann, later recalled that LaVey warned Jayne that if she continued to see Brody, she too could face a tragic death.

Anton LaVey recalled the incidents with Brody and the curse a little differently than other accounts. According to his story, Jayne became an active member of the Church of Satan and the curse had been a spell to protect her, rather than because LaVey was simply angry. In an interview, LaVey said that the curse was placed on Sam Brody because, "He'd been giving her [Jayne] a rough time and even embarrassing her in public. At the San Francisco Film Festival, he threw liquor all over her dress. He had blackened her eyes and beaten her up on many occasions."

He tried to protect Jayne, LaVey claimed. "Brody followed Jayne everywhere she went, despite her attempts to shake him. Jayne unloaded her problems with Brody on me daily. When she returned home from San Francisco, furniture would be missing from her home or she'd find bills for services that had not been authorized or in some cases not even performed. Brody padded his statements and sometimes double-billed her. He had her in a very delicate position. Supposedly, he represented her legally but he had her so compromised that she couldn't leave him. He arranged it so that she was so deeply in debt to him for legal services that if he had demanded payment, the consequences would have been terrible. And if she didn't conform to his personal wishes, he threatened to have custody of her children withdrawn and have her declared an unfit mother."

According to LaVey, the incidents that provoked the curse were different than in other accounts. One night, Jayne had telephoned LaVey, screaming and crying because Brody had been beating her. She was calling for help and weeping. Brody took the phone away from her and ordered LaVey to never speak to Jayne again. He said that if the church leader continued to befriend her, then Brody would see that he was exposed as a charlatan and instigate legal actions against the church.

At this point, LaVey had finally had enough of Brody's abuse. "I warned him that he was dealing with greater powers than he had ever dreamed of and that all of his threats would amount to nothing," LaVey recalled. "I told him to go ahead, expose and attack me because in one year, you'll be dead." Brody slammed down the phone without saying another word.

Jayne called back a few minutes later to plead with LaVey to remove the curse, but he refused. "I warned her to stay away from him," LaVey said. "I explained that Brody was traveling under a dark cloud and there was no way that he could escape. But she wouldn't listen... she just wouldn't listen."

Not long after, Jayne and Brody were involved in two separate auto accidents. The first occurred at the intersection of Sunset and Whittier in Beverly Hills. Although Jayne was not injured, Brody suffered a broken leg, a broken elbow and thumb and two cracked teeth. His Mercedes was destroyed. A few weeks later, when Brody's arm and leg were still in casts, they were involved in another accident. This time they were in San Francisco. Brody refused to let Jayne ride in LaVey's Jaguar, insisting that she ride with him instead. Neither of them was injured in this mishap, and Jayne still refused to heed LaVey's warning to stay away from the attorney.

About a month later, Jayne's five-year-old son, Zoltan, accompanied her to Jungleland, in Thousand Oaks, where she had agreed to pose for publicity photos. While she looked on in horror, a supposedly tame lion suddenly jumped onto the little boy and began mauling him. As the boy underwent several emergency surgeries, Jayne flew to San Francisco to plead with Anton LaVey to try and help her son. According to friends, LaVey donned a ceremonial robe and climbed to the top of Mount Tamalpais, outside of the city, in the driving rain to perform a ceremony that would provide assistance for the boy. Whether you believe in such things or not, Zoltan survived and Jayne credited LaVey for saving the boy's life.

And while the children may have been able to avoid the curse that hung over the heads of the actress and her attorney, Jayne's troubles were just beginning. A short time later, while on tour in Japan, a collection of prized diamonds that Jayne had bought at the height of her career were stolen. Soon after, in England, she was publicly humiliated and her performance canceled when she was falsely accused of skipping out on her hotel bills. She was also hit by a charge of income tax evasion from the Venezuelan government, robbed in Las Vegas, and attacked at Carnival in Rio de Janeiro by a crazed mob that stripped her of her clothing.

On June 22, Sam Brody was on his way to pick up Jayne for a charity luncheon when his vehicle was stuck by another car. It was badly damaged and Brody was again hospitalized with a broken leg and cracked ribs.

A week later, in the early morning hours of June 29, Jayne left Gus Steven's Supper Club in Biloxi, Mississippi, to drive to New Orleans, where she was scheduled to appear on a television talk show later that morning. She was accompanied by Sam Brody, the supper club's 19-year-old driver, Ron Harrison, and three of her children, Miklos, Zoltan, and Mariska.

According to those who were on the scene, Jayne stood nearby as the children and her trademark pink luggage were loaded into the car. She looked tired and haggard as she climbed in next to Brody in the front seat. The attorney sat in the middle next to Ron Harrison and Jayne sat next to the door. The children were all sleeping in the back seat as they started driving west on Route 90. The road was slick from a light rain that had fallen earlier. Ahead of the car, Harrison spotted a white cloud that was coming from a mosquito-spraying truck on the highway. He slowed down and followed the truck for several minutes until becoming impatient. He accelerated and drove around the truck into the fog. It was now 2:25 a.m.

Harrison did not know that a slow-moving trailer truck was ahead of the mosquito truck until the front of the supper club's Buick slammed under it. The Buick's roof was sheared off and rolled backwards like an opened can. Sam Brody died instantly when he was thrown from the car and Harrison suffered the same fate. The children, lying down in the back seat, sustained injuries, but they survived the crash.

The wreckage of the car that Jayne was riding in when she was killed.

When the truck driver, who was unhurt, jumped down from his cab, he immediately spotted the bodies of the two men on the pavement. Glancing back through the Buick's windshield, he saw the battered body of a woman in blood-soaked clothing. Legends state that Jayne was decapitated in the crash, but later reports

220

from police officers who investigated the scene discovered that what the truck driver thought was her severed head was actually one of Jayne's blonde, and now bloody, wigs.

Anton LaVey later declared that, "Jayne was a victim of her own frivolity." California occultists were of the opinion that the Satanist's curse killed both the believer and the victim alike. Shortly after Jayne's death, a memorial service was held at the Church of Satan in her honor. About thirty people were present and saw several amber-colored light bulbs suddenly flare up without explanation. The sudden glare lasted for less than a minute and left the bulbs undamaged, something considered impossible at the time. One of the bulbs remained with its filaments in the shape of a heart, Jayne's favorite design. Many of the possessions in her home, including the swimming pool, bathtubs and furnishings were heart-shaped. LaVey denied causing the bizarre light show. "Anyone can rig bulbs to flare like that, but to do so without damaging them is impossible," he said. "I think that Jayne wanted to let us know that she was still with us."

The publicity that followed Jayne Mansfield's death attracted what LaVey felt were the "wrong sort of people" to the church. These were the people that even LaVey feared – the sick, the mentally ill and the ones mad enough to believe that they could commit crimes and have the protection of the Devil himself. LaVey saw himself as a "true" Satanist, a shameless schemer, much like he believed the Devil to be. He held his "Black Masses" for the entertainment of the media, but no human blood was ever spilled in Satan's name. It was pure theater for the curious, who were treated to the sight of a naked girl tied down on an altar while people in black robes chanted and sang. Invocations were accompanied by individual demands for whatever the members desired – a better-paying job, the attentions of a pretty girl or riches. LaVey confessed to journalists that his own black magic rituals were limited to requests for good parking spaces and success in business, with the odd mischievous prank on the side.

Devout Christians and moralists were outraged by LaVey's shameless self-promotion and the inflammatory nature of his widely publicized beliefs, but the truth of the matter was that they needed a "devil" like him to complain about. They needed LaVey to be a real "evil" or their own existence would lose its meaning. LaVey might have been Satan's best promoter but he made a valid point when he wrote, "Satan has been the best friend the Church has ever had. He's kept them in business all these years."

The Christians lost their adversary on October 29, 1997, when LaVey died at St. Mary's Hospital in San Francisco of pulmonary edema. For reasons open to speculation, the time and date of his passing were listed incorrectly on his death certificate - stating that he died on Halloween. LaVey's funeral was a secret, by-invitation-only satanic service held in Colma, California. His body was cremated, with his ashes eventually divided among his heirs.

THE TEMPLE OF SET

The type of Satanism created by Anton by LaVey is the most accepted form among the general public today, but it's certainly not the only one. In fact, practitioners of traditional Satanism see it as a watered-down, mainstream version of what they truly believe in – the literal worship of Satan. They see the Church of Satan as a farce and utterly corrupt. One such practitioner was a man who actually began his immersion into the works of the Devil with LaVey, but soon went off in another direction altogether.

Michael Aquino is proof that Satanists can be found in unusual places. This former Eagle Scout (in fact, he was the national commander of the Eagle Scout Honor Society) was born in Santa Barbara, California. In 1964, he ranked ten th in his high school graduating class. A volunteer soldier in uneasy times, he served nine months in Vietnam as a lieutenant in the Army's 82nd Airborne unit. Back home in the states, looking forward to a San Francisco wedding in 1968, he saw an advertisement for Anton LaVey's Church of Satan in the Berkeley University newspaper. Intrigued, he wound up at LaVey's home on a whim, taking his fiancée and several friends along with him.

Aquino was immediately impressed with LaVey and they became good friends. Aquino was ordained as a satanic priest in 1970, heading up a small "grotto" in Kentucky, where he was stationed with the military. On the side, he lectured about Satanism at the University of Louisville and had an estimated dozen followers – mostly military personnel – convening at his home for rituals aimed, in Aquino's words, at "destroying the influence of conventional religion in human affairs." In August 1973, Aquino was elevated to the status of Magister Templi, the only Church of Satan member besides LaVey to hold the title.

Michael Aquino

But all was not well in the church. Aquino came to see LaVey's creation as increasingly corrupt, while LaVey was put off by Aquino's massive ego and intellectual snobbery. It was true that Aquino might have been the best-educated Satanist in modern times. He had earned a Master of Public Administration degree from George Washington University and would later earn a Ph.D. in political science from UC Santa Barbara, submitting a dissertation on tactical deployment of the neutron bomb in Europe. By mid-1975, dissension had reached the point that Aquino decided to leave the church, followed by his wife-to-be, Lilith Sinclair, and several members of her "Lilith Grotto" in Spotswood, New Jersey.

On the night of June 21, 1975, the Summer Solstice, Aquino allegedly performed a magical working that produced a manuscript called *The Book of Coming Forth by Night*. According to the book, Aquino received a visitor who was none other than Set, the Egyptian god of the dead. In the course of their chat, Set formally terminated LaVey's "Age of Satan" and anointed Aquino as "Magus V of the Age of Set." From that time on, he would be known as the "Second Beast" with Aleister Crowley (who had claimed a visit from Set's mouthpiece, Aiwass in 1904) being the first. Like LaVey, Aquino groomed himself for his new role, plucking his eyebrows and cutting his hair into a severe widow's peak. He also had the numbers "666," the biblical "mark of the beast" tattooed on his scalp.

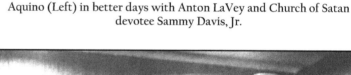

Aquino (Left) in better days with Anton LaVey and Church of Satan devotee Sammy Davis, Jr.

Church and military duties competed for Aquino's time throughout the late 1970s. In 1979, he stepped down as high priest of the temple, resuming the office three years later in a dispute for his replacement, whose "restrictive policies" interfered with the "free dialogue of ideas." In the meantime,

Devil Worshiper Holds Sensitive Army Post and Top Brass Say 'No Problem'

EX-GREEN BERET Lieut. Col. Michael Aquino is a high priest of a satanic church.

By CHRIS FULLER

A senior U.S. military intelligence officer with a secret security clearance admits he's also the founder and high priest of a satanic church — and amazingly, the Army says "no problem"!

Lieut. Col. Michael Aquino, a 41-year-old former Green Beret, confirmed to The ENQUIRER that he's been involved in devil worship for 22 years.

He said he formed his own satanic church, the Temple of Set, in 1975 after belonging to another sect, the Church of Satan, for the previous 10 years.

"My religion has been no secret in the Army," said Col. Aquino, who served as a psychological warfare specialist in Vietnam and is now a reserve officer working full-time on extended duty at the Army's reserve personnel center in St. Louis. He admitted satanic terminology is used in his church's rituals, adding: "We are quite proud of that."

But William Gill, executive director of the Catholic War Veterans, fumed:

"This is outrageous and a national disgrace!

"It's unbelievable that an admitted devil worshiper should be allowed to hold a senior and sensitive post in the U.S. Army. This abominable situation insults the memory of those who have fought and often died to uphold the traditional values of our great country.

"Citizens have a right to expect our military to uphold the traditional values of God and country — not the evil ramblings of some satanic sect."

Col. Aquino's satanic church is advertised in the yellow pages in San Francisco, where he was stationed from 1981 to 1986. He says most members are in the U.S. and Canada, although "we have a sprinkling of members in places like Western Europe and the Pacific."

The Constitution's guarantee of freedom of religion protects Col. Aquino from action by the Army, said Lieut. Col. Greg Rixon, an Army public affairs officer in Washington, D.C.

"As long as an individual's religious practice remains within the limit of the law, there is no problem," Col. Rixon said.

But Catholic War Veterans director Gill blasted that stand. "For the Army to say 'no problem' is mind-boggling," he said. "This disturbing situation is a problem for everyone who is concerned about national security and morality.

"The U.S. Army is no place for worshipers of the Prince of Darkness!"

Aquino had received Top Secret clearance from the Army in June 1981, and began reporting directly to the Joint Chiefs of Staff that same year, with the rank of lieutenant colonel – which was something that would have unsettled a lot of people if they knew.

During that time, Aquino's public statements stressed his desire to keep his religious beliefs separated from his military career, but there is every reason to suspect that his satanic philosophies influenced his performance in uniform. A glance at the official Temple of Set reading list revealed Aquino's fascination with ESP – dubbed "Metamind" in temple jargon – and the application of mind-control techniques, which he called "lesser black magic." He pushed for their use in "appropriate situations." The military uses of mind-control techniques (his "lesser black magic") were explored in an article co-authored by Aquino for the Army's *Military Review*, titled "From PSYOP to MindWar: The Psychology of Victory." America lost the Vietnam War, Aquino wrote, "not because we were out-fought, but because we were out-PSYOPed." In future conflicts, he suggested, the U.S. military could avoid defeat by utilizing the "national will to victory" as a kind of ESP weapon against its enemies.

Copies of the *Military Review* article were distributed within the Temple of Set, complete with a cover sheet that identified the source as "Headquarters Imperial Stormtroop Force / Office of the Chief of Staff / MindWar Center/ Hub Four." A joke perhaps, but during 1985 the U.S. Army commissioned a two-year, $425,000 study by the National Research Council on military applications of biofeedback, psychokinesis, ESP and "remote viewing." The December NRD report dismissed such techniques as "scientifically unsupportable," but the army continued to spend millions of dollars in pursuit of the "MindWar" for years.

Another pet topic for Aquino was Nazi Germany, specifically the occult beliefs of Heinrich Himmler and other ranking fascists. As Aquino described Nazi magic: "Many of the techniques perfected by the Nazis continue to be used/abused – generally in a superficial and ignorant fashion – by every country in the world in one guise or another. The magician who can recognize and identify these techniques and the principles behind them can thus control or avoid their influence as desired."

Obsessed with the Nazis' brand of the occult, Aquino interrupted an October 1984 tour of NATO bases in Europe so he could stop at Himmler's Wewelsburg Castle in Westphalia. There, in the "Hall of the Dead," where Himmler and his SS cronies once performed their own black magic rituals, Aquino devoted ninety minutes to a ritual of his own. He later described the experience for his followers: "The reality of the chamber rushed in upon me. This was no Hollywood set, no ordinary room painted and decorated to titillate the senses. Twelve hundred thirty-five inmates of the Niederhagen concentration camp died during the reconstruction of the Wewelsburg for the SS. If the Marble Hall and Walhalla were memorials to a certain unique quality in mankind, they also serve as grisly reminders of the penalty mankind pays for that quality."

A year later, Aquino's fascination with the "unique quality" of Nazism was cited as a major complain by defectors who left the temple to form the competing Temple of Nephthys. Published denials notwithstanding, Aquino's deliberately ambiguous treatment of Nazism, tinged with an obvious admiration for "a state based on magical rather than conventional principles," became a bone of contention for his former followers. The reader should keep in mind that this was a man with a high rank in the United States military...

At this point, Aquino was largely unknown to the general public. However, in January 1986, a *Penthouse* magazine article on Satanism "outed" him by described his role in the Temple of Set and his position in the military. This led to Aquino's appearance on one of television journalist Geraldo Rivera's notorious "exposés" on Satanism. The events that followed probably had the army wishing that they had never heard of the suddenly infamous Satanist.

During the 1980s, television talk show hosts had their audiences agog over the supposed nefarious deeds of Satanists. Satanic Panic and the Satanic Ritual Abuse scandals caused an uproar in American society (see more in the next chapter). Aquino found himself at the center of a modern-day witch hunt. A three-year-old girl, reportedly molested at the Army's Presidio day-care center in San Francisco, accused Aquino of being the "Mikey" who had photographed her in the nude and sexually abused her in a black-painted room with a cross on the ceiling. The accusations had come as part of an investigation into the principal suspect in the molestation, a Baptist minister named Gary Hambright. He was indicted on charges that he committed "lewd and lascivious acts" with six boys and four girls, ranging in age from three to seven years, during September-October 1986. At the time of the alleged sex crimes, Hambright was employed at the child care center on the Army base at Presidio.

According to an article in the *San Francisco Examiner*, one of the victims identified Aquino and his wife as participants in the molestation. The child's description of the house, which was also the headquarters of Aquino's Satanic Temple of Set, was so detailed, that police were able to obtain a search warrant. On August 14, 1987, Aquino's home was raided by police detectives, FBI agents and members of the Army's Criminal Investigation Division. Several carloads of "evidence" were seized from the house, but no charges were filed against Aquino or any members of his church. Aquino claimed that he had been in Washington, D.C., at the time of the alleged rape, enrolled in a year-long reserve officers' course at the National Defense University. However, he did admit that he made frequent visits back to the Bay Area and to his church/home. The public flap over the Hambright indictment prompted the army to transfer Aquino from the Presidio, where he was the deputy director of reserve training, to the U.S. Army Reserve Personnel Center in St. Louis.

On April 19, 1988, the indictment against Hambright was dropped by U.S. Attorney Joseph Russoniello, on the grounds that, while there was clear evidence of child abuse (six of the children contracted the venereal disease, chlamydia), there was insufficient evidence to link Hambright (or the Aquinos) to the crimes. In spite of this, Aquino and his wife were questioned again by army investigators about charges of child molestation by the couple in two northern California counties, Sonoma and Mendocino. A nine-year-old girl in Santa Rosa and an 11-year-old boy in Fort Bragg separately identified Aquino as the rapist in a series of 1985 incidents, after they had seen him on television. But were they legitimate complaints, or simply part of the "witch hunt" atmosphere of the times?

In April 1989, Aquino filed formal complaints against two San Francisco detectives involved in the raid on his home. Police commissioners sustained the complaints in November 1990 – long after the Satanic Panic period had peaked. One of the detectives was "counseled" to avoid derogatory comments about Aquino's church or lifestyle, while the other was given a written reprimand for his role in the 1987 raid.

Aside from bookings on Geraldo Rivera's and Oprah Winfrey's shows, Aquino's brush with the law provided him with material for endless letters to newspapers, bemoaning the cruel persecution of innocent Satanists by hysterical Christians. In time, interest in him and the Temple of Set began to fade. While he is still active in occult circles today, there is little current information available about him. As could be said about his long career in the U.S. military, however, he may simply remain a devil, hiding in plain sight.

THE PROCESS CHURCH OF THE FINAL JUDGMENT: THE MANSON FAMILY AND BEYOND

No satanic cult in modern times has enjoyed a more sinister reputation – or been linked to as many sensational crimes – than the Process Church of the Final Judgment, created by Robert and Mary Ann DeGrimston in 1963 and officially dissolved just twelve years later. But so powerful was the group's aura of evil, and its diabolical links to some of the most horrific crimes of the 1960s and 1970s, that tales of its resurgence and revival still circulate today, more than three decades after the cult disappeared from public view.

Robert DeGrimston Moore was born in Shanghai in 1935, the son of a British engineer and grandson of a vicar. He was taken home to England in the first year of his life, and by 1963 he was an advanced student at L. Ron Hubbard's London Scientology Institute. There, he met Mary Anne MacLean in one of his classes. Four years older than Robert, Mary Anne had a colorful past that included a brief engagement to boxer Sugar Ray Robinson and a time spent working as a prostitute. The two would-be Scientologists were instantly attracted to one another and, finding themselves so well attuned, they soon split from Hubbard's cult and started their own "therapy" group under the title of "Compulsion Analysis." By 1964, this name had been discarded in favor of a new, suitably mystical-sounding name: "The Process."

As with Scientology, Process "therapy" cloaked itself in religious trappings, with new recruits surrendering a major portion of their worldly goods to Robert and Mary Anne DeGrimston (Mary Anne had disposed of Robert's surname of "Moore" as too common). In essence, followers were offered a choice of deities to worship: Jehovah called for strict obedience and sexual abstinence while Lucifer encouraged his followers to do whatever they wanted. Ardent worshippers of Jehovah resorted to self-flagellation at times to expiate whatever sins they felt they had committed. Mary Anne DeGrimston especially enjoyed the disciplinarian side of cult management, giving free rein to what some have referred to as her "control perspective." In fact, cult members were actively encouraged to grovel in fear before the DeGrimstons, addressing them as "God" and "Goddess."

By March 1966, the cult had obtained enough of their followers' funds to lease a mansion in London's exclusive Mayfair district. The DeGrimstons moved in with about twenty-five of their disciples and a pack of German Shepherds – each dog possessing its own cult title, pursuant to a special canine oath. The house was luxurious, but England was starting to seem rather small to the DeGrimstons. Robert was already cultivating his hair and beard in an impersonation of images of Christ, while Mary Anne was referring to herself variously as "Hecate," "Circe," "the Oracle," or as the reincarnation of Nazi propaganda minister Joseph Goebbels.

In June, the DeGrimstons, their dogs, and a select group of followers embarked for Nassau in the Bahamas. Six weeks later, they showed up in Yucatan, Mexico, attempting to start a commune near the coastal fishing village of Sisal. They called the place "Xtul," creating a whole nonsense lexicon of "magic" words that all started with the letter "X." It was in Mexico that Robert picked up a third deity for the church in the person of Satan, meanwhile adopting the title of "Christ" for himself. The commune survived a hurricane in late September 1966, but British attorneys showed up on the scene two months later, hired by the families of Process recruits to bring home three of the brainwashed members.

Momentarily daunted by their clash with legal forces, the Process members moved back to London. They cleaned up the Mayfair mansion and began making determined efforts to recruit members of rock bands like the Rolling Stones and the Beatles. When that plan fell through, Robert and Mary Anne – billing themselves as "The Omega" – departed for Greece, Israel and Turkey in April 1967. Somehow, they eventually ended up in Miami, Florida, and by August had put down roots in New Orleans, operating under the cover of a three-month tourist's visa. In January 1968, the cult was formally incorporated in the United States as the Process Church of the Final Judgment. The New Orleans chapter officially closed its doors two months later (although Process members remained in New Orleans for up to six years) and the cult moved to California, riding the coattails of the hippie movement.

Robert DeGrimston, co-founder of the Process Church and Below, his wife, Mary Anne.

The DeGrimstons arrived in San Francisco that spring, but their message had preceded them, with Process "evangelists" first showing up during 1967's "Summer of Love," when as many as 100,000 young people flocked to the Haight-Ashbury neighborhood of San Francisco. One early member in San Francisco was a leather craftsman named Victor Wild (a.k.a. "Brother Ely") who rode with the Gypsy Jokers motorcycle club when he wasn't turning out hand-tooled wallets and belts. Wild is generally credited with introducing the DeGrimstons to the idea of recruiting outlaw bikers as shock troops for the coming apocalypse. It is worth noting that Wild's home, which became a Process chapel, was just two blocks from a crash pad occupied by another fledgling cult, this one headed by Charles Manson.

War – specifically a kind of hodgepodge racial war to end all wars – was very much on the minds of Process members in 1968 and 1969. One member of the cult, questioned by Los Angeles police about his link to a pair of biker murders, described the "natural hate" that Process members had for blacks, but the cult was also willing to use minorities, when feasible, "to begin some kind of militant thing."

Robert DeGrimston, meanwhile, talked of war in the guise of various deities. In *Satan on War*, he advised his people to "Release the fiend that lies dormant within you, for he is strong and his power if far beyond the bounds of human frailty." If anyone was

curious how that power might be used, DeGrimston supplied the answer in his sequel, *Jehovah on War*. "My prophecy upon this wasted earth," he wrote, "and upon the corrupt creation that squats upon its ruined surface is: thou shalt kill."

Mary Anne was engrossed in her own activities – a kind of psychic terrorism that she dubbed "The Fear." It was something that cult members apparently regarded as a beneficial growth experience, or so they said. She also endorsed the writings of Mendez Castle in the Process newsletter, which urged readers to sample necrophilia and grave robbing, "if it turned them on."

226

DeGrimston and the Process Church, like other such cults at the time, often staged publicity photos. Below, one of the Process Church's "awesome" recruiting posters.

THE PROCESS
CHURCH OF THE FINAL JUDGEMENT

Meanwhile, the U.S. Immigration Service was finally catching up with the British Process members. Deportation orders were issued in May 1968. Some of them promptly went underground and disappeared, while the DeGrimstons found it a convenient time to visit Europe. Back in England, the Anglican Church was speaking out against the Process, stating that they were a group that showed "two faces to the world. One is that of pious respectability and the other is one of self-indulgent depravity." But the old adage of there being no such thing as bad publicity proved true once again. That summer saw short-lived Process chapters started in Rome, Paris, Amsterdam, Munich and Hamburg. By late 1968, the DeGrimstons were safely back in London, but their popularity in America was stronger than ever. Chapters of varying size were reported in New York, Boston, Chicago and Toronto, but the most activity could still be found in California.

Research by journalist Ed Sanders, who wrote one of the first books on Charles Manson, entitled *The Family*, later revealed that Manson was first exposed to Process teachings in the spring or early summer of 1967. At that time, he rubbed shoulders with a group calling itself the Final Church of the Judgment – a.k.a. the Companions of Life – at San Francisco's infamous "Devil House." It is believed that he also attended some of Robert DeGrimston's lectures at the Esalen Institute at Big Sur. In any case, by the time he moved his followers to southern California in 1968, Manson was referring to his "family" as the "Final Church," and working overtime to recruit outlaw bikers and instill "The Fear" in his loyal disciples. Indeed, Manson's whole "Helter Skelter" rant on race war, Armageddon and the Beatles was an obvious rip-off of Process dogma, with a strong dose of Manson insanity added to spice things up.

227

Charles Manson was not only tied into the Process Church, but with other satanic activities as well. Most think of him and his "family" as the killers behind the Tate-LaBianca murders, but cult members were involved in many more crimes than they were ever charged with.

Born Charles Maddox to unmarried, 16-year-old Kathleen Maddox in Cincinnati in 1934, Manson never knew his real father. For a time, after her son's birth, Kathleen Maddox was married to a laborer named William Manson and the boy was given his last name. Manson's mother, allegedly a heavy drinker, once sold him for a pitcher of beer to a childless waitress, from whom his uncle retrieved him a few days later. When his mother was sentenced to five years in prison for robbing a Charleston, W.Va., service station in 1939, Manson was placed in the home of an aunt and uncle. His mother was paroled in 1942 and he was returned to her, faced with a life of run-down hotel rooms and flophouses. Kathleen could only handle the boy for about five years and in 1947, she tried to have him placed in a foster home. With no spaces available, the court sent him to the Gibault School for Boys in Terre Haute, Indiana. After ten months there, he fled and returned to his mother, who wanted nothing to do with him.

Charles Manson

Manson ended up living on the streets, making his way by committing petty thefts. Arrested in Indiana, he escaped from the local juvenile center after one day's confinement. Recaptured and sent to Father Flanagan's Boys Town, he lasted four days before his next escape, fleeing in a stolen car to see relatives in Illinois. He committed more robberies while on the road and then was arrested again at age 13. Confined for three years at a boy's school in Plainfield, Indiana, he later recalled abuse by older boys and guards alike. He was tested by psychiatrists and social workers who found Manson to have a high I.Q., but labeled him "aggressively antisocial." After being transferred from one institution after another, each more secure than the next because of continued disciplinary problems, he finally became a model prisoner and was paroled from his last reformatory, in Ohio, in 1954.

After temporarily honoring a parole condition that he live with his aunt and uncle in West Virginia, Manson sought out his mother again. He moved in with her for a time, and then in January 1955, he married Rosalie Jean Willis, 17, a waitress with whom, by his own account, he found genuine, but short-lived happiness. He supported them by working at a series of low-paying jobs that included parking lot attendant and bus boy – and by stealing cars. In October of that same year, Manson stole a car and moved his pregnant wife to Los Angeles. The unlucky Manson was caught again, and charged with interstate theft. After a psychiatric evaluation, he received five years' probation. His subsequent failure to appear at a Los Angeles hearing on an identical charge filed in Florida resulted in his March 1956 arrest. His probation was revoked and he was sentenced to three years' imprisonment at Terminal Island in San Pedro, Calif.

Charles Manson, Jr., Manson's son by Rosalie, was born while Manson was behind bars. During his first year at Terminal Island, Manson received visits from his wife and his mother, who were now living together in Los Angeles. In March 1957, the visits ceased and Manson's mother informed him that Rosalie was living with another man. Manson was caught trying to escape less than two weeks before a scheduled parole hearing. Needless to say, his parole was denied.

Manson was released in September 1958 to find himself divorced and once again, in trouble with the law. By November, he was pimping a 16-year-old girl and was receiving additional money from another girl with wealthy parents. In September 1959, he entered a guilty plea to attempting to cash a forged U.S. Treasury check

Bobby Beausoleil

Susan Atkins

but received a 10-year suspended sentence after a young woman with a history of prostitution arrests tearfully told the court that she and Manson were in love and would get married if he were freed. The young woman, whose name was Leona, actually did marry Manson before the year was out. Manson took her and another woman from California to New Mexico to work as prostitutes. There, Manson was held and questioned for violation of the Mann Act, which prohibited taking women across state lines for the purposes of prostitution. Though he was released, Manson was convinced he was still being investigated and he disappeared. Now in violation of his probation, a bench warrant was issued and he was arrested in Laredo, Texas, when one of his girls was picked up for prostitution. Manson was returned to Los Angeles and for violating his probation for the check-cashing charge, he was ordered to serve his 10-year sentence.

Manson spent a year trying to appeal the revocation of his probation and ended up being transferred from the Los Angeles County Jail to the federal penitentiary at McNeil Island. In 1963, Leona was granted a divorce. During the proceedings, she alleged that she and Manson had a son, Charles Luther.

In June 1966, Manson was sent to Terminal Island in preparation for an early release. By the time he got out, on March 21, 1967, he had spent more than half of his 32 years incarcerated in one institution or another. He later claimed that he requested to be allowed to stay at Terminal Island, as the prison had become his home.

After his release, Manson was allowed to move to San Francisco, where, with the help of a prison friend, he obtained an apartment in Berkeley. It was here, during the famed "Summer of Love" that Manson began to develop the influence that he had over women, which had started to emerge a few years before. He would also begin the early formation of the "Family." Manson was mostly panhandling in San Francisco, until he met Mary Brunner, an assistant librarian at UC Berkeley. They moved in together and in a short time, Manson overcame her resistance to bringing other women into bed with them. Before long, they were sharing Brunner's apartment with eighteen other young women. Manson quickly established himself as a guru of sorts in San Francisco's Haight-Ashbury. Using his age (he was several years older than most of his followers) and some of the Scientology techniques that he studied in prison, he soon had his first group of cult followers, most of them young and female, with a mixture of easily manipulated young men thrown in for good balance. They came from all levels of society. Some, like Mary Brunner, were college graduates. Others, like Susan Atkins and Robert Beausoleil, were already involved with satanic cults. Atkins had previously danced topless in a show called the Witches' Sabbath that was organized by Anton LaVey. Most of the Family members weren't practicing Satanists; just hopelessly confused about their lives. They adopted Manson as a combination mentor, lover, father figure and Christ incarnate. They drifted in from all over the state, with the Family topping fifty members at its peak, following their chosen leader through a dreamy summer that would soon turn into a waking nightmare.

From Scientology to Satanism, Manson collected ideas and doctrines, blending the best – or worst – of what he learned into a bizarre, hodgepodge philosophy of his own. In 1967, hanging around the San Francisco landmark that came to be known as the "Devil House" (LaVey's headquarters of the Church of Satan), he first met Robert DeGrimston and the members of the Process Church. A former Family member described the scene to Ed Sanders: "They said it was a religious order, and it went under many ancient names, one of them being the Companions of Life, another being the Final Church of the Judgment. The Final Church is the name Manson chose for the church he would eventually found." Aside from the name, Manson also borrowed the concept of keeping converts in line by use of "The Fear" from Mary Anne DeGrimston, along with the cult's methods of recruiting outlaw bikers to "terrorize society" on the eve of the apocalypse.

Near the end of 1967, Manson and a group of his followers piled into an old school bus that had been renovated in hippie style. The seats had been removed and colored rugs and pillows were placed on the floor. Hitting the road, they roamed through California, Mexico and the Southwest. When they returned to L.A., they continued to move from place to place, living in Topanga Canyon, Malibu, and Venice.

In Topanga Canyon, Manson met an even more sinister cult at a house called the "Spiral Staircase" because of the circular stairs at the home's entrance. Apparently, no one called the house by that name at the time, the nickname came later. Most referred to it as the "Snake Pit," because of all of the bizarre things that were going on there in 1967 and 1968. The house, a tumbledown Victorian structure, was demolished in 1968. Manson himself described the scene at the house:

Each time I returned, I would observe and listen to all of the practices and rituals of the different groups that visited the place. I'm not into sacrificing some animal or drinking its blood to get a better charge out of sex. Nor am I into chaining someone and whipping them to get my kicks like some of those people were.

The day we first drove up, we were innocent children compared to some of those we saw during our visits there. In looking back, I can honestly say our philosophy – fun and games, love and sex, peaceful friendship for everyone – began changing into madness that eventually engulfed us in that house.

It was around this time that Manson's Family began associating with black magic groups like the homicidal "Four P Movement," itself a spin-off of the Process Church of the Final Judgment.

The "Four P Movement" would not come to light until 1969, when Ed Sanders encountered reports of a sinister satanic cult that was alleged to practice human sacrifice in several parts of California, luring youthful members from colleges throughout the western half of the United States. The cult originally boasted fifty-five members, of whom fifteen were middle-aged, the rest consisting of young men and women in their twenties. The group's leader, dubbed the "Head Devil" was said to be a wealthy California businessman who exercised his power by compelling younger members of the cult to act as his slaves and murder random people on his command.

Organized in 1967, the cult began holding its meetings in the Santa Cruz Mountains, south of San Francisco. Rituals that included sacrificing dogs were conducted on a stellar timetable. Beginning in June 1968, authorities in San Jose, Santa Cruz and Los Gatos began reporting the discovery of butchered canines, skinned and drained of blood for no apparent reason. The director of the Santa Cruz animal shelter told Sanders that whoever was doing the killing was an expert with a knife. He added, "the really strange thing is that these dogs have been drained of blood."

If the stories were true, the blood was being drunk by the cultists during their ceremonies. So, several alleged eyewitnesses claimed, was human blood, obtained from sacrificial victims who were murdered on a ritual altar. They were first stabbed to death with a custom-made, six-bladed knife. The knife was designed with blades of various length in order to penetrate a victim's stomach first, before the heart was skewered, bringing merciful release. Each sacrifice climaxed with the removal of the heart, which cultists divided up amongst themselves to eat. The corpses were then burned, leaving no trace behind. Members of the "Four P

The Spahn Movie Ranch, where Manson and his Family came to live in August 1968.

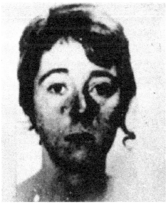

(Left) Charles "Tex" Watson
(Right) Lynette "Squeaky" Fromme

Movement" who later talked to news reporters stated that victims were mostly hitchhikers, drifters and runaways, with an occasional volunteer from the ranks.

In 1969, the cult moved southward, shifting operations to the O'Neil Park region of the Santa Ana Mountains, near Los Angeles. The move caused a factional dispute within the group, one segment striving to deemphasize the satanic rituals and concentrate more on kinky sex, while more traditional adherents clung to Satan and human sacrifices. The group apparently survived its schism and expanded nationally into the late 1970s. Those who have attempted to follow the activities of the cult point to the deaths and ritual skinning of eighty-five large dogs in New York between October 1976 and October 1977.

The "Four P Movement" would be linked to not only Charles Manson but to convicted killer David Berkowitz, the infamous "Son of Sam" serial killer who claimed six victims in New York City in the late 1970s. Berkowitz professed membership in the "Four P" cult, backing up his claims with inside information about unsolved California homicides committed by the group.

By the middle part of 1968, Manson was calling himself Christ and Satan, with the titles used interchangeably. By that time, the Family was living at the Spahn Movie Ranch, not far from Topanga Canyon. The ranch had once been a location for shooting Western films but by 1968, the old sets were deteriorating and largely abandoned. It was primarily doing business offering horseback rides and Manson convinced the elderly, nearly blind owner, George Spahn, to allow the Family to live at the ranch in return for doing work around the place. It was not hard to convince Spahn. Manson had Lynette Fromme, one of his girls, act as Spahn's eyes. She, along with other girls, serviced the old man sexually. Because of the tiny squeal that Lynette would emit when Spahn pinched her thigh, she acquired the nickname "Squeaky." The Family was joined at Spahn's Ranch by Charles Watson, a Texan who had quit college and moved to California. Watson's drawl earned him the nickname "Tex" from George Spahn.

At the ranch, Manson was busy recruiting outlaw bikers, concentrating on gangs like the Straight Satans and Satan's Slaves. One Straight Satan, Danny DeCarlo, moved in with the Family and became Manson's personal gunsmith. On the side, Manson orchestrated weird rituals for the faithful, later recalled secondhand by a cellmate of Susan Atkins in Los Angeles:

She described to me that on various occasions Charlie would put himself on a cross, and a girl would kneel at the foot of the cross, and that he would moan, cry out as though he was being crucified. They would sacrifice animals and drink their blood as a fertility rite.

From killing animals, it was a short step to human beings.

On October 13, 1968, two women were found beaten and strangled to death near Ukiah, California. One of them, Nancy Warren, was the pregnant wife of a highway patrol officer. The other victim, Clida Delaney, was Warren's 64-year-old grandmother. The murders were ritualistic in nature, with thirty-six leather thongs tied around each woman's throat. Several members of the Manson Family – including two later convicted of unrelated murders – were in Ukiah at the time.

Two months later, on December 30, 17-year-old Marina Habe was abducted from outside her West Hollywood home. Her body was recovered on New Year's Day with multiple stab wounds in the back and chest. Investigators learned that Habe was friendly with various Family members. Police came to believe that her ties with the Manson group led to her disappearance and subsequent death.

On July 17, 1979, Mark Walts, 16, disappeared while hitchhiking from Chatsworth, California, to do some fishing at the Santa Monica Pier. His battered body, shot three times and possibly run over by a car, was found the next morning in Topanga Canyon. Walts was a frequent visitor to the Spahn Ranch and the dead boy's brother publicly accused Manson of the murder, though no charges were ever filed.

Around the time of Walt's death, an unidentified female corpse was discovered near Castaic, northeast of the Spahn Ranch. It was tentatively identified as Susan Scott, a Family member once arrested with a group of Manson's women in Mendocino. Scott was living at the Spahn Ranch when she dropped out of sight. While the corpse was never officially identified, Susan was never seen again.

During this time, Manson had become obsessed with death and "Helter Skelter," his race war to end all wars. One day, Manson and Tex Watson visited a friend who lived in Topanga Canyon. The friend played the Beatles' White Album for them, which had recently been released. Manson was obsessed with the band and some of the songs on the album played right into some of the crazed rhetoric that he had been spouting for some time: that America was going to become embroiled in a race war between blacks and whites. He excitedly told the Family that the social turmoil he had been predicting was also foreseen by the Beatles. The White Album songs, he said, spoke to him in code. In fact, he said, the album had been specifically intended for the Family, a carefully selected group that was being instructed to preserve the world from the coming disastrous events. Within a couple of months, Manson's vision was complete. The Family would create an album with songs that would trigger the predicted chaos. Ghastly murders of white people by black attackers would be met with retaliation and a split between the racist and non-racist whites would bring about the white race's annihilation. The blacks would then turn to the Family to lead them after the storm had cleared. The Family would survive by riding out the conflict in a mysterious cave called the Devil's Hole in Wingate Pass, hidden away in Death Valley. Legend had it that an underground city was below the earth there, and the family planned to stay there until the war had ended.

The Family members worked on vehicles and studied maps, preparing to make their escape when the war began. They also worked on songs for their "world-changing album." When they were told Terry Melcher, a music producer that Manson had met during his short friendship with Beach Boy Dennis Wilson, agreed to hear their material, the girls cleaned up and prepared a huge meal, but Melcher never arrived.

(Left) Terry Melcher and his mother, actress Doris Day (Right) The house at 10050 Cielo Drive, which Manson believed was still the residence of Melcher. He was not aware that it had been rented to Sharon Tate and her husband, Roman Polanski.

Manson went looking for Melcher at 10050 Cielo Drive. The house was owned by Rudy Altobelli and Melcher had once been a tenant but no longer lived there. The new tenants were actress Sharon Tate and her husband, film director Roman Polanski.

At some point, Manson managed to track down Melcher, who visited the Spahn Ranch to hear a performance by Manson and the girls. Melcher came back again a short time later and brought a friend who owned a mobile recording unit. However, he himself never recorded the group.

By June, Manson was telling the Family that they might have to show the blacks how to start "Helter Skelter." When Manson gave Tex Watson the job of getting money together to help the Family with the conflict to come, Watson ripped off a black drug dealer named Bernard "Lotsapoppa" Crowe. The dealer responded with a threat to wipe out everyone at the Spahn Ranch, but Manson got to Crowe first and shot him at his Hollywood apartment on July 1. Manson assumed that Crowe was dead and this mistake was seemingly confirmed by a news report that announced the discovery of the body of a Black Panther member in Los Angeles. Although Crowe was not a member of the group, Manson concluded that he had been and expected retaliation from the radical group. He turned the Spahn Ranch into an armed camp, putting out night guards and passing weapons around. The Family was convinced that "Helter Skelter" was coming.

Still looking for money, Manson sent Bobby Beausoleil, along with Mary Brunner and Susan Atkins, to the house of acquaintance Gary Hinman on July 25, 1969. Manson had heard rumors that Hinman had recently inherited some money and Manson wanted it. The three Family members held an uncooperative Hinman hostage for two days, during which Manson showed up with a sword to slash his ear. After that, Beausoleil stabbed Hinman to death, acting on Manson's instructions. Before leaving the Topanga Canyon residence, Beausoleil, or one of the girls, used Hinman's blood to write "Political piggy" on the wall and to draw a panther paw, a Black Panther symbol.

Beausoleil was arrested on August 6, 1969, driving Hinman's car. The murder weapon was found in the tire well. Two days later, Manson told the Family members at Spahn Ranch, "Now is the time for Helter Skelter."

On the night of August 8, Manson directed Watson to take Susan Atkins, Linda Kasabian and Patricia Krenwinkel to "that house where Melcher used to live" and "destroy everyone... as gruesome as you can." The girls were instructed to do whatever Watson told them to do. When the four of them arrived at the entrance to the Cielo Drive property, Watson (who had been to the house before on Manson's orders) climbed a telephone pole and cut the telephone lines. It was now just after midnight on August 9, 1969.

They parked at the bottom of the hill and walked up to the gate. Assuming that it might be alarmed or electrified, they climbed up an embankment and dropped onto the grounds. Just then, headlights came their way from within the property and Watson ordered the girls to hide in the bushes. He stopped the approaching car and shot the driver, 18-year-old Steven Parent, to death. After cutting the screen of an open window of the main house, Watson told Kasabian to keep watch down by the gate. He removed the screen, entered through the window, and let Atkins and Krenwinkel in through the front door.

The first person to encounter the intruders was a friend of Polanski, Wojciech Frykowski, who was sleeping on the living room couch. When he awoke, Watson kicked him in the head. The man asked who he was and what he was doing there and Watson replied, "I'm the Devil, and I'm here to do the Devil's business."

Sharon Tate in 1969

Susan Atkins found the house's three other occupants and, with Krenwinkel's help, brought them into the living room. The three were Sharon Tate, who was eight-and-a-half months pregnant; her friend, Jay Sebring, a celebrity hairstylist, and Frykowksi's girlfriend, Abigail Folger, heiress to the Folgers Coffee fortune. Roman Polanski was in London at the time, working on a film project.

Watson tied Tate and Sebring together by their necks with a rope that he'd brought along and he threw it up over a ceiling beam. When Sebring protested about his rough treatment of the pregnant Tate, Watson shot him in the face. After Folger was taken back into the bedroom to get her purse, which held about $70, Watson beat and stabbed the wounded Sebring.

Frykowski, whose hands had been tied together with a towel, managed to get free and he began struggling with Atkins, who stabbed him in the legs with the knife she was carrying. Frykowski got loose and began running for the front door, but Watson caught up with him on the porch and struck him several times with the gun (breaking the gun's right grip in the process), stabbed him repeatedly, and then shot him twice. Around this time, Linda Kasabian came up from the driveway after hearing "horrifying sounds." In a vain effort to halt the massacre, she lied to Atkins, telling her that someone was coming.

(Left) Patricia Krenwinkel
(Right) Linda Kasabian

(Left) The front door to 10050 Cielo Drive, with the word "PIG" written on the door in blood.
(Right) The blood-spattered front doorway.

A horrific crime scene photograph of Sharon Tate and Jay Sebrig, tied together and murdered in the living room of the 10050 Cielo Drive House.

Abigail Folger's bloody corpse was found on the lawn of the house. She had been stabbed 28 times.

Inside the house, Abigail Folger escaped from Krenwinkel and ran out a bedroom door to the pool area. Krenwinkel pursued her and tackled her in the yard. Folger was stabbed several times by Krenwinkel and then Watson joined in with his own knife. Abigail Folger died after being stabbed twenty-eight times. Frykowski had been stabbed fifty-one times. Atkins, Watson, or both of them, killed Sharon Tate, who was stabbed sixteen times. She pleaded with her killers to let her live long enough to have her baby and she cried, "mother... mother..." until she finally died.

Earlier that night, as the four Family members had left Spahn Ranch, Manson told the girls to "leave a sign... something witchy," at the house. After the murders, Atkins wrote "Pig" on the front door of the house in Sharon Tate's blood. Then they fled, changing out of their gore-soaked clothing and dumping the clothes, along with the weapons, in the hills.

Leno and Rosemary La Bianca, the next victims of the Manson Family

The La Bianca Home in 1969

The next night, six Family members, including the four from the previous night's murders plus Leslie Van Houten, and Steve "Clem" Grogan, were sent out with instructions from Manson. This time, Manson went along with them. He gave Kasabian directions to 3301 Waverly Drive, home of supermarket executive Pasqualino "Leno" LaBianca and his wife, Rosemary, who was co-owner of an upscale women's clothing store. Located in the Los Feliz section of L.A., the LaBianca home was next door to a house at which Manson and Family members had attended a party the year before.

Manson and Watson went into the house first and, according to Watson's later version of the events, Manson ordered him to bind Leno LaBianca's hands with a leather cord. Rosemary LaBianca was brought into the living room and Watson followed Manson's instructions to put pillowcases over the couple's heads. Manson then left, sending Krenwinkel and Leslie Van Houten into the house with instructions to kill the couple.

Rosemary was sent back into the bedroom with the girls and Watson began stabbing Leno LaBianca with a bayonet, which had been given to him by Manson when Watson complained about the inadequate weapons that had been provided for the previous night's murders. Watson's first thrust went into LaBianca's throat. Suddenly, he heard noises in the bedroom and he went in to find Rosemary

LaBianca was keeping the girls away from her by swinging a lamp that they had tied to her neck. Watson charged forward and stabbed the woman several times with the bayonet, sending her to the floor. He then went back into the living room and renewed his attack on Leno LaBianca, stabbing him a total of twelve times. He then carved the word "War" on the man's abdomen.

Returning to the bedroom, where Krenwinkel was attacking Rosemary LaBianca with a kitchen knife, Watson, who had been told by Manson that each of the girls needed to play a part in the murders, ordered Van Houten to stab her, too. She did so, jamming the knife into the woman's back and buttocks. Rosemary LaBianca died after being stabbed forty-one times.

While Watson cleaned off the bayonet and showered in the LaBianca's bathroom, Krenwinkel used the victims' blood to scrawl "Rise" and "Death to Pigs" on the walls and "Healter Skelter" on the refrigerator door (she was not sure how to spell it). She also stabbed Leno LaBianca fourteen times with an ivory-handled, two-tined carving fork, which she left jutting out of his abdomen. She jammed a steak knife into his throat and left it there when she and her companions left the house.

Planning to carry out two murders on the same night, Manson sent Kasabian to the Venice home of an actor acquaintance of hers. Manson dropped off the second set of Family members at the man's apartment building and then drove back to the Spahn Ranch, leaving all of them to hitchhike home. Kasabian deliberately thwarted this murder by knocking on the wrong apartment door and waking a stranger. The group abandoned the murder plan and left.

The words "Death to Pigs" were scrawled on the walls of the La Bianca house in blood. Manson had instructed his killers to try and incite a race war with the murders.

On August 10, as the bodies from the Tate murders were being autopsied and the LaBiancas' bodies were yet to be found, detectives from the L.A. County Sheriff's Department, which had jurisdiction in the Hinman case, informed LAPD detectives assigned to the Tate case of the bloody writing that had been found at the Hinman house. They even mentioned that their suspect, Beausoleil, hung out with a group of hippies led by "a guy named Charlie." The detectives on the Tate case, believing that the murders were connected to a drug deal gone bad, ignored the information.

Steven Parent, the young man who had been killed in the Tate driveway, had no connection to the other victims. He was an acquaintance of William Garretson, who had been hired by Rudi Altobelli to watch over the property while Altobelli was out of town. When the killers arrived, Parent had been leaving Cielo Drive, after visiting Garretson. Held for a short time as a possible murder suspect, Garretson told the police that he was living in the guesthouse but had neither seen nor heard anything on the night of the murders. He was released on August 11, after a polygraph exam showed that he was not involved in the crimes.

On August 12, the LAPD announced to the news media that it had ruled out any connection between the Tate and LaBianca murders. On August 16, sheriff's deputies raided the Spahn Ranch and arrested Manson and twenty-five others – but not for murder. They were picked up as suspects in an auto theft ring that had been stealing Volkswagens and converting them into dune buggies. Weapons were seized, but because the warrant had been misdated, the Family was released a few days later.

Manson was back on the street August 26. That night, he directed the torture slaying of Donald "Shorty" Shea, a movie stuntman and Family hanger-on who "knew too much" and was suspected of discussing Family business with the police.

By the end of August, virtually all leads in both cases had gone nowhere. As it turned out, a report by LaBianca detectives (younger than those assigned to the Tate murders), noted a possible connection between the bloody writings at the LaBianca house and the latest album by "the singing group of the Beatles" but nothing further was done to follow up on this.

In mid-October, the LaBianca team, still working separately from the Tate team, checked with the sheriff's office about any possible similar crimes and learned of the Hinman murder, which had been ignored by the detectives on the Tate case. They also learned that detectives working on the case had spoken with Beausoliel's girlfriend, Kitty Lutesinger, who had been arrested a few days earlier with members of the Manson Family.

Ironically, the downfall of Charlie Manson came about because of a relatively petty crime. On the night of September 18, 1969, members of the cult burned a piece of road-grading equipment that was owned by Death Valley National Monument because it was obstructing one of their desert dune buggy trails. Arson investigators traced the evidence to Manson and new arrests were ordered. A joint force of National Park rangers and officers from the California Highway Patrol and the Inyo County Sheriff's Office had raided the Family's location. The officers found stolen dune buggies and other vehicles and arrested two dozen persons, including Manson. A Highway Patrol officer found Manson hiding in a cabinet under a bathroom sink.

A day later, Susan Atkins was picked up in Ontario, California. She made the mistake of talking to her cellmates. One of them informed the LAPD of the Family's involvement in the Tate and LaBianca murders.

Manson himself was out of circulation, but even though he was in jail, it didn't stop the carnage. On November 5, 1969, Family member John Haught – a.k.a. "Zero" – was shot and killed in Venice, California. Eleven days later, another unknown woman – tentatively identified as Family member Sherry Cooper – was found dead near the site where Marina Habe's body had been found earlier in the year. On November 21, Scientologists James Sharp and Daureen Gaul were found dead in a Lose Angeles alley, stabbed more than fifty times with a long-bladed knife. Detectives learned that Gaul had been the girlfriend of Bruce Davis, a Family member subsequently convicted of first-degree murder.

And some believed that Manson's reach was very long. Joel Pugh, husband of Family member Sandra Good, flew to London in late 1968, accompanied by Bruce Davis. Their mission included the sale of some rare coins and the establishment of connections with satanic groups in Britain. Davis returned to the United States in April 1969, but Pugh stayed behind. His body was found in a London hotel room on December 1. His throat had been slit and his blood used to paint "backwards writing" and "comic book drawings" on a nearby mirror. In the absence of suspects, police ruled the strange death a suicide. Pugh's wife, though, was not convinced. She later told a friend, "I would not want what happened to Joel to happen to me."

On the same day that Pugh died in London, the LAPD announced warrants for the arrest of Watson, Krenwinkel, and Kasabian in the Tate case. The suspects' involvement in the LaBianca murders was also noted. Manson and Atkins, already in custody, were not mentioned. At this point, it was not known that Leslie Van Houten, who was also arrested in the raid that had picked up Manson, had been involved in the LaBianca case. Watson and Krenwinkel had also been arrested. Both had fled from L.A. but authorities in McKinney, Texas, and Mobile, Alabama, had picked them up after being notified by the LAPD. Informed that there was a warrant out for her arrest, Linda Kasabian voluntarily surrendered to authorities in Concord, New Hampshire, on December 2.

Soon, physical evidence like Krenwinkel's and Watson's fingerprints, which had been found at Cielo Drive, was enhanced by evidence recovered by the public. On September 1, 1969, the distinctive .22-caliber Hi Standard Buntline Special revolver Watson used to shoot Parent, Sebring, and Frykowski had been found and given to the police by a 10-year-old who lived near the Tate home. In December, when the Los Angeles Times published an account of the crimes based on information from Susan Atkins, the boy's father made several telephone calls to the police and they finally connected the gun to the murders. Acting on the same article, a local ABC television crew quickly located the bloody clothing that had been discarded by the killers.

At the trial, which began on June 15, 1970, the prosecution's main witness was Linda Kasabian, who, along with Manson, Atkins, and Krenwinkel, was charged with seven counts of murder and one count of conspiracy. Since she did not take part in the actual killings (and even tried to stop some of them), she was granted immunity in exchange for testimony that detailed the events that occurred on the nights of the crimes.

Because of his conduct, including violations of a gag order and submission of "outlandish" and "nonsensical" pretrial motions, Manson's permission to act as his own attorney (which had been reluctantly granted in the first place) was withdrawn by the court before the trial started. His strange behavior continued once the trial actually began. On Friday, July 24, the first day of testimony, Manson appeared in court with an "X" carved into his forehead and issued a statement that stated that since he was considered to be inadequate to represent himself, he had placed an "X" on his head to cross himself out of the "establishment's" world. That weekend, all of the female defendants duplicated the marks on their own foreheads and within a day or two, most of the other Family members did, too.

Prosecutor Vincent Bugliosi named Manson's interpretation of "Helter Skelter" as the main motive in the murders. The crime scenes' bloody White Album references were correlated with testimony about Manson's predictions that the murders that blacks committed at the outset of the race war would involve writing the word "pigs" in their victims' blood. Testimony that Manson said, "Now is the time for Helter Skelter" was backed up by Kasabian's testimony that, on the night of the LaBianca murders, Manson considered leaving Rosemary LaBianca's wallet lying on the street in a black neighborhood. His plan was for someone to pick up the wallet and use the credit cards inside it, making it seem that "some sort of organized group killed these people." Manson directed Kasabian to leave the wallet in the ladies room of a gas station near a black neighborhood. "I want to show blackie how to do it," Manson told Family members after the LaBianca murders.

During the trial, Family members lurked in the entrances and corridors of the courthouse. To keep them out of the courtroom itself, the prosecution subpoenaed them as prospective witnesses. That way, they were unable to enter the courtroom while others were testifying. The Family established a vigil on the sidewalk outside. Each of them carried a large, sheathed hunting knife. Since it was carried in plain sight, it was legal. The knives, along with the "X" carved into their foreheads, made Family members easily identifiable.

On August 4, despite precautions taken by the court, Manson flashed the jury a front page from the *Los Angeles Times*, with a headline that read "Manson Guilty, Nixon Declares," a reference to a statement made the previous day when President Richard Nixon complained about what he saw as the media's glamorization of Manson. When questioned by the judge, the jury members stated that the headline did not influence them. The next day, the female defendants stood up and announced in unison that in light of Nixon's opinion, there was no point in going on with the trial.

And this was not the end of the disruptions. On October 5, after the court refused to allow the defense to question a prosecution witness whom they had earlier declined to cross-examine, Manson jumped over the defense table and tried to attack the judge. He was wrestled to the floor by court bailiffs and was removed from the courtroom, along with the female defendants, who had risen to their feet after Manson's outburst and began chanting in Latin.

On November 19, the prosecution rested its case – and so did the defense, without ever calling a witness. Lawyers for the women were unwilling to let their clients testify and assume all of the guilt, believing that Manson had instructed them to do this. The next day, Manson was permitted to testify, but because his statements would possibly violate a California statute by implicating his co-defendants, the jury was removed from the courtroom. Manson spoke for more than an hour, blaming everything on rock and roll music, which was instructing young people to rise up against the establishment. He also stated that he didn't ever recall telling the girls to "get a knife and a change of clothes and go do what Tex says."

Members of the Manson Family lurked outside of the courthouse during the trial. Eventually, the girls shaved their heads in support of their leader.

As the trial was concluding, attorney Ronald Hughes, who had been representing Leslie Van Houten, disappeared during a weekend trip. Hughes had tried to separate the interests of his client from those of Manson, a move that angered Manson and may have cost Hughes his life. He hoped to show that Van Houten was not acting independently, but was controlled in her actions by Manson. Despite Hughes' disappearance, Judge Charles Older ordered the trial to proceed and appointed a new attorney, Maxwell Keith, for Van Houten. Keith was appointed to represent Van Houten during Hughes' absence but this caused a two-week delay as Keith familiarized himself with the case. The girls angrily demanded the firing of all their lawyers, and asked to reopen the defense. The judge denied the request and the trial resumed just before Christmas. However, disruptions caused by the defendants during the closing arguments forced the judge to ban them from the courtroom. Not long after this, Ronald Hughes' decomposed body was found wedged between two boulders in Ventura County. Due to severe decomposition, he had to be identified by dental records. The cause of his death was ruled as "undetermined."

One thing that the authorities did know was that Hughes had last been seen in the company of two Family members named "James" and "Lauren" – whose fate was later traced by Vincent Bugliosi. On November 8, 1972, hikers found the decapitated body of James Willett, 26, in a shallow grave near Guerneville, California. Three days later, Willett's station wagon was spotted outside a house in Stockton. Police arrested two members of the Aryan Brotherhood inside, along with three Manson women. The body of Lauren Willett, James' wife, was found buried in the basement.

On January 25, 1971, guilty verdicts were returned against Manson, Krenwinkel and Atkins on all counts. Van Houten was convicted on two counts of murder and one count of conspiracy. During the trial's penalty phase, Manson shaved his head and told the press that he was the Devil. Once the jury retired to weigh the state's request for the death penalty, the female defendants shaved their heads, as well. On March 29, 1971, the jury returned verdicts of death against all four defendants. The judge agreed with their findings and on April 19, sentenced them to death.

The lengthy proceedings to extradite Charles Watson from Texas, where he had returned a month before he was arrested, resulted in his being tried separately for the murders. The trial began in August 1971 and by

A recent photo of Charles Manson, who remains safely behind bars today. Despite numerous attempts at parole, it's unlikely he will ever be released.

October, he had been found guilty on seven counts of murder and one of conspiracy. He, too, was sentenced to death.

The death penalties were never carried out. In February 1972, the sentences of all five parties were automatically reduced to life in prison by California v. Anderson, a case in which the California Supreme Court abolished the death penalty in the state.

In a 1971 trial that was held after his convictions in the Tate and LaBianca murders, Manson was found guilty in the murders of Gary Hinman and Donald "Shorty" Shea and was given a life sentence for those crimes. In separate trials, Family members Bruce Davis and Steve "Clem" Grogan were also found guilty of Shea's murder.

With the Tate and LaBianca murders solved and the defendants safely locked behind bars, it seemed the Family would fade away for good. But neither Manson, nor many members of the Family, could remain out of the spotlight. On September 5, 1975, the Family was back in the news when Lynette "Squeaky" Fromme attempted to assassinate President Gerald Ford. The attempt took place in Sacramento, where she and fellow Manson girl Sandra Good had moved to be near Manson while he was incarcerated at Folsom State Prison. A subsequent search of the apartment shared by Fromme, Good, and a Family recruit turned up evidence that, coupled with later actions on the part of Good, resulted in Good's conviction for conspiring to send death threats through the U.S. mail. The threats were against corporate executives and government officials for what she saw as their neglect of the environment.

Manson himself seemed to enjoy being seen as the "crazed cult leader" and made a number of notable television appearances in the 1980s. He appeared on all three major networks from the California Medical Facility, a state prison hospital, and San Quentin. He was interviewed by Tom Snyder, Charlie Rose, and Geraldo Rivera, the last of whom spoke with Manson as part of a prime-time special on Satanism.

On September 25, 1984, while imprisoned at the California Medical Facility, Manson was seriously burned by a fellow inmate who poured paint thinner on him and then set him on fire. The prisoner later stated that Manson had threatened him. Despite suffering second and third-degree burns, Manson recovered from his injuries.

Although it seems unlikely that he will ever be released, Charles Manson, now 78, became eligible for parole after California v. Anderson nullified the death sentences in the state in 1972. This made Manson eligible to apply for parole after just seven years in prison. His first parole hearing was held in 1978 and on May 23, 2007, he was turned down for parole for the eleventh time. He failed to win his release again in 2012 after he bragged to a prison psychologist, "I am a very dangerous man."

He remains an inmate today in the Protective Housing Unit at California's Corcoran State Prison, relishing his continued notoriety and the attention that he receives on websites, in books, and within the underground culture of America.

Oddly, Manson's "Helter Skelter" motive in August massacres has long puzzled many students of the Family. Evidence of other, possibly more compelling motivations surfaced many years later when several Los Angeles informants told Ed Sanders (along with journalist Maury Terry) that the LaBiancas had been linked to drug trafficking in the city. In fact, Rosemary LaBianca, they claimed, was an established LSD dealer. FBI agents also described Vojtek Frykowski as a dealer, with an operation bankrolled by heiress Abigail Folger. Beyond the

241

drug connection, Leno LaBianca owed $230,000 to Los Angeles bookies on the night he died. He also served on the board of directors of a Hollywood bank linked to organized crime.

Nor was Sharon Tate the innocent that most headline articles made her out to be. Initiated as a witch by British occultist Alex Sanders before her marriage to Polanski, Tate had drifted into drugs and sordid sexual affairs around Hollywood. As actor Dennis Hopper described the Tate-Polanski set, "They had fallen into sadism and masochism and bestiality – and they recorded it all on videotape, too. The L.A. police told me this. I know that three days before they were killed, twenty-five people were invited to that house for the mass whipping of a dealer from the Sunset Strip who'd given them bad dope." In 1987, Manson asked an interviewer: "Don't you think those people deserved to die? They were involved in kiddie porn."

Still, the primary motive comes back to Frykowski and drugs.

A Family member told Maury Terry: "Frykowski was the motive. He had stung his own suppliers for a fair amount of money, and that didn't go down well at all with the people at the top of the drug scene here. And to make it worse, he was upsetting the structure of the LSD marketplace by dealing independently, outside of the established chain of supply. He was a renegade."

Journalist Ed Sanders, the first to writer to probe the connections between the Manson Family and the Process Church

A decade after the slaughter in California, "Son of Sam" David Berkowitz provided independent confirmation of the story from prison through a cell block confidant: "When Manson had the Tate murders done, he was not doing it out of some Helter Skelter fantasy. That was part of it, he believed in that shit. But there was a real motive, Berkowitz told me. He said Manson was working for somebody else when those crimes were committed. He said Manson volunteered to do the killings for somebody else. Manson was a puppet."

If that was true, then who was pulling the strings? According to Berkowitz, Manson was – like Berkowitz himself – a member of the malicious "Four P Movement," which was immersed in drugs, pornography, prostitution and ritual murder. Ed Sanders believed that Manson was indoctrinated into the group while he was hanging around the "Spiral Staircase" / "Snake Pit" house in Topanga Canyon, hanging out with killers and blood-drinking Satanists. Sanders learned this information from two prison informants, one in New York and the other in Florida – both of whom were murdered before year's end.

While this was going on, the Process Church of the Final Judgment was working overtime to distance itself from Charles Manson. In May 1971, Process members, "Father John" and "Brother Matthew," flew to L.A. from Cambridge, Massachusetts, to visit prosecutor Vincent Bugliosi and deny any links that the Process might have to the Family. A day later, they met with Manson in his cell and, according to Bugliosi; he suddenly became very evasive when asked about the cult.

The mysterious Process members also turned up at FBI headquarters in Los Angeles. An FBI memo on May 25 noted: "They explained they were ministers of a religious cult and preached about Satan and that Charles Manson had been a follower of a similar cult."

Later that year, when Ed Sanders published his book on the Manson Family, including a detailed analysis of how Manson was linked to the Process Church, cult members threatened his publisher with a libel suit. The American editors folded, deleting mention of the Process from future editions. British publishers stood firm, though, and won their case when it finally went to trial in March 1974.

By that time, the public image of the Process Church was beginning to unravel. Rumors and bad publicity from the Manson trial and from the Church's alleged links to Sirhan Sirhan prompted the DeGrimstons to try and clean up their image in 1971 and 1972. A "faith-healing tour" of Canada added new members, which had the cult claiming 100,000 members by mid-1972 – a doubtful figure since the church's largest chapter, in Chicago, had only 150 members. Splinter movements and offshoots had started to appear across the country, from the murderous "Four P Movement" in California (which drew its name from the swastika-like Process "power sign" – to the Luciferians in New Orleans, who were led by "Pope Satan I" and had a "true holy trinity" of God, Satan and the Serpent. A major, ultimately fatal rift occurred in the cult in early 1974, but it is unknown what the cause of the split was, or even its final results.

Some believe that the Process members devoted to Christ or Jehovah were fed up with Robert DeGrimston's emphasis on Satan by March 1974, dumping their founder to pursue a path of high-minded morality. Other sources say that the rift occurred between Robert and Mary Anne DeGrimston, with either Robert being kicked out by his wife, or leaving her for a life of his own. In any case, the end result was a new cult, dubbed the Foundation Church of the Millennium, later re-named the Foundation Faith of the Millennium in 1977, and the Foundation Faith of God in 1980. Mary Anne apparently led the new church for a time before dropping out of sight. Robert, meanwhile, tried to rally original members from a base in New Orleans, including a handful of chapters in Boston, Toronto, Chicago, New York, San Francisco and London. Various sources agree that he returned to England in the late 1970s.

But the movement that he started was not quite dead. In New York, for instance, David "Son of Sam" Berkowitz was seen in the company of one "Father Lars," a spokesman for a known Process splinter group. Berkowitz later confessed his membership in a satanic cult, described as an "offshoot of Scientology," which hated blacks, idolized deceased Nazis and practiced canine blood sacrifice. A continuing string of murders connected to alleged Process groups suggests that members may still be active in America today, committing crimes that range from rape and murder to animal and even human sacrifice.

Robert DeGrimston returned to New York in 1990 and worked as a business consultant there for many years. Oddly, Mary Anne's faction of the church later became the Best Friends Animal Society (which still exists today). Mary Anne DeGrimston currently lives in Utah.

6. DECEIVED BY SATAN

IS THE DEVIL REALLY LURKING IN THE DETAILS?

This is not the chapter that I initially planned to write.

I'm sure that if you, the reader, have gotten this far, you have also likely asked yourself – does he really believe all of this stuff? I confess that much of it does stretch the limits of believability. Do I honestly believe that black magicians were invoking demons from inside of magic circles? Were they really raising the dead to ask them about the whereabouts of lost treasure? Was the Devil really once an angel who was kicked out of Heaven for being too rebellious? Is Hell truly a place, as fundamentalist preachers would have us believe? And the list of the book's questionable contents goes on...

No, of course I don't – I don't believe that every myth and legend recounted in the preceding pages is true. But I do believe that they created the foundation of a belief system that is very important to millions of people around the world. I'm not even convinced that the "Devil" is a solitary figure, responsible for all of the horrible things that happen in our world. However, I do believe in a great evil – a darkness that is personified by a central character and one that people believed in for centuries.

My writing and research into the Devil – and all his works – has proven to be a contradictory affair. On one hand, I dismiss a millennium or more of beliefs in devils and demons, but on the other, I've been forced to take a hard look at the evil that men do – evil that they have perpetrated on other human beings for the sake of greed, lust, power, or simply because they believed that the Devil wanted them to.

This chapter was one of the most difficult to write. It was originally designed to take a look at things (and perhaps even chuckle about them a bit) that were connected to Satan on the surface, but really had nothing to do with the Devil at all. It was an easy list, starting with Hellfire Clubs, which began in the eighteenth century as an excuse for wealthy and titled Englishmen to carry on sex orgies, and ending with heavy metal music, with the "satanic messages" that were allegedly revealed in the recordings when you played them backwards. There was nothing funny about people who abused their kids and claimed that they did it because they were possessed by demons, but this was just as ridiculous as believing you would start worshipping the Devil by playing records backward.

And of course, one of my favorite topics – the Satanic Panic of the 1980s, when tabloids and television talk show hosts tried to convince us that seemingly ordinary people had "repressed memories" of being forced as children to participate in devil worship. Self-proclaimed "experts" insisted that satanic cults were carrying out human sacrifices all over the country on a daily basis. Satanists, they told us, were around every corner, just waiting to snatch us off the street.

Ridiculous stuff, right? The first stories like this broke back when I was still in high school and lasted for several years. They seemed scary at the time, but soon the "repressed" memories began to be called into question, the best-selling books turned out to be largely fictional, and the television talk-shows lost their credibility. Before long, it was easier to accept that nothing like that ever happened. Children weren't being given to Satan in diabolical rites and hitchhikers weren't being kidnapped and turned into human sacrifices.

None of that could be real, I knew, and I felt compelled to do a chapter of this book on such silly stuff, just to make sure that everyone knew that there was nothing to be afraid of. But then my research began, and the interviews, and the first-hand accounts... None of this could be real, or could it? Did those stories get started for a reason, only to spin out of control so that the truth was lost amid the urban legends and outright lies?

Would it frighten you to know that I think there is truth to such accounts, often buried deep under the lies? If it doesn't scare you, it should. In this chapter (and the one that follows), you'll get a good look at the depravity that can be found inside the human mind and just how far someone will go when they believe that they are doing the work of the Devil.

THE HELLFIRE CLUBS

Most people today are unfazed by satanic imagery and devices. We see them in movies and they appear in books. Such images are especially prevalent in the music world. Pentagrams and devilish images began appearing on the album covers of heavy metal artists in the early 1970s and scores of musicians still use them widely today.

But in eighteenth-century England, it was very rare to find anyone who claimed an association with the Devil. Of course, secret societies, like the Freemasons were rampant in those days and almost every gentleman in society belonged to at least one, or more, of them. Occult societies, too, began springing up, but Hellfire Clubs were something else altogether. While Freemasonry taught moderation, the Hellfire Clubs promoted excess; while Freemasonry bound its members to obey moral law and to be productive citizens, the Hellfire Clubs encouraged drunkenness, debauchery and a disregard for social convention.

Why did such clubs come about? It's a complicated question but it seems to have much to do with the political stability – one could almost say stagnation – in England during the early part of the eighteenth century. There were few social outlets for dissent in those days. London street gangs, the most famous of which were the Mohocks, first began to be mentioned in newspapers in March 1712. These were not your typical street gangs, though. The Mohocks were politically stifled Whigs who encouraged revolt through outrageous behavior. These rakes were gentlemen of talent and breeding who drank, gambled and womanized with flamboyance. The sons of landed gentry, merchants and minor aristocracy, they had more free time than the average laborer and the means to enjoy it. It was out of this leisure time that the Hellfire Clubs were born.

Phillip, Duke of Wharton

(Right) A painting of one of Phillip's original Hellfire Clubs, which was an excuse for lascivious behavior.

Little is known about the first Hellfire Club that it began around 1720. It is uncertain whether its founder, Phillip, Duke of Wharton, came up with the idea on his own or borrowed it from an earlier body. The club met for the specific purpose of "drinking, gambling and blaspheming," and became immediately popular. There may have been three societies—the Hellfire Club and two others like it—or just one. They met at three houses: one in Westminster, one in Conduit Street near Hanover Square, and one at Somerset House. The total membership amounted to forty-odd. Surprisingly, their goal – at least not their primary one -- wasn't partying but blasphemy. They came to meetings dressed "as revered figures from the Bible, or saints, and played them for laughs. They staged mock rituals making fun of Christian dogmas such as the Trinity." There is nothing to suggest in those early days that the club indulged in orgies, Satanism or occult rituals, but all of that was to change.

Wharton, the founder and president of the original club, had contacts, if not sympathies, with the Jacobites. They were a political movement in Great Britain and Ireland to restore the Stuart King James II of England and his heirs to the thrones of England, Scotland and Ireland. Wharton's view was that the Revolution of 1688 had been betrayed, leaving England saddled with a permanent army, press censorship, a corrupt Parliament and a Church that took orders from the monarchy. Wharton was potentially a spokesman for the dissenting Whigs, who wanted parliament to allow true liberty and freedom from patronage. The Hellfire Clubs were a way to resist the government in those days, but soon other ideas came to mind. Wharton started a second club in 1723 that was dedicated to sex, rather than blasphemous pursuits. He finally left England in 1725, going first to Vienna, then Madrid, where he gained an appointment as a Colonel in the Spanish army. Indicted for treason in England, Wharton drifted to France in 1728. Creditors drove him back to Spain, where he died in a Bernardine monastery in 1731.

The eccentric Sir Francis Dashwood

Wharton's unrestrained sex life, his flouting of Protestant respectability, his crazy spending, and his almost comic rebellion against the standards of the day made him a legend that lived on in the minds of later rebels. His introduction of the Hellfire Club would soon be copied by other Englishmen.

Such clubs spread quickly, largely among the lower ranks of the aristocracy, in England, Ireland and Scotland. According to one writer, "a wave of blasphemy swept over the small close-knit world of the Anglo-Irish." In Ireland the Hellfire clubs were obviously inspired by Wharton but they tended to be more harmful, with their members committing petty crimes and flirting with devil-worship. Limerick had a Hellfire Club, as did Dublin from about 1735. Lord Santry, Simon Luttrell, who was known as "the wicked madman," Colonels Clements, Ponsonby and St George, were all members of the Dublin Hellfire Club, which held orgies at the Eagle Tavern on Cork Hill, at Daly's Club on College Green, and at a hunting lodge on Montpelier Hill until the lodge burnt down and they relocated to the Killakee Dower House farther down the same hill. They gathered to drink hot scaltheen, a mixture of whisky and butter laced with brimstone, and to toast Satan. There were rumors of orgies, Black Masses and mock crucifixions, but no one knows if such stories were true. Black magic was enjoying resurgence in Europe at the time and it spread to the rakish set in Britain and Ireland.

The most famous of all of the British Hellfire Clubs was one founded by Sir Francis Dashwood, likely in the 1730s. By that time, such clubs had become so notorious that they had been banned by Royal Proclamation – which, of course, made them even more exciting to their members. Dashwood and his friend, the Earl of Sandwich, began meeting at a Hellfire Club in London at the George & Vulture Inn in the 1730s and soon started a club of their own. The subsequent club was the first to adopt the philosophy *"Fais Ce Que Voudras,"* or "Do What Thou Wilt," which was later embraced by Aleister Crowley and Anton LaVey.

Dashwood's club was never originally known as a Hellfire Club; it was given that name much later by his detractors. His club in fact used a number of other names, such as the Brotherhood of St. Francis of Wycombe, the Order of Knights of West Wycombe and the Order of the Friars of St. Francis of Wycombe. Later, after moving their meetings to Medmenham Abbey in Buckinghamshire, they called themselves the Monks of Medmenham. Although the names given to the various incarnations of the club sounded like they were inspired by Catholicism, Dashwood preferred the free-spirited paganism of antiquity to dour Christianity. Prior to starting the club, Dashwood and some of his friends took several "Grand Tours" around Europe, Russia and the Near East. They visited royal courts and bordellos and toured museums and archaeological sites, paying particular attention to those where there were artifacts of an erotic nature. Dashwood and his companions acquired various grimoires and books of spells, and spent time in Italy, which was then seeing a revival of interest in the black arts.

Back home, membership in the club was initially limited to twelve (thirteen, including Dashwood, the traditional number of a coven), but soon increased. Of the original twelve, some are regularly identified: Robert Vansittart; Thomas Potter; Francis Duffield; Edward Thompson; Paul Whitehead and John Montagu, 4th Earl of Sandwich. The list of supposed members is immense; among the more probable candidates are George Bubb Dodington; William Hogarth has been associated with the club after painting Dashwood as a Franciscan Friar, and John Wilkes, though much later, under the pseudonym John of Aylesbury. Benjamin Franklin is known to have occasionally attended the club's meetings during 1758 as a non-member during his time in England. But since there are no records left, many of these men are just assumed to have been members.

Dashwood owned a large estate in West Wycombe in Buckinghamshire and meetings were soon moved to his home. The first was held on Walpurgis Night in 1752 but the stories say that it was something of a failure and no large-scale meetings were ever held there again. In 1751, Dashwood had leased nearby Medmenham Abbey, a ruined twelfth-century monastery on the banks of the Thames, from a friend, Francis Duffield. Meetings were then moved to the Abbey, but not before Dashwood had some extensive – and curious – remodeling work carried out on the building. The structure was rebuilt by architect Nicholas Revett in Gothic Revival style and a tower and cloister were added. At this time, the "Do What Thou

Dashwood's Estate in West Wycombe in Buckinghamshire

Wilt" motto was placed above a doorway in stained glass. An Italian artist was hired to decorate the walls with frescoes, with his son later continuing the work. While it is thought that William Hogarth may have executed murals for this building, none survive. Underneath West Wycombe Hill, Dashwood had workmen carve out a tunnel and a series of caves that branched out from an existing cave. The walls were carved with an eclectic mix of mythological themes and phallic symbols as well as niches for statues. Dashwood's garden at West Wycombe also contained numerous statues, many of them copies of those he had admired during his trips to Greece, as well as shrines to different gods: Daphne and Flora, Priapus, Venus and Dionysus.

Quite simply, Dashwood had plenty of money and the resources with which to bring his fantasies to life. The caves ran down from a 200-foot entrance into the center of the hill. There was an underground stream that was meant to represent the River Styx. A boat ferried club members to an area of the caves where they boozily paid homage to Demeter, Greek goddess of fertility, by re-enacting a version of the Eleusian Mysteries. The caves also contained a large banqueting hall and a number of smaller chambers the size of monks' cells that were used for private assignations.

Meetings occurred twice a month, with a longer meeting taking place during the June solstice that lasted a week or more. According to Horace Walpole, each gathering of members was "rigorously pagan: Bacchus and Venus were the deities to whom they almost publicly sacrificed; and the nymphs and the hogsheads that were laid in against the festivals of this new church, sufficiently informed the neighborhood of the complexion of those hermits."

The members addressed each other as "Brother" and the leader, which changed regularly, as "Abbot." During meetings, members wore white trousers, jacket and cap, while the "Abbot" wore a red ensemble of the same style. Poet and satirist Paul Whitehead kept the club's records, but he ordered all of his papers destroyed shortly before his death so whatever actually went on when the "Brothers" got together is unknown. Carousing, certainly, and a great deal of feasting and general hilarity but whether the rumors of Black Masses and demon worship are true or just the stuff of legends can't be confirmed. Dashwood enjoyed tweaking the nose of conventional society and he loved pranks, so the tales of club members entertaining prostitutes who were dressed as nuns seem likely, unlike the stories that sprang up in the 1970s of them kidnapping and sacrificing local children.

The downfall of Dashwood's Hellfire Club was drawn-out and complicated. In 1762, Dashwood was appointed Chancellor of the Exchequer, despite his being widely held to be incapable of understanding "a bar bill of five figures."Dashwood resigned the post the next year, having raised a tax on cider which caused near-riots. He next sat in the House of Lords after taking up the title of Baron le Despencer after the previous holder died. Then there was the attempted arrest of John Wilkes for seditious libel against the king in early 1763. During a search authorized by a general warrant, a version of *The Essay on Woman* was discovered set up on the press of a printer whom Wilkes had likely used. It was scurrilous, blasphemous, libelous, and bawdy, and although not pornographic, it was still unquestionably illegal under the laws of the time. The government used it to drive Wilkes into exile. Between 1760 and 1765, a book called *Chrysal, or the Adventures of a Guinea* by Charles Johnstone was published. It contained stories easily identified with Medmenham, one in which Lord Sandwich was ridiculed as having mistaken a monkey for the Devil. This book sparked the association between the Medmenham Monks and the Hellfire Club. By this time, many of the Friars were either dead or living too far away for the club to continue as it did before. Medmenham was finished by 1766.

Paul Whitehead was the last lingering member of the Club. He had served for years as the secretary and steward of the group. When he died in 1774, his will specified that his heart be placed in an urn at West Wycombe. It was sometimes taken out to show to visitors, some of whom are recorded as having tossed it playfully back and forth, but was lost or stolen in 1829.

The Hellfire Club had lasted for some thirty-five years. Whether it ever lived up to Sir Francis Dashwood's fantasies is not known, although he and his friends must have enjoyed themselves for them to have continued meeting for so long. Despite the lurid stories, it was really more of an eighteenth-century version of the Playboy Club than a sinister gathering of devil-worshippers.

The Hellfire Clubs were a parody of the traditional Black Mass. In the early chapters of the book, the history of the Black Mass was described; having turned from the Sabbaths that worshipped the old gods to what the Church saw a perversion of its own rites. But the transition from those days to the Black Masses of modern times has not been recounted. It might be useful to do so at this point, so that readers understand how the original Black Mass became the repeated subject of "repressed memories" in the 1980s.

The actual form of the Black Mass changed greatly from the old Sabbaths. Those were celebrations of the harvest, of fertility rites and Solstices. Things took a darker turn as the power of the Church in Europe began to grow. There are a varied number of rituals that became known as Black Masses, but the first recorded event took place in the seventh century when the Church Council of Toledo condemned an office known as the Mass of the Dead.

The Mass of Saint-Sécaire is a classic example and was a ritual supposed to have been performed in Gascony, France. The best-known account of the Mass is that of James George Frazer in his 1890 book, *The Golden Bough*. Frazer described the ritual as what would become known as the Black Mass. According to the account, the Mass could only be said in a ruined or deserted church. At precisely 11:00 p.m., the corrupt priest, with only his lover as attendant, would begin to recite the Mass backwards, being sure to finish at precisely the last stroke of midnight. Among other details intended to parody the normal practice of the Catholic Mass, the host used would be triangular and black, rather than round and white, with three points instead of the usual four; the priest would not consecrate wine but instead drink water from a well into which an unbaptized infant had been thrown. It was also said that the sign of the cross would only be made by the priest with his left foot on the ground before him. At the end, the priest would pronounce the name of a victim, who, it was believed, would soon waste away and die, for no identifiable cause.

Continuous prosecutions and the continuous association of the Black Mass with witchcraft have made the ceremony notorious throughout the centuries. Satanists of all sorts still practice it today and despite many localized variations, the Black Mass is basically a blasphemous ceremony that reverses everything in the Christian / Catholic version of the mass. The altar is covered with a black cloth instead of a white one; the crucifix is hung upside-down; hymns and prayers are sung and recited backward; the candles are black, rather than white; and whenever the name of God or Christ is used, it is spat upon and abused. Satan takes the place of God and water (or blood) replaces wine in the sacrament, where a turnip or similar satirical item is used in place of the host. Sexual rites have long been a part of the ritual, even dating back to its origins as a pagan practice.

One of the most extraordinary accounts of a Black Mass and its repercussions appears in Moncure Daniel Conway's *Demonology* from 1870. It recounts a 1669 investigation of two villages in Sweden, Mohra and Elfdale, when thirty-three adults and fifteen children were executed for practicing witchcraft. Dozens more were punished for their part in the crimes. The "confession" began as follows:

We of the province of Elfdale do confess that we used to go to a gravel-pit which lay hard by a crossway, and there we put on a vest over our heads, and then we danced around, and after this ran to the crossway, and called the Devil thrice, first with a still voice, the second somewhat louder, and the third time very loud, with these words – Antecessor, come and carry us to Blockula.

Whereupon immediately he used to appear, but in different habits, but for the most part we saw him in a grey coat and red and blue stockings: he had a red beard, a high-crowned hat, with linen of divers colours wrapt about it, and long garters upon his stockings.

The villagers were then asked by Satan if they would serve him with soul and body. When he received their agreement, he placed them aboard a great beast that carried them over a number of churches and high walls. They eventually came to a high meadow where there was a satanic placed called "Blockula." There, the villages had to obtain scrapings of altars and pieces of church clocks. Then the Devil gave them a horn with salve in it so that they could anoint themselves. He also gave them a saddle, a hammer, and a wooden nail with which to fix the saddle. After these preparations had been made, they were to continue the journey. The confessions continued:

For their journey, they said they made use of all sorts of instruments, of beasts, of men, of spits, and posts, according as they had opportunity: if they do ride upon goats and have many children with them, that all may have room, they stick a spit into the backside of a goat, and then they are anointed with the aforesaid ointment. What the manner of their journey is, God only knows. Thus much was made out, that if the children did at any time name the names of those that had carried them away, they were again carried by force either to Blockula, or to the crossway, and there miserably beaten, insomuch that some of them died of it.

One young girl confessed that as she was being carried away by the Devil, she shouted the name of Jesus. Immediately afterward, she fell to the ground with a great wound in her side. Apparently, the Devil closed the wound and continued to abduct her. At the time of her confession, she still complained of pain in her side.

All of the villagers agreed that the sinister Blockula was located in a meadow that was so large that they could not see the other side of it. There was a house that fronted the meadow with a brightly painted gate and beyond the gate was a yard where the beasts were grazed that were used in the satanic rites. Inside of the house, the masters lived, and in one large room was a long table. In another room were "lovely and delicate beds."

The first ritual observed at this strange place was the Black Mass, followed by a satanic pact. This had to be sworn, and each villager cut a finger and wrote their name in blood in the Devil's Book They were also baptized in the Devil's name and assured that the final Day of Judgment was at hand. On that day, they would face a more monstrous creature than the one that had carried them away, a dragon that was surrounded by fire and bound with an iron chain. The Devil told them that if the villagers returned home and confessed anything of what they had seen or done, the dragon would be loosed upon them, plunging all of Sweden into demonic horror.

The villagers went on to confess (despite the Devil's threats) that he often entertained them with music from a harp and would take many of the women into a chamber and have sex with them. Eventually, the villagers claimed, sons and daughters were produced for the Devil. He then proceeded to have incestuous relations with his sons and daughters and their progeny were toads and serpents. After sexual intercourse, a meal was had where those most favored were seated at the Devil's right hand, while the children had to stand by the door to be fed with meat and drink by the Devil. After dining, dancing began, and in the midst of it, the villagers were encouraged to fight among themselves.

The villagers who admitted to having sex with the Devil were looked on as witches by the commissioners who investigated the crimes. The interrogators asked the villagers to demonstrate their powers of witchcraft, but they were unable to do so. They claimed that once they had confessed, all of their powers had disappeared. The Devil had appeared to them after their confessions, they said, in a particularly vengeful mood. His appearance was hideous, with claws on his hands and feet, horns on his head and a long, serpent-like tail. He conjured up visions for them of a burning pit with a desperate hand rising out of it, which the Devil mercilessly shoved back down again. He told the confessors that this would be their fate if they continued to tell his secrets.

It's pretty clear from the extraordinary fantasy concocted by the villagers that such startling images could not have created with ease. While some believe that the images were suggested to them by the witch-finders, it's my opinion that there was a powerful personality among them who preyed on them and fed these visions to them in the midst of depravity and abuse. The entire fantasy likely came out of the only element of truth in the story – the sinister celebration of the Black Mass. Coerced, or merely invited, into the ritual, the leader (posing as the Devil) created the stories in a wild mixture of sex, alcohol, burning herbs and drugs – hence, the "ointment" that was applied. While the villagers were high on hallucinogens, it was easy for him to create whatever mood he wanted, take advantage of them, and have sex with men, women and children alike. By picking apart the "confession," it's easy to see that the "trip" they took to Blockula was very likely a drug-induced nightmare that included sex, bestiality and horror.

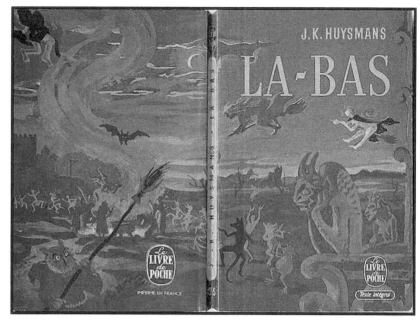

Strangely, many of the images conjured up from the 1669 accounts would remain consistent with "Satanic Ritual Abuse" cases in the 1980s.

A more recent account of a Black Mass was offered in *Là Bas* (Down There or The Damned), a novel by French writer Joris-Karl Huysmans, first published in 1891. The novel dealt with Satanism in contemporary France, and the novel stirred a certain amount of controversy on its first appearance. The book was first published in serial form by the newspaper *L'Écho de Paris*, with the first installment appearing on February 15, 1891. It came out in book form in April of the same year. Many of *L'Écho de Paris'* more conservative readers were shocked by the subject matter and urged the editor to halt the serialization, but he ignored them.

The plot of *La Bas* concerned a novelist who is disgusted by the emptiness and vulgarity of the modern world. He seeks relief by turning to the study of the Middle Ages and begins to research the life of the notorious fifteenth-century child-murderer Gilles de Rais. Through his contacts in Paris, he discovers that Satanism was not simply a thing of the past, but is alive and well in turn-of-the-century France. He embarks on an investigation of the occult underworld with the help of his lover, Madame Chantelouve. The novel culminated with a description of a Black Mass, which many researchers now believe was taken from real life. Huysmans claimed that he attended such a ceremony and he used the book to describe it with startling realism.

The hero of the story, Durtal, was taken to a ruined chapel by a woman named Hyacinthe. There, he found a conventional altar, dominated by an obscene Christ. The neck was stretched upward and there was a sneering smile on his face. The figure was also naked and sexually aroused. The altar was draped in black cloth and decorated with black candles. Meanwhile, the toxic smell of bitumen and resin increased the foulness of the atmosphere. Instead of incense, myrtle, rue, henbane and dried nightshade were burned, as well as thorn apple, a narcotic.

The officiant was an old and corrupt priest, wearing a dark red vestment and scarlet cap, to which two horns of red cloth had been sewn. Underneath his outfit, he was naked. When he began the Black Mass, the worshippers inhaled the pungent fumes and worked themselves into a frenzy. Durtal noticed that the

communion chalice was was filled with dark red blood. Before the altar, a black goat was tied, surrounded by a garland of saffron, pine cones, deadly nightshade and other poisonous plants.

Huysmans described a Black Mass with all of the most dramatic elements of Satanism. It would be a scene that would be widely copied in Europe for years to come.

In the 1950s and 1960s, Black Masses were reported in Italy, France and England. One was held in a Sussex church (which had to be re-sanctified afterward), while another, in Clophill in Bedfordshire, involved necromancy. A skeleton was found inside the church, while in the churchyard, the graves of six women were found to have been opened.

Richard Cavendish, a respected author on the history of the occult, wrote in his book *The Powers of Evil:*

In the Black Mass ritual of one of the present-day Satanist groups, Christ is again denounced as a do-nothing king and coward. God is cursed as "the pig" and "that nefarious foul-mouthed Jew" and that "foul imposter" who would deny the pleasures of Almighty Satan's realm and condemn humanity to a life of piety and want, and he is ordered to vanish into the void of his empty heaven.

Traditional Satanist conviction is that Christ is a false God and that everything he stands for is evil. This is the reason for the turning of the Catholic Mass obscenely on its head. The dualism of Christianity made it highly convenient for the practitioners of the Black Mass to create Satan as a figurehead and the ruler of the Earth. The Black Mass has appealed to a variety of different classes, ranging from the idle rich to the disillusioned poor, from the religiously fanatic to the sexually frustrated. The drugs and sex element only serves to fuel a hysteria that is already present in the blasphemy of the service.

In *La Bas*, Huysmans described the frantic behavior that occurred near the end of the Black Mass:

... the women threw themselves down and rolled on the carpet, one of them, as if moved by springs, threw herself on her stomach and beat the air with her feet, another squinting hideously, first made a clucking noise, then became voiceless, her jaws wide, her tongue sticking to the roof of her mouth. Another, her face swollen, the pupils of her eyes dilated, let her head fall to her shoulders and then, lifting it abruptly, began to tear her throat with her nails. Yet another stretched out on her back, undid her skirt, showing a naked stomach, huge with flatulence, twisted her face into hideous grimaces; from her blood-filled mouth, she thrust out her tongue, bitten at the edges, and could not get it back in.

All of this is very reminiscent of hysterical possession among primitive tribes and even of the conditions that result from extreme forms of Christian worship ceremonies. The Black Mass whips its followers up into a frenzy of emotion and leaves them limp and exhausted, both physically and mentally. To the Satanist, the ritual is the ultimate expression of all he believes in and there is no doubt that it echoes the long-held philosophy of "Do What Thou Wilt."

Even though Satanists see the Devil as the ruler of the Earth, God is still strangely worshipped in the Black Mass. It is an indirect worship and he is regarded more as a talisman against the unbridled evil of Satan than anything else. Protection was needed against the power of the Devil, and what better to put it against it than the power of God. Of course, the Devil is not merely worshipped at the Black Mass – the whole power of evil is also sought after. In the grimoires, the traditional ritual is clearly laid down and followed today in the same way that it was a century or more ago. The Grimoire of Honorius, for instance, relies heavily on the Christian Mass as a springboard toward the Black Mass. This book states emphatically that the Christian Mass is used to protect and empower the officiant.

In most cases, the officiant should be an ordained priest (but presumably a defrocked or non-practicing one) and the ritual should begin with the celebrating of a Mass of the Holy Ghost on the first Monday of the month in the early morning hours. This is the mass for the Pentecost, commemorating the occasion when the disciples of Christ received the gift of speaking in tongues. As a result, the practitioners of the Black Mass hope to gain further power through their own commemoration of the Christian miracle. After the consecration of the host, the satanic priest holds it in his left hand and prays to Christ. Part of the prayer reads: "...give to thy unworthy servant, holding thy living body in his hands, the strength to use that power which is entrusted to him against the rebellious spirits."

At sunrise, the priest takes a black rooster and kills it, ripping out its heart, eyes and tongue. They are dried and turned into a powder. The remainder of the corpse is buried in a secret place. At the next sunrise, the priest recites the Mass of the Angels, which is part of the passion of St. Michael – the great fighter against Satan. This is meant to protect the priest in case the demonic powers that he summons become too strong for him to handle.

On the altar, one of the black rooster's feathers is placed. The priest takes this, sharpens the point, dips it into consecrated wine and writers a series of magical characters on a blank piece of parchment. Two days later, at midnight, he lights a candle of yellow wax that is made in the form of a cross, and recites Psalm 78. This is followed by the Mass for the Dead. At the same time, the priest calls on God to free him from the fear of Hell and to make demons obedient to him. After the candle is extinguished, a young male lamb is sacrificed by having its throat cut. The powdered remains of the hearts, eyes and tongue of the black rooster are ground into the skin of the lamb and the corpse is buried with the following prayer, which identifies the slaughtered lamb with Christ:

Sacrificed Lamb, be Thou a pillar of strength against the demons! Slain Lamb, give me power over the powers of darkness! Sacrificed Lamb, give me strength to subdue the rebellious spirits! So be it.

More magical symbols are drawn on the parchment, more psalms are read and the priest then says another Mass for the Dead. This concluded with the chanting of the seventy-two names of great power and, at last, the incantation for the spirits to appear at the Black Mass. This long and complicated process makes the culminating Mass itself a highly charged and exciting event for the priest and the worshippers.

Once the preparations are concluded, the worshippers form a cross, or a semi-circle, around the altar. Each is given a part of the host to eat and, instead of communion wine, they drink a foul-tasting and deadly cold mixture of blood, wine and various drugs. Their "worship" concludes with a free-for-all orgy, after which many are convinced that they engaged in sex with the Devil himself.

The Black Mass widely varies in how it's carried out, but the basics remain the same as they have been for many years. One account, collected in Spain in 1942, concerned six men and three women who met at a farm, had a huge feast and then stripped. They boiled a cat in a cauldron of soup, drank the soup while reciting incantations, made an altar of wooden planks and then celebrated Black Mass, using slices of sausage as the host. In similar situations, a particular concoction was substituted for bread and wine – the standard recipe containing menstrual blood and semen.

In reality, Devil worship and the Black Mass have been, and still are, an expression of hatred against Christianity, orthodox religion and conventional society as a whole. The Church takes it very personally. They are outraged by the fact that consecrated hosts are burned, consecrated wine is poured on the floor and the crucifixion is mocked. But, with all due respect, what do they expect?

The Church brought the Devil to life when they sought to provide an adversary for God – a figure of such terror that sinners would have someone to fear. Because of this, Church authorities can hardly complain when Satan is worshipped in the Black Mass. If only they had avoided personalizing the Devil, then there would have been no one to worship. It is so much easier to pray to a figure – even if he is the Devil – than to the real dark force that exists inside of everyone, which is the true source of evil.

THE DEVIL MADE ME PLAY IT: SATAN AND HIS LOVE FOR HEAVY METAL MUSIC

You must have the Devil in you to succeed in any of the arts.
Voltaire

He did not see any reason why the devil should have all the good tunes.
Rowland Hill

One of the more ridiculous aspects of the Devil's "works" has to involve the alleged satanic aspects that can be found in the music of heavy metal bands, the mysterious backwards messages found in their music and the way they use their talents to lure the youth of America to the dark side.

Rock music has enjoyed a strange, symbiotic relationship with the occult since the 1960s when the Beatles included a photograph of Aleister Crowley on their *Sgt. Pepper* album and the Rolling Stones credited Anton LaVey and Voodoo priests for their inspiration in creating "Sympathy for the Devil," "Goat's Head Soup" and "Their Satanic Majesties Request." It was perhaps inevitable that the hippie era of the late 1960s, with its emphasis on "acid rock" and Eastern mysticism would initiate a change in classic rock and roll, evolving over time into the current "heavy metal" scene.

Heavy metal, which gets its name from its reliance on electric guitars cranked to ear-splitting decibels, has become inextricably linked to Satanism in the public eye, thanks in equal parts to lyrics, deliberate marketing strategy, and the exaggerated claims of some Christian fundamentalist groups. Beyond the stage lights and amplifiers, in the daily lives of the rabid fans who become obsessed with heavy metal, the police and religious groups claim that the music has a disastrous effect. They claim that fans commit crimes ranging from petty vandalism to murder – all directly inspired by the message of occult-oriented bands.

But such claims are nothing new and not all of them can be attributed to the blasting chords of heavy metal.

Music has been a part of life since the beginning of recorded time, and likely before. The earliest songs offered a welcome respite to simple villagers and monastic liturgies often had Earthly, secular themes. By the early days of the twentieth century, jazz music was being blamed for inciting lewd and lascivious acts, even though now jazz is seen as pleasantly sophisticated.

And then came the blues.

It was said that the Devil himself presided over the birth of the blues in the Mississippi Delta in the 1920s, and he has kept a grip on the offspring of the blues ever since. It was not just the fact that blues players were black and therefore were considered a threat to the white population of still-segregated region. No, it was the fact that the blacks of those days were determined to enjoy what little life had to offer them and that often meant dancing, drinking, sex and of course, music. But there was another, rarely acknowledged, reason why white society and the religious authorities were suspicious, even fearful, of black music – the blues sounded otherworldly to the whites, smacking of Voodoo and African rhythm that could only be the music of the Devil.

One of the most enduring legends of blues history tells how Robert Johnson, the "King of the Delta Blues Singers," sold his soul to the Devil at a crossroads on Mississippi's Highway 61 at midnight in exchange for some amazing guitar skills and a handful of tunes. An awkward young man, he had been booed off stage only nine months earlier and so when he returned to the local juke joints after making his pact with the Devil, the crowd was spooked by his transformation. His fame spread quickly, but at night Johnson was haunted by dreams in which

Robert Johnson

the Devil pursued him down a long dirt road leading to a cemetery. These nightmares inspired his classic songs "Crossroad Blues," "Me and the Devil Blues" and "Hellhound on my Trail."

The Devil only allowed Johnson to live until his twenty-seventh birthday. He was apparently poisoned by a club owner who suspected the singer of seducing his wife. He was buried in an unmarked grave by the locals, who refused to put him in consecrated ground for fear that the Devil would come to claim his own.

When the blues artists left their rural backwaters for Chicago, searching for record contracts and regular gigs, they soon found that they needed to amplify their guitars to be heard above the rattle of the elevated trains and the noise of the traffic. Electric guitars, bass, drums and amplified vocals made for a raunchier, rhythm-driven sound and with it came ever earthier lyrics, which enhanced the music's reputation for promoting debauchery, drinking and drugs.

But the religious groups did not come out in force against the new "race music" until it threatened to corrupt a white audience through the records of Elvis Presley, Chuck Berry, Little Richard, Carl Perkins, Jerry Lee Lewis and many others. As rock and roll was unleashed upon a generation of teenagers who had never heard anything like it before, it was condemned from pulpits across America as "jungle music." Society blamed it for the subsequent rise in drunkenness, vandalism, violence and juvenile delinquency. Rock music and the Devil have been inseparable ever since.

The rockabilly of the 1950s and the "beat combos" of the early 1960s eventually gave way to the psychedelic movement, whose foremost exponents experimented with mind-altering substances and promoted the exotic philosophies of the East. The Rolling Stones initially tuned in and tripped out on acid until they realized that it made their music soft and self-indulgent. They discarded the love beads and came up with "Sympathy for the Devil," the first explicitly satanic song that had ever been released. They were inspired by the media's self-righteous rage surrounding Anton LaVey's newly founded Church of Satan. Satanism became a fashionable

Mick Jagger

indulgence for the band and many of their followers. In 1969, lead singer Mick Jagger had collaborated with California underground filmmaker Kenneth Anger on an eleven-minute movie called *Invocation of My Demon Brother*. It included footage of the cast smoking hashish from a human skull and conducting a satanic funeral for a dead dog. Anger was an avowed disciple of Aleister Crowley and a close friend of Anton LaVey. He went on to later collaborate with another Crowley follower, Jimmy Page of Led Zeppelin, on a second film called *Lucifer Rising* in 1972.

The press labeled Jagger the "Lucifer of Rock" because the Rolling Stones were more interested in sex, drugs and music than worshipping the Devil. Their satanic image was nothing more than a clever marketing ploy during a time period when the public was titillated by the occult. But the Stones found out that even playfully evoking a Satanic image could prove fatal. At the Altamont Music Festival in 1969, a group of Hell's Angels that they had hired to provide security fatally stabbed a fan in front of the stage while Jagger was performing. Shocked by the event, the band dropped the satanic references from their music. The Rolling Stones went on to become a multi-million dollar corporate act that is a harmless parody of their former rebellious selves.

Other less mainstream bands, however, found the satanic imagery too tempting to resist and as the late 1960s came around, bands like Black Widow and Coven summoned the faithful to the Black Mass. The Chicago band Coven can lay claim to being the first overtly satanic band to release an album. The closing track of *Witchcraft Destroys Minds and Reaps Souls* is a thirteen-minute Black Mass that uses a Latin chant that the sleeve notes claim is authentic. The cover of their 1969 debut album also featured what might have been the first appearance of the "Devil's sign," a hand gesture that was later popularized by Ronnie James Dio, who replaced Ozzy Osbourne in Black Sabbath. He claimed that he learned it from his Italian grandmother, who told him it was a traditional protection against the "evil eye." The gesture was subsequently used en masse by metal fans as a way of showing tribute to the performers. Incidentally, Dio also fronted Ritchie Blackmore's band Rainbow, another group with a passing interest in the occult.

Black Widow's debut album, *Sacrifice*, also featured several songs with satanic themes, including "Conjuration," "Come to the Sabbat" and the title track. Their stage act included a faux ritual, complete with a naked female dancer, which they claimed was choreographed by Alex Sanders, the so-called "King of the Witches." As it turned out, though, you needed more than just a good stage act to make it in rock and roll. Their music proved to be too unremarkable to make much of a lasting impression.

In contrast, British metal band Black Sabbath embraced the "schlock horror" aspect of witchcraft and devil worship wholeheartedly. They named themselves after a stylish Italian horror film starring Boris Karloff and they served up the musical version of Hammer horrors in tracks like "The Wizard," "Children of the Grave," "War Pigs" and "Paranoid."

But Black Sabbath soon realized that they had inadvertently started something that couldn't be stopped. Fans began reading invocations to Satan into every lyric. "N.I.B.," for example was interpreted to mean "Nativity in Black," but it had actually been a reference to the drummer's nickname, Nibby. The negative attention that they attracted from seriously disturbed fans led the group to write songs that warned against dabbling in the occult. They later admitted that they had been uncomfortable with the subject from the start.

In 1966, bassist Geezer Butler began reading black magic magazines and Dennis Wheatley novels. Raised as a Catholic, he believed in the existence of the Devil and so when he started having precognitive dreams, he wondered if they had been sent to him by dark forces. He started putting upside-down crosses on his walls, painted his apartment black and decorated the place with pictures of Satan. But his avid interest would some come to an end.

One of Geezer's supernatural experiences inspired the title track of the band's debut album. He had been lying in bed one night after reading a book on the occult when he sensed what he called a "malign presence." When he opened his

Black Sabbath – seemingly one of history's most sinister heavy metal bands, but in truth, it was merely their image

eyes, he was terrified to see a large black shape that looked like a hooded monk standing at the end of his bed. After a moment or two, it disappeared, but it left behind an unsettling atmosphere. The next morning, Geezer discovered that the occult book he had been reading was gone. He knew that the thing, whatever it was, had been drawn by the book and he vowed never to read anything on the subject again.

Ozzy Osbourne, a bandmate who also made the most of Black Sabbath's satanic image has since become one of America's favorite eccentric uncles as he shuffles through his Hollywood mansion in his slippers, struggling to cope with his reality show. As a working-class lad from Birmingham, Ozzy always had his tongue firmly wedged in his cheek when it came to being the "Prince of Darkness." He seemed a frightening figure until TV viewers saw him struggling with television remotes and taking abuse from his kids. After that, he hardly seemed like a threat to the nation's youth. As for the rest of the band, he now admits that the members of Black Sabbath were so shaken after watching *The Exorcist* that they had to sleep in the same bed. "That's how satanic we were!" he now laughs.

Black Sabbath might have been a "hell of a band" in their prime, but they could barely reach the level of success of Led Zeppelin – who allegedly signed a pact with Satan in exchange for fame and fortune. Whether there is any truth to this legend, it is a matter of record that after scoring a string of platinum albums and record-breaking concert tours, the band suffered a number of personal tragedies, which culminated in the death of drummer John Bonham and their decision to call it quits. Rock scribes and superstitious fans who had bought into the occult myth blamed it all on the curse of Aleister Crowley, with whom member Jimmy Page was obsessed. Page had even purchased Crowley's old home near Loch Ness and had hired Satanist Charles Pace to decorate the house in a motif depicting various aspects of ritual magic. He also owned a priceless collection of Crowley manuscripts and first editions, which was said to be the finest in the world. Years later, Page was asked about how intense his interest in the occult had been at the time and he replied, "I was living it. That's all there is to it. It was my life – that fusion of magick and music."

Page confirmed that the occult symbols featured on the *Led Zeppelin IV* album cover and the embroidered designs of his stage costumes were not mere decorations but expressions of talismanic magic. Page had once

258

Led Zeppelin member, occult bookstore owner and Aleister Crowley devotee, Jimmy Page

owned an occult bookstore and publishing house in London, but he sold it once Led Zeppelin took off and his family life became more demanding. However, his interest in the occult never waned and with his royalties from record sales, he was able to send his assistants out to scour bookstores for rare manuscripts and first editions.

Lead Singer Robert Plant also professed a fascination with witchcraft and it comes as no surprise that Led Zeppelin was one of the first bands charged with inserting subliminal prayers to Satan in their recorded tunes. Outwardly, though, the band's albums only contain fleeting, obscure references to the occult and even those are ambiguous and open to interpretation. Jimmy Page might have been under Crowley's spell but he was astute enough to realize that overt references to magic and the Devil would only appeal to a minority of listeners.

Other bands of the era knew this as well. Alice Cooper is regarded today as the godfather of Gothic rock and was at one time the purveyor of the most perversely pleasurable stage show in the business. Cooper, born Vincent Furnier, allegedly borrowed his stage name from a seventeenth-century witch, after consulting a Ouija board. He used a satanic image in his shows and advertising, but in reality, he is a born-again Christian who loves golf. He is far from the image of every parent's worst nightmare that he was in the 1970s.

By the 1970s, showmanship was clearly the key for heavy metal bands, epitomized by the fire-spitting, tongue-wagging performances of KISS. Guitarist Gene Simmons described the band's style to an interviewer: "We wanted to look like we crawled out from under a rock somewhere in Hell. We wanted parents to look at us and instantly want to throw up."

Within a few short years, satanic emblems, lyrics and tattoos became the standard trappings of successful heavy metal bands. Taking their cue from Black Sabbath, would-be successes began calling themselves Iron Maiden, Venom, Slayer, Sodom, Anti Christ, Hellhammer, Nocticula, Megadeth and Possessed. A small-time band from Denver, Satan's Host, boasted performers with stage names like Satan Patrick Evil, Belial, D. Lucifer Steele and Leviathan Thisiren. Publicists worked overtime to exploit the "witchy" angle of their bands, creating Black Metal, Death Metal and Thrash Metal – each louder, faster and perhaps more profitable than anything that had come before. The vocals were an unintelligible growl, the guitars were a screaming level of distortion and the drummers needed the stamina and speed of an Olympic athlete to keep up the insanely fast tempo. This was the unholy sound of bands like Acheron, Angel Witch, Anaal Nathrakh, Bathory, Cloven Hoof, Cradle of Filth, December Moon, Hecate, Hell Satan, King Diamond (Mercyful Fate), Lord Belial, Megiddo Bal Sagoth, Onslaught, Pagan Altar, Reign of Erebus, Sabbat, Venom, Warhammer, Witchfynde and many other so-called legions of the damned. It was not like music anymore, it was more like war. Some began to feel like the apocalypse had finally arrived.

Critics of this new wave of demonic music noted its preoccupation with satanic themes and kinky sex, brute force and bloodshed. On the Christian talk show circuit, word began to circulate that certain heavy metal bands (as opposed to the ones that were blatantly demonic with their names and images) were hiding secret messages in their names and lyrics. Thus, it was suggested that KISS *really* stood for "Knights in Satan's Service." AC/DC's logo was said to be shorthand for "Anti-Christ / Devil's Child." By the same logic, WASP became "We Are Satan's People." Heavy metal performers denied the claims, but by the time the "secrets" were announced, it was too late.

It is difficult, if not impossible, to gauge the true measure of occult / satanic belief among heavy metal performers. For some bands, like Motley Crue, pentagrams and inverted crosses were simply part of the act, along with lipstick, eye shadow and women's underwear. At the other end of the spectrum was King Diamond from the band Mercyful Fate, who openly proclaimed his devotion to Satan. This was a rare thing in the fading days of the 1980s, but by the 1990s, the horrific side of metal was slapping people right in the face.

Band members of Venom stated, "We are not here to entertain you but to preach the ways of Satan." Their manifesto was declared in the song "Possessed," which stated, "I am possessed by all that is evil. The death of your God I demand I... I sit at Lord Satan's right hand."

But what they critics failed to take into account was that artists perform "in character." Their lyrics don't necessarily represent their personal beliefs. Did Mick Jagger really believe that he was Lucifer incarnate when he asked for sympathy for the devil? No, he was acting the part for the sake of the song. And when Vincent Furnier beheaded dolls and sang "No More Mr. Nice Guy" he did it as his alter ego and stage persona, Alice Cooper. Only someone who believes that rock is the Devil's music would assume that the spirit that moves and inspires artists in mysterious ways is anything other than their figurative muse.

That said, some of the Black Metal bands took themselves very seriously indeed. Acheron recruited Peter Gilmore from the Church of Satan to act as master of ceremonies for their album *The Rites of the Black Mass*, but then again, how evil is the Church of Satan? LaVey's creation was sort of the religious equivalent of most heavy metal bands. But then Morbid Angel boasted that they were "Satan's sword" on a mission to "rid the world of the Nazarene" and frontman Trey Azagthoth claimed to be a genuine vampire. He proved it by biting himself on stage and drinking his own blood.

Showmanship or insanity? Who can say? But in reality, if the bands had been serious practitioners of the black arts they might have released some pretty incredible forces with the energy conjured up by the number of leather and black t-shirt clad fans who came to "worship" them every week. Whipped into a frenzy, horrific things would have occurred in the course of what should have been satanic rituals – but of course, nothing did. However, this didn't stop the religious fanatics from "crucifying" the bands for everything they did. Little did they know, but their criticism simply brought the artists more attention, more press and a legion of new fans.

By the middle 1980s, occult symbols and satanic song titles were everywhere. Every metal band seemed to be laboring under the impression that having a pentagram on the cover of their album, or the number 666 in a lyric, was a more effective marketing gimmick than posing with a naked model in leather and chains. As the bands became more outrageous in their celebration of satanic imagery, society's moral watchdogs became increasingly indignant about what they saw as their insidious influence on impressionable fans. Finally, the righteous could repress their rage no longer and launched an aggressive campaign against a score of iconic rock acts accusing them of deliberately planting subliminal satanic messages in their music. Of course, the messages were said to be audible only when the albums were played backward.

"Backmasking," or the process of bands deliberately recording words or music backward on records, became the hot topic of the day with evangelists, politicians and right-wing parents' groups alleging deliberate attempts to "brainwash" young people with hidden advertisements for sex, drugs and, of course, Satan.

It's true that backmasking (sometimes mistakenly called backwards masking) *does* exist and has for many years. In 1969, the Beatles planted backwards lyrics on their *Abbey Road* album that hinted at Paul McCartney's death – a morbid publicity stunt that went awry. Popular singers like David Bowie and Meatloaf acknowledged using the technique on their albums, but denied any sinister intent. Musicians who acknowledged its use defended it as an enhancement of their musical range or, more practically, as a sales gimmick to help sell more records, like Styx did with their *Paradise Theater* album. Fundamentalist Jacob Aranza, on the other hand, cited "expert sources" in his 1984 book *Backward Masking Unmasked* in defense of the contention that subliminal persuasion was intended to convert fans of rock and roll to the occult without their conscious knowledge.

Ozzy Osbourne

In support of their claims, the enemies of backmasking produced a list of songs that contained "hidden messages" – messages that strain both the ear and the imagination of the listener. Led Zeppelin's "Stairway to Heaven" played backward presented a very garbled "Hail to my Sweet Satan." Snowblind" by Styx allegedly contained the command, "Satan, move in our voices." Black Oak Arkansas was targeted for their song "When Electricity Came to Arkansas," which reportedly hid the message, "Satan, Satan, Satan. He is God, God, God." In April 1986, evangelist Jim Brown convinced Ohio teenagers to burn their records of television's *Mister Ed* theme song (how many copies could there have been?) because he somehow persuaded them that a reversal of "A Horse is a Horse" contained the words "Someone sung this song for Satan." And so it went.

Some "hidden" messages were less garbled than others, but how many were deliberate, much less demonic? Was there ever any proof that a conspiracy existed to brainwash fans of heavy metal music? No – but that doesn't mean that a lot of people believed it and were serious enough about it to file a case in court.

In October 1984, John McCollum, 19, shot himself in the head with a .22-caliber handgun after listening to a number of Ozzy Osbourne albums, including *Blizzard of Oz*, which features the song "Suicide Solution." When the police arrived on the scene, they found the young man still wearing headphones, gun still in his hand, which suggested that his death was spontaneous and had a direct link with the music that he was listening to at the time. It was said that he had been suffering from depression and had an alcohol problem. Grief-stricken and angry at what they believed to be the rock star's irresponsible and reckless indifference to the effects of his music, McCollum's parents initiated legal proceedings against Ozzy Osbourne and his label, CBS records. It was one of three similar lawsuits that Ozzy was forced to defend himself against at the time.

Two other teenagers had killed themselves in similar circumstances, also allegedly under the influence of Osbourne's satanic spell. When the McCollum case came to trial in January 1986, the media – as well as the radical religious right – saw it as a critical test case.

Dressed conservatively in a tailored suit, Osbourne took the stand to protest that the song was in fact inspired by his own self-destructive drinking habit and was intended as a warning against over-indulgence. The word "solution" in the title, he said, referred to alcohol, not the ending of one's life as a solution to life's problems. In other words, alcoholism was a form of suicide. Osbourne also argued that his image as a devil-worshipping occultist was just a part of his act. He had no wish to convert the youth of America to Satanism. Rock was entertainment, nothing more.

Unimpressed, the prosecution alleged that Osbourne had hidden subliminal messages in an instrumental section of the song, which encouraged listeners to "Get the gun – shoot," a suggestion that the singer strenuously denied. Under pressure from relentless questioning, Ozzy barked at the prosecutor, "I swear on my kid's life I never said 'get the fucking gun!'"

Neither the judge nor the jury could make out what was being said in the passage in question, which was totally obscured by guitar feedback, bass and drums, so they turned to the experts from the Institute for Bio-Acoustics Research to dig into it a little deeper. The IBAR techs subjected "Suicide Solution" to intense scrutiny in their laboratory, filtering it through state-of-the-art sound equipment to isolate Ozzy's mumblings, which they claimed had been recorded at one and a half times the normal rate of speech, presumably to avoid detection by the casual listener. Their report concluded that the "meaning and true intent" of the subliminal lyrics "becomes clear after being listened to over and over again." The offending lines were said to be "Why try, why try? Get the gun and try it! Shoot, shoot, shoot," followed by a demonic laugh. Anticipating the argument that the defense might offer, that these words were ad-libs, the scientific experts revealed that they had identified something far more sinister in the track – the presence of high frequency signals had been detected. These signals are a patented process that was developed to aid the assimilation of information by the human brain. They could not have been incorporated into the recording accidentally.

This was disputed by the defense, who argued that Ozzy had been messing around at the mixing desk, so the so-called "lyrics" were merely a sound effect. Besides, he was free under the First Amendment of the U.S. Constitution to write and record anything that he wished, unencumbered by the worry that someone might misinterpret what he had said.

The judge agreed and the court of appeal concurred that the Devil might have all of the best tunes, but his lyrics are unintelligible, so there's no risk to any of his fans.

The acquittal in Osbourne's trial didn't stop a civil action from being brought against Judas Priest in 1990. According to the prosecution, James Vance, 20, and Raymond Belknap, 18, attempted to end their lives with a shotgun after listening to Judas Priest's music. Belknap was successful, but Vance only managed to blow away part of his face.

When the case came to court in Nevada, part of the prosecution's case was that one of the band's songs contained the command "do it" when played backwards. The bands defense team responded by demonstrating that the same song – again played backwards – also contained what sounded like, "I asked for a peppermint, I asked her to get me one."

At the end of the trial, the judge dismissed the case. He told the court that when the speech is played backwards those who wished to hear intelligible phrases will interpret the garbled sounds into whatever they want to hear. However, it was unintentional on the part of the artist. The point was simple – no artist can be held responsible for what their listeners might hear—or do – when in a disturbed state of mind.

By the middle 1990s, the first generation of Black Metal bands were history, having split up or been sidelined by the next big thing. Their demise was no doubt hastened by the Satanic Ritual Abuse scandal (more, later in this chapter) that tainted bands by association, even those who protested that their devil worship was all just an act. However, after the dust had settled, satanic rock became louder than ever before in the form of Marilyn Manson, Slip Knot, Rob Zombie, Slayer and even a resurrected Ozzy Osbourne, whose reality show had made him even bigger than ever before.

As in the past, the image of being a Satanist was more about marketing than reality. However, some artists professed to believe in what they sang about. One of them was Marilyn Manson, who was reputedly ordained as a priest in the Church of Satan and had close ties with the late Anton LaVey.

For most bands, though, Satanism is all part of the branding and marketing of their music, which is something that religious groups and moral watchdogs have always failed to understand. No true Satanists or black magicians would ever publicize their methods or indulge in self-promotion. The simple reason would be that the attention of outsiders would be an unwelcome distraction.

Success in the art of magic depends on the ability to focus the will on what the magician wishes to bring into being. The same could be said for the artist. Music and the Devil may go hand in hand, but don't be fooled into thinking that just because something looks and sounds satanic that is necessarily is.

"DEMON CHILDREN"

Although accounts of children possessed by demons have been with us for many years, the 1970s began to see an epidemic of children whose parents came to believe that they were possessed.

Of course, the theme of possessed children is as old as man's written records. In the Gospel of Mark, Christ was approached by a man who brought his teenage son to him, stating that the boy was possessed by a spirit that made him speechless. Whenever it attacked him, it would throw him to the ground, where he would foam at the mouth, grind his teeth and go rigid. Christ's disciples had tried to oust the spirit from the boy, but had failed. Now, Jesus himself saw the spirit as it "threw the boy into convulsions," so that he "fell to the ground and rolled about, foaming at the mouth." Diabolic, or demonic possession, or possession by an "evil" or "unclean" spirit were often used interchangeably in early Christian writings – a bad habit that continues today.

When Christ saw the boy suffering, he asked the father how long he had been that way. The father replied that he had suffered the attacks since childhood and often, he added, the possessing entity had tried to kill him "by throwing him into the fire or water." He pleaded with Jesus and asked him to take pity on them. Jesus replied that anything was possible to someone who has faith.

Then, while a crowd milled about, Christ "rebuked" the demon and said, "Deaf and dumb spirit, I command you to come out of him, and never go back." According to Mark, the possessing spirit first cried aloud and shook the boy's body "fiercely," but finally gave up and "came out." The boy remained on the ground, unmoving, and one of the onlookers feared that he was dead. But "Jesus took his hand and raised him to his feet, and he stood up."

The image of a demon-possessed child is doubly dramatic, because a young boy or girl has an undeveloped personality, something seemingly easily controlled by a nonhuman entity. This theme, that of a child acting as a mere shell for the personality and destructive schemes of another entity, permeates the plots of novels and motion pictures. The mastery of evil over innocence, at least temporarily, captured the imagination of readers and film audiences all over the world, especially in the 1970s when films like *The Exorcist*, *The Omen* and scores of others appeared on the big screen. Possessed children seemed to be everywhere back then – and many believe they can be found across the country today.

But look at the story of Christ and the possessed boy in another way – what if his "possession" was actually epilepsy? What if he had a medical condition that caused all of the symptoms described in the account? In other words, perhaps he was not possessed at all. Of course, in this story, Christ's "exorcism" was harmless – perhaps even helpful to his condition – but far too many "exorcisms" were not.

In far too many cases, the "demon children" ended up dead.

In May 2010, a convicted child murderer named Blaine Milam was sentenced to death in Conroe, Texas. If there was anyone who deserved to pay the highest price imaginable for his crime, it was Milam. He, along with the child's mother, Jesseca Carson, had beaten 13-month-old Amora Carson to death. The little girl's offense? She had been possessed by a demon, they believed. The only way to cleanse her soul was to beat the spirit out of her. And so they did...

When the police were called to the couple's Rusk County home, they found the baby on the floor and immediately knew that something was wrong. Lieutenant Reynold Humber of the County Sheriff's Office said the couple told detectives conflicting stories of how the child suffered the injuries, including a fabricated auto accident and then a story of how the child was attacked by the family's dogs. The couple then told investigators they had left the child unattended and someone else must have gone into the home and harmed her. Carson and Milam even said the child beat herself in the head with the hammer. "They had multiple stories they went through before they told us they had beaten the child to death," Humber said. "It is their version of the truth."

Humber said that the couple then told deputies that the child was possessed and that they were trying to rid her of demons. According to the arrest affidavit, Milam performed the "exorcism" while Carson looked on. After they realized the exorcism had not gone as planned, they decide to hire a priest and drove into Henderson to "pawn some items to pay for an exorcism."

When asked if he bought the couple's story about what happened, Humber replied, "The child had been beaten so much we couldn't tell how many times it was hit and then there were more than twenty bite marks on her body. The bottom line, regardless of any stories, is that they killed that sweet little innocent child."

Tragically, little Amora was not the first – and undoubtedly will not be the last – to suffer such a cruel fate.

David Weilbacher, named after his father, was an adorable two-year-old with dark blond hair and big eyes when his mother brought him to live in a house on South 12th Street in Yakima, Washington, near the end of 1975. The old ramshackle house was set back on a narrow lot in a neighborhood of crumbling buildings, dirt alleys, broken streets and one-room shacks, a ghetto of poverty that existed on the city's southeast side. It was a bad place to live – and an even worse place to die.

Debra Marie Weilbacher was only 19 when she began taking David to the old house. She had been an Army brat, born at Fort Benning, Georgia, later moving with her family to Utah, then Washington. On March 25, 1972, 16-year old Debbie dropped out of school and got married. On January 4 of the following year, her only child was born. But her marriage was already failing. Debbie and her Marine husband spent only two months out of their four years of marriage together. Two weeks after little David's third birthday, their divorce was final.

By then, Debbie and David had moved out of their small Yakima apartment and into the house on South 12th Street. Debbie had been told about it by a former classmate, Lorraine Edwards, whom Debbie had sought out for comfort and friendship. The young, lonely woman was turning toward religion and someone told her that Lorraine knew of a family that might help her. One day in early September 1975, Lorraine invited her to the old house. Debbie's reaction to what she found there was immediate. She felt loved and wanted nothing more than to return. It was not just a house there on South 12th Street – it was a church and a family whose existence revolved around the Bible and God. The next time that Debbie came back, she formally dedicated her life to God. In a ceremonial rite, presided over by the head of the family, Debbie was saved. Of course, this left her worried too. She feared that if she went back out into the world, she might not make it on her own.

She asked the family if she could move into the house with them. They agreed and by December, the family had grown by two. Debra and David were now not only close to God, but lived with a man through whom He spoke. Edward Leon Cunningham, 51, had convinced her that he was a messenger of God.

Cunningham went by his middle name of Leon. He came out of Oklahoma, as did his wife, Velma, but they didn't meet until their paths crossed in California in the 1930s. Velma was not long out of grade school and Leon was just out of his teens. When they wed, in early January 1946, Leon was 21 and Velma was 14. The following November, she gave birth to the first of seven children.

For many years, Leon was a heavy drinker and gambler, especially during his rowdy Army days. He once won $88 on a $2 bet and he never forgot it. What little money he had was often wasted on chasing the dream of winning big again. But Leon was unhappy with himself and felt there was no meaning in his life. In the middle 1950s, he began to change. His father, like his grandfather, was a strict Baptist and both worked as lay ministers. Leon's father urged him to turn back to the God that he had forgotten. His change at first was gradual, then dramatic. One day, two years later, Leon heard God's voice and later, when he spoke, it was as if God's own voice were speaking through him. Like his father and grandfather, he also became a minister.

Occasionally, the stubby, overweight man with short gray hair and a scarlet rash on his right cheek and nose would speak at churches, delivering casual sermons. Mostly, though, he ministered at home, preaching to his family and raising his children in a grim spiritual world dedicated to God, dictated by the Bible and specifically, defending them against the Devil. Leon knew all about the Devil – he had seen him once. Another time, his daughter Marilyn had been possessed by the Devil. Through prayer, Leon had driven the demon from her.

Years later, he would decide that it would take more than prayer to exorcise the Devil from the house on South 12th Street.

Other family and friends kept the house full, at times crowded, through late winter and into the spring. At times, there were as many as nine people staying in the wood-frame six-room house and makeshift church. The principal occupants were Debbie, Leon, Velma and their unmarried daughter, Carolyn, 27, a large, square-faced woman who had dropped out of school after eighth grade. Another mostly full-time resident was Lorraine, who had joined the family after giving birth to a baby fathered by one of Leon's sons, who later married another woman. And, of course, there was little David.

Later, the family was not able to remember when the "change" began to come over David. He had seemed a normal boy, but he was not very friendly toward other children. He had spent most of his time around adults. Leon was the first to notice there was something wrong with David. He felt uneasy around him starting after a spring day when the girls had taken the little boy with them on a stroll around the neighborhood, passing the shells of three burned-out houses.

At home later, while his mother was fixing food in the kitchen, David babbled about the burned houses. They seemed to fascinate him, perhaps because his grandfather was fireman – or perhaps because of something else.

The boy's talk about the houses stuck in Leon's mind. Previously, Leon had been concerned with other things, including the end of the world. The part-time used car salesman, mechanic, odd-jobber and minister had received visions from God that led him to pick various dates when an Antichrist would arise and destroy all who failed to believe as Leon believed. On November 22, 1975, the twelfth anniversary of the assassination of John F. Kennedy, a spiritual change swept through the household. That was when Leon received his vision that the Antichrist would rise in August 1976 and would be the reincarnation of President Kennedy. Other family members had their own visions, one seeing a barn, another saw a farm. Leon saw Texas. Eventually, the picture in his head was a Texas farm where the family would be safe from the new, evil Kennedy. In December, they began selling their household goods and other property to pay for the move. Leon ended up with $1,700 in cash.

The family's thoughts and daily lives revolved around God and religion – or at least Leon's version of it. They held twice-a-week services that were open to anyone, and occasionally strangers would drift in. The neighbors heard the singing and praying, but paid little attention. The family paid attention only to one of the neighbor's trucks, which had a shack built onto the back of it. It would be perfect, they thought, for their end-of-days escape to Texas. Having sold their furniture, the family began living frugally, preparing for the move. Except now, there was this problem with David.

It took some time, but the family began to add it all up. Leon pointed all of it out to them, starting with David's excited comments about the burned houses. It just wasn't right for a child to act that way. Then there was David's unfriendly attitude toward other children, and the fact that he wet his pants and smeared excrement on the bedroom wall. Once he put pieces of broken glass in his shoes and wore them. David acted as though he'd rather be an adult than a child, although he had a foolish laugh that seemed to be neither young nor old. And there was the cough, something he would seem to work up all by himself. It kept his mother awake at night, on purpose it seemed to Leon, and once she remembered waking up suddenly because David had bitten her on the shoulder. She finally made him sleep in a room by himself after she woke up to find him staring at her one morning. In the end, it was clear, particularly to Leon: David Weilbacher, age three, was possessed by the Devil.

The spankings began in April. Leon had pointed to something in the Bible that he believed was the answer. It was in Proverbs: "Withhold not correction from the child, for if thou beatest him with a rod he shall not die. Thou shalt deliver his soul from Hell." Twice a day, with David in his underwear, they started beating him to drive the Devil out of him. David would not die; the Bible said so.

The spankings consumed the household. Leon had a special place to sit when they took place – on the end of the couch, one of the few pieces of furniture that they hadn't sold. Debbie would sit across from him, in a rocking chair. The others sat around the room, Velma often on the couch next to Lorraine, and Carolyn sat in another chair. The paddles, sanded boards about a foot-and-a-half long, were passed around. Each adult took a turn swatting David many times on his legs, his rear, his back, his arms – almost everywhere except the genitals and the kidney area. Leon said to always beware of the kidney area.

After the beating, Leon would ask David if he had love in his heart. David said that he did and when asked to show it, David would hug and kiss his abuser. But Leon did not think the boy was being honest. David had the Devil in him; he could see it in his face. He knew that was why David hated people, why David misbehaved and why David did not show love when he hugged Leon. David received more spankings after his "lies," each family member taking their turn.

For four months, this continued, sometimes daily, sometimes only weekly, but Leon began to realize that the spankings were not having the effect that the Bible said they would. David's case was unusual, Leon understood, in that it was not so much that the Devil possessed David, but that David – when the Devil was temporarily driven out by the spankings – would call the Devil back into him again. That was when the "humblings" began. Leon and Debbie pushed David to the floor and then ordered him to get up. They spanked him when he didn't get up quickly enough. Leon was pleased with this; he could see the results almost instantly. The devilish look would leave David's face when he was humbled.

On the hot morning of July 22, 1976, David was given his morning spankings. They apparently had no effect. By the afternoon, Leon could see that the Devil was still in David. It seemed that David liked to be whipped. Later, Carolyn would remember that David had an extra-long session of spanking that afternoon. After it was over, he passed out. But Debbie remembered David fighting with her when she picked him up off the floor. She turned around, swinging David by his arms and legs – and then he "fell." There was blood on his lips. As Debbie, Carolyn and Leon watched, they swore that they saw the little boy raise his fists and growl at them. A few seconds later, his chest rose and fell twice and then he stopped breathing.

There was no question of taking David to a doctor – only God could heal, they believed. Carolyn and Debbie picked the boy up and put him in the back bedroom. God could take care of him there, they said. His mother changed his underwear and left him – seemingly dead, maybe alive -- on his bed. Two hours later, she pulled the covers up over him after bathing his body with a sponge. She did this each day for the next three days.

On the fourth day, the family, led by Leon, entered the room and said their final prayers over the boy. Leon lifted the body from the bed and cried out, "In the name of Jesus, arise!" When nothing happened, the child's body was returned to the bed. Then the windows of the room were painted so no one could see in. Rags were stuffed in the cracks and the doors were shut and taped. That night was the last time that Leon and the family saw David Weilbacher and his demon.

The family kept a vigil to prevent the Devil from returning to the old house on 12th Street. One person always stayed up all night while the others slept. For two months, they prayed and awaited David's ressurection. They had decided to re-name him Seth David when he came back.

On September 19, though, someone else arrived. A knock on the door announced the presence of Yakima Police Sergeant Robert Langdale. Velma had gone to the police and told them what had happened. Armed with a search warrant, the officer checked the house and discovered the back bedroom. Family members had sprayed deodorant around the door when he was searching another part of the house. Langdale broke open the door and got the shock of his life. After retrieving a gas mask, he discovered David's body under the blankets on the bed. It was bloated and black with decay. A pathologist would later say that there was no way to be certain about how David had died, but he surmised that the boy had been beaten to death.

The family was arrested. Their escape to Texas would never take place. After their trials, Debbie Weilbacher and Leon and Carolyn Cunningham were convicted of second-degree assault and first-degree manslaughter. Velma Cunningham and Lorraine Edwards were convicted of second-degree assault and second-degree manslaughter. All of them received sentences of between 10 and 20 years in prison.

As for David, his remains were buried two weeks later, laid to rest in a desolate section of the Tacoma Cemetery. All that is left of the poor little boy today is a small stone marker over his grave that reads "David Wellbacker." The name on the stone is misspelled. Sadly, it is almost as if David never really existed at all.

In April 1997, Rosa Wilkerson, 46, and her daughter, Angelic Burney, 25, were charged with killing Angelic's five-year-old daughter, Amy Burney. They fatally poisoned the girl and then placed her body in the trash out in front of their Bronx, New York, apartment building. A police official stated that the killing had been an "exorcism."

In an attempt to drive out the demons that caused Amy to have tantrums, the two women tied her down, forced her to swallow a lethal potion of ammonia, vinegar, cayenne pepper, black pepper and olive oil and taped her mouth shut so that she wouldn't spit it out. After she died, the women kept her body in the apartment for a week before leaving it at the curb in a garbage bag. Police charged the women with second-degree murder and depraved indifference.

No one knew why the two women thought the child was possessed by evil spirits. But 17 years before, the grandmother made a similar claim about her oldest daughter, Julia. According to her sister, Mary Burney, Rosa made this unusual claim and then gave her four children to her brother, Willie, Mary Burney's husband. The couple raised the children in Miami, Florida. Julia, who was nine years old then, "was as normal as the other children," Mary Burney said. And Angelic, who was seven, was slow in school but had a sweet voice and sometimes sang in the church choir. She quit school in the 12th grade and moved to Lakeland, Florida, where she had two children. On weekends, Angelic would take the children to Miami, where they played in Mary Burney's house. In 1996, Angelic decided to move to New York to get to know the mother she had not seen in sixteen years. She and her children moved into Rosa's apartment.

What happened after that – and what drove the two women to perform the exorcism – is unknown.

In November 2001, a woman who lived in the Washington Heights section of Manhattan was charged with the drowning death of her four-year-old daughter after she had repeatedly dunked her under water to exorcize the demons from her body.

After the discovery of the murder, the authorities were trying to determine how Sabina Wright, 29, had come into contact with her daughter, Signifagance Oliver, and her twin sister, Ellagance. She had lost custody of the twins and two older children in July 1997 after the city's Administration for Children's Services found evidence of physical abuse, an agency spokeswoman said. It was unclear to anyone at the agency how long the twins had been living with her. "There is a joint investigation between the A.C.S. and N.Y.P.D. into how these two little girls ended up in the custody of their mother," said Children's Services spokeswoman, Jennifer Falk.

Ms. Falk said that the twins, who had been placed in foster care shortly after their birth in 1997, were placed in the care of an out-of-state aunt in April 1999. The agency had assumed the children were still living with the aunt.

Officers had been called to Wright's apartment on West 160th Street shortly before 5:00 a.m. When they arrived, they found Signifagance dead and Ellagance in good condition, they said. Wright was taken into custody and sent to a local hospital for evaluation after she told detectives the child was possessed by demons.

Neighbors had some unusual things to say about the family – but not about the allegedly "possessed" girl; their strange statements were about the mother. They recalled a woman prone to swearing loudly, picking fights with neighbors and shifting moods abruptly.

"She had two faces," said Ramona Garcia, who lived on the same block as Wright. She said her son, Raymond, had knocked on Wright's door a few days before the murder to play with the twins, but was sent away with Wright screaming and throwing salt at him. Garcia added, "Sometimes she would be nice, and other times she would be scary."

Some neighbors reported seeing the twins for the past year and a half, while others said the pair moved in with Wright during the summer. Most expressed shock at the polite, respectful little girl's death and wondered why the city had not stepped in to investigate.

According to Children's Services spokeswoman Falk, her agency first investigated Ms. Wright in December 1992 on charges of physical abuse and had removed her two older children. In July 1997, three months after the twins were born, the two oldest children were returned to Wright on a trial basis. After several days, however, there was another report of domestic violence and all four children were placed in foster care, she said. Wright's parental rights to the two older children were dissolved and they remained in foster care. In the case of the twins, a paternal aunt petitioned for custody, which was granted in February 1999, she said. The twins then moved in with the aunt, and child welfare officials in that state found in two reports, in April and December of that year, that the twins were doing well. The case was then closed – far before it should have been.

In August 2004, a Milwaukee minister named Ray Hemphill was sent to prison for two years and spent seven more years under state supervision for his part in the suffocation death of an eight year old named Terrance Cottrell, Jr. who was "possessed by the Devil."

Terrance had been diagnosed as autistic at the age of two. At some point, his mother, a fundamentalist Christian, became convinced that the boy was possessed. She went to Hemphill for help. Hemphill, a former maintenance worker with no formal religious schooling, was ordained as a pastor of the Faith Temple Church of the Apostolic Faith by his brother, Bishop David Hemphill, who founded the church in 1977.

In a statement that he gave to the police, Hemphill said that on the night of August 22, 2003, he had been holding a series of special prayer services, described by some as "exorcisms," during the previous three weeks to remove "evil spirits" of autism from the boy. Hemphill described how he would sit or lay on the boy's chest for up to two hours at a time, whispering into his ear for the "demons" to leave his body.

Three women -- including the child's mother, Patricia Cooper -- described to police how they sat on the boy's arms and legs while Hemphill sat on his chest. One woman said she pushed down on the child's diaphragm several times during the service. They said that they were trying to press the demons out of him, but they killed him instead. At some point during the service, he stopped struggling and was no longer breathing. An autopsy later determined that Cottrell suffocated.

Hemphill was arrested for his part in the "exorcism." He had had faced a maximum penalty of 10 years in prison and a $25,000 fine. Prosecutors chose not to file murder charges, because it would have been difficult to prove that Hemphill intended to kill Cottrell. He never admitted any sort of guilt. He told the court, "Your honor, I'm truly sorry for what happened to Terrance Cottrell, Jr. That is what I would like to say. Thanks."

The prosecutors were stunned by the case. Assistant District Attorney Mark Williams said Hemphill and his brother continued to insist that Cottrell was possessed by demons.

In April 2008, a young mother in Waukegan, Illinois, confessed to slashing her daughter to death because she believed the child – who had a history of sleepwalking – was possessed by the Devil. Nelly Vasquez-Salazar, 25, was arrested and charged with first-degree murder.

Authorities responded to Vasquez-Salazar's apartment at 4:40 a.m. on April 11 after the young woman went to a neighbor's house, badly bleeding from slashes to her own hands and wrists. Officers found the body of Vasquez-Salazar's six-year-old daughter, Evelyn Vasquez, in the family's apartment. The child, who died of multiple stab wounds to her neck and upper chest, according to the coroner, was found on the floor of her bedroom. She had been stabbed eleven times. A butcher knife, believed to be the murder weapon, was recovered at the scene, as was a religious picture featuring St. Joseph, Mary and an infant Jesus. The artwork had been cut up by a knife.

Vasquez-Salazar initially told investigators that she killed her daughter in self-defense after the child came at her with a knife, according to Stephen Scheller, an assistant state's attorney in Lake County. The woman later admitted to being fearful that her daughter was possessed by the devil. "The first statement we received from the defendant was that it was an act of self-defense," Scheller said. "After she made the statement to detectives, she later recanted it, made a second statement, which she admitted in fact she had stabbed her daughter multiple times about the body."

According to Waukegan Chief of Police William Biang, "She had had conversations with her mother because Evelyn had been sleepwalking and [Vasquez-Salazar] would wake up and her daughter would be standing by her bed. The theory was that the daughter was possessed."

Domenic Cappelluti, a detective for the Waukegan police, cited a recent call between the suspect and the suspect's mother in Mexico that could have, in part, prompted the killing. Cappelluti explained, "In summary, Nelly said, 'My daughter is sleepwalking.' She called mom for advice, her mom said she might be possessed and then Nelly took it for whatever she took it for."

Unfortunately, this is merely a handful of cases of children that have been killed during religious rituals and exorcisms that are designed to drive demons out of their bodies. A complete list would go on and on, stretching into the pages of another book entirely.

For those who think that such beliefs are a thing of the past, they're not correct. Cases like these come from the very time of the writing of this book:

Last January, authorities in Washington, D.C., discovered the bodies of four children ages 5 to 16 decomposing in a row house. Their mother told police that her daughters were possessed and that they had died in their sleep. She was charged with four counts of murder.

Not long after, Lawrence Douglas Harris, Sr. was charged with two counts of first-degree murder after his two stepdaughters were found fatally stabbed and strangled inside a burning house in Sioux City, Iowa. Harris told authorities that the girls died during a religious ritual inside the house.

And while they may be the most tragic cases, such deaths are not limited to children. In February, Jan David Clark was arrested after his wife died during what he described as an "exorcism" inside their Texas home. Clark told authorities that the devil entered her body during the religious ritual and caused the death.

And the nightmare continues.

"SATANIC PANIC"

The hysteria of the Salem Witch Trials marked a definitive point in American history, when a group of innocent people were so overwhelmed by the witch-hunting fervor of the day that they were sent to their deaths for crimes they had not committed. Most believe that nothing like what occurred in Salem, Massachusetts, in the seventeenth century could happen in these modern times, but that's an assumption that turned out to be false. In the 1980s, the idea ran rampant that Satanists were everywhere. The hysteria was spread by fundamentalist Christians, radical religious groups, television talk show hosts and many otherwise well-intentioned people and organizations who lived in fear that a vast satanic underground network was infiltrating the country. They claimed that satanic groups were spreading their evil message through rock and roll music, kidnapping and abusing children and could even be responsible for murdering thousands of people who went missing in America every year, never to be seen again. Those missing persons, they believed, had fallen victim to satanic cults who used them for blood sacrifices to the Devil. The evidence for such an underground was obvious, they claimed, and pointed to a handful of murders carried out by pseudo-Satanists in black t-shirts, child abuse cases that would turn out to be more than a little questionable and, of course, "recovered memories" of what came to be known as Satanic Ritual Abuse.

The end result of the "witch hunts" of the 1980s and early 1990s were scores of people being accused of crimes they did not commit, the destruction of families causes by "repressed" memories of things that never happened, a nationwide panic that cultists were waiting on every corner to kidnap children – and the tragic dismissal of genuine cases of child abuse that were swept up into the climate of the day and then forgotten when the vast majority of false cases were finally seen for what they were.

As I stated at the start, this was not the chapter that I originally intended to write. It started off to be a sardonic (perhaps even smug) look at how superstitious and ignorant people can be when they start seeing the Devil around every corner. This section was meant to be an I'm-shaking-my-head-can-you-believe-how-gullible-people-can-be look at the "satanic" child abuse cases that appeared in the 1980s, but instead, as my stacks of research grew larger, I began to find cases of what may have actually have been real ritual abuse, carried out by people who really thought they were doing the Devil's work – warped, confused, ignorant freaks who think that it's okay to hurt children if you're doing it for the "glory" of Satan. Unfortunately, in the midst of all of the controversy over the cases that turned out to be fake, these authentic cases vanished into the trash too, forgotten and ignored and heartbreakingly dismissed as more "crazy" stuff.

Don't get me wrong, people definitely went overboard in the 1980s when it came to Satan, but I hate to break the news to you that a lot of things went on that you never heard about.

If there was a single thing that can truly credited with starting what became known as Satanic Panic in the 1980s, it was the publication of a book called *Michelle Remembers*, co-written by a Canadian psychiatrist named Dr. Lawrence Pazder and his patient, Michelle Smith. I discovered this book when I was starting my first year of high school and confess to being terrified by the contents. Not only did I believe that what I was reading was possible, I was convinced that it had all taken place. Like so many others at the time, I was fooled by the startling, horrific contents of the book, but my gullibility would not last for long. Within a few years, I began to realize, as many others also did, that the satanic hysteria of the 1980s had very little basis in truth. Unfortunately, though, the movement was only just beginning. It was just too colorful and too sensational for the talk show hosts and television evangelists to relinquish and they found that by ignoring the facts and spreading half-truths, they could keep their audiences glued to their seats – and utterly terrified that devil-worshipping boogiemen were around every corner waiting to get them.

Michelle Remembers was published in 1980 and became an almost instant bestseller. It was truly the first book of its kind and the first to deal with Satanic Ritual Abuse, a phenomenon that would soon take the psychiatric community – and the tabloid world – by storm. The book chronicled Dr. Pazder's 1970s-era treatment of Michelle Smith. He had first started treating her in 1973 at his private practice in Victoria, British Columbia. In 1976, Smith began suffering from depression after a miscarriage, and confided in Pazder that she felt that she had something very important to tell him, but could not remember what it was. Shortly thereafter, Pazder and Smith had a session where Smith screamed hysterically for almost twenty-five minutes, then began speaking in a voice that sounded like that of a five-year-old child. Over the next fourteen months, Pazder spent over 600 hours using hypnosis to help Smith recover alleged memories of Satanic Ritual Abuse that she suffered when she was a child. The abuse spanned the years 1954 and 1955 and it was carried out at the hands of her mother, Virginia Proby, and others. Smith claimed they were part of an underground "satanic cult" in the Victoria area.

The book is put together as a narrative, flashing back and forth between the past and present, and offers the version of events that Smith remembers during her therapy. It documents her mother's involvement with the cult, the many satanic rituals that the young Michelle was forced to attend and participate in, and the many horrifying events that occurred during a time when she was literally held prisoner by the cult. During the rites, Smith was allegedly tortured, locked in cages, sexually assaulted, witnessed several murders and was covered in the blood of slain infants and adults. Pazder maintained that Smith was abused by the Church of Satan, which he stated was a worldwide organization that pre-dated the Christianity. The first ritual that Smith was forced to attend was in 1954 and the final event that was documented was an 81-day ritual in 1955 that summoned the Devil himself and involved the intervention of Jesus, the Virgin Mary and the archangel Michael. The angel (conveniently) removed all of the scars that Smith received during her year of abuse and repressed all of her memories of the events "until the time was right."

Michelle Remembers was first publicized in the tabloids, including the *National Enquirer*, and in *People* magazine. It was immensely popular and earned Pazder and Smith a hefty hardcover advance, paperback rights, royalties, and a potential movie deal. Pazder was a credentialed psychiatrist in Canada and the book stated that the source material (the therapy tapes) was carefully scrutinized. Despite this, questions about the accuracy of the book's allegations were raised shortly after it was published. One of the first problems was raised by Church of Satan founder Anton LaVey, who threatened to sue for libel if references to abuse by members of the church were not removed from subsequent editions. LaVey stated that his organization had not been in any way involved with any of the alleged events. This was the first issue raised about the book, but it was far from the last.

In an October 27, 1980, article in the Canadian weekly news magazine, *Macleans*, reporter Paul Glescoe interviewed Smith's father, Jack Proby, who denied all of the allegations that had been made against Smith's mother, Virginia, who had died in 1964. He stated that he could refute all of the claims that had been made in the book. Glencoe also interviewed the mother of a childhood friend of Smith, who described Virginia Proby as a kind, caring woman. He also noted that the book failed to make any mention of Smith's two sisters, Charyl and Tertia, and that Pazder and Smith had divorced their spouses and had married each other.

Unfortunately, the article did not garner much attention in Canada and was not seen in the United States at all. For this reason the allegations in the book were still considered to be true, which gained Pazder a reputation as an expert in the area of what had come to be called Satanic Ritual Abuse. As more and more abuse cases began to be recovered through treatment of so-called "repressed memories," Pazder's expertise was frequently called upon. He acted as a consultant for several high-profile cases and in 1985 he appeared on the first major news report on Satanism for the ABC news program *20/20*. He became a part of the CCIN (Cult Crime Impact Network) and lectured to police agencies about Satanic Ritual Abuse during the late 1980s, reporting that he spent nearly one-third of his time consulting on such cases. In September 1990, Pazder reported that he had acted as a consultant "in more than 1,000 'ritual abuse' cases." With people suddenly being prosecuted for Satanic Ritual Abuse, district attorneys used *Michelle Remembers* as a guide when preparing cases against alleged Satanists.

It was not long, though, before the veracity of the events chronicled in *Michelle Remembers* began to fall apart. In 1990, reporters were finally exposing further inconsistencies and problems with the book. Many who were involved with the events described in the book were interviewed and described *Michelle Remembers* as "the hysterical ravings of an uncontrolled imagination." Jack Proby was interviewed again and maintained that the book was filled with lies. Although he indicated that he had decided not to sue, he did file a notice of intent to sue against the book's publisher if *Michelle Remembers* was ever made into a movie. Smith's childhood family doctor said that, "I believe it was ... an over-active imagination." A former neighbor of the Proby family said, "I dismissed the book as crazy. The mother was a nice, gracious lady. A little girl could not have been tortured without someone hearing." A former childhood friend of Smith told reporters, "Virginia was like a second mother to me. I certainly never had a bad feeling about her." Smith's ex-husband said that, "Not once during our marriage or the birth of our daughter did Michelle ever mention her experience."

As this new information began to surface, the local Catholic Church and Bishop Remi De Roo began to distance themselves from Pazder and Smith. Bishop De Roo now claimed that he had asked for details about the abuse years before, but the information that he requested was never supplied. It was also reported that the Royal Canadian Mounted Police stated there had never been a single prosecution in Victoria for satanic practices.

Even Pazder began to back-pedal. When asked what was more important – if the story was true, or if Michelle believed that it was true, he replied: "It is a real experience. If you talk to Michelle today, she will say, 'That's what I remember.' We still leave the question open. For her it was very real. Every case I hear I have skepticism. You have to complete a long course of therapy before you can come to conclusions. We are all eager to prove or disprove what happened, but in the end it doesn't matter."

The truth of the story may not have mattered to Pazder, but it certainly mattered to those who had believed in the book, and to those who lives had been ruined by others who suddenly began to recall instances of Satanic Ritual Abuse that may, or may not have, taken place.

In 1995, more inconsistencies in the story came out. In the book, a car accident is described but no record of the crash could be found, despite the fact that the local newspaper reported on all vehicle accidents at the time. Former friends, neighbors and teachers were interviewed and yearbooks from Smith's elementary school were reviewed. There was no indication that Smith had been absent for any length of time, including during the alleged 81-day ceremony. No one who knew Smith in the 1950s could corroborate any of the details in her allegations.

A 2002 article by Canadian occult author and Detective Constable Charles Ennis not only explored the inconsistencies in Smith's story, it also looked into the unlikely nature of her allegations. Among other things, he noted that it was improbable that a cult that had secretly existed for generations could be outwitted by a five-year-old; that the cult's rituals in Ross Bay Cemetery could go unnoticed since it was surrounded on three sides by a residential neighborhood; that an 81-day, non-stop ritual involving hundreds of participants in a massive round room could have gone unnoticed and that none of Smith's abusers (except for her mother) have ever been identified, especially since some of them had cut off their middle fingers to symbolize their allegiance to Satan. Ennis noted that Smith's "recovered memories" were nothing more than reflections of the popular culture of the time, notably the film *The Exorcist* and its many imitators. He also made notes about how Pazder's own religious beliefs and experiences while living in Africa in the early 1960s seeped into the narrative. During that time, there had been widespread concern about secret, blood-drinking cannibal cults – which sounded a lot like Smith's so-called "Satanists."

To this day, the book's contents have remained unsubstantiated, other than by Smith's recollections. Even though there are still people out there who believe that the contents of *Michelle Remembers* are the truth and that there is a vast, underground conspiracy of devil worshippers who are abusing and murdering children and adults, most see the book for what it is – the colorful product of an overactive imagination and the manipulations of therapy involving "repressed memories."

Michelle Remembers was the first book of its kind, but its success would inspire dozens of copy-cat titles and it would become an important part of the controversies regarding Satanic Ritual Abuse and repressed memories. Satanic Ritual Abuse first made headlines after the publication of the book and referred to physical and sexual abuse that reportedly occurred during occult or satanic ceremonies. The phenomenon began in the early 1980s, mostly in the United States, but spread to other parts of the world, impacting how the legal, therapeutic and social work professions dealt with allegations of abuse.

Books about repressed memories that followed included *Suffer the Child* by Judith Spencer, *Satan's Underground* by Lauren Stratford and far too many others. In the hysteria that followed these publications, no one thought to ask why earlier cases of ritual abuse had not come to light. Before reason could prevail, the flames of moral indignation were fanned once again when a former member of a satanic cult, Mike Warnke, offered to expose

"Satanic High Priest" Mike Warnke
in the 1970s

the crimes that had been committed in the name of Satan – and take his own place in the spotlight of the talk show circuit.

Warnke claimed to be a high priest of Satan in San Bernardino, California. He had attempted to profit from his experiences in 1972 (when interest in the occult was peaking with *The Exorcist*) with the publication of a book called *The Satan Seller*. His disclosures brought him instant notoriety and lucrative speaking engagements on the evangelical revival circuit, but those fees paled in comparison to the money that he began making during the panic days of the 1980s.

No one questioned Warnke's account of a nationwide occult conspiracy to corrupt children or his claims to have led over 1,500 Satanists in California. His appearances on talk shows like *Larry King Live* and *The Oprah Winfrey Show* endorsed his reputation as a self-appointed expert on the occult and led to his being invited to act as a consultant to the police on what appeared to be occult crime cases. But Warnke's "expertise" began to unravel in 1991 when the Christian magazine *Cornerstone* published the results of its exhaustive investigation into his stories, as well as others who were reaping the benefits of satanic hysteria. In addition to looking into many of the reports of Satanic Ritual Abuse that were making news, the magazine also looked into the claims that were the basis for books like Lauren Stratford's *Satan's Underground*. They concluded that their claims were unfounded and magazine investigators accused Stratford of having lied about giving up her newborn baby for sacrifice. In fact, they questioned if the baby had ever existed.

Warnke claimed that he had been a long-haired, drug-taking Satanist in the late 1960s, but photographs taken of him at the time showed that this was not the case. His claim to have attended a satanic ritual with Charles Manson on a particular date was also proven false, because Manson was incarcerated at the time. Accounting irregularities, marital scandals and his own begrudging admission to have "exaggerated" his experiences severely damaged his image. He failed to name even a single member of his California coven, which he had dramatically downsized from 1,500 to just 13. Overnight, the Christian community turned against him. In 2002, he published a rebuttal called *Friendly Fire: A Recovery Guide for Believers Battered by Religion* and went on a low-key tour as a "Christian comedian" – but most people weren't laughing.

The book *Michelle Remembers* was the first to link the abuse of children to satanic rituals and it provided the model for the ritual abuse allegations that followed. The book not only influenced later allegations of ritual abuse, but many believe that such allegations only existed because of it. In the early 1980s, during the implementation of mandatory reporting laws, there was an increase in the number of child protection investigations in the United States and an increased public awareness about child abuse. The investigation of incest allegations in California was also changed, and many cases were submitted by social workers who could use leading and coercive interviewing techniques that could not be used by the police. The result was a greater number of confessions by abusers, offered in exchange for plea bargains. Shortly thereafter, some children in child protection cases began making allegations of physical and sexual abuse that took place during organized rituals that used satanic images. Such allegations were labeled Satanic Ritual Abuse in the media and among professionals. Not long after, memories of similar abuse began to appear during psychotherapy sessions with adults, who often stated that the memories had been "repressed" until being recalled by stress or by hypnotic techniques.

In 1983, charges were filed in what became known as the McMartin Preschool Trial in California. The case received nationwide attention and contained allegations of Satanic Ritual Abuse. The effect on people across the country was immediate and startling. Soon, more than ten preschools across the country were faced with similar sensationalistic allegations, all of which were eagerly reported by the press. Throughout the McMartin trial, the media coverage against the defendants was unrelentingly negative. Michelle Smith and Dr. Lawrence Pazder, co-authors of *Michelle Remembers*, along with other alleged abuse survivors met with the parents involved during the trial and it's believed their presence influenced the testimony that was heard in the courtroom.

The McMartin case began when Judy Johnson, mother of one of the Manhattan Beach, California, preschool's students, complained to the police that her son had been sodomized by her estranged husband and by McMartin teacher Ray Buckey, grandson of school founder Virginia McMartin and son of school administrator Peggy McMartin Buckey. Johnson's belief began when he son had some painful bowel movements, but what happened next is still in dispute. Some sources reported that he denied her suggestion that had had been molested, but another source stated that during a hospital exam, he confirmed that he was sodomized and accused a teacher at school of abusing him. Johnson soon made a number of other startling accusations, including that teachers at the daycare center had sex with animals, that Peggy had "drilled a child under the arms" and that "Ray flew in the air." Buckey was questioned but was released due to lack of any evidence. Unbelievably, though, the police sent an open letter to about 200 parents of children at the McMartin school – stating that abuse might have taken place at the school and asking parents to question their children. In the letter, parents were supposed to check and see if their children had been involved in oral sex, fondling of the genitals, sodomy, and child pornography. Ray Buckey was named in the letter as a suspect.

The letter, not surprisingly, created an uproar; in the end, it should have never been sent at all. Judy Johnson was hospitalized after being diagnosed with acute paranoid schizophrenia. In 1986, she was found dead in her home from complications of chronic alcoholism. Although the prosecution asserted that Johnson's mental illness was caused by the events in the case, Johnson admitted that she was mentally ill beforehand, which begs the question as to why her claims, including those that Ray Buckey could fly, were taken seriously by the authorities. Evidence of Johnson's mental state was withheld from the defense in the case for three years and when it was provided, was only available in the form of sanitized reports, edited by the prosecution. One of the original state's attorneys in the case, Glenn Stevens, left the case due to the way that the prosecution had withheld evidence – and over the fact that Johnson's son was unable to identify Ray Buckey in a series of photographs. He also accused the deputy district attorney in the case of lying and of withholding evidence from the court and from defense lawyers. But the trial's problems were still to come...

Long before this, in spite of the continued lack of any hard evidence, several hundred children had been interviewed by the Children's Institute International, a Los Angeles-based abuse therapy clinic. The interviewing techniques used during the investigations were highly suggestive and misleading and by the spring of 1984, claims were being made that as many as 360 children had been abused. The children were asked repetitive, leading questions that almost always yielded positive results, making it impossible to know what the alleged victims actually experienced. Some have stated that they believe that the suggestive questioning led the children to "remember" events that never took place. The interviews were later criticized as being improper, coercive, and directed in a way that forced the children to follow a rigid script that was run by the examiner. The interviews contained far more speech by the adult questioners than by the children and the situation created vivid and dramatic testimonies that likely had nothing to do with any actual abuse being suffered. Ultimately, only forty-one of the original three hundred and sixty children testified during the grand jury and pre-trial hearings and less than a dozen appeared at the actual trial.

Not surprisingly, the often "bizarre" accusations included elements of Satanic Ritual Abuse, a panic that was just starting to gain momentum in the United States at the time of the McMartin case. It was alleged that, in addition to having been sexual abused, the children saw witches fly, traveled in a hot air balloon, and were taken through underground tunnels. When shown a series of photographs by Danny Davis, the McMartins' attorney, one child identified actor Chuck Norris as one of the abusers. Some of the abuse was said to have occurred in secret tunnels under the school. Several investigations turned up evidence of old buildings on the site and debris from before the school was built, but the mysterious tunnels were never found. There were also claims of orgies taking place at car washes and at airports, and of children being flushed down toilets to secret rooms where they would be abused, cleaned up and then given back to their unsuspecting parents.

On March 22, 1984, Virginia McMartin, Peggy McMartin Buckey, Ray Buckey, Ray's sister Peggy Ann Buckey and teachers Mary Ann Jackson, Bette Raidor, and Babette Spitler were charged with 115 incidents of child abuse, later expanded to 321 incidents of child abuse involving forty-eight children. Over the course of twenty months of preliminary hearings, the prosecution presented its case, which included inconsistent statements by the alleged victims and meetings between the parents in the case and Michelle Smith and Dr. Lawrence Pazder, which prosecutor Glenn Stevens believed influenced the children's testimony. In 1986, a new district attorney called the evidence "incredibly weak," and dropped all charges against Virginia McMartin, Peggy Ann Buckey, Mary Ann Jackson, Bette Raidor and Babette Spitler. Peggy McMartin Buckey and Ray Buckey remained in custody awaiting trial.

In 1989, Peggy Anne Buckey appealed to have her teaching credentials re-instated and the judge in her hearing ruled that there had been no credible evidence to lead to the license being suspended in the first place. A review of the videotaped interviews with the McMartin children led the judge to issue a statement saying that they "reveal a pronounced absence of any evidence implicating [Peggy Ann] in any wrongdoing and... raise additional doubts of credibility with respect to the children interviewed or with respect to the value of CII interviewing techniques themselves." The state licensing board agreed with the judge's ruling and restored Buckey's license – adding further doubts about the entire case.

In 1990, after three years of testimony and nine weeks of deliberation by the jury, Peggy McMartin Buckey was acquitted on all counts. Ray Buckey was cleared on 52 of the 65 counts against him, and was finally freed on bail after five years behind bars. During a press conference after the trial, ten of the jurors admitted they had voted to acquit Ray Buckey of all charges but the refusal of the remaining two to vote for a not guilty verdict resulted in a deadlock on the last charges. The media overwhelmingly focused on the two jurors who voted guilty. Buckey was retried later on six of the remaining thirteen counts, which produced another hung jury. The prosecution then gave up trying to obtain a conviction, and the case was closed with all charges against Ray Buckey dismissed. He had been jailed for five years without ever being convicted of anything.

It was the media and social workers who helped to fan the flames of the witch hunt in the McMartin case and they continued to spread the word about so-called Satanic Ritual Abuse in the months and years to come. Kee McFarlane of Children's Institute International, an unlicensed social worker, had recently developed a new way to interrogate children using anatomically correct dolls while in the process of writing a book on child sexual abuse. McFarlane tested their use when interviewing the McMartin children. Using the dolls, and by asking leading questions, she diagnosed sexual abuse in almost all of the children. She was accused of using coercion in lengthy interviews that rewarded the children for discussions about abuse and punished those who denied it. But McFarlane alone could not be blamed. She had assistance when it came to allegations of satanic abuse, both from the prosecution and by Smith and Pazder, who were called to testify as "experts" in the case. Strangely, the initial charges in the case featured claims of satanic abuse, but those features were later dropped. Thanks to the media, however, they would soon surface again in other cases and claims of ritual abuse began to take on even greater proportions.

The witch hunt continued as the McMartin case was still going on. Psychiatrist Roland Summit spoke at conferences while the case was in progress that depicted Satanic Ritual Abuse as part of a nationwide conspiracy. He stated that anyone who denied the existence of the abuse, as well as an underground satanic movement, was part of the conspiracy. In 1986, a social worker named Carol Darling argued in a grand jury hearing that the conspiracy reached into the highest levels of the government. Her husband, Brad Darling, gave conferences about the satanic conspiracy, which he alleged dated back for centuries.

By the late 1980s, the recognition that mental health workers had given to Satanic Ritual Abuse led to the formation of Christian psychotherapy groups, exorcisms, multiple personality claims and the development of groups for "survivors'" of abuse. Thanks to all of the attention, federal funding was increased for research on child abuse, with large portions of the funds going towards studying sexual abuse. Funding was also provided for conferences supporting the idea of Satanic Ritual Abuse, offering an opportunity for prosecutors to exchange ideas on the best ways to secure convictions on cases that might be many years old. Many cases were prosecuted based on an adult's "recovered memories" of alleged childhood assaults.

Perhaps predictably, given its "wacky" reputation and its history of weird cults, California generated the majority of the ritual abuse reports. In Concord, a mechanic was named by his stepdaughter as part of a cult that forced her to eat feces and murder a baby. His trial ended with a hung jury. Nearby, in Antelope Valley, three children horrified their foster mother with stories of their father having taken part in ritual murder and cannibalism. No bodies were ever found, but the accused was convicted of felony child abuse. Several children at a fundamentalist Christian preschool in Mendocino claimed they had been raped, tied to crosses and forced to chant, "Baby Jesus is dead!" In Pico Rivera, a 10-year-old named David Tackett accused six neighbors of being involved in orgies, urine-drinking and the sacrifice of infants. Nine other children supported the story, but no charges were ever filed. Similar investigations in Torrance, Whittier and Covina failed to produce any hard evidence. In Fremont, a five-year-old boy complained of being removed from his preschool by strangers who took him to a church where he was injected with drugs, sexually abused and forced to watch the candlelit mutilation of humans and animals. At Fort Bragg, five children from a church daycare center claimed bizarre activities took place at the center involving drugs, pornography, black candles, pentagrams and pets were being sacrificed. In Redwood City, two victims described adults wearing black robes and cremating a sacrificed infant, whose burned body "really stunk." In Atherton, a 17-year-old girl outlined abuse rituals performed by her stepfather and ten strangers.

In San Francisco, Police Detective Sandi Gallant was contacted by a frightened mother in May 1984. The woman had been watching television with her eight-year-old daughter when she saw a news report about a missing child. The girl remarked, "My daddy and I picked up a little boy named Kevin the other day, and he looks like him." As it happened, the caller's ex-husband already had a child abuse charge on file, but he still had visitation rights. The woman had noted what she called her daughter's "spacey" behavior after visits with her father. In therapy, the girl refused to speak but constantly drew swastikas, pentagrams and pictures of robed figures burning babies in blazing fires. Now, the mother listened, stunned, as her child began to tell a graphic tale of ritual abuse that involved chanting people and slaughtered animals. The claims went nowhere and no charges were ever filed.

In January 1985, five Sacramento men were jailed on 150 counts of child molestation. The alleged ringleader, Arthur Dill, 33, was accused by nine children – including four of his own – of ritual abuse that included rape, murder of infants and the production of "snuff" films. Incidents reportedly dated back to 1982, finally surfacing in the summer of 1984, when Dill's children started therapy for aberrant behavior after their parent's divorce. Authorities followed numerous leads in the search for physical evidence, but found nothing. Dill blamed his ex-wife and former mother-in-law for "brainwashing" the children to make false accusations. The case soon fizzled out and prosecutors dismissed all of the charges in September 1985.

Meanwhile, allegations of abuse were spreading beyond California. In Parker, Arizona, four children regaled the police with stories of satanic sex and drug abuse, but no charges were filed. In Memphis, Tennessee, a routine pediatric check-up exposed charges of ritual abuse when a three-year-old girl told her doctor that a preschool teacher had fondled her genitals. The girl named three other victims for the police, and those children in turn named others, all from the church-run Georgian Hills Early Childhood Center. Prosecutors ultimately charged a 54-year-old female staff member, her son, and Reverend Paul Shell with sexually abusing 26 children, torturing some and baptizing others in "the Devil's name." Reports from the children included the now-familiar descriptions of black robes and masks, burning candles, plus mutilations of gerbils, hamsters and a human infant. What might have been a legitimate report of abuse spun out of control during the frenzy of the times and likely led to people who had nothing to do with any sort of abuse becoming targets of the investigation. The congregation of the church stood behind the accused minister, but the prosecution refused to abandon the case. Bewildered jurors deadlocked on the case in 1987, causing a mistrial.

In October 1984, in Chicago, multiple charges of child molestation were filed against Deloartic Parks, a janitor at the Rogers Park Jewish Community Center, where several children complained of abuse at the daycare located there. The allegations included the by-now-familiar satanic rituals and black robes, with two teachers named as participants and two more suspended by administrators for failing to report ongoing abuse. Of 88 children in the daycare program, doctors claimed that 32 of them showed signs of being molested. State investigators decided that "most" of the allegations were unsupported by "credible evidence" and Parks was acquitted at his trial on charges of raping a seven-year-old girl. In an ironic footnote to the story, it was discovered that Allen Friedman, the "expert" that led the state's investigation, had grossly falsified his résumé to claim expertise in the field of child abuse. Friedman's work experience, various college credits and professional affiliations were all proven to be false upon examination. However, his committee's findings that Satanic Ritual Abuse had occurred were allowed to stand.

Another bizarre case came from Evansville, Indiana. A two-year investigation into ritual abuse charges was finally abandoned by prosecutor Steve Levco, who called the charges "inherently unbelievable." The probe folded without indictments in July 1991 with critics saying that it was a "political decision" that catered to public apathy. Levco didn't care. There was nothing to the charges and most agreed with him. As a sideshow to the main event, an elderly Evansville couple filed suit against the tabloid TV show *A Current Affair* after their home was featured in a broadcast about satanic cults.

The media continued to add fuel to the fire. In 1987, Geraldo Rivera produced a national television special on satanic cults, claiming that "estimates are that there are over one million Satanists [in the United States] linked in a highly organized, secretive network." This show, along with others that began appearing at the time, were subsequently used by religious groups, psychotherapists, social workers and law enforcement agencies to promote the idea that satanic cults were engaged in a conspiracy to commit serious crimes across the country.

Perhaps the groups that benefited the most from the claims of satanic conspiracies were conservative Christian organizations, which were enthusiastic in promoting rumors of Satanic Ritual Abuse. Just as the Church had been quick to condemn the accused during the witchcraft scares of hundreds of years before, religious fundamentalists in the late 1980s were using Satanic Panic to frighten believers and to bring new members into their churches. Christian psychotherapists began working with patients to "recover" lost and repressed memories and soon after, accounts similar to those in *Michelle Remembers* began to appear. Religious groups were instrumental in starting, spreading and maintaining rumors about Satanic Ritual Abuse through sermons about its dangers, by way of lectures by purported experts, and by prayer sessions and special showings of programs like Geraldo Rivera's 1987 "exposé."

Eventually, though, even the sensationalistic media couldn't ignore the fact that there was little in the way of hard evidence that would confirm the thousands of alleged accounts of satanic abuse, or that a vast underground conspiracy existed that was covering everything up. Media coverage began to turn negative toward the end of the 1980s and the Panic finally came to an end between 1992 and 1995. By the end of the 1990s, allegations of ritual abuse were finally being met with skepticism and belief in Satanic Ritual Abuse finally stopped being given much credence in mainstream professional psychological circles.

But, here's the problem: In the midst of all of the furor and negative press that eventually (and belatedly) focused on the ridiculousness of widespread Satanic Ritual Abuse, many genuine cases of child abuse were tragically ignored. Let's face it; there are a lot of crazy people out there and a lot of people who believe that they are doing evil in the name of the Devil. Far too much of the evil they commit is aimed at the most helpless among us – the children.

There were scores of fanciful and far-fetched stories being reported. There were also many other children who had been obviously coached by psychologists and by separated and divorced parents with a grudge against their former partners. But there were also stories of abuse that defied all efforts to dismiss them.

In Contra Costa County in California, a nine-year-old girl told stories of satanic abuse to a psychologist who accepted her report as "truthful." This might not have given the stories much legitimacy in the 1980s, when far too many psychologists were jumping on the Satanic Ritual Abuse bandwagon, but this one took the time to check out the claims. The therapist later recalled, "This happened in her father's home. She was able to recite for me what she called their Egyptian names, to sing for me the chants and the songs they sang. She described every conceivable sex act you can imagine. She described their playing with live snakes. She talked about young women in their teens who were sacrificed. Her description of how guts pop out when you slit open a live abdomen does justice to a Vietnam War veteran." Could she have seen all of those things on television? It's possible, but the therapist and the authorities didn't believe so.

Unfortunately, the sensational charges were too far-fetched for the jury to believe. Reports of other abuse cases that were being dismissed were already in the news by that time and a country prosecutor blamed this fact for the girl's father remaining free. He said, "They were as detailed as they were, I hate to use the word 'unbelievable' because at least to some degree, I believed them, although I had some questions about some of it. I question how much of it was exaggeration or misunderstanding, and how much of it was fact. There's no doubt in my mind that she was a participant in satanic worship, but she also described at one point how her father put his hand around her hand holding a knife and the two of them plunged the knife into the chest of an infant. There was some question in my mind about whether that was an actual sacrifice or possibly a simulated sacrifice, and that's what I said to the jury. I argued that the case wasn't about devil worship, and that whether they believed or disbelieved the child about the satanic stuff, there should be no question that she was a victim of child molestation."

Strange incidents reportedly occurred at West Point, the famed military academy in 1984. Mixed in with the other wild tales of the era, the reports were eventually ignored. In this case – based on other sexual abuse reports – these incidents probably should not have been forgotten.

In July 1984, the wife of an army sergeant stationed at West Point noted that her three-year-old daughter was bleeding from her vagina after her second day at the West Point Child Development Center. At the hospital, doctors found her vaginal canal was lacerated with small punctures and the girl described a teacher probing her genitals with a pen. By September, when the case was making news, eleven children had complained of being "hurt down there" by two of their teachers – one of whom fled the state after being indicted. One girl reported that she had been driven to a nearby high school, where she was allegedly photographed nude in the school's darkroom. Photos of the darkroom and other sites on the high school campus – including a burned tree that was inexplicably wrapped with cables – were snapped by investigators and shown to several of the other children without any comment. Several of the children reacted violently, crying out about their own traumatic experiences at the school and describing seeing children being bound to the tree while they were abused. A West Point physician, Dr. Walter Grote, turned down a scheduled promotion after learning that his own daughter had been abused at the daycare center. In an open letter to the Secretary of the Army, Grote wrote, "By the time I left West Point. I knew of approximately three dozen children who were ritually abused there."

Oddly, there seemed to be an established history of sexual abuse at West Point. In 1984, a senior commissioned officer at the post – later implicated in ritual abuse charges – was convicted of enticing two children to pose for pornographic photos. A year later, a civilian employee at the West Point Officer's Club was also convicted of sexually abusing several boys on the academy grounds. The U.S. attorney probing the charges later told reporters, "there isn't much question" that children were molested at the daycare center, with staff members "probably responsible"... but no indictments were ever returned in the case. Thanks to the climate of the times, prosecutors didn't think a jury would believe them.

The West Point cases were not alone. In the hundreds of Satanic Ritual Abuse cases that emerged, the vast majority of them could be dismissed as wild imagination or – more likely—coaching by parents and therapists who were swept up in the hysteria at the time. The authorities who were *not* interested in pursuing the satanic angle of abuse cases were the majority of police officers and prosecutors. Stereotypically, charges of ritual abuse were believed to have been filed by right-wing fundamentalist detectives and corrupt district attorneys trying to profit from the windfall of publicity. Ironically, though, the evidence is overwhelming that police and prosecutors actively attempted to bury cult-related claims in many cases, fearful that the bizarre allegations would destroy their case with the jury. In some cases, detectives ridiculed children who talked about pornographic films and rituals. In another, they refused to pursue such claims altogether. In the words of one detective who got mixed up in a satanic case, "This was not out finest moment. We had one simple case with one offender and we felt uncomfortable with the nature of the [ritual] allegations. To be honest with you, I didn't want to hear this. This was going to destroy our case."

And in far too many instances, it did. Child molesters began to go free because ritual abuse was brought in during otherwise straightforward cases and jumbled things up so badly that juries refused to believe it – usually for good reason. In some cases, though, there were molesters who really did fill the character of a ritual abuser, thinking that he was abusing kids for some sort of spiritual, satanic reason. But who would believe it? An FBI agent who worked as a "cult expert" in the 1980s, Ken Lanning, wrote, "Ritualistic crime may fulfill the cultural, spiritual, sexual and psychological needs of the offender." He warned the police that while child molesting "may be criminal if performed for sexual gratification," they enter a whole new ball game when "the ritualistic activity and child abuse may be integral parts of some spiritual belief system." More to the point, Lanning cautioned that once "acts of ritualistic abuse are performed for spiritual indoctrination, potential prosecution may be jeopardized." In other words, if there was even a hint of satanic mumbo-jumbo in your case, you might as well give up. The case would never survive a jury.

And thanks to the fact that few of them ever did make it through a jury trial, far too many child abusers escaped justice in the 1980s and early 1990s, all because a handful of people thought that profit, fame and notoriety were more important than telling the truth. One has to wonder if those who started the Satanic Ritual Abuse craze ever had any idea of the damage that they had really done.

HUMAN SACRIFICE AND THE "SATANIC CONSPIRACY"

There is no question that television talk show hosts have a far too powerful sway over the hearts and minds of the ordinary citizen, as evidenced by the number of bestsellers that Oprah Winfrey made out of otherwise mundane books by merely placing them in her monthly "book club" at the height of her popularity. In the late 1980s, people like Winfrey, Sally Jesse Raphael, Geraldo Rivera and a handful of others were just starting to see the power that they had over the American media and the public at large. People were tuning in by the millions to hear their opinions on everything from religion to race and to embrace them in a way that had once been reserved for popular politicians and religious leaders.

Because of this, it caused quite a stir in 1987 when Geraldo Rivera hosted his now infamous special about how Satanism had infiltrated every corner of our society, from police departments to political offices, schools and even churches. In addition, he stated that those same Satanist groups, which he claimed boasted over one million members across the country, had conspired to establish a secret underground network for the ritual abuse of children and were responsible for the murders of hundreds – perhaps thousands – of people every year in nefarious instances of human sacrifice. There was a reason that so many people disappeared every year and were never seen again – they were abducted by devil worshippers and sacrificed to Satan! People believed every word of it. The nation was terrified and outraged. They began tuning in by the millions as Rivera's ratings skyrocketed.

And it didn't stop there. Good research on crime and criminal enterprises by journalists like Maury Terry was hijacked and used to feed the frenzy. Rival talk shows could not afford to miss such sensational stories and they followed up with "special" shows of their own, each more lurid than the last.

Interestingly, if any of these talk show hosts would have made an accusation like this about any other ethnic or religious group in the country, they would have been denounced and taken off the air. But since the shows were about Satanism, there were few voices raised in protest. Little was known about the actual belief of Satanists but much was assumed, mostly gleaned from low-budget horror movies and the rantings

Research done by journalists like Maury Terry was hijacked by the talk show hosts of the late 1980s to prove their allegations of nationwide satanic "conspiracies."

of rock bands, who thought the symbolism was cool, but who were as ill-informed about the real beliefs of Satanists as their teenage audiences and their parents. It was enough to be told that satanic sects attracted anti-social types and that their beliefs were opposed to God-fearing Christian family values.

More importantly, few questioned the facts behind the statements of these shows. Had the subject been thoroughly researched, the show's researchers would have learned that official satanic churches in America could barely muster 10,000 members. There were perhaps another 10,000 or others who practiced Satanism in private and definitely no more than a few thousand teenagers who fooled around with pseudo-Satanism for a few months before getting tired of it when it didn't magically bring the results they wanted. Few of these people were known to have killed or harmed animals in their rituals and they certainly hadn't killed or injured any humans. Those who did so would better be labeled as psychopaths, not Satanists.

It was deliberately misleading for the shows, particularly Geraldo Rivera's exposé, to suggest that the FBI had Satanists under surveillance in anticipation of child abductions and ritual sacrifices. This could not have been further from the truth. The FBI had started exhaustive investigations into the allegations of organized Satanic murders and child abuse as far back as 1981, but had concluded the incidents were isolated, unorganized and were part of sexual and criminal activity, rather than occult behavior.

But that didn't stop people from believing that Satanists were everywhere. The general public was more fascinated with talk show claims and the wild incidents connected to Satanic Ritual Abuse that were almost daily making headlines in the late 1980s. If grave markers were knocked over in a cemetery, it wasn't simply vandalism, it was cult activity. If a child was abused and later recalled memories that they had "repressed" about black robes and candles, it must have been abuse by a group of Satanists. If a murder occurred that might be linked to local miscreants who listened to heavy metal music, then it must have been a sacrifice to the Devil. In the late 1980s and early 1990s, Satan was firmly entrenched in the public consciousness, especially when it came to crime. A modern-day witch hunt was still in progress – as three young men from West Memphis, Arkansas, were about to find out.

On the morning of May 6, 1993, the bodies of three young friends – Chris Byers, Michael Moore and Stevie Branch – were discovered face-down in a drainage ditch in Robin Hood Hills, a wooded area just off the interstate. The terrible rumors started almost immediately, claiming that the boys had been mutilated and that satanic symbols had been found at the scene. In truth, the boys had not been disfigured at all. They had been stripped naked, hogtied with their own shoelaces and then bludgeoned to death. There was nothing to indicate that the murders involved any sort of ritual, or had any occult overtones, but the rumors persisted. The stories were fueled by the local media, which was obsessed with occult killings and were determined to find devil worshippers somehow involved. The media stories were a product of the times, when television shows and newspapers were still under the spell of the Satanic Panic that had been concocted a few years before.

With no clues to work with, the West Memphis Police Department decided to call in FBI profilers from the Behavioral Science Unit, but the FBI had little to add except to assure the local detectives that there was no evidence of occult activity being involved in the murders. As pressure intensified on the police to make an arrest, the department turned to West Memphis juvenile officer Jerry Driver, who had been keeping an eye on several young men who did not conform to the image of what the community thought of as "good citizens."

Antisocial delinquents with a taste for heavy metal music, Jesse Misskelley, 17, Jason Baldwin, 16, and Damien Echols, 18, looked like the perfect suspects for the crime. Had they been regular churchgoers with good grades and short hair, it's likely safe to say that they would have never been suspected. But once the police started looking in the young men's backgrounds, and particularly when they searched the homes of Echols and Baldwin and found a stash of occult literature, their presumptions and prejudices seemed valid.

Even before his arrest, Damien Echols heard the rumors that he was one of the people involved in the murders. The police heard the same stories, which ended up directing the investigation. Although there was no forensic evidence to connect the three teenagers to the crime scene or to the bodies, the police hauled them in and subjected them to an intense and prolonged interrogation. After being hammered by intense questioning for hour after hour, denied sleep, water and food, Jesse finally confessed – to something. In his statement, he described how Damien and Jason had abused the boys as part of a satanic ritual, but his story was riddled with inconsistencies. The fact that he had been diagnosed as borderline intellectually challenged was not taken into account. The confused and exhausted young man was willing to say anything to end the grilling by the police.

When Damien heard about the confession, he later admitted to feeling powerless, angry and frightened. He had good reason to be. Despite a lack of any physical proof, the "West Memphis Three," as they became known, were convicted by a mixture of circumstantial and hearsay evidence. For example, when a knife was found in the lake behind Jason's house, expert witnesses testified that it could have made the wounds found on the bodies, yet it was almost certainly not the murder weapon. Recently, the wounds were re-examined by seven prominent forensic pathologists who agreed unanimously that they had been caused by animals after the boys' deaths.

It was also claimed that Damien had been heard confessing to the crime, but he later admitted that he had no recollection of having said anything that could be construed as a confession. Even if he had said something, he said, it would have been sarcastic.

More damning was the police mismanagement of the case. Dan Stidham, the defense attorney for Jesse Misskelley, cited multiple substantial police errors at the crime scene, characterizing it as "literally trampled, especially the creek bed." The bodies, he said, had been removed from the water before the coroner arrived to examine the scene and determine the state of rigor mortis, allowing the bodies to decay on the creek bank, and to be exposed to sunlight and insects. The police did not telephone the coroner until almost two hours after the discovery of the floating shoe. Officials failed to drain the creek in a timely manner and secure possible evidence in the water. There was a small amount of blood found at the scene that was never tested. According to HBO's documentaries *Paradise Lost: The Child Murders at Robin Hood Hills* (1996) and *Paradise Lost 2: Revelations* (2000), no blood was found at the crime scene, indicating that the location where the bodies were found was not necessarily where the murders occurred. After the initial investigation, the police failed to control disclosure of information about the crime scene.

The so-called "West Memphis Three, " a group of young men who were railroaded into prison by a poor judicial system and charges of "satanic crime." (Left to Right) Jason Baldwin, Damien Echols and Jesse Misskelley.

According to Mara Leveritt, an investigative journalist and the author of a book on the case called *Devil's Knot*, "Police records were a mess. To call them disorderly would be putting it mildly." Leveritt speculated that the small local police force was overwhelmed by the crime, which was unlike any they had ever investigated. Police refused an unsolicited offer of aid and consultation from the violent crimes experts of the Arkansas State Police, and critics suggested this was due to the WMPD being investigated by the Arkansas State Police for suspected theft from the Crittenden County drug task force. When police speculated about the assailant, Jerry Driver, the juvenile probation officer assisting at the scene of the murders, was overheard saying, "It looks like Damien Echols finally killed someone."

To make matters worse, the police almost completely ignored any alternate suspects in the case once they fixated on Misskelley, Baldwin and Echols. On the evening of the murders, workers in the Bojangles' restaurant about a mile from the crime scene in Robin Hood Hills reported seeing a black male who seemed "mentally disoriented" inside the ladies' room of the restaurant. The man was bleeding and had brushed against the walls of the restroom. Officer Regina Meeks responded to the call, taking the restaurant manager's report through the restaurant's drive-through window. By then, the man had left and police never went into the restroom. The following day, after the victims' bodies were found, Bojangles' manager Marty King, thinking there was a possible connection to the bloody man found in the bathroom, repeated the incident to police officers who then inspected the ladies room. King gave the police a pair of sunglasses that he thought the man had left behind and detectives took scrapings of blood stains left on the walls. Police detective Bryn Ridge testified that he later lost those blood scrapings. A hair identified as belonging to a black male was later recovered from a sheet which was used to wrap one of the victims.

In spite of all this, the three young men were found guilty at trial and Damien was sentenced to death. His friends each received a life sentence. All of them maintained their innocence. In May 1994, the three appealed

Pearl Jam's Eddie Vedder and Natalie Maines of the Dixie Chicks were two of the celebrities that were instrumental in supporting the West Memphis Three and getting them released from prison.

their convictions. The convictions were upheld on direct appeal. In 2007, Echols petitioned for a retrial based on a statute permitting post-conviction testing of DNA evidence due to technological advances made since 1994 that might provide exoneration for the wrongfully convicted. However, the original trial judge, Judge David Burnett, disallowed presentation of this information in his court.

The legal system in Arkansas might not have been listening – but other people were.

Film makers, celebrities and ordinary people began to rally to the cause of the West Memphis Three. Documentaries were made, hoping to shed light on the problems in the case and director Peter Jackson funded an investigation on behalf of the three men. Pearl Jam singer Eddie Vedder and Natalie Maines of the Dixie Chicks got involved in the story and made frequent appearances in court in support of Misskelley, Baldwin and Echols. Other celebrities that gave support included Henry Rollins, Johnny Depp, members of Metallica and many others.

New DNA evidence and tests were submitted, stories changed, witnesses recanted and "expert testimony" from a highly dubious "occult expert" was finally challenged. After weeks of negotiations on August 19, 2011, Echols, Baldwin and Misskelley were released from prison as part of an Alford plea deal, a rare legal mechanism in which "no contest" pleas are entered but innocence is nevertheless maintained. An Alford plea concedes that prosecutors have sufficient evidence to secure a conviction but reserves the right to assert innocence. Under the deal, Judge David Laser vacated the previous convictions, including the capital murder convictions for Echols and Baldwin, and ordered a new trial. Each man then entered an Alford plea to lesser charges of first and second degree murder while verbally stating their innocence. Judge Laser then sentenced them to time served, a total of 18 years and 78 days, and they were given a suspended sentence that could send them back to prison if they are ever convicted of a crime.

It was an unusual plea deal, but one that allowed the three men to walk free after nearly two decades in prison.

The story of the West Memphis Three was obviously a miscarriage of justice, swirling around the idea that the murder of the three boys had been some sort of ritual sacrifice to Satan. In this case, it was a ridiculous claim that came at a time when Americans were being deluged with wild tales of Satanist kidnappers and national conspiracies that were causing the disappearances of people across the country. Needless to say, no proof of such a conspiracy has ever been found – but there are parts of the story that cannot easily be dismissed.

Human sacrifice, for instance, has been with us since before the dawn of recorded history.

Without regard to race, creed or geography, it is a simple fact that residents of every continent, at one time or another, have indulged in ceremonial murder. The ancient Greeks dismembered and cannibalized a child each year atop Mount Lykaion and their Roman counterparts elevated ritual bloodshed to an art form. The Old Testament places recurring emphasis on sacrifice of the firstborn, both animal and human, a command from Jehovah that the Jews honored in festivals at their Great Temple on Mount Moriah. Druids sacrificed human victims and buried their charred bones at Stonehenge, while Celtic witch covens executed their own leaders in nine-year cycles. Sanskrit and Vedic texts required human sacrifice to ensure prosperity and sanctify new buildings. Mayan priests were decapitating victims, carving out their hearts and rolling the corpses down pyramid steps centuries before the Aztecs and Incas followed their example.

No one should assume that human sacrifice was eliminated by the spread of Christianity or the exploration of the New World by "civilized" Europeans. Indian disciples of the goddess Kali slaughtered millions of victims between the mid-thirteenth century and their eventual suppression in the 1840s. Medieval witch cults sacrificed and cannibalized infants, according to the numerous confessions they made. Before her exposure in the late seventeenth century, a mistress of King Louis XIV hired renegade priests to sacrifice children during stylized Black Masses. As recently as 1841, Italian treasure hunters sacrificed a young boy to a demon they believed would help them find a buried fortune in gold. In 1910, sheriff's deputies in Oklahoma interrupted the crucifixion of a young woman who was planned as a sacrifice to Halley's Comet. In Thailand, Sila Wongsin's cult of devil worshippers was broken up in 1959, its leader executed for human sacrifices. Similar charges were filed against elderly Indian Laxman Giri in 1980. In Spain, a self-styled witch was put to death in 1912 for murdering children and using their remains in "magic" potions. In 1962, at Figueras, Spanish officials blamed the disappearance of a young girl on a local satanic cult.

In Africa, practitioners of ju-ju typically sacrifice goats and other animals, but also have rituals for the murder of a man – "the animal that eats salt." Rampant promiscuity encouraged periodic harvest festivals that sacrificed "throwaway babies" that were donated to cults by unmarried mothers. The babies were sacrificed by ju-ju priests and processed into various potions, powders, soaps and lotions. Adult victims were used in the ritual of *iko-awo*, in which a man or woman was flayed alive, then gutted, the liver preserved in a box, while the corpse was washed and hung in a wardrobe before being taken home as a "spirit slave" by the client who sponsored the sacrifice.

In the west, ju-ju traditions survive in such variants as Voodoo, Santeria, Abaqua, Macumba and others, while the Bantu religion of Palo Mayombe took root with rituals that involved human sacrifice. Reports of ritual murder emanate periodically from Haiti, where Voodoo has long been the dominant religion. Offshoots of Voodoo were blamed for the ritual murder of a young Cuban girl in 1903. More recently, in 1978, devotees of Abaqua murdered the entire twenty-member cast of a play that publicized their cult's secret rituals.

Mexico, home of the Aztecs, has also experienced its share of human sacrifice in modern times, from the ritual bloodletting of the Hernandez brothers in the 1960s, to the grisly murders of Adolfo Constanzo, linked to at least 23 sacrificial murders between 1987 and 1989. Police in Mexico City investigated ritual slayings of 60 adults and 14 infants during the same period, with more deaths reported around Veracruz. With the exposure of Constanzo's cult in 1989, many blamed him for all of the crimes, but the ceremonies (and discovery of bodies) continued after his death at the hands of the police.

Farther south, in Peru, human sacrifice dates back to the days of the Incas – and continues today. For some practitioners, the ritual offering of human lives is believed to ensure bountiful crops, control the weather, and prevent such natural catastrophes as floods and earthquakes. Such rituals, called "paying the Earth," are employed by wealthy businessmen, ranging from mine owners to beer distributors, to ensure continued prosperity. Various local festivals call for human sacrifice and regional drug smugglers – in Mexico and elsewhere – rarely make a move without spilling blood to appease the gods in advance.

While isolated human sacrifices have been documented throughout Peru from the 1940s to the present day, some practicing shamans have traditional killing grounds of their own. One location, near Puno, is Mount Santa Barbara, the site of several sacrifices in the early 1980s. A female victim, killed there in 1982, was found with her breasts cut off, her vagina slashed open, and her face painted black. Around Yunguyo, ritual murders became so common that Mayor Horcaio Benavides circulated a petition in May 1988 that called on the provincial prosecutor's office to investigate. Signed by local nuns, civil and military authorities, the petition charged that "around these places there are abnormal elements or people who are practicing paganism or perhaps the narcotrafficker *pistacos* [vampires]." Several well-publicized cases that resulted in convictions followed, but the murders continued for years.

In neighboring Chile, human sacrifice became such an established tradition that the courts recognized "compulsion by irresistible psychic forces" as grounds for acquittal in cases of ritual murder. When the police tried to discourage the practice, Mapuche Indians complained of frequent droughts and earthquakes, events that began after fewer children were offered to the gods. In 1960, following a series of earthquakes near Puerto Dominguez, Clara Huenchillan decapitated two of her own children as a sacrifice. Remarkably, prosecutors declined to press charges when she blamed the murders on a dream inspired by the "many witches" in the neighborhood. A quarter-century later, at Lago Budi, Juana Namuncura was suspected – but never charged – with sacrificing her great-grandchild to appease the elements. A year later, in August 1986, cultists in Vista Hernose blamed Osvaldo Salamanca's chronic illness on a "vampire demon," which they exorcised by a driving a wooden stake through the heart of his nine-year-old nephew.

But human sacrifices don't just occur in modern-day Africa, Mexico and South America – they happen in the United States, as well. Many of these cases began to appear after the influx of Cuban refugees in the early 1980s and continued in the wake of record illegal immigration from Mexico and Central America in more recent years. Spokespeople for Santeria, Palo Mayombe and other religions staunchly deny involvement in human sacrifices, but investigations, informants and grim facts speak for themselves. In February 1981, a man named Leroy Carter was found decapitated in San Francisco's Golden Gate Park, with typical Santeria offerings of fried corn and mutilated chickens nearby. Five years later, in Miami, a murdered infant was discovered with its tongue and eyelids severed as an offering to appease the Afro-Caribbean *orishas*, the gods of Santeria. A similar case was reported in Fairfield, Connecticut, in March 1986, when a day-old infant was found in a city park, smothered and mutilated, its body surrounded by pennies, fruit and other Santeria offerings. In 1987, three bodies were dredged from the Miami River, shot to death and bound to a sacrificial goat. Around the same time, in Fort Myers, Florida, a search of a drug dealer's home turned up a *nganga* – a traditional Palo Mayombe cauldron of blood – with the severed heads of two men and the internal organs of a third human body inside. Houston, Texas, narcotics officers blamed cult-related killers for at least a dozen murders in their city, and officers of the New Jersey Port Authority, investigating a child pornography ring in 1988, discovered a Santeria altar with jars of human blood in one suspect's home. Four months after the discovery of Adolfo Constanzo's heart-eating cult in Matamoros, Mexico, a similar case was reported in the Florida Keys. In July 1989, Sherry Perisho, 39, was found floating in the ocean with her heart cut out. A short time earlier, Lisa Sanders, 20, had been found in a rock grotto at No Name Key. She had been strangled and her heart was removed. Detectives told the press, "All we can determine is that someone killed her for her heart."

But what do any of these murders have to do with the Devil? Modern Satanists adopt contradictory attitudes on the subject of ritual murder. Anton LaVey devoted four pages of his *Satanic Bible* to the "choice of a human sacrifice," with readers halfway through the chapter before discovering that LaVey's human sacrifice is merely "symbolic," amounting to his version of a "death curse." Even so, LaVey's language was ambiguous enough that a number of killers chose to take him literally.

The writings of Aleister Crowley were more to the point: "For the highest spiritual working one must accordingly choose that victim which contains the greatest and purest choice. A male child of perfect innocence and high intelligence is the most satisfactory and suitable victim." Crowley's rhetoric took root in the modern cultist and in the imaginations of people who claimed to have "repressed memories" as well. Many alleged victims of ritual abuse claimed to have seen infants murdered in ritual sacrifices and others told of "breeders," young women impregnated in satanic rituals who donated their offspring to the cult.

But how authentic are such stories? The vast majority of Satanic Ritual Abuse cases can, of course, be dismissed, but what about the accounts of ritual sacrifices – people literally murdered in the name of Satan? Do such things really happen?

Not according to the skeptics. In 1992, FBI forensic behaviorist Kenneth V. Lanning released a comprehensive report on the subject of satanic ritual killings and noted that "there are no bodies and there is not one conviction." This ignored the fact that there were numerous unsolved murders that could easily fit into the category of "ritual" or "occult-related," but since the crimes were not solved, they were deleted from the list. It's no surprise that Lanning's report came at the time that it did, for it came as a direct response to the wild overreaction on the part of law enforcement and religious organizations to the Satanic Panic of the time. Lanning's report was the voice of reason during a volatile time when many people believed that murderous devil worshippers were lurking everywhere, but did it go too far in the opposite direction?

Admittedly, it was unlikely that a national group of cultists was killing hitchhikers in the name of Satan, but a litany of murders over the years has shown that far too many depraved individuals have come to *believe* that they are doing the work of the Devil.

Satan may not have been guiding their hand – but they certainly believed that he was.

7. IN THE NAME OF SATAN

MURDER AND MAYHEM ON BEHALF OF THE DEVIL

At one time, the Devil was believed to be behind every evil act, but modern psychiatric professionals tend to explain deviant behavior in more prosaic ways. Crime is seen as a mild form of insanity, a temporary aberration in otherwise ordinary people, a lack of empathy or simple selfishness. Blaming the Devil for their own actions is the last resort of the criminally insane, a last-ditch defense made popular in cases like that of Ronald DeFeo, the young Long Island man who killed his parents and four siblings in a case that led to a series of movies based on Jay Anson's 1977 book, *The Amityville Horror: A True Story.*

"The Devil Made Me Do It," went the popular phrase... Some killers claimed it was so, but others really believed it.

Still others believed that they were carrying out a murder – or series of murders – as glorification of the Devil, perhaps earning them a greater place in Hell. While perhaps these murders do not fit into a category of "true" satanic ritual killings, there is no question that the perpetrators involved believed they were doing the work of the Devil, which makes them just as terrifying.

And what's even more terrifying? What follows is merely a sampling of killers who murdered in the name of Satan – there are many more out there that we don't even know about.

1929: THE EVANGELISTA "OCCULT MURDERS"

The story of the Detroit "Occult Murders" is one of the strangest in American crime. It's a story of black magic, murder and a clever and enterprising man who came to Detroit with a strange dream and who made use of the opportunities he found in a city that was bursting at the seams in those days. Immigrants from around the world had flocked to Detroit, hoping to capture their piece of the American dream in the factories that had brought the city to life. Sadly, many of them found overcrowded wooden tenements, brutal working conditions – and death.

Born in Naples, Italy, in 1885, Benjamino Evangelista was best-known as Bennie Evangelist, a self-proclaimed "Divine Prophet." Benny came to America in 1904 and invested his savings in real estate, soon emerging as a prosperous realtor and landlord. On the side, he supplemented his income by the sale of herbs, hexes and "spiritual remedies," performing chants, dances and animal sacrifices for paying customers for the purpose of either cures or curses.

But he hadn't started out in America as a "hex man." The first place that he lived in the New World was Philadelphia, where he joined his older brother, Antonio. But Antonio, by his own accounts, disowned Benjamino when he began having mystic visions of a very non-Catholic nature and sent him on to York, Pennsylvania, and a job on a railroad construction crew. Bennie's best friend in York, another immigrant from Naples, was a man named Aurelius Angelino. The two of them began to dabble in the occult. Something snapped in Angelino and in 1919, he attacked his family with an ax and killed two of his children. He was sent to a prison for the criminally insane and Bennie, unsettled by what had occurred, moved to Detroit.

Bennie went to work as a carpenter and began to dabble in real estate. Settled comfortably into his new life, he returned to his interest in the occult. Bennie began performing psychic healings on those who paid his fees, which went as high as $10 (the equivalent of two days' pay on the assembly line). He did quite well for himself, having taken on a wife, and along with their four children they had settled into a house at the corner of St. Aubin and Mack avenues. Benjamino Evangelista now called himself Bennie Evangelist, without the foreigner's "a" at the end. Their home was a large and comfortable one, painted green with a wide front porch. It was said that if a passerby cocked his head just right, he could see inside a basement window and view Bennie's "Great Celestial Planet Exhibition." Using papier-mâché, wires and wood, he had built nine planets and a sun with an electric eye that sat in the center.

But what passersby could not see was the basement chamber where Bennie practiced his infernal rituals. In that place, where he mixed up spells, hexes and potions, and carried out his magical sacrifices, he kept a crude altar along with knives, bottles and jars. Copies of his self-published book, *The Oldest History of the World Discovered by Occult Science in Detroit, Mich.*, were stacked around the room. Bennie claimed to have produced the book through a series of nightly trances, beginning in 1906. He said it was the first in a series of four books that would reveal previously unknown information relayed to him from God. Unfortunately for Bennie and his family, fate had another plan in store.

On the morning of July 4, 1929, many would ponder if it was Bennie's dabbling in the occult that caused his murder. On that sunny morning, the *Detroit Free Press* broke the news to the stunned city that Evangelist and his family had been brutally slain. The headline read: "Divine Prophet, Wife, 4 Children Hacked to Death. Wholesale tragedy laid to fanatics, humble St. Aubin Avenue home is scene of murders."

A man named Vincent Elias had come to the home on July 3 at about 10:30 a.m. to discuss a real estate deal with Bennie. When he got there, he found Bennie sitting behind his desk, his hands across his chest – and his head severed from his body! The corpse was mildly slumped forward on the desk and the head was on the floor next to the chair. The three older children, Angeline, Margaret and Jean, were found in a room on the second floor, their heads crushed with an axe. Bennie's wife, Santina, was found in the master bedroom with the youngest child, Mario, at her side. Their skulls had also been crushed with an ax.

Nearly the entire Detroit homicide division was dispatched immediately to the crime scene. When the police arrived, they searched the house and made notes of some of the odd things they found. One of the strangest discoveries was that someone had surrounded Bennie's severed head with three large framed photographs of a child in a coffin. It was later determined to be a post-mortem photograph of Evangelist's son who had died several years before. There was no explanation as to what message the photographs were intended to convey. The newspaper noted some other odd discoveries:

Several pieces of women's undergarments, each tagged with the name of its owner, police point out, reveal that the so-called mystic indulged in practices of "voodoosim," or devil worship. Such garments, "voodooism" has it, can lead to the finding of a missing person, when they are properly handled by one versed in the mystic arts of that belief.

No one had any clue as to what this meant, either.

The police failed to keep newspaper reporters and the dozens of gawkers who gathered around the house from contaminating the crime scene and from destroying any potential clues except for one -- a bloody fingerprint on the front doorknob. To make matters even more difficult, most of Evangelist's neighbors and "clientele" were recent Sicilian and Italian immigrants who were reticent to provide information to law enforcement. Detectives were unable to compel even one of them into making an official statement that could have provided at least some starting point from which to launch their investigation. Evangelist's own records and the collection of personal trinkets found in the home proved that hundreds of people had come to him for "services," but scarcely a handful of those questioned admitted to even having known him.

The police used what few clues they had to pursue three very different theories. One of them revolved around several notes found in the home that suggested Bennie had once been threatened by the "Black Hand," a criminal group that preyed on wealthy Italian immigrants. The most recent letter was six month old and warned, "This is your last chance." The problem with the Black Hand theory was that by 1929 it was an outdated, defunct enterprise that had long since evolved into the traditional Mafia structure of organized crime. Crude extortion schemes were a thing of the past, dating back to the years before Prohibition became the law of the land. It seems unlikely that Bennie took the notes very seriously. Whoever was trying to extort money from him was almost certainly an amateur looking for an easy mark, not someone who could have carried out the grisly murders of an entire family.

The second theory was significantly more plausible. A 42-year-old local man named Umberto Tecchio had visited the Evangelist home on the night before the bodies were found. He was making the final payment on a house Bennie had sold him. Tecchio, along with a friend named Angelo Depoli who had accompanied him to the house on the night before the murders, were brought in for questioning the next day when an ax, a "keen-edged" banana knife, and a pair of suspiciously clean work boots were found in the barn behind the boarding house where they lived. Tecchio and Depoli claimed to know nothing about the murders. They both stated that nothing unusual had happened during the visit and that they had gone out drinking after dropping off the last payment on Tecchio's home to Evangelist. But the newspapers – largely thanks to prejudice against Italian immigrants – cast suspicion on Tecchio. Accounts mentioned that, just three months prior to the massacre, Tecchio had knifed his brother-in-law to death in an argument. How he escaped prosecution for that is unclear, but it certainly gave investigators a reason to make him a prime suspect. However, with no physical evidence and no confession, Tecchio was let go. He died a few years later in 1934.

After Tecchio's death, the continuing investigation into Detroit's largest mass murder uncovered a newspaper delivery boy who told police he had seen Tecchio on Evangelist's front porch on the morning of the murders. But what kind of weight could this recollection hold in the face of no motive and no evidence?

The police also briefly suspected one of Evangelist's tenants, posthumously accused of the murders by a vengeful ex-wife, but the dead man's thumbprint didn't match the bloody fingerprint on the doorknob, which brings us to the third theory...

In 1923, Bennie's old friend Aurelius Angelino (who murdered two of his children with an ax) escaped from the Pennsylvania prison for the criminally insane where he was incarcerated — and was never seen again. Had Angelino somehow made his way to Detroit, where his old friend had set up his eerie basement room? It is certainly possible, but was there any proof of this?

The Detroit police seemed to have invested more of their time in the pursuit of Umberto Tecchio, but looking back after more than eighty years, the nature of the crime itself seems the most damning evidence against

Aurelius Angelino. The murders seem to most closely match the crime Angelino committed back in York and it's not hard to imagine him slowly making his way west to Detroit, and finally tracked down his old partner in "voodooism," the code word for satanic activities that the police and the newspapers used in those days. Upon arriving at the door of the now-prosperous Evangelist, isn't it possible that Angelino thought back over the horrors of the previous nine years and felt rage boil up inside of him? It isn't hard to imagine the escaped madman and convicted ax-murder slithering in an open window while Bennie sat at his desk during the early morning hours of July 3. And once inside the house, how difficult would it have been for him to murder the family of the man who had left him behind in York to rot in the insane asylum while he practiced his magic and grew fat off selling spells and potions? It's not hard to imagine at all.

And yet, after Angelino's escape from the state of Pennsylvania's custody in 1923, no record of his existence, whether in Detroit, or anywhere else, can be found. Could a family of six be slaughtered so easily and the killer simply disappear? It's certainly possible, as history has proven time and time again.

This murder will never be solved but for the purposes of bringing an end to the tale, we'll simply say that an evil spirit of some sort exacted retribution of some kind upon Evangelist and his unwitting family. When he was finished, he disappeared into the humid July night, leaving his bloody fingerprint on the door knob when he let himself out of a house filled with death.

1970: LOOKING FOR THE "HEAD DEVIL"

Strung out on barbiturates, Southern California native Steven Hurd was a rootless drifter who never stayed in one place for long. Little is known about his early life, other than that he was born in 1950, but by his late teens, he was a homeless wanderer who scavenged for food and slept in open fields and highway culverts. What little money that he managed to scrounge up was usually spent on drugs. Somewhere along the way from childhood to oblivion, he discovered the Devil and he preached the

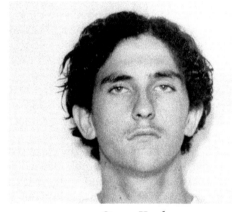

Steven Hurd

ways of Satan with such zeal that he managed to win himself a small group of disciples from the streets.

When they got tired of chanting, burning things and mutilating small animals, the cult decided that they would get a bigger kick from human sacrifice. As Hurd later told the police, he believed that it would okay to "snuff people out," as long as certain body parts were saved for Satan. Hurd's experimentations with murder turned out to be what some say are among Orange's County's "50 Most Notorious Crimes."

The cult's first murder began as a simple robbery. Hurd had decided that he wanted to go to San Francisco for a private consultation with "Head Devil" Anton LaVey, but was predictably short of cash – and gas. Thinking that he could come up with pocket money and gas at the same time, Hurd and his followers decided to visit a Santa Ana service station on the night of June 2, 1970. They confronted an attendant named Jerry Carlin who was working the graveyard shift and Hurd and follower Arthur "Moose" Hulse forced him into the station's restroom, where they butchered him with a hatchet. The cult fled with a tank of gas, a pocketful of cash, Carlin's jacket and a can of motor oil.

Steven Hurd walks with an officer during the jury tour of the crime scene that occurred during his trial. He was initially sent to a mental hospital and then convicted of two counts of murder. (Orange County Register)

But Hurd's run of back luck continued. Before he could get ready to leave on his trip, his car broke down. He went in search of a replacement, accompanied by his flock. On June 3, the cult hijacked a station wagon driven by Florence Brown, 31, a mother of four. She was stopped at the intersection of Interstate 5 and Sand Canyon Boulevard when three cultists jumped into her car and drove her to an orange grove near the Irvine campus of the University of California. There, she was stabbed twenty-one times in the back, her right arm was severed, her heart and lungs removed, along with three ribs from her back and strips of flesh from her right leg. The cult members were nearly captured that night when they were pulled over by a police officer with the woman's body wrapped in a blanket in the back seat of the car. The officer somehow failed to notice that three drug-crazed maniacs were driving a stolen car with the body of a murder victim in the back. Hurd and his companions buried Brown's body in a shallow grave near Ortega Highway. Hurd later told authorities that he and his followers cannibalized parts of the corpse before they buried it. His defense attorney William Gamble later commented, "He said it tasted like chicken."

Hikers found the pitiful remains of the young woman on June 15.

Hurd and the cult began moving north after the murders, driving first to San Quentin to visit with incarcerated cronies and then on to Los Gatos, where they split up after torching the stolen car. In early July, the police were still stymied with their investigation into the murder of gas station attendant Jerry Carlin when an informant told detective John McClain that he had spent a night in jail with a man wearing Carlin's bloodstained jacket. McClain traced the jacket to a drifter, who in turn told him that he had gotten it from Steven Hurd. Arrested in Corona on July 9, Hurd quickly fell apart during questioning, admitting his role in the Carlin homicide. As he was signing his confession, Hurd paused and said, "You guys have been pretty nice. I guess I should tell you about the other one."

Hurd named the other members of his cult, which included Melanie Daniels, 31, Christopher Giboney and Herman Taylor, both 17, and 16-year-old Moose Hulse. Daniels was already serving ninety days for a narcotics conviction when Hurd gave her name to the police, but there was no evidence to link her to the murders. Hulse was named as the hatchet man in Carlin's murder and the two other boys were blamed for the murder of Florence Brown. In the absence of a coherent eyewitness to support murder charges against Hurd's teenage followers, the boys were remanded to the California juvenile system.

Hurd, however, was happy to take the blame for his part in the murders. He did add that he and his followers had been visited – and given pointers by – the Church of Satan's Anton LaVey, a claim that an outraged LaVey was quick to deny from his San Francisco headquarters.

Diagnosed as a schizophrenic prior to trial, Hurd spent five years at the Atascadero State Mental Hospital. He continued to report frequent visits from "Father Satan," whom he described as "a man wearing a gold helmet, with the skin of a pine cone." He was eventually tried in Orange County in May 1975, convicted of two counts of first-degree murder and sentenced to life in prison, with parole possible after seven years. There was no death penalty when his crimes were committed. When Hurd did come up for parole, the Orange County District Attorney's Office successfully opposed it seven times, starting in 1981.

Hurd died from a brain hemorrhage on May 28, 2005 at a local hospital near the Mule Creek State Prison in Amador County. He had spent the majority of his life in prison.

1970: "I'M A CANNIBAL"

This wasn't the first time I'd heard this story. Long before I began my research into killers who claim to murder for Satan, I was chilled by the story of Stanley Baker, a seemingly harmless hippie drifter who got picked up by the police on a summer night in 1970. I first read the story in a comic book that was given to me by my parents in the late 1970s (believe it or not, I was raised in a pretty stringent religious family). The comic followed the adventures of a couple of Christian missionaries called "The Crusaders." It was drawn by Jack Chick, a fundamentalist cartoonist turned publisher who was famous for his hellfire-and-brimstone religious tracts. Anyway, this particular story appeared in an issue called "The Broken Cross." It was a hair-raising cautionary tale for Christian kids about the horrors that awaited them if they ever fell into the clutches of Satan worshippers.

Needless to say, I never gave the warning much attention but years later, I found out that at least part of the book was true – Stanley Baker was real and he really was arrested with a human finger in his pocket. How much truth there was to the rest of his story remains in debate, but I can tell you one thing for sure: Stay away from those Christian comics, they'll give you nightmares.

On July 13, 1970, California Highway Patrol officers began receiving reports about a hit-and-run accident at Big Sur. Three people had been injured in one car, while two men with long hair sped away in another vehicle, fleeing the scene of the crash. Patrolmen who answered the call spotted two long-haired men walking down a nearby road and noted that their descriptions were very similar to the men reported in the car that left the scene of the accident. Under questioning, one of the men readily admitted to having been involved. He admitted to causing the crash and then startled police by adding, "I have a problem. I'm a cannibal."

To prove his point, Stanley Baker, 22, turned out his pockets and produced a copy of Anton LaVey's *The Satanic Bible* and a human finger bone – the latter object, he claimed, having come from his latest victim in Montana. Baker's companion, Harry Allen Stroup, 20, was also carrying a human finger in his pocket. Baker and Stroup were quickly taken into custody on suspicion of homicide. A stolen car was found nearby, registered to a Montana man named James Schlosser, and Montana detectives soon followed Baker's directions to a lonely spot on the Yellowstone River. There they found Schlosser's body, missing the heart and several fingers.

The case was gruesome enough, but once locked up, Baker had more stories to tell. According to his statement, he had been recruited by satanic cultists on a college campus in his home state of Wyoming. He had joined up with the homicidal "Four P Movement" (their history was detailed in an earlier chapter) and swore allegiance to the cult's leader, an enigmatic businessman from the San Francisco area. Baker claimed that he had murdered a number of people on the cult's behalf. There had been human sacrifices, he said, in the Santa Ana Mountains, south of Los Angeles.

Displaying cult tattoos, Baker also claimed to have participated in the April 19, 1970 murder of Robert Salem, a 40-year-old lighting designer from San Francisco. Salem lived and worked in a residence/studio in the 700 block of Stevenson Street, an alley behind The San Franciscan Hotel at 1231 Mission Street. On April 19, police responded to a complaint from people living in the rooms at the back of the hotel of a horrible smell coming from the alley. When they investigated, they found Salem's nude body sprawled inside his apartment in the midst of a bloody scene reminiscent of a slaughterhouse. The killer – or killers, if Baker is to be believed – had turned up the thermostat to 90 degrees and had apparently used the shower after the murder. And for good reason – Salem had cut to pieces. He had been stabbed twenty-seven times and nearly decapitated. His left ear had been severed and removed from the scene, following orders that Baker claimed came from the "Four P Movement's" mysterious leader. On the wall, smeared in the victim's blood, were the words "Satan Saves" and "Zodiac." An Egyptian ankh was drawn near the name and the same symbol was drawn in blood on the victim's stomach. The police almost immediately decided that the murder had nothing to do with the work of the Zodiac killer, who had become infamous in recent years, but was a copycat effort to stir up panic in an atmosphere already tense from revelations in the ongoing Manson murder trial. How they came to this conclusion is anyone's guess, but if we believe Baker's story, it was correct.

Some reports state that bloody fingerprints found in Salem's apartment were matched to Baker's, but San Francisco prosecutors gave Montana first crack at the cannibal killer, losing their man forever when a California court ruled that the delay violated Baker's right to a speedy trial.

Baker and Stroup were returned to Montana on July 20, where they were subsequently convicted of murder and sent to prison. Behind bars, Baker continued his efforts on behalf of the cult. Authorities reported that he actively solicited other inmates to join a satanic coven. Full moons seemed to bring out the worst in him, prompting him to crouch in his cell and howl like a wolf. He also threatened guards and was relieved of homemade weapons on eleven separate occasions before he was finally moved to a maximum-security prison in Illinois. Under these stricter conditions, Baker became a model inmate, counseling other prisoners on the fine points of transactional analysis, a type of psychology that teaches that each person has validity, importance and is worthy of respect and that each man has control over his own story and destiny. Throughout this time, though, Baker remained devoted to the Devil, although the Church of Satan officially rejected his application for membership in 1976.

Harry Stroup completed his sentence and was released from prison in 1979. Stanley Baker was paroled in 1985, requesting that his whereabouts remain confidential. Journalists tracked him to Minneapolis about six years later and in a television interview, he denied any knowledge of satanic murders, and then lapsed into an Indian accent to describe himself as a "good man." In the interview, he blamed the Schlosser murder on drug abuse and "that outfit in California" that Baker said "used powerful prayers in an incorrect manner."

What happened to him after that remains unknown, but suffice it to say, he is probably still out there somewhere. We can only hope that his appetites have changed over the years.

1976: "SON OF SAM"

New Yorkers are regrettably accustomed to reports of violent death in every form, from the mundane to the frightening and bizarre. They take this in stride, accepting the carnage as a small price to pay for living in what they believed is the greatest city in America. But local residents were unprepared for the all-out reign of terror that began in the summer of 1976. For the next thirteen months, New York was a city under siege, its female residents afraid to venture out at night while a homicidal maniac was waiting in the shadows, seeking his next victims.

When the killer was finally caught, the story became one that nearly impossible to believe, only to become even stranger after claims emerged of the role that a satanic cult played in the slayings – claims that have yet to be investigated by the authorities.

The first shooting attributed to the killer that became known as Son of Sam took place in the Pelham Bay area of New York City's northernmost borough, the Bronx. At about 1:10 a.m. on July 29, 1976, Donna Lauria, 18, and her friend Jody Valenti, 19, were sitting in Valenti's Oldsmobile, discussing their evening at the Peachtree, a New Rochelle disco. As Lauria was getting out of the car, she noticed a man quickly walking toward them. She was startled by his sudden appearance, but before she could speak, he pulled a pistol from the paper bag he was carrying. The man went into a crouch, braced one elbow on his knee, aimed his weapon with both hands, and fired three times. Lauria was struck by one bullet and died instantly. Valenti was shot in the thigh. A third bullet missed both women. The gunman never spoke. He simply turned and walked away.

Valenti, who survived her injuries, said she did not recognize the killer. She described him as a white male in his thirties with a fair complexion, standing about 5 feet 9 inches and weighing about 160 pounds. His hair was short, dark and curly.

Police detectives were able to determine that the murder weapon

Jody Valenti and (Right) Donna Lauria

was a pistol chambered for the .44 Special cartridge, manufactured by Charter Arms and called the Bulldog model. A five-shot revolver intended for use in close quarters, the .44 Bulldog was easily identified by ballistics tests, but that was about the only clue investigators had. In the absence of other evidence, the police surmised that the man was a spurned lover of Lauria, or that the shooting was a mistaken assassination of the wrong person. The neighborhood had seen recent mob activity and police even hinted that Lauria's father, a member of the Teamsters union, might be involved in organized crime.

The shooting was a tragic incident, but in itself not that unusual for New York. There was scattered sympathy, but no alarm among the residents of the city – until the next attack.

On October 23, 1976, a second shooting occurred in Queens. In a secluded residential area of Forest Hills Gardens, Carl Denaro, 25, and Rosemary Keenan, 38, were sitting in Keenan's parked car when the windows suddenly shattered: "I felt the car exploded," Denaro said later. Keenan quickly started the car and sped off for help. The panicked couple did not realize that someone had been shooting at them, even as Denaro was bleeding from a bullet wound to his head. Keenan had only superficial injuries from the broken glass, but Denaro eventually needed a metal plate to replace a portion of his skull. Neither victim saw the attacker.

Police determined that the bullets embedded in Keenan's car were .44 caliber, but they were so damaged and deformed that they thought it was unlikely that they could ever be linked to a particular weapon. Denaro had shoulder-length hair and police would later speculate that the shooter had mistaken him for a girl. Keenan's father was a 20-year veteran NYPD detective, spurring an in-depth investigation. As with the earlier shooting, however, there seemed to be no motive and no progress was made in the case. Even though it was very similar to the July attack, investigators did not initially make a connection between them, partly because the shootings occurred in different boroughs and were investigated by different police precincts.

Just over one month later, on November 27, two young girls – Donna DeMasi, 16, and Joanne Lomino, 18 – walked home from a movie and were chatting on the porch of Lomino's home in Queens. A blonde man in his early twenties, dressed in military fatigues, approached them and asked for directions. Before he could complete his question, he drew a pistol and opened fire at the girls. He shot each of them once and, as they fell to the ground, he fired several more times, striking the apartment building, before running away. Having heard the gunshots, a neighbor rushed out of the apartment building and saw a blond man run by, gripping a pistol in his left hand.

DeMasi had been shot in the neck, but the wound was not life-threatening. Lomino was hit in the lower spine and was permanently paralyzed. Based on testimony from the girls and one of their neighbors, the police produced several composite sketches of the shooter. Police also determined the gun was a .44 caliber, but the slugs were too damaged to link them to any particular gun.

Donna Demasi and (Right) Christine Freund

The Christmas season passed without another shooting, but the killer was far from finished. In the early morning of January 30, 1977, an engaged couple, Christine Freund, 26, and John Diel, 30, were sitting in Diel's car parked in Station Square in Forest Hills Gardens, Queens, preparing to go dancing after having been to the movies. They were embracing when three bullets shattered their windshield. In a panic, Diel drove away for help. He suffered minor injuries, but Freund was shot twice and died several hours later at the hospital. Neither victim had seen their attacker.

In the wake of the shooting, the police made the first public announcement that the most recent attack was similar to the earlier incidents, and that the crimes might be connected. All the victims had been struck with .44 caliber bullets, and the shootings seemed to focus on young women with long, dark hair. Composite sketches of two shooters – one with dark hair, and one blonde – were released. The police were looking for multiple suspects, not just one.

But the investigation went nowhere and the police were no closer to finding the killers on March 8, 1977 when Barnard College student Virginia Voskerichian, 19, was walking home from school around 7:30 p.m. A man suddenly approached her and pulled out a gun. Voskerichian tried to shield herself with her textbooks, but the bullet pierced the books and stuck her in the head, killing her instantly. She was found dead 100 yards from where Freund was slain.

Moments after the shooting, a neighborhood resident who had heard the gunshots was rounding the corner onto the street. He nearly collided with a person he described as a short, husky boy, 16 to 18 years old and clean-shaven, wearing a sweater and a knitted watch cap. The boy was sprinting away from the scene but had pulled the cap over his face, making him impossible to identify. Other neighbors would later claim to have seen the "teenager," as well as another person who matched the dark-haired shooter's description, loitering separately in the area for about an hour before the shooting.

There were no direct witnesses to the Voskerichian murder, which happened on the victim's own street. The Voskerichian shooting differed from the other recent crimes in several respects. All the other victims were couples, and were shot on weekends late at night or in the early morning, but on March 10, NYPD officials and New York City Mayor Abe Beame declared that the same .44 Bulldog revolver had fired the shots that killed Lauria and Voskerichian. The same day, the Operation Omega task force made its public debut. Charged solely with investigating the .44 caliber shootings, the task force was led by Deputy Inspector Timothy J. Dowd, backed up by over 300 police officers.

The shootings made newspaper headlines on a daily basis, in New York and across the country. A sense of panic gripped the city, stoked by the sensational reports that appeared in the newspapers. Mayor Beame, meanwhile, helped funnel unprecedented amounts of money to the NYPD to help solve the case, but even with the task force in place, the investigation was going nowhere.

Around 3:00 a.m. in the early morning hours of April 17, 1977, Alexander Esau, 20, and Valentina Suriani, 18, were in the Bronx, only a few blocks from the scene of the Lauria-Valenti shooting. They were sitting in Suriani's car near her home, when a man approached the car and opened fire. They were each shot twice. Suriani died at the scene, and Esau died in the hospital several hours later without being able to describe his attacker.

But this time, the killer left something behind. Detectives found a crudely printed letter lying in the street near Suriani's car. Written mostly in block capital letters with some lower-case letters, it was addressed to NYPD Captain Joseph Borrelli. It was in this letter that the name "Son of Sam" was revealed for the first time. In the press, the killer had previously been dubbed the ".44 Caliber Killer" because of his signature weapon. Although the letter was initially withheld from publication, some of its contents leaked to the press and the Son of Sam moniker rapidly grabbed the public's attention.

With its rambling and feverish tone, the letter expressed the killer's determination to continue his work, and taunted police for their fruitless efforts to capture him. In full, with misspellings intact, it read:

Valentina Suriani and Alexander Esau

I am deeply hurt by your calling me a wemon hater. I am not. But I am a monster. I am the "Son of Sam." I am a little 'brat.' When father Sam gets drunk he gets mean. He beats his family. Sometimes he ties me up to the back of the house. Other times he locks me in the garage. Sam loves to drink blood. "Go out and kill" commands father Sam. Behind our house some rest. Mostly young — raped and slaughtered — their blood drained — just bones now. Papa Sam keeps me locked in the attic, too. I can't get out but I look out the attic window and watch the world go by. I feel like an outsider. I am on a different wave length then everybody else — programmed too kill. However, to stop me you must kill me. Attention all police: Shoot me first — shoot to kill or else. Keep out of my way or you will die! Papa Sam is old now. He needs some blood to preserve his youth. He has had too many heart attacks. Too many heart attacks. "Ugh, me hoot it hurts sonny boy." I miss my pretty princess most of all. She's resting in our ladies house but I'll see her soon. I am the "Monster" — "Beelzebub" — the 'Chubby Behemouth.' I love to hunt. Prowling the streets looking for fair game — tasty meat. The wemon of Queens are z prettyist of all. I must be the water they drink. I live for the hunt — my life. Blood for papa. Mr. Borrelli, sir, I dont want to kill anymore no sir, no more but I must, 'honour thy father.' I want to make love to the world. I love people. I don't belong on Earth. Return me to yahoos. To the people of Queens, I love you. And I wa want to wish all of you a happy Easter. May God bless you in this life and in the next and for now I say goodbye and goodnight. Police — Let me haunt you with these words; I'll be back! I'll be back! To be interrpreted as — bang, bang, bang, bank, bang — ugh!! Yours in murder Mr. Monster

The killer's unusual behavior towards the police and the media received widespread scrutiny. Psychologists observed that many serial killers crave recognition and seem to get gratification from challenging their pursuers. After consulting with several psychiatrists, police released a psychological profile of their suspect on May 26, 1977. He was described as neurotic and probably suffering from paranoid schizophrenia, believing himself to be a victim of demonic possession. The writer was apparently irrational – or else he had a message for the city that detectives were unable to figure out.

Columnist Jimmy Breslin of the *New York Daily News* received a second hand-written letter from the man calling himself "Son of Sam" on May 30, postmarked Englewood, New Jersey. On the advice of police, the paper published it, along with a plea from Breslin for the killer to turn himself in. The *Daily News* sold 1.1 million copies that day, as desperate New Yorkers frantically read and re-read the letter to try and figure what was behind the shootings and where Son of Sam might strike next..

The police questioned fifty-six owners of .44 Bulldog revolvers that were legally registered in New York, and forensically tested each gun, ruling them all out as the murder weapon. Among other unsuccessful ideas, police created traps with undercover officers posing as lovers parked in isolated areas, hoping to lure the shooter.

Nothing worked and in the meantime, New York's panic continued. The police received thousands of tips, all of which proved baseless. Since all of the shooting victims so far had long dark hair, thousands of women in New York acquired short cuts or dyed their hair blonde. Beauty supply stores had trouble meeting the demand for wigs.

On June 26, the gunman struck again. Sal Lupo, 20, and Judy Placido, 17, had left the Elephas Disco on Northern Boulevard in the Bayside section of Queens. The young couple was sitting in their car at about 3:00 a.m. when three gunshots blasted through the window. Both of them were struck by bullets, but their injuries were relatively minor, and both survived. Neither Lupo nor Placido had seen who had fired the shots, but witnesses reported a tall, stocky, dark-haired man sprinting from the area, as well as a blonde man with a mustache who drove away in a Chevy Nova without turning on its headlights.

Early on July 31, 1977, Stacy Moskowitz and Robert Violante, both 20, were in Violante's car, which was parked under a streetlight near a city park in the Brooklyn neighborhood of Bath Beach. They were kissing when a gunman approached to within about three feet of the passenger side of the car and fired four times. Both victims were wounded in the head. Moskowitz died several hours later. Violante survived, though one of his eyes was destroyed and he retained only very limited vision in the other eye. Whoever their attacker had been, he disappeared from the park.

The shooting – which would turn out to be the last, although police obviously didn't know it at the time – produced more witnesses than any of the other Son of Sam murders. At the time of the shooting, Tommy Zaino, 19, was parked with his date three cars in front of Violante's. Moments before the shooting, Zaino got a glimpse of the shooter's approach and happened to glance in his rear view mirror just in time to see the crime occur. Due to the bright street light, Zaino clearly saw the perpetrator for several seconds, later describing him as 25 to 30 years old, of average height with shaggy hair that was dark blond or light brown — "it looked like a wig," Zaino said.

About a minute after the shooting, a woman seated next to her boyfriend in his car on the other side of the park saw a "white male [who was wearing] a light-colored, cheap nylon wig" sprint from the park and enter a "small, light-colored" auto, which drove away quickly. She managed to write down a few of the numbers from the license plate.

Other witnesses included a woman who saw a light-colored car speed away from the park about twenty seconds after the gunshots, and at least two witnesses who described a yellow Volkswagen driving quickly from the neighborhood with its headlights off. A neighborhood resident heard the gunshots and Violante's calls for help, and glancing from her apartment window, she saw a man who was walking casually away from the crime scene as many others were rushing towards the scene to try and help. Another man, driving near the park a few minutes after the shooting, was nearly struck by a yellow Volkswagen Beetle that sped through the intersection, against the red light and without headlights, with the driver holding his door shut with his left arm. Angered and alarmed, he followed the Volkswagen for several minutes before losing sight of the vehicle. He failed to notice the car's license plate but described the driver as a white male in his late 20s or early 30s, with a narrow face; dark, long, stringy hair; several days' growth of dark whiskers and wearing a blue jacket.

The police did not learn of the shooting until almost thirty minutes had passed and Deputy Inspector Dowd did not think it was a "Son of Sam" shooting until an officer on the scene reported the large-caliber bullets that had been used. About an hour after the shooting, police set up a series of roadblocks, stopping hundreds of cars to question drivers and inspect vehicles, but too much times had passed. Based on the reports of the Volkswagen speeding away from the crime scene, the police came to believe that the shooter owned or drove such a vehicle. In subsequent days, they determined there were over 900 Volkswagens in New York or New Jersey, and they made plans to track down each of these cars and their owners. Luckily, they never had to.

At the scene of the last shooting, a local resident named Cecilia Davis had been walking her dog when she saw a parked car being ticketed near a fire hydrant. Moments after the traffic officer had left, a young man walked past her from near the car. She was nervous because she spotted something dark in his hand, but the man passed by. A few moments later, she heard shots fired down the street. Davis stayed silent about this experience for four days until she contacted police, who closely checked every car that had been ticketed in the area that night. As it turned out, that's how they found David Berkowitz – by pure luck.

David Berkowitz

Among the cars ticketed on the street that night was Berkowitz's four-door yellow Ford Galaxy. Initially, he was sought as a possible witness, not as a suspect, but that soon changed. On August 9, 1977, NYPD detective James Justis called the Yonkers police and asked for help in finding Berkowitz to schedule an interview. Mike Novotny was a sergeant at the Yonkers Police Department. According to Novotny, the Yonkers police had their own suspicions about Berkowitz, in connection with other strange crimes in Yonkers, crimes they saw referenced in the "Son of Sam" letter. Novotny believed that it was possible that Berkowitz was Son of Sam.

The next day, August 10, 1977, police investigated Berkowitz's car parked on the street outside his Pine Street apartment in Yonkers. Seeing a rifle in the backseat, they searched the car and found a duffel bag filled with ammunition, maps of the crime scenes, and a threatening letter addressed to Sgt. Dowd of the Omega task force. Police decided to wait for Berkowitz to leave the apartment and when he did, he was immediately arrested. They discovered he was carrying a .44 Special Bulldog in a paper sack. His first words to them were reported to be, "Well, you got me. How come it took you such a long time?"

Investigators searched his apartment and found it in disarray, with satanic graffiti covering the walls. They also found diaries he had kept since he was 21 years old – three nearly full stenographer's notebooks in which Berkowitz had scrawled notes about hundreds of fires he claimed to have set throughout the New York area.

After the arrest, Berkowitz was briefly held in a Yonkers police station before being transported directly to Police Headquarters in New York City. At about 1:00 a.m., Mayor Beame arrived to see the suspect personally. After a brief and silent encounter, he announced to the media: "The people of the City of New York can rest easy because of the fact that the police have captured a man whom they believe to be the Son of Sam."

David Berkowitz was born Richard David Falco on June 1, 1953. His mother, Betty Broder, grew up in an impoverished Jewish family and later married Tony Falco, an Italian-American Catholic. The couple ran a fish market together. His parents separated before David was born. His father left for another woman, and his mother later had an affair with a married real estate agent, Joseph Kleinman. When she became pregnant, Kleinman threatened to abandon her if she kept the baby, so she put the child up for adoption and listed Falco as the father. Within a few days of his birth, the infant boy was adopted by Pearl and Nathan Berkowitz of the Bronx. The childless Jewish couple were hardware store retailers of modest means. They reversed the order of the boy's first and middle names and gave him their own surname, raising young David Richard Berkowitz as their only son.

Despite being raised by caring parents in a loving home, Berkowitz had a troubled childhood. Although smart, he lost interest in school at an early age and began a career of petty larceny and arson. Neighbors and relatives would recall Berkowitz as difficult, spoiled and bullying – his adoptive parents consulted at least one psychotherapist due to his misconduct – but his misbehavior never resulted in legal intervention or serious mention in his school records. Berkowitz's adoptive mother died of breast cancer when he was 13 and his home life became strained in later years, particularly because he disliked his father's second wife.

In 1971, at the age of 18, Berkowitz joined the Army and served in the U.S. and South Korea. After an honorable discharge in 1974, he located his birth mother, Betty Falco. After a few visits, she disclosed the details of his illegitimate birth, which greatly disturbed him, particularly because his birth father was deceased. His sense of identity shattered, he lost contact with his birth mother, but stayed in touch with his half-sister, Roslyn. He subsequently held several blue-collar jobs, and at the time of his arrest he was working as a letter sorter for the U.S. Postal Service.

Berkowitz had led what might be called a life of "quiet desperation." He was unknown, ignored and disenfranchised – the perfect dupe, some might say, who could be easily influenced by others. But was he? That still remains to be seen.

After his arrest, Berkowitz was interrogated for about one-half hour during the early morning hours of August 11, 1977. He quickly confessed to the shootings, but the story that he told seemed tailor-made for an insanity defense in court. Berkowitz claimed that his neighbor's dog was one of the reasons that he killed, stating that the dog demanded the blood sacrifice of pretty young girls. He said that that the "Sam" referred to in his letter was his former neighbor, Sam Carr. Berkowitz claimed that Carr's black Labrador retriever, Harvey, was possessed by an ancient demon and that it issued irresistible commands that Berkowitz must kill people. Berkowitz said he once tried to kill the dog, but was unsuccessful due to supernatural interference and the dog recovered from his wounds.

A few weeks after his arrest and confession, Berkowitz was permitted communication with the press. In a letter to the *New York Post* dated September 19, 1977, Berkowitz alluded to his original story of demonic possession but closed with a warning that has been interpreted by some investigators as an admission of criminal accomplices: "There are other Sons out there, God help the world."

Berkowitz was examined by a number of psychiatrists and all but one described him as a paranoid schizophrenic, suffering from delusions and therefore, incompetent to stand trial. The lone exception was Dr. David Abrahamson, who found that Berkowitz was sane and capable of understanding that his actions were criminal. Berkowitz filed a guilty plea at his court appearance and on June 12, 1978, he was sentenced to 25 years to life in prison for each murder, to be served consecutively.

After his arrest, Berkowitz was initially confined to a psychiatric ward in Brooklyn's Kings County Hospital where staff reported that he appeared remarkably untroubled by his new environment. On the day after his sentencing, he was taken first to Sing Sing Correctional Facility in Ossining and then to the upstate Clinton Correctional Facility for psychiatric and physical examinations. Two more months were spent at the Central New York Psychiatric Center in Marcy before his admission to Attica prison. Berkowitz served about a decade in Attica until he was moved to Sullivan Correctional Facility in Fallsburg, New York, where he has remained ever since.

Life in Attica Penitentiary was described by Berkowitz as a "nightmare." On July 10, 1979, there was an attempt on his life and the wound took 56 stitches to close. He refused to identify the person who attacked him with a homemade knife, but suggested that the act was directed by a cult that he used to belong to. It was soon after that strange allegations began to be made about the murders, the cult and the other people involved in the slayings.

It was shortly before this, in early 1979 that Berkowitz mailed a booked about witchcraft to the police in Minot, North Dakota. He had underlined several passages and written a few marginal notes in it, including the phrase: "Arliss [sic] Perry, Hunted, Stalked and Slain. Followed to Calif. Stanford University." The reference was about Arlis Perry, a 19-year-old North Dakota newlywed who had been murdered at Stanford on October 12, 1974.

Arlis was a devout Christian and was involved in many school activities and organizations while attending Bismarck High School, where she met her future husband, Bruce Perry. After she attended what was then Bismarck Junior College for a year, Arlis married Bruce in August 1974 prior to moving to Palo Alto, where Bruce was already an undergraduate student at Stanford. By October 1, Arlis landed a job as a receptionist at a law firm called Spaeth, Blase, Valentine and Klein.

It was at the law firm's office where she was visited by a mystery guest the day before she was killed, an incident that continues to puzzle those who attempted to solve the crime. Witnesses described the man as being in his early twenties and five-foot 10-inches tall. He wore jeans, a plaid shirt and had blonde, curly hair. Co-workers reported that Perry seemed upset by the visitor, who they thought was her husband. However, the identity of the visitor remains unknown to this day.

On the night of October 12, a Saturday, Arlis and Bruce were walking out to mail a letter and got into an argument about air pressure in their car's tires, according to sheriff's reports. Arlis went off by herself around 11:50 p.m. to pray at Stanford Memorial Church. That was the last time Bruce saw her alive.

Arlis Perry – Was her murder proof that the "Son of Sam" killings extended far beyond David Berkowitz?

Around 3:00 a.m., Bruce called campus security after Arlis failed to return home. Shortly before dawn, her body was discovered in the church, partially hidden under the pews. She had been choked, beaten and sexually assaulted using candles from the altar. Detectives found semen at the scene, and retrieved a partial handprint from a candle that was used in the assault. An autopsy later revealed that Arlis was killed by a blow from an ice pick punched just behind her ear. The way her body was positioned led detectives to believe it was a ritualistic killing. At that time, it was recognized as one of the worst crimes ever committed on a college campus.

At first, Bruce Perry was the primary suspect, but detectives soon became convinced he had nothing to do with the murder. The investigation later turned into an unsolved mystery due to a lack of leads – but five years later, Berkowitz suggested that he knew something about the murder.

He mentioned the Perry murder in other letters, suggesting that he knew details of it from the perpetrator himself. Local investigators interviewed him, but his claims were dismissed and the case remains unsolved today. Berkowitz's revelations about the Perry murder were mixed with other stories that he began to tell after his transfer to Sullivan Correction Facility. In 1987 he declared himself a born-again Christian.

According to Berkowitz, he had joined a satanic cult (with connections to the Process Church started by the DeGrimstons) in 1975. He had met some of its members at a party, and initially thought the group was involved only in harmless occult activities such as séances and fortune telling; the group, however, gradually introduced him to drug use, sadism, crime and murder. Berkowitz stated that he knew roughly two dozen core members in New York, but the group had a national membership, mixed up with drug smuggling and other illegal activities.

Berkowitz's alleged connections to satanic activities were announced at the same time that he stated to the press that he had only killed three of the Son of Sam victims: Donna Lauria, Alexander Esau and Valentina Suriani. The rest of the murders were carried out by other shooters, but Berkowitz and several other cult members were involved in every incident by planning the events, providing early surveillance of the victims, and acting as lookouts and drivers at the crime scenes. He refused to divulge the names of his accomplices, because doing so would put his family at risk. Berkowitz claimed that he had once planned to reveal everything he knew but the attack on him at Attica convinced him that doing so might cost him his life. He offered a small amount of information in a letter:

..I was a member of an occult group. Being sworn to secrecy or face death I cannot reveal the name of the group, not do I wish to. This group contained a mixture of satanic practices which included the teachings of Aleister Crowley and Eliphaz [sic] Levi. It was (still is) totally blood-oriented and I am certain you know just what I mean. The Coven's doctrines are a blend of Druidism, the teachings of the Secret Order of the Golden Dawn, Black Magick and a host of other unlawful and obnoxious practices.

As I said, I have no interest in revealing the Coven, especially since I have almost met death on several occasions (once by half an inch) and several others have already perished under mysterious circumstances. There people will stop at nothing, including murder. They have no fear of man-made laws or the Ten Commandments.

Among Berkowitz's unnamed associates was a female cult member whom he claimed fired the gun at Denaro and Keenan. The intended victims survived, he said, because she was unfamiliar with the powerful recoil of the handgun. Berkowitz declared that "at least five" cult members were at the scene of the Freund-Diel shooting, but the actual shooter was a prominent cult associate who had been brought in from outside New York with an unspecified motive. He identified this cult member only by his nickname, "Manson II." Another unnamed figure was the gunman in the Moskowitz-Violante case, a male cult member who had arrived from North Dakota for the occasion, also without explanation.

The only cult members that Berkowitz would name were already deceased – John and Michael Carr, the sons of dog-owner Sam Carr. Both of these other "sons of Sam" were long dead: John had fled New York in February 1979 and "committed suicide" in Minot, North Dakota, two days later and Michael had been in a fatal car accident in October of that same year. Berkowitz claimed that the actual perpetrator of the DeMasi-Lomino shooting was John Carr, and added that a Yonkers police officer, also a cult member, was involved in the crime. He also claimed that Michael Carr fired the shots at Lupo and Placido, adding that cult members had long wanted to kill someone at the Elephas Disco because of the similarity of its name to that of nineteenth-century occultist Eliphas Levi.

Most found Berkowitz's claims to be far-fetched and dismissed them as simply more ramblings from a mentally unbalanced convicted murderer who already had a bizarre reputation. But not everyone was so quick to ignore the stories. Journalist Maury Terry spent six years investigating the Son of Sam case and came to believe that there were at least five different gunmen involved in the attacks, including Berkowitz, John Carr and several others. Terry also noted (perhaps erroneously) that six of the seven shootings fell in close proximity to recognized satanic holidays, the March 8 Voskerichian attack emerging as the sole exception to the pattern. In Terry's opinion, Berkowitz was chosen as the scapegoat by the other members of the cult, who then "decorated" his apartment with occult graffiti and doctoring the "arson ledger" – which includes peculiar, out-of-order entries – to support an insanity plea.

Even skeptical journalists like John Hockenberry asserted that, all satanic cult claims aside, many officials doubted the single-shooter theory, writing, "[w]hat most don't know about the Son of Sam case is that from the beginning, not everyone bought the idea that Berkowitz acted alone." John Santucci, Queens District Attorney at the time of the killings, and police investigator Mike Novotny both expressed their convictions that Berkowitz had accomplices.

Other contemporaries have voiced their belief in the satanic cult theory, including Donna Lauria's father. Hockenberry's report was covered on network news and given in-depth coverage by *Dateline NBC* in 2004. In the report, he discussed Maury Terry, who started investigating the Son of Sam shootings before Berkowitz was arrested. Terry published a series of investigative articles in the Gannett newspapers in 1979, which challenged the official explanation of a lone gunman. Vigorously denied by police at the time, Terry's articles were widely read and were later assembled in book form as *The Ultimate Evil*. Largely impelled by these reports of accomplices and satanic cult activity, the Son of Sam case was reopened by Yonkers police in 1996, but no new charges were filed. Due to the lack of findings, the investigation was eventually suspended – but it remains open.

1979: THE "DEVIL" CAME TO FALL RIVER

For students of American crime, the town of Fall River, Massachusetts, will always be known as the home of Lizzie Borden, who was tried and acquitted of hacking her father and step-mother to death in 1892. However, an even more grisly, twisted and macabre case occurred in the town some ninety years later. This time, there were three victims instead of two, and the killers were self-professed members of a satanic cult.

On October 13, 1979, a couple of joggers out for a morning run discovered the corpse of Doreen Levesque, 17, underneath some bleachers at Fall River High School. Doreen's wrists and ankles were bound and her skull had been crushed with stones. An autopsy later discovered that she had been stabbed several times in the back of the head. The investigation soon brought to light the young girl's troubled history, with drinking and drug charges dating back to age 12, interspersed with several juvenile arrests for shoplifting and petty larceny. Shortly before her death, she had been working as a prostitute. The police were unable to find any suspects in the case.

Three months later, on January 26, 1980, a hunter stumbled upon the battered, decomposing corpse of Barbara Ann Raposa, who had been missing since November. Like Doreen Levesque, her wrists were bound together and her skull had been pulverized by a series of heavy blows that suggested that she had also been beaten by rocks. The missing person report that was on file for Barbara had been filed by Andre Maltais, 43, who was already familiar to the state police because of a call he had made in October, claiming knowledge about the Levesque murder. When he met with detectives at the time, Maltais brought along two prostitutes -- Karen Marsden, 20, and Robin Murphy, 17 -- whom he named as his sources of information. Murphy was reluctant to speak with the police but Marsden claimed that Doreen's killer was a man named Cark Drew, a local pimp and a die-hard Satanist.

By this time, the authorities in Fall River were well-acquainted with the local occult scene. Undercover officers attended cult gatherings at the apartment of prostitute Maureen Sparda, noting the appeal that Satanism seemed to have for pimps and hookers. Stories of gruesome animal sacrifices were recorded, along with stories that humans were being used for rituals from time to time.

Carl Drew was avidly immersed in Satanism. His criminal record included three armed robbery charges between December 1974 and February 1975. Pimping required less work, but Drew had a violent temper and kept his women in line with threats of beatings, mutilation and death. In February 1978, Drew was arrested for beating a customer, but he escaped from the Fall River jail and fled through a blizzard. He was finally recaptured near the Canadian border by New Hampshire state troopers, but by this time, the case against him had fallen apart. Detectives had neglected to question the beaten customer before he died and they had nothing to hold Drew on. Two years later, Drew had turned to the occult with a passion, wearing tattoos of the Devil on his chest and left arm, the latter sporting writing that read "Satan's Avengers."

The police still had no evidence to support a murder charge against Drew. Karen Marsden had stopped talking to the police a few months earlier, stating that she was terrified of Drew – whom she called "The Devil" – and that he made threats to kill her for what little she had already said. On January 30, another prostitute told detectives that Marsden knew details about Barbara Raposa's death, but Marsden refused to discuss it, repeating that she was too terrified to talk because of Drew's threats.

The case went in a bizarre direction on February 5. Andre Maltais approached detectives with claims of a "psychic vision" that revealed to him details of the Raposa murder. By the time that he finished leading investigators on a tour of the crime scene, Maltais found himself charged as a suspect. On February 9, Robin Murphy came forward and stated that she had watched Maltais beat Raposa to death in November.

On the same day, Karen Marsden was reported missing by her grandmother, who confirmed the threats that Marsden had received from Carl Drew. The following day, February 10, Carl Drew was again questioned by the police. Drew, 26, proudly admitted to worshipping Satan, but denied any role in the recent homicides and disappearances. His satanic tattoos were photographed for the record and Drew was released for the lack of any solid evidence against him.

On February 16, 1980, the police found a crude, handmade altar in the woods outside Fall River. Nearby, they found the burned-out remains of a car that had been stolen on February 6, two days before Karen Marsden was last seen alive. Piece of bone were found in the trunk, but their size and condition made them useless as forensic evidence. Meanwhile, rumors continued to surface about Carl Drew's involvement in the recent murders, stories describing the ritual murders of several women and at least one unidentified man who had allegedly been tortured to death with a baseball bat shoved up his rectum. Another member of the cult, some whispered, was another pimp, 24-year old Carl Davis.

On April 13, a partial human skull was found in the woods in nearby Westport, Massachusetts. New searches of the area found pieces of scalp with hair still attached, articles of women's clothing and the rotting carcasses of three dead cats. In time, the partial skull was identified as belonging to Karen Marsden, using x-rays taken in 1978, when she was treated for a sinus ailment.

Meanwhile, on April 14, Robin Murphy confessed her role in Marsden's murder to a girlfriend. Grilled by the police, she named the other participants in the crime as Carl Drew and Carl Davis, both alleged to be members of the local satanic cult. She had also witnessed the murder of Doreen Levesque, which had been committed by Drew and "a black man named Willie," who police later identified as 31-year-old William Smith.

On May 9, 1980, Drew, Davis and Murphy were indicted for the murder of Karen Marsden. The formal charge stated that Carl Drew "participated with others in the prearranged, ritualistic slaying of the victim and the dismemberment of the victim's body." Davis was already in jail, serving 30 days on an assault and battery charge, when the indictments were handed down, and all three defendants were held without bail.

In January 1981, Robin Murphy turned state's evidence against Andre Maltais, pleading guilty to second-degree murder in the Raposa case and drawing a life in prison term, with eligibility for parole in 15 years. Maltais' courtroom display of Bibles and portraits of Jesus failed to convince jurors of his piety and he was convicted of first-degree murder, earning a sentence of life without parole. He served six years, still proclaiming his innocence, before a series of strokes killed him in 1987.

Carl Drew's trial for the murder of Karen Marsden began on March 2, 1981. Prosecutors did their best to stay away from the satanic cult issues that ran through the case, believing that it was too inflammatory for the court. Fall River detectives objected to this tactic, stating that Drew's occult rituals were the heart of the case. Robin Murphy's testimony for the state was grim enough. She described how Marsden was stoned by her killers, tortured by having her hair and fingernails ripped out, beaten savagely and slashed with a knife before Drew broke her neck. While Marsden was being tortured, Murphy was ordered to perform oral sex on her as a sign of obedience to Drew. Unsatisfied, Drew had Murphy slash Marsden's throat, after which he severed her head and kicked it around like a soccer ball. Marsden's fingers were cut off in an effort to steal her rings and Drew finished by having sex with the headless corpse, carving an "X" on her chest, and smearing Marsden's blood on Murphy's forehead as a symbol of membership in the cult.

Carl Drew testified in his own defense, blandly denying any occult ties, taking part in rituals or participating in any criminal activities whatsoever. By the time of his trial, he had removed a portion of the tattoo from his arm so that it merely read "Avengers," but this was not enough to cancel out the horror of Murphy's testimony. Convicted of first-degree murder on Friday, March 13, Drew was sentenced to life imprisonment without parole. Murphy was convicted of second-degree murder in Marsden's killing in exchange for her testimony against Drew. She was paroled in 2004.

Indictments for the murder of Donna Levesque were returned in March 1981, while Drew's first trial was still in progress. The indictments named the killers as Drew, Robin Murphy, William Smith and the late Karen Marsden. In May 1982, on the eve of Smith's murder trial, Murphy recanted her story of watching the murder take place and Smith was released for lack of evidence. That November, without Murphy's testimony, the case against Drew for the murder of Levesque was dropped when a judge ruled that his right to a speedy trial had been violated. Prosecutors had been stalling as they tried to gather more evidence, but eventually called the whole thing "an exercise in futility."

Carl Davis – Drew's fellow murderous pimp – was never tried for murder in Fall River. However, he was convicted in 1982 for assaulting prostitute and fellow Satanist, Maureen Sparda, with a deadly weapon, drawing a prison term of seven years. He was released after serving the minimum possible time and vanished into history.

1981: CHICAGO'S "RIPPER CREW"

Chicago is a city that has seen more than its share of horror over the decades, from the unknown number of murder victims lured to the "Murder Castle" by H.H. Holmes in the 1890s to the atrocities perpetrated by John Wayne Gacy in the 1970s, but few were as strange as the Ripper murders of the early 1980s. A serial killer, predictably dubbed "Jack the Ripper" by the press, was stalking young women and prostitutes in the Windy City and discarding their mutilated corpses like garbage. Homicide detectives had no ideas about the killer's motive or identity and they couldn't even manage to agree on an actual body count. The speculation, which appeared each day in the Chicago newspapers was bad, but the truth, when it was finally revealed, was even worse.

On May 23, 1981, Linda Sutton, 21, was abducted in Elmhurst, a Chicago suburb, by persons unknown. Ten days later, her mutilated body was recovered from a field in Villa Park, adjacent to the Rip Van Winkle Motel. But the discovery of the body – and realizing that it was Linda Sutton – was not as easy as it seemed.

The aging motor lodge was located in a seedy area that was filled with second-hand shops, fast-food joints, and bars where shady characters hung out. The body had technically been discovered by a motel maid, who had noticed a bad odor near the motel that grew worse with each passing day. She told the motel's manager about it and he walked out into the field to see if he could get rid of whatever was causing the smell. It was not, as he expected, a dead animal. It was a woman whose remains consisted largely of bones and some clinging flesh. He ran for the office and called the police.

Three detectives arrived on the scene and they could see that the victim had been there quite a while. She was so decomposed that they could see her skeletal structure, but the maggots were still there, doing their work—an unusual combination of postmortem characteristics. The woman clearly had been murdered, because she had been bound with handcuffs before being dumped in the field. She also had cloth stuffed in her mouth, and still wore a sweater and panties, which had been pulled down to her thighs. In one of her socks was a small wad of dollar bills, so robbery had probably not been a motive.

The key issue at the moment was to first establish the corpse's identity and then figure out when she had died. In the condition the body was in, that would be difficult. Police first examined the scene and then sent the body to the county coroner. They then searched the missing person reports but found no one who could have been the woman in the field. A detective with the Chicago Police Department suggested that the practice of rolling money inside socks probably indicated that the victim had been a prostitute – making identification even more difficult. Prostitutes often drifted from place to place and didn't keep in regular contact with their families. The only people who might notice that a prostitute was missing would be other hookers or their pimps or drug dealers, none of whom would be likely to go to the police. But fingerprints and dental records helped, and in less than two weeks, they had an ID: Linda Sutton, 21. As they had suspected, she was a prostitute with a string of arrests. She was also the mother of two children, both of whom lived with Sutton's mother.

But a twist in the case came from the coroner -- despite the body's advanced state of decomposition, he had determined that she had been dead for only three days. The remains' advanced rate of decomposition was caused by the fact that both breasts had been removed. This had allowed for an invasion of parasites that had devoured her flesh in record time.

Linda Sutton had been brutally mutilated and murdered – and she would not be the last.

On February 12, 1982, a 35-year-old cocktail waitress was abducted from her car. The fuel gauge showed that the tank was empty, implying that she had run out of gas and had possibly been trying to flag down a passing motorist when she was abducted. Her purse was on the front seat and the keys were still in the ignition. A search turned up her nude body on an embankment near the road. She had been raped, tortured and mutilated. The press was asked not to report that one of her breasts had been amputated, so that the police could retain that detail for interrogation purposes.

A few days later, the body of a Hispanic woman wearing an engagement ring was discovered. She had also been raped and strangled. While her breasts were not removed, they had been badly bitten. Her killer had also masturbated over her body.

On May 15, 1982, another young woman Lorraine Borowski, 21, was scheduled to open the Elmhurst realtor's office where she worked. Employees who turned up for work that morning found the office locked. Borowski's shoes and the scattered contents of her purse were strewn outside the door. She had apparently been abducted as she crossed the parking lot. The police were called at once, but five months passed before her corpse was found on October 10 in the Clarendon Hills Cemetery, south of Villa Park. She had been repeatedly raped and then subjected to having one of her breasts sliced off with a piece of wire. Finally, one of her attackers killed her with a hatchet.

Two weeks later, on May 29, Shui Mak was abducted on as she was returning home from her family's restaurant in Streamwood. She had been riding in her brother's car, but after they argued, he dropped her off to wait for a ride with other relatives, whom he believed were following them. They never saw her alive again. She was abducted moments later, although her body was not found until September 30, dumped at a construction site in Barrington. She had also been mutilated; her left breast sliced from her body.

The police now had a number of similar killings to deal with and the link seemed obvious: young women who all had lost a breast in a similar grotesque manner. They had a difficult time finding any leads, however, until another victim turned up. But this one, Angel York, a young prostitute, had survived. On June 13, she reported that two men were using a red van to abduct women and handcuffs them inside, where they were raped and tortured. They had even forced her to use a large knife to cut her own breast, which she said drove one man into a frenzy. He cut her more and then masturbated into the wound before closing it with duct-tape and dumping her into the streets.

The police now had something to go on but they were unable to stop the men from killing another woman. On August 28, Sandra Delaware was found dumped along the side of the Chicago River. Her wrists were bound together behind her with a shoelace and her left breast had been amputated in the same fashion as the prior victims. Her bra was knotted around her throat.

On September 8, Rose Davis, 30, was found stabbed, raped and strangled behind a stairway of a North Lake Shore apartment building. A black sock was tied around her neck and her clothing was in disarray. Her face was crushed and blood pooled beneath her. It turned out later that she had been beaten with a hatchet. Her breasts had been slashed and cut and her abdomen was full of small punctures.

Chicago's "Ripper Crew" from left to right: Andrew Kokoraleis, Tommy Kokoraleis, Robin Gecht and Edward Spreitzer. Gecht was the sadistic "mastermind" of the group but his friends were terrified to testify against him.

On October 6, detectives in the case got their first real break. Another prostitute, Beverly Washington, 20, was abducted from off the street, mutilated, raped, and dumped. Her abductors had left her for dead, but she survived and was taken to the hospital. She was able to give the police a description of the gang of men in the van. The driver had been a slender white man who looked to be around 25, wearing a flannel shirt and square-toed boots. He had greasy brown hair and a mustache. Washington said he had offered more money than she'd asked for and had seemed unaccountably nervous. When she climbed into the back of the van with him, he produced a gun. He ordered her to remove her clothes. Then he handcuffed her, forced her to perform oral sex, and threatened her with violence if she did not swallow the handful of pills that he held out to her. As she passed out, she saw him holding a cord over her, and she feared that she was going to die. The man dumped her into the trash, one breast severed and the other nearly so, but someone discovered her and called the police. She told police that the man who attacked her was driving a red van with tinted windows and a wooden divider behind the driver's seat.

The details provided by Washington led to an arrest. On October 20, the police pulled over a red van and questioned the driver. He had red hair and did not resemble Washington's description of her assailant, but the van was a perfect match to the one she described. The driver told officers his name was Eddie Spreitzer, and that the van belonged to his boss, Robin Gecht. The police directed Spreitzer to drive to Gecht's house and had him get Gecht to come outside. When he walked out, they knew he matched the description that Washington's had given, right down to his flannel shirt and square-toed boots. Gecht greeted the officers, acting as if he had no worries at all. Detectives knew that they either had the wrong man – or Gecht was utterly arrogant, confident that he was untouchable.

Later, Beverly Washington picked Gecht out of a photo array as the man who had assaulted her, but when detectives brought him in for an interview, he had a lawyer with him. It was clear that he was going to be quite careful in his dealings with the police – something he had learned from experience. Gecht was an odd character, who had been ousted from his home as a teenager for molesting his younger sister. A few years later, he worked for contractor and serial killer John Wayne Gacy, who had been arrested for the murders of nearly three dozen young men and boys just a few years earlier. Gecht was known to remark to friends that Gacy's "only mistake" had been burying his victims under his home, where the bodies were easily found. In other words, Gecht showed no awareness of the wrongness of Gacy's brutality -- he just thought the man had gone about it the wrong way.

At first, little information was obtained from Spreitzer and Gecht, but after some time had passed, detectives came to believe that Spreitzer might break down. He seemed to be genuinely afraid of Gecht. The detectives leaned on him and his guilt finally got the better of him. Spreitzer's interrogation produced a 78-page statement.

Spreitzer first admitted to driving the van as Gecht committed a drive-by shooting in which a man died and another was left paralyzed. Investigators quickly identified the incident as the shooting of a drug dealer named Rafael Torado. After that, his story got even darker. Spreitzer was driving and Gecht directed him to slow down to pick up a black prostitute. Gecht had sex with her and then took her into an alley and used a knife to remove her left breast, which he then tossed on the floor of the van. The more he talked, the more upset Spreitzer seemed to get, claiming that he didn't like all of the blood. He said that during such incidents, Gecht sometimes had sex with the breast on the spot. He also described how Gecht had shot a black woman in the head, chained her up, and used bowling balls to weight her down in water. He believed that she had never been found. Later, Spreitzer would confess to taking part in these blood-soaked incidents. He admitted cutting off a woman's breasts, but said she was dead at the time. On another occasion, Gecht forced him to have sexual contact with the woman's gaping wounds.

By the time Spreitzer was finished, he had offered details for seven outright murders and one aggravated battery. His interrogators were shaken by the aberrant nature of the acts, yet they believed they now had some leverage with Gecht, who was in another interrogation room. They collected photographs of known victims and laid them before him. He looked at them without much interest and denied knowing any of the women. Using a tried and true detective's trick, they took him to an area where he could plainly see Spreitzer showing something to other officers, hinting that Gecht that if he didn't make a deal, Spreitzer was bound to make one first. But Gecht didn't waver, continuing to act as if he had nothing to hide. The detectives were frustrated. Spreitzer had clearly implicated him, so why didn't Gecht react?

But Gecht knew something the detectives didn't. His closeness had an odd effect on Spreitzer. He suddenly changed his story, as if afraid, and said that Gecht hadn't murdered anyone. His account became so confusing that his interrogators did not know what to believe. Spreitzer now said that another man, his girlfriend's brother, Andrew Kokoraleis, had been the killer, but he could not offer many details about him. When asked, Gecht confirmed that he knew Kokoraleis and even provided police with an address for him. He appeared to be undisturbed by this new development.

Still frustrated, the police went in search of Kokoraleis and found that he and his brother, Thomas, had been recent tenants at the same hotel in Villa Park where the body of Linda Sutton had been found. They had left a forwarding address for any mail that they might receive. When they found Kokoraleis, they found his answers to questions were so erratic that they took him downtown for further questioning. The detectives wondered if three men could really kill together in such a horrendous manner.

They did not yet know the half of it.

It wasn't long before Kokoraleis also confessed. In his statement, he talked about how they had kidnapped women off the streets, raped them, and stabbed them with knives, razors, tin can lids, and can openers. They used piano wire to amputate one or both breasts and masturbated onto the open wounds. He admitted to the murders of Rose Davis and Lorraine Borowski, and inadvertently confessed that he had been involved in the deaths of eighteen women. As he described the assault on Sandra Delaware, he said that he had shoved a rock into her mouth to keep her from screaming, forced a wine bottle into her that made her bleed badly, and stabbed her with a knife. An autopsy report confirmed these horrific details.

Meanwhile, as the interrogations continued, detectives were also asking acquaintances about their personalities and habits. It soon became clear that Gecht had a breast fetish, asking girls he knew to let him stab them with pins. He allegedly forced his wife to endure much more, including inflicting wounds that became infected, but she never turned him in. But when the detectives began questioning Kokoraleis's slow-witted brother, Tommy, they were in for another unpleasant surprise. He indicated that he, too, had been on this "Ripper Crew." Shortly, he broke down and confessed, adding even more gruesome details about sex, blood — and Satan.

It was Tommy who first spoke of the "satanic chapel" in the attic of Gecht's Northwest Side home, where captive women were tortured with knives and ice picks, gang-raped and then sacrificed to the Devil by the crew. The killers gathered there during the evening hours after Gecht's wife had left for work. Supposedly, Gecht had painted six red-and-black crosses on the walls and covered the altar with a red cloth.

Tommy told the police that they would all kneel together around the altar and Gecht would produce the freshly-removed breasts. He would read passages from occult books as each man masturbated into the body part. When everyone was finished, Gecht would cut it up and hand around the pieces for them to eat. Tommy said that he had witnessed two murders and had participated in nearly a dozen such rituals. When the detectives asked him why he had done such macabre and illegal activities, he told them in all seriousness that Gecht had the power to make them do whatever he wanted. "You just have to do it," he said with conviction. Apparently he was convinced that Gecht had some supernatural connection with the Devil, and he was afraid of what Gecht might do to him if he did not do as he was told.

A search of the residences of the "Ripper Crew" did reveal the "satanic chapel," which was as Tommy described, as well as a large amount of occult literature. The killers had followed a popular trend of the time, delving into Satanism and heavy metal, but unlike most restless teenagers who claimed to be "devil worshippers," they had taken things to another level.

After the interrogations, the killers were held at the Pontiac Correctional Center on $1 million bond on a variety of charges. Gecht adamantly refused to admit to the charges, but the evidence against him continued to mount. As the police interviewed more people, they learned that Spreitzer and the Kokoraleis brothers were not alone in their fear of Gecht or their belief in his powers. Others also claimed that he had a real ability to draw people to him and get them to do his bidding. One person warned detectives to never look into Gecht's eyes. No matter how sick or disgusting an act might be, he could inspire others to get involved. He got his start by molesting his sister, then working for Gacy and finally developing a keen interest in Satanism and its secret rituals.

Needless to say, the newspapers grabbed the story and ran with it, using headlines that linked the "Ripper Crew" or the "Chicago Rippers" with the notorious Jack the Ripper who slaughtered prostitutes in London's Whitechapel district in 1888. Each member of this deadly crew faced his own separate trial.

Gecht attempted to avoid trial by offering an insanity plea, but after a psychiatric evaluation, he was found to be competent to stand trial. He was also considered to have been sane at the time of the offenses – sick and depraved, but still sane. He did have a mistrial, so his second trial began on September 20, 1983.

The prosecutor presented a lot of startling, and compelling, evidence. They presented what the police had found when they discovered the "chapel," as well as a rifle used in a shooting. They also found satanic literature and a "trophy" box owned by Gecht in which Andrew had described seeing as many as fifteen pieces of female breast. From victim reports, the way the crew operated was detailed for the jury: Women had been kidnapped, held against their will, tortured, raped and then had their breasts cut off for satanic sacrifice. Most of the women died, but they had likely suffered horrendous pain before they finally expired. The few that survived would relive their ordeal for their rest of their lives.

Gecht took the stand to speak in his own defense. He had previously admitted to having attacked Beverly Washington, but in court, he insisted that he had killed no one and was innocent of rape and aggravated battery. He protested that during the time when most of the murders had occurred, he was not even acquainted with the other defendants. Despite compelling eyewitness testimony, as well as testimony from women who claimed that Gecht had asked them to cut off their nipples for him, the confessions of the others implicating Gecht were not admissible against him. With no physical evidence linking him to murder, he could not be prosecuted for any of the killings, and his accomplices were not willing to testify against him.

308

Nevertheless, the jury found Gecht guilty on all of the counts with which he was charged: attempted murder, rape, deviate sexual assault, aggravated battery, and armed violence. He was sentenced to 120 years at the Menard Correctional Center.

The other trials followed. Edward Spreitzer and Andrew Kokoraleis were sentenced to death. On March 16, 1999, Kokoraleis was executed by lethal injection at Tamms Correctional Center in southern Illinois for the murder of Lorraine Borowski. Edward Spreitzer's death sentence was commuted in George H. Ryan's last-minute commutation of all death sentences in Illinois in 2003. Incidentally, Andrew Kokoraleis' was Governor Ryan's only execution, just over two months into his administration. Kokoraleis was also the last inmate executed in Illinois, almost twelve years before Governor Pat Quinn signed legislation to abolish the death penalty on March 9, 2011, and commuted fifteen death sentences to life imprisonment without parole.

Tommy Kokoraleis was convicted of Lorraine Borowski's murder and received a life sentence. His sentence was later commuted and he is now scheduled to be released on September 30, 2017. He is currently in Illinois River Correctional Center.

One of the most frightening parts of the story is that, despite the fact that he was sentenced to serve 120 years in prison, Robin Gecht may be released from behind bars someday. Even though he was obviously the ringleader of the so-called "Ripper Crew," he could not officially be linked to any of the murders – and he will someday be eligible for parole.

We can only hope that he never gets out.

1984: THE "NIGHT STALKER"

From June 1984 to August 1985, Richard Ramirez, a vagrant from El Paso, Texas, terrorized the people of Los Angeles. He entered homes in the middle of the night (the media dubbed him the "Night Stalker" after an AC/DC song) and shot or strangled the men present so that he could rape and murder the females and children in the house. The year of terror that he brought to Southern California in the 1980s was unlike anything ever experienced in the region before.

And, not surprisingly, he claimed to do it all in honor of Satan.

Ricardo Munoz Ramirez was born in El Paso, the youngest of five children to working-class Mexican immigrants Julian Ramirez and Mercedes Munoz. Those who knew him always referred to him as a loner, even as a childhood. Ramirez received early inspiration for his later crimes from his cousin, Mike, a Vietnam veteran who enthralled Ramirez with photographs of Vietnamese women that he had tortured and killed during the war. The two spent a lot of time together, often driving around and smoking pot, and Ramirez later claimed that Mike showed him the best ways to cut and kill people. Ramirez was only a boy when Mike murdered his wife, further enhancing his fascination with blood and death.

In the years that followed, Ramirez began getting into trouble. He started skipping school, smoking marijuana and sniffing glue. He attended Thomas Jefferson High School in El Paso, but dropped out in the ninth grade after being arrested twice for drug possession. He continued to use drugs and was arrested several times for possession and minor incidents of theft. He eventually ended up in California, where he was arrested two more times for auto theft in 1981 and 1984. During this time, Ramirez began cultivating a "demonic personality," inspired by his drug use, interest in rock music and the pseudo-Satanism that became a part of the heavy metal culture of the late 1970s and 1980s. He often etched five-pointed pentagrams on his body and years later, at his trial, he would shout "Hail Satan!" in open court. At some point in 1984, Ramirez began to put all of his passions for death, murder, bloodshed and chaos into practice and his murder spree began.

On June 28, 1984, Ramirez removed a window screen and crept into the home of a 79-year-old woman named Jennie Vincow of Glassell Park in Los Angeles. Her body was discovered by her son, Jack, the next morning. She had been sexually assaulted, stabbed repeatedly, and her throat slashed so savagely that she was nearly decapitated. Ramirez also ransacked the place and made off with any valuables that he could find.

Ramirez stayed quiet for the next ten months until on March 17, 1985, Angela Barrios, 22, was attacked as she got out of her car in the garage of the condominium that she shared with a roommate, Dayle Ozazaki, 34. Barrios described the man who assaulted her as tall and dressed entirely in black, with a baseball cap pulled down low on his head. He came at her with a gun in his hand and shot at her face as she raised her hands in self-defense. The bullet hit her in the hand and was deflected by her car keys, which she still gripped in her fist. As Barrios fell to the ground, Ramirez pushed his way into the condominium. She lay there without moving for some time and then went out the garage door and around to the front door. She hid when she saw Ramirez leaving, but he spotted her and raised the gun to shoot her again. She asked him not to kill her and he lowered the gun and ran away.

Moments later, Barrios entered the house though the open front door. She found Okazaki lying dead on the kitchen floor. She had been shot in the forehead at close range and her blouse had been pulled up to expose her breasts. Hernandez called the police and on the ground outside, investigators found a baseball cap with AC/DC on the front of it.

Within an hour of the attack on Angela Barrios and murder of Dayle Okazaki, a car driven by Tsia-Lian Yu, 30, was forced to a stop near Monteray Park by a car driven by a man later identified as Ramirez. Ramirez jumped out and pulled Yu out of her car. Joseph Duenas stepped out onto the balcony of his nearby apartment after hearing a woman screaming for help. When he saw what was happening, he ran inside and called the police, then stepped back onto the balcony. Duenas saw the man push Yu away, get into her car and drive away. As Yu's attacker sped away from the scene, he passed a car containing Jorge Gallegos and his girlfriend. Gallegos saw the driver's profile and noted the number of the license plate of the car. Both men later testified at Ramirez's trial. Meanwhile, Yu crawled a short distance and then collapsed on the ground. When the police arrived, she was still alive, but barely. She stopped breathing moments later and when the ambulance arrived it was too late. She died before she could be taken to the hospital. An autopsy revealed that she had been shot twice in the chest at close range. The .22-caliber bullet recovered from Yu's body was fired by the same gun that had killed Dayle Okazaki.

Ramirez's next victims were found ten days later, on the morning of March 27. Vincent Zazzara, 64, was a retired investment banker who had opened a pizzaria. His son, Peter, came to visit that morning and after ringing the bell several times with no answer, he let himself into the house. His father's body was lying on a couch in the den. He had been shot in the head. Vincent Zazzara's wife, Maxine, 44, was found naked on the bed. Her eyes had been gouged out and she had been stabbed repeatedly in the face, neck, stomach, and groin. She had also been shot in the head. The coroner believed that she was already dead from the gunshot wound before her slayer began stabbing and mutilating her. The house had been ransacked and burglarized.

On April 15, Ramirez returned to Monterey Park and broke into the home of William and Lillian Doi, entering their bedroom while they slept. Ramirez first shot William Doi in the face, the bullet passing through his tongue and becoming lodged in his throat. Then Ramirez beat him into unconsciousness. Lillian Doi was slapped into submission and then Ramirez bound her hands behind her back as he searched the house. Before he left, he returned to the bedroom and raped her. However, he had not killed her husband, who managed to crawl from his bed and dial the police. He was unable to tell the dispatcher what had happened, but the call was traced and an ambulance and patrol car were dispatched to the address. William Doi died in the ambulance on the way to the hospital. Lillian Doi was treated for her injuries and was able to give the police a description of the couple's attacker.

As the attacks continued, Los Angeles was plunged into a state of panic. One police official referred to the murderous rapist as the "Valley Intruder," while newspapers initially referred to him as the "Midnight Stalker." Meanwhile, Ramirez was just getting started with his bloody spree.

On May 29, police officers found Malvia Keller, 83, and her invalid sister, Blanche Wolfe, 80, in their Monrovia home. Both women had been beaten with a hammer and Wolfe had a puncture wound above one ear. Keller had been raped and an inverted pentagram had been drawn in lipstick on her inner thigh. A second pentagram was found on the bedroom wall over Wolfe's body. Perhaps most horribly, forensics showed that the sisters had been attacked about two days before they were found. Doctors were able to revive Wolfe, but Keller died soon afterwards.

On May 30, Ramirez entered the Burbank home of Ruth Wilson, 41, and awakened her by shining a flashlight in her face. He ordered her out of bed at gunpoint and marched her to the bedroom of her 12-year-old son. Ramirez put the gun to the child's head, warning Wilson not to make a sound. He then handcuffed the boy and locked him in a closet. Assuming that he only intended to burglarize the house, Ruth tried to cooperate but Ramirez tied her up with pantyhose and raped her on her bed. Bravely, she told Ramirez that he must have had a "very unhappy life" to have done this to her. He reportedly told her that she looked "pretty good" for her age and said he was going to let her live although he had killed many others. She complained that the pantyhose that he tied her up with was cutting off the circulation in her arms and Ramirez loosened them, and then brought her a robe before releasing her son from the closet. He handcuffed them side-by-side and departed. The boy was able to get to the phone and call 911.

On July 2, the body of Mary Louise Cannon, 75, was found in her Arcadia home. She had been beaten and her throat slit. The house had been ransacked.

On July 5, Ramirez returned to Arcadia and savagely beat Whitney Bennett, 16, a junior at La Cañada High School, with a tire iron. Whitney required 478 stitches after the attack, but she survived. Two days later, on July 7, the body of Joyce Lucille Nelson was found in her home in Monterey Park. She had been beaten to death with a blunt object.

Later that same night in Monterey Park, Sophie Dickman, 63, was awakened at around 3:30 a.m. by a "tall, skinny man dressed in black." The man ordered her out of bed at gunpoint and locked her in the bathroom. After he ransacked the house, he returned and pushed her back onto the bed. He attempted to rape and sodomize her but could not maintain an erection. Frustrated and humiliated, he screamed at her and then gathered up her valuables and left. Sophie was amazed that she had survived the encounter.

On July 20, Ramirez showed up in Glendale. He entered the home of Max and Lela Kneiding, both 66, who had been following the crimes in the news. Like thousands of other Los Angeles area residents who were terrified by the thought of the homicidal maniac who was slipping into houses while the occupants slept, the Kneidings had locked all their doors and windows. Despite their precautions, Ramirez cut through a screen on a sliding door and unlocked it. He entered the bedroom, turned on the lights and began to scream. With a machete, he hacked at Max's neck and then swung at Lela, but missed. He pulled his .22-caliber pistol from his pocket and pulled the trigger, but the gun jammed. As his victims begged for their lives, Ramirez cleared the gun and shot them to death. Then, he cut them apart and mutilated them with the machete. He robbed the house and this time, Ramirez had a police scanner with him and fled when a report of shots being fired came over the radio.

On August 6, Ramirez targeted another couple, Christopher and Virginia Petersen, ages 38 and 27. He entered again through a sliding door and slipped into the house. Just before he entered the bedroom, he cocked a .25 caliber automatic pistol. Virginia, a light sleeper, awoke to the sound. As Ramirez walked toward her, she screamed and he shot her in the face. The bullet went through the roof of her mouth and down her throat, exiting out the back of her neck. Christopher Petersen awoke to the commotion and Ramirez shot him in the temple. However, the ammunition in the gun was old and had lost its potency. The bullet only glanced off Petersen's skull. He jumped up and attacked Ramirez, who shot at him two more times. Both shots missed and as they fought, Petersen was thrown onto the floor. Ramirez fled through the open sliding door. The Petersens both survived the attack.

Two nights later, Ramirez attacked again. He broke into the home of Elyas and Sakina Abowath, 35 and 29. He immediately shot Elyas in the head and killed him, and then attacked Sakina. He raped and sodomized her and forced her to perform oral sex on him. He left the house after robbing it, leaving Sakina battered but alive.

Los Angeles County was terrorized by the brutal attacks and murders. The Night Stalker crimes were becoming more frequent and each attack seemed bloodier than the last. Detectives had no doubt that he would strike again – and soon. But as it turned out, Ramirez decided to abandon familiar territory after the attack on the Abowaths. He headed north to San Francisco.

On August 18, Peter and Barbara Pan were found in their blood-soaked bed in a housing development in San Francisco. Both had been shot in the head. Peter, 66, was pronounced dead at the scene but Barbara, 64, survived, although she was an invalid for the rest of her life. Ramirez had scrawled another inverted pentagram on the wall, along with the words "Jack the Knife," which was from a song called "The Ripper" by heavy metal band Judas Priest. Fearing that the Night Stalker had traveled north, San Francisco detectives sent a bullet that had been removed from Peter Pan to a forensic team in L.A. The bullet matched those recovered from earlier Los Angeles crime scenes.

Night Stalker panic had now spread to San Francisco. Hoping to allay the fears of the public, Mayor Dianne Feinstein spoke publicly about the hunt for the killer, angering detectives who felt that she had impeded the investigation by giving out too much information about the crimes. But the San Francisco police caught a break when the manager of the Bristol Hotel, a cheap dive in the Tenderloin District, came forward with information about a young man who fit the Night Stalker's description and who had stayed in the place several times over the past year. Detectives searched the room he had last stayed in (he had checked out on August 17) and found a pentagram drawn on the bathroom door. Investigators then located a man who said that he had purchased some jewelry – a diamond ring and a pair of cufflinks – from a man who fit the killer's description. The items had belonged to Peter Pan.

On August 24, while San Francisco cops were scrambling to find the mysterious tenant of the Bristol Hotel, Ramirez was targeting new victims in Mission Viejo, about fifty miles south of Los Angeles.

Bill Carns and his 29-year-old fiancée had just fallen asleep when they were suddenly shocked into consciousness by the sound of gunshots in their bedroom. Instinctively, the young woman reached for her fiancée, but he had already been seriously wounded. Before she could react, the intruder grabbed her by the hair and dragged her into another bedroom, where he tied her wrists and ankles. He rummaged through the house, looking for items to steal, but found little that was portable. Angry, Ramirez returned to the bedroom and raped the young woman two times.

Afraid of what he might do to her next, she tried to get him to take some money that Carns had in a dresser drawer. Ramirez forced her to "swear to Satan" that she was telling the truth about the money. She did as he asked and Ramirez found the money. He then demanded that she swear her love for Satan. Terrified, she mumbled, "I love Satan." He ordered her to say it again and again. He yanked her by the hair, made her kneel and then forced her to perform oral sex on him. When he was finished, Ramirez pushed her back on the floor and left her there. As soon as she could free herself from her bindings, she immediately called the police.

Ramirez didn't know it yet, but his days of chaos were numbered.

Richard Ramirez

Earlier that night, a teenager who had been working on his motorcycle in his parents' garage had noticed an unfamiliar orange Toyota driving around the neighborhood. He noticed it again later on. Something about the car and the driver made him suspicious, so he wrote down the license plate number. The next morning, he called the police and it was discovered that the 1976 Toyota had been stolen in L.A.'s Chinatown while the owner was having dinner. An alert was put out for the car and, two days later, it was located in the Rampart section of Los Angeles. The police kept the car under surveillance in hopes that the Night Stalker would return for it, but he didn't. A forensics team scoured the car and came up with a fingerprint that was matched a few hours later. The print belonged to Ricardo "Richard" Ramirez and it matched a print that had been lifted from the windowsill of the Pan's home in San Francisco. The police finally had an identity for the dreaded Night Stalker – now they needed to find him before he killed again.

While all of this was going on, Ramirez had gone to Arizona to visit his brother. He returned to Los Angeles on August 31, arriving at the Greyhound bus station. As he was leaving the station, he noticed that the area was flooded with cops but managed to slip away unnoticed. He had no idea that he had been identified as the Night Stalker. However, as he walked into a corner store, the owners recognized him and shouted in alarm. Ramirez turned to run and saw a rack of newspapers that had his photograph on the front. He grabbed one and fled.

Ramirez ran for the next two miles, heading east from downtown. He hopped fences and ended up in the yard of Faustino Pinon. Spotting a Ford Mustang in the driveway with the keys in the ignition, he jumped in and started the engine. He didn't notice that the car's owner was underneath it, working on the transmission. As soon as Pinon heard the car start up, he rolled out from under it. Angry, he reached through the window and grabbed Ramirez by the neck. Ramirez cried out that he had a gun, but the furious Pinon ignored him. Ramirez put the Mustang into gear and tried to drive away, but Pinon hung on and refused to let go. The car crashed into a fence, then into the garage.

Pinon got the door open, pulled Ramirez out, and threw him onto the ground. Ramirez crawled away and then scrambled to his feet. He fled into the street just as a young woman named Angelina de la Torres was getting into her Ford Granada. Ramirez ran to the car and stuck his head into the driver's window. He yelled at de la Torres to give him the keys, threatening to kill her if she didn't. Angelina screamed for help and her husband, Manuel, came running from the backyard. He grabbed a piece of metal fence post as he passed through the gate next to the house.

At the same time, Jose Burgoin, who had heard the struggle in Faustino Pinon's driveway, had called the police. He ran outside to help Pinon, and when he heard Angelina's scream, he called to his sons, Jaime and Julio, for assistance. As the brothers ran to help Angelina, they saw a stranger climbing across the front seat of her car. Jaime recognized him from photographs on television and yelled that this was the killer, and the men made a mad dash to catch him. Ramirez ran, but Manuel de la Torres caught up with him and hit him across the neck with the metal post he was still carrying. Ramirez tried to get away but Manuel hit him again and again. Jaime Burgoin caught up with Ramirez and punched him. Ramirez stumbled and fell, but quickly got up and continued running with Manuel and the two Burgoin boys right behind him. Finally, one of Manuel's swings struck him in the head and the Ramirez collapsed on the ground. Jaime and Jose kept him there until the police arrived. The Night Stalker turned out to be no match for these stubborn and determined men.

One day after Ramirez's face was presented to the public, the Night Stalker was behind bars. When he was arrested, Ramirez was charged with fourteen murders and thirty-one other felonies related to his 1985 crime spree. He was also charged with a fifteenth murder in San Francisco and rape and attempted murder in Orange County.

Ramirez was brought to trial on July 22, 1988 and on September 20, 1989, he was found guilty on thirteen counts of murder, five attempted murders, eleven sexual assaults, and fourteen burglaries. During the penalty phase of the trial on November 7, 1989, he was sentenced to death in California's gas chamber. It was one of the most difficult and longest criminal trials in American history. Nearly 1,600 prospective jurors were interviewed and more than 100 witnesses testified. Ramirez seemed to enjoy his notoriety, performing for the press throughout the proceedings, and playing up the satanic angle of his crime spree. He flashed the palm of his hand, where he had etched a pentagram, and on other occasions, as he sat listening to the prosecutors, he placed two upturned fingers on either side of his head to indicated horns and chanted, "evil... evil... evil."

By the time of his trial, Ramirez had accumulated a following of dozens of twisted fans who were writing to him and paying him visits. A freelance magazine editor named Doreen Lioy wrote him more than 75 letters. She told the *Los Angeles Times* that she was smitten with Ramirez when she saw his mug shot on television the night before he was apprehended. Despite intense competition from other women who sent him letters and photographs and who visited him in jail, Lioy succeeded in her quest to become Mrs. Richard Ramirez. In 1988, he proposed to her and on October 3, 1996, they were married in the main visiting room at San Quentin State Prison. Lioy told interviewers that she was raised a Roman Catholic but considers herself an agnostic. She said she had no objection to Ramirez being a Satanist; in fact she purchased a platinum wedding band for him after he told her that Satanists don't wear gold jewelry.

Lioy has stated that she plans to commit suicide when Ramirez is executed. When that will occur is unknown at this time. Death penalty cases are automatically appealed in California, and Ramirez exhausted all his state appeals in 2006. However, he is still entitled to appeal to the U.S. Supreme Court, a process that would likely take two years. Executions have been on hold in California in recent years due to legal challenges. Ramirez's attorney will not file a federal appeal until California resumes executing prisoners. Meanwhile, the Night Stalker remains one of 729 men and women on California's Death Row.

1989: HORROR IN MATAMOROS

No matter what you may have read in the pages that came before this, if you're like most people, you probably refuse to believe that it's possible that people – even children – can be sacrificed in satanic rituals to gain wealth or power. It's hard to imagine how anyone, aside from a deranged serial killer, could target someone, lure them to a quiet spot and then sacrifice them to the Devil in hopes of gaining favors. And yet, it's happened far too many times to count. Such things are part of the dark underbelly of civilized society. We don't want to believe that it can happen – and yet it does, and often in places where we would least expect it.

Mark Kilroy

Every year during spring break, American college students cross the Mexican-United States border to indulge in some fun in the slum town of Matamoros. They hit the strip of ramshackle bars and nightclubs stuck between the whorehouses and drug dens and surrounded by poverty and hunger. Spring break remains a national event and has been the subject of endless teen comedies over the years. Parents never worried about their kids crossing the border to party. They knew the kids wouldn't be doing anything that they didn't do when they were young. No one thought anything terrible could happen. No one worried – until the spring of 1989.

Like a lot of other students, Mark Kilroy, a pre-med student at the University of Texas at Austin, was eagerly looking forward to having a good time during his March vacation. A friend who went with him recalled, "The whole semester, that was all he talked about." No one suspected that the handsome, dark-haired Kilroy would come to any harm. All he was going to do was spend a few nights partying and blowing off some steam across the border. College kids had been doing it since the 1930s and nothing bad had ever happened before.

On the first evening in Mexico, Kilroy and three of his Lambda Chi Alpha Fraternity brothers met up with some girls from Kansas. They drank cold Mexican beer and listened to music. At the end of the night, Kilroy and his buddies returned to their rooms at the Sheraton Hotel on South Padre Island, Texas, about twenty miles away. Their second night of revelry and beer-drinking went equally well. Around 2:00 a.m. on the morning of March 14, the four young men decided to call it a night. They began walking toward the river, a fifteen-minute stroll that would take them across the bridge over the Rio Grande to Brownsville on the U.S. side of the border, where they had left their car.

Two of the boys walked ahead of the others. Kilroy and Bill Huddleston, both 21, followed about twenty feet behind them. Huddleston stopped for a moment to relieve himself in an alley and Kilroy waited for him on the street. By the time Huddleston came out of the alley, Kilroy was gone. Huddleston called for his friend, thinking Kilroy was playing a prank on him, but he got no response. The police were called. Kilroy's family had various connections, including an uncle who worked for the U.S. Customs Service, so everything possible was done to find him. A $15,000 reward was offered for information leading to the young man's safe return or for the arrest of his kidnappers. But no useful leads appeared and Kilroy's whereabouts became a nagging mystery.

A month later, however, an unexpected incident put investigators onto a new trail. In the bleak plains of Mexico's Rio Grande Valley – about twenty miles from where Kilroy disappeared – drug smuggling was the region's most profitable trade. For this reason, Mexican authorities occasionally mounted anti-drug campaigns, putting up roadblocks in random spots and sweeping the border district for smugglers. When a car driven by a young man who worked for a local drug lord failed to stop at one of the roadblocks, the police gave chase. They pursued him to a nearby rundown cattle ranch where a quick search turned up 75 pounds of marijuana. It was a routine seizure, but the investigation took a darker turn when the authorities casually showed the ranch's caretaker a photograph of Mark Kilroy. It was something they had regularly been doing since the young man vanished. As with every other time they had shown the photo, they expected nothing to come of it. This time, however, they were surprised when the caretaker replied, "Yeah, I saw him," and pointed to a rust-colored wooden shack in a corral.

As the officers walked through the dusty, windblown yard, they made a ghastly discovery. In and around the corral, where the stench of death hung in the air, they found several makeshift graves. After extensive digging, the corpses of twelve young men were uncovered (later, a thirteenth was unearthed), the youngest only 14 years old. Several of the victims had been slashed with knives; others bludgeoned on the head. One had been hanged, another burned to death. At least two of the bodies were riddled with bullets. Some had been tortured with razor blades or had their hearts ripped out. Nearly all had been severely mutilated: ears, nipples and testicles removed, the eyes gouged from one victim, the head missing from another. Among the victims, the police discovered the body of Mark Kilroy.

When officers entered the darkness of the shack, they found a squat iron pot. Its contents suggested that more than just a band of ruthless killers had been at work. Inside the pot, resting in dried blood, was a charred human brain, a spinal column, other human bones, a turtle shell and a horseshoe. Also in the pot were sticks called "*palos*," which practitioners of Palo Mayombe use to communicate with spirits in the afterlife. Other containers inside the nightmare shack held human hair, a goat's head and various chicken parts.

Mexican police arrested and questioned four suspects, including the drug baron's lackey who had led them to the ranch. The horrifying truth soon became clear: The authorities were dealing with a cult of drug smugglers who believed that human sacrifices would win diabolic protection for their weekly marijuana shipments into the United States.

"They felt that all the killing would draw a protective shield around them," Said Texas Attorney General Jim Mattox. "It was religious craziness."

Mark Kilroy – like all but two of the victims – was picked at random. It was his brain and spinal column that were found in the black magic cauldron. Fate had dealt him a hideously bad hand. His spring break revelry had ended with his bloody demise. Further questioning of suspects revealed what had happened to him. While he was waiting for his friend, he was lured to a red pick-up truck by a man who offered him a ride. Unbeknownst to Kilroy, the men in the truck had been sent out with orders to find and capture "an Angelo spring-breaker." Two thugs threw him into the back and sped off. Five blocks away, Kilroy attempted to escape, but was recaptured and driven to the ranch. There he was gagged and blindfolded with tape and shoved into the shack. Kilroy's captors brought him bread and water and assured him that he was in no danger. A few hours later, though, he was abruptly led outside and executed with a machete to the back of his neck. The man who wielded the weapon was the cult's leader, a 26-year-old Cuban-American named Adolfo de Jesus Constanzo, one of the most sinister satanic cultists to ever wreak havoc in the annals of American crime.

Adolfo Constanzo was born in Miami on November 1, 1962, the son of a teenaged Cuban immigrant. He was still an infant when his widowed mother moved to Puerto Rico and married for a second time. There, Constanzo was baptized as a Catholic and served the church as an altar boy, appearing to accept the teachings of the faith. He was 10 years old when his family moved back to West Miami, and his step-father died about a year later, leaving the boy and his mother financially well off.

By that time, neighbors in Little Havana had started to notice that there was something odd about Aurora Constanzo and her son. Some said that she was a witch, and those who angered her were liable to find headless goats or chickens on their doorsteps in the morning. Adolfo's mother had introduced her son to Santería around the age of nine and took him along to Haiti for instruction in Voodoo. But there were more secrets to be learned and in 1976, he was apprenticed to a practitioner of Palo Mayombe, a man who was already rich from selling "protection" to local drug dealers.

It is important to realize that Palo Mayombe is not all bad; there is, after all, good and bad in all religions. Many practitioners perform rites of healing and spells for the good of local communities – but it should also be pointed out that many of them use human bones stolen from graveyards. And that is the problem. It's hard to get away from the dark side of Palo Mayombe. Even as far back as 1903, there is a record of a practitioner sacrificing a young girl for a Palo Mayombe rite. And in more recent times, there have been many incidents pointing to murder and black magic rituals. In 1986, for example, a baby in Miami was found murdered, its tongue and

Adolfo Constanzo – soon to become one of the most feared men in Mexico

eyelids cut off and offered to various deities. The same year, in Fort Myers, Florida, a search of a drug dealer's home and shrimp boat turned up a cauldron containing two human skulls. In March 2005, police in Florida launched a manhunt for six armed people after discovering human skulls and bones inside a shed. They also found cocaine, handguns, a goat's head, live chickens, pigeons and guinea pigs. "It gives me the creeps," one neighbor said.

And for good reason.

It was around the same time as Constanzo's introduction to the dark side that his mother noted that her son began displaying psychic powers, scanning the future to predict such events as the 1981 shooting of President Ronald Reagan. True or not, Constanzo had problems foretelling his own future, including two arrests for shoplifting – one involving the theft of a chainsaw. In addition, he also began to display bisexual inclinations around this same time, showing a strong preference for young male lovers.

Modeling work took the handsome young man to Mexico City in 1983, where he spent his free time telling fortunes with tarot cards in the city's infamous Zona Rosa prostitution district. Before returning to Miami, Constanzo collected his first Mexican disciples, including Martin Quintana, homosexual "psychic" Jorge Montes and Omar Orea Ochoa, who had been deeply immersed in the occult since the age of 15.

In mid-1984, Constanzo moved to Mexico City full-time. He gained followers throughout the city as his "magic" reputation grew. It was said that Constanzo could read the future and he offered *limpias* – ritual "cleansings" – for those who believed they had been cursed by their enemies. Of course, those who required his

Omar Orea Ochoa and (Right) Martin Quintana

services paid dearly. Constanzo's journals, recovered after his death, documented at least 31 customers who paid up to $4,500 for a single ceremony. He charged separately for sacrificial animals, including goats, chickens, boa constrictors, zebras and even African lion cubs. As his mentor in Miami had done, Constanzo went out of his way to charm wealthy drug dealers, helping them schedule shipments and meetings on the basis of his predictions and the magic he offered for protection. For a price, he offered spells that would make dealers and gunmen invisible to the police and bulletproof against their enemies. It was all nonsense, of course, but most smugglers came from Mexican peasant stock, with backgrounds in folk magic, and were strongly inclined to believe. According to Constanza's ledger, one dealer in Mexico City paid him $40,000 for magical services rendered over a three-year period.

At those rates, customers demanded something in return and Constanzo recognized the folly of disappointing ruthless crime lords who carried automatic weapons. His magic required first-rate ingredients and in mid-1985, he and three of his disciples raided a Mexico City cemetery for human bones to start his *nganga* – the traditional cauldron of blood employed by practitioners of Palo Mayombe. The spooky rituals and air of mystery surrounding Constanzo were powerful enough to lure a cross-section of Mexican society, with his immediate circle of disciples including a physician, a real estate speculator, fashion models and several transvestite nightclub performers.

At first glance, the most peculiar aspect of Constanzo's career was the appeal he seemed to have for ranking law enforcement officers. At least four members of the Federal Judicial Police joined Constanzo's cult in Mexico City. One of them, Salvador Garcia, was a commander in charge of narcotics investigations. Another, Florentino Ventura, retired from the police to lead the Mexican branch of Interpol. In a country where bribery permeates all levels of law enforcement and federal officers sometimes serve as triggermen for drug smugglers, corruption is not unusual, but the devotion of Constanzo's followers ran deeper than mere money. Whether in uniform or out of it, they worshipped him as a minor god in his own right, their living conduit to the dark side.

In 1986, Florentino Ventura introduced Constanzo to the Caldaza drug family, then one of Mexico's dominant cartels. Constanzo won over the leaders with his charm and promises of magical protection, profiting immensely from his contacts with them. By early 1987, he was about to pay cash for a luxury Mexico City condominium and a fleet of high-priced cars. When not working magic for the Caldazas or other clients, Constanzo worked scams of his own, once posing as a DEA agent to rip off a cocaine dealer in Guadalajara. He sold the stash through his police contacts for $100,000.

At some point around this time, Constanzo began to feed his *nganga* with offerings of human sacrifice. No final tally for his victims has ever been found, but thirty-three ritual murders are well-documented. Mexican authorities point to a rash of unsolved mutilation killings around Mexico City and elsewhere, suggesting that Constanzo's known victims may only represent the tip of a blood-soaked iceberg. In any case, his willingness to torture and kill total strangers – as well as close friends – impressed the ruthless cartel members who were his most important clients.

In the course of his year of association with the cartel, Constanzo started to believe his own press, fooling himself into thinking that his magical powers alone were responsible for the Calzada cartel's continued success and survival. In April 1987, he demanded a full partnership in the syndicate and was curtly refused. On the surface, Constanzo seemed to take the rejection in stride, but in his mind, he was plotting revenge.

On April 30, Guillermo Calzada and six members of the cartel vanished under mysterious circumstances. They were reported missing on May 1 and during the investigation, the police noted the melted candles and other evidence of strange religious ceremony left behind in Calzada's office. Six more days passed before officers began pulling mutilated human remains from the Zumpango River. Seven corpses were found over the course of the next week, all bearing signs of sadistic torture – fingers, toes and ears chopped off, hearts and sex organs cut out, part of the spine ripped from one body, two others missing brains.

The missing body parts, as it turned out, were used to feed Constanzo's cauldron of blood. He believed they were working an infernal magic for greater conquests still to come.

Sara Aldrete

In July 1987, Salvador Garcia introduced Constanzo to another cartel, this one led by brothers Elio and Ovidio Hernandez. At the end of that month, in Matamoros, Constanzo also met Sara Aldrete, 22. Aldrete was a Mexican national with resident alien status in the United States, where she was a honor student at Texas Southmost College in Brownsville, Texas. Constanzo charmed the young woman, who was dating a Brownsville drug smuggler named Gilberto Sosa at the time, and soon she found herself in Constanzo's bed. She plunged full-tilt into his dark world, emerging as the "head witch" of his cult, adding her own twists to the torture of his sacrificial victims.

Constanzo's rituals became more elaborate and more sadistic after he moved his headquarters to Rancho Santa Elena in a lonely stretch of desert, twenty miles from Matamoros. There, on May 28, 1988, smuggler Hector de la Fuente and farmer Moises Castillo were executed by gunfire, but the sacrifice was a disappointment to Constanzo. Back in Mexico City, he directed his followers to dismember a transvestite named Ramon Esquivel, and dump his grisly remains on a street corner where they were found by local children. Soon after, his "magical luck" held as Constanzo narrowly escaped a Houston police raid on a drug house in June 1988. The officers seized not only the city's largest-ever shipment of cocaine, but numerous items of occult paraphernalia.

On August 12, Ovidio Hernandez and his two-year-old son were kidnapped by members of a rival cartel and the family turned to Constanzo for help. That night, another human sacrifice was staged at the ranch and the hostages were released unharmed on August 13. Constanzo claimed full credit for their return. His star rising, he barely noticed when Florentino Ventura committed suicide in Mexico City on September 17, killing his wife and a friend before shooting himself.

In November 1988, Constanzo sacrificed disciple Jorge Gomez, who was accused of using cocaine in direct violation of Constanzo's ban on drug use. A month later, Constanzo's ties to the Hernandez cartel were cemented with the initiation of Ovidio Hernandez as a full-fledged member of the cult, complete with ritual bloodletting and prayers to the *nganga*.

On February 14, 1989, Constanzo ordered the torture sacrifice of a competing smuggler named Ezequiel Luna and when two other dealers, Ruben Garza and Ernesto Diaz, showed up at the ceremony uninvited, they promptly wound up being sacrificed too. On another occasion, when Constanzo ordered a sacrifice on the spur of the

The shed on the ranch outside Matamoros that Constanzo used for black magic. Investigators that raided the ranch had never seen anything like the horror on the ranch before.

moment, Ovidio Hernandez gladly joined a hunting party and turned his own 14-year-old cousin, Jose Garcia, into a subject for the bloody ritual.

The authorities reveal some of the items discovered during the raid on the ranch, including Constanzo's "cauldron of blood."

On March 13, 1989, Constanzo sacrificed yet another victim at the ranch near Matamoros, but was gravely disappointed when his prey did not scream and plead for mercy the way that his victims usually did. Disgruntled, he ordered that his men bring him an American the next time --- and his men abducted Mark Kilroy from the streets of Matamoros. The sacrifice was followed two weeks later by the slaughter of Sara Aldrete's former boyfriend, Gilberto Sosa. Targeting an American college student from a middle-class family was a misstep in what had been a ghoulishly successful dance of death. Kilroy's disappearance marked the beginning of the end for Constanzo and his homicidal cult.

The magic was beginning to unravel.

On April 9, returning from a Brownsville meeting with Constanzo, cult member Serafin Hernandez failed to stop at a police roadblock, ignoring the police cars that quickly followed in pursuit. Hernandez believed that what Constanzo told him about being invisible was true and he seemed surprised when the police officers trailed him to his destination in Matamoros. Even so, the smuggler was arrogant, inviting the police to shoot him since he knew the bullets would merely bounce off.

They arrested him instead, along with cult member David Martinez. Soon after, Elio Hernandez and Sergio Martinez were arrested as well and all four were interrogated through the night, revealing tales of black magic, torture and human sacrifice with a perverse kind of pride. They admitted to their grisly deeds with no remorse whatsoever. When paraded before reporters in Matamoros, the shirt of one of the suspects was pulled back to show a series of scars in the form of inverted crosses, an apparent sign that he was selected to kill. Later, police dispensed their own brand of punishment. Having discovered from their interviews that there was one further

The authorities spent days unearthing the human remains that had been buried on the ranch.

body buried at the ranch, they hauled one of the drug traffickers back to the grave site and forced him to dig in the blazing sun, without water, until he uncovered it.

Lawmen searched the border in vain for Constanzo and what remained of his cult. On April 17, they arrested another gang member, Serafin Hernandez, in Houston. Searching the house where he had been hiding, they seized weapons and cash, but no evidence of blood rituals. Constanzo and his closest aides, meanwhile, had moved on. The following day, Constanzo, still believing in his occult gifts, read betrayal in his tarot cards. He knew that informers must have betrayed Serafin and now he eyed his friends more warily. He kept a gun close at hand and rarely slept for more than a few minutes at a time. Increasingly, he threatened those around him with power that he promised exceeded that of the police. "They cannot kill you," he warned, "but I can."

On April 22, the ranch was scoured for evidence and the police tore apart the shed where Constanzo kept his sinister *nganga*. Finally, the officers burned the shed to the ground, performing their own sort of "cleansing" of the area. Commander Juan Benitez Ayala, head of the Mexican anti-narcotics squad, who was in charge of the hunt for Constanzo, muttered angrily under his breath: "You see, I'll bury the son of a bitch. I'll kill him. I'll kill him." He admitted that burning the shed was an act that was designed to "drive Constanzo crazy."

The next morning, Constanzo flew into a rage when he saw on television that the police conducted a full-scale exorcism at the ranch, sprinkling holy water over the emptied graves and the smoldering ruins of the shack. He tore apart the small apartment where he was hiding out, smashing lamps and overturning furniture.

On April 24, the police arrested another cultist, Jorge Montes. Like the others arrested before him, Montes spilled everything that he knew, naming Constanzo as the leader of the cult and the man behind the string of horrific homicides. Three days later, Constanzo and his four remaining cohorts moved to their last hideout, an apartment house on Rio Sena in Mexico City.

Sara Aldrete was one of the last to remain with Constanzo. On May 2, perhaps fearing for her life, she wrote a note and tossed it from the bedroom window to the street below. It read:

Please call the judicial police and tell them that in this building are those they are seeking. Tell them that a woman is being held hostage. I beg this, because what I want most is to talk – or they're going to kill the girl.

A passerby found the note a few minutes later. He read it, but kept it to himself, believing that it was someone's poor attempt at a joke. Upstairs in the cramped apartment, Constanzo began making plans to flee

Mexico with his remaining disciples. They would start fresh, he said, where no one knew them. He did not fear the police. "They'll never take me," he assured them.

But his plans fell apart on May 6 when the police arrived in Rio Sena, doing door-to-door inquiries. They were asking questions everywhere – but not about Constanzo. It was a completely unrelated case, involving a missing child, but Constanzo didn't know this. When he glimpsed a policeman from a window, he panicked and opened fire with a machine gun. Within moments, there were 180 officers surrounding the apartment building, returning fire in a fierce exchange that lasted for nearly forty-five minutes. Miraculously, the only person wounded was a police officer who was struck by Constanzo's first shots.

It didn't take long for Constanzo to accept the fact that escape was impossible. Without hesitation, he handed his weapon to cult member Alvaro de Leon Valdez – a hired killer known as "El Duby" – with bizarre new orders. Valdez later told the police, "He told me to kill him and Martin [Quintana]. I told him I couldn't do it, but he hit me in the face and threatened me that everything would go bad for me in hell. Then he hugged Martin, and I just stood in front of them and shot them with a machine gun."

Constanzo was dead when the police stormed the apartment. They arrested El Duby and Sara Aldrete and rushed them off to jail. In custody, El Duby cheerfully informed the police that Constanzo "would not be dead for long." Mexican authorities were less concerned with Constanzo's impending resurrection than with making charges stick against the surviving cult members. El Duby's case was open and shut: His confession recorded two murder counts. But Sara Aldrete insisted that she was a victim, claiming that the gang took her as a hostage. She later betrayed herself by inadvertently disclosing intimate knowledge about the cult's bloody rituals.

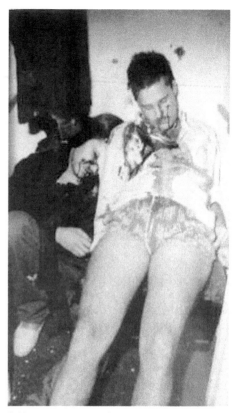

Adolfo Constanzo and Martin Quintana were found shot to death in the closet of the apartment.

In the wake of the Mexico City shoot-out, fourteen cult members were rounded dup. They were indicted on various charges, including multiple murder, weapons and narcotics violations, conspiracy and obstruction of justice. Sara Aldrete continued to protest her innocence, but jurors didn't believe her. In 1994, Aldrete and four male accomplices were convicted of multiple slayings at the ranch. Aldrete was sentenced to sixty-two years in prison. The others drew terms of sixty-seven years. If any of them live long enough to be released from custody in Mexico, U.S. authorities stand ready to prosecute them.

The evil started by Constanzo and his cult may not be over, even now.

A grisly list of cult-related crimes remains unsolved in Mexico. From prison, Sara Aldrete told reporters, "I don't think the religion will end with us, because it has a lot of people in it. They have found a temple in Monterrey that isn't even related to us. It will continue."

Between 1987 and 1989, police in Mexico City recorded seventy-four unsolved, suspected ritual murders, fourteen of them involving infant victims. Constanzo's cult is thought to have been involved in at least sixteen of those cases, all involving children and teenagers. But authorities never had enough evidence to pursue charges.

When asked about the cases, prosecutor Guillermo Ibarra told reporters: "We would like to say, yes, Constanzo did them all, and poof, all those cases are solved. And the fact is, we believe he was responsible for some of them, though we'll never prove it now. But he didn't commit all those murders. Which means someone else did. Someone who is still out there."

A lot of paranoia surrounded the Matamoros case, which is not surprising considering the sheer horror of it. Parents were terrified of sending their teenagers away for spring break. The economy of the small Mexican town of Matamoros, which depended on the money spent by partying college students, was shattered. It was terrifying to think that some of Constanzo's people might still be out there, seeking new victims. Could more people be in danger? No one could say for sure, but what was certain was that much of the paranoia was exacerbated by the general wave of Satanic Panic that was sweeping the United States at the time.

The Matamoros case proved that all of the stories about an undercover satanic conspiracy operating across America were true, didn't it? Numerous Christian groups had been saying this for years. They believed that a massive Devil-worshipping network was entrenched across the country. Despite their accusations, no evidence was ever found to substantiate such beliefs. Was the Matamoros horror evidence that such a conspiracy existed?

In some ways, the Matamoros killings were like a gift to fundamentalist Christians and self-appointed cult watchdogs. It validated their views and brought them a level of credence that they didn't previously have, probably extending the Satanic Panic longer than it would have continued on its own.

That said, though, in October 1989, after memories of Matamoros had started to fade, FBI agents working on a drug case in Brownsville made a sinister discovery. While serving a search warrant on a suspected drug dealer's house, they found a back room with walls and ceiling painted crimson red. This could have been written off as a poor decorating choice if there had not been a noxious odor coming from a refrigerator in the room. Inside were vials of blood and unidentified fluids. Each contained a tiny slip of paper with a person's name scrawled on it, along with a curse or spell of control. At the other end of the room was an altar. On it were three figures made from twigs that were painted black, with pins sticking in them. Next to them were three glass-encased candles with the words "Law Be Gone" written on each of them. Most chilling of all was that in the center of the altar was a black-and-white photograph of Commander Juan Benitez Ayala of the Mexican anti-narcotics squad, the man who hunted down Constanzo's cult. A large pin had been thrust through the photograph, pinning it to the altar.

The officers who made the discovery stood back in horror. Some were reported to have voiced the fear that Constanzo's evil still lived on. But the truth was the people behind the room might not have had any connection to Constanzo at all. Many drug dealers believe in the black magic of Palo Mayombe and believe that working spells will prevent them from being caught. It's scary to think that there may be others out there who believed in the same things that Constanzo did --- but just how far do they take those beliefs?

Is there another burial ground out there somewhere, where the bones of the missing have yet to be found?

That is a question that should keep all of us awake at night.

BIBLIOGRAPHY
AND RECOMMENDED READING

Ashley, Leonard R.N. – *Complete Book of Devils & Demons*; 1996

Baker, Phil – *The Devil is a Gentleman*; 2009

Barton, Blanche – *Secret Life of a Satanist*; 1990

Baskin, Wade – *Dictionary of Satanism*; 1972

Black, Candice – *Satanica Sexualis*; 2006

Cavendish, Richard – *The Black Arts*; 1969

-------------------------- - *Man, Myth and Magic: An Illustrated Encyclopedia of the Superanatural*; 1970

Chaplin, J.P. – *Dictionary of the Occult and the Paranormal*; 1976

Constantine, Nathan – *History of Cannibalism*; 2006

Demos, John – *The Enemy Within*; 2008

Durschmied, Erik – *Whores of the Devil*; 2006

Ebon, Martin - *Demon Children*; 1978

----------------- - *Devil's Bride*; 1974

Ennemoser, Joseph – *The History of Magic*; 1970

Flowers, Stephen E. Ph.D – *Lords of the Left-Hand Path*; 1997

Guiley, Rosemary Ellen – *Encyclopedia of Demons & Demonology*; 2009

---------------------------- - *Encyclopedia of Witches & Witchcraft*; 1999

Haining, Peter – *The Secret History of Cults*; 1999

Hill, Douglas & Pat Williams -- *The Supernatural*; 1965

King, Francis X. – *Satan and the Swastika*; 1976

Kirsch, Jonathan – *The Grand Inquisitor's Manual*; 2008

Lamb, Geoffrey – *Magic, Witchcraft and the Occult*; 1977

LaVey, Anton – *Satanic Bible*; 1969

---------------- - *Satanic Rituals*; 1972

---------------- - *Satanic Witch*; 1970

Lord, Evelyn – *The Hell-Fire Clubs*; 2008

Laurence, Theodor – *Satan, Sorcery & Sex*; 1974

Lewis, Brenda Ralph – *Ritual Sacrifice*; 2001

Mannix, Daniel P., *History of Torture*; 1964

Masello, Robert – *Fallen Angels*; 1994

-------------------- - *Raising Hell*; 1996

Masters, Anthony – *The Devil's Dominion*; 1978

McGovern, Una (Editor) – *Chambers Dictionary of the Unexplained*; 2007

Michelet, Jules – *Satanism & Witchcraft*; 1939
Mikul, Chris – *The Cult Files*; 2009
Newman, Paul – *History of Terror*; 2000
Newton, Michael – *Encyclopedia of Unsolved Crimes*; 2009
---------------------- *Raising Hell*; 1993
Ramsland, Katherine -- *Robin Gecht & the Notorious Chicago Rippers*; Crime Library; 2006
Rhodes, H.T.F – *The Satanic Mass*; 1954
Robbins, Russell Hope – *Encyclopedia of Witchcraft & Demonology*; 1959
Robson, Peter – *The Devil's Own*; 1966
Roland, Paul – *Dark History of the Occult*; 2011
---------------- *The Nazi's and the Occult*; 2012
Ruickbie, Dr. Leo – *The Supernatural*; 2012
Russell, Jeffrey Burton – *Witchcraft in the Middle Ages*; 1972
Savage, Candace – *Witch*; 2000
Seligman, Kurt – *History of Magic and the Occult*; 1948
Seth, Ronald – *In the Name of the Devil*; 1969
Shreeve, Jimmy Lee – *Human Sacrifice*; 2008
Smith, Michelle & Lawrence Pazder, MD, *Michelle Remembers*; 1980
Spence, Lewis – *Encyclopedia of Occultism*; 1960
Steiger, Brad – *Sex and Satanism*; 1969
Summers, Montague – *Popular History of Witchcraft*; 1973
------------------------------ *Witchcraft & Black Magic*; 1974
Tannahill, Reay – *Flesh and Blood*; 1975
Taylor, Troy – *Devil Came to St. Louis*; 2006
---------------- *Sex & the Supernatural*; 2009
Turner, Alice K. – *History of Hell*; 1993
Waite, Arthur Edward – *Book of Ceremonial Magic*; 1913
Wheatley, Dennis – *The Devil & All his Works*; 1971
Wikipedia References
Wilson, Colin – *The Occult*; 1971
------------------- *Witches*; 1989

Personal Interviews & Correspondence

Copyright 1905
By Souvenir Post Card Co. N.Y.

Special Thanks to:
Jill Hand (Editor)
April Slaughter
(Cover Design, Suggestions and Essential Details)
Elyse Horath (E-Book Design)
Rene Kruse
Orrin Taylor
Janet Morris
and Helayna Taylor

About the Author
TROY TAYLOR

Troy Taylor is an occultist, crime buff, supernatural historian and the author of more than 90 books on ghosts, hauntings, history, crime and the unexplained in America.

He is also the founder of the American Ghost Society and the owner of the American Hauntings Tour company.

Taylor shares a birthday with one of his favorite authors, F. Scott Fitzgerald, but instead of living in New York and Paris like Fitzgerald, Taylor grew up in Illinois. Raised on the prairies of the state, he developed an interest in "things that go bump in the night" at an early age and as a young man, began developing ghost tours and writing about hauntings and crime in Chicago and Central Illinois. His writings have now taken him all over the country and into some of the most far-flung corners of the world.

He began his first book in 1989, which delved into the history and hauntings of his hometown of Decatur, Illinois, and in 1994, it spawned the Haunted Decatur Tour -- and eventually led to the founding of his Illinois Hauntings Tours (with tours in Alton, Chicago, Decatur, Lebanon, Springfield & Jacksonville) and the American Hauntings Tours, which travel all over the country in search of haunted places.

Along with writing about the unusual and hosting tours, Taylor has also presented on the subjects of ghosts, hauntings and crime for public and private groups. He has also appeared in scores of newspaper and magazine articles about these subjects and in hundreds of radio and television broadcasts about the supernatural. Taylor has appeared in a number of documentary films, several television series and in one feature film about the paranormal.

When not traveling to the far-flung reaches of the country in search of the unusual, Troy resides part-time in Decatur, Illinois.

WHITECHAPEL PRESS

Whitechapel Productions Press is a division of Apartment #42 Productions and a small press publisher, specializing in print and electronic books about ghosts and hauntings. Since 1993, the company has been one of America's leading publishers of supernatural books and has produced such best-selling titles as *Haunted Illinois, The Ghost Hunter's Guidebook, Ghosts on Film, Confessions of a Ghost Hunter, The Haunting of America, Sex & the Supernatural* the *Dead Men Do Tell Tales* crime series and many others.

With more than a dozen different authors producing high quality books on all aspects of ghosts, hauntings and the paranormal, Whitechapel Press has made its mark with America's ghost enthusiasts.

You can visit Whitechapel Productions Press online and browse through our selection of ghostly titles, plus get information on ghosts and hauntings, haunted history, spirit photographs, information on ghost hunting and much more by visiting the internet website at:

WWW.WHITECHAPELPRESS.COM

Find out more about tours, and make reservations online, by visiting the internet website at:

WWW.AMERICAN HAUNTINGS.ORG

Milton Keynes UK
Ingram Content Group UK Ltd.
UKHW051330301123
433559UK00020B/904